MEMORY

MEMORY

Critical Concepts in Psychology

Edited by Jackie Andrade

Volume II

Memory Processes

Routledge
Taylor & Francis Group

LONDON AND NEW YORK

First published 2008
by Routledge
2 Park Square, Milton Park, Abingdon, Oxon OX14 4RN, UK

Simultaneously published in the USA and Canada
by Routledge
270 Madison Avenue, New York, NY 10016

*Routledge is an imprint of the Taylor & Francis Group,
an informa business*

Editorial material and selection © 2008 Jackie Andrade;
individual owners retain copyright in their own material

Typeset in Times by RefineCatch Limited, Bungay, Suffolk
Printed and bound in Great Britain by
TJI Digital, Padstow, Cornwall

British Library Cataloguing in Publication Data
A catalogue record for this book is available from the British Library

Library of Congress Cataloging in Publication Data
A catalog record for this book has been requested

ISBN10: 0–415–41323–0 (Set)
ISBN10: 0–415–41325–7 (Volume II)

ISBN13: 978–0–415–41323–7 (Set)
ISBN13: 978–0–415–41325–1 (Volume II)

Publisher's Note
References within each chapter are as they appear
in the original complete work.

CONTENTS

CONTENTS

CONTENTS

ACKNOWLEDGEMENTS

The Publishers would like to thank the following for permission to reprint their material:

The University of Illinois Press for permission to reprint Hiroshi Minami and Karl M. Dallenbach, 'The effect of activity upon learning and retention in the cockroach, *Periplaneta americana*', *American Journal of Psychology* 59 (1946): 1–58. Copyright © 1946 by the Board of Trustees of the University of Illinois Press.

Taylor & Francis Ltd for permission to reprint John Brown, 'Some tests of the decay theory of immediate memory', *Quarterly Journal of Experimental Psychology* 10 (1958): 12–21. www.tandf.co.uk/journals

The American Psychological Association for permission to reprint Benton J. Underwood, 'Interference and forgetting', *Psychological Review* 64(1) (1957): 49–60. Copyright © 1957 by the American Psychological Association.

The American Psychological Association for permission to reprint Harry P. Bahrick, 'Semantic memory content in permastore: Fifty years of memory for Spanish learned in school', *Journal of Experimental Psychology: General* 113(1) (1984): 1–29. Copyright © 1984 by the American Psychological Association.

Elsevier for permission to reprint John D. Bransford and Marcia K. Johnson, 'Contextual prerequisites for understanding: Some investigations of comprehension and recall', *Journal of Verbal Learning and Verbal Behavior* 11 (1972): 717–726.

Elsevier for permission to reprint Fergus I. M. Craik and Robert S. Lockhart, 'Levels of processing: A framework for memory research', *Journal of Verbal Learning and Verbal Behavior* 11 (1972): 671–684.

Elsevier for permission to reprint C. Donald Morris, John D. Bransford and Jeffery J. Franks, 'Levels of processing versus transfer appropriate processing', *Journal of Verbal Learning and Verbal Behavior* 16 (1977): 519–533.

AAAS for permission to reprint Anthony D. Wagner, Daniel L. Schacter, Michael Rotte, Wilma Koutstaal, Anat Maril, Anders M. Dale, Bruce R. Rosen and Randy L. Buckner, 'Building memories: Remembering and forgetting of verbal experiences as predicted by brain activity', *Science* 281 (1998): 1188–1191.

Cambridge University Press for permission to reprint Fredrick C. Bartlett, 'Experiments on remembering: (b) The method of repeated reproduction', in *Remembering: A Study in Experimental and Social Psychology*, 1932, pp. 63–94. © Cambridge University Press.

The American Psychological Association for permission to reprint Allan M. Collins and Elizabeth F. Loftus, 'A spreading-activation theory of semantic processing', *Psychological Review* 82 (1975): 407–428. Copyright © 1975 by the American Psychological Association.

The American Psychological Association for permission to reprint James L. McClelland and David E. Rumelhart, 'Distributed memory and the representation of general and specific information', *Journal of Experimental Psychology: General* 114 (1985): 159–188. Copyright © 1985 by the American Psychological Association.

The American Psychological Association for permission to reprint Donald Homa, Sharon Sterling and Lawrence Trepel, 'Limitations of exemplar-based generalization and the abstraction of categorical information', *Journal of Experimental Psychology: Human Learning and Memory* 7 (1981): 418–439. Copyright © 1981 by the American Psychological Association.

The Psychonomic Society, Inc. for permission to reprint Lawrence W. Barsalou, 'Context-independent and context-dependent information in concepts', *Memory & Cognition* 10(1) (1982): 82–93.

The American Psychological Association for permission to reprint David E. Meyer and Roger W. Schvaneveldt, 'Facilitation in recognizing pairs of words: Evidence of a dependence between retrieval operations', *Journal of Experimental Psychology* 90 (1971): 227–234. Copyright © 1971 by the American Psychological Association.

The *British Journal of Psychology* for permission to reprint Duncan R. Godden and Alan D. Baddeley, 'Context-dependent memory in two natural environments: On land and underwater', *British Journal of Psychology* 66 (1975): 325–331. © The British Psychological Society.

Cambridge University Press for permission to reprint Geoffrey G. Lloyd and William A. Lishman, 'Effect of depression on the speed of recall of pleasant and unpleasant experiences', *Psychological Medicine* 5 (1975): 173–180. © Cambridge University Press.

The American Psychological Association for permission to reprint Eric Eich, 'Mood as a mediator of place dependent memory', *Journal of Experimental Psychology: General* 124(3) (1995): 293–308. Copyright © 1995 by the American Psychological Association.

The American Psychological Association for permission to reprint Endel Tulving and Donald M. Thomson, 'Encoding specificity and retrieval processes in episodic memory', *Psychological Review* 80 (1973): 352–373. Copyright © 1973 by the American Psychological Association.

The Psychonomic Society, Inc. for permission to reprint John M. Gardiner, 'Functional aspects of recollective experience', *Memory & Cognition* 16(4) (1988): 309–313.

Elsevier for permission to reprint Murray Glanzer and Anita R. Cunitz, 'Two storage mechanisms in free recall', *Journal of Verbal Learning and Verbal Behavior* 5 (1966): 351–360.

The American Psychological Association for permission to reprint Arthur M. Glenberg and Naomi G. Swanson, 'A temporal distinctiveness theory of recency and modality effects', *Journal of Experimental Psychology: Learning, Memory, and Cognition* 12 (1986): 3–15. Copyright © 1986 by the American Psychological Association.

The American Psychological Association for permission to reprint Lydia Tan and Geoff Ward, 'A recency-based account of the primacy effect in free recall', *Journal of Experimental Psychology: Learning, Memory, and Cognition*, 26 (2000): 1589–1625. Copyright © 2000 by the American Psychological Association.

Disclaimer

Part 5

FORGETTING

22

THE EFFECT OF ACTIVITY UPON LEARNING AND RETENTION IN THE COCKROACH, *PERIPLANETA AMERICANA*

Hiroshi Minami and Karl M. Dallenbach

Source: *American Journal of Psychology*, 59 (1946): 1–58.

In 1924, Jenkins and Dallenbach,[1] using the method of retained members, found that retention after 1, 2, 4, and 8 hr. of sleep was far better than after corresponding periods of normal waking activity, and further that there was practically no greater loss in retention after 8 hr. of sleep than after 2 hr. They considered their results as significant enough to account for the discrepancy in Ebbinghaus' curve of forgetting between the 8.8-hr. and the 24-hr. periods[2]—a discrepancy that prompted their study; and to warrant their conclusion that "forgetting is not so much a matter of the decay of old impressions and associations as it is a matter of interference, inhibition, or obliteration of the old by the new."

Though the Ss in the Jenkins and Dallenbach study went to bed immediately after learning the series of nonsense syllables in the night experiments, they did not immediately fall asleep. An indetermined time was spent in going to sleep. The fact that the Ss did not immediately cease all mental and physical activities may in part at least account for the losses found at the 1- and 2-hr. intervals of sleep.

If it were possible to put the Ss into a dreamless sleep immediately after learning, so that no new experiences would have an opportunity to interfere with, inhibit, or obliterate the old, a perfect retention might be expected. Because of the dangers of drugs, anesthetics, and other methods of inducing unconsciousness quickly, no one has thus far attempted to realize those conditions with human Ss, but with animals the case is different.

Hunter, in 1932, accepting the suggestion of Jenkins and Dallenbach that forgetting is mainly due to interpolated activity, undertook an investigation with cockroaches, which are readily and quickly immobilized by cold, with the expectation that "almost perfect retention might be secured if the subject's physiological processes could be held practically in quiescence during the period of rest interpolated between learning and relearning."[3] He tested the effect of inactivity produced by temperatures of 3°–6°C. upon the learning and retention of the avoiding response to darkness. He found, contrary to expectation, that the performance of the quiescent Ss was worse, not better, than that of the controls which were held at normal temperatures and permitted normal activity during the interim between learning and relearning. Realizing that cold may have a deleterious effect upon his Ss, and that inactivity due to cold need not have the same effect upon learning and retention as inactivity due to sleep, he was cautious in his conclusions and merely stated his findings; namely, that exposure to cold (with time for subsequent recovery) retards learning and decreases retention and that the retardation is greater after an exposure to cold of 4 hr. than after 2 hr.

Following this study, Hunter and Russell in 1937 attacked the general problem again by testing the effect of inactivity produced by sodium amytal on the retention of partially learned maze-habits of albino rats.[4] The experimental group of Ss was under that anesthetic for from 8–17 hr. of a 24-hr. interval interpolated between partial and complete learning of a maze. The authors found no significant difference between the performances of the experimental and control groups as that was expressed by the mean and the median error of the two groups. Furthermore, they found no correlation between the length of time under amytal and the retention-scores. The authors did not, however, consider their results as conclusive because of the possibility, since the control rats seemed to have a stronger thirst drive than the experimental group, that the amytal animals were still physiologically affected by their anesthesia at the time of relearning.

The effect of anesthetization upon the retention of insects has been studied by numerous investigators. Phillips,[5] Von Buttel-Reepen,[6] and Tirala[7] found that bees required a longer time to return to their hives after exposure to tobacco smoke, ether, and chloroform, but Eldering,[8] Plath,[9] Rösch-Berger,[10] Grabensberger,[11] and Kalmus,[12] failed with bees, wasps, and cockroaches to find the detrimental effect.

Another method of testing the hypothesis advanced by Jenkins and Dallenbach is to compare the effect upon retention of interpolated activities of different degrees, ranging from a relatively inactive state to an activity far greater than normal. Hoagland,[13] in 1931, tested the effect of an 18-hr. exposure to temperatures below and above a critical temperature (25° C.) upon retention of a maze-habit in ants. He found no effect with temperatures varying from 15° to 25.1° C., but exposures at 28.3° C. and 29.4° C., had detrimental effects since many more than the initial number of trials were required in relearning. Original learning was also, he found, retarded by exposures at high temperatures.

More recently, in 1942, French[14] conducted a similar experiment with goldfish. His Ss were divided into three groups: one group was kept in water at 4° C., a second group at 16° C., and the third group at 28° C. The group averages of the total errors on the original learning of a maze and on 4 days of successive relearning were compared. French found that the 4°-C. group of Ss was best in retention, the 28°-C. group the worst, and the 16°-C. group about midway between the other two groups. Since the record of relative activity showed that the 16°-C. group was most active, the author discarded the possibility of a retroactive inhibition due to general activity during the intervals.

As the preceding survey shows, the favorable effects of sleep upon retention in man—effects obtained by many experimenters[15]—seem to be the only supporting evidence for Jenkins and Dallenbach's hypothesis that forgetting is due to retroactive inhibition. The studies with animals, however, were not decisive. The experimenters were themselves cautious in their conclusions since the methods used to produce quiescence during the intervals interpolated between learning and relearning may have had other deleterious effects. For example, Hunter's cockroaches may have suffered lasting physiological changes as the result of their chilling, and the anesthetization of the insects may have produced physiological changes, as in the case of Russell and Hunter's rats, that were of long duration and did not end with the immediacy of awaking from sleep.

Problem

The present study stems from Hunter's work with cockroaches and Hoagland's and French's experiments with ants and fishes. It was conducted to test further the hypothesis that forgetting is a function of retroactive inhibition. If unambiguous results cannot be obtained when cockroaches are rendered inactive by means of cold—an ingenious method of escaping the lag of normal sleep—perhaps, taking the cue from Hoagland and French, a greatly increased activity, interpolated immediately after the original learning, might accomplish that result.

If activity, increased greatly over normal, yields clear-cut results, if the retention of cockroaches compulsorily exercised is found to be inferior to those normally active—as theory dictates—then it may be worth while to seek some other method than chilling of accomplishing Hunter's desired end; namely, 'of placing and of holding the S's physiological processes in a quiescent state during the period of rest interpolated between learning and relearning.'

This study is accordingly divided into two parts. The first, Experiment I, deals with the effect of compulsory physical activity upon learning and

5

retention; and the second, Experiment II, with the effect of inactivity upon those processes.

Experiment I. The effect of compulsory physical activity upon learning and retention

The effect of interpolated activity upon retention in animals has been extensively studied and the results on the whole indicate slight evidence of retroactive inhibition. Hunter,[16] Hunter and Yarbrough,[17] Webb,[18] and Pechstein,[19] with rats as the experimental animals, reported only a small amount of retroactive inhibition; and Brockbank[20] reported none. Ho,[21] to complete the gamut of possibilities, found, with interpolated practice on a different maze, a facilitory effect in the relearning of the original maze. All of these investigations, however, used learning as the interpolated activity.

The effect of forced physical exercise during the interim between learning and relearning was first employed by Corey.[22] Using white rats, he tested the effect of daily exercises in a rotating drum of 1-, 3-, and 5-hr. durations upon learning and relearning of an elevated maze. He found that his experimental animals made in general slightly better—not worse—scores than his controls. Corey's results were confirmed by Gray[23] with white rats and a multiple T-maze. As measured by time-scores, Gray found that forced activity did not have a deleterious effect; and, as measured by error-scores, that it was slightly beneficial.

Although the results of the experiments with animals stand in opposition to the interference or inhibitory theory of forgetting, they are not decisive enough to close the chapter nor even to warrant an unequivocal statement. Further work in this field is still needed.

Subjects

The Ss used in this experiment were American cockroaches, *Periplaneta americana*. They were obtained from the Department of Entomology at Cornell University, and were kept together in three large colonies before individuals were isolated for study. These colonies and also individuals kept in separate jars were housed in a cupboard in the experimenter's room. Room temperature was kept between 25°C and 28°C. Bread-and-water was the diet throughout the experimental period. Care was taken to avoid injury such as broken legs or antennae. Only full-grown Ss, about 3 cm. in body-length, of both sexes, were used.

Apparatus

The apparatus, taken in the main from Hunter, consisted of five separate pieces: (a) a practice-box and (b) a learning-box, both of which were placed side by side in a glass corral (see Fig. 1); (c) a resting-cage; (d) an activity treadmill; and (e) a trapping and transporting device.

(a) Practice-box

The practice-box (B in Fig. 1) was 18 in. long, 3½ in. wide, and 2½ in. high. It was constructed of glass, the inside walls and ends of which were coated with vaseline to discourage the Ss from climbing. If the Ss did succeed in escaping the box they were still confined within the corral, the inside walls of which were also coated with vaseline.

(b) Learning-box

The learning-box (A in Fig. 1) was of the same dimensions and construction as the practice-box. It differed from the practice-box, however, in two respects. One end was made into a dark compartment, 4 in. in length, and the remaining part was divided longitudinally by a glass partition, 8 in. long and 2½ in. high. The partition was placed 1½ in. from the dark compartment. It thus extended to within 4½ in. of the opposite end wall. The partition and all of the inside walls were greased with vaseline. An electrical punishment-grill, made of brass strips 2 mm. wide, connected to an inductorium and a 1½-v. battery, was placed on the floor of the dark compartment.

The glass corral was illuminated by a single 75-w. bulb suspended 30 in. above its floor. The floor of the dark compartment was in consequence cast in a sharply contrasting dark shadow.

(c) Resting cage

The Ss were kept in the resting cage during the intervals of normal rest. Since the roach is inclined to stay in a corner of a square cage and remain inactive

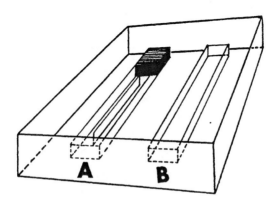

Figure 1 Glass corral showing learning-box (A) and practice-box (B) in position.

for a long period of time, a circular container was chosen to keep the Ss out of corners and normally active during the interval between the learning and relearning. This cage was 8 in. in diameter, and 4 in. in height.

(d) Activity treadmill

The activity treadmill (Fig. 2) was specially designed to exercise S continually during the interpolated interval.[24] The cage, a box made of celluloid, was 5 in. long, 2½ in. wide and 3 in. high. A paper belt, 2½ in. wide and 22½ in. long moved under the bottom of the cage at the rate of 6 r.p.m., *i.e.* 135 in. per min., thus providing a moving floor to the cage. This apparatus as well as the resting cage were placed near the learning apparatus on the same table.

(e) Trapping device

This was a small box made of celluloid to trap and to transport the Ss. A long glass tube, with a piece of cotton wool attached at one end was used to push the S gently into the trapping device or to start it in the learning apparatus.

General method

An S was taken from a colony at a given hour on the first day and put into a separate glass jar which contained bread and water. The jar was numbered and kept in a cupboard. After 24 hrs., S was taken out and put into the practice-box for 10 min. At this time the bodily condition of the roach was

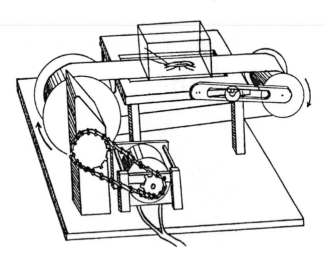

Figure 2 Activity Treadmill.

examined and its strength was tested by a gentle push, and then put back into the jar. At the same hour on the third day the initial learning took place. The method was as follows:

(1) S was put into the practice-box for 10 min. to adapt to the experimental situation. Care was taken not to excite it by rough handling when transported from the jar. The bodily condition and strength were again examined.

(2) S was then put into the learning-box at the corner of the illuminated part. Usually S ran rapidly into the dark compartment. Whenever it entered the dark area, a shock was given immediately by closing the circuit and S ran out. If, after several trials, S did not run voluntarily toward the dark corner it was given a light push and was forced to move. Frequently S stood quietly at the entrance of the dark compartment. In such a case a gentle push again made it either return to the illuminated end or enter the dark corner. Whenever S went as far as the end of the glass partition and turned back without entering the dark corner, the performance was counted as a 'correct' response. The criterion for complete learning was nine correct responses out of ten successive trials, the one used by Hunter.[25]

(3) After the completion of the original learning, S was given intervals of activity or rest according to the following experimental schema. (a) The experimental Ss were put into the forced-activity apparatus for periods of 10, 20 or 30 min. (b) The control Ss were put into the resting cage for similar intervals. No food or water was provided the Ss of either group during their intervals of activity or rest. The illumination was constant during the adaptation, original learning, activity or rest, and relearning period.

(4) Following the activity or rest periods, relearning took place in exactly the same manner as the original learning but without an adaptation-period in the practice-box.

(5) After relearning, S was put back into its separate jar and kept there until the next experimental period.

S's performance at every learning and relearning period was measured in terms (a) of the number of trials required until the learning was complete (excluding the last ten trials); and (b) of the total number of shocks received.

Experiment I consists of three parts; Part A, the Main Experiment, on the effect of forced activity on relearning; and Parts B and C, two problems that arose in connection with the main work. Specifically, Part B is concerned with the effect on retention and relearning of compulsory activity interpolated at different points in the rest-period between learning and relearning;

and Part C, a check experiment, deals with the effect of activity upon learning.

Part A. Retention and relearning after forced activity

Our first and main concern in Experiment I was to discover the effect of compulsory physical activity upon retention and relearning in *Periplaneta americana*. Part A of this study is accordingly devoted to that problem.

Subjects

The number of *S*s used in Part A was 24; 12 male and 12 female. Since Turner[26] reported a sex difference in the capacity of cockroaches to learn, we used the same number of each sex.

Method

Care was taken in planning the procedure to avoid the effects of diurnal variation and of practice. To eliminate diurnal variation the *S*s were divided into morning and night groups. Each group consisted of 6 males and 6 females. As regards the practice effect, Gates and Allee[27] found no evidence of retention from day to day in the learning of a simple maze by American cockroaches. Still, since every *S* in our experiment was tested with 6 different intervals (10-, 20-, and 30-min. of normal activity and 10-, 20,- and 30-min. of compulsory activity) and the learning took place on every other day, a practice effect due to the preceding learning might be expected. In order to counteract this, the rest and activity periods of different durations were alternated according to a planned haphazard order in which every temporal interval of activity and of rest should be alternated and should occur equally often before and after every other interval in the sequence of experiments (see Table I).

Results

The results of the Main Experiment are given in Tables II and III. Table II shows, for the Control and Activity experiments and for every interpolated interval, the average number of trials required and the average number of shocks received by the *S*s in the original learning and the relearning of the avoidance response to darkness. The range of the individual measures and the S.D. of their averages are also given. Table III shows the Saving Scores[28] calculated from number of trials and of shocks for the Control and Activity Experiments at every relearning interval together with the Scores of Relative Retroaction.[29]

Table I Schedule of main experiments showing for every *S* the order in which the interpolated intervals of rest and activity were employed

Sequence	*S*	Experimental period					
		1	*2*	*3*	*4*	*5*	*6*
RRRAAA	1	10R	20R	30R	10A	20A	30A
	2	20R	30R	10R	20A	30A	10A
	3	30R	10R	20R	30A	10A	20A
RARARA	4	10R	10A	30R	30A	20R	20A
	5	20R	20A	10R	10A	30R	30A
	6	30R	30A	20R	20A	10R	10A
AAARRR	7	10A	20A	30A	10R	20R	30R
	8	20A	30A	10A	20R	30R	10R
	9	30A	10A	20A	30R	10R	20R
ARARAR	10	10A	10R	30A	30R	20A	20R
	11	20A	20R	10A	10R	30A	30R
	12	30A	30R	20A	20R	10A	10R
RRRAAA	13	10R	30R	20R	10A	30A	20A
	14	20R	10R	30R	20A	10A	30A
	15	30R	20R	10R	30A	20A	10A
RARARA	16	10R	10A	20R	20A	30R	30A
	17	20R	20A	30R	30A	10R	10A
	18	30R	30A	10R	10A	20R	20A
AAARRR	19	10A	30A	20A	10R	30R	20R
	20	20A	10A	30A	20R	10R	30R
	21	30A	20A	10A	30R	20R	10R
ARARAR	22	10A	10R	20A	20R	30A	30R
	23	20A	20R	30A	30R	10A	10R
	24	30A	30R	10A	10R	20A	20R

(1) Effect of forced activity

These tables reveal that forced activity had, at every time-interval employed, a detrimental effect upon retention and relearning.[30] In the Control Experiments the average number of trials required and shocks received by the *S*s in relearning is considerably less at every interval than in the original learning, whereas in the Activity Experiments the averages of both measures in relearning are, contrariwise, greater than in the original learning. At the 10-min. interval, for example, the *S*s relearned in the Control Experiments on an average of 3.52 trials and 2.91 shocks whereas in the Activity Experiments they required 25.25 trials and 17.50 shocks. As with the 10-min. interval so also with the others; relearning after forced activity is definitely worse than after equal intervals of normal rest—such as the *S*s were permitted in the control experiments. These results, which are consistent

Table II Average number of trials and of shocks for the control and activity groups

Relearning interval		Control		Activity		Diff.rel.	C.R.
		Learn.	Relearn.	Learn.	Relearn.		
10 min.	Trials	17.43	3.52	16.25	25.25		
	Range	0–49	0–18	0–27	1–59	21.73	6.94
	S.D.	12.45	4.32	10.20	14.33		
	Shocks	13.65	2.91	12.95	17.50		
	Range	0–45	0–9	1–27	2–44	14.59	6.16
	S.D.	8.77	2.46	8.61	11.10		
20 min.	Trials	15.09	4.48	14.92	27.17		
	Range	2–35	0–22	1–37	8–52	22.69	7.88
	S.D.	8.90	4.93	8.79	13.03		
	Shocks	12.00	4.26	11.46	20.13		
	Range	2–26	0–15	2–24	4–38	15.87	8.06
	S.D.	7.00	4.07	6.36	8.38		
30 min.	Trials	17.38	7.21	19.46	31.17		
	Range	2–39	0–25	5–47	14–60	23.96	7.65
	S.D.	11.56	7.72	10.59	12.89		
	Shocks	13.25	5.50	14.15	21.88		
	Range	3–31	0–15	5–32	11–36	16.38	7.58
	S.D.	8.58	4.68	8.80	9.61		

Table III Saving scores and scores of relative retroaction of the control and activity groups computed from table II

Relearning interval	Calculated from	Saving Scores		R.R. Scores
		Control	Activity	
10 min.	Trials	79.80	−55.38	169.27
	Shocks	78.68	−35.14	144.66
20 min.	Trials	70.31	−82.10	216.77
	Shocks	64.50	−75.65	178.13
30 min.	Trials	58.52	−60.17	202.82
	Shocks	58.49	−54.63	194.40

throughout, clearly indicate that the *S*s could not relearn to avoid darkness as readily as they learned it. This result is shown in Table III by the fact that the Saving Scores in the Control Experiments are positive and in the Activity Experiments, negative. The scores of Relative Retroaction (R.R.) show the same result. They are all greater than 100, and the amount they exceed 100 indicates how much relearning is worse than original learning.

(2) Effect of time

The effect of time, that is the effect of the length of the interval interpolated between learning and relearning, is shown in Tables II and III but it is depicted more clearly in Fig. 3. In the Control Experiments the Saving Scores yield curves for trials and for shocks which follow closely the normal curve of forgetting; sharp initial declines which tend to become progressively less. In the Activity Experiments, on the other hand, very different curves are obtained. The Saving Scores, which are negative, yield results which fall for all temporal intervals below the 0% baseline of retention into an area denoted as the detrimental effect on relearning. The curves in this area are not regular. From a detrimental effect of −55.38% for trials and −35.14% for shocks at the 10-min. interval, the curve falls to −82.10% for trials and −75.65% for shocks at the 20-min. interval to rise to −60.17% for trials and −54.63% for shocks at the 30-min. interval. We have no explanation for the irregularity of the activity curves at the 20-min. interval. If, however, the results of one S, which were completely out of line, had been omitted from the computations at the 20-min. activity-interval, the decrement would have been about equal to that of the 30-min. activity-interval. This S learned in one trial but required 25 trials to relearn after 20 min. of activity. It may have been unusually excited upon that occasion, as its results on the other days are in line.

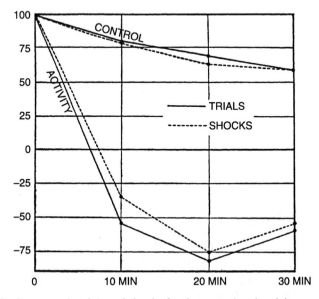

Figure 3 Saving scores in trials and shocks for the control and activity experiments.

(3) Behavior during learning and relearning

Before discussing the causes of the marked decrement in relearning in the Activity Experiments, a general description of the Ss' behavior in the various situations is given to show the qualitative changes in their responses. The Ss' behavior in the original learning can be divided into the following stages.

(A) ORIGINAL LEARNING

(i) Initial stage. After being placed in the learning-box, S usually runs immediately into the dark compartment only to rush out on being shocked. After a short pause at the illuminated end, S repeats this sequence of acts. As a rule this stage is characteristic of the first 5–10 trials. There is, of course, no correct response in this period.

(ii) Intermediate stage. Following the rather vigorous reactions in the initial stage, S is less active, resting for a long time in the illuminated part of the box and going forward slowly along the alley toward the dark end. At the same time, S begins actively to touch the floor and walls with its antennae. It stops at the entrance of the dark compartment, using its antennae actively to explore the floor and walls. Then after a short pause S puts one of its front legs on the floor of the compartment, receives a slight shock, steps back a little and then enters again. Following a few of these responses it finally turns back to the illuminated end and stays there again for a long time. Thereafter it moves very slowly, even when it gets a light push with a piece of cotton.

(iii) Final stage. At the final stage S goes slowly until it reaches the dark compartment and then turns back slowly without entering. Once it learns to avoid darkness it rarely fails on later trials. This sudden insightful learning is characteristic of the original learning.

(B) RELEARNING AFTER REST-INTERVALS

Relearning after the intervals of rest is essentially the same in pattern as the first learning, except that the initial stage consists of only few trials and S reaches the final stage quickly after a short period in the intermediate stage. A perfect retention without the first two stages was also observed in several cases. A typical record is shown for S 6 in Fig. 4A. In the first experiment with this S the final stage was quickly reached and learning occurred suddenly in an insightful manner. S's behavior for the first eight trials was of the type of the initial stage, and the next four of the intermediate. Relearning after a 30-min. interval of rest was completed with only four trials. Of these, the behavior of this S for the first two trials was of the type of the initial stage and for the next two was of the intermediate stage.

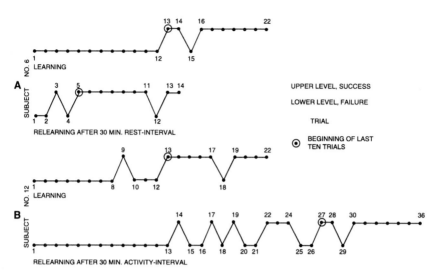

Figure 4 Typical records of learning and relearning in the control and activity experiments (A, Control experiments; B, Activity experiments.)

(C) RELEARNING AFTER ACTIVITY-INTERVALS

Relearning after intervals of activity showed a quite different picture. Three stages, however, were again distinguished.

(i) Initial stage. After being transferred from the activity treadmill to the learning-box, *S* shows a marked restlessness and runs immediately into the dark compartment. After receiving a shock it turns back to the illuminated part of the box with such speed that it often bumps into the end wall. This violent response is repeated many times almost without pause. The initial stage in relearning is always longer than that of the original learning. As shown for *S* 12 in Fig. 4 B, 13 trials were necessary for this *S* to reach the first correct response. The behavior of this *S* throughout these trials was of the initial stage. In extreme cases of slow learning, the number of trials in the initial stage may amount to 30. In these instances there are long pauses among the later trials. In spite of the violent responses, the *S*s show no apparent weakness. Their behavior may be characterized as "excessive irrit-ability"; defecation and urination were often observed. They also become very sensitive to external stimuli such as light touches or accidental air-currents.

(ii) Intermediate stage. In the intermediate stage, *S* becomes less irritable and runs toward the dark corner with a slower speed than in the initial stage and stops at the entrance of the dark compartment. Then it either runs into the compartment or turns back suddenly to the illuminated

15

end. Thus the correct and incorrect responses are often alternated until the final stage is reached. For example, in the first experiment with S 12, the intermediate stage began with the fourteenth and ended at the twenty-sixth trial.

(iii) Final stage. The final stage is essentially the same as that of the original learning, except that S is often very active and the response of avoiding the dark corner is made by a sudden turning back.

Discussion of results

As indicated in the above description of the Ss' behavior in the relearning situation, certain physiological effects caused by the interpolated exercise seem to be responsible for the greatly impaired capacity to relearn. Although a marked retardation of learning and relearning of a simple maze after cutting the antennae was reported by Brecher[31] with cockroaches, this explanation, since our animals retained their antennae intact, cannot serve in the present experiment. About all that is known positively concerning the effect of activity upon the bodily condition of insects is that there is an acceleration of metabolism, an increase in heart beat and in oxygen intake.[32] We may of course assume that an accompanying change must also take place in the nervous system of the animal.

Other explanations in terms of fatigue or emotion may, however, be considered. Since there was no apparent sign of weakness or slowness in the Ss' movements after the activity-intervals, the detrimental effect on relearning cannot be laid to the effect of fatigue. This is obvious in the initial stage of the relearning because the animal is still very active. The fluctuating (trial-and-error) character of the learning curve, as in our intermediate stage—shown in the relearning of S 12 (Fig. 4 B)—was interpreted by Szymanski[33] as the result of fatigue. He likened this fluctuation in the learning-curve to the fluctuation in Kraepelin's work-curve, and ascribed it to an antagonism between fatigue and the learning capacity. Apart from the question of the validity of this interpretation, the fluctuation in our experiment seems rather to be due to the gradual decline of the excessive irritability of the initial stage during the course of the intermediate stage. If there is no gradual decline in the activity of the animal, the fluctuation does not occur. This can be seen in the following extreme case. S 23 showed a marked restlessness throughout the relearning-period and there was only one correct response in the intermediate stage. Thus the relearning curve of this S showed no typical fluctuation, and the decline in activity took place rather abruptly. We cannot, therefore, explain the result by fatigue.

We are also not justified in explaining the retardation of the relearning in terms of emotion. A retroactive inhibition caused by interpolated emotional disturbances in human Ss was reported by Tait,[34] Harden,[35] Frank and Ludvigh,[36] and White.[37] May we assume that the excessive activity of our animals was emotional? The word "emotion" was indeed used by Piéron[38] to designate the excited state in insects due to an "excessive discharge of nervous energy." The mechanism underlying the excessive irritability in the lower animals has not, however, been studied enough to justify calling it emotion. We think it safe only to say that marked retardation of relearning after the active intervals was caused by physiological changes which explain the excessive and gradually diminishing irritability throughout the relearning period.

If this be true, we might expect that a recovery period interpolated after the forced activity and before the relearning might reduce the physiological after-effect upon the relearning. We can not, however, guess how long the recovery period would have to be. This possibility can be tested by measuring the relearning scores after an activity period interpolated at different points during the interval between the first learning and relearning. This would result in variable intervals between the activity and relearning periods. Part B, which follows, was conducted to test this possibility.

Part B. Retention after intervals of activity interpolated at different points in the rest-period

In Part B, five different series of experiments were conducted under conditions set to determine the effect of forced activity interpolated at different points in a 3-hr. period of rest between learning and relearning. The apparatus and procedure, with the exceptions noted below, were the same as described in the Main Experiments.

The specific experimental conditions of Part B, which are graphically shown in Fig. 5, were as follows.

Condition A (control): 10 min. light-adaptation in practice-box; learning to avoid darkness; 3 hr. rest in darkness; 5 min. light-adaptation in practice-box; relearning to avoid darkness.

Condition B: 10 min. light-adaptation in practice-box; learning to avoid darkness; 10 min. in activity-treadmill in darkness; 2 hr. 50 min, rest in darkness; 5 min. light-adaptation; relearning.

Condition C: 10 min. light-adaptation; learning to avoid darkness; I hr. rest in darkness; 10 min. in darkened treadmill; 1 hr. 50 min. rest in darkness; 5 min. light-adaptation; relearning.

Condition D: 10 min. light-adaptation; learning; 2 hr. rest in darkness; 10 min. in darkened treadmill; 50 min. rest in darkness; 5 min. light-adaptation; relearning.

Condition E: 10 min. light-adaptation; learning; 2 hr. 50 min. rest in darkness; 10 min. in darkened treadmill; 5 min. light-adaptation; relearning.

The Ss in all five series were given, at the beginning of the experiments, a 10-min. period of light-adaptation in the practice-box so as to accustom

17

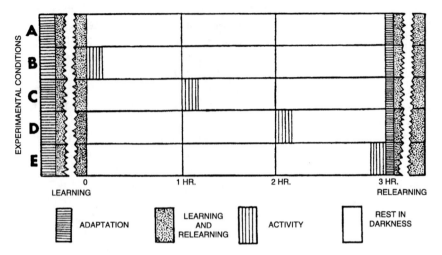

Figure 5 Graphic representation of the experimental conditions in Part B. This diagram shows the position in the 3-hr. interval between learning and relearning at which the 10-min. period of activity was interpolated. Condition A in which forced activity did not occur was the control.

them to the illumination of the learning-experiments. Following learning, the *S*s in all the series spent the 3-hr. intervals before relearning in darkness. They were placed in darkness during that interval so as to avoid that long exposure to light and the unknown effects that it might have upon them. Except for the 10-min. activity-intervals in a darkened treadmill, they spent the 3-hr. interval in a rest-cage in a dark cupboard. After this interval and before the relearning experiments, the *S*s were again given a period of light-adaptation in the practice-box. This period was 5 min. in length. It was shorter than the light-adaptation period at the beginning of the experiment because the *S*s came to it with a shorter period of darkness-adaptation—specifically 3 hr.—whereas when brought to the experiment they had had many hours and even days of darkness-adaptation. In any case the 5-min. re-adaptation period to light sufficed.

Subjects

In Part B, 60 *S*s, divided into five groups of 12 each, were used. Every group contained 6 males and 6 females. The experiments with them were, with a few exceptions, conducted during the afternoon. A few *S*s were run at 11 A.M. and at 5 P.M.

Results

The results of Part B are given in Tables IV, V, and VI. Table IV shows the average number of trials required and shocks received by the members of

18

Table IV Average number of trials and of shocks for the various experimental conditions

	A (Control)		B		C		D		E	
	Learn	Re-learn	Learn	Re-learn	Learn	Re-learn	Learn	Re-learn	Learn	Re-learn
Trials	17.50	8.92	18.58	12.33	17.75	9.42	18.17	13.25	16.92	17.00
Range	9–27	5–19	12–28	7–19	9–32	3–19	11–29	5–18	7–27	6–28
S.D.	4.27	3.09	5.39	3.09	6–18	4.35	4.54	4.03	4.97	6.90
Shocks	14.34	7.58	16.67	11.58	16.08	8.33	16.08	12.08	14.75	15.83
Range	8–27	3–19	9–25	7–17	10–30	4–15	7–29	6–18	6–25	5–26
S.D.	4.87	3.68	4.52	2.99	5.48	3.40	6.63	4.44	4.85	6.51

every group of *S*s in the learning and relearning experiments, together with the ranges of the individual scores and their S.D. Table V gives the average Savings Scores for trials and shocks for every experimental condition, their S.D., and their Scores of Relative Retroaction. Table VI gives the difference, and its significance, between the Saving Scores of every two of the five experimental conditions used. Since the number of *S*s used in each Condition was small, *i.e.* 12, the significance of these differences is expressed in terms of Fisher's t,[39] instead of the C.R.

As these tables show, the control group of *S*s, *i.e.* those serving under Condition A, relearned with a saving of approximately 46% in trials and 45% in shocks. These results stand in close agreement with those obtained at the 10-, 20-, and 30-min. intervals of normal rest in the Main Experiments (see Tables II and III, and Fig. 3, pp. 11, 12, and 13). They show a proportional drop in the curve of forgetting which conforms to the results of previous investigations. The results of this group serve very well, therefore, as a basis of comparison of the results of four other groups. The behavior of the *S*s in the relearning-situation after the rest-period was the same as in the original learning.

A comparison of the results of the other Conditions with those of Condition A reveals that the 10-min. period of forced activity was least deleterious to relearning in Condition C, most deleterious in Condition E, and inter-mediate in its effect in Conditions B and D (see Fig. 6). In Condition C, in which the period of activity was interpolated 1 hr. after learning and 1 hr. 50 min. before relearning, there was little if any effect. Indeed, from the Saving Scores for both trials and shocks given in Table V, Condition C is shown to be superior to Condition A. The differences in both measures of performance are so slight, however, that they are, as the *t* values in Table V show, insignificant. The behavior of the *S*s in relearning in Condition C was

19

Table V Saving scores and scores of relative retroaction for every one of the various experimental conditions (Not computed from Table IV but from the average of the individual saving scores.)

Calculated from		A (Control)		B		C		D		E	
		Saving	R.R.	Saving	R.R.	Saving	R.R.	Saving	R.R.	Saving	R.R.
Trials	Av.	46.46	0.00	30.33	34.72	47.92	-3.14	27.95	39.84	1.94	6.47
	S.D.	13.44		20.10		14.95		11.61		31.32	
Shocks	Av.	45.24	0.00	26.98	40.36	48.27	-6.70	23 67	47.07	-4.91	110.85
	S.D.	19.74		21.37		13.01		14.18		35.03	

Table VI Significance of difference between the saving scores of the various experimental conditions (Computed by Fisher's *t*)

Conditions	Trials		Shocks	
	Diff.	*t*	*Diff.*	*t*
A-B	16.13	2.21	18.26	2.08
A-C	−1.46	0.24	−3.03	0.42
A-D	18.51	**3.45***	21.57	**3.07**
A-E	44.52	**4.33**	50.15	**4.14**
B-C	17.59	**2.33**	21.29	**2.82**
B-D	2.38	0.34	3.31	0.43
B-E	28.39	**2.53**	31.89	**2.58**
C-D	16.97	**2.97**	24.60	**4.24**
C-E	45.98	**4.00**	53.18	**4.72**
D-E	26.01	**2.58**	28.58	**2.51**

* This and the following values in boldfaced type are statistically significant.

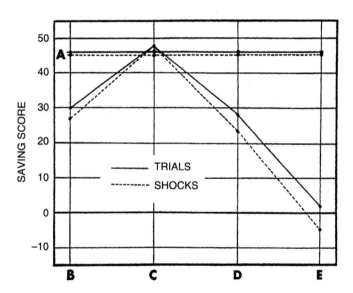

(The horizontal lines running across the diagram near the top represent the results for Condition A.)

Figure 6 Saving scores for trials and shocks in the various conditions of Part B.

not unlike that in Condition A. Insofar as this study is concerned, the *S*s under Conditions A and C yielded the same results.

In Condition B, in which the activity was interpolated immediately after learning, at the beginning of the 3-hr. rest-period, relearning was affected adversely. The Saving Scores for trials and shocks are 30% and 27%

21

respectively as against 46% and 45% in Condition A. The differences between these Saving Scores, which are 16.13% for trials and 18.26% for shocks, have t values of 2.21 and 2.08 respectively, indicating that these differences would occur about 98 times in 100. There was no appreciable difference, however, between the behavior of the Ss in these two groups in relearning. Because of the long rest after the forced activity (2 hr. 50 min), the Ss in Condition B came to the relearning period in approximately the same physical state as those in Condition A.

Condition D showed a more marked effect upon relearning. Though the forced activity was not given until 2 hr. after learning, the Saving Score for trials and shocks dropped to approximately 28% and 24% respectively. The differences between these scores and those made by the control Ss (Condition A) are 18.51% for trials and 21.57% for shocks and their t values indicate that they are statistically significant. Though coming to the relearning-situation with only 50 min. of rest, the Ss in Condition D showed no restlessness nor signs of excitement. Their behavior was again similar to that of the controls. One of the 12 Ss serving under this Condition, did, however, show the fluctuation in its relearning, the trial-and-error pattern, that was observed in all the activity groups in the Main Experiment (see Fig. 4B).

In Condition E, in which the 10-min. period of forced activity was given immediately before relearning at the end of the 3-hr. rest-period, there was a marked deterioration in the Ss' ability to learn. On an average, as Table IV shows, the Ss required more trials and shocks to relearn the avoidance response to darkness than to learn it: 17.00 trials and 15.83 shocks in relearning as against 16.92 trials and 14.75 shocks in learning. The average individual Saving Scores (Table V) was 1.94% for trials and −4.91% for shocks; 44.52% and 50.15% respectively smaller than the Saving Scores of Condition A, the control. The t values of these differences (Table VI), 4.33 and 4.14 respectively, show that the differences have high statistical significance. The behavior of the Ss in Condition E was also different from that in Condition A. They were on the whole more active in the relearning-situation but still they did not show excitement nor irritability such as the Ss in the Main Experiment showed in their relearning after activity. Three of the 12 Ss serving in Condition E relearned in the trial-and-error pattern, that is they fluctuated for a considerable number of trials between success and failure.

In addition to showing the difference and their t values between the Saving Scores of Condition A and the other four experimental Conditions, Table VI gives the differences and their t values between every two of the other four Conditions: B, C, D, and E. Except for the differences between Conditions B and D, which are small and statistically insignificant both for trials and shocks, all the differences are large and statistically significant. They corroborate among themselves the results obtained from their comparison with the control experiments under Condition A.

Discussion

Contrary to expectation that relearning would be improved as the recovery-period following forced activity was lengthened, the results of Part B indicate that the relation between the temporal position of the interpolated activity in the rest-period and relearning is not a simple one. So far as the results of Conditions C, D, and E are concerned, they may be explained in terms of the expected relation between the physiological after-effects of forced activity and the length of the recovery-period.

The poor relearning-scores of the Ss in Condition E may, for example, be explained as being due to the physiological changes induced by the forced exercise that was interpolated immediately before relearning. Although Whitely[40] found that physical exercise did not have a detrimental effect on relearning in human Ss, it is doubtful whether the 5-min. period of calisthenics which he employed had as great a physiological after-effect as did our 10-min. period of forced activity. A detrimental effect of activity interpolated just before relearning has, moreover, been reported by Whitely[41] himself, and by Houlahan,[42] Müller,[43] Bunch,[44] Newman,[45] Sisson,[46] and Maeda.[47] In these corroborating studies, however, we must take into account, as Skaggs has pointed out, the fact that the interpolated task was always of the same general nature as the original learning, hence "there is always the possibility that the degree of similarity may have played some part."[48] That the interpolated activity had a physiological effect is borne out, however, by the differences in the behavior of the Ss in Condition E and the control group (Condition A) in the relearning situation.

The results of Condition D may be similarly explained. The Ss were still affected physiologically by the forced activity when they came to relearning but to a lesser degree, because of the 50-min. recovery-period, than the Ss in Condition E. So also for Condition C. Once again it may be said that the Ss were affected physiologically by the forced activity but in this instance the effect was obscured by the rest-period (1 hr. 50 min.), which was sufficiently long for them completely to recover.

With the results of Condition B, however, this explanation fails. If relearning varied directly as the length of the recovery period, Condition B should yield better not worse results than Condition C. We must, therefore, look for some other explanation. Proximity to original learning may suffice.

The detrimental effect upon relearning of an activity interpolated immediately after original learning was first reported by Müller and Pilzecker.[49] Their results showed that the earlier an activity was interpolated the greater the degree of retroactive inhibition. From this they concluded that following original learning there was a gradual diminution of the physiological processes which served to intensify the established associations and further that these processes were inhibited by the interpolation of activity when given immediately after original learning. Retention is consequently worse when original learning is immediately followed by an interpolated activity than when there is a normal interval of rest between the original learning and relearning. According to their results, the detrimental effect of an interpolated activity upon relearning will vary as the interval between original learning and the interpolated activity is increased. This theory of retroactive inhibition, called the perseveration theory, was experimentally corroborated by Heine,[50] Skaggs,[51] White,[52] and Sisson.[53]

Since the appearance of Müller and Pilzecker's study and the formulation of the perseveration-theory of retroactive inhibition, many conflicting studies and objections to the theory have been published. As mentioned above, some authors found that retroactive inhibition was greater when the activity was interpolated just before relearning than immediately after the original learning. Still other authors[54] have found no consistent differences in the amount of retroactive inhibition with different temporal positions. All of these results, however, involve a possible confusion between the original and the interpolated material at the time of relearning. Thus they cannot be considered as evidence against the consolidation- or perseveration-theory.

The perseveration-theory implies that retroactive inhibition is a function of either the intensity or nearness of the interpolated activity to the original learning. Contrary to this assumption, the studies of Webb,[55] Robinson,[56] McGeoch,[57] Skaggs,[58] Johnson,[59] Gengerelli,[60] and Gibson and Gibson,[61] showed that the similarity between the original and interpolated learning is more important than the intensity of the interpolated activity. As DeCamp[62] suggested, however, the amount of retroactive inhibition due to the similarity factor "would vary directly as the relative identity of the neurological groups" involved in the original and interpolated learning varied. This would mean that the effect of similarity is neurologically similar to that of intensity. Consequently, we need not discard the possibility of the importance of the similarity factor.

The perseveration-theory also implies that a consolidation process lasts a short time after the original learning. This seems to be contradicted by the experiments of Bunch and McTeer,[63] who found retroactive inhibition when the interpolated activity was given 3 weeks after original learning and 3 weeks before relearning. Since, however, these authors used two similar types of stylus mazes in the original and interpolated learning, we might expect a possible confusion at the time of relearning between those two mazes even after the 3-wk. interval. Their results, therefore, can not be considered as crucial evidence against the existence of a consolidation process.

From the above discussion, we may conclude that the interference with the consolidating process by the interpolated activity is a factor in determining the amount of retroactive inhibition. The detrimental effect of the interpolated activity when close to the original learning may, however, depend upon the following conditions. (1) The interpolated activity must be strong enough to involve a general excitement. For example, White[64] showed that a detrimental effect upon retention of electric shock, given during the interval between learning and relearning, varied directly as the 'emotional' disturbances, measured by the galvanic skin-resistance, increased. (2) Original learning must not be too well established. When *S* overlearns, the detrimental effect may not be as great as when *S* barely learns. In our experiment, the 10-min. activity was strong enough and the original learning was not overlearned. Consequently a marked detrimental effect of the interpolated activity was to be expected. Since the neural mechanism underlying the consolidation process has not yet been directly demonstrated, the present interpretation is only tentative.

Interpretation

In the light of the above discussion, the results of the present study are interpreted as follows.

(1) We assume that two factors X and Y determine the retroactive inhibition; that X acts as an "anti-consolidation" factor, and that Y appears as excitement or irritability. Since the interpolated activity in our study is a non-learning exercise, the similarity factor need not be considered.

(2) Factor X is assumed to become less effective as the interval between the first learning and relearning is increased, and Factor Y also becomes less effective as the recovery-period is prolonged.

(3) Factor X must be strongest in Condition B where the interpolated activity was introduced immediately after the first learning. The poor relearning under that condition may be due to this effect alone, since there is a long recovery-period and since Factor Y is negligible.

(4) Factor X is not effective 1 hr. after the first learning because the process of consolidation is complete by this time. Furthermore, the 1-hr. 50-min. recovery-period is sufficient to prevent the action of Factor Y. The relearning under Condition C is, therefore, about the same as that under normal conditions.

(5) Factor Y is effective when the recovery period is reduced to 50 min. and its strength at that point (Condition D) may be as great as the maximal strength of Factor X at Condition B. The relearning scores under Condition D are, therefore, about the same as those of Condition B. There is, of course, no effect of Factor X.

(6) Factor Y is great when the activity was interpolated at the end of the recovery period and its strength is far greater than the maximal strength of Factor X at Condition B. A marked retardation under Condition E is due to this effect.

Thus the interpolated activity had a detrimental effect upon relearning when the interval between the first learning and relearning is filled with activity as in the Main Experiment, where both Factors X and Y act together, and also when the activity-period is given at certain points during the interval as in the present experiment.

Since the Ss made a worse score in the relearning than in the original learning in Part A, it is obvious that the interpolated activity had a detrimental effect not only upon retention but also upon the ability to learn.

Part C. Effect of forced activity upon learning

The experiments in Part C of this study were conducted to determine to what extent the activity forced upon our Ss affected their ability to learn. The results of Part A, and those of Condition E in Part B, showed unquestionably that forced activity affected relearning; as the Ss in those experiments required more trials and shocks to relearn the avoidance of darkness than they did in the original learning—which was accomplished before the activity was forced upon them. We wished in Part C specifically to compare learning before with learning after a 10-min. period of forced activity in our treadmill.

Method and procedure

The apparatus and procedure were the same as those employed in Parts A and B of this study. Two experimental conditions, Conditions F and G, were used. In Condition F, forced activity (10 min. in the treadmill, running 135 in. per min.) was given the Ss immediately before being placed in the learning-box. They were not permitted a recovery-period. In Condition G, the forced activity was given them 50 min. before the beginning of the learning experiments. For control, that is for learning without previous activity, we used the results of the 60 Ss in Part B and of the first experiments with the 24 Ss in Part A.[65] These 84 Ss, as it will be recalled, learned to avoid darkness before they were subjected to forced activity. The detailed procedures used in the control and experimental conditions were as follows.

Control: 10 min. light-adaptation in practice-box; learning to avoid darkness.

Condition F: 10 min. light-adaptation in practice-box; 10 min. activity in treadmill; learning to avoid darkness. The illumination was constant throughout this Condition.

Condition G: 10 min. light-adaptation in practice-box; 10 min. activity in treatmill; 50-min. recovery-period spent in rest-cage in dark cupboard; 5 min. light-adaptation; learning to avoid darkness.

Subjects

In Condition F, 6 Ss were used: 3 male and 3 female. In Condition G, there were 12 Ss, 6 male and 6 female. The experiments under both conditions were conducted during the early afternoon.

Results

The results of Part C are shown in Tables VII and VIII. Table VII gives the average number of trials required and shocks received by the various groups of Ss (the Control, and those serving under Conditions F and G) in learning to avoid darkness, and Table VIII gives the differences among these three groups together with Fisher's *t*-values showing their statistical significance.

As these tables show, the average number of trials and shocks required by the Control group of Ss to learn the avoidance response to darkness was considerably smaller than the average number required by either of the groups given a 10-min. period of forced activity. The learning performance averaged 18.91 trials and 16.00 shocks for the Control group as against 33.50 trials and 28.83 shocks for the Ss in Condition F and 23.41 trials and 21.92 shocks for those in Condition G. These numerical differences among the three groups are parallelled by behavioral differences. The Control Ss came

Table VII Average number of trials and of shocks for the various experimental groups in original learning

| | Condition | | |
	Control (84Ss)	F(6Ss)	G(12Ss)
Trials	18.91	33.50	23.41
Range	6–42	28–41	14–30
S.D.	6.21	4.11	5.74
Shocks	16.00	28.83	21.92
Range	5–32	20–34	13–28
S.D.	6.28	4.64	5.63

Table VIII Significance of differences between the number of trials and of shocks for the various experimental groups (Computed by Fisher's *t*)

| | Trials | | Shocks | |
Groups	Diff.	t	Diff.	t
Control-F	14.59	**7.44***	12.83	**5.86**
Control-G	4.50	1.69	5.92	2.23
F-G	10.09	**3.99**	6.91	**2.58**

* This and the following values in boldface type are statistically significant.

27

to the learning experiment, after 10 min. in the adaptation-box, in a relatively unexcited condition, as described above (pp. 14–15). The *S*s in Conditions F and G were, however excited and irritable, and those in Condition F to a higher degree than those in Condition G. All the *S*s in Condition F evinced the trial-and-error type of learning, *i.e.* fluctuation between success and failure and the gradual elimination of the failures, and only 3 of the 12 *S*s in Condition G evinced it.

As the differences among the numerical averages of performance are statistically significant to a high degree (see Table VIII), and as those differences are parallelled by behavioral differences, we feel justified in concluding: (1) that forced activity given as long as 50 min. before learning affects adversely the American cockroach's ability to learn; and (2) that the effect of the activity varies inversely with the length of the recovery period. The second conclusion is based upon the fact that the averages in Condition F, in which the activity occurred immediately before learning, are larger than those in Condition G, in which there was a 50-min. recovery period; and that the differences between those averages (see Table VIII) are statistically significant.

Discussion

As the results of Part C show, forced activity preceding learning has a detrimental effect upon the *S*s' ability to learn. Two possible causes may be assumed to explain this effect.

(1) The increase in the strength of the photo-negative tendency might be brought about by certain physiological changes resulting from the preceding activity. Szymanski[66] found that some insects and other lower animals showed a stronger tropistic reaction when they were in heightened activity, and suggested that this result might be due to an increased sensitivity. According to Brecher,[67] who studied the spatial orientation in the American cockroach with the visual organ removed, the photo-negative tendency depends mainly on the photo-sensitivity of the whole body-surface. If this is true, it is probable that the physiological changes due to the activity might so affect the body-surface that the photo-negative tendency would be increased. Although there is no evidence of this possibility, we need not discard it.

(2) The excessive irritability might hinder the establishment (fixation) of the correct response. Testing the learning capacity of the goldfish, canary, white mouse, and dog, Szymanski[68] found that the more active the animals were at the time of learning, the slower the learning. Similarly, Higginson[69] and Gagné and Graham[70] reported a retardation of the learning in rats when they were excited before the learning started. These results may, as Hunt[71] has suggested, be due to the interference of the uncoördinated

responses brought about by the preceding excitement. Our results may also be interpreted in the same way.

These two causes—an increased photo-negative tendency and the excessive irritability—may combine to give rise to a marked retardation in learning and relearning. Excessive irritability seems, however, to be the more important.

General discussion of the results of Experiment I

Since our Ss' ability to learn in Part C was affected by forced activity, the results at the relearning-period in Parts A and B were also affected. If we determine—as is common practice in experiments involving diurnal variations in learning—the deterimental effect of forced activity upon the ability to form associations (*i.e.* to learn), and make the proper correction at the relearning-period, we should be able to state definitely what part of the loss at relearning was due to forgetting (loss in retention), and what part was due to the decreased ability to learn. One learning-trial before forced activity may, as far as forming associations is concerned, be worth several trials after that activity.

The Control Ss in Part C learned in 18.91 trials, the Ss in Condition F learned immediately after a 10-min. period of forced activity in 33.50 trials. If the effect of the activity be computed by the formula: 100 (C—A)/C, in which C is the average number of trials required by the Control Ss to learn, and if A is the average number required by the Activity Ss, then we should obtain a value which would enable us to make comparisons directly with the Saving Scores in the relearning experiments. In this particular case the "activity-effect" is −77.15%. If the effect of activity were the only determining factor present in the relearning-experiments after the 10-min. activity-period in Part A, then the Ss in that part of the study should show a similar value in their average Saving Score. As Table II shows, however, their Saving Score is −55.38%. The Ss were not so adversely affected in that experiment by forced activity as they should have been. Something, which we believe to be retention, alleviated their loss by 21.77%. In the Control experiments at the 10-min. interval in Part A, the Ss relearned with a saving of 79.80% (see Table II), which may be regarded, for the present at least, as the retention-score, as the Ss were not forcibly exercised during that interval. If these assumptions are sound, then the difference between the retention-score of the Control experiments (79.80%) and the Activity experiments (21.77%), *i.e.* 58.03%, would represent the detrimental effect of forced activity upon retention. In this particular case 20.20% is the loss due to normal activity (100% −79.80%, the retention-score in the Control Experiment); 58.03% is the loss in retention due to the detrimental effect of forced activity; making a total of 78.23%. The difference between this value and the total loss sustained

(155.38%) is 77.15%, which is the loss due to the decreased ability of the Ss to learn immediately after forced activity.

Since we do not know the effect of 20 and 30 min. of forced activity upon learning, similar corrections cannot be made for the 20- and 30-min. activity-intervals in Part A.

A similar correction may, however, be made in the results under Condition D of Part B by a comparison with the results under Condition G of Part C. The forced activity in both of these Conditions was followed by a 50-min. recovery-period and a 5-min. light-adaptation period. The "activity-effect" computed by the formula suggested above from the average trial-scores of the Control Ss and those of Condition G (Table VII) is −23.79%. If the effect of activity were the only determining factor in the relearning scores in Condition D, the Ss serving under it should show a similar decrement in their average Saving Score. Their Saving Score, however, is 27.95% for trials (Table V). The difference between the "activity" value and the Saving Score, i.e. 51.74%, is the true retention-score at Condition D. This score is not significantly different from the Saving Score of the Control group in Part B and indicates that retention itself is not impaired by forced activity introduced 50-min. before relearning.

As mentioned in the discussion of the results in Experiment B, we assumed Factors X ("anti-consolidation") and Y (irritability) in the detrimental effect of activity upon relearning. We may consider Factor X as responsible for the impairment of retention itself, and Factor Y for the decrement in the learning capacity. If that is the case, the detrimental effect of activity on learning demonstrated in Experiment C is due to Factor Y alone. Consequently, the correction we made for the relearning-score in the above discussion is to exclude the decrement due to Factor Y from the total amount of decrement in relearning due to both Factors X and Y. Thus we obtain the detrimental effect of Factor X alone, i.e. the effect on retention itself.

If a forced activity interpolated between learning and relearning has a detrimental effect upon retention and relearning, what is the effect of normal activity during the rest-interval? Since the Ss are active during the normal rest-period, this activity might also interfere with retention and relearning. If we could, as McGeoch suggested, introduce a "psychological vacuum or a period of complete absence of activity"[72] between original learning and relearning, we might expect perfect retention, as Jenkins and Dallenbach's theory implies. Experiment II was introduced to test this possibility.

Experiment II. Effect of inactivity upon learning and retention

In Experiment I we discovered that activity forced upon Ss had, in comparison with Ss normally at rest, a detrimental effect upon learning and retention. Since the Ss normally at rest engaged in some activity, our comparison was between much and little activity. Does the little activity have an effect? If we could discover some means of producing quiescence during the rest-interval between learning and relearning that would not at the same time be deleterious to the physical organism, we would have not only an answer to that simple question but crucial evidence for or against the Jenkins-Dallenbach hypothesis that "forgetting . . . is a matter of interference, inhibition, or obliteration of the old [associations and impressions] by the new."[73] The present study is concerned with that problem. We wished specifically to determine what effect, in comparison with normally resting Ss, inactivity has upon learning and retention; that is, what is the difference between a "little" activity and none?

As mentioned above in the historical review (pp. 1–4), several attempts have been made with low temperatures and various anesthetics to induce a state of quiescence during the interval between learning and relearning. All of them, however, are subject, as we pointed out above, to the criticism that other effects in addition to quiescence were induced which were still effective at the time of relearning. Temperature, anesthetics, and drugs are definitely not to be considered. Some method must be discovered of inducing an inactive state without producing an abnormal S. The obvious condition is natural sleep, such as has been used with human Ss.[74]

Many methods of inducing sleep or a sleep-like condition were tried and discarded. For example, S was turned on its back and held in that position until it became quiet. It moves its legs vigorously in that condition for an indefinite length of time, and after the legs become immobile the antennae continue to move for an indeterminate period. The duration of inactivity obtained in this way is not long and it is extremely variable. Moreover, it is doubtful whether we should have a normal S after it had spent a period of from 1–3 hr. on its back.

Working from the well-known fact that insects, when in bodily contact with external objects, tend to become inactive and to remain in the same position for a long period of time (a state of akinesis sometimes regarded as "animal hypnosis"),[75] we finally developed the following method. A small box, approximately 3 in. long, ½ in. high, and ½ in. wide, was lined at the top and bottom with wedges of tissue paper so that the further S crawled into the open end of the box the greater would be its bodily contact.

S was induced to crawl into the box in the following manner. A conical tube of tissue paper was attached to the open end of the box. The box and the S were both placed under a bright light, and S was permitted to enter at its own volition. When it did, it crawled, with antennae folded over its back, as far into the box as it could and then became immobile. When S was in the box, the open end was covered with wire mesh, and the box and insect were placed in a dark cupboard to await the relearning experiment.

With this method, inactivity was induced without difficulty. Care had to be taken not to excite the S. otherwise it will not readily enter the box. When the

S is in the box, it will remain immobile for long periods of time. At the end of the interval of inactivity, *S* may be removed without injury or harm by gently pulling out the tissue paper.

Experiment II, like Experiment I, is divided into three parts. In Part A, we compare the ability of normally active and inactive *S*s to learn and to retain the avoidance response to darkness after intervals of 1, 2, and 3 hr. In Part B, the relearning intervals are extending to 8 and 24 hr. In Part C, a check experiment, the effect of preceding inactivity upon original learning is determined.

Part A. Retention and relearning after short intervals of inactivity

Having devised a method of inducing inactivity in cockroaches (*Periplaneta americana*) that had no deleterious physical after-effects, we sought in Part A of the present study to determine the effect of inactivity upon retention and relearning after intervals of 1, 2, and 3 hr.

Method and procedure

The same method and procedure were used as in Part A of Experiment 1. After a 10-min. adaptation-period in the illuminated practice-box, *S* was transferred to the learning-box. When it had learned to avoid darkness, it was put either in a resting-cage or in an inactivity-box and placed in a dark cupboard. At the end of a predetermined interval, it was transferred for a 5-min. light-adaptation period to the practice-box, and then placed in the learning-box for the relearning experiments.

Subjects

We used 24 *S*s, 12 male and 12 female, in this part of the study. Every *S* served in both the normal rest and the inactivity experiments, performing three experiments (one at each of the three temporal intervals) under each condition. The experiments with the different *S*s were so arranged, as shown in Table IX, as to counterbalance the effects of normal rest and inactivity. To eliminate the effect of diurnal variation, the experiments with half of the *S*s (6 male and 6 female) were conducted in the morning from 8–12 A.M., and half in the evening from 8–12 P.M. The trials with a given *S* were conducted every other day.

Results

(a) Retention and relearning

The numerical results of Part A are given in Tables X and XI. Table X shows the average number of trials and of shocks required by the *S*s in the normal

Table IX Schedule of normal rest and inactivity intervals in hours for Part A or the experiment

(R = Rest; I = Inactivity)

Order	S	Experimental period					
		1st	*2nd*	*3rd*	*4th*	*5th*	*6th*
	1	1 R	2 R	3 R	1 I	2 I	3 I
	2	2 R	3 R	1 R	2 I	3 I	1 I
	3	3 R	1 R	2 R	3 I	1 I	2 I
R I							
	4	1 R	1 I	3 R	3 I	2 R	2 I
	5	2 R	2 I	1 R	1 I	3 R	3 I
	6	3 R	3 I	2 R	2 I	1 R	1 I
	7	1 I	2 I	3 I	1 R	2 R	3 R
	8	2 I	3 I	1 I	2 R	3 R	1 R
	9	3 I	1 I	2 I	3 R	1 R	2 R
I R							
	10	1 I	1 R	3 I	3 R	2 I	2 R
	11	2 I	2 R	1 I	1 R	3 I	3 R
	12	3 I	3 R	2 I	2 R	1 I	1 R
	13	1 R	3 R	2 R	1 I	3 I	2 I
	14	2 R	1 R	3 R	2 I	1 I	3 I
	15	3 R	2 R	1 R	3 I	2 I	1 I
R I							
	16	1 R	1 I	2 R	2 I	3 R	3 I
	17	2 R	2 I	3 R	3 I	1 R	1 I
	18	3 R	3 I	1 R	1 I	2 R	2 I
	19	1 I	3 I	2 I	1 R	3 R	2 R
	20	2 I	1 I	3 I	2 R	1 R	3 R
	21	3 I	2 I	1 I	3 R	2 R	1 R
I R							
	22	1 I	1 R	2 I	2 R	3 I	3 R
	23	2 I	2 R	3 I	3 R	1 I	1 R
	24	3 I	3 R	1 I	1 R	2 I	2 R

and inactivity experiments to learn and to relearn the avoidance response to darkness, together with the differences between their relearning scores and the C.R. of those differences. Table XI shows the saving scores calculated, not from the group averages given in Table X, but from the results of the individual *S*s.

A comparison of the results of the control and of the inactivity experiments given in Table X reveals no significant differences in the number of trials or shocks required to learn the avoidance response to darkness; but in relearning the case is very different. At every relearning interval, the number

Table X Average number of trials and of shocks for the control and inactivity experiments for learning and relearning intervals together with the differences between the relearning results and the C.R. of the differences

Relearning interval		*Control*		*Inactivity*		$Diff_{rel.}$	*C.R.*
		Learn	*Relearn*	*Learn*	*Relearn*		
	Trials	19.38	8.04	18.67	2.33		
	Range	12–43	1–21	7–37	0–7	5.71	4.80
	S.D.	8.69	5.08	7.17	2.61		
1 hr.							
	Shocks	15.26	6.43	15.69	2.63		
	Range	7–41	2–19	7–37	0–7	3.80	4.18
	S.D.	7.83	3.90	6.96	1.93		
	Trials	18.29	9.08	17.79	3.13		
	Range	6–40	2–31	6–40	0–15	5.95	4.25
	S.D.	7.76	5.55	8.08	3.75		
2 hr.							
	Shocks	14.04	7.42	13.63	3.29		
	Range	5–38	2–28	7–39	0–9	4.13	3.36
	S.D.	7.55	5.30	8.30	2.64		
	Trials	18.61	9.87	19.00	3.21		
	Range	12–37	2–23	9–41	0–13	6.66	4.63
	S.D.	6.04	5.66	8.27	3.70		
3 hr.							
	Shocks	13.96	8.13	15.12	3.50		
	Range	7–38	3–22	6–41	0–12	4.63	3.73
	S.D.	6.84	5.08	8.45	2.93		

Table XI Saving scores for the control and inactivity groups together with the differences between the relearning results and the C.R.

Relearning intervals	Calculated from	Control	Inactivity	Diff.	C.R.
1 hr.	Trials	58.74±19.78	88.71±10.75	29.97	6.43
	Shock	56.65±15.60	86.85±9.87	30.20	7.59
2 hr.	Trials	48.13±17.51	85.40±14.37	37.27	7.90
	Shocks	44.02±19.74	77.13±14.25	33.11	6.52
3 hr.	Trials	47.06±17.91	84.36±12.30	37.30	8.11
	Shocks	40.10±23.86	77.15±14.20	37.05	6.39

of trials and shocks is much smaller, and the differences in every instance are statistically significant.

Table XI simply makes these results more precise: the saving scores in the inactivity experiments are greatly superior to those in the control, and the differences in all cases are highly significant. The saving scores of the control experiments (those performed after intervals of normal rest) decline with the length of the interpolated interval, but the scores of the inactivity experiments, particularly at the 2- and 3-hr. intervals, show but little change.

A comparison of the saving scores of the inactivity experiments with those obtained after 10, 20 and 30 min. of normal rest in Part A of Experiment I, reveals that the saving after 3-hr. of inactivity (84.36% for trials and 77.15% for shocks) is of the same order as after 10 min. of normal rest (83.39% for trials and 75.34% for shocks).

(b) Behavior

The *Ss's* behavior after normal intervals of rest was similar to that described in Part A of Experiment I. The three stages observed in original learning were telescoped in relearning. They could be distinguished but in abbreviated form. Their behavior after inactivity intervals was markedly different. They showed neither weakness nor irritability in the relearning experiments. The first behavioral stage was omitted and the second was greatly abbreviated. It was almost as if they had started at the third stage.

Summary and conclusions

(1) Relearning of the darkness-avoidance response after 1-, 2-, and 3-hr. intervals of inactivity was markedly superior to that after corresponding intervals of normal rest.

(2) The relearning scores for the inactivity experiments showed no noticeable decline as the length of the intervals was increased, and they are approximately of the same order as the relearning scores after 10 min. of normal rest.

(3) *Ss* showed neither weakness nor irritability at the time of relearning after intervals of inactivity.

(4) The above results indicate that the inactivity induced by our method has no adverse physiological after-effects at the time of relearning, and may be compared to the state of natural sleep in its favorable effect upon retention and relearning demonstrated in human experiments.

Part B. Retention and relearning after long intervals of inactivity

In the preceding part of this Experiment, the effect of inactivity proved to be favorable for retention and relearning at 1-, 2-, and 3-hr. intervals. In the following part the intervals of inactivity were extended to 8- and 24-hr. in order to determine the effect of these longer intervals.

Subjects

Forty-eight Ss, divided into four groups of 12 each (6 male and 6 female) were used in this part of the experiment. Two of these groups, a control and an experimental, served at each of the two temporal intervals, 8- and 24-hr., which were interpolated between learning and relearning. The control Ss spent these intervals in resting-cages which permitted normal activity, and the experimental Ss in inactivity-boxes which confined them and induced an immobile, sleep-like state.

Method

The method and procedure were the same as in the preceding experiment. The original learning was started about 11 A.M. for both the 8- and 24-hr. intervals. As far as we were able to discern, the experimental Ss remained quietly in the inactivity-box throughout both of these long intervals.

The schedule of events in this part of the study was as follows: 10 min. light-adaptation in practice-box; learning the avoidance response to darkness; 8 or 24 hr. in resting-cage or inactivity box; 10 min. light-adaptation in practice-box; relearning the avoidance response.

During the interpolated intervals, all the Ss, those in the inactivity box as well as in the resting-cage, were placed in a dark cupboard.

Results

(a) Retention and relearning

The numerical results of Part B are given in Tables XII and XIII. Table XII shows the average number of trials and of shocks required in the control and inactivity experiments, together with the differences between their relearning scores and Fisher's t of those differences. Table XIII shows the saving scores, calculated not from Table XII but from the individual scores. The differences between control and inactivity groups and Fisher's t are also given in the same table.

A comparison of the relearning scores for the normal and inactivity groups in Table XII reveals that the number of trials and of shocks required by the inactivity group is much smaller at both the 8- and the 24-hr. intervals

Table XII Average number of trials and of shocks for the control and inactivity groups in Part B, Experiment II

Relearning interval		Control		Inactivity		$Diff_{rel.}$	t
		Learn	Relearn	Learn	Relearn		
8 hr.	Trials	19.83	13.33	20.08	3.42		
	Range	11–31	5–27	10–30	0–9	0.91	4.70
	S.D.	7.88	6.47	7.55	2.63		
	Shocks	17.42	12.17	17.50	4.08		
	Range	7–31	4–27	7–27	1–8	8.09	3.99
	S.D.	7.42	6.35	6.37	2.27		
24 hr.	Trials	19.42	14.25	18.58	4.25		
	Range	12–27	6–25	13–28	1–8	10.00	5.52
	S.D.	4.46	5.42	3.97	2.55		
	Shocks	17.25	12.67	17.25	4.50		
	Range	11–26	6–25	11–27	2–8	8.17	4.67
	S.D.	4.58	5.51	4.14	1.85		

Table XIII Saving scores for the control and inactivity groups in Part B

Relearning intervals	Calculated from	Control	Inactivity	Diff.	t
8 hr.	Trials	33.60±19.17	85.06±9.79	51.46	7.93
	Shocks	30.02±20.11	78.92±6.59	48.90	7.66
24 hr.	Trials	27.92±17.87	75.94±15.39	48.02	7.11
	Shocks	28.07±21.90	72.14±13.06	44.07	5.73

than by the normal group, and further that the differences are statistically significant. Similarly, as shown in Table V, the saving scores for the inactivity group are markedly superior to those of the control group for both intervals and the differences are highly significant.

The saving scores of both control and inactivity groups show a slight decline between the 8- and 24-hr. intervals.

A comparison of the saving scores of this and the preceding part (Part A) reveals that the saving after 24-hr. of inactivity (75.94% for trials and 72.14% for shocks) is slightly inferior to that after 2 hr. of inactivity (85.40% for trials and 77.13% for shocks). A similar comparison with Part A Experiment I reveals that the saving after 24 hr. of inactivity is of the same order as that after 10 min. of normal rest (83.39% for trials and 75.34% for shocks), and is superior to that after 20 min. of normal rest (73.39% for trials

37

and 65.31% for shocks). These comparisons show the marked beneficial effect of the sleep-like state in the inactivity experiments on relearning and retention.

(b) Behavior

The Ss showed neither apparent weakness nor excitement at the time of relearning, and their behavior was the same as in the relearning after the shorter intervals of inactivity in the immediately preceding part (Part A, Experiment II).

Summary and conclusions

(1) Relearning of the avoidance response to darkness after 8- and 24-hour intervals of inactivity was markedly superior to that after corresponding intervals of normal rest.

(2) The relearning scores of both control and inactivity groups showed only a slight decline between the 8- and 24-hr. intervals.

(3) The relearning after 24-hr. of inactivity is but slightly inferior to that after 2-hr., and superior to that after 20 min. of normal rest.

(4) No apparent physiological after-effect was observed in the Ss' behavior at the time of relearning.

(5) The results of Part B indicate that long periods of inactivity have a markedly favourable effect upon retention and relearning.

Part C. Effect of inactivity upon learning

In the preceding divisions (Parts A and B), we have found that the relearning of the darkness-avoidance response, as measured by the saving scores for trials and shocks, was far better after the various intervals of inactivity than after corresponding intervals of normal rest—from 30–37% better at the shorter intervals (1-, 2-, and 3-hr.) to 44–51% at the longer (8- and 24-hr.). These differences may be due entirely to better retention during the intervals of inactivity, but again they might be due, in part at least, to an increased capacity to learn which was produced by the sleep-like state of inactivity that the Ss maintained during the inactivity intervals. That is, the Ss made better records after intervals of inactivity, not because they retained more, but because their capacity to learn had been increased by the sleep-like rest. Recalling the results of the check runs in Experiment I (Part C), in which we found that forced activity had a pronounced deleterious effect upon learning, it seemed desirable to make similar tests in order to determine whether inactivity had, contrariwise, a beneficial effect upon learning. The present experiment was conducted to test this possibility.

Subjects

The Ss were 6 in number; 3 male and 3 female.

Method

The same method and procedure were used as before. Since relearning after intervals of inactivity ranging from 2- to 24-hr. showed no significant difference, a 2-hr. interval of inactivity was used *before original learning*. The schedule of events for this study was as follows: 10 min. light-adaptation; 2 hr. inactivity; 5 min. light-adaptation; learning to avoid darkness.

The Ss were placed in the cupboard during the interval of inactivity. The experiments were conducted in the afternoon for all Ss.

Results

The numerical results are shown in Table XIV. The learning scores in average of trials and of shocks for normal learning are the scores obtained from the learning on the first day of all Ss in this study, 144 in number. As will be seen in this table, the average number of trials required for the learning after the 2-hr. period of inactivity (18.33 ± 4.33) is almost the same as that for the normal learning (19.06 ± 6.31). In number of shocks, the learning is better after the inactive period (14.16 ± 4.38) than under normal conditions (16.48 ± 6.10). Both scores, however, yield differences which are not statistically significant, hence we feel justified in concluding that our sleep-like inactivity has no appreciable effect upon the cockroach's capacity to learn the avoidance response to darkness.

The Ss showed neither weakness nor irritability at the time of learning, *i.e.* after the 2-hr. period of inactivity.

Summary and conclusion

(1) The learning after the 2-hr. period of inactivity is only slightly better than that under normal conditions, and the differences are not significant.
(2) There are no noticeable physiological after-effects at the time of learning after the inactive period.
(3) From the above results we may conclude that the state of inactivity induced before the learning has no noticeable effect, beneficial or other-

Table XIV Average number of trials and of shocks for learning under normal conditions and after a period of inactivity

	Normal (144 Ss)	*Inactivity (12 Ss)*	*Diff.*	*t*
Trials	19.06±6.31	18.33±4.33	0.73	0.52
Shocks	16.48±6.10	14.16±4.318	2.32	1.63

wise, upon the Ss' capacity to learn the avoidance response to darkness, and that the superiority of relearning after intervals of inactivity over relearning after corresponding intervals of normal rest, demonstrated in Parts A and B of Experiment II is, therefore, due mainly to the *beneficial effect of inactivity upon retention.*

Summary and discussion of the results of Experiment II

Experiment II was concerned with the effect of quiescence, that is of a sleep-like state of inactivity, on the retention and relearning of the avoidance response of cockroaches to darkness.

(a) In Part A, we wished to determine the effect for intervals of 1-, 2-, and 3-hr. We found that relearning, after intervals of inactivity, showed a marked and a statistically significant superiority to relearning after corresponding intervals of normal rest. The saving scores for the inactivity experiments were high at the 1-hr. interval (88.71% for trials and 86.85% for shocks), dropped slightly at the 2-hr. interval (85.40 and 77.13), and there was little or no change at the 3-hr. interval (84.36 and 77.15). The differences among those scores, however, are not statistically significant. The scores at all those intervals are approximately of the same order as those after 10-min. of normal rest (83.39 and 75.34)—Part A, Experiment I. In the control, the scores showed a sharp drop at the 1-hr. interval (58.74 and 56.65), a further decline at the 2-hr. interval (48.13 and 44.02), and a lesser decline at the 3-hr. interval (47.06 and 40.10).

(b) In Part B, the intervals were extended to 8- and 24-hr. to test the effect of long intervals of inactivity. Saving scores for the inactive groups were markedly superior to those for the control groups at both intervals, and the differences have high statistical significance. The 8-hr. scores of the inactivity group are 85.06 and 78.92, and the 24-hr. scores are 75.94 and 72.14. The latter scores are still superior to the scores after 20-min. of normal rest (73.39 and 65.31)—Part A, Experiment I. The scores for the control group dropped at the 8-hr. interval to 33.60 and 30.02 and at the 24-hr. interval to 27.92 and 28.07.

(c) In Part C, we tested the effect of our sleep-like state upon the Ss' capacity to learn. Following a 2-hr. period of inactivity the Ss were brought to the learning situation. The inactivity group (18.33 trials and 14.16 shocks) showed slightly better learning scores than those of the normal group (19.06 trials and 16.48 shocks), but the differences are not statistically significant. Thus our inactivity has no marked effect upon learning capacity itself.

(d) None of the Ss in any of the experiments showed any apparent physiological after-effects of inactivity in their behavior at the time of learning or relearning.

(*e*) The foregoing results indicate that a sleep-like, inactive state has a markedly beneficial effect upon retention.

(*f*) Although sleep in cockroaches[76] and other insects is attested,[77] we can not say that the inactivity produced in our experiment is the same as that of natural sleep. We can state, however, that insofar as the effect of our inactivity is concerned, it is similar to that of natural sleep in human *S*s. Very little is known about the physiology of our inactive, sleep-like state, but from the fact that it is beneficial to retention it must be very different from the inactive states produced by low temperature or anesthetics, which are detrimental to retention.

(*g*) The explanation of the favorable effect of inactivity on retention may be as follows. As soon as the *S*s had learned the avoidance response to darkness they were placed in resting-cage or inactivity-boxes. The normally active or control *S*s moved about freely in the resting-cages. The random movements which they made during the interpolated intervals interfered, in terms of the perseveration-theory, with the normal consolidation-process which continues after learning. The inactive or experimental *S*s, on the other hand, made no movements— or very restricted ones; hence in their cases the consolidation-process continued without interruption. The inferiority of retention after normal rest to that after inactivity is mainly due, as we believe, to the anti-consolidation factor (Factor X), mentioned in Experiment I, which operated at a higher level in the normal activity state (control) than in the inactive state.

Supplementary results

In this section of the study we present results which are ancillary to our main experiments. These results are discussed under four general headings. The first three are concerned with variations in the learning-capacity due (1) to sex-differences, (2) to diurnal rhythm, and (3) to practice effects. The fourth (4) deals with the curve of obliviscence, ranging from 10-min. to 24-hr. intervals of normal rest and from 1-hr. to 24-hr. intervals of inactivity.

(1) Sex difference in learning

Little is known regarding the sex difference in the learning capacity of cockroaches. Turner,[78] in an experimental investigation of the reversal response to light by *Periplaneta orientalis L.*, found a slight difference in favor of the males. He did not calculate the significance of the difference, hence we do not know whether it is a real or a chance result.

Hunter,[79] working with *Blatella germanica* upon a similar problem, did

41

not mention the subject of sex difference. It is reasonable to suppose, there-fore, that it was either negligible or nonexistent for, had a real difference existed, he would have noticed and reported it. Since our Ss (*Periplaneta americana*) were a sufficiently large sample (144, equally divided as to sex) upon which to base conclusions, we examined the results of all our studies to that purpose.

Table XV gives, for the two sexes, the average number of trials and shocks required for the original learning of the avoidance response to darkness in the first experiment with every S. The data are also divided according to the time of day (morning, afternoon, or night) in which the learning occurred. The male Ss learned in fewer trials and shocks than the female in the morn-ing and night groups (17.72 trials and 14.39 shocks in the morning groups as against the female Ss' averages of 18.72 and 15.81 respectively; and 19.25 trials and 16.65 shocks against 20.10 and 17.23 in the night groups). In the afternoon groups, however, the female Ss were slightly superior (18.43 trials and 16.40 shocks for the female as against 18.88 trials and 16.97 shocks for the male). The differences between the sexes are throughout small and none of them is statistically reliable. Indeed, as the totals for the two sexes in Table XV show, the scores of the male (18.62 trials and 16.00 shocks) and of the female (19.49 trials and 16.95 shocks) are of the same order. We feel justified in concluding, therefore, that the differences are due to chance, and that our Ss do not show a sex difference in their ability to learn to avoid darkness.

(2) Diurnal variation in learning

In order to take account of the diurnal variation in learning, if one existed, we divided the Ss in the various parts of this study into morning, afternoon, and night groups, at which times the experiments were conducted with them. The results of these different groups are given in Table XV. As may be seen there, the learning scores for the morning and afternoon groups are

Table XV Sex difference and diurnal variation in learning capacity

Sex		Morning (18 Ss of each sex)		Afternoon (34 Ss of each sex)		Night (20 Ss of each sex)		Total average	
		Av.	S.D.	Av.	S.D.	Av.	S.D.	Av.	S.D.
Male	Trials	17.72	6.51	18.88	5.39	19.25	6.33	18.62	5.99
	Shocks	14.39	6.62	16.97	5.69	16.65	5.71	16.00	5.96
Female	Trials	19.72	6.78	17.79	6.13	20.95	6.99	19.49	6.63
	Shocks	17.22	6.66	15.82	6.01	17.80	6.02	16.95	6.23
Total average	Trials	18.72	6.65	18.34	5.76	20.10	6.66	19.06	6.31
	Shocks	15.81	6.64	16.40	5.85	17.23	5.87	16.48	6.10

almost identical. The morning group, as Table XV shows, required 18.72 trials and 15.81 shocks and the afternoon group, 18.34 trials and 16.40 shocks—differences of +0.38 trials and −0.59 shocks for the morning group. The night group, however, gave results that were poorer than either of the other two: 20.10 trials and 17.23 shocks. The S.D. of the averages of the three groups are so large, from 30–40%, and the differences among the groups are so small that we feel justified in concluding that our Ss showed no diurnal variation in learning the avoidance response to darkness.

This result is corroborated by Hunter in his experiment with the cockroach. Though diurnal variation was not mentioned in his study, he states, in a personal letter written to Van Ormer in response to an inquiry "whether diurnal variation of learning performance was controlled," that it had been checked, "and none was found."[80]

Daily rhythm of activity in cockroaches was first recorded by Szymanski[81] and later by Wille.[82] They found that on the average there were about 3 hr. out of the 24 in which the roaches were most active—generally during the first half of the night. A recent study by Gunn,[83] however, showed that activity is great during darkness regardless of the time of the day and that continuous darkness or continuous light abolished the normal rhythm. Since our Ss were kept in a dark cupboard, except for the actual time they were engaged in our experiments, the diurnal rhythm of activity must have been abolished when they were used. As Mellanby[84] reported, the normal rhythm occurred regardless of natural changes in temperature and humidity, although light may change the rhythm and extreme temperature may abolish it temporarily. The rhythm of activity, therefore, seemed to be due to an internal mechanism. In this sense, the inactivity induced in our experiment is also a modification of the normal rhythm of activity.

(3) Effect of practice

As may be seen opposite "Range" in Tables II and X the ranges of trials and shocks vary in the Control and Activity Experiments both in learning and relearning from 0 upwards. These and other low ranges of 1, 2, etc., particularly in the original learning, are due to the effects of practice. The Ss, it will be recalled, served on 6 alternate days. The effect of one day's learning was in many instances carried over to subsequent days. Learning in 0 trials and with 0 shock, which was obtained three times in the original learning, (Table II), occurred once on the third day and twice on the fifth day.

Considering only trials and the original learning, we obtain the following results. In all there were 23 instances in which learning was accomplished in 5 or less trials. Of these cases, 1 occurred on the first day, 2 on the second, 4 on the third, 5 on the fourth, 7 on the fifth, and 4 on the sixth. When we turn to the total number of trials required by the Ss at the different learning periods we again find evidence of the effect of practice. Table XVI gives

Table XVI Total number of trials required in original learning by all Ss at every experimental period

| | Experimental period | | | | | | Total | |
	1st	2nd	3rd	4th	5th	6th	1–3	4–6
Part A, Exp. I (24 Ss)	481	386	442	375	337	382	1309	1094
Part A, Exp. II (24 Ss)	442	473	445	464	444	417	1360	1325

separately for Experiments IA and IIA the total number of trials required in original learning by all the *S*s at every experimental period. Though the numbers vary considerably among the experimental periods, there is a tendency, particularly in Experiment IA, for the trials to decrease. From an initial total of 481 trials the number falls to 386 at the second period, rises to 442 at the third, falls to 375 at the fourth, to 337 at the fifth, and rises again to 382 at the last period—a range of 144 trials which vary from 481 at the first period to 337 at the fifth. The improvement is more clearly shown when the total of the first three periods (1309) is set against that of the last three periods (1094)—a difference in favor of the latter of 215 trials. In Experiment IIA, however, the tendency is not so clearly shown. From 442 trials on the first day the total rises to 473, falls to 445, rises again to 464 and then falls to 444 and 417—a range of 56 trials varying from 473 at the second period to 417 at the last. The total of the first three periods is 1360 and of the last three 1325—a slight difference (35) but one that lies in the same direction as the difference in Experiment IA.[85]

The results reported here justify, as we believe, the statement that the American cockroach retains from one experimental period to the next (2 days) a learned response to avoid darkness, Gates and Allee's results to the contrary notwithstanding.[86]

(4) Curves of obliviscence

The curves of obliviscence obtained from the average saving scores in the various parts of this study are brought together in Fig. 7. Except for the first three points in the control curve, which were obtained from Part A, Experiment I (Table III) all the points in the curves (control as well as inactivity) were obtained from Parts A and B, Experiment II (Tables X and XIII above).

The results shown in the curves in Fig. 7 were obtained, as it will be recalled, under slightly different conditions. In Parts A, Experiments I and II, which give the points in the curves at 10, 20, and 30 min., and 1, 2, and 3 hr. respectively, the *S*s served both as control and experimental animals. In Part B, Experiment II, a control and an experimental group served at each interval (8 and 24 hr.). Moreover, in Part A, Experiment I, the *S*s in

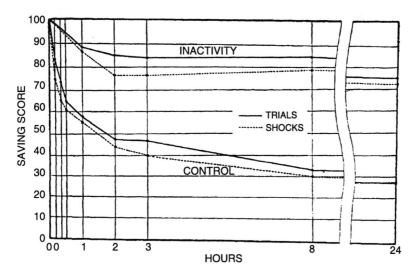

Figure 7 Saving scores for trials and shocks at the various time-intervals of normal activity (control) and inactivity.

the normal rest experiments spent the short periods (10, 20, and 30 min.) interpolated between learning and relearning in an illuminated resting-cage and, since they were light-adapted, they were not given a 10-min. light-adaptation period at the conclusion of the interpolated intervals but were immediately replaced in the learning-box.[87] In Parts A and B, Experiment II, on the other hand, the *S*s in the control experiments spent the interpolated periods (1, 2, 3, 8 and 24 hr.) in a resting-cage that was placed in a dark cupboard and, since they were completely dark-adapted when returned to the relearning situation, they were given a 10-min. light-adaptation period before being replaced in the learning-box.[88]

Despite the differences among the conditions, the results of the several experiments yield fairly uniform curves. The control curves, for both trials and shocks, take the familiar form: a sharp decline which becomes progressively flatter at the longer time-intervals. The first three intervals, however, are slightly out of line with the later five.[89] The losses at the first three are greater than the modulus of the curve derived from the last five would indicate. Indeed, the losses after the ½- and 1-hr. intervals are not very different. These results are due, as we believe, to the differences in procedure mentioned above. The *S*s of the 10, 20, and 30 min. intervals served alternately between the normal rest (the control) and the forced-activity experiments; the latter of which, as we have seen (Part C, Experiment I), have pronounced deleterious effects upon learning. Moreover, the *S*s serving at these short periods were under strong illumination during the experimental periods. The *S*s of the 1-, 2-, and 3-hr. intervals served alternately also, but the experiments (inactivity) alternating with normal rest (control) did not have deleterious effects. Indeed, as shown above (Part C), the inactivity experiments had a slight, but insignificant, beneficial effect upon learning. In the 8- and 24-hr. intervals, different groups of Ss served in the control and inactivity experiments. The holdover on subsequent control experiments of the deleterious effects of the earlier forced activity experiments, or the illumination, or the greater activity of the Ss under illumination, or a combination of these factors, is responsible, as we believe, for the disproportionate losses at the three shortest intervals in the control curves.

The form of the inactivity curves, for both trials and shocks, is very different from that of the control. After a sharp initial drop at the 1- and 2-hr. intervals, the inactivity curves flatten and a high constant level is thenceforth maintained. Indeed, from the 2-hr. interval on, the inactivity curves are practically horizontal lines as none of the differences among the saving scores, from which the points of the curves were plotted, are statistically significant; all are chance.

The inactivity curves of our Ss are similar in form to the retention curves in sleep for human Ss that were obtained by Jenkins and Dallenbach, and by Van Ormer.[90] The initial drop in the inactivity curves is not so great as those in the curves of human sleep (ca. 20% as against Jenkins and Dallenbach's 45% and Van Ormer's 55%) and the plateaus are at correspondingly higher levels, but the differences do not conceal the similarities. The differences, moreover, may in part be explained by the fact that the cockroaches passed into the inactive state sooner after learning than the human Ss and had consequently less time for new experiences to interfere with the consolidation of the "memory traces" just established. The cockroaches passed into the inactive state in a few minutes after learning —just as soon as they entered the inactivity-box; whereas the human Ss, though they went to bed immediately after learning, remained awake and mentally active for indetermined intervals—as long as 10 min., as Van Ormer reports.

General summary and discussion

In this study we sought to determine the effect of activity upon the retention and relearning of the avoidance response to darkness by the American cockroach (*Periplaneta americana*). Three degrees of activity were employed: (a) forced activity, during which the Ss were required to run in a motor-driven treadmill at the rate of 135 in. per min.; (b) normal resting activity—the control—in which the Ss normally moved about when placed in circular resting-cages, 8 in. in diam., that offered no corners at which they could make bodily contact and come to rest; and (c) inactivity, a sleep-like, immobile state, obtained by inducing the Ss to crawl into a small dark resting-box in which tissue paper came in close bodily contact from below and above.

Learning and relearning were measured in terms of the number of trials required and shocks received by the *S*s for them to make 9 correct responses out of 10 successive trials—the criterion of learning.

The intervals between learning and relearning were 10, 20, 30 min., 1, 2, 3, 8, and 24 hr.

The study was divided into two major parts: Experiments I and II. In the first part, the effect of forced activity was investigated, and in the second, the effect of inactivity.

Experiment I was itself divided into three parts: Parts A, B, and C. (*1*) In Part A, we studied the effect of forced activity of 10, 20, and 30 min. duration on retention and relearning. We found that the scores in relearing at all of those intervals were much poorer after forced activity than after corresponding intervals of normal rest, and further that they were even poorer than those made in learning. The behavior of the *S*s was also altered. After being forced they were more irritable and active than after the normal resting-state. It is obvious, from the results for Part A, that forced activity affects relearning as well as retention, and that the decrement in both is due chiefly to the physiological after-effects of activity.

(*2*) Part B was undertaken to determine how rapidly, if at all, the *S*s recovered from the physiological after-effects of forced activity, and incidentally to discover the relationship between the temporal position of the interpolated activity and the magnitude of the decrement in retention and relearning. Five series of experiments, a control and four experimental series, were conducted. In the control series (Condition A), no activity was interpolated in a 3-hr. interval between learning and relearning. In the experimental series, a 10-min. period of forced activity was interpolated immediately after learning (Condition B), after 1 hr. (Condition C), after 2 hr. (Condition D), and after 2 hr. 50 min. (Condition E). Since the time between learning and relearning was spent in darkness, the *S*s were given a 5-min. light-adaptation period before relearning.

We found (a) that the conditions ranked, according to their relearning scores, from best to poorest, as follows: C, A, B, D, and E; and (b) that the behavior of the *S*s was unaffected and normal in Conditions A, B, and C; showed some increase in activity in Condition D; and a considerable increase in Condition E. The relearning scores were practically identical in Conditions A and C—control and forced activity after 1 hr. Forced activity, given 1 hr. after learning and 2 hr. before relearning, has no more effect upon retention and relearning than a 3-hr. interval of normal rest. The interval of 1 hr. apparently exceeds the effective span of the anti-consolidation factor (Factor X) and the 2-hr. recovery-period apparently eliminates the irritability-factor (Factor Y).

In Condition B, in which the forced activity was interpolated immediately after learning, the anti-consolidation factor was at its maximum and was alone effective. Since Condition D yielded relearning-scores that were poorer than those of Condition B, the conclusion is unescapable that Factor X, at its maximum, has less effect on the score than Factor Y has 1 hr. before relearning.

Condition E shows the effectiveness of Factor Y. The relearning and learning scores are almost identical, *i.e.* apparently nothing was retained from the original learning, as the *S*s required practically as many trials and shocks to relearn the avoidance response to darkness as they did to learn it. That the decrement in Condition E was not so great as in the 10-min. forced-activity interval in Part A was due, as we believe, to the 5-min. light-adaptation period given the *S*s just before relearning.

The results of Part B corroborate those of Part A and lead us to reaffirm the conclusion that forced activity has a detrimental effect upon our *S*s' capacity to relearn as well as upon their retention.

(3) Part C, a check experiment, was conducted to test the conclusion that activity affects relearning and retention. A 10-min. period of forced activity was given 0 min. (Condition F), and 50 min. (Condition G) before learning. The learning under Condition F was greatly retarded in comparison to that under normal conditions, and the *S*s showed excessive irritability in the learning situation. The learning scores under Condition G were much better than those under Condition F, although still inferior to those under normal conditions. The *S*s in Condition G were less irritable than those in Condition F, but they were more active than normal *S*s. The results indicate that forced activity had a detrimental effect upon learning due to the factor of irritability (Factor Y).

As shown in the foregoing experiments, the relearning scores of our *S*s after intervals of forced activity are determined by Factor X (anti-consolidation factor) and Factor Y (irritability). Factor X is responsible for the decrement in retention itself by interfering with consolidation and maintenance of the memory trace, whereas Factor Y has a detrimental effect upon the *S*s' learning-capacity at the time of relearning. The decrement in the saving scores after forced activity, therefore, is a sum total of decrements due to those two factors. Hence, if we exclude the decrement solely due to Factor Y from the total decrement in the saving, we obtain the decrement due to Factor X only, *i.e.* decrement in retention itself or the amount of forgetting in its true sense. In applying this fractionation to our results we find that savings due to retention at the 10-min. activity-interval amounts to 21.77%; the balance of the decrement at that interval, that is, 77.15%, being due to the deleterious effect of the forced activity upon the *S*s' capacity to learn at the time of relearning.

Experiment II was also divided into three parts, A, B, C. *(1)* In Part A, we tested the effect of inactivity of 1-, 2-, 3-hr. duration on retention and relearning. The results showed that the scores for relearning after intervals of inactivity were greatly superior to those after corresponding intervals of normal rest, and that they were approximately of the same order as those after 10-min. of normal rest (Part A, Experiment I). The *S*s showed neither weakness nor excessive irritability at the time of relearning after intervals of inactivity. Thus the sleep-like, inactive state has a markedly beneficial effect upon retention and relearning.

(2) In Part B, intervals were extended to 8 and 24 hr. to test the relearning after longer intervals of inactivity. We found that the relearning scores after both intervals of inactivity were much better than those after corresponding intervals of normal rest, and that they were superior even to those after 20-min. of normal rest. Again the *S*s showed no apparent physiological after-effects in their behavior after the intervals of inactivity.

(3) Part C, a check experiment, was conducted to test the possibility that the superiority of relearning in the inactivity experiments is partly due to the increased capacity to learn at the time of relearning after intervals in the inactive state. A 2-hr. inactivity-period was given before the *S*s started to learn. We found that the learning-scores after the period of inactivity were slightly better than those under normal conditions, but that the differences were not statistically significant, being of a chance order. From this result we conclude that our inactive state has a markedly beneficial effect upon retention itself.

The foregoing experiments indicate that the superiority of retention and relearning after intervals of inactivity is mainly due to the lack of Factor Y (excessive irritability) and to the extremely low level of Factor X (anti-consolidation).

Subordinate results regarding sex differences, diurnal variation, practice effect, and the curve of obliviscence during the normal and inactive (quiescent) state were obtained in this Study. No sex difference nor significant diurnal variations were found. Slight practice effect was observed. A normal curve of obliviscence was obtained from the several parts of the Study for the Control *S*s (those normally at rest), but a very different curve, one similar to the retention-curves of human *S*s in sleep, was obtained for the quiescent *S*s (those that were inactive).

Notes

1 J. G. Jenkins and K. M. Dallenbach, Obliviscence during sleep and waking, this JOURNAL, 35, 1924, 605–612.

2 H. Ebbinghaus, *Ueber das Gedächtnis: Untersuchungen zur experimentellen Psychologie*, 1885, 103 f.; esp. the table on 103. Ebbinghaus showed experimentally that forgetting is a function of time: rapid at first and progressively slower. The difference between the amount retained at the 8.8-hr. and the 24-hr. periods was not, however, of the same order as the differences between the values of his other successive periods—it was not as large as was expected and was out of line with his other results. "Such a relation," Ebbinghaus wrote, "is not credible, since, according to all the other figures, the decrease in the after-effect suffers a marked retardation with increasing time." He did not credit his figures even under the plausible assumption that sleep (the state in which the greater part of the interval between the two periods in question was spent) materially retarded forgetting—a suggestion that he himself made. He sought rather to find an explanation of the discrepancy among the accidental errors of his experiment and thus he neglected the true cause of the error.

3 W. S. Hunter, The effect of inactivity produced by cold upon learning and retention in the cockroach, *Blatella Germanica, J. Genet. Psychol.*, 41, 1932, 254.

4 R. W. Russell and W. S. Hunter, The effect of inactivity produced by sodium amytal on the retention of the maze habit in albino rats, *J. Exper. Psychol.*, 20, 1937, 426–436.

5 E. F. Phillips, *Beekeeping: A Discussion of the Life of the Honeybee and the Production of Honey*, 1916, 179.

6 H. von Buttel-Reepen, Zur Psychobiologie der Hummein, *Biol. Zentbl.*, 27, 1907, 579–587, 604–613.

7 L. Tirala, Ueber den Einfluss der Äthernarkose auf die Heimkehrfähigkeit der Bienen, *Arch. f. exp. Pathol. u. Pharmakol.*, 97, 1923, 433–440.

8 F. J. Eldering, Acquisition d'habitudes par les insectes, *Arch. néerland. Physiol.*, 3, 1919, 469–490; Sur les habitudes acquises chez les insectes (d'apres des expériences sur *Periplaneta americana*), *ibid.*, 5, 1921, 129.

9 O. E. Plath, Do anesthetized bees lose their memory? *Amer. Natur.*, 58, 1924, 162–166.

10 K. Rösch-Berger, Das Gedächtnis der Bienen nach der Narkose, *Zsch. f. vergl. Physiol.*, 18, 1933, 474–480.

11 W. Grabensberger, Experimentelle Untersuchungen über Zeitgedächtnis von Bienen und Wespen nach Verfütterungen von Euchinin und Jodthyreoglobulin, *Zsch. f. vergl. Physiol.*, 20, 1934, 338–342.

12 H. Kalmus, Ueber die Natur des Zeitgedächtnisses der Bienen, *Zsch. f. vergl. Physiol.*, 20, 1934, 405–419.

13 H. Hoagland, A study of the physiology of learning in ants, *J. Gen. Psychol.*, 5, 1931, 21–41.

14 J. W. French, The effect of temperature on the retention of a maze habit in fish, *J. Exper. Psychol.*, 31, 1942, 79–87.

15 Before Jenkins and Dallenbach's study, by W. A. Lay (Über das Morgan-und Abendlerner, *Zsch. f. Erforsch. u. Behandl. jugendl. Schwachsinns*, 5, 1912, 285–292), Rosa Heine (Ueber Wiedererkennen und rückwirkende Hemmung, *Zsch. f. Psychol.*, 68, 1914, 225–234), and F. Nicholai (Experimentelle Untersuchungen über das Haften von Gesichtseindrucken und dessen zeitlichen Verlauf, *Arch. ges. Psychol.*, 42, 1922, 137); and following it by A. Dahl (Ueber den Einfluss des Schlafens auf das Wiedererkennen, *Psychol. Forsch.*, 11, 1928, 290–311), E. B. van Ormer (Retention after intervals of sleep and waking, *Arch. Psychol.*, 21, 1932, no. 137, 1–49), and E. B. Newman (Forgetting of meaningful material during sleep and waking, this JOURNAL, 52, 1939, 65–71).

16 W. S. Hunter, The auditory sensitivity of the white rat, *J. Anim. Behav.*, 5, 1915, 312–329, esp. 324–325.

17 W. S. Hunter and J. U. Yarbrough, The interference of auditory habits in the white rat, *J. Anim. Behav.*, 7, 1917, 49–65.

18 L. W. Webb, Transfer of training and retroaction; a comparative study, *Psychol. Monog.*, 24, 1917, no. 104, 1–90.

19 L. A. Pechstein, Whole vs. part methods in motor learning; a comparative study, *Psychol, Monog.*, 23, 1917, no. 99, 1–80.

20 T. W. Brockbank, Redintegration in the albino rat; a study in retention, *Behav. Monog.*, 4, 1919, no. 18, 1–66.

21 Y. H. Ho, Transfer and degree of integration, *J. Comp. Psychol.*, 8, 1928, 87–99.

22 S. M. Corey, The relationship between compulsory physical exercise and the ability of the white rat to learn and relearn an elevated skeleton maze, *J. Comp. Psychol.*, 11, 1931, 291–318.

23 W. L. Gray, The effect of forced activity on the maze performance of white rats, *J. Comp. Psychol.*, 23, 1937, 475–512.

24 This apparatus was devised by Dr. J. W. Macmillan to whom grateful acknowledgement is made.

25 Hunter, *op. cit., J. Genet. Psychol.*, 41, 1932, 255 f.

26 C. H. Turner, An experimental investigation of apparent reversal of response to light of the roach *(Periplaneta orientalis), Biol. Bull.*, 23, 1912, 371–386.

27 M. F. Gates and W. C. Allee, Conditioned behavior of isolated and grouped cockroaches on a simple maze, *J. Comp. Psychol.*, 15, 1933, 331–358.

28 Calculated by the formula: 100 (L—RL) / L; in which L equals the number of trials or shocks in the original learning, and R L the number in the relearning.

29 This score was proposed by J. A. McGeoch (Studies in retroactive inhibition; iv. Temporal point of interpolation and degree of retroactive inhibition, *J. Comp. Psychol.*, 15, 1933, 410), who computed this value by the formula 100 (Rest minus Work)/Rest. In applying this formula to our study, we used the following: 100 (Control Saving Score—Activity Savings Score)/Control Savings Score. This score gives a zero value when there is no retroactive inhibition, and a value which increases as retroactive inhibition increases until 100 is reached, at which point complete loss of memory is indicated.

30 If the savings score of the activity experiments has a negative sign, as it does in our case, the value of McGeoch's score will exceed 100.

31 G. Brecher, Beitrag zur Raumorientierung der Schabe, *Periplaneta americana, Zsch. wiss. Biol., Abt. C., Physiol.*, 10, 1929, 497–526.

32 V. B. Wigglesworth, *Principles of Insect Physiology*, 1939, 226, 340 f.

33 J. S. Szymanski, Modification of the innate behavior of cockroaches, *J. Anim. Behav.*, 2, 1912, 81–90.

34 W. D. Tait, The effect of psycho-physical attitudes on memory, *J. Abnorm. Psychol.*, 8, 1913, 10–37.

35 L. M. Harden, The effect of emotional reactions upon retention, *J. Gen. Psychol.*, 3, 1930, 197–221.

36 J. D. Frank and E. J. Ludvigh. The retroactive effect of pleasant and unpleasant odors on learning, this JOURNAL, 43, 1931, 102–108.

37 M. M. White, Influence of an interpolated electric shock upon recall, *J. Exper, Psychol.*, 15, 1932, 752–757.

38 H. Piéron, Les formes élémentaires de l'émotion dans le comportement animal, *J. de Psychol.*, 17, 1920, 937–945; Emotions in animals and man, in *Feelings and Emotions: The Wittenberg Symposium*, edited by M. L. Raymert, 1928, 284–294.

39 Calculated by the formula: $t = $ Diff. $/ [(\sigma_1^2 / N_1 - 1) + (\sigma_2^2 / (N_2 - 1)]^{1/2}$, in which Diff. is the difference between the two scores, σ_1 and σ_2 are their S.D., and N_1 and N_2 the number of *Ss*.

40 P. L. Whitely, The dependence of learning and recall upon prior mental and physical conditions, *J. Exper. Psychol.*, 7, 1924, 420–428.

41 P. L. Whitely, The dependence of learning and recall upon prior intellectual activities, *J. Exper. Psychol.*, 10, 1927, 489–508.

42 F. J. Houlahan, Retroactive inhibition as affected by the temporal position of interpolated activities in elementary school children, *Catholic Univ. Amer. Educ. Res. Monog.*, 10, 1937, no. 3, 1–27.

43 I. Müller, Zur Analyse der Retentionsstörung durch Häufung, *Psychol. Forsch.*, 22, 1937, 180–210.

44 M. E. Bunch, The efficiency of retention of a rational learning problem under (1) normal conditions and (2) conditions of interpolated learning, for long intervals of time, (abstract in) *Psychol. Bull.*, 35, 1938, 691.

45 E. B. Newman, Forgetting of meaningful material during sleep and waking, this JOURNAL, 52, 1939, 65–71.

46 E. D. Sisson, Retroactive inhibition; the temporal position of interpolated activity, *J. Exper. Psychol.*, 25, 1939, 228–233.
47 Y. Maeda, On the retroactive inhibition, *Jap. J. Psychol.*, 15, 1940, 181–206, 261–281.
48 E. B. Skaggs, Discussion of the temporal point of interpolation and degree of retroactive inhibition, *J. Comp. Psychol.*, 16, 1933, 411.
49 G. E. Müller and A. Pilzecker, Experimentelle Beiträge zur Lehre vom Gedächtnis, *Zsch. f. Physiol. d. Sinnes., Ergt. 1*, 1900, 174–198.
50 Heine, *op. cit.*, 225–234.
51 E. B. Skaggs, Further studies in retroactive inhibition, *Psychol. Monog.*, 34, 1925, no. 161, 1–60.
52 White, *op. cit.*
53 Sisson, *op. cit.*
54 E. S. Robinson, Some factors determining the degree of retroactive inhibition, *Psychol. Monog.*, 28, 1920, no. 128, 1–57; J. A. McGeoch, Studies in retroactive inhibition: i. The temporal course of the inhibitory effects of interpolated learning, *J. Gen. Psychol.*, 9, 1933, 24–43; ii. Relationships between temporal point of interpolation, length of interval and amount of retroactive inhibition, *ibid.*, 44–57; J. A. McGeoch and M. E. Nolen, Studies in retroactive inhibition: iv. Temporal point of interpolation and degree of retroactive inhibition, *J. Comp. Psychol.*, 15, 1933, 407–417.
55 L. W. Webb, *op. cit.*
56 E. S. Robinson, *op. cit.*, *Psychol. Monog.*, 28, 1920, no. 128, 1–57; The similarity factor in retroaction, this JOURNAL, 39, 1927, 297–312.
57 J. A. McGeoch, The influence of four different interpolated activities upon retention, *J. Exper. Psychol.*, 14, 1931, 400–413.
58 Skaggs, *op. cit.*
59 H. M. Johnson, Similarity of meaning as a factor in retroactive inhibition, *J. Gen. Psychol.*, 9, 1933, 377–389.
60 J. A. Gengerelli, Similarity and retroaction, *J. Exper. Psychol.*, 17, 1934, 680–690.
61 E. J. Gibson and J. J. Gibson, Retention and the interpolated task, this JOURNAL, 46, 1934, 603–610.
62 J. E. DeCamp, A study of retroactive inhibition, *Psychol. Monog.*, 19, 1915, no. 84, 1–69.
63 M. E. Bunch and F. D. McTeer, The influence of punishment during learning upon retroactive inhibition, *J. Exper. Psychol.*, 15, 1932, 473–495.
64 White, *op. cit.*
65 Six learning and relearning experiments were conducted with every *S* in Part A. We used the results only of the first experiment with every *S*, as we did not wish to contaminate our control with the results of practice, as we should have done had we included the learning-scores of the other five experiments.
66 J. S. Szymanski, Ein Beitrag zur Frage über tropische Fortbewegung, (Pflügers) *Arch. f. d. ges. Physiol.*, 154, 1913, 343–363.
67 G. Brecher, *op. cit.*
68 J. S. Szymanski, Abhandlungen zum Aufbau der Lehre von den Handlungen der Tiere, *Arch. f. d. ges. Physiol.*, 170, 1918, 159–177.
69 G. D. Higginson, The after-effects of certain emotional situations upon maze learning among white rats, *J. Comp. Psychol.*, 10, 1930, 1–10.
70 R. M. Gagné and C. H. Graham, The effect of an "emotional state" on the initial stages of acquisition in a conditioned operant response, *Proc. Nat. Acad. Sci.*, 26, 1940, 297–300.
71 W. A. Hunt, Recent developments in the field of emotion, *Psychol. Bull.*, 38, 1941, 267–268.

72 J. A. McGeoch, *The Psychology of Human Learning*, 1942, 477.
73 J. G. Jenkins and K. M. Dallenbach, Obliviscence during sleep and waking, this JOURNAL, 25, 1924, 612.
74 R. Heine, Über Wiedererkennen und rückwirkende Hemmung, *Zsch. f. Psychol.*, 68, 1914, 161–236; J. G. Jenkins and K. M. Dallenbach, Obliviscence during sleep and waking, this JOURNAL, 25, 1924, 605–612; A. Dahl, Über den Einfluss des Schlafens auf das Wiedererkennen, *Psychol. Forsch.*, 11, 1928, 290–311; E. B. van Ormer, Retention after intervals of sleep and of waking, *Arch. Psychol.*, 21, 1932, no. 137, 1–49.
75 F. Steiniger, Die Biologie der sogennanten "tierischen Hypnose," *Erg. d. Biol.*, 13, 1936, 348–451.
76 P. Rau, Auditory perception in insects, with special reference to the cockroach, *Quart. Rev. Biol.*, 15, 1940, 137–155.
77 K. Fiebrig, Schlafende Insekten, *Zsch. Naturwiss.*, 48, 1912, 315–364; P. Rau and N. Rau, The sleep of insects: an ecological study, *Ann. Entomol. Soc. Amer.*, 9, 1916, 227–274; R. T. Young, "Sleep" aggregation in the beetle, *Altica bimarginata, Science*, 81, 1935, 435–436.
78 C. H. Turner, An experimental investigation of an apparent reversal of response to light of the roach *(Periplaneta orientalis L.)*, *Biol. Bull.*, 23, 1912, 371–386.
79 W. S. Hunter, *op. cit.*
80 E. B. van Ormer, Sleep and retention, *Psychol, Bull.*, 30, 1933, 432, footnote 18, in which Hunter's letter is quoted.
81 J. S. Sxymanski, Eine Methode zur Untersuchungen der Ruhe und Aktivitätsperioden bei Tieren, *Arch. ges. Physiol.*, 158, 1914, 343–385, esp. 350–359.
82 J. Wille, Biologie und Bekämpfung der deutschen Schabe *(Phillodromia germanica L.)*, *Monog. z. angew. Entomol.*, 1920, 1–140. (Cited by Gunn.)
83 D. L. Gunn, The daily rhythm of activity of the cockroach, *Blatta orientalis L.*: i. Aktograph experiments, especially in relation to light, *J. Exper. Biol.*, 17, 1940, 267–277.
84 K. Mellanby, The daily rhythm of activity of the cockroach, *Blatta orientalis L.:* II. Observations and experiments on a natural infestation, *ibid.*, 278–285.
85 That the practice-effect was more in evidence in Experiment IA than in Experiment IIA was at first surprising. In Experiment IA, in which the experimental conditions alternated between forced activity and normal rest, forced activity had a deleterious effect upon the *Ss'* retention and ability to learn, and it made them irritable. Under those circumstances the effect of practice might have been obscured—but it was clearly indicated. In Experiment IIA, in which the experimental conditions alternated between inactivity and normal rest, inactivity was beneficial to the *Ss'* retention and it did not make them irritable. Under those circumstances the effect of practice should have been maximum—it was almost totally obscured. What caused these apparently discrepant results? We do not know but our guess is 'overlearning.' The *Ss* subjected to forced activity, Experiment IA, required many trials (see Table II) in relearning to reach our criterion of success, whereas the inactive *Ss*, Experiment IIA, required only a few (see Table X). If the *Ss* overlearned in the first case and just barely learned in the second, we should expect the results obtained.
86 Gates and Allee, *op. cit., J. Comp. Psychol.*, 15, 1933, 358.
87 These *Ss* were kept in the light during the normal rest experiments so their interpolated intervals would be the same, insofar as illumination was concerned, as the interpolated intervals of the activity experiments; and the *Ss* in the activity experiments were kept in the light that their activity in the treadmill might be observed. We wished to observe our *Ss'* behavior and also to be certain that they were exercised and that no bodily harm came to them in the treadmill.

88 The *S*s were placed in darkness for the long interpolated intervals because we did not know what effect, if any, long illumination would have upon them. We did not wish at that point of the experiment to risk defeating its main purpose by introducing any condition, the effects of which were unknown, even though it meant a slight variation in the procedure at the longer interpolated intervals. It is reasonable to suppose that bright illuminations of 8- and 24-hr. durations would have some deleterious effects upon such marked nocturnal insects as the cockroach.

89 The points plotted in Fig. 7 for the first three intervals (10, 20, and 30 min.) are not the same as those plotted in Fig. 3 for the corresponding intervals. In Fig. 7 these points are plotted from the averages of the individual saving scores; in Fig. 3 they are plotted from group saving scores, *i.e.* from the averages given in Table II. We used these different methods of computing the saving scores so as to conform in each instance with the method used to obtain the other scores in the respective experiments. It was necessary in Part A, Experiment I (the results of which are shown in Fig. 3) to compute the saving scores in the forced activity experiments from group averages because of the excessively large individual variations. If that were done for the experimental series it should also be done with the control series with which comparisons were to be made. All the saving scores in Experiment II, on the other hand (the results of which are shown in Fig. 7), are the averages of individual scores. If a comparison is to be made between the results of the control experiments in Part A, Experiment I, and those of Parts A and B, Experiment II, the same method of computing the results should be, and was, used.

90 For a discussion of these curves, see Van Ormer, *op. cit., Psychol. Bull.*, 30, 1933, 423 ff., 429 ff.

23

SOME TESTS OF THE DECAY THEORY OF IMMEDIATE MEMORY

John Brown

Source: *Quarterly Journal of Experimental Psychology*, 10 (1958): 12–21.

Abstract

The hypothesis of decay of the memory trace as a cause of forgetting has been unpopular. The reasons for this unpopularity are criticized and a theory of the memory span, based on this hypothesis, is put forward. Three experiments which test the hypothesis are described. In each, two kinds of stimuli are presented to the subject, viz., "required" stimuli, which he attempts to remember, and "additional" stimuli, to which he merely makes responses. The first experiment will show that even when the number of required stimuli is well below the memory span, forgetting occurs if the presentation of additional stimuli delays recall for several seconds. The second shows that the effect of the additional stimuli depends only slightly on their similarity to the required stimuli: it also shows that their effect is negligible when they precede, instead of follow, the required stimuli. The third shows that the effect of additional stimuli interpolated before recall remains considerable even when there is an interval of several seconds between presentation of required and additional stimuli.

Introduction

The experiments reported below concern memory over a period of a few seconds, when only a single presentation of the material has been given. It is convenient to describe such memory as "immediate." The experiments form part of a series described in an unpublished Ph.D. dissertation (Brown, 1955): two of the series have already been published (Brown, 1954, 1956).

Immediate memory usually operates under conditions very different from those provided in conventional immediate memory tests. Typically, it is necessary to retain information while continuing to carry out other activities. In a lecture delivered in Cambridge in 1950, Sir Frederic Bartlett suggested that forgetting may be extremely rapid under these circumstances. The series of experiments began as an attempt to put this suggestion to an experimental test, with highly positive results. However, the three experiments described below, while they illustrate rapid loss of information in immediate memory when other activity intervenes before recall, were designed to test a particular theory of immediate memory. The basic hypothesis of this theory is that when something is perceived, a memory trace is established which decays rapidly during the initial phase of its career. (By memory trace is meant only the neural substrate of retention, whatever this may be.) Some decay of the trace is assumed to be compatible with reliable recall just as partial fading of print may be compatible with perfect legibility. But recall will cease to be reliable if decay of the trace proceeds beyond a critical level.

Two fundamental problems of immediate memory are (1) the origin and nature of the immediate memory span, and (2) why we forget when this span is exceeded. One solution to these problems is to postulate a special mechanism for short-term retention. The memory span can then be regarded as the capacity of this special mechanism. When the span is exceeded, forgetting will occur because retention becomes dependent on a mechanism which is less efficient. The hypothesis of rapid decay of the memory trace, however, also provides a possible solution to these problems and one which has the merit of simplicity. The hypothesis leads to a theory of the memory span which in outline runs as follows: When a sequence of items is presented, the interval between the perception of each item and the attempt to recall that item will depend on the length of the sequence. If the sequence exceeds a certain length, decay of the memory traces of some of the items will proceed too far for accurate recall of the sequence to be possible. This length is the memory span. Thus the trace-decay hypothesis can explain both the origin of the span and why forgetting occurs when the span is exceeded.

The hypothesis that decay of the memory trace is an important cause of forgetting has been unpopular. However, theories of forgetting have developed almost entirely in relation to forgetting over relatively long periods. Where forgetting over very short periods has been specifically considered, there has been greater readiness to postulate a decay process. Thus the "stimulus trace" which plays an important rôle in Hull's explanations of serial learning phenomena (Hull, 1940) is assumed to decay rapidly. Decay of the trace has also been invoked from time to time to explain negative time errors in psychophysical judgement (e.g. Pratt, 1933). The two main reasons for the unpopularity of the decay theory are the existence of distortions in remembering and the importance of the similiarity factor in P.I. and R.I. (pro- and retro-active inhibition). These facts have seemed to some to imply a more dynamic theory of forgetting than is provided by decay of a static trace (notably to Bartlett, 1932, and to Koffka, 1935). To others they have seemed to show that a competition-in-recall theory of forgetting is adequate (e.g. McGeoch, 1942, and Underwood, 1957). But it is possible to argue that distortions in remembering are due to the constructive and inferential character of recall, made necessary by decay of the memory trace (Brown 1956). In like manner, competition-in-recall may itself be a manifestation of such decay, a point which seems to have been overlooked and which merits discussion.

Competition-in-recall may mean one of two things. It may mean that a competing response inhibits recall of the required response. In this case, the competition theory is a genuine theory of forgetting and belongs to that class of theories according to which, for some reason, not dependent on the state of the trace itself, the trace fails to lead to effective recall. Alternatively, it may mean that both responses tend to be elicited and that the organism is unable to distinguish which of the two responses is correct. It is important to recognize that such failure of discrimination, i.e. confusion between responses, cannot be regarded as a primary cause of forgetting. Failure of discrimination presupposes forgetting of that which determines which of the responses is correct. It is thus a possible *effect* of forgetting, however caused, but is not itself a primary cause of forgetting. Now experiments which have demonstrated the importance of the similarity factor on R.I. and P.I. have invariably used an interfering material which could be confused with the required material; very often, for example, both materials have consisted of nonsense syllables. Properly considered, therefore, the results of such experiments do *not* constitute evidence against the decay of the trace theory of forgetting.

Experiment I

On the hypothesis of decay of the memory trace, recall will become unreliable if decay proceeds too far, i.e. if the retention interval exceeds a certain length. This will apply whether or not the amount the subject attempts to retain lies within the memory span. One way to test the hypothesis of decay of the trace, therefore, is to see whether if recall is delayed for several seconds forgetting occurs even when the amount of material is well within the memory span. However, if the subject is left free to rehearse the material during the delay, no forgetting is to be expected. For rehearsal is itself a form of recall, albeit implicit, and is likely to counteract the effect of decay, either directly, or through the establishment of a new trace. Thus, in order to test the hypothesis, it is necessary to require the subject to perform an additional activity during the delay period so that rehearsal is prevented. And it must be arranged that this activity involves a high information rate, if prevention of rehearsal is to be really effective. In the following experiment, between 1 and 4 pairs of stimuli were presented for the subject to remember and there was an interval of just under 5 sec. before recall. Under one condition, the subject was required to make immediate responses to 5 pairs of additional stimuli during this interval in order to prevent rehearsal; under a second condition, the interval was empty.

Method

Condition I: On each trial two sets of stimuli were presented in immediate succession. The subject was instructed to read out the stimuli of both sets during presentation and to attempt to remember the stimuli of the first set. The first set will therefore be called the required or "M" stimuli and the second set the additional or "X" stimuli. The required stimuli consisted of between 1 and 4 pairs of consonants (excluding the consonant Y), which were randomly selected except that no consonant was repeated in the stimuli for any one trial. The additional stimuli consisted of 5 pairs of number digits copied directly from tables of random numbers. Both sets of stimuli were recorded on a paper strip, the required stimuli in black and the additional stimuli in red. This strip was passed behind a screen in which there was a viewing window so that the stimuli appeared pair by pair (for details of apparatus, *see* Brown, 1954). The sequence of events on each trial was as follows. The experimenter said "ready" and a warning line appeared in the window. Then, after 0.5 sec., the pairs of stimuli followed at intervals of 0.78 sec. (all the M pairs were presented before the X pairs). As soon as presentation was over, the subject attempted to write down the required stimuli. Each consonant was scored correct if, and only if, it was reproduced in the correct position in the sequence.

Condition II: This was the control condition and differed in that the additional stimuli were omitted, i.e. there was still an interval (4.7 sec.) before recall, but it was unfilled.

Six stimulus strips were prepared, three for each condition. Each strip carried stimuli for 3 trials with 1 pair of M stimuli, followed by 3 trials with 2 pairs, 3 with 3 pairs and 3 with 4 pairs (but trials with only 1 pair were omitted under Condition II). Ten university students were tested and each was first given a practice strip. Condition I and Condition II strips were given alternately. Half the subjects started with Condition I and half with Condition II.

Two of the original 10 subjects made an unacceptable number of errors in reading out the stimuli during presentation. Accordingly, two substitutes were tested instead. With the other subjects reading errors were rare. Reading errors were also rare in the other two experiments.

Results

Table I shows the scores for the subject as a group under the two conditions. In Figure I, these scores are shown as percentages. The most striking feature

Table I Pooled recall scores

| | Number of pairs of required stimuli | | | |
	1	2	3	4
Condition I	176	244	221	181
Condition II	—	358	505	471
Maximum possible	180	360	540	720

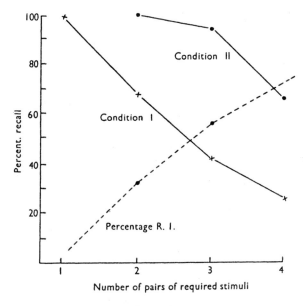

Figure I

of the results is that only a single pair of stimuli were retained without error when the additional stimuli intervened before recall. The dotted line in Figure I represents the effect of this activity as percentage R.I. It will be seen that the effect increases with the number of pairs of required stimuli. Table II shows that percentage recall for the last pair of required stimuli was much higher when there was only one pair of required stimuli than when there were four pairs: the difference is significant for each subject individually on a χ^2 test ($p < 0.05$).

Discussion

The results confirm what was expected on the hypothesis of decay of the memory trace: a delay of several seconds before recall could produce

Table II Recall of last pair

Number of pairs	1	2	3	4	5	6	7	8	9	10
1	18	18	18	18	15	18	18	18	17	18
4	11	10	14	4	0	10	7	9	9	12

considerable forgetting, if rehearsal was prevented, even when the number of stimuli was within the memory span, as shown by a control condition.

Figure I shows that the effect of preventing rehearsal varied with the number of required stimuli. This can be partly attributed to the increase in the mean interval between presentation of stimuli and the start of the recall period which occurs as their number increases (since the stimuli are presented successively). But this is not the whole explanation. Table II shows that recall of the last pair of required stimuli, for which the interval was constant, was not independent of whether there were previous pairs. Several factors may contribute to this result. Firstly, since the subject attempts recall of the stimuli in the order of their presentation, recall of the last pair is delayed by recall of earlier pairs. And as one might expect on the trace decay theory, this can lead to further forgetting (Brown, 1954). Secondly, prevention of rehearsal may not be fully effective when there is only a single pair of stimuli to rehearse.

Experiment II

This experiment tests two further deductions from the decay of the trace hypothesis about the effect of additional stimuli, to which the subject is asked merely to make responses, on the recall of required stimuli. The first concerns the effect of similarity between required and additional stimuli. The second concerns the effect of additional stimuli presented immediately before the required stimuli.

(1) On the trace-decay hypothesis, the similarity factor should be important only in so far as it leads to confusion in recall. This has already been argued in the Introduction. On certain other theories of forgetting, the similarity factor can be a crucial one. For example, according to Koffka (Koffka, 1935), similarity determines the extent to which perceptions interfere with pre-existing traces and to which traces interfere with one another.

(2) Stimuli presented immediately before the required stimuli should have little effect on recall on the trace decay hypothesis, since they cannot prevent rehearsal of the required stimuli during retention. Again on other theories of forgetting, interference is possible or even likely. For if incidental learning of the additional stimuli occurs, the traces so established may interact with the traces subsequently established by the required stimuli or may lead to

blocking of recall. Even on the decay hypothesis however, such incidental learning may have a slight effect. For it may lead to confusion of the additional and required stimuli in recall. Accordingly, in the experiment, the effect of additional stimuli which precede the required stimuli is studied, both where such confusion is possible (i.e. both sets of stimuli belong to the same class) and where it is not possible (i.e. one set consists of digits and the other of consonants).

Previous work: Several experiments have concerned the similarity factor in immediate memory. Robinson (1927) found, as one might expect, that recall increased with the degree of percentage identity between the two halves of a list. Harden (1929) and Young & Supa (1941) found that, if one half of the list consisted of consonants and the other of digits, recall was higher than when the whole list consisted of items of the same kind. This result is held to show that intra-serial R.I. and P.I. in immediate memory are a function of the similarity factor. But it is a result which seems readily explicable in terms of reduced intra-serial confusion when the two halves differ. Thus 8 consonants, for example, can be arranged in 40,320 ways: whereas 4 consonants followed by 4 digits can be arranged in only 576 ways. It is therefore quite compatible with the trace-decay hypothesis. An experiment by Pillsbury & Sylvester (1940)—to which little attention has been paid—makes questionable any assumption that R.I. in immediate memory is a function of similarity to a marked extent. They studied the effect of different activities interpolated during a 10-sec. retention interval. Comparison between the effects of these activities is a little difficult, since there was no control of the rates at which they were performed Nevertheless, it is noteworthy that all activities produced considerable R.I., irrespective of whether there was much similarity between original and interpolated materials.

Method

Only differences from the method of Experiment I will be described. The required, M, stimuli consisted of four pairs of consonants. The additional, X, stimuli consisted of either three pairs of consonants or of three pairs of digits: these two types of X will be referred to as Xs and Xd respectively (i.e. similar to or different from M). No consonant or digit was repeated in the stimuli for any one trial. The additional stimuli were presented either immediately before or immediately after the required stimuli. Thus there were four experimental conditions which will be labelled Xs (before), Xd (before), Xs (after), Xd (after). In addition there was a control condition under which no additional stimuli were presented. The pairs of stimuli were presented at intervals of 1.33 sec. This relatively slow rate was chosen so that subjects would not have any tendency to make mistakes in reading out M stimuli when they had been immediately preceded by X stimuli. The interval between the start of each trial and the presentation of M and the interval between the presentation of M and the start of the recall period were both 5·33 sec. under all conditions. Five paper strips were prepared: each carried eight trials under one of the five conditions. After a practice strip, with samples of all conditions, each subject was given the strips in a different order. Each strip was taken equally often at each stage of the experiment. The 15 subjects were university students.

Results

Table III shows percentage recall of the required stimuli by the subjects as a group under the various conditions. An analysis of variance of individual scores was performed, after transforming each score, s, to $\sin^{-1}{}_s$ in order to improve the stability of the error variance. The variance attributable to conditions was highly significant ($p < 0.001$). The residual variance of this analysis was then used to calculate "t" for each of the comparisons (in transformed scores) shown in Table IV. From Tables III and IV it will be seen that (i) both Xs (after) and Xd (after) produced very large amounts of interference, (ii) Xs (after) produced slightly but significantly ($p < 0.05$) more interference than Xd (after), (iii) Xs (before) produced slight interference (p (0·01) but Xd (before) did not.

The extent to which subjects inadvertently gave additional stimuli in their recall attempts, when both sets of stimuli consisted of consonants, is of interest. No consonant was repeated in the stimuli for each trial and the letter Y was not used. On each trial, of the 20 possible consonants, 8 were used for M stimuli, 6 for X stimuli and 6 were not used on each trial. Thus on a chance basis, intrusions from Xs should form about half the total number of intrusions. With Xs (after), 122 out of a total of 234 intrusions, i.e. a little over one half, were Xs stimuli. This is not significantly more than chance expectation on a χ^2 test, which provides an approximate test of significance.

Table III Percentage recall scores

Control	Xs (before)	Xs (after)	Xd (before)	Xd (after)
67.3	58.6	25.6	65.5	30.6

Table IV

Comparison	t *(with 56 d.f.)	Significance
1. Control with Xs (before)	3.39	$p < 0.01$
2. Control with Xd (before)	< 1.0	not significant
3. Xd (after) with Xs (after)	2.03	$p < 0.05$

* Derived from analysis of variance: *see* text.

But with Xs (before), 76 out of a total of 194 intrusions, i.e. *less* than one half, were Xs stimuli. This is significantly less than chance expectation on a χ^2 test ($p < 0.01$).

Discussion

Both deductions from the trace-decay hypothesis appear to be confirmed. When the additional stimuli intervened before recall, their similarity to the required stimuli was of minor importance in determining the amount of interference produced. When they preceded the required stimuli, the interference was slight, and occurred only when the two sets of stimuli could be confused in recall. Several points require discussion, however.

The effects of consonants and digits as additional stimuli may differ intrinsically, irrespective of their similarity to the required stimuli. This could distort the apparent importance of the similarity factor. Another experiment of the series (Brown, 1955)—which is primarily concerned with a different problem—shows, in conjunction with the results of the present experiment, that there is in fact little difference in the intrinsic effects of the two kinds of stimuli. It is therefore safe to accept the conclusion that the similarity factor is of minor importance (at any rate for the type of similarity studied).

On the trace-decay hypothesis, it was expected that any effect of similarity would be attributable to confusion in recall. In conformity with this expectation, intrusions from these stimuli were a little higher than would be expected on a chance basis, when similar stimuli intervened before recall. But when similar stimuli preceded the required stimuli, intrusions were significantly *less* than would be expected on a chance basis, although slight interference was produced by these stimuli. This is certainly puzzling. A possible explanation is that, if the unwanted stimuli intrude in the process of recall, this will tend to delay recall of required stimuli, even when the subject recognizes them as intrusions and does not include them in his overt recall attempts. This would impair recall, on the trace-decay hypothesis, and yet lead to fewer intrusions than would be expected on a chance basis, since no consonant was used twice in the stimuli for any one trial.

Experiment III

If an interval is introduced between the required stimuli and the additional stimuli which intervene before recall, the subject is likely to rehearse the stimuli during this interval. Everyday experience—of trying to remember telephone numbers, for example—suggests that the effect of such rehearsal may be to counteract decay of the trace rather than to strengthen it much, since continuing rehearsal tends to be necessary to prevent forgetting. If this is so, an interval between the required and additional stimuli should not drastically reduce the interference produced by the latter on the trace-decay hypothesis. On a theory which ascribes the effect of intervening stimuli to interference with the traces of the required stimuli, however, this interval might prove to be very critical, for there is much evidence to suggest that the lability of the memory trace—at least to gross cerebral disturbance—is highest immediately after learning and declines rapidly with its age. Thus a blow on the head often produces a short-term retrograde amnesia and the various forms of shock therapy have the same effect. Some of the most interesting evidence comes from experiments on the effect of electro-convulsive shock on learning. Duncan (1949), for example, studied the effect of different time intervals between learning trials and the administration of shock for rats learning a simple avoidance response. There was little evidence of learning if the interval was under 20 sec. and little interference with learning if it exceeded 60 sec.

It is of interest that Muller & Pilzecker (1900), who introduced the misleading expression "retroactive inhibition" (ruckwirkende Hemmung), believed that an activity interpolated during retention interferes with a process of consolidation in the memory trace. Consolidation was believed to depend on a sort of after-discharge of the neural elements involved in learning (it is not, therefore, to be identified with rehearsal, which consists of successive voluntary recall). The idea of a perseverating neural activity following learning, which consolidates a (presumably) structural trace, is not unlike the dual trace mechanism of Hebb (1949) and others.

Method

Again only differences from the method of Experiment I will be described. The required, M, stimuli consisted of three pairs of consonants and the additional, X, stimuli of three pairs of digits. The pairs were presented at intervals of 0.78 sec. However, the interval between the last M pair and the first X pair was varied and was either 0.78, 2.34 or 4.68 sec.: these will be referred to as Intervals I_1, I_2 and I_3 respectively. The total length of the retention interval was held constant at 7 sec. A practice strip was prepared and three test strips. Each test strip carried stimuli for three I_1, three I_2 and three I_3 trials. The orders of I_1, I_2 and I_3 in the different strips formed a Latin square. After the practice strip, different subjects took the different strips in different orders. At the start of each trial, the subject was told the position of the X stimuli. Twelve university students were tested.

Results

Table V shows mean percentage recall scores for the group for different sizes of the interval between the required and additional stimuli. As in the previous experiment, individual scores were subjected to analysis of variance. The variance attributable to variation of the interval was highly significant

Table V Interval in seconds

0.78 (I_1)	2.34 (I_2)	4.68 (I_3)
41	54	59

(percentage recall scores).

(p < 0.001). The analysis also showed that the effect of increasing the size of the interval was non-linear (p < 0.05). It will be seen from Table V that as the interval increased from 0.78 to 4.68 sec. recall rose from 41 to 59 per cent. It will also be seen that the increase in the interval from 0.78 to 2.34 sec. was relatively more important than the increase from 2.34 to 4.68. Another experiment of the series under comparable conditions gave similar results. Nearly all subjects spontaneously reported "going over" the letters during the longer two intervals. Some subjects also reported searching for interpretations of the letters such as "National Debt" for ND.

Discussion

Recall was 59 per cent. when the interval between the required and additional stimuli was about 4 sec. and about 41 per cent. when the interval was less than 1 sec. With similar subjects, recall was 94 per cent. in Experiment I when there were no additional stimuli, but conditions were otherwise almost identical. Thus even when the interval was about 4 sec., the additional stimuli must still have produced considerable interference to keep recall as low as 59 per cent. The conclusion is that increase in the interval from less than I sec. to about 4 sec. only moderately reduces the interference produced by the additional stimuli. This reduction can plausibly be attributed to the effect of rehearsal during the interval, without postulating any additional effect such as diminished interference with traces. A rough check—based on asking subjects to rehearse aloud—suggests that two or three complete rehearsals of the required stimuli are possible during an interval of 4 sec. It is not impossible that the moderate strengthening of learning which did occur was due, not to rehearsal as such, but to finding interpretations of the letters, in the manner spontaneously reported by some subjects (e.g. "National Debt" for ND). If so, this raises the interesting problem of why immediate rehearsal has no permanent effect on learning.

General discussion

The results of the individual experiments have already been discussed. They fit well with the hypothesis of rapid decay of the memory trace when it is first established. It is not claimed that they are incompatible with alternative theories of forgetting. The merit of the decay hypothesis lies in its simplicity and its ability to explain the results without arbitrary auxiliary hypotheses. Results of other recent experiments can also be readily explained on the hypothesis. Brown (1954) found that the delay produced by recalling earlier members of a sequence impairs recall of later members. Conrad (1957) has reported that, if the rate of recall of the sequence as a whole is reduced, recall is likewise impaired. Broadbent (1956, 1957) presents results on a two-channel intake of information which can be interpreted, as he points out, as an effect of trace-decay, although in this case a subsidiary hypothesis is also required (1957, p. 6).

Any theory about forgetting in immediate memory, if it is to be acceptable, must take account of the memory span. A theory of the memory span, based on the hypothesis of trace-decay, was outlined in the introduction. However, the main problem is not the mere existence of a limit to the amount which can be fully recalled following a single presentation: it is the fact that this limit is on a number of disconnected items or "chunks" (Miller, 1956) rather than on information content. Can the trace-decay hypothesis provide a solution to this problem? This will now be considered.

Partial decay of the memory trace of an item is assumed to be compatible with reliable recall because the trace may adequately specify the item, even when it has lost some of its initial features—in other words, because of initial "redundancy" in the trace. The extent of this redundancy should be inversely related to the information content of the item (cf. a chalk mark remains legible after more smudging if it can only be "A" or "B" than if it can be "A" or "B" or "C" or "D"). This means that the critical interval, after which recall becomes unreliable, will be longer for items of low information content than for items of high information content. Consequently one might expect the span to vary directly with the information content of the items. But this does not take account of the fact that the items have to be recalled in a sequence. If the redundancy of those aspects of the traces which mediate retention of the order of the items is low, it is primarily the information content of the order which will determine the size of the span: This could explain why the span is a relatively fixed number of items irrespective of the information content of the items, since the order information depends only on the number of items, provided the items are all different and the order is random (the order information in such a sequence of n items is $\log_2 n!$ "bits"). One way to test this hypothesis would be to see whether the size of the span becomes much larger if the subject is not required to recall the order of the items. But unless he recalls the items in order of presentation, the retention interval will be disproportionately long for some items. Moreover, recall in the order of presentation may well aid recall of what the items are. A better test, therefore, would be to see whether the span is greatly increased if the order information is reduced or eliminated. It is significant and probably not just accidental that the span is high for words in a meaningful passage, since here the constraints of language partly predetermine the order of the words and hence greatly reduce the order, information.

My thanks are due to Professor G. C. Drew, of Bristol University, in whose department the experiments were performed, and to Dr. A. Carpenter and to Dr. D. E. Broadbent for helpful discussion.

References

BARTLETT, F. C. (1932). *Remembering.* Cambridge.

BROADBENT, D. E. (1956). Successive responses to simultaneous stimuli. *Quart. J. exp. Psychol.*, **8**, 145–152.

BROADBENT, D. E. (1957). Immediate memory and simultaneous stimuli. *Quart. J. exp. Psychol.*, **9**, 1–11.

BROWN, J. (1954). The nature of set to learn and of intra-material interference in immediate memory. *Quart. J. exp. Psychol.*, **6**, 141–8.

BROWN, J. (1955). Unpublished Ph.D. thesis. Cambridge.

BROWN, J. (1956). Distortions in immediate memory. *Quart. J. exp. Psychol.*, **8**, 134–9.

CONRAD, R. (1957). Decay theory of immediate memory. *Nature*, **179**, 4564.

DUNCAN, C. P. (1949). The retroactive effect of electroshock on learning. *J. comp. physiol. Psychol.*, **42**, 32–44.

HARDEN, L. M. (1929). The quantitative study of the similarity factor in retroactive inhibition. *J. gen. Psychol.*, **2**, 421–30.

HEBB, D. O. (1949). *The Organization of Behaviour.* New York.

HULL, C. L. *et al.* (1940). *Mathematico-deductive Theory of Rote Learning.* New Haven.

KOFFKA, K. (1935). *Principles of Gestalt Psychology.* New York.

McGEOCH, J. A. (1942). *The Psychology of Human Learning.* New York.

MILLER, G. A. (1956). The magical number seven, plus or minus two. *Psychol. Rev.*, **63**, 81–97.

MULLER, C. E. and PILZECKER, A. (1900). Experimentelle Beiträge zur Lehre vom Gedächtnis. *Z. Psychol. Ergb.*, **1**, 1–288 (Quoted in McGeoch, 1942):

PILLSBURY, W. B. and SYLVESTER, A. (1940). Retroactive and proactive inhibition in immediate memory. *J. exp. Psychol.*, **27**, 532–45.

PRATT, C. C. (1933). Time errors in the method of single stimuli. *J. exp. Psychol.*, **16**, 798–814.

ROBINSON, E. S. (1927). The similarity factor in retroaction. *Amer. J. Psychol.*, **39**, 297–312.

UNDERWOOD, B. J. (1957). Interference and forgetting. *Psychol. Rev.*, **64**, 49–60.

YOUNG, C. W. and SUPA, M. (1941). Mnemic inhibition as a factor in the limitation of the memory span. *Amer. J. Psychol.*, **54**, 546–52.

24

INTERFERENCE AND FORGETTING

Benton J. Underwood[1]

Source: *Psychological Review*, 64(1) (1957): 49–60.

I know of no one who seriously maintains that interference among tasks is of no consequence in the production of forgetting. Whether forgetting is conceptualized at a strict psychological level or at a neural level (e.g., neural memory trace), some provision is made for interference to account for at least some of the measured forgetting. The many studies on retroactive inhibition are probably responsible for this general agreement that interference among tasks must produce a sizable proportion of forgetting. By introducing an interpolated interfering task very marked decrements in recall can be produced in a few minutes in the laboratory. But there is a second generalization which has resulted from these studies, namely, that most forgetting must be a function of the learning of tasks which interfere with that which has already been learned (19). Thus, if a single task is learned in the laboratory and retention measured after a week, the loss has been attributed to the interference from activities learned outside the laboratory during the week. It is this generalization with which I am concerned in the initial portions of this paper.

Now, I cannot deny the data which show large amounts of forgetting produced by an interpolated list in a few minutes in the laboratory. Nor do I deny that this loss may be attributed to interference. But I will try to show that use of retroactive inhibition as a paradigm of forgetting (via interference) may be seriously questioned. To be more specific: if a subject learns a single task, such as a list of words, and retention of this task is measured after a day, a week, or a month, I will try to show that very little of the forgetting can be attributed to an interfering task learned outside the laboratory during the retention interval. Before pursuing this further, I must make some general comments by way of preparation.

Whether we like it or not, the experimental study of forgetting has been largely dominated by the Ebbinghaus tradition, both in terms of methods and materials used. I do not think this is due to sheer perversity on the part of several generations of scientists interested in forgetting. It may be noted that much of our elementary knowledge can be obtained only by rote learning. To work with rote learning does not mean that we are thereby not concerning ourselves with phenomena that have no counterparts outside the laboratory. Furthermore, the investigation of these phenomena can be handled by methods which are acceptable to a science. As is well known, there are periodic verbal revolts against the Ebbinghaus tradition (e.g., 2, 15, 22). But for some reason nothing much ever happens in the laboratory as a consequence of these revolts. I mention these matters neither by way of apology nor of justification for having done some research in rote learning, but for two other reasons. First, it may very well be true, as some have suggested (e.g., 22), that studies of memory in the Ebbinghaus tradition are not getting at all of the important phenomena of memory. I think the same statement—that research has not got at all of the important processes—could be made about all areas in psychology; so that the criticism (even if just) should not be indigenous to the study of memory. Science does not deal at will with all natural events. Science deals with natural events only when ingenuity in developing methods and techniques of measurement allow these events to be brought within the scope of science. If, therefore, the studies of memory which meet scientific acceptability do not tap all-important memorial processes, all I can say is that this is the state of the science in the area at the moment. Secondly, because the bulk of the systematic data on forgetting has been obtained on rote-learned tasks, I must of necessity use such data in discussing interference and forgetting.

Returning to the experimental situation, let me again put in concrete form the problem with which I first wish to deal. A subject learns a single task, such as a list of syllables, nouns, or adjectives. After an interval of time, say, 24 hours, his retention of this list is measured. The explanatory problem is what is responsible for the forgetting which commonly occurs over the 24 hours. As indicated earlier, the studies of retroactive inhibition led to the theoretical generalization that this forgetting was due largely to interference from other tasks learned during the 24-hour retention interval. McGeoch (20) came to this conclusion, his last such statement being made in 1942. I would, therefore, like to look at the data which were available to McGeoch and others interested in this matter. I must repeat that the kind of data with which I am concerned is the retention of a list without formal interpolated learning introduced. The interval of retention with which I am going to deal in this, and several subsequent analyses, is 24 hours.

First, of course, Ebbinghaus' data were available and in a sense served as the reference point for many subsequent investigations. In terms of percentage saved in relearning, Ebbinghaus showed about 65 per cent loss over 24 hours (7). In terms of recall after 24 hours, the following studies are representative of the amount forgotten: Youtz, 88 per cent loss (37); Luh, 82 per cent (18); Krueger, 74 per cent (16); Hovland, 78 per cent (11); Cheng,

65 per cent and 84 per cent (6); Lester, 65 per cent (17). Let us assume as a rough average of these studies that 75 per cent forgetting was measured over 24 hours. In all of these studies the list was learned to one perfect trial. The percentage values were derived by dividing the total number of items in the list into the number lost and changing to a percentage. Thus, on the average in these studies, if the subject learned a 12-item list and recalled three of these items after 24 hours, nine items (75 per cent) were forgotten.

The theory of interference as advanced by McGeoch, and so far as I know never seriously challenged, was that during the 24-hour interval subjects learned something outside the laboratory which interfered with the list learned in the laboratory. Most of the materials involved in the investigations cited above were nonsense syllables, and the subjects were college students. While realizing that I am viewing these results in the light of data which McGeoch and others did not have available, it seems to me to be an incredible stretch of an interference hypothesis to hold that this 75 per cent forgetting was caused by something which the subjects learned outside the laboratory during the 24-hour interval. Even if we agree with some educators that much of what we teach our students in college is nonsense, it does not seem to be the kind of learning that would interfere with nonsense syllables.

If, however, this forgetting was not due to interference from tasks learned outside the laboratory during the retention interval, to what was it due? I shall try to show that most of this forgetting was indeed produced by interference—not from tasks learned outside the laboratory, but from tasks learned previously in the laboratory. Following this I will show that when interference from laboratory tasks is removed, the amount of forgetting which occurs is relatively quite small. It then becomes more plausible that this amount could be produced by interference from tasks learned outside the laboratory, although, as I shall also point out, the interference very likely comes from prior, not interpolated, learning.

In 1950 a study was published by Mrs. Greenberg and myself (10) on retention as a function of stage of practice. The orientation for this study was crassly empirical; we simply wanted to know if subjects learn how to recall in the same sense that they learn how to learn. In the conditions with which I am concerned, naive subjects learned a list of ten paired adjectives to a criterion of eight out of ten correct on a single trial. Forty-eight hours later this list was recalled. On the following day, these same subjects learned a new list to the same criterion and recalled it after 48 hours. This continued for two additional lists, so that the subjects had learned and recalled four lists, but the learning and recall of each list was complete before another list was learned. There was low similarity among these lists as far as conventional symptoms of similarity are concerned. No words were repeated and no obvious similarities existed, except for the fact that they were all adjectives and a certain amount of similarity among prefixes, suffixes, and so on must inevitably occur. The recall of these four successive lists is shown in Fig. 1.

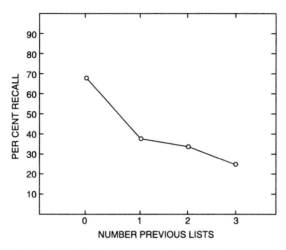

Figure 1 Recall of paired adjectives as a function of number of previous lists learned (10).

As can be seen, the more lists that are learned, the poorer the recall, from 69 per cent recall of the first list to 25 per cent recall of the fourth list. In examining errors at recall, we found a sufficient number of intrusion responses from previous lists to lead us to suggest that the increasing decrements in recall were a function of proactive interference from previous lists. And, while we pointed out that these results had implications for the design of experiments on retention, the relevance to an interference theory of forgetting was not mentioned.

Dr. E. J. Archer has made available to me certain data from an experiment which still is in progress and which deals with this issue. Subjects learned lists of 12 serial adjectives to one perfect trial and recalled them after 24 hours. The recall of a list always took place prior to learning the next list. The results for nine successive lists are shown in Fig. 2. Let me say again that there is no laboratory activity during the 24-hour interval; the subject learns a list, is dismissed from the laboratory, and returns after 24 hours to recall the list. The percentage of recall falls from 71 per cent for the first list to 27 per cent for the ninth.

In summarizing the more classical data on retention above, I indicated that a rough estimate showed that after 24 hours 75 per cent forgetting took place, or recall was about 25 per cent correct. In viewing these values in the light of Greenberg's and Archer's findings, the conclusion seemed inescapable that the classical studies must have been dealing with subjects who had learned many lists. That is to say, the subjects must have served in many conditions by use of counterbalancing and repeated cycles. To check on this I have made a search of the literature on the studies of retention to see if

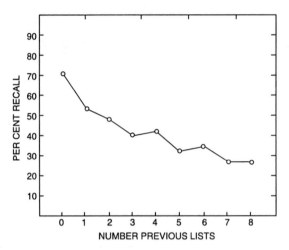

Figure 2 Recall of serial adjective lists as a function of number of previous lists learned. Unpublished data, courtesy of Dr. E. J. Archer.

systematic data could be compiled on this matter. Preliminary work led me to establish certain criteria for inclusion in the summary to be presented. First, because degree of learning is such an important variable, I have included only those studies in which degree of learning was one perfect recitation of the list. Second, I have included only studies in which retention was measured after 24 hours. Third, I have included only studies in which recall measures were given. (Relearning measures add complexities with which I do not wish to deal in this paper.) Fourth, the summary includes only material learned by relatively massed practice. Finally, if an investigator had two or more conditions which met these criteria, I averged the values presentation in this paper. Except for these restrictions, I have used all studies I found (with an exception to be noted later), although I do not pretend to have made an exhaustive search. From each of these studies I got two facts: first, the percentage recalled after 24 hours, and second, the average number of previous lists the subjects had learned before learning the list on which recall after 24 hours was taken. Thus, if a subject had served in five experimental conditions via counterbalancing, and had been given two practice lists, the average number of lists learned before learning the list for which I tabulated the recall was four. This does not take into account any previous experiments in rote learning in which the subject might have served.

For each of these studies the two facts, average number of previous lists learned and percentage of recall, are related as in Fig. 3. For example, consider the study by Youtz. This study was concerned with Jost's law, and had several degrees of learning, several lengths of retention interval, and the subjects served in two cycles. Actually, there were 15 experimental conditions

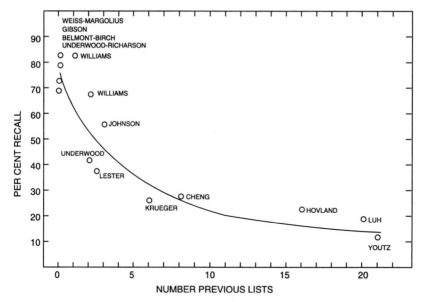

Figure 3 Recall as a function of number of previous lists learned as determined from a number of studies. From left to right: Weiss and Margolius (35), Gibson (9), Belmont and Birch (3), Underwood and Richardson (33), Williams (36), Underwood (27, 28, 29, 30), Lester (17), Johnson (14), Krueger (16), Cheng (6), Hovland (11), Luh (18), Youtz (37).

and each subject was given each condition twice. Also, each subject learned six practice lists before starting the experimental conditions. Among the 15 conditions was one in which the learning of the syllables was carried to one perfect recitation and recall was taken after 24 hours. It is this particular condition in which I am interested. On the average, this condition would have been given at the time when the subject had learned six practice lists and 15 experimental lists, for a total of 21 previous lists.

The studies included in Fig. 3 have several different kinds of materials, from geometric forms to nonsense syllables to nouns; they include both paired-associate and serial presentation, with different speeds of presentation and different lengths of lists. But I think the general relationship is clear. The greater the number of previous lists learned the greater the forgetting. I interpret this to mean that the greater the number of previous lists the greater the *proactive* interference. We know this to be true (26) for a formal proactive-inhibition paradigm; it seems a reasonable interpretation for the data of Fig. 3. That there are minor sources of variance still involved I do not deny. Some of the variation can be rationalized, but that is not the purpose of this report. The point I wish to make is the obvious one of the relationship between number of previous lists learned—lists which presumably had no intentionally built-in similarity—and amount of forgetting. If you like to think in correlational terms, the rank-order correlation between the two variables is – .91 for the 14 points of Fig. 3.

It may be of interest to the historian that, of the studies published before 1942 which met the criteria I imposed, I did not find a single one in which subjects had not been given at least one practice task before starting experimental conditions, and in most cases the subjects had several practice lists and several experimental conditions. Gibson's study (1942) was the first I found in which subjects served in only one condition and were not given practice tasks. I think it is apparent that the design proclivities of the 1920s and 1930s have been largely responsible for the exaggerated picture we have had of the rate of forgetting of rote-learned materials. On the basis of studies performed during the 1920s and 1930s, I have given a rough estimate of forgetting as being 75 per cent over 24 hours, recall being 25 per cent. On the basis of modern studies in which the subject has learned no previous lists— where there is no proactive inhibition from previous laboratory tasks—a rough estimate would be that forgetting is 25 per cent; recall is 75 per cent. The values are reversed. (If in the above and subsequent discussion my use of percentage values as if I were dealing with a cardinal or extensive scale is disturbing, I will say only that it makes the picture easier to grasp, and in my opinion no critical distortion results.)

Before taking the next major step, I would like to point out a few other observations which serve to support my general point that proactive inhibition from laboratory tasks has been the major cause of forgetting in the more classical studies. The first illustration I shall give exemplifies the point that when subjects have served in several conditions, forgetting after relatively short periods of time is greater than after 24 hours if the subject has served in only one condition. In the Youtz study to which I have already referred, other conditions were employed in which recall was taken after short intervals. After 20 minutes recall was 74 per cent, about what it is after 24 hours if the subject has not served in a series of conditions. After two hours recall was 32 per cent. In Ward's (34) well-known reminiscence experiment, subjects who on the average had learned ten previous lists showed a recall of only 64 per cent after 20 minutes.

In the famous Jenkins-Dallenbach (13) study on retention following sleep and following waking, two subjects were used. One subject learned a total of 61 lists and the other 62 in addition to several practice lists. Roughly, then, if the order of the conditions was randomized, approximately 30 lists had been learned prior to the learning of a list for a given experimental condition. Recall after eight waking hours for one subject was 4 per cent and for the other 14 per cent. Even after sleeping for eight hours the recall was only 55 per cent and 58 per cent.

I have said that an interpolated list can produce severe forgetting. However, in one study (1), using the A-B, A-C paradigm for original and interpolated learning, but using subjects who had never served in any previous conditions, recall of the original list was 46 per cent after 48 hours, and in another comparable study (24), 42 per cent. Thus, the loss is not nearly as great as in the classical studies I have cited where there was no interpolated learning in the laboratory.

My conclusion at this point is that, in terms of the gross analysis I have made, the amount of forgetting which might be attributed to interference from tasks learned outside the laboratory has been "reduced" from 75 per cent to about 25 per cent. I shall proceed in the next section to see if we have grounds for reducing this estimate still more. In passing on to this section, however, let me say that the study of factors which influence proactive inhibition in these counterbalanced studies is a perfectly legitimate and important area of study. I mention this because in the subsequent discussion I am going to deal only with the case where a subject has learned a single list in the laboratory, and I do not want to leave the impression that we should now and forevermore drop the study of interference produced by previous laboratory tasks. Indeed, as will be seen shortly, it is my opinion that we should increase these studies for the simple reason that the proactive paradigm provides a more realistic one than does the retroactive paradigm.

When the subject learns and recalls a single list in the laboratory, I have given an estimate of 25 per cent as being the amount forgotten over 24 hours. When, as shown above, we calculate percentage forgotten of lists learned to one perfect trial, the assumption is that had the subjects been given an immediate recall trial, the list would have been perfectly recalled. This, of course, is simply not true. The major factor determining how much error is introduced by this criterion-percentage method is probably the difficulty of the task. In general, the overestimation of forgetting by the percentage method will be directly related to the difficulty of the task. Thus, the more slowly the learning approaches a given criterion, the greater the drop on the trial immediately after the criterion trial. Data from a study by Runquist (24), using eight paired adjectives (a comparatively easy task), shows that amount of forgetting is overestimated by about 10 per cent. In a study (32) using very difficult consonant syllables, the overestimation was approximately 20 per cent. To be conservative, assume that on the average the percentage method of reporting recall overestimates the amount forgotten by 10 per cent. If we subtract this from the 25 per cent assumed above, the forgetting is now re-estimated as being 15 per cent over 24 hours. That is to say, an interference theory, or any other form of theory, has to account for a very small amount of forgetting as compared with the amount traditionally cited.

What are the implications of so greatly "reducing" the amount of forgetting? There are at least three implications which I feel are worth pointing out. First, if one wishes to hold to an interference theory of forgetting (as I do), it seems plausible to assert that this amount of forgetting could be produced from learning which has taken place outside of the laboratory. Furthermore, it seems likely that such interference must result primarily from proactive interference. This seems likely on a simple probability basis. A 20-year-old college student will more likely have learned something during his 20 years prior to coming to the laboratory that will interfere with his retention than he will during the 24 hours between the learning and retention test. However, the longer the retention interval the more important will retroactive interference become relative to proactive interferences.

The second implication is that these data may suggest greater homogeneity or continuity in memorial processes than hitherto supposed. Although no one has adequately solved the measurement problem of how to make comparisons of retention among conditioned responses, prose material, motor tasks, concept learning, and rote-learned tasks, the gross comparisons have indicated that rote-learned tasks were forgotten much more rapidly than these other tasks. But the rote-learning data used for comparison have been those derived with the classical design in which the forgetting over 24 hours is approximately 75 per cent. If we take the revised estimate of 15 per cent, the discrepancies among tasks become considerably less.

The third implication of the revised estimate of rate of forgetting is that the number of variables which appreciably influence rate of forgetting must be sharply limited. While this statement does not inevitably follow from the analyses I have made, the current evidence strongly supports the statement. I want to turn to the final section of this paper which will consist of a review of the influence of some of the variables which are or have been thought to be related to rate of forgetting. In considering these variables, it is well to keep in mind that a variable which produces only a small difference in forgetting is important if one is interested in accounting for the 15 per cent assumed now as the loss over 24 hours. If appropriate for a given variable, I will indicate where it fits into an interference theory, although in no case will I endeavor to handle the details of such a theory.

Time

Passage of time between learning and recall is the critical defining variable for forgetting. Manipulation of this variable provides the basic data for which a theory must account. Previously, our conception of rate of forgetting as a function of time has been tied to the Ebbinghaus curve. If the analysis made earlier is correct, this curve does not give us the basic data we need. In short, we must start all over and derive a retention curve over time when the subjects have learned no previous materials in the laboratory. It is apparent that I expect the fall in this curve over time to be relatively small.

In conjunction with time as an independent variable, we must, in explanations of forgetting, consider why sleep retards the processes responsible for forgetting. My conception, which does not really explain anything, is that since forgetting is largely produced by proactive interference, the amount of time which a subject spends in sleep is simply to be subtracted from the total retention interval when predicting the amount to be forgotten. It is known that proactive interference increases with passage of time (5); sleep, I believe, brings to a standstill whatever these processes are which produce this increase.

Degree of learning

We usually say that the better or stronger the learning the more or better the retention. Yet, we do not know whether or not the *rate* of forgetting differs for items of different strength. The experimental problem is a difficult one. What we need is to have a subject learn a single association and measure its decline in strength over time. But this is difficult to carry out with verbal material, since almost of necessity we must have the subject learn a series of associations, to make it a reasonable task. And, when a series of associations are learned, complications arise from interaction effects among associations of different strength. Nevertheless, we may expect, on the basis of evidence from a wide variety of studies, that given a constant degree of similarity, the effective interference varies as some function of the strength of associations.

Distribution of practice

It is a fact that distribution of practice during acquisition influences retention of verbal materials. The facts of the case seem to be as follows. If the subject has not learned previous lists in the laboratory, massed practice gives equal or better retention than does distributed practice. If, on the other hand, the subject has learned a number of previous lists, distributed practice will facilitate retention (32). We do not have the theoretical solution to these facts. The point I wish to make here is that whether or not distribution of learning inhibits or facilitates retention depends upon the amount of interference from previous learning. It is reasonable to expect, therefore, that the solution to the problem will come via principles handling interference in general. I might also say that a theoretical solution to this problem will also provide a solution for Jost's laws.

Similarity

Amount of interference from other tasks is closely tied to similarity. This similarity must be conceived of as similarity among materials as such and also situational similarity (4). When we turn to similarity within a task, the situation is not quite so clear. Empirically and theoretically (8) one would expect that intratask similarity would be a very relevant variable in forgetting. As discussed elsewhere (31), however, variation in intratask similarity almost inevitably leads to variations in intertask similarity. We do know from a recent study (33) that with material of low meaningfulness forgetting is significantly greater with high intralist similarity than with low. While the difference in magnitude is only about 8 per cent, when we are trying to account for a total loss of 15 per cent, this amount becomes a major matter.

Meaningfulness

The belief has long been held that the more meaningful the material the better the retention—the less the forgetting. Osgood (21) has pointed out that if this is true it is difficult for an interference theory to handle. So far as I know, the only direct test of the influence of this variable is a recent study in which retention of syllables of 100 per cent association value was compared with that of zero association value (33). There was no difference in the recall of these syllables. Other less precise evidence would support this finding when comparisons are made among syllables, adjectives, and nouns, as plotted in Fig. 3. However, there is some evidence that materials of very low meaningfulness are forgotten more rapidly than nonsense syllables of zero association value. Consonant syllables, both serial (32) and paired associates (unpublished), show about 50 per cent loss over 24 hours. The study using serial lists was the one mentioned earlier as knowingly omitted from Fig. 3. These syllables, being extremely difficult to learn, allow a correction of about 20 per cent due to criterion overestimation, but even with this much correction the forgetting (30 per cent) is still appreciably more than the estimate we have made for other materials. To invoke the interference theory to account for this discrepancy means that we must demonstrate how interference from other activities could be greater for these consonant syllables than for nonsense syllables, nouns, adjectives, and other materials. Our best guess at the present time is that the sequence of letters in consonant syllables are contrary to other well-established language habits. That is to say, letter sequences which commonly occur in our language are largely different from those in consonant syllables. As a consequence, not only are these consonant syllables very difficult to learn, but forgetting is accelerated by proactive interference from previously well-learned letter sequences. If subsequent research cannot demonstrate such a source of interference, or it some other source is not specified, an interference theory for this case will be in some trouble.

Affectivity

Another task dimension which has received extensive attention is the affective tone of the material. I would also include here the studies attaching unpleasant experiences to some items experimentally and not to others, and measuring retention of these two sets of items. Freud is to a large extent responsible for these studies, but he cannot be held responsible for the malformed methodology which characterizes so many of them. What can one say by way of summarizing these studies? The only conclusion that I can reach is a statistical one, namely, that the occasional positive result found among the scores of studies is about as frequent as one would expect by sampling error, using the 5 per cent level of confidence. Until a reliable body of facts is established for this variable and associated variables, no theoretical evaluation is possible.

Other variables

As I indicated earlier, I will not make an exhaustive survey of the variables which may influence rate of forgetting. I have limited myself to variables which have been rather extensively investigated, which have immediate relevance to the interference theory, or for which reliable relationships are available. Nevertheless, I would like to mention briefly some of these other variables. There is the matter of *warm-up* before recall; some investigators find that this reduces forgetting (12); others, under as nearly replicated conditions as is possible to obtain, do not (23). Some resolution must be found for these flat contradictions. It seems perfectly reasonable, however, that inadequate set or context differences could reduce recall. Indeed, an interference theory would predict this forgetting if the set or context stimuli are appreciably different from those prevailing at the time of learning. In our laboratory we try to reinstate the learning set by careful instructions, and we simply do not find decrements that might be attributed to inadequate set. For example, in a recent study (33) subjects were given a 24-hour recall of a serial list after learning to one perfect trial. I think we would expect that the first item in the list would suffer the greatest decrement due to inadequate set, yet this item showed only .7 per cent loss. But let it be clear that when we are attempting to account for the 15 per cent loss over 24 hours, we should not overlook any possible source for this loss.

Thus far I have not said anything about forgetting as a function of characteristics of the subject, that is, the personality or intellectual characteristics. As far as I have been able to determine, there is not a single valid study which shows that such variables have an appreciable influence on forgetting. Many studies have shown differences in learning as a function of these variables, but not differences in rate of forgetting. Surely there must be some such variables. We do know that if subjects are severely insulted, made to feel stupid; or generally led to believe that they have no justification for continued existence on the earth just before they are asked to recall, they will show losses (e.g., 25, 38), but even the influence of this kind of psychological beating is short-lived. Somehow I have never felt that such findings need explanation by a theory used to explain the other facts of forgetting.

Concerning the causes of forgetting, let me sum up in a somewhat more dogmatic fashion than is probably justified. One of the assumptions of science is finite causality. Everything cannot influence everything else. To me, the most important implication of the work on forgetting during the last ten years is that this work has markedly *reduced* the number of variables related to forgetting. Correspondingly, I think the theoretical problem has become simpler. It is my belief that we can narrow down the cause of forgetting to interference from previously learned habits, from habits being currently learned, and from habits we have yet to learn. The amount of this interference is primarily a function of similarity and associative strength, the latter being important because it interacts with similarity.

Summary

This paper deals with issues in the forgetting of rote-learned materials. An analysis of the current evidence suggests that the classical Ebbinghaus curve of forgetting is primarily a function of interference from materials learned previously in the laboratory. When this source of interference is removed, forgetting decreases from about 75 per cent over 24 hours to about 25 per cent. This latter figure can be reduced by at least 10 per cent by other methodological considerations, leaving 15 per cent as an estimate of the forgetting over 24 hours. This estimate will vary somewhat as a function of intratask similarity, distributed practice, and with very low meaningful material. But the overall evidence suggests that similarity with other material and situational similarity are by far the most critical factors in forgetting. Such evidence is consonant with a general interference theory, although the details of such a theory were not presented here.

Note

1 Most of the data from my own research referred to in this paper were obtained from work done under Contract N7 onr-45008, Project NR 154–057, between Northwestern University and The Office of Naval Research.

References

1. ARCHER, E. J., & UNDERWOOD, B. J. Retroactive inhibition of verbal associations as a multiple function of temporal point of interpolation and degree of interpolated learning. *J. exp. Psychol.*, 1951, **42**, 283–290.
2. BARTLETT, F. C. *Remembering: a study in experimental and social psychology.* London: Cambridge Univer. Press, 1932.
3. BELMONT, L., & BIRCH, H. G. Re-individualizing the repression hypothesis. *J. abnorm. soc. Psychol.*, 1951, **46**, 226–235.
4. BILODEAU, I. McD., & SCHLOSBERG, H. Similarity in stimulating conditions as a variable in retroactive inhibition. *J. exp. Psychol.*, 1951, **41**, 199–204.
5. BRIGGS, G. E. Acquisition, extinction, and recovery functions in retroactive inhibition. *J. exp. Psychol.*, 1954, **47**, 285–293.
6. CHENG, N. Y. Retroactive effect and degree of similarity. *J. exp. Psychol.*, 1929, **12**, 444–458.

7. EBBINGHAUS, H. *Memory: a contribution to experimental psychology.* (Trans. by H. A. Ruger, and C. E. Bussenius) New York: Bureau of Publications, Teachers College, Columbia Univer., 1913.

8. GIBSON, ELEANOR J. A systematic application of the concepts of generalization and differentiation to verbal learning. *Psychol. Rev.,* 1940, **47**, 196–229.

9. GIBSON, ELEANOR J. Intra-list generalization as a factor in verbal learning. *J. exp. Psychol.,* 1942, **30**, 185–200.

10. GREENBERG, R., & UNDERWOOD, B. J. Retention as a function of stage of practice. *J. exp. Psychol.,* 1950, **40**, 452–457.

11. HOVLAND, C. I. Experimental studies in rote-learning theory. VI. Comparison of retention following learning to same criterion by massed and distributed practice. *J. exp. Psychol.,* 1940, **26**, 568–587.

12. IRION, A. L. The relation of "set" to retention. *Psychol. Rev.,* 1948, **55**, 336–341.

13. JENKINS, J. G., & DALLENBACH, K. M. Oblivescence during sleep and waking. *Amer. J. Psychol.,* 1924, **35**, 605–612.

14. JOHNSON, L. M. The relative effect of a time interval upon learning and retention. *J. exp. Psychol.,* 1939, **24**, 169–179.

15. KATONA, G. *Organizing and memorizing: studies in the psychology of learning and teaching.* New York: Columbia Univer. Press, 1940.

16. KRUEGER, W. C. F. The effect of overlearning on retention. *J. exp. Psychol.,* 1929, **12**, 71–78.

17. LESTER, O. P. Mental set in relation to retroactive inhibition. *J. exp. Psychol.,* 1932, **15**, 681–699.

18. LUH, C. W. The conditions of retention. *Psychol. Monogr.,* 1922, **31**, No. 3 (Whole No. 142).

19. McGEOCH, J. A. Forgetting and the law of disuse. *Psychol. Rev.,* 1932, **39**, 352–370.

20. McGEOCH, J. A. *The psychology of human learning.* New York: Longmans, Green, 1942.

21. OSGOOD, C. E. *Method and theory in experimental psychology.* New York: Oxford Univer. Press, 1953.

22. RAPAPORT, D. Emotions and memory. *Psychol. Rev.,* 1943, **50**, 234–243.

23. ROCKWAY, M. R., & DUNCAN, C. P. Pre-recall warming-up in verbal retention. *J. exp. Psychol.,* 1952, **43**, 305–312.

24. RUNQUIST, W. Retention of verbal associations as a function of interference and strength. Unpublished doctor's dissertation, Northwestern Univer., 1956.

25. RUSSELL, W. A. Retention of verbal material as a function of motivating instructions and experimentally-induced failure. *J. exp. Psychol.,* 1952, **43**, 207–216.

26. UNDERWOOD, B. J. The effect of successive interpolations on retroactive and proactive inhibition. *Psychol. Monogr.,* 1945, **59**, No. 3 (Whole No. 273).

27. UNDERWOOD, B. J. Studies of distributed practice: VII. Learning and retention of serial nonsense lists as a function of intralist similarity. *J. exp. Psychol.,* 1952, **44**, 80–87.

28. UNDERWOOD, B. J. Studies of distributed practice: VIII. Learning and retention of paired nonsense syllables as a function of intralist similarity. *J. exp. Psychol.,* 1953, **45**, 133–142.

29. UNDERWOOD, B. J. Studies of distributed practice: IX. Learning and retention of paired adjectives as a function of intralist similarity. *J. exp. Psychol.,* 1953, **45**, 143–149.

30. UNDERWOOD, B. J. Studies of distributed practice: X. The influence of intralist similarity on learning and retention of serial adjective lists. *J. exp. Psychol.*, 1953, **45**, 253–259.

31. UNDERWOOD, R. J. Intralist similarity in verbal learning and retention. *Psychol. Rev.*, 1954, **3**, 160–166.

32. UNDERWOOD, B. J., & RICHARDSON, J. Studies of distributed practice: XIII. Interlist interference and the retention of serial nonsense lists. *J. exp. Psychol.*, 1955, **50**, 39–46.

33. UNDERWOOD, B. J., & RICHARDSON, J. The influence of meaningfulness, intralist similarity, and serial position on retention. *J. exp. Psychol.*, 1956, **52**, 119–126.

34. WARD, L. B. Reminiscence and rote learning. *Psychol. Monogr.*, 1937, **49**, No. 4 (Whole No. 220).

35. WEISS, W., & MARGOLIUS, G. The effect of context stimuli on learning and retention. *J. exp. Psychol.*, 1954, **48**, 318–322.

36. WILLIAMS, M. The effects of experimentally induced needs upon retention. *J. exp. Psychol.*, 1950, **40**, 139–151.

37. YOUTZ, ADELLA C. An experimental evaluation of Jost's laws. *Psychol. Monogr.*, 1941, 53, No. 1 (Whole No. 238).

38. ZELLER, A. F. An experimental analogue of repression: III. The effect of induced failure and success on memory measured by recall. *J. exp. Psychol.*, 1951, **42**, 32–38.

25

SEMANTIC MEMORY CONTENT IN PERMASTORE

Fifty years of memory for Spanish learned in school

Harry P. Bahrick

Source: *Journal of Experimental Psychology: General*, 113(1) (1984): 1–29.

Retention of Spanish learned in school was tested over a 50-year period for 733 individuals. Tests of reading comprehension, recall, and recognition vocabulary and grammar were administered together with a questionnaire to determine the level of original training, the grades received, and rehearsals during the retention interval in the form of reading, writing, speaking, or listening to Spanish. Multiple regression analysis shows that retention throughout the 50-year period is predictable on the basis of the level of original training. The great majority of subjects rehearse so little that the data reveal no significant rehearsal effects. The analysis yields memory curves which decline exponentially for the first 3–6 years of the retention interval. After that retention remains unchanged for periods of up to 30 years before showing a final decline. Large portions of the originally acquired information remain accessible for over 50 years in spite of the fact the information is not used or rehearsed. This portion of the information in a "permastore" state is a function of the level of original training, the grades received in Spanish courses, and the method of testing (recall vs. recognition), but it appears to be unaffected by ordinary conditions of interference. The life-span frequency distribution of learned responses is discontinuous; one portion of the response distribution has life spans of 0–6 years, the other portion, life spans in excess of 25 years, and no responses have life spans of 6–25 years. This suggests a discrete transition into a permastore state during the extended period of original training. Analysis of successive relearning processes over extended

> time periods is deemed essential for an understanding of the
> acquisition of permanent semantic memory content.

Acquisition of knowledge is the objective of education, and the organization and acquisition of semantic knowledge have been important foci of psychological research. In contrast, questions concerned with the permanence of knowledge have been neglected. It is clear that much of the knowledge acquired in schools is eventually lost, but we have failed to investigate these losses systematically, and hence we know little about how they are affected by conditions of original learning or of later rehearsals. A few investigators have established how much is forgotten during the period immediately following learning (Cohen, 1976; Smythe, Jutras, Bramwell, and Gardner, 1973; Spitzer, 1939) but such research has never been extended to cover significant portions of the human life span. This dearth of information is reflected in textbooks concerned with memory. The leading texts, for example, Baddeley (1976), Wickelgren (1977), Klatzky (1980), Zechmeister and Nyberg (1982), and Ellis and Hunt (1983), give extensive coverage to losses of episodic memory content and to questions regarding the organization of semantic content, but they include no information about the long-term retention of semantic memory content. Neisser (1978) comments critically that higher education depends heavily on the assumption that students remember something valuable from their educational experience. One might expect psychologists to leap at the opportunity to study a critical memory problem so close at hand, but they never do. It is difficult to find even a single study, ancient or modern, of what is retained from academic instruction. Given our expertise and the way we earn our livings, this omission can only be described as scandalous! (p. 5)

The reasons for this neglect are methodological. Dependable conclusions regarding the loss of memory content require accurate assessments of the level of original knowledge and of rehearsals during the retention interval, and it is difficult to obtain such assessments in naturalistic memory research covering long time spans. Furthermore, conditions of learning and of rehearsals tend to change during long time periods, making it even more difficult to establish how much information has been lost. To overcome these problems a method of cross-sectional adjustment was applied in two previous investigations (Bahrick, 1983; Bahrick, Bahrick, and Wittlinger, 1975) that dealt, respectively, with retention of names and faces of high school classmates, and retention of the cognitive map of a city. The merits and shortcomings of this method have been discussed elsewhere, (Bahrick, 1979; Bahrick & Karis, 1982) and will be reviewed in later sections of this article. The present study deals with acquisition and retention of knowledge of Spanish learned in high school or college. The content is naturalistic and semantic in the sense that it is learned in real life and over a prolonged period, but unlike the two preceding investigations the content is acquired through study and rehearsal rather than as the incidental by-product of interacting with peers or with the spatial environment. For this reason the present research has direct implications for the technology of teaching and learning and for questions concerned with what I have called the maintenance of knowledge.

The purpose of this investigation was two-fold: (a) to provide normative data regarding long-term retention of this semantic memory content, and (b) to project estimates of the types and amounts of periodic rehearsal needed to maintain various levels of performance (Bahrick, 1979). The investigation fails to accomplish the second goal because the subjects of this research rehearsed their acquired knowledge so little that the data reveal no significant rehearsal effects. This failure turns out to be fortuitous because it leads to significant conclusions regarding the semipermanent nature of unrehearsed knowledge, and to important inferences regarding previously undocumented characteristics of the memory system. A method of transforming retention curves into life-span frequency distributions of responses reveals that this memory content has a dichotomous life-span distribution. One portion of the content is lost in accordance with an exponential decay function within 6 years after learning terminates. The other portion survives more than 25 years, and most of that content has a life span of more than 50 years. The implications are that during an extended acquisition period, portions of the long-term memory content acquire a semi-permanent character. This content is maintained indefinitely without rehearsals, and is immune to ordinary interference effects. Understanding the circumstances of this transformation is critical for an understanding of long-term memory and for advances in the technology of education.

Method

Subject characteristics and recruitment procedures

There were 773 participants in the study. Of these, 146 were students who at the time of testing were enrolled in a high school- or college-level Spanish course, or who had recently completed such a course. The tests were administered during the last week of course attendance, or within 2 months thereafter. A total of 587 individuals had taken one or more Spanish courses during their attendance at high school or college, and their Spanish instruction had occurred from 1 to 50 years prior to being tested. These subjects were assigned to one of eight groups in accordance with the time elapsed since their last Spanish course. The remaining 40 individuals had no instruction in Spanish. They were included in the study in order to establish a baseline for performance that differentiates knowledge acquired in Spanish classes from knowledge acquired incidentally, as well as from correct answers based upon guessing. Twenty of these individuals (C1) ranged in age from 17 to 22 and their performance provides a control for individuals currently enrolled in Spanish classes. The other 20 (C2) ranged in age from 41 to 62 (M = 51), and their performance provides a control for the inference of long-term memory from Spanish instruction.

The mean of the retention interval, and the level of Spanish training for the eight retention groups are presented in Table 1. For purposes of this classification and subsequent data analyses, a full year of high school Spanish instruction is equated with a term or semester course in college. Thus individuals classified at Level 3 in Table 1 include those who took three college courses of Spanish and no high school courses, as well as those with three years of high school Spanish instruction and no college courses. Subjects with a combination of high school and college instruction were assigned to a level determined by the highest level college course taken, regardless of the amount of prior high school instruction. Thus subjects who completed 2 years of Spanish in high school and followed this by taking two courses in college, were assigned to Level 2 if the college courses were beginning Spanish, but to Level 4 if the two college courses were intermediate Spanish. The decision to equate high school and college instruction in this way was based on data available from college language placement examinations. Students with high school language instruction are typically assigned to an appropriate level college course on the basis of their performance on a placement examination. Separate analyses of knowledge acquired in high school and college were not carried out because most subjects had taken courses at both the high school and college level.

Students enrolled in Spanish courses at the time of testing were recruited from Ohio Wesleyan University; Hayes High School in Delaware, Ohio; and

Table 1 Number of subjects at each level of training

Group	Mean interval (months)	Training level									
		1	2	3	4	5	6	7	8	9	10
Current students	0.1	52	27	39	18	3	2	0	0	0	5
1	14.5	12	26	34	53	0	2	1	0	0	2
2	37.8	15	61	21	11	0	2	0	0	0	0
3	69.1	27	36	15	23	2	4	0	3	0	2
4	114.0	5	16	8	11	2	3	0	0	0	2
5	175.1	11	6	10	11	2	1	0	0	1	3
6	300.6	4	32	4	10	2	5	0	2	0	2
7	415.2	6	23	7	10	1	0	0	1	0	1
8	596.4	1	16	4	6	0	3	0	2	1	0

The Ohio State University. Some Ohio Wesleyan University students satisfied a course requirement in introductory psychology by taking the test; the remaining subjects were paid. Subjects not enrolled in Spanish courses were recruited by newspaper advertisement and with the help of local churches and community service organizations. Most of these subjects were volunteers who donated their pay to the service organization that helped to recruit them. The control subjects (C1 and C2) were tested 2 years after the other subjects. They were recruited by the same methods and from the same populations as the remaining subjects.

Test construction and administration

In addition to taking a test of knowledge of Spanish, subjects completed a questionnaire designed to provide information about Spanish instruction; grades obtained in Spanish courses; and various opportunities to read, write, speak, or listen to Spanish and other Romance languages during the retention interval. Each subject supplied the dates of these experiences and signed a statement authorizing the high school or college attended to release information concerning the grades earned in Spanish courses. A summary of the questionnaire and portions of each subtest appear in Appendixes A and B. The test consists of the following 10 subtests: Reading comprehension; Spanish–English recall vocabulary; Spanish–English recognition vocabulary; English–Spanish recall vocabulary; English–Spanish recognition vocabulary; grammar recall; grammar recognition; idiom recall; idiom recognition; and word order. The decision to develop a test for the purpose of this study was reached after consideration of existing language tests indicated that available tests, for example, the CLOZE tests, were reliable (Oller, 1973) but would not yield the subscores desired for obtaining analytic learning and memory data. The subtests were constructed in such a way as to minimize "built in" interdependence. Thus the meaning of all words was supplied in subtests measuring knowledge of grammar, idioms, and word order, and the sequence of subtests was arranged in such a way as to minimize facilitation effects among the subtests. The tests were assembled on the basis of vocabulary lists and reading exercises available in textbooks or contributed by language teachers. The test was revised several times on the basis of pilot data, so as to achieve a difficulty level suitable for reflecting improvement throughout a sequence of four college-level Spanish courses, and a total length that would permit completion of both the test and questionnaire within 1 hour.

The test was administered to individuals or groups of up to 40 subjects, without strict adherence to time limits. Most individuals completed test and questionnaire within 1 hour, but they were allowed to continue as long as they chose. The decision not to impose time limits was based on the fact that the concern of this investigation is the amount of knowledge retained rather than the speed of retrieval. Subjects ranged in age from 17 to over 70 years, and adherence to strict time limits could have adversely affected the performance of older subjects (Burke & Light, 1981).

Verification of questionnaire data

It is important to determine the accuracy of information given on the questionnaire since the independent variables in this investigation are derived by scoring answers provided on the questionnaire. To determine the extent to which these data are subject to error because of faulty memory or other causes, we verified answers regarding the number of Spanish courses taken, the time elapsed since the last Spanish course, and the grades received in Spanish courses. This was done for 14% of the subjects, selected on the basis of accessibility of the data. The verification was obtained by checking answers against the records of the registrar at Ohio Wesleyan University and at The Ohio State University. Although the selection of data for verification was not random, subjects belonging to the various retention intervals were represented proportionately in the verified data, and the results can be generalized with confidence to the remaining subjects.

Verification of the number of Spanish courses taken showed that 81% of all subjects reported the number accurately. Subjects belonging to Time Groups 1 and 2 reported no errors; after that the error rate remained constant at 22%. Most errors were errors of one course, and subjects were twice as likely to understate the number of Spanish courses taken than to overstate that number. Verification of the retention interval reported by subjects indicated that 57% of all subjects stated the interval correctly, 89% reported an interval which fell within 10% of the correct interval, and 96% of subjects reported an interval which placed them within the same group to which they were assigned on the basis of the verified interval. Those subjects who committed errors were somewhat more likely to report an interval shorter than the verified interval, and the average error increased approximately proportionately to the retention interval.

Verification of reported grades showed that 78% were reported correctly, 97% reported average grades within 0.5 of the verified average. These data showed no systematic variation with the retention interval. Of those subjects who reported erroneously, a somewhat larger amount overstated their grades, and the average error of overstatement was twice as large as the average understatement (0.54 vs. 0.27). Thus, in contrast to memory of the retention interval, the accuracy of memory reports of grades does not decline with time. In a sense these data provide a study within a study; that is, they constitute a miniature study of the accuracy of reports based on long-term memory. These data are also of some general interest as they give an indication of the validity of other nonverified autobiographical memory reports here and elsewhere.

Scoring of questionnaire data

All of the variables entered into the analysis of data are presented in Table 2. Variables 1–10 are the dependent variables based on the scores obtained from the 10 subtests. Variables 11–42 are independent variables based on information taken from the questionnaire. The time elapsed between completion of the last Spanish course and the date of the test was calculated to the nearest month, and the assignment to groups was based upon this score.

Table 2 Abbreviations and names of all variables

Abbreviation	Variable	Abbreviation	Variable
PARCOM	(1) Reading comprehension	RECENG	Recency of visits using English in months
VSEREC	(2a) Vocabulary Spanish–English recall	RECSP	Recency of visits using Spanish in months
VSEREG	(2b) Vocabulary Spanish–English recognition	LSTRAD	Listening to radio (minutes per year)
VESREC	(2c) Vocabulary English–Spanish recall	LSTTV	Listening to television (minutes per year)
VESREG	(2d) Vocabulary English–Spanish recognition	LSTFLM	Listening to films (minutes per year)
GRMREC	(3a) Grammar recall		
GRMREG	(3b) Grammar recognition	LSTCNV	Listening to conversation (minutes per year)
IDREC	(4a) Idiom recall		
IDREG	(4b) Idiom recognition	READNW	Reading of newspapers (minutes per year)
WRDORD	(5) Word order		
RETENT	Retention interval in months	READMG	Reading of magazines (minutes per year)
LEVEL	Highest level of courses	READBK	Reading of books (minutes per year)
HIGH	Level of high school courses		
COLLEG	Level of college courses	READCR	Reading of correspondence (minutes per year)
TAPE	Level of courses using tapes	SPEAK	Speaking (minutes per year)
MEAN	Mean grade in courses	WRITE	Writing (minutes per year)
GRDREC	Most recent grade	TOTLST	Total listening (minutes per year)
TRVLEG	Travel using English (1 = yes, 0 = no)		
TRVLSP	Travel using Spanish (1 = yes, 0 = no)	TOTRED	Total reading (minutes per year)
FREQEG	Frequency of visits using English	TOTROM	Total of Romance language courses
FREQSP	Frequency of visits using Spanish	FRENCH	Level of French courses
		PORT	Level of Portuguese courses
DURENG	Duration of visits using English in days	ITALAN	Level of Italian courses
DURSP	Duration of visits using Spanish in days	LATIN	Level of Latin courses

The level of Spanish training was established as reported earlier. Letter grades on all Spanish courses were converted into the conventional scale with A = 4; B = 3, and so forth, and an average grade was computed for each subject. Travel to Spanish-speaking countries was scored in terms of frequency, duration, and recency of trips. Frequency was scored in terms of the number of separate trips, regardless of duration. Duration was scored in terms of the aggregate number of days spent in Spanish-speaking countries, and recency, in terms of the number of months elapsed since the most recent trip. Separate subscores for these three variables were established for travel in the company of English-speaking people, and travel in which most or all conversation was in the Spanish language. Individuals who spent more than 1 year travelling in Spanish-speaking countries were excluded from the study as were those who reported extensive childhood experiences with the Spanish language based either on being raised in a Spanish-speaking home, prolonged residence in a Spanish-speaking country, or in a foreign-language elementary school program. The data regarding rehearsals during the retention interval in the form of listening to, reading, speaking, or writing in Spanish were scored by estimating the number of minutes per year spent in each category of activity. Separate scores were entered for the various subcategories, for example, reading newspapers, magazines, listening to TV, and so forth. To transform the frequency data of the questionnaire into estimates of minutes of rehearsal per year it was necessary to assign estimates of mean frequency to each frequency category. The category "once a year or less" was scored 0 or 1 depending on whether or not a duration of rehearsal was indicated. The frequency category of "2–11 times per year" was scored 6, the category "several times each month" was scored 30, and the category "several times each week" was scored 150. These estimated frequency-per-year scores were then multipled by the indicated average duration of the rehearsal activity to arrive at the estimated aggregate number of minutes per year spent in the activity.

The level of training in other Romance languages was scored in terms of the total number of courses taken in high school and college, using the same method of combining high school and college work as was used in determining the level of Spanish training.

Scoring the language test

Although the test is objective, a variety of scoring problems arose in regard to answers that were nearly correct or partly correct. These problems were most challenging in the reading comprehension subtest, but also occurred in tests of recall vocabulary. Two college teachers of Spanish examined pilot data and classified answers into the categories of correct, partly correct, and wrong. Guidelines for classifying answers to each question were established on the basis of agreement between the raters, and of dictionary definitions for individual words. The answers of *boyfriend, lover,* or *fiancee,* for example, were classified as a correct translation of the Spanish word *novio,* but the answer of *girlfriend* was classified as partly correct. In order to avoid fractional scores, the subtests in which partial credit was to be awarded were scored on the basis of 2 points for correct answers and 1 point for answers that were partly correct, yielding a maximum score of twice the number of questions in the subtest. This scoring applied to the reading comprehension test yielded a maximum score of 40, and applied to subtests for recall of vocabulary and grammar yielded maximum scores of 30 points. No such ambiguities were present in the scoring of recognition tests, where the maximum score remained equal to the number of items on the test. Some subjects failed to answer individual questions on the five alternative recognition subtests in spite of instructions that encouraged guessing. In order to establish comparability of scores with those who received the benefits of guessing, unanswered recognition questions were awarded 1/5 point. The fractional points were summed for each subtest, and a correction was made if the aggregate point score could be rounded to a whole number. Thus subjects who omitted the answers to 3–7 questions on a recognition subtest were awarded 1 additional point.

Data analysis and results

Acquisition data

Means for all dependent variables for students at each level of Spanish instruction are shown in Table 3, along with the means for the control subjects C1 who had no Spanish instruction. Acquisition functions for the

Table 3 Subtest performance by students at various training levels

| Variable | *Level of training* | | | | | | *Possible score* |
	C1	1	2	3	4	8.3	
PARCOM	2.1	14.7	24.9	25.2	29.6	34.3	40
VSEREC	0.3	7.3	17.0	17.2	18.0	28.2	30
VSEREG	3.3	6.5	8.2	9.3	10.2	13.6	15
VESREC	0.3	12.7	22.0	19.8	23.1	29.3	30
VESREG	4.8	7.0	10.2	10.3	10.9	13.9	15
GRMREC	0.0	11.8	17.7	17.2	14.0	22.8	30
GRMREG	2.6	4.6	8.4	8.4	7.5	13.0	15
IDREC	0.0	1.9	2.9	3.6	3.2	6.7	10
IDREG	1.3	3.7	5.6	5.8	6.0	8.0	10
WRDORD	0.3	3.1	5.1	4.8	5.0	5.6	8

Note. See Table 2 for explanation of abbreviations.

10 dependent variables appear in Figures 1 and 2. The control subjects C1 provide the data for the initial points for all subtests. The data for plotting Figures 1 and 2 were obtained by dividing the mean raw score for each subtest by the maximum obtainable score on that subtest, and multiplying the quotient by 100. This yields a percentage score that permits certain comparisons. Subjects at Level 5 of Spanish instruction were grouped with those at higher levels of training, because the number of subjects per group was too small to yield reliable data. The average training level for these subjects (8.3) is used in Table 3 and Figures 1 and 2. The test remains reasonably sensitive to continued improvement, and ceiling effects have little influence on performance at least through Training Level 4. Direct comparisons of recall and recognition performance are not appropriate since the words used for recall and recognition subtests are not the same. The difficulty level of each subtest was adjusted on the basis of pilot data so as to remain sensitive to improvements throughout the acquisition period. It is appropriate, however, to compare relative progress at various stages of training among the subtests. It is apparent, for instance, that the recall for the English equivalents of Spanish words is relatively low at Training Level 1, but for students at Training Level 8, performance on this subtest is high. In other words this subtest is not generally more difficult than the other subtests; it is relatively difficult during the early stages of learning the language, but not during the later stages. The subtest for English recall for the meaning of Spanish idioms,

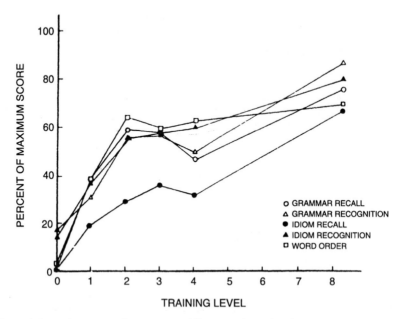

Figure 1 Learning curves for grammar, idioms, and word order.

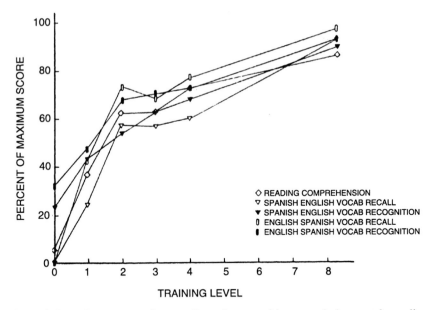

Figure 2 Learning curves for recall and recognition vocabulary and reading comprehension.

on the other hand, is a relatively difficult test, that is, performance on this test remains lower than performance on the other tests throughout the learning period. It must be noted that the groups at various levels of training are not equated in regard to independent variables, and the values of Figures 1 and 2 are influenced by such inequalities. Thus subjects at Level 1 achieved a mean grade of 2.8 in Spanish whereas subjects at Level 8 achieved a mean grade of 3.5. No statistical adjustments were made to correct this inequality because the grading patterns in beginning courses differ from those in advanced courses. This difference may reflect general leniency of the instructor, and/or subject characteristics resulting from self-selection on the part of those individuals who chose to take advanced courses. However, these methodological problems do not directly apply to the retention data, permitting more sophisticated statistical treatment of the latter.

Retention data

The mean scores on all variables for the eight retention groups and for the control group C2 appear in Table 4. It is apparent that the eight retention groups differ considerably on several independent variables likely to affect the amount of knowledge of Spanish. Training level varies from 2.3 for Group 2 to 3.6 for Group 5, and the level of training in other Romance languages varies from 0.7 to 2.7, with the older alumni groups generally

Table 4 Unadjusted mean scores for nine groups

Variable	Group								
	1	*2*	*3*	*4*	*5*	*6*	*7*	*8*	*C2*
PARCOM	24.2	15.2	17.7	20.4	20.3	16.4	14.9	12.1	2.0
VSEREC	14.1	6.6	8.8	9.4	10.3	7.8	6.9	6.7	0.1
VSEREG	8.5	6.0	7.2	7.0	8.1	6.9	6.9	7.1	3.4
VESREC	15.6	7.0	8.1	7.6	9.8	7.9	6.8	6.5	0.1
VESREG	9.9	7.0	7.5	8.2	8.5	7.6	7.2	7.2	4.9
GRMREC	12.4	6.3	7.1	7.4	7.4	5.0	3.7	4.2	0.0
GRMREG	6.1	3.8	4.9	5.4	5.6	4.6	3.9	3.7	2.7
IDREC	2.9	1.6	2.2	2.4	2.7	2.2	1.9	1.9	0.4
IDREG	4.7	3.3	3.7	3.6	3.7	3.2	2.6	2.6	1.3
WRDORD	3.7	2.2	2.9	3.5	3.4	2.3	2.1	1.7	0.2
RETENT	14.5	37.8	69.1	114.0	175.1	300.6	415.2	596.4	
LEVEL	3.3	2.3	2.9	3.4	3.6	3.3	2.9	3.4	
HIGH	2.5	2.1	2.0	2.1	1.7	1.5	1.4	1.5	
COLLEG	1.6	0.6	1.2	1.5	1.9	1.9	1.6	2.1	
TAPE	1.4	1.9	2.0	2.5	1.9	1.2	0.1	0.0	
MEAN	3.2	3.1	3.1	3.0	3.1	3.1	3.0	2.7	
GRDREC	3.1	3.0	3.0	2.9	3.0	3.0	2.9	2.8	
TRVLEG	0.2	0.2	0.2	0.2	0.2	0.3	0.4	0.4	
TRVLSP	0.1	0.0	0.1	0.0	0.0	0.0	0.0	0.0	
FREQEG	0.7	0.2	0.3	0.3	0.4	0.6	0.7	1.0	
FREQSP	0.1	0.0	0.1	0.0	0.0	0.0	0.0	0.1	
DURENG	5.1	2.0	5.4	10.2	8.0	4.6	6.0	7.7	
DURSP	8.3	0.0	7.0	0.0	0.5	0.3	0.0	1.3	
RECENG	4.4	7.1	7.9	16.4	20.4	33.8	36.4	58.6	
RECSP	2.0	0.0	5.2	0.0	3.7	2.0	0.0	2.6	
LSTRAD	103.0	43.4	33.3	10.7	13.5	2.7	3.5	9.2	
LSTTV	77.5	66.7	14.9	10.7	12.0	1.8	5.8	9.6	
LSTFLM	18.2	11.7	7.4	13.4	2.7	1.3	4.3	0.5	
LSTCNV	470.7	91.7	136.5	87.3	11.6	20.5	15.4	6.3	
READNW	390.5	13.4	27.8	15.5	6.8	15.1	5.6	3.1	
READMG	458.6	14.0	30.2	15.7	10.8	16.5	1.9	1.8	
READBK	590.7	14.0	159.1	19.0	40.9	24.2	10.8	2.5	
READCR	429.9	20.8	27.9	70.7	4.6	3.5	15.9	2.4	
SPEAK	380.4	44.0	108.9	56.3	39.1	23.0	15.0	8.8	
WRITE	4.9	1.7	0.9	0.4	1.6	1.2	12.0	0.0	
TOTLST	625.9	223.2	269.2	122.1	39.8	26.3	29.0	25.6	
TOTRED	1,800.6	62.2	244.6	120.9	63.2	59.2	34.2	9.8	
TOTROM	1.0	0.7	1.5	1.5	2.4	2.1	2.4	2.7	2.4
FRENCH	0.5	0.5	1.0	0.6	1.1	0.8	0.9	0.7	
PORT	0.0	0.0	0.0	0.0	0.1	0.0	0.0	0.0	
ITALAN	0.1	0.0	0.1	0.0	0.1	0.2	0.2	0.0	
LATIN	0.3	0.2	1.1	0.8	1.1	1.1	1.3	2.0	

Note. See Table 2 for explanation of abbreviations.

having more training than the younger groups. To obtain estimates of retention which are free of these inequities, it is necessary to adjust the data. Two procedures were used to obtain the adjusted estimates. The first of these regression procedures closely follows the one used in the earlier investigations (Bahrick, 1983; Bahrick, et al., 1975). In this method of adjustment the data for all retention groups (excluding C2) are pooled and intercorrelations are established among all variables, with indicator variables designating time groups (Neter & Wasserman, 1974). Variables are then entered into the regression program in accordance with some fixed order, for example, the magnitude of the correlation with the dependent variable, and they are maintained in the regression equation if they add significantly to the portion of variance accounted for on the dependent variable. This approach yields common partial regression coefficients for the regression equations applicable to all time groups, and separate intercept values for the equation of each group. The adjusted scores are calculated for each group by multiplying the partial regression coefficient of each included variable by the desired value of that variable for the projected retention estimate. These products are then added to the intercept value appropriate for that group.

The partial regression coefficients calculated for each of the 10 dependent variables and the intercept values applicable to each group appear in Table 5. In this case the same 14 variables were added to the regression program, in the order listed, for each of the 10 dependent variables. It is apparent that only the variables of level of Spanish training, mean grade received, and the level of training in other Romance languages contribute significantly to the variance accounted for on any dependent variable. This was true regardless of the order in which the variables were entered into the regression program. Adjusted retention functions for all dependent variables based on this procedure are shown in Figures 3 and 4. In calculating these adjusted scores the mean grade in Spanish courses was set at 3, the level of Spanish training was set at 3, and the level of training in other Romance languages was set at 0. These adjusted scores together with the portion of variance accounted for on each dependent variable are presented in Table 6. In order to render the retention functions for the various dependent variables comparable, Figures 3 and 4 are expressed as a percentage of the original scores for that same variable. The original scores for each variable are the values attained by the student group trained at Level 3 (Table 3, column 3) with minor regression adjustments to reflect a mean grade of 3, and to discount training in other Romance languages. The 10 retention functions exhibit common as well as divergent characteristics. All functions show a rapid loss of information during the first 3 years of the retention interval, followed by a very long period of relatively stable or even improved performance. Thus performance declines as a linear function of the logarithm of time, only for an initial period.

Table 5 Partial regression weights and intercept values for 8 groups and 10 dependent variables

Dependent variable

Predictors	PARCOM	VSEREC	VSEREG	VESREC	VESREG	GRMREC	GRMREG	IDREC	IDREG	WRDORD
INTERCEPT	-7.14	-7.45	1.588	-7.37	1.78	-7.09	-0.22	-1.02	-0.63	-1.81
IND. 1	11.36	6.43	1.19	8.11	2.42	7.26	2.33	0.78	2.08	1.87
IND. 2	4.74	1.01	-0.54	1.58	0.20	2.91	0.78	-0.10	1.08	0.85
IND. 3	5.72	2.09	0.13	1.52	0.26	2.77	1.48	0.26	1.24	1.21
IND. 4	7.44	1.96	-0.27	0.36	0.79	2.52	1.63	0.27	0.97	1.69
IND. 5	6.53	2.33	0.54	2.08	0.81	2.19	1.58	0.51	0.85	1.48
IND. 6	3.37	.48	-0.39	0.78	0.16	0.20	0.84	0.17	0.49	0.46
IND. 7	2.95	.42	-0.20	0.72	0.09	-0.14	0.39	0.02	0.13	0.44
LEVEL	2.16	1.77	0.56	1.79	0.62	1.46	0.57	0.38	0.41	0.37
MEAN	4.05	2.87	1.59	2.79	1.14	2.30	0.60	0.59	0.59	0.74
TOTROM	0.29	0.07	0.16	0.05	0.05	0.01	0.11	0.02	0.07	0.07
TOTRED	0.06	0.00	0.00	0.00	0.00	0.00	0.00	0.00	0.00	0.00
TOTLST	0.00	0.00	0.00	0.00	0.00	0.00	0.00	0.00	0.00	0.00
WRITE	0.02	0.01	0.00	0.00	0.00	0.02	0.00	0.00	0.00	0.00
SPEAK	0.00	0.00	0.00	0.00	0.00	0.00	0.00	0.00	0.00	0.00

Note. See Table 2 for explanation of abbreviations. Ind. = indicator variable.

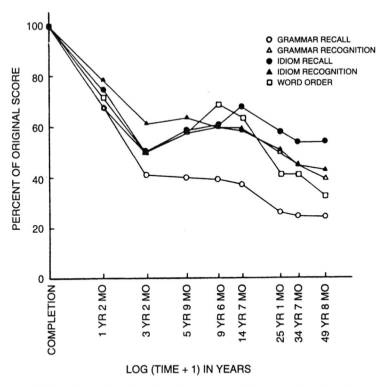

Figure 3 Adjusted retention functions for grammar, idioms, and word order.

Comparisons among the four functions related to knowledge of individual words show that recognition performance is maintained at a higher level than recall performance, and that the directions of search from English to Spanish and Spanish to English yield nearly identical retention functions for recognition, but not for recall. The Spanish-to-English recall direction is maintained at a higher level. The superiority of recognition performance to recall must be interpreted in relation to the control baseline provided by the C2 data. These data support the conclusion that performance on subtests for recall reflects almost entirely memory of Spanish training, while performance on recognition subtests reflects, in part, the benefits of guessing, of memory from instruction in other Romance languages, and of information about Spanish acquired incidentally. It is worth noting that such incidental information makes a significant contribution to performance on the subtests for recognition vocabulary, where performance of both C1 and C2 groups significantly exceeds chance success ($p < .01$). In contrast, performance on the idiom recognition subtest falls significantly short of the expected chance level ($p < .01$). The latter result reflects the fact that certain foils on the idiom

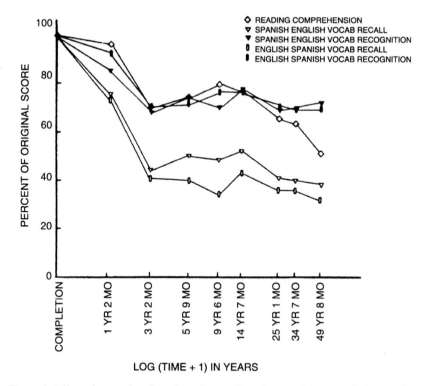

Figure 4 Adjusted retention functions for recall and recognition vocabulary and for reading comprehension.

recognition test are chosen with high frequency because they contain English cognates for portions of the Spanish idiom.

In comparing the recall and recognition functions one must keep in mind that the two types of tests are not based on the same words, and that all retention scores are expressed as a percentage of the performance attained on that same indicant at the end of training.

At the end of 50 years subjects trained at Level 3 perform approximately at Acquisition Level 1 in reading comprehension and recognition vocabulary. However, they perform considerably below that level in recall for Spanish words, in regard to knowledge of proper word order, and particularly in recall for grammar rules. This suggests that reading comprehension is comparatively less affected by a decline of these latter indicants, and is maintained largely on the basis of recognition vocabulary and knowledge of grammar at the recognition level.

An examination of the intercorrelations among all variables yields conclusions in keeping with the results which have been presented. Intercorrelations among all dependent variables and selected independent variables pooled for

Table 6 Adjusted retention scores for 8 groups and 10 dependent variables

Dependent variable	Time group									R^2
	0	1	2	3	4	5	6	7	8	
PARCOM	25.2	24.16	17.5	18.53	20.25	19.34	16.18	15.76	12.81	42
VSEREC	17.2	12.96	7.54	8.62	8.26	8.86	7.01	6.95	6.53	47
VSEREG	9.3	7.94	6.20	6.87	6.46	7.28	6.35	6.54	6.74	38
VESREC	19.8	14.48	8.17	7.89	6.73	8.45	7.15	7.09	6.37	46
VESREG	10.3	9.48	7.26	7.32	7.85	7.87	7.22	7.15	7.06	40
GRMREC	17.2	11.45	7.10	6.96	6.71	6.38	4.39	4.05	4.19	50
GRMREG	8.4	5.63	4.08	4.78	4.93	4.88	4.14	3.69	3.30	38
IDREC	3.6	2.67	1.80	2.09	2.16	2.40	2.06	1.91	1.89	39
IDREG	5.8	4.52	3.51	3.68	3.41	3.29	2.93	2.57	2.44	36
WRDORD	4.8	3.39	2.36	2.73	3.22	3.00	1.98	1.95	1.52	33

Note. See Table 2 for explanation of abbreviations.

all retention groups are presented in Table 7. It is apparent that intercorrelations among the dependent variables are quite high and that the dependent variables do not correlate highly with those independent variables reflecting rehearsal during the retention interval. The dependent variables do correlate with independent variables defining original training, for example, the level of Spanish training, the mean grade received in Spanish courses, and the level of training in other Romance languages. The low correlation between retention of Spanish and rehearsal variables such as reading, listening to, or speaking Spanish during the retention interval, reflects the fact that scores on these rehearsal variables are extremely low for the great majority of subjects. Thus it is not appropriate to conclude from our data that practice does not help in the retention of knowledge. Rather, we find that our subjects rehearse their knowledge minimally or not at all, and that the data therefore reflect no important influence of the rehearsal variables. Those subjects who rehearse tend to do so only during the first year of the retention interval (see Table 4). After that time the mean number of minutes spent in reading Spanish ranges from 10 min to 240 min per year for the various groups. The mean number of minutes of listening to Spanish ranges from 25 min to 253 min per year, and for speaking Spanish, from 9 min to 70 min per year. There is good reason to believe that even these low numbers are overestimates caused by the nature of our questionnaire, which emphasized rehearsal, and by the nature of our calculation, which assumed that the midpoint values of rehearsal frequency categories best represented the data in these categories. The absence of rehearsal effects must also be interpreted in relation to the amount of knowledge to be rehearsed. The probability of reexposure to individual words or items on our test is quite small when subjects rehearse 1 or 2 hours per year to cover a vocabulary of several thousand words. It is therefore not surprising that the correlations of indicated rehearsals with the dependent variables are negligible. For these reasons the regression equations for predicting retention do not include variables related to the amount or type of practice during the retention interval. The fact that most of our subjects failed to rehearse was at first a most disappointing finding because it precludes attaining one of the objectives of this investigation, that is, to estimate the type and amount of rehearsal needed to maintain various levels of language performance. It will be shown in the General Interpretation and Discussion section, however, that this finding is basic to the major theoretical conclusion of this investigation, and thus it turns out to be most fortuitous.

Two considerations led to the decision to apply a second, somewhat different method of analysis to the retention data. (a) Scattergrams constructed for individual correlations of the level of training variables and retention variables showed strong indications of nonlinear regression, and (b) the possibility of systematic differences among the subject populations sampled in various time groups made it desirable to minimize such effects by a method that is not based on the assignment of subjects to groups and that permits

Table 7 Intercorrelations among dependent and selected independent variables

Independent and dependent variables	Dependent variable									
	PARCOM	VSEREC	VSEREG	VESREC	VESREG	GRMREC	GRMREG	IDREC	IDREG	WRDORD
PARCOM	1.00	0.79	0.71	0.76	0.76	0.74	0.59	0.72	0.67	0.70
VSEREC	0.79	1.00	0.77	0.88	0.79	0.80	0.68	0.79	0.74	0.68
VSEREG	0.71	0.77	1.00	0.73	0.74	0.67	0.60	0.70	0.64	0.59
VESREC	0.76	0.88	0.73	1.00	0.77	0.82	0.68	0.75	0.72	0.68
VESREG	0.76	0.79	0.74	0.77	1.00	0.74	0.58	0.71	0.65	0.65
GRMREC	0.74	0.80	0.67	0.82	0.74	1.00	0.72	0.72	0.71	0.69
GRMREG	0.59	0.68	0.60	0.68	0.58	0.72	1.00	0.64	0.60	0.59
IDREC	0.72	0.79	0.70	0.75	0.71	0.72	0.64	1.00	0.66	0.63
IDREG	0.67	0.74	0.64	0.72	0.65	0.71	0.60	0.66	1.00	0.62
WRDORD	0.70	0.68	0.59	0.68	0.65	0.69	0.59	0.63	0.62	1.00
LEVEL	0.50	0.55	0.51	0.51	0.50	0.51	0.53	0.54	0.48	0.44
MEAN	0.41	0.42	0.39	0.39	0.39	0.41	0.31	0.38	0.34	0.36
SPEAK	0.12	0.18	0.12	0.17	0.13	0.20	0.16	0.17	0.14	0.14
WRITE	0.11	0.15	0.16	0.10	0.13	0.09	0.14	0.15	0.14	0.10
TOTLST	0.12	0.17	0.14	0.18	0.13	0.22	0.18	0.18	0.15	0.15
TOTRED	0.08	0.14	0.13	0.14	0.11	0.14	0.17	0.14	0.14	0.08

Note. See Table 2 for explanation of abbreviations.

some smoothing. The revised analysis corrected for these problems by (a) entering higher order terms for all independent variables in the regression analysis, and maintaining these terms in the regression equation if their inclusion led to significant increases in the predictable portion of the variance of any of the dependent variables; and (b) treating retention time as an independent quantitative variable, rather than as an indicator variable. Thus, instead of adjusting mean retention performance of each group upward or downward to correct for inequalities among the groups in regard to independent variables; the assignment of subjects to groups was disregarded, and the retention interval pertaining to each subject was expressed as log (1 + retention interval) and entered as an additional independent variable in the analysis. The partial regression weights resulting from this analysis are shown in Table 8 for each of the 10 dependent variables together with the portion of the variance accounted for. It can be seen that the same independent variables are represented in this analysis as in the analysis based on cross-sectional adjustment of group means, but higher order terms are included for the variables of retention time, level of Spanish training, and mean grade. Comparing column 10 in Table 6 with row 11 of Table 8 shows that this method of analysis yields a higher portion of variance accounted for in the case of every dependent variable. The increments range from 5% to 12% and average 7%. What may be termed contour retention curves for each of the 10 dependent variables, based upon the regression weights in Table 8, appear in Figures 5–10. To obtain the functions shown in Figures 5–10, the regression equation for each dependent variable was evaluated for successive retention intervals corresponding to the mean intervals of each of the 8 time groups. These intervals were chosen in order to obtain comparable reference points; the equations can, of course, be evaluated for any retention interval. At each retention interval the equations were evaluated for three levels of Spanish training (1, 3, and 5), and in Figure 10, for two mean grade levels (A and C). The graphs in Figures 5–9 show three retention curves reflecting the effect of level of training, with the mean grade fixed at C, and the graphs in Figure 10 show two retention curves reflecting the effect of the mean grade, with the level of training fixed at 3. The level of training in non-Spanish Romance languages was set at 1.41, the mean value for all subjects. Retention performance is expressed as a predicted raw score for each variable, rather than as a percentage of the original score. This makes it possible to illustrate the effects of level of training and mean grade. Inspection of Figures 5–10 supports most of the previous conclusions reached on the basis of the linear, group adjustments, but there are significant additional findings. The reading comprehension function again shows losses for the first 3 years of the retention interval, followed by a 20-year period of relative stability. Pronounced losses occur again between 35 and 50 years after training. The effects of level of training and of the mean grade are quite strong, and because the absolute amount of these effects remains the same throughout the retention interval

Table 8 Partial regression weights with time as an independent variable, and higher order terms included in the regression program

	Dependent variable									
Predictors	PARCOM	VSEREC	VSEREG	VESREC	VESREG	GRMREC	GRMREG	IDREC	IDREG	WRDORD
INTERCEPT	12.65	6.30	6.84	11.46	6.84	10.46	7.40	2.49	3.40	2.70
LOG RET	-0.17	0.94	-1.51	-7.98	0.22	-9.40	-4.64	-0.96	-1.77	-3.02
(LOG RET)^2	-6.88	-6.09	-0.39	-2.24	-2.76	2.96	2.42	-0.23	0.47	1.63
(LOG RET)^3	3.78	2.96	0.45	2.23	1.40	-0.30	-0.44	0.31	0.00	-0.30
(LOG RET)^4	-0.58	-0.41	-0.08	-0.35	-0.20	-0.02	0.01	-0.06	-0.01	0.01
LEVEL	4.50	3.88	1.14	3.03	1.31	2.08	0.92	0.61	0.71	0.66
(LEVEL)^2	-0.18	-0.14	-0.04	-0.10	-0.05	-0.06	-0.02	-0.02	-0.02	-0.02
(MEAN GRADE)	-5.30	-5.86	-2.18	-3.33	-1.61	-3.04	-2.74	-1.52	-1.16	-0.87
(MEAN GRADE)^2	1.64	1.55	0.58	1.10	0.47	0.98	0.62	0.38	0.31	0.29
TOTROM	0.36	0.15	0.18	0.17	0.09	0.11	0.14	0.05	0.08	0.09
R^2	0.47	0.53	0.43	0.58	0.47	0.58	0.46	0.44	0.44	0.38

Note. See Table 2 for explanation of abbreviations. LOG RET = Natural log of retention interval (in years) plus one.

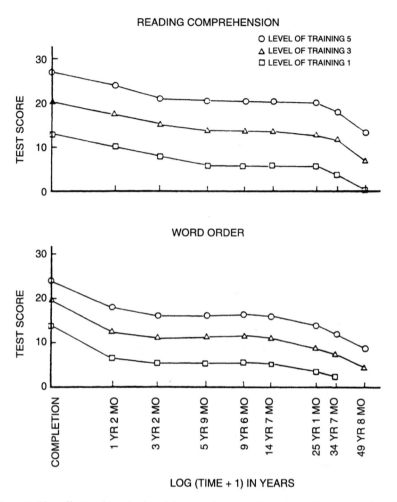

Figure 5 The effects of level of training on the retention of reading comprehension and word order.

in accordance with homogeneity of regression, the effects become relatively more important as time passes. There is some evidence that the correlations of dependent variables with levels of training and mean grade diminish somewhat toward the end of the retention interval. Because this diminution was not statistically significant, homogeneity of regression was assumed and the predicted retention curves for various levels of training and for various grades do not converge. If this diminution of correlation were reflected in Figures 5–10, the contour functions would converge somewhat during the last 15 years and this would also correct for the anomaly of projected negative scores at the end of the retention interval.

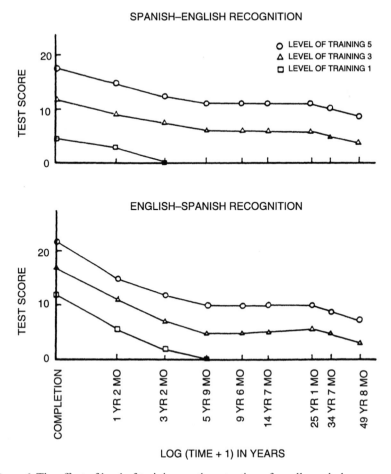

Figure 6 The effect of level of training on the retention of recall vocabulary.

Comparison of retention for recall versus recognition subtests must again take into account the baseline performance reflected by the C2 data. Recognition vocabulary for students trained at Level 1 who earn a grade of C declines approximately to the baseline level 3–6 years after training. This is quite comparable for most subtests including those for recall vocabulary, where the baseline is close to zero. Recall vocabulary stabilizes somewhat later, and the level of stabilization is relatively higher for recalling the English equivalents of Spanish words than for retrieval in the reverse direction. Individuals who receive grades higher than C, or who are trained beyond Level 1, maintain permanent knowledge above the respective baselines in all subtest areas.

The recall for grammar declines most precipitously and is one of the two subscores which shows no clear evidence of stabilizing during the retention

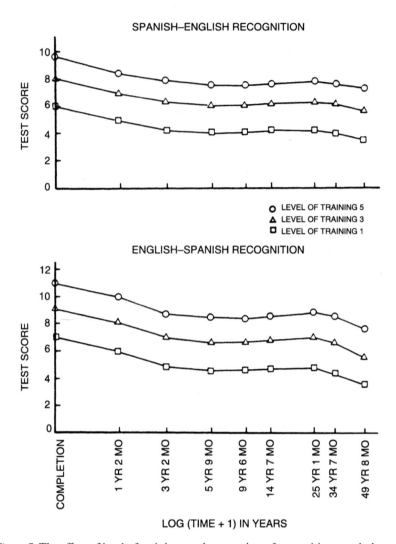

Figure 7 The effect of level of training on the retention of recognition vocabulary.

interval. At the end of 50 years C students have lost virtually all of the grammar information they once had at the recall level, and the scores of A students decline within 1 year to the original level of performance of C students. Recognition for grammar fares relatively better. Performance stabilizes 3 years after training, and those trained at Level 5 retain substantial knowledge for about 20 years before showing a further pronounced decline. The function for the recall for English equivalents of Spanish idioms closely parallels the function for the recall for individual Spanish words, and the effects of earned

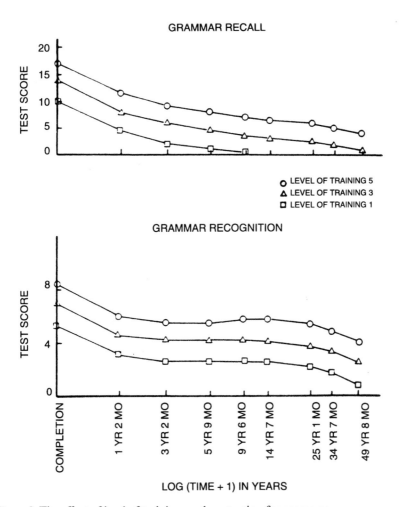

Figure 8 The effect of level of training on the retention for grammar.

grade are also quite comparable for these functions. The recognition for Spanish idioms shows more pronounced and continuous decline than the recognition for individual Spanish words. There is no clear period of stability, and it is perplexing that the relative losses are more severe than for the recall for idioms, particularly during the later portion of the retention interval. It is possible that the use of cognate foils on this subtest is responsible not only for performance below the chance level for control subjects but also for a continuous decline of the performance of other subjects during the retention interval. Knowledge of word order stabilizes for a period of at least 20 years after the initial losses, but ultimately there are additional

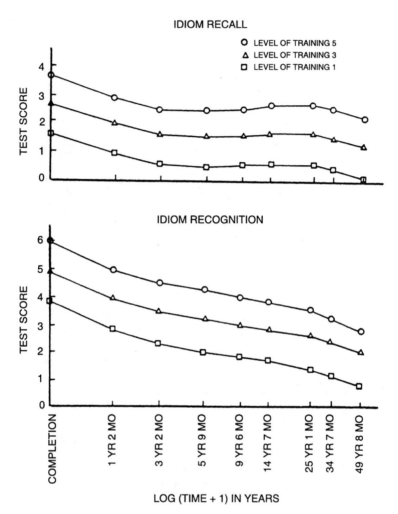

Figure 9 The effect of level of training on the retention for idioms.

losses which leave C students with very little of the original knowledge at the end of 50 years.

Methodological caveats

A variety of problems may affect the validity of cross-sectional research. These problems have been discussed by Lachman, Lachman, and Taylor (1981), Schaie (1977), Bahrick and Karis (1982), and others. We have already presented data to reveal the magnitude of errors affecting scores based on subjects' long-term memory reports. In addition, there may be variables

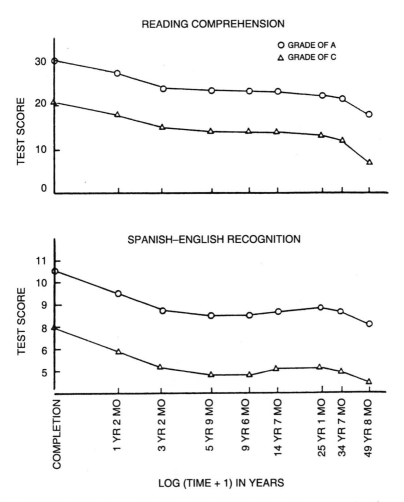

Figure 10 The effect of earned grade on the retention for reading comprehension and recognition vocabulary.

confounded with the retention interval which may affect the data but remain unassessable. Thus the methods of teaching Spanish may change, so that Training Level 3 may not reflect the same amount of knowledge now as it did 50 years ago; grade inflation may occur so that an A does not stand for the same amount of knowledge as it did 50 years ago, and the talent of students selecting Spanish courses may change so that individuals belonging to various time groups may represent different populations.

The bottom line for evaluating the validity of the use of the adjustment method in a particular cross-sectional investigation is the multiple correlation yielded by the regression equations which predict dependent variables from independent variables. The multiple correlations obtained in this investigation range from .61 to .77 for the 10 dependent variables, with a median correlation of .69. These correlations are based on a very large sample, and are therefore subject to only small statistical errors. The multiple correlations establish validity, and therefore also the reliability of the data, taking into account the aggregate effects of all error sources that have been mentioned. In other words, the multiple correlations between independent variables and retention performance indicate how well the amount of knowledge retained at any point in time can be predicted on the basis of the subject's report of level of training, time of training, and grade received, in spite of changes in grading standards, errors in reporting, and changes of talent among those who selected Spanish courses. For most of our dependent variables, the regression analysis accounts for approximately 50% of variance, a proportion which must be considered high in light of the complexity of the phenomena investigated and the variety of error sources that have been discussed. The acceptability of findings in laboratory investigations is not usually evaluated in terms of the proportion of variance of dependent variables accounted for by independent variables, although such evaluations would have substantial merit. Rather, the minimum standard of acceptability is met if the independent variables produce statistically significant effects on the dependent variables, regardless of the proportion of variance they account for. This latter test is obviously met for the major effects examined in this investigation, but it is not an appropriate way of evaluating validity here. Continued experience with large-scale investigations of naturalistic memory will help to establish standards and further improve methodology in this area, so that these methods can be used more extensively in memory research.

General interpretation and discussion

When retention curves represent the number, or the percentage, of correct responses on the ordinate, the slope of the retention function can easily be related to the frequency distribution of the life span of responses. A retention function of constant slope indicates that a constant number of responses are lost per unit of time, and this implies a flat frequency distribution for the life span of responses, that is, a distribution in which an equal number of responses fall into each life-span interval. An exponentially declining retention function indicates that a diminishing number of responses are lost in successive, equal intervals of time. This requires a frequency distribution for the life span of responses which is skewed in the direction of a longer life span, that is, the highest frequency corresponds to responses with short life spans, and diminishing frequencies are associated with responses of longer life spans. A related analysis has been discussed in an earlier paper (Bahrick, 1965) and the preceding examples are illustrated in

Figure 11, which shows the frequency distributions corresponding to a straight line and an exponentially declining retention function. It is, of course, the exponential retention function and its corresponding frequency distribution that have typically been obtained in episodic memory research conducted in the laboratory. However, memory research usually terminates before all of the tested information is lost, and in that case there is no way of knowing what eventually happens to the remaining information. Gradual losses may continue indefinitely, or they may end as the retention curve approaches an asymptote above the base line of zero knowledge.

The concept of a permastore

The retention functions obtained in this investigation are not of the type illustrated in Figure 11. Rather, 8 of the 10 functions shown in Figures 5–10

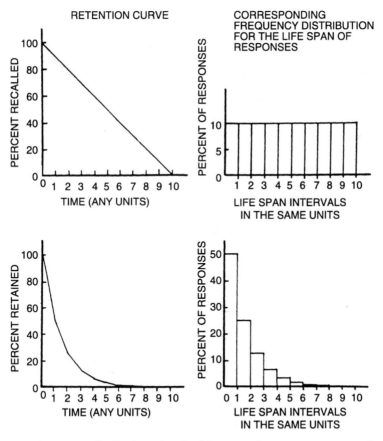

Figure 11 Frequency distributions for the life span of responses corresponding to straight-line and logarithmic retention functions.

fall exponentially for a period of 3 to 6 years. They then remain flat for several decades, after which they show an additional positively accelerated decline. Based on a response life-span analysis these retention functions correspond to a frequency distribution of responses that is discontinuous. One portion of the distribution has life spans of 0 to 6 years, with relative frequencies distributed similarly as has been found in episodic memory research, except for the fact that the mean life span is much longer here. The other portion I will call the "permastore." This memory content has a distribution of life spans of 25 years or longer, and the distribution is skewed in the direction of shorter life spans. The largest number of these responses survives 50 years or longer, and diminishing numbers are lost during the two preceding decades. The two portions of the distribution are discontinuous, that is, there is a period from approximately 5 to 25 years after training during which no responses appear to be lost, and the frequency of responses with life spans within these limits is therefore near zero. Figure 12 shows a life-span frequency distribution typical for the data which have been reported here.

The portion of the distribution in permastore varies with the level of training, the mean grade achieved, and the nature of the required response. Individuals trained at Level 1 who earned a grade of C retain very little of their original knowledge in permastore. Those trained at higher levels and those who earned higher grades retain increasing portions: Individuals with a mean grade of A retain approximately 52%, 72%, and 80% of Spanish–English recall vocabulary for Training Levels 1, 3, and 5 respectively; individuals with a mean grade of C retain only 0%, 53%, and 73% at the three training levels.

This life-span analysis applies directly only to those dependent variables for which individual responses are reasonably independent of each other. The analysis therefore applies to recall and recognition vocabulary, but not to the scores for reading comprehension. Correct answers to questions regarding the meaning of a sentence or a paragraph depend not only on knowledge of vocabulary but also on knowledge of grammar, word order, and so forth, and success or failure in answering the questions can therefore not be directly related to the life span of a response. It will be noted, however, that the memory functions obtained for reading comprehension do closely parallel the memory functions for recognition vocabulary, and that the correlation between reading comprehension scores and the various analytical scores is high. It would therefore appear that the decline and maintenance of reading comprehension can be adequately predicted on the basis of the analysis of the life-span frequency distribution of individual responses, and the concept of permastore remains applicable, although the analysis into a life-span frequency distribution is not directly applicable.

It does not really come as a surprise that semantic memory contains much semipermanent information. Everyone knows that we rarely forget the

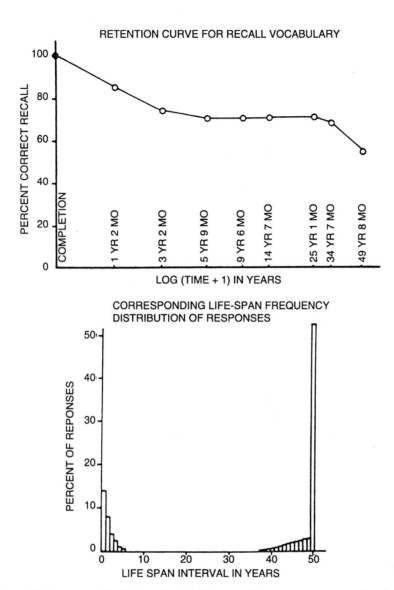

Figure 12 Frequency distribution for the life span of responses corresponding to the retention of Spanish-English recall vocabulary.

meaning of most words in our native language, the rules of arithmetic, and many other facts about the world. However, psychological research has not dealt directly with the process by which knowledge becomes permanent, so that the necessary conditions for this transition are not well understood. It is not clear, for example, to what extent the maintenance of knowledge in permastore depends on periodic access or rehearsal. If retention measurement stops several days, weeks, or years after original training, the fate of any remaining knowledge is conjectural. The most noteworthy finding of this investigation is almost certainly the fact that a very large amount of information is maintained in permastore under conditions of minimal rehearsal. This conclusion is possible because of the fortuitous circumstance that the great majority of individuals who were subjects in this investigation rehearsed very little or not at all, and that their retained knowledge bears no significant relation to the small amount of reported rehearsal. Our results show that very significant portions of semantic knowledge remain perfectly accessible for decades without being used at all.

We are now able to reconcile the strikingly divergent results obtained in two earlier investigations of long-term memory for names and faces. Data obtained from Bahrick et al. (1975) and from Bahrick (in press) are combined in Figure 13. The earlier study shows that the names and faces of high school classmates are recognized at about the same level of accuracy 25 years after original exposure as they are immediately after graduation,

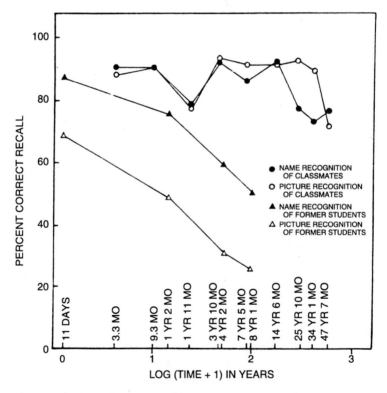

Figure 13 Comparison of retention of former classmates and former students, based on data from Bahrick et al. (1975) and Bahrick (in press).

even when the estimated effects of rehearsals are statistically removed. In contrast, the later study shows that the accuracy of recognizing the names and faces of former students by their college instructors declines with the logarithm of time. The decline begins very soon after exposure, and relatively little information survives beyond 8 years. Memory for the names and faces of high school classmates is based on a 4-year period of interaction during which most of the information necessary for recognition has apparently attained permastore status. In contrast, memory for the names and faces of former students was based on 10 weeks of much more restricted interaction in the classroom. It appears that comparatively little of that information has become permanent. These findings indicate that dichotomous durability distributions may characterize a variety of semantic memory content.

There are various sources of evidence to suggest that the concept of permastore may not be limited to semantic memory content. Brown and Kulik (1977) reported long enduring memory for salient episodic experiences called "flashbulb" memories, and reports by Penfield and Perot (1963) based on findings obtained through brain stimulation indicate that certain images may be preserved for long periods with great clarity. Neisser (1967) cites motor skills, for example, bicycle riding or piano playing, and well-rehearsed verbal performances by old actors, as illustrations of other memories which endure without the benefit of intervening rehearsals.

It is important to point out that the term permastore has been used here without any intended structural implications. It simply refers to the finding that much of the information in memory has a life span of several decades, apparently without requiring periodic access or relearning.

Implications for the acquisition process

Significant questions regarding the maintenance of information in permastore concern the relative importance of the acquisition process versus the effect of conditions prevailing during the retention interval. Variance of the life span of responses might result from conditions present during the period of acquisition, from conditions present during the retention interval, or from some combination of both. It has already been shown that rehearsal during the retention interval played no important role in maintaining knowledge of Spanish. The data support the further inference that variation of conditions of interference encountered during the retention interval did not play a major role in determining the portion of information retained in permastore. It is difficult to conceive of conditions of interference that would yield the discontinuous life-span frequency distribution characteristic of much of the present data. The amount of interference affecting various portions of a large recognition vocabulary is likely to follow a normal or at least a continuous distribution.

The sharp contrast between recognition for names and faces of high school classmates versus the recognition for names and faces of former students is also best explained on the basis of differences in the degree of original learning, rather than differences in the degree of interference sustained during the retention interval. At the end of original exposure, name recognition is slightly below 90% correct in both investigations. This level is maintained for at least 25 years in the study of high school classmates, but the level has fallen to about 50% within 8 years in the study of memory for the names of former students. This is equally true for instructors who retire soon after teaching their classes, and for younger instructors who continue to teach and are subject to the additional interference associated with learning names and faces of new students. Thus the interference due to learning new names and faces does not affect recognition of the names and faces of former classmates for at least 25 years, but comparable interference is associated with continued decline in recognizing names and faces of former students because this information never attained permastore status. All of these considerations support the conclusion that discontinuity of the life-span frequency distribution is determined during the acquisition period, and is relatively unaffected by normal interference encountered during the retention interval.

Semantic memory content is typically acquired over extended time periods during which exposure or active rehearsal is limited to relatively short periods spaced at intervals. This is true of knowledge acquired in formal learning sessions, for example, foreign-language classes, but it also applies to the casual learning of names and faces of people we meet repeatedly. Practice sessions may be more or less clearly defined, but in most instances intervals intercede between sessions, and without repeated exposure only a small portion of the information acquired during the first exposure would endure (Bahrick, 1979). Acquisition is the cumulative result of successive relearning sessions, with a portion of the material forgotten during the intervals between sessions. Melton (1963) showed that this same process operates in traditional laboratory learning of episodic content, during the alternation of trials and intertrial intervals, but in that case the whole process is compressed into a short time span, whereas the acquisition of semantic knowledge may continue over a period of several months or years. It has long been known that the distribution of practice sessions is an important variable determining the durability of acquired knowledge, and the results of this investigation suggest that extension of the reexposure to information over long time periods produces a cumulative effect which eventually gives permanence to responses and renders them invulnerable to most interference effects.

It would appear that the transition to this state of permanence occurs during acquisition and is discrete, rather than continuous, even though the transition reflects the cumulative effect of successive relearning sessions. If successive reexposure would gradually increase the life span of responses, we would expect a continuous frequency distribution of the life span with many responses of an intermediate longevity. The obtained distribution indicates such an effect only for the portion of the distribution with life spans of less than 6 years. The life span of the remaining responses does not appear to have been extended gradually. Had this been the case one would expect many responses to show intermediate life spans of 10, 15, or 20 years. The fact that there are no responses with these intermediate life spans indicates a discrete transition during acquisition from long-term storage to permastore. This interpretation differs from the position taken by Rock (1957) regarding the discrete acquisition of paired-associate responses, in that the discrete process is assumed here only for the transition to permastore status, not for increments in the life span of responses up to approximately 6 years.

The thrust of this research is directed at the large amount of information that constitutes permanent knowledge of the individual. Neither the conditions of acquisition of permanent knowledge, nor the conditions of its maintenance have been the direct object of psychological research. It is apparent that although a portion of the information in long-term memory remains there only if it is periodically used or rehearsed, another very significant portion attains permastore status during acquisition and requires no further access or rehearsal during the life span of the individual. Research directed at the first portion must concentrate on conditions of maintenance; research directed at the second portion must concentrate on conditions of acquisition. It is clear that both types of research are essential for the development of a more integrative conceptualization of memory, and for the development of educational programs based on sound psychological knowledge.

Note

This research was supported by U.S. Public Health Service Research Grant HD00926–16 from the National Institute of Child Health and Human Development. The author is indebted to his colleagues Pilar Concejo, Conrad Kent, and Roy Wittlinger for valuable help and advice; to Phyllis Bahrick, Melva Hunter, and Maryanne Stewart who supervised the recruitment of subjects and the analysis of data; to Mike Vetter, Brenda Hay, Cassie Hicks, and Scott Henkel who were student assistants; and to the 733 individuals who volunteered to take the test and answer the questionnaire.

Appendix A

Portions of each subtest of Spanish

Reading comprehension

Directions: Read the following selections and answer the question in the space provided. Answer in English.

117

La politica en la casa (Modern Language Association, 1973)

Ramón: Pues digan lo que digan Vargas
Campo es el hombre del diá.

Padre: No digas tonterías. Es un loco idealista que todo lo quiere cambiar.
¡Nuestro pueblo jamás lo va a aceptar!

Ramón: A pesar de lo que tú digas, papá, no estoy de acuerdo contigo.

Madre: Les ruego que no discutan más de política. Cambiemos de tema.

Ramón: ¿De qué quieres que hablemos, mamá?
¿De vestidos?

Madre: Es que ustedes dos nunca se ponen de acuerdo. Siempre terminan en un pleito.

Padre: Dejemos ese tema. De todos modos, quería hablarte de otra cosa más importante, tus estudios.

Ramón: Por favor, no insistan en que estudie medicina.

Padre: No nos vamos a oponer a lo que tú escojas. Tú eres el que decides. Pero . . .

Madre: Lo único que te pedimos es que no estudies para abogado.

Ramón: ¿Qué hay de malo en eso?

Madre: Es que hay tantas abogados que es muy difícil destacarse en ese campo.

Padre: A menos que uno se meta en la política y ojalá que tu no te dediques a eso. Que lo hagan otros.

Madre: Bueno, sigan ustedes hablando de eso.
Voy a ver como anda lo de la comida.

Ramón: . . . Mira, papa, Volviendo a lo otro.

1. Why doesn't Father like Vargas Campo?
2. Why doesn't Mother want the family to talk politics?
3. What topic does Father want to discuss?
4. Why doesn't Mother want Ramon to be a lawyer?
5. What did Mother have to do?

Vocabulary: Spanish to English recall

Directions: Write the English meaning of the Spanish word in the appropriate place on this page.

Answer

1. llamar   1. _____
2. ojo   2. _____
3. razon   3. _____

Vocabulary: Spanish to English recognition

Directions: Write the number of the correct English meaning of the Spanish word in the answer column.

1. _____ feliz
   1) happy 2) fault 3) feet 4) new 5) clean
2. _____ mandar
   1) to make 2) to mend 3) to yell 4) to command 5) to arrange
3. _____ romper
   1) to roam 2) to break 3) to look 4) to roar 5) to search

Vocabulary: English to Spanish recall

Directions: Write the Spanish meaning of the English word in the appropriate place on this page.

		Answer
1.	time	1. _____
2.	to hear	2. _____
3.	to read	3. _____

Vocabulary: English to Spanish recognition

Directions: Write the number of the correct Spanish meaning of the English word in the answer column.

1. _____ to reach
   1) sentar 2) cambiar 3) recoger 4) alcanzar 5) cumplir
2. _____ lady
   1) dama 2) hermano 3) semana 4) marques 5) sistema
3. _____ date
   1) mesa 2) fecha 3) cuenta 4) niña 5) fina

Grammar recall

Directions: Write the correct form of the verb given in the blank provided.

1. El _____ español.   (estudiar)
   He studies Spanish.
2. Yo _____ la menor.   (ser)
   I am the youngest.
3. Ellos _____ ir conmigo.   (poder)
   They are able to go with me.

119

Grammar recognition

Directions: Write the *number* of the correct form of the verb in the answer column.

1. _____ They are going there for the holidays.
Ellos _____ allí para los dias feriados.
1) vayan 2) iban 3) van 4) fueron 5) va

2. _____ Enter the room.
_____ ustedes al cuarto.
1) pasen 2) pasan 3) passaron 4) passarían 5) pasaban

3. _____ Yesterday they gave me 10 pesos.
Ayer me _____ diez pesos.
1) dan 2) den 3) dieron 4) daron 5) daban

Idiom recall

Directions: Write the correct English meaning of the Spanish idiom in the answer column.

Idiom		Answer
1. hace mal tiempo	1.	_____
2. hasta la vista	2.	_____
3. en vez de	3.	_____

Idiom recognition

Directions: Choose the correct English meaning of the Spanish idiom and write the number in the answer column.

1. _____ sin embargo
1) without restriction 2) almost 3) an embargo 4) nevertheless 5) sometimes

2. _____ tal vez
1) perhaps 2) many times 3) certain times 4) all the time 5) once upon a time

3. _____ desde luego
1) from then on 2) as soon as 3) later than 4) of course 5) at a later time

Word order

Directions: The Spanish words are not in the correct sequence. Put the Spanish words into the correct order *on this page* by using the numbers associated with the words. For example, a possible answer for the first question might be 12534678.

1. Henry did not explain to me clearly all the problems.
    Enrique no explicó me claramente todos los
      1   2   3   4   5   6   7
    problemas.
      8
    Answer: _____
2. When the letter arrived, Carlos had left.
    Cuando la carta Ilegó Carlos habia partido.
       1   2 3   4   5   6   7
    Answer: _____
3. Helen did not like the play.
    Elena a no (le) gustó la comedia.
     1 2 3 4 5 6 7
    Answer: _____

Appendix B

Summary of the questionnaire

Language training

Subjects provided information concerning the number of years of Spanish taken in high school and the number and level of Spanish courses taken in college. They indicated the letter grades received in each course, the dates of completion of each course, and the name and location of the school where the work was taken. They identified courses in which frequent use was made of a listening laboratory. Similar information was obtained for courses taken in Latin, French, Italian, and Portuguese, and subjects were asked to indicate any other learning opportunities for Romance languages, such as residence abroad, or residence in a bilingual area.

Rehearsal opportunities during the retention interval

Rehearsal opportunities were grouped into the categories of exposure through listening, reading, speaking or writing Spanish, or traveling in countries where Spanish is spoken. The format of the questions is illustrated for the categories of listening and reading.

Listening to Spanish (other than travel)

	Once a year or less	2–11 times per year	several times each month	several times each week
Radio	_____	_____	_____	_____
Television	_____	_____	_____	_____
Films	_____	_____	_____	_____
Conversation of others	_____	_____	_____	_____
Estimated average length of listening times _____				

Please check whether the above answers apply:

1. For all years since your last Spanish course
2. For a period of time from approximately _____ to _____

Reading of Spanish

	Once a year or less	2–11 times per year	several times each month	several times each week
Newspapers	_____	_____	_____	_____
Magazines	_____	_____	_____	_____
Books	_____	_____	_____	_____
Correspondence	_____	_____	_____	_____
Estimated average length of reading times _____				

Please check whether the above answers apply:

1. For all the years since your last Spanish course
2. For a period of time from _____ to _____ with the following significant changes: _____ .

References

Baddeley, A. D. (1976). *The psychology of memory*. New York: Basic Books.

Bahrick, H. P. (1965). The ebb of retention. *Psychological Review, 72*, 60–73.

Bahrick, H. P. (1979). Maintenance of knowledge: Questions about memory we forgot to ask. *Journal of Experimental Psychology: General, 108*, 296–308.

Bahrick, H. P. (1983). The cognitive map of a city—50 years of learning and memory. In G. Bower (Ed.), *The psychology of learning and motivation: Advances in research and theory* (Vol. 17, pp. 125–163). New York: Academic Press.

Bahrick, H. P. (in press). Memory and people. In J. Harris (Ed.), *Everyday memory, actions, and absentmindedness*. New York: Academic Press.

Bahrick, H. P., Bahrick, P. O., & Wittlinger, R. P. (1975). Fifty years of memories for names and faces: A cross-sectional approach. *Journal of Experimental Psychology: General, 104*, 54–75.

Bahrick, H. P., & Karis, D. (1982). Long-term ecological memory. In C. Puff, (Ed.), *Handbook of research methods in human memory and cognition* (pp. 427–465). New York: Academic Press.

Brown, R., & Kulik, J. (1977). Flashbulb memories. *Cognition, 5*, 73–99.

Burke, D. M., & Light, L. L. (1981). Memory and aging: The role of retrieval processes. *Psychological Bulletin, 90*, 513–546.

Cohen, A. D. (1976). The Culver City Spanish immersion program: How does summer recess affect Spanish speaking ability. *Language Learning, 24*, 55–68.

Ellis, H. C., & Hunt, R. R. (1983). *Fundamentals of human memory and cognition* (3rd ed.). Dubuque, 1A: Wm, C. Brown.

Klatzky, R. L. (1980). *Human memory structures and processes.* San Francisco: Freeman.

Lachman, J. L., Lachman, R., & Taylor, D. W. (1981). Reallocation of mental resources over the productive lifespan: Assumptions and task analyses. In F. I. M. Craik & S. E. Trehub (Eds.), *Aging and cognitive processes* (pp. 279–308). New York: Plenum Press.

Melton, A. W. (1963). Implications of short-term memory for a general theory of memory. *Journal of Verbal Learning and Verbal Behavior, 2*, 1–21.

Modern Language Association. (1973). *Modern Spanish* (3rd ed.). New York: Harcourt Brace Jovanovich.

Neisser, U. (1967). *Cognitive psychology.* New York: Appleton-Century-Crofts.

Neisser, U. (1978). Memory: What are the important questions? In M. M. Gruneberg, P. E. Morris, & H. N. Sykes (Eds.), *Practical aspects of memory* (pp. 3–24). London: Academic Press.

Neter, J., & Wasserman, W. (1974). *Applied linear statistical models.* Homewood, IL: Irwin.

Oller, J. W., Jr. (1973). Cloze tests of second language proficiency and what they measure. *Language Learning, 23*, 105–118.

Penfield, W., & Perot, P. (1963). The brain's record of auditory and visual experience. A final summary and discussion. *Brain, 86*, 595.

Rock, I. (1957). The role of repetition in associative learning. *American Journal of Psychology, 70*, 186–193.

Schaie, K. W. (1977). Quasi-experimental research designs in the psychology of aging. In J. E. Birren & K. W. Schaie (Eds.), *Handbook of the psychology of aging* (pp. 39–58). New York: Van Nostrand Reinhold.

Smythe, P. C., Jutras, G. C., Bramwell, J. R., & Gardner, R. C. (1973). Second language retention over varying intervals. *Modern Language Journal, 57*, 400–405.

Spitzer, H. (1939). Studies in retention. *Journal of Educational Psychology, 30*, 641–657.

Wickelgren, W. A. (1977). *Learning and memory.* Englewood Cliffs, NJ: Prentice-Hall.

Zechmeister, E. B., & Nyberg, S. A. (1982). *Human memory: An introduction to research and theory.* Monterey, CA: Brooks/Cole.

Part 6

ENCODING

26

CONTEXTUAL PREREQUISITES FOR UNDERSTANDING

Some investigations of comprehension and recall[1]

John D. Bransford and Marcia K. Johnson

Source: *Journal of Verbal Learning and Verbal Behavior*, 11 (1972): 717–726.

The present paper presents a series of studies showing that relevant contextual knowledge is a prerequisite for comprehending prose passages. Four studies are reported, each demonstrating increased comprehension ratings and recall scores when Ss were supplied with appropriate information before they heard test passages. Supplying Ss with the same information subsequent to the passages produced much lower comprehension ratings and recall scores. Various explanations of the results are considered, and the role of topics in activating cognitive contexts is discussed.

The present paper sketches a general approach to some problems of comprehension and memory. Several studies are reported which employ an experimental paradigm that seems particularly adaptable to such problems and that has been useful in developing the point of view proposed here.

Probably the most well-developed approach to comprehension stems from theories based on transformational linguistics (e.g., Chomsky, 1957, 1965, 1968; Postal, 1964). Sentences are assumed to have both superficial and underlying (deep) structures. The surface structure characterizes the phonological shape of the sentence, but the deep structural information is presumed necessary for characterizing sentence meaning (see Katz & Postal, 1964). According to Katz & Postal (p. 12), the semantically interpreted deep structural relations underlying sentences constitute a full analysis of their cognitive meaning. Comprehension thus involves the recovery and interpretation of the abstract deep structural relations underlying sentences, and sentence memory involves retention of the deep structural but not necessarily the surface structural forms. Many studies have demonstrated the importance of deep structure in sentence perception and memory tasks (e.g., Bever, Lackner, & Kirk, 1969; Blumenthal, 1967, Blumenthal & Boakes, 1967; Perfetti, 1969; Rohrman, 1968; Sachs, 1967; Wanner, 1968).

However, several lines of research support the notion that performance in comprehension and memory tasks has a broader base than simply the semantically interpreted deep structural relations underlying linguistic inputs. Kintsch (1972), for example, has shown that Ss often know more than a sentence specifies directly. The results of experiments by Bransford and Franks (1971), Bransford, Barclay, and Franks (1972) and by Johnson, Bransford, & Solomon (in press) indicate that the information Ss use in a sentence memory task may originate from the integration of information from several related sentences and may include ideas not directly expressed in the acquisition materials.

For example, Johnson, Bransford, and Solomon (in press) presented Ss with short passages like either (a) "The river was narrow. A beaver hit the log that a turtle was sitting beside and the log flipped over from the shock. The turtle was very surprised by the event" or (b) "The river was narrow. A beaver hit the log that a turtle was sitting on and the log flipped over from the shock. The turtle was very surprised by the event." After acquisition, the Ss were read a list of recognition sentences and asked to indicate which sentences they had actually heard during the acquisition task. Those Ss hearing passage (b) were much more likely to think they had heard the novel sentence, "A beaver hit the log and knocked the turtle into the water," than those hearing passage (a). The Ss' understanding of the acquisition sentences apparently involved a realization of the probable consequences of the situations suggested by the input sentences; Ss frequently thought they had heard information which could only have been inferred.

The experiments mentioned above lend considerable support to the idea that Ss do not simply interpret and store the meanings of sentences per se. Rather, Ss create semantic products that are a joint function of input information and prior knowledge. The present paper focuses directly on the role played by prior knowledge in comprehension. Its purpose is to show that not only is prior knowledge reflected in the S's performance in tasks involving the comprehension of linguistic information, but that certain knowledge may be necessary for the meaningful processing of the information in the first place. In the experiments presented below, the availability of prior knowledge is manipulated in order to assess its influence on Ss' ability to comprehend and remember linguistic materials.

Experiment I

The information presented to the *S*s consisted of a passage in which the sentences followed rules of normal English construction and the vocabulary items were used in nonmetaphorical ways. The prediction tested was that *S*s who received the appropriate prerequisite knowledge would be able to comprehend the passage quite easily, and hence would subsequently be able to recall it relatively well. On the other hand, *S*s who did not have access to the appropriate knowledge should find the passage difficult to understand and recall. The prerequisite knowledge was in the form of a picture that provided information about the context underlying the stimulus passage. The passage did not simply describe the contextual picture, but instead described various events that could happen given the context as a conceptual base.

Method

The experiment consisted of an acquisition phase, followed by two tasks— comprehension rating and recall. There were five independent groups of *S*s with 10 *S*s per group. In addition to the No Context (1) *S*s (who simply heard the passage) and the Context Before *S*s (who saw the appropriate context picture before they heard the passage), there were three other groups of *S*s. Context After *S*s first heard the passage and then saw the appropriate picture. Since it was assumed that contextual information is necessary for the ongoing process of comprehension, the Context After *S*s were expected to assign lower comprehension ratings and recall less than the Context Before *S*s. Partial Context *S*s were shown a picture before the passage was presented. The partial context picture contained all of the objects represented in the appropriate context picture, but the objects were rearranged. It was assumed that the availability of concrete representations of the objects would be equal for the Partial Context and Context Before groups. However, the comprehension and recall performances of the former group were expected to be lower since the relations among the objects in the partial context picture constituted an inappropriate conceptual base for the passage. Finally, No Context (2) *S*s heard the passage twice. This group was included to assess the effects of repetitions in the absence of context.

Materials

The passage was as follows:
If the balloons popped, the sound wouldn't be able to carry since everything would be too far away from the correct floor. A closed window would also prevent the sound from carrying, since most buildings tend to be well insulated. Since the whole operation depends on a steady flow of electricity, a break in the middle of the wire would also cause problems. Of course, the

fellow could shout, but the human voice is not loud enough to carry that far. An additional problem is that a string could break on the instrument. Then there could be no accompaniment to the message. It is clear that the best situation would involve less distance. Then there would be fewer potential problems. With face to face contact, the least number of things could go wrong.

The appropriate- and partial-context pictures are shown in Figures 1 and 2, respectively.

Procedure

The *S*s assigned to a given condition were tested as a group in a single session. All *S*s were told that they were going to hear a tape-recorded passage

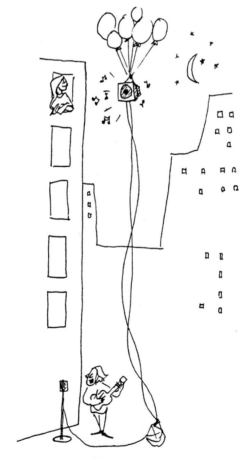

Figure 1 Appropriate context picture for Experiment I.

Figure 2 Partial context picture for Experiment I.

and were asked to attempt to comprehend and remember it. They were informed that they would later be asked to recall the passage as accurately as they could. The Context Before and Partial Context Ss were given 30 seconds to inspect their respective pictures before the start of the recorded passage. The No Context (2) group heard the same recording twice. After acquisition, there was a 2-minute delay before Ss rated the passage. During this interval, Ss received recall sheets, Context After Ss were allowed 30 sec. to inspect the appropriate picture, and instructions about how to use the comprehension scale were given. A seven-point scale was used, with 1 indicating the passage was very difficult to comprehend, 4 indicating moderate, and 7 indicating very easy. Immediately after the rating task, Ss were asked to recall the passage as accurately as they could and were told that if they could not remember it word for word, they should write down as many ideas as possible. Seven minutes were allowed for recall.

Subjects

The Ss were 50 male and female high school students who volunteered to participate in the experiment.

Results

We have adopted the following standard procedure for scoring recall protocols of sentence materials or prose passages: Idea units are designated a priori and correspond either to individual sentences, basic semantic propositions, or phrases. Maximum possible scores for the materials used in Experiments I–IV are given in the appropriate tables. The protocols, which cannot be identified as to condition, are scored independently by two judges against the list of idea units. Paraphrases are allowed. Interjudge reliability for materials such as those used in the present experiments ranges from .91 to .99. Any differences in the assignment of scores to Ss are resolved by a third judge. These adjusted scores are then used in the final analysis of the data.

The mean comprehension rating and the mean number of ideas recalled for each group in Experiment I are given in Table 1. For both comprehension and recall scores, Dunnett's test was used to compare the Context Before condition with each of the other four conditions. The comprehension ratings were higher in the Context Before condition than in each of the other four conditions; all values of $d(5, 45) \geq 4.19$, $p < .005$. The Ss in the Context Before condition also recalled a greater number of ideas than Ss in each of the other four conditions; all values of $d(5, 45) \geq 4.12$, $p < .005$. An inspection of the data in Table 1 suggests that, relative to the No Context (1) condition, hearing the passage twice, receiving the context after or receiving the partial context before, increased comprehension ratings somewhat. Relative to the No Context (1) condition, these manipulations had little effect on recall scores.

Table 1 Mean comprehension ratings and mean number of ideas recalled, Experiment I

	No context (1)	No context (2)	Context after	Partial context	Context before	Maximum score
Comprehension	2.30 (.30)[a]	3.60 (.27)	3.30 (.45)	3.70 (.56)	6.10 (.38)	7
Recall	3.60 (.64)	3.80 (.79)	3.60 (.75)	4.00 (.60)	8.00 (.65)	14

[a] Standard error in parentheses.

Discussion

The presentation of the appropriate semantic context had a marked effect on both comprehension ratings and recall. All *S*s presumably knew the lexical meanings of the words and were familiar with the sentence structures used in the passage. Comprehension ratings and recall were relatively low, however, when *S*s did not receive the appropriate context before they heard the passage.

The large difference in recall between the Context Before and the No Context (1) groups could be due to various factors. For example, knowledge of the appropriate context could simply provide information that allowed *S*s to generate (at recall) ideas based on pre-experimental experiences, and many of these ideas could have overlapped with those in the passage. If this were an important factor, the Context After *S*s should also have been able to augment recall by guessing or generating ideas from the picture. Providing the *S*s with the appropriate context after they heard the passage did not, however, produce an increment in recall.

One might also argue that the Context Before group benefited from a more available set of retrieval cues (i.e., the elements of the picture—balloons, wire, window, etc.) relative to the No Context group. There are data to suggest that retrieval cues are important for recall and that it is important that these cues be present at input (e.g., Tulving & Osler, 1968). The elements of the picture were available to the Partial Context *S*s before they heard the passage, yet their recall was far below that of the Context Before group. What the partial context picture lacked was the appropriate information about the relations among the concrete elements. Understanding the relations in the appropriate context was a prerequisite for understanding the events suggested by the passage. Although considerable research is needed to assess the relative contributions of comprehension vesus retrieval processes to remembering, it seems clear that there is little reason to expect retrieval cues to augment recall for prose appreciably if *S*s have not understood the meaning of a passage. On the other hand, comprehension per se does not necessarily guarantee subsequent recall. Pilot studies using the passage in Experiment I indicate that recall scores for the Context Before *S*s can be increased by supplying them with key words as retrieval cues.

The comparison of the No Context (2) and Context Before groups can be viewed as a transfer of training design, where the No Context (2) group receives Learn A, Learn A, Test A and the Context Before group receives Learn B, Learn A, Test A where Learn B represents time taken to study the prerequisite context. For *S*s in the present experiment, it was more beneficial to transfer from B to A than it was to spend time trying to learn A. Generally, this should be the case if the context in question is truly a prerequisite for comprehension.

The finding that neither Context After, nor Partial Context, nor No Context (2) groups showed augmented recall relative to No Context (1) *S*s

133

was somewhat surprising, although these groups were expected to be clearly inferior to the Context Before group. Eventually, it will be important to characterize those situations under which these types of treatments will benefit the *S*s' performance. For present purposes, however, the major points are the clear advantage of the Context Before group and the resulting picture of the comprehension process that is supported by the general pattern of the results.

In Experiment I, it was very unlikely that the appropriate prerequisite context was (in all its details) part of the preexperimental knowledge of the *S*s. If one generally characterizes comprehension as a process requiring appropriate semantic contexts, then the conditions under which existing structures become activated are extremely important. If a passage does not provide sufficient cues about its appropriate semantic context, the *S* is in a problem-solving situation in which he must find a suitable organization of his store of previous knowledge. Experiments II, III, and IV involve materials for which the appropriate contexts should be part of the pre-experimental knowledge of most *S*s. Some *S*s are given a cue (a topic for the passage) that should help activate a suitable context.

It should be noted that the experiments to follow are similar to a set of studies that became available in the literature at the time the present paper was being written: Dooling and Lachman (1971) found that providing the topic of a passage affected subsequent recall. The present studies are included here, however, because (*a*) the passages used are relatively straightforward linguistic descriptions whereas those used by Dooling and Lachman were explicitly metaphorical; and (*b*) the present studies include conditions where *S*s receive knowledge of the topic after hearing the passage in order to determine whether recall increments are simply due to *S*s' abilities to generate probable statements about familiar topics.

Experiments II, III, and IV

The results of Experiments II, III, and IV will be presented and discussed after the procedures have been described since the three studies were similar in design.

Method

These experiments were similar to Experiment I in that the acquisition phase, consisting of a single auditory presentation of the materials, was followed by comprehension rating and recall tasks. The rating scale was the same as that used in Experiment I. The conditions in each of the studies were as follows. *Experiment II:* A No Topic group (17 *S*s) heard a passage and received no additional information; a Topic After group (17 *S*s) received the topic of the passage after acquisition and prior to the rating and recall tasks; a Topic

Before group (18 Ss) received the topic prior to the presentation of the passage. *Experiment III:* Topic After (10 Ss) and Topic Before (11 Ss) conditions. *Experiment IV:* No Topic (9 Ss), Topic After (11 Ss), and Topic Before (11 Ss) conditions.

Materials

Materials for Experiments II and III consisted of passages A and B, respectively. Passage B is a slightly longer version of Passage A. Experiments II and III were conducted under different conditions and no comparisions of Ss' performance on Passage A and B were planned or conducted.

Passage A:

The procedure is actually quite simple. First you arrange things into different groups depending on their makeup. Of course, one pile may be sufficient depending on how much there is to do. If you have to go somewhere else due to lack of facilities that is the next step, otherwise you are pretty well set. It is important not to over do any particular endeavor. That is, it is better to do too few things at once than too many. In the short run this may not seem important, but complications from doing too many can easily arise. A mistake can be expensive as well. The manipulation of the appropriate mechanisms should be self-explanatory, and we need not dwell on it here. At first the whole procedure will seem complicated. Soon, however, it will become just another facet of life. It is difficult to foresee any end to the necessity for this task in the immediate future, but then one never can tell.

Passage B:

The procedure is actually quite simple. First you arrange things into different groups. Of course, one pile may be sufficient depending on how much there is to do. If you have to go somewhere else due to lack of facilities that is the next step, otherwise you are pretty well set. It is important not to overdo things. That is, it is better to do too few things at once than too many. In the short run this may not seem important but complications can easily arise. A mistake can be expensive as well. At first the whole procedure will seem complicated. Soon, however, it will become just another facet of life. It is difficult to foresee any end to the necessity for this task in the immediate future, but then one never can tell. After the procedure is completed one arranges the materials into different groups again. Then they can be put into their appropriate places. Eventually they will be used once more and the whole cycle will then have to be repeated. However, that is part of life.

The materials used in Experiment IV were less like a paragraph than those used in Experiments I–III and the sentences were presented as sentences, rather than in paragraph form. In order of presentation, the sentences were: A newspaper is better than a magazine/ A seashore is a better place than the street/ At first it is better to run than to walk/ You may have to try several times/ It takes some skill but it's easy to learn/ Even young children can enjoy it/ Once successful, complications are minimal/ Birds seldom get too close/ Rain, however, soaks in very fast/Too many people doing the same thing can also cause problems/ One needs lots of room/ If there are no complications, it can be very peaceful/ A rock will serve as an anchor/ If things break loose from it, however, you will not get a second chance/

EXPERIMENT II PROCEDURE

All *S*s were tested simultaneously. Assignment of *S*s to conditions was made by randomizing the instruction sheets in blocks of the three experimental treatments and passing the resulting stack of booklets out in normal class-room fashion. The written instructions told the *S*s to listen carefully to the passage that *E* would read to them and that they would later be asked to recall it as accurately as possible. The instruction sheet for the Topic Before *S*s included the additional sentence, "The paragraph you will hear will be about washing clothes." Immediately after the passage was read, *S*s opened their comprehension rating instructions. For the Context After *S*s, these instructions included the sentence, "It may help you to know that the paragraph was about washing clothes." Approximately 2 minutes after the end of acquisition, *S*s were reminded to recall as accurately as possible and instructed to write down at least the essential ideas. Five minutes were allowed for recall.

EXPERIMENT III PROCEDURE

The *S*s were tested in groups corresponding to the two conditions. Both groups heard the same tape recording of Passage B. All instructions and the topic (again, "washing clothes") were given verbally by *E*. Acquisition instructions informed *S*s that they would later be asked to recall all the essential ideas of the passage. There was a 1-minute interval between the end of acquisition and the comprehension rating and a 1-minute interval between the rating and recall tasks. Six minutes were allowed for recall.

EXPERIMENT IV PROCEDURE

All *S*s were tested simultaneously with a procedure similar to that used in Experiment II. The topic (which was presented on the acquisition instruction sheet and on the comprehension rating instruction sheet for Topic Before and Topic After groups, respectively) was "making and flying a kite." The sentences were read by *E* and there was a 2-second interval between the end of one sentence and the beginning of the next. Six minutes were allowed for recall.

Subjects

In Experiment II the Ss were 52 male and female students enrolled in a course in human learning at the State University of New York, Stony Brook. The Ss for Experiments III ($N = 21$) and IV ($N = 31$) were male and female high school student volunteers.

Results

Mean comprehension ratings and mean recall scores for conditions in Experiments II and III are presented in Table 2 and those for Experiment IV are presented in Table 3.

Experiment II

Comprehension ratings were higher in the Topic Before condition than in either the No Topic or the Topic After conditions, Dunnett's test $(3, 49) = 4.46$ and 4.80, $p < .005$, respectively. Likewise, recall was greater in the Topic Before condition than in the No Topic or Topic After conditions, $d(3, 49) = 3.97$ and 4.20, $p < .005$, respectively.

Experiment III

Both comprehension ratings and recall scores were higher in the Topic Before condition than in the Topic After condition: the Fs $(1, 19)$ were 12.24 for comprehension and 20.03 for recall, $p < .005$ in both cases.

Experiment IV

In the analysis of the comprehension ratings, the Topic Before scores were higher than the No Topic scores, $d(3, 28) = 2.01$, $p < .05$. However, there was no significant difference between ratings of the Topic Before and Topic After Ss, $p > .05$. Recall of the Topic Before Ss was superior to that of both No Topic and of Topic After Ss, $d(3, 28) = 2.49$ and 2.68, $p < .05$, respectively.

Discussion

The results of Experiments II, III, and IV indicate that prior knowledge of a situation does not guarantee its usefulness for comprehension. In order for prior knowledge to aid comprehension, it must become an activated semantic context. As in Experiment I, it appears that for maximum benefit the

Table 2 Mean comprehension ratings and mean number of ideas recalled

	Experiment II				Experiment III			
	No topic	Topic after	Topic before	Maximum score		Topic after	Topic before	Maximum score
Comprehension	2.29 (.22)[a]	2.12 (.26)	4.50 (.49)	7		3.40 (.48)	5.27 (.27)	7
Recall	2.82 (.60)	2.65 (.53)	5.83 (.49)	18		3.30 (.66)	7.00 (.43)	20

[a] Standard error in parentheses.

Table 3 Mean comprehension ratings and mean number of ideas recalled, Experiment IV

	No topic	*Topic after*	*Topic before*	*Maximum score*
Comprehension	2.44 (.47)[a]	3.82 (.52)	4.00 (.59)	7
Recall	3.22 (.55)	3.18 (.57)	5.54 (.76)	14

[a] Standard error in parentheses.

appropriate information must be present during the ongoing process of comprehension. Comprehension and recall scores of the Topic After groups were generally much lower than those of the Topic Before groups. In short, the effect of topic in Experiments II, III, and IV was similar to that of context in Experiment I.

Lachman and his associates (Pompi & Lachman, 1967; Dooling & Lachman, 1971) suggested that knowledge of the topic facilitates retention by functioning as a mnemonic device. In recognition, Ss score higher on theme-related words because they match test words to the theme. In recall, a reconstructive process (with the theme as the mediating schema) is emphasized. The present writers view the role of the topic as something more than a schema for generating lexical matches or associations, however. Its critical role appears to be in helping Ss create contexts that can be used to comprehend the passages in the first place. At least in the present experiments, Topic After groups were at a considerable disadvantage relative to Topic Before groups. Most importantly, knowledge of the topic of a passage may be neither necessary nor sufficient for optimal comprehension. Note, for example, that the context supplied in Experiment I did not contain information about the topic of the stimulus passage. The topic would be something like "Possible breakdowns in communication during a serenade." The picture simply supplied information about a basic situation that could have been developed in many different directions. The stimulus passage discussed just one of the many possible sets of events that could have taken place. The picture greatly improved comprehension and recall scores, despite the fact that Ss in the Context Before group had no more explicit prior information about the topic than Ss in the other groups. Moreover, knowledge of the topic alone is not sufficient for optical comprehension of the passage in Experiment I. Pilot studies indicate that Ss receiving the topic of this passage before hearing it were still clearly inferior to Context Before Ss. The topic "possible breakdowns in communication during a serenade" is not sufficient to suggest the kind of contextual information communicated by the appropriate context picture.

It is interesting that in all the experiments, the absence of an appropriate semantic context seemed to have an effect on memory that is similar to that found when *S*s are led to focus on nonsemantic apects of linguistic inputs. For example, attention to the orthographic properties of sentences or words (rather than attention to their semantic features) causes a considerable decrement in recall (Bobrow & Bower, 1969; Hyde & Jenkins, 1969). In the present experiments all *S*s presumably tried to process the information semantically, yet attention to semantic properties alone will not guarantee the availability of an adequate context for comprehension of prose.

Additional evidence that contexts are important for processing incoming information is that many of the *S*s in the present experiments who were not provided with the context or topic prior to hearing the passage reported that they actively searched for a situation that the passage might be about; generally they were unable to find one suitable for understanding the entire passage, although they could make parts of it make sense. The extent to which context availability becomes a problem will certainly vary with the circumstances. Many sentences provide cues that allow one to create contextual structures that are sufficient for processing sentences seemingly in isolation. In other cases one will need additional information, such as that built up by perceptual context or previous linguistic context, in order to comprehend.

The notions that certain cognitive structures may be prerequisites for knowledge acquisition, or that such structures may influence perception and recall, have, of course, been discussed by many investigators (e.g., Arnheim, 1971; Ausubel, 1960; Bartlett, 1932; Gombrich, 1961, Piaget, 1950; and Winograd, 1971). Although at present it is not possible to provide a precise statement synthesizing these views and specifying mechanisms and processes operating during the acts of comprehending and remembering, the present results do emphasize the crucial role of semantic contexts. The experimental manipulation of context availability may constitute a useful strategy for investigating the interaction of prior knowledge and present input events.

Note

1 This research was supported in part by a Research Foundation of the State University of New York summer research fellowship to the second author. Senior authorship was decided by tossing a coin. We wish to thank Brian O'Callaghan, guidance counselor, and the students of Ward Melville High School, East Setauket, New York, for their cooperation.

References

ARNHEIM, R. *Visual thinking.* Berkeley: University of California Press, 1971.

AUSUBEL, D. P. *Educational psychology: A cognitive view.* New York: Holt, Rinehart and Winston, Inc., 1968.

BARTLETT, F. C. *Remembering.* Cambridge: Cambridge University Press, 1932.

BEVER, T. G., LACKNER, J. R., & KIRK, R. The underlying structures of sentences are the primary units of immediate speech processing. *Perception and Psychophysics,* 1969, **6,** 225–234.

BLUMENTHAL, A. Prompted recall of sentences. *Journal of Verbal Learning and Verbal Behavior*, 1967, **6**, 203–206.

BLUMENTHAL, A. & BOAKES, R. Prompted recall of sentences: A further study. *Journal of Verbal Learning and Verbal Behavior*, 1967, **6**, 674–675.

BOBROW, S. A., & BOWER, G. H. Comprehension and recall of sentences. *Journal of Experimental Psychology*, 1969, **80**, 455–461.

BRANSFORD, J. D., BARCLAY, J. R., & FRANKS, J. J. Sentence memory: A constructive versus interpretive approach. *Cognitive Psychology*, 1972, **3**, 193–209.

BRANSFORD, J. D., & FRANKS, J. J. The abstraction of linguistic ideas. *Cognitive Psychology*, 1971, **2**, 331–350.

CHOMSKY, N. *Syntactic structures*. London: Mouton and Company, 1957.

CHOMSKY, N. *Aspects of the theory of syntax*. Cambridge: M.I.T. Press, 1965.

CHOMSKY, N. *Language and mind*. New York: Harcourt, Brace and World, 1968.

DOOLING, D. J., & LACHMAN, R. Effects of comprehension on retention of prose. *Journal of Experimental Psychology*, 1971, **88**, 216–222.

GOMBRICH, E. H. *Art and illusion*, New York: Pantheon Books, 1961.

HYDE, T. S., & JENKINS, J. J. Differential effects of incidental tasks on the organization of recall of a list of highly associated words. *Journal of Experimental Psychology*, 1969, **82**, 472–481.

JOHNSON, M. K., BRANSFORD, J. D., & SOLOMON, S. Memory for tacit implications of sentences. *Journal of Experimental Psychology*, in press.

KATZ, J. J., & POSTAL, P. M. *An integrated theory of linguistic descriptions*. Cambridge: M.I.T. Press, 1964.

KINTSCH, W. Notes on the structure of semantic memory. In E. Tulving and W. Donaldson (Eds.), *Organization of memory*. New York: Academic Press, 1972.

PERFETTI, C. R. Lexical density and phrase structure depth as variables in sentence retention. *Journal of Verbal Learning and Verbal Behavior*, 1969, **8**, 719–724.

PIAGET, J. *The psychology of intelligence*. London: Routledge and Kegan Paul, Ltd., 1947.

POMPI, K. F., & LACHMAN, R. Surrogate processes in the short-term retention of connected discourse. *Journal of Experimental Psychology*, 1967, **75**, 143–150.

POSTAL, P. M. Underlying and superficial linguistic structure. *Harvard Educational Review*, 1964, **34**, 246–266.

ROHRMAN, N. L. The role of syntactic structure in the recall of English nominalizations. *Journal of Verbal Learning and Verbal Behavior*, 1968, **7**, 904–912.

SACHS, J. Recognition memory for syntactic and semantic aspects of connected discourse. *Perception and Psychophysics*, 1967, **2**, 437–422.

TULVING, E., & OSLER, S. Effectiveness of retrieval cues in memory for words. *Journal of Experimental Psychology*, 1968, **77**, 593–601.

WANNER, H. E. On remembering, forgetting and understanding sentences: a study of the deep structure hypothesis. Unpublished doctoral dissertation. Harvard University, 1968.

WINOGRAD, T. Procedures as a representation for data in a computer program for understanding natural language. Report No. MAC TR-84, Massachusetts Institute of Technology, Project MAC, 1971.

LEVELS OF PROCESSING

A framework for memory research[1]

Fergus I. M. Craik and Robert S. Lockhart

Source: *Journal of Verbal Learning and Verbal Behavior*, 11 (1972): 671–684.

This paper briefly review the evidence for multistore theories of memory and points out some difficulties with the approach. An alternative framework for human memory research is then outlined in terms of depth or levels of processing. Some current data and arguments are reexamined in the light of this alternative framework and implications for further research considered.

Over the past decade, models of human memory have been dominated by the concept of stores and the transfer of information among them. One major criterion for distinguishing between stores has been their different retention characteristics. The temporal properties of stored information have, thus, played a dual role: Besides constituting the basic phenomenon to be explained, they have also been used to generate the theoretical constructs in terms of which the explanation is formulated. The apparent circularity has been avoided by the specification of additional properties of the stores (such as their capacity and coding characteristics) thereby characterizing them independently of the phenomena to be explained. The constructs, thus formulated, have been used to account for data across a variety of paradigms and experimental conditions. The essential concept underlying such explanations is that of information being transferred from one store to another, and the store-to-store transfer models may be distinguished, at least in terms of emphasis, from explanations which associate different retention characteristics with qualitative changes in the memory code.

In the present paper we will do three things: (*a*) examine the reasons for proposing multistore models, (*b*) question their adequacy, and (*c*) propose an alternative framework in terms of levels of processing. We will argue that the memory trace can be understood as a by-product of perceptual analysis and that trace persistence is a positive function of the depth to which the stimulus has been analyzed. Stimuli may also be retained over short intervals by continued processing at a constant depth. These views offer a new way to interpret existing data and provide a heuristic framework for further research.

Multistore models

The case in favor

When man is viewed as a processor of information (Miller, 1956; Broadbent, 1958), it seems necessary to postulate holding mechanisms or memory stores at various points in the system. For example, on the basis of his dichotic listening studies, Broadbent (1958) proposed that information must be held transiently before entering the limited-capacity processing channel. Items could be held over the short term by recycling them, after perception, through the same transient storage system. From there, information could be transferred into and retained in a more permanent long-term store. Broadbent's ideas have been developed and extended by Waugh and Norman (1965), Peterson (1966), and Atkinson and Shiffrin (1968). According to the modal model (Murdock, 1967), it is now widely accepted that memory can be classified into three levels of storage; sensory stores, short-term memory (STM) and long-term memory (LTM). Since there has been some ambiguity in the usage of terms in this area, we shall follow the convention of using STM and LTM to refer to experimental situations, and the terms "short-term store" (STS) and "long-term store" (LTS) to refer to the two relevant storage systems.

Stimuli can be entered into the sensory stores regardless of whether or not the subject is paying attention to that source; that is, sensory stores are "preattentive" (Neisser, 1967). The input is represented in a rather literal form and can be overwritten by further inputs in the same modality (Neisser, 1967; Crowder & Morton, 1969). Further features which distinguish the sensory registers from later stores are the modality-specific nature and moderately large capacity of sensory stores and the transience of their contents.

Attention to the material in a sensory register is equivalent to reading it out and transferring it to STS. Here, verbal items are coded in some phonemic fashion (Shulman, 1971) or in auditory–verbal–linguistic terms (Atkinson & Shiffrin, 1968). The STS is further distinguished from sensory memories by virtue of its limited capacity (Miller, 1956; Broadbent, 1958), by the finding that information is lost principally by a process of displacement (Waugh & Norman, 1965), and by the slower rate of forgetting from STS: 5–20 seconds as opposed to the ¼–2-second estimates for sensory storage. While most research has concentrated on verbal STS, there is evidence that more literal "representational" information may also be held over the short term (Posner,

1967), although the relationship between such modality-specific stores and the verbal STS has not been made clear.

The distinctions between STS and LTS are well-documented. Whereas STS has a limited capacity, LTS has no known limit; verbal items are usually coded phonemically in STS but largely in terms of their semantic features in LTS (Baddeley, 1966); forgetting from STS is complete within 30 seconds or less while forgetting from LTS is either very slow or the material is not forgotten at all (Shiffrin & Atkinson, 1969). In the free-recall paradigm, it is generally believed that the last few items are retrieved from STS and prior items are retrieved from LTS; it is now known that several variables affect one of these retrieval components without affecting the other (Glanzer, 1972). Further persuasive evidence for the STS/LTS dichotomy comes from clinical studies (Milner, 1970; Warrington, 1971). The distinguishing features of the three storage levels are summarized in Table 1.

The attractiveness of the "box" approach is not difficult to understand. Such multistore models are apparently specific and concrete; information flows in well-regulated paths between stores whose characteristics have intuitive appeal; their properties may be elicited by experiment and described either behaviorally or mathematically. All that remains, it seems, is to specify

Table 1 Commonly accepted differences between the three stages of verbal memory (see text for sources)

Feature	Sensory registers	Short-term store	Long-term store
Entry of information	Preattentive	Requires attention	Rehearsal
Maintenance of information	Not possible	Continued attention	Repetition
		Rehearsal	Organization
Format of information	Literal copy of input	Phonemic	Largely semantic
		Probably visual	Some auditory and visual
		Possibly semantic	
Capacity	Large	Small	No known limit
Information loss	Decay	Displacement Possibly decay	Possibly no loss Loss of accessibility or discriminability by interference
Trace duration	¼–2 Seconds	Up to 30 seconds	Minutes to years
Retrieval	Readout	Probably automatic Items in consciousness Temporal/phonemic cues	Retrieval cues Possibly search process

the properties of each component more precisely and to work out the transfer functions more accurately.

Despite all these points in their favor, when the evidence for multistore models is examined in greater detail, the stores become less tangible. One warning sign is the progressively greater part played by "control processes" in more recent formulations (for example, Atkinson & Shiffrin, 1971). In the next section we consider the adequacy of multistore notions more critically.

The case against

The multistore approach has not been without its general critics (Melton, 1963; Murdock, 1972). Other workers have objected to certain aspects of the formulation. For example, Tulving and Patterson (1968) argued against the notion of information being transferred from one store to another. Similarly, Shallice and Warrington (1970) presented evidence against the idea that information must necessarily "pass through" STS to enter LTS.

In our view, the criteria listed in the previous section do not provide satisfactory grounds for distinguishing between separate stores. The adequacy of the evidence will be considered with reference to the concepts of capacity, coding, and finally, the retention function itself.

Capacity

Although limited capacity has been a major feature of the information flow approach, and especially a feature of STS in multistore models, the exact nature of the capacity limitation is somewhat obscure. In particular, it has been unclear whether the limitation is one of processing capacity, storage capacity, or is meant to apply to some interaction between the two. In terms of the computer analogy on which information flow models are based, the issue is whether the limitation refers to the storage capacity of a memory register or to the rate at which the processor can perform certain operations. The notion of a limited-capacity channel (Broadbent, 1958) appears to emphasize the second interpretation while later models of memory, such as that of Waugh and Norman (1965), appear to favor the storage interpretation. Both interpretations are present in Miller (1956) but the relationship between the two is not explicitly worked out.

Attempts to measure the capacity of STS have leant towards the storage interpretation, and considered number of items to be the appropriate scale of measurement. Such attempts have provided quite a range of values. For example, recent estimates of primary memory size (Baddeley, 1970; Murdock, 1972) have yielded values between two and four words. However, measures of memory span (which have been said to reflect the limited capacity of the STM box) are typically between five and nine items, depending on whether the items in question are words, letters or digits (Crannell & Parrish, 1957). Finally, if the words in a span test form a sentence, young subjects can accurately reproduce strings of up to 20 words (Craik & Masani, 1969). Thus, if capacity is a critical feature of STM operation, a box model has to account for this very wide range of capacity estimates.

The most widely accepted explanation of this variation is that capacity is limited in terms of chunks, and that few or many items can be recoded into a chunk depending on the meaningfulness of the material. Apart from the difficulty of defining a chunk independently from its memorial consequences, this view entails a rather flexible notion of STS as a storage compartment which can accept a variety of codes from simple physical features to complex semantic ones.

From the standpoint of the present paper, the concept of capacity is to be understood in terms of a limitation on processing; limitations of storage are held to be a direct consequence of this more fundamental limitation.

Coding

Working with verbal material, Conrad (1964) and Baddeley (1966) provided one plausible basis for distinguishing STS and LTS. They concluded that information in STS was coded acoustically and that coding was predominantly semantic in LTS. Further research has blurred this distinction, however. First, it has been shown that STS coding can be either acoustic or articulatory (Levy, 1971; Peterson & Johnson, 1971). Second, recent papers by Kroll and his colleagues (Kroll *et al.*, 1970) have demonstrated that even with verbal material, STS can sometimes be visual. Apparently STS can accept a variety of physical codes.

Can STS also hold semantic information? The persistence of contradictory evidence suggests either that the question has been inappropriately formulated or that the answer depends on the paradigm used. When traditional STM paradigms are considered, the answer seems to be "no" (Kintsch & Buschke, 1969; Craik & Levy, 1970), although Shulman (1970, 1972) has recently presented persuasive evidence in favor of a semantic STS. While type of coding may originally have seemed a good basis for the distinction between short-term and long-term memory, the distinction no longer appears satisfactory. A defender of the multistore notion might argue that STS coding is flexible, but this position removes an important characteristic by which one store is distinguished from another.

We will argue that the coding question is more appropriately formulated in terms of the processing demands imposed by the experimental paradigm and the material to be remembered. In some paradigms and with certain material, acoustic coding may be either adequate or all that is possible. In other circumstances processing to a semantic level may be both possible and advantageous.

Forgetting characteristics

If memory stores are to be distinguished in terms of their forgetting charac-teristics, a minimal requirement would seem to be that the retention function should be invariant across different paradigms and experimental conditions. While this invariance has not been rigorously tested, there are cases where it clearly breaks down. We will give two examples. First, in the finite-state models of paired-associate learning, the state commonly identified as STS shows forgetting characteristics which are different from those established for STS in other paradigms (Kintsch, 1970, p. 206). In the former case, STS retention extends over as many as 20 intervening items while in the free-recall and probe paradigms (Waugh & Norman, 1965), STS information is lost much more rapidly. As a second example, the durability of the memory trace for visual stimuli appears to depend on the material and the paradigm. According to Neisser (1967), the icon lasts 1 second or less, Posner (1969) and his colleagues have found evidence for visual persistence of up to 1.5 seconds, while other recent studies by Murdock (1971), Phillips and Baddeley (1971) and by Kroll *et al.* (1970) have yielded estimates of 6, 10, and 25 seconds, respectively. Estimates are even longer in recognition memory for pictures (Shepard, 1967; Haber, 1970). Given that we recognize pictures, faces, tunes, and voices after long periods of time, it is clear that we have long-term memory for relatively literal nonverbal information. Thus, it is difficult to draw a line between "sensory memory" and "representational" or "pictorial" memory.

We will argue that retention depends upon such aspects of the paradigm as study time, amount of material presented and mode of test; also upon the extent to which the subject has developed systems to analyze and enrich particular types of stimuli; that is, the familiarity, compatibility, and meaningfulness of the material.

Although we believe that the multistore formulation is unsatisfactory in terms of its capacity, coding, and forgetting characteristics, obviously there are some basic findings which any model must accommodate. It seems cer-tain that stimuli are encoded in different ways within the memory system: A word may be encoded at various times in terms of its visual, phonemic, or semantic features, its verbal associates, or an image. Differently encoded representations apparently persist for different lengths of time. The phenom-enon of limited capacity at some points in the system seems real enough and, thus, should also be taken into consideration. Finally, the roles of perceptual, attentional, and rehearsal processes should also be noted.

One way of coping with the kinds of inconsistencies we have described is to postulate additional stores (see, Morton, 1970; Sperling, 1970). However, we think it is more useful to focus on the encoding operations themselves and to consider the proposal that rates of forgetting are a function of the type and depth of encoding. This view is developed in the next section.

147

Levels of processing

Many theorists now agree that perception involves the rapid analysis of stimuli at a number of levels or stages (Selfridge & Neisser, 1960; Treisman, 1964; Sutherland, 1968). Preliminary stages are concerned with the analysis of such physical or sensory features as lines, angles, brightness, pitch, and loudness, while later stages are more concerned with matching the input against stored abstractions from past learning; that is, later stages are concerned with pattern recognition and the extraction of meaning. This conception of a series or hierarchy of processing stages is often referred to as "depth of processing" where greater "depth" implies a greater degree of semantic or cognitive analysis. After the stimulus has been recognized, it may undergo further processing by enrichment or elaboration. For example, after a word is recognized, it may trigger associations, images or stories on the basis of the subject's past experience with the word. Such "elaboration coding" (Tulving & Madigan, 1970) is not restricted to verbal material. We would argue that similar levels of processing exist in the perceptual analysis of sounds, sights, smells and so on. Analysis proceeds through a series of sensory stages to levels associated with matching or pattern recognition and finally to semantic-associative stages of stimulus enrichment.

One of the results of this perceptual analysis is the memory trace. Such features of the trace as its coding characteristics and its persistence thus arise essentially as byproducts of perceptual processing (Morton, 1970). Specifically, we suggest that trace persistence is a function of depth of analysis, with deeper levels of analysis associated with more elaborate, longer lasting, and stronger traces. Since the organism is normally concerned only with the extraction of meaning from the stimuli, it is advantageous to store the products of such deep analyses, but there is usually no need to store the products of preliminary analyses. It is perfectly possible to draw a box around early analyses and call it sensory memory and a box around intermediate analyses called short-term memory, but that procedure both oversimplifies matters and evades the more significant issues.

Although certain analytic operations must precede others, much recent evidence suggests that we perceive at meaningful, deeper levels before we perceive the results of logically prior analyses (Macnamara, 1972; Savin & Bever, 1970). Further elaborative coding does not exist in a hierarchy of necessary steps and this seems especially true of later processing stages. In this sense, "spread" of encoding might be a more accurate description, but the term "depth" will be retained as it conveys the flavor of our argument.

Highly familiar, meaningful stimuli are compatible, by definition, with existing cognitive structures. Such stimuli (for example, pictures and sentences) will be processed to a deep level more rapidly than less meaningful stimuli and will be well-retained. Thus, speed of analysis does not necessarily predict retention. Retention is a function of depth, and various factors, such as the amount of attention devoted to a stimulus, its compatibility with the analyzing structures, and the processing time available, will determine the depth to which it is processed.

Thus, we prefer to think of memory tied to levels of perceptual processing. Although these levels may be grouped into stages (sensory analyses, pattern recognition, and stimulus elaboration, for example) processing levels may be more usefully envisaged as a continuum of analysis. Thus, memory, too, is viewed as a continuum from the transient products of sensory analyses to the highly durable products of semantic-associative operations. However, super-imposed on this basic memory system there is a second way in which stimuli can be retained—by recirculating information at one level of processing. In our view, such descriptions as "continued attention to certain aspects of the stimulus," "keeping the items in consciousness," "holding the items in the rehearsal buffer," and "retention of the items in primary memory" all refer to the same concept of maintaining information at one level of processing. To preserve some measure of continuity with existing terminology, we will use the term primary memory (PM) to refer to this operation, although it should be noted that our usage is more restricted than the usual one.

We endorse Moray's (1967) notion of a limited-capacity central processor which may be deployed in a number of different ways. If this processing capacity is used to maintain information at one level, the phenomena of short-term memory will appear. The processor itself is neutral with regard to coding characteristics: The observed PM code will depend on the processing modality within which the processor is operating. Further, while limited cap-acity is a function of the processor itself, the number of items held will depend upon the level at which the processor is operating. At deeper levels the subject can make greater use of learned rules and past knowledge; thus, material can be more efficiently handled and more can be retained. There is apparently great variability in the ease with which information at different levels can be maintained in PM. Some types of information (for example, phonemic features of words) are particularly easy to maintain while the main-tenance of others (such as early visual analyses —the "icon") is apparently impossible.

The essential feature of PM retention is that aspects of the material are still being processed or attended to. Our notion of PM is, thus, synonymous with that of James (1890) in that PM items are still in consciousness. When attention is diverted from the item, information will be lost at the rate appropriate to its level of processing—slower rates for deeper levels. While PM retention is, thus, equivalent to continued processing, this type of processing merely prolongs an item's high accessibility without leading to formation of a more permanent memory trace. This Type I processing, that is, repetition of analyses which have already been carried out, may be contrasted with Type II processing which involves deeper analysis of the stimulus. Only this second type of rehearsal should lead to improved memory performance. To the extent that the subject utilizes Type II processing, memory will improve with total study time, but when he engages in Type I processing, the "total time hypothesis" (see Cooper & Pantle, 1967) will break down. Stoff and Eagle (1971) have reported findings in line with this suggestion.

To summarize, it is suggested that the memory trace is better described in terms of depth of processing or degree of stimulus elaboration. Deeper analysis leads to a more persistent trace. While information may be held in PM, such maintenance will not in itself improve subsequent retention; when attention is diverted, information is lost at a rate which depends essentially on the level of analysis.

Existing data reexamined

Incidental learning

When memory traces are viewed as the product of a particular form of processing, much of the incidental learning literature acquires a new significance. There are several reviews of this literature (Postman, 1964; McLaughlin, 1965), and we will make no attempt to be comprehensive. An important characteristic of the incidental learning paradigm is that the subject processes the material in a way compatible with or determined by the orienting task. The comparison of retention across different orienting tasks, therefore, provides a relatively pure measure of the memorial consequences of different processing activities. According to the view of the present paper, and in agreement with Postman (1964), the instruction to learn facilitates performance only insofar as it leads the subject to process the material in a manner which is more effective than the processing induced by the orienting task in the incidental condition. Thus, it is possible, that with an appropriate orienting task and an inappropriate intentional strategy, learning under incidental conditions could be superior to that under intentional conditions.

From the point of view of this paper, then, the interesting thing to do is to systematically study retention following different orienting tasks within the incidental condition, rather than to compare incidental with intentional learning. Under incidental conditions, the experimenter has a control over the processing the subject applies to the material that he does not have when the subject is merely instructed to learn and uses an unknown coding strategy.

We will consider several examples which illustrate this point. Tresselt and Mayzner (1960) tested free recall after incidental learning under three different orienting tasks: crossing out vowels, copying the words, and judging the degree to which the word was an instance of the concept "economic". Under the last condition, the number of words recalled was four times higher than that of the first and twice that of the second condition. Similar results using the free-recall paradigm have been obtained by Hyde and Jenkins (1969), and Johnston and Jenkins (1971). The experiments by Jenkins and his colleagues showed that with lists of highly associated word pairs, free recall and organization resulting from an orienting task which required the use of the word as a semantic unit, was equivalent to that of an intentional control group with no incidental task, but both were substantially superior to an incidental group whose task involved treating the word structurally (checking for certain letters or estimating the number of letters in the word). These results are consistent with those of Mandler (1967) who showed that incidental learning during categorization of words yielded a similar recall level to that of a group who performed the same activity but who knew that their recall would be tested.

Experiments involving the incidental learning of sentences (Bobrow & Bower, 1969; Rosenberg & Schiller, 1971) have shown that recall after an orienting task that required processing the sentence to a semantic level was substantially superior to recall of words from equivalently exposed sentences which were processed nonsemantically.

Schulman (1971) had subjects scan a list of words for targets defined either structurally (such as words containing the letter A) or semantically (such as words denoting living things). After the scanning task, subjects were given an unexpected test of recognition memory. Performance in the semantically defined target conditions was significantly better than that in the structurally defined conditions although scanning time per word was approximately the same in most cases.

These results support the general conclusion that memory performance is a positive function of the level of processing required by the orienting task. However, beyond a certain stage, the form of processing which will prove optimal depends on the retrieval or trace utilization requirements of the subsequent memory test. There is clear evidence in the incidental learning literature that the relative value of different orienting tasks is not the same for all tests of memory.

This conclusion is supported by comparisons of the differential effects of orienting tasks on recognition and recall. Eagle and Leiter (1964) found that whereas free recall in an unhindered intentional condition was superior to that of an incidental group and to a second intentional group who had also to perform the orienting task, these latter two conditions showed superior recognition performance. Such a result poses no difficulty provided it is assumed that optimal processing does not take the same form for both memory tests. In the Eagle and Leiter (1964) experiment, the orienting task, while almost certainly involving some degree of semantic analysis, might have served to prevent the kind of elaborative processing necessary for later access to the stored information. On the other hand, such elaborative coding might hinder subsequent discrimination between target words and the associatively related distractors used in this experiment. Results consistent with this kind

151

of analysis have also been reported by Dornbush and Winnick (1967) and Estes and DaPolito (1967).

While the orienting tasks used by Wicker and Bernstein (1969) in their study of incidental paired-associate learning all required analysis to a semantic level, they did not facilitate subsequent performance to the same degree. When the orienting task involved the production of mediating responses, performance was equal to that of unhindered intentional learning and superior to when the orienting task was rating words for pleasantness. In single-trial free recall, this latter orienting task produces performance equal to that of intentional learning (Hyde & Jenkins, 1969). Identical orienting tasks do not seem to have equivalent effects across different paradigms. The interaction between initial encoding and subsequent retrieval operations is worth emphasizing. Although the distinction between availability and accessibility (Tulving & Pearlstone, 1966) is a useful one, the effectiveness of a retrieval cue depends on its compatibility with the item's initial encoding or, more generally, the extent to which the retrieval situation reinstates the learning context.

Selective attention and sensory storage

Moray (1959) showed that words presented to the nonattended channel in a dichotic listening test were not recognized in a later memory test. Similarly, Neisser (1964) has shown that nontarget items in a visual search task left no recognizable trace. Thus, if stimuli are only partially analyzed, or processed only to peripheral levels, their record in memory is extremely fleeting. This point was neatly demonstrated by Treisman (1964). When the same prose passage was played to both ears dichotically, but staggered in time with the unattended ear leading, the lag between messages had to be reduced to 1.5 seconds before the subject realized that the messages were identical. When the attended (shadowed) ear was leading, however, subjects noticed the similarity at a mean lag of 4.5 seconds. Thus, although the subjects were not trying to remember the material in either case, the further processing necessitated by shadowing was sufficient to treble the durability of the memory trace. Treisman also found that meaningfulness of the material (reversed speech versus normal speech, and random words versus prose) affected the lag necessary for recognition, but only when the attended channel was leading. If the message was rejected after early analyses, meaningfulness played no part; but when the message was attended, more meaningful material could be processed further and was, thus, retained longer. The three estimates of memory persistence in these experiments (1.5 seconds for all nonattended material, 3 seconds for attended reversed speech and attended strings of random words, and 5 seconds for attended prose) can be attributed to the functioning of different stores, but it is more reasonable, in our view, to postulate that persistence is a function of processing level.

152

While further studies will not be reviewed in such detail, it may be noted that the findings and conclusions of many other workers in the area of sensory memory can also be accommodated in the present framework. Neisser (1967, p. 33) concluded that "longer exposures lead to longer-lasting icons." Studies by Norman (1969), Glucksberg and Cowen (1970), and Peterson and Kroener (1964) may all be interpreted as showing that non-attended verbal material is lost within a few seconds.

Massaro (1970) suggested that memory for an item is directly related to the amount of perceptual processing of the item, a statement which is obviously in line with the present proposals, although his later arguments (Massaro, 1972), that echoic memory inevitably lasts only 250 milliseconds, are probably overgeneralizations. Shaffer and Shiffrin concluded from an experiment on picture recognition that "it might prove more fruitful to consider the more parsimonious view that there is just a single short-term visual memory. This short-term visual memory would decay quickly when the information content of the visual field was high and more slowly when the information content was greatly reduced" (Shaffer & Shiffrin, 1972, p. 295). Plainly this view is similar to our own, although we would argue that the continuum extends to long-term retention as well. We would also suggest that it is processing level, rather than information content, which determines the rate of decay.

The STS/LTS distinction

The phenomenon of a limited-capacity holding mechanism in memory (Miller, 1956; Broadbent, 1958) is handled in the present framework by assuming that a flexible central processor can be deployed to one of several levels in one of several encoding dimensions, and that this central processor can only deal with a limited number of items at a given time. That is, items are kept in consciousness or in primary memory by continuing to rehearse them at a fixed level of processing. The nature of the items will depend upon the encoding dimension and the level within that dimension. At deeper levels the subject can make more use of learned cognitive structures so that the item will become more complex and semantic. The depth at which primary memory operates will depend both upon the usefulness to the subject of continuing to process at that level and also upon the amenability of the material to deeper processing. Thus, if the subject's task is merely to reproduce a few words seconds after hearing them, he need not hold them at a level deeper than phonemic analysis. If the words form a meaningful sentence, however, they are compatible with deeper learned structures and larger units may be dealt with. It seems that primary memory deals at any level with units or "chunks" rather than with information (see Kintsch, 1970, pp. 175–181). That is, we rehearse a sound, a letter, a word, an idea, or an image in the same way that we perceive objects and not constellations of attributes.

As pointed out earlier, a common distinction between memory stores is their different coding characteristics; STS is said to be predominantly acoustic (or articulatory) while LTS is largely semantic. According to the present argument, acoustic errors will predominate only insofar as analysis has not proceeded to a semantic level. There are at least three sources of the failure of processing to reach this level; the nature of the material, limited available processing capacity, and task demands. Much of the data on acoustic confusions in short-term memory is based on material such as letters and digits which have relatively little semantic content. The nature of this material itself tends to constrain processing to a structural level of analysis and it should be no surprise, therefore, that errors of a structural nature result. Such errors can also occur with meaningful material if processing capacity is diverted to an irrelevant task (Eagle & Ortoff, 1967).

A further set of results relevant to the STS/LTS distinction are those that show that in free recall, variables such as presentation rate and word frequency, affect long-term but not short-term retention (Glanzer, 1972). Our interpretation of these findings is that increasing presentation rate, or using unfamiliar words, inhibits or prevents processing to those levels necessary to support long-term retention, but does not affect coding operations of the kind that are adequate for short-term retention. It follows from this interpretation that diverting processing capacity as in the Eagle and Ortoff (1967) experiments should result in a greater decrement in long-term than in short-term retention and, indeed, there is good evidence that such is the case (Murdock, 1965; Silverstein & Glanzer, 1971).

Conversely, manipulations that influence processing at a structural level should have transitory, but no long-term, effects. Modality differences (Murdock, 1966) provide a clear example. Finally, long-term recall should be facilitated by manipulations which induce deeper or more elaborative processing. We suggest that the encoding variability hypothesis as it has been used to account for the spacing effect in free recall (Madigan, 1969; Melton, 1970) is to be understood in these terms.

The serial position curve

Serial-position effects have been a major source of evidence for the STS/LTS distinction (see Broadbent, 1971, pp. 354–361; Kintsch, 1970, pp. 153–162). In free recall, the recency effect is held to reflect output from STS while previous items are retrieved from LTS (Glanzer & Cunitz, 1966). Several theoretical accounts of the primacy effect have been given, but perhaps the most plausible is that initial items receive more rehearsals and are, thus, better registered in LTS (Atkinson & Shiffrin, 1968; Bruce & Papay, 1970). We agree with these conclusions. Since the subject knows he must stop attending to initial items in order to perceive and rehearse subsequent items, he subjects these first items to Type II processing; that is, deeper semantic processing. Final list items can survive on phonemic encoding, however, which gives rise to excellent immediate recall (since they are still being processed in primary memory) but is wiped out by the necessity to process interpolated material. In fact, if terminal items have been less deeply processed than initial items, the levels of processing formulation would predict that in a subsequent recall attempt, final items should be recalled least well of all list items. The finding of negative recency (Craik, 1970) supports this prediction. An alternative explanation of negative recency could be that recency items were rehearsed fewer times than earlier items (Rundus, 1971). However, recent studies by Jacoby and Bartz (1972), Watkins (1972), and Craik (1972) have shown that it is the type rather than the amount of processing which determines the subsequent recall of the last few items in a list.

In serial recall, subjects must retain the first few items so that they can at least commence their recall correctly. The greatly enhanced primacy effect is thus probably attributable, in part at least, to primary-memory retention. The degree to which subjects also encode initial items at a deeper level is likely to depend on the material and the task. Using a relatively slow (2.5 seconds) presentation rate and words as visually presented stimuli, Palmer and Ornstein (1971) found that an interpolated task only partially eliminated the primacy effect. However, Baddeley (1968) presented digits auditorily at a 1-second rate and found that primacy was entirely eliminated by the necessity to perform a further task.

Repetition and rehearsal effects

One suggestion in the present formulation is that Type I processing does nothing to enhance memory for the stimulus; once attention is diverted, the trace is lost at the rate appropriate to its deepest analyzed level. Thus, the concept of processing has been split into Type I or same-level processing and Type II processing which involves further, deeper analysis of the stimulus and leads to a more durable trace. Similarly, the effects of repeated presentation depend on whether the repeated stimulus is merely processed to the same level or encoded differently on its further presentations. There is evidence, both in audition (Moray, 1959; Norman, 1969), and in vision (Turvey, 1967), that repetition of an item encoded only at a sensory level, does not lead to an improvement in memory performance.

Tulving (1966) has also shown that repetition without intention to learn does not facilitate learning. Tulving's explanation of the absence of learning in terms of interitem organization cannot easily be distinguished from an explanation in terms of levels of processing. Similarly, Glanzer and Meinzer (1967) have shown that overt repetition of items in free recall is a less effective strategy than that normally used by subjects. Although both Waugh and Norman (1965), and Atkinson and Shiffrin (1968) have suggested that rehearsal has the dual function of maintaining information in primary memory and transferring it to secondary memory, the experiments by Tulving (1966) and by Glanzer and Meinzer (1967) show that this is not necessarily so. Thus, whether rehearsal strengthens the trace or merely postpones forgetting depends on what the subject is doing with his rehearsal. Only deeper processing will lead to an improvement in memory.

Concluding comments

Our account of memory in terms of levels of processing has much in common with a number of other recent formulations. Cermak (1972), for example, has outlined a theoretical framework very similar to our own. Perceptually oriented attribute-encoding theories such as those of Bower (1967) and Norman and Rumelhart (1970) have a close affinity with the present approach as does that of Posner (1969) who advocates stages of processing with different characteristics associated with each stage.

If the memory trace is viewed as the by-product of perceptual analysis, an important goal of future research will be to specify the memorial consequences of various types of perceptual operations. We have suggested the comparison of orienting tasks within the incidental learning paradigm as one method by which the experimenter can have more direct control over the encoding operations that subjects perform. Since deeper analysis will usually involve longer processing time, it will be extremely important to disentangle such variables as study time and amount of effort from depth as such. For example, time may be a correlate of memory to the extent that time is necessary for processing to some level, but it is possible that further time spent in merely recycling the information after this optimal level will not predict trace durability.

Our approach does not constitute a theory of memory. Rather, it provides a conceptual framework—a set of orienting attitudes—within which memory research might proceed. While multistore models have played a useful role, we suggest that they are often taken too literally and that more fruitful questions are generated by the present formulation. Our position is obviously speculative and far from complete. We have looked at memory purely from the input or encoding end; no attempt has been made to specify either how items are differentiated from one another, are grouped together and organized, or how they are retrieved from the system. While our position does not imply any specific view of these processes, it does provide an appropriate framework within which they can be understood.

Note

1 This research was supported by Grants A8261 and A0355 from the National Research Council of Canada to the first and second author, respectively. We thank

our colleagues who read a preliminary version of the paper and made many helpful suggestions.

References

ATKINSON, R. C., & SHIFFRIN, R. M. Human memory: A proposed system and its control processes. In K. W. Spence and J. T. Spence (Eds.) *The psychology of learning and motivation: Advances in research and theory*, Vol. II. New York: Academic Press, 1968. Pp. 89–195.

ATKINSON, R. C., & SHIFFRIN, R. M. The control of short-term memory. *Scientific American*, 1971, **224**, 82–89.

BADDELEY, A. D. Short-term memory for word sequences as a function of acoustic, semantic, and formal similarity. *Quarterly Journal of Experimental Psychology*, 1966, **18**, 362–365.

BADDELEY, A. D. How does acoustic similarity influence short-term memory? *Quarterly Journal of Experimental Psychology*, 1968, **20**, 249–264.

BADDELEY, A. D. Estimating the short-term component in free recall. *British Journal of Psychology*, 1970, **61**, 13–15.

BOBROW, S. A., & BOWER, G. H. Comprehension and recall of sentences. *Journal of Experimental Psychology*, 1969, **80**, 455–461.

BOWER, G. H. A multicomponent theory of the memory trace. In K. W. Spence and J. T. Spence (Eds.) *The psychology of learning and motivation: Advances in research and theory*, Vol. 1. New York: Academic Press, 1967. Pp. 230–325.

BROADBENT, D. E. *Perception and communication*. New York: Pergamon Press, 1958.

BROADBENT, D. E. *Decision and stress*. New York: Academic Press, 1971.

BRUCE, D., & PAPAY, J. P. Primacy effect in single-trial free recall. *Journal of Verbal Learning and Verbal Behavior*, 1970, **9**, 473–486.

CERMAK, L. S. *Human memory. Research and theory*. New York: Ronald, 1972.

CONRAD, R. Acoustic confusions in immediate memory. *British Journal of Psychology*, 1964, **55**, 75–84.

COOPER, E. H., & PANTLE, A. J. The total-time hypothesis in verbal learning. *Psychological Bulletin*, 1967, **68**, 221–234.

CRAIK, F. I. M. The fate of primary memory items in free recall. *Journal of Verbal Learning and Verbal Behavior*, 1970, **9**, 143–148.

CRAIK, F. I. M. A 'levels of analysis' view of memory. Paper presented at the 2nd Erindale Symposium on Communication and Affect, March, 1972.

CRAIK, F. I. M., & LEVY, B. A. Semantic and acoustic information in primary memory. *Journal of Experimental Psychology*, 1970, **86**, 77–82.

CRAIK, F. I. M., & MASANI, P. A. Age and intelligence differences in coding and retrieval of word lists. *British Journal of Psychology*, 1969, **60**, 315–319.

CRANNELL, C. W., & PARRISH, J. M. A comparison of immediate memory span for digits, letters, and words. *Journal of Psychology*, 1957, **44**, 319–327.

CROWDER, R. G., & MORTON, J. Precategorical acoustic storage. *Perception and Psychophysics*, 1969, **5**, 365–373.

DORNBUSH, R. L., & WINNICK, W. A. Short-term intentional and incidental learning. *Journal of Experimental Psychology*, 1967, **73**, 608–611.

EAGLE, M., & LEITER, E. Recall and recognition in intentional and incidental learning. *Journal of Experimental Psychology*, 1964, **68**, 58–63.

EAGLE, M., & ORTOFF, E. The effect of level of attention upon "phonetic" recognition errors. *Journal of Verbal Learning and Verbal Behavior*, 1967, **6**, 226–231.

ESTES, W. K., & DaPOLITO, F. Independent variation of information storage and retrieval processes in paired-associate learning. *Journal of Experimental Psychology*, 1967, **75**, 18–26.

GLANZER, M. Storage mechanisms in recall. In G. H. Bower (Ed.) *The psychology of learning and motivation: Advances in research and theory*. Vol. 5. New York: Academic Press, 1972. Pp. 129–193.

GLANZER, M., & CUNITZ, A. R. Two storage mechanisms in free recall. *Journal of Verbal Learning and Verbal Behavior*, 1966, **5**, 351–360.

GLANZER, M., & MEINZER, A. The effects of intralist activity on free recall. *Journal of Verbal Learning and Verbal Behavior*, 1967, **6**, 928–935.

GLUCKSBERG, S., & COWEN, G. N. Memory for nonattended auditory material. *Cognitive Psychology*, 1970, **1**, 149–156.

HABER, R. N. How we remember what we see. *Scientific American*, 1970, **222**, 104–112.

HYDE, T. S., & JENKINS, J. J. The differential effects of incidental tasks on the organization of recall of a list of highly associated words. *Journal of Experimental Psychology*, 1969, **82**, 472–481.

JACOBY, L. L., & BARTZ, W. H. Encoding processes and the negative recency effect. *Journal of Verbal Learning and Verbal Behavior*, 1972, **11**, 561–565.

JAMES, W. *Principles of psychology*. New York: Holt, 1890.

JOHNSTON, C. D., & JENKINS, J. J. Two more incidental tasks that differentially affect associative clustering in recall. *Journal of Experimental Psychology*, 1971, **89**, 92–95.

KINTSCH, W. *Learning, memory, and conceptual processes*. New York: Wiley, 1970.

KINTSCH, W., & BUSCHKE, H. Homophones and synonyms in short-term memory. *Journal of Experimental Psychology*, 1969, **80**, 403–407.

KROLL, N. E. A., PARKS, T., PARKINSON, S. R., BIEBER, S. L., & JOHNSON, A. L. Short-term memory while shadowing. Recall of visually and aurally presented letters. *Journal of Experimental Psychology*, 1970, **85**, 220–224.

LEVY, B. A. Role of articulation in auditory and visual short-term memory. *Journal of Verbal Learning and Verbal Behavior*, 1971, **10**, 123–132.

MACNAMARA, J. Cognitive basis of language learning in infants. *Psychological Review*, 1972, **79**, 1–13.

MADIGAN, S. A. Intraserial repetition and coding processes in free recall. *Journal of Verbal Learning and Verbal Behavior*, 1969, **8**, 828–835.

MANDLER, G. Organization and Memory. In K. W. Spence and J. T. Spence (Eds.) *The psychology of learning and motivation: Advances in research and theory*, Vol. 1. New York: Academic Press, 1967. Pp. 328–372.

MASSARO, D. W. Perceptual processes and forgetting in memory tasks. *Psychological Review*, 1970, **77**, 557–567.

MASSARO, D. W. Preperceptual images, processing time, and perceptual units in auditory perception. *Psychological Review*, 1972, **79**, 124–145.

MCLAUGHLIN, B. "Intentional" and "incidental" learning in human subjects: The role of instructions to learn and motivation. *Psychological Bulletin*, 1965, **63**, 359–376.

MELTON, A. W. Implications of short-term memory for a general theory of memory. *Journal of Verbal Learning and Verbal Behavior*, 1963, **2**, 1–21.

MELTON, A. W. The situation with respect to the spacing of repetitions and memory. *Journal of Verbal Learning and Verbal Behavior*, 1970, **9,** 596–606.

MILLER, G. A. The magical number seven, plus or minus two: Some limits on our capacity for processing information. *Psychological Review*, 1956, **63,** 81–97.

MILNER, B. Memory and the medial temporal regions of the brain. In K. H. Pribram and D. E. Broadbent (Eds.) *Biology of memory*. New York: Academic Press, 1970. Pp. 29–50.

MORAY, N. Attention in dichotic listening: affective cues and the influence of instructions. *Quarterly Journal of Experimental Psychology*, 1959, **9,** 56–60.

MORAY, N. Where is capacity limited? A survey and a model. In A. Sanders (Ed.) *Attention and performance*. Amsterdam: North-Holland, 1967.

MORTON, J. A. functional model of memory. In D. A. Norman (Ed.) *Models of human memory*. New York: Academic Press, 1970. Pp. 203–254.

MURDOCK, B. B. JR. Effects of a subsidiary task on short-term memory. *British Journal of Psychology*, 1965, **56,** 413–419.

MURDOCK, B. B. JR. Visual and auditory stores in short-term memory. *Quarterly Journal of Experimental Psychology*, 1966, **18,** 206–211.

MURDOCK, B. B. JR. Recent developments in short-term memory. *British Journal of Psychology*, 1967, **58,** 421–433.

MURDOCK, B. B. JR. Four channel effects in short-term memory. *Psychonomic Science*, 1971, **24,** 197–198.

MURDOCK, B. B. JR. Short-term memory. In G. H. Bower (Ed.) *Psychology of learning and motivation*, Vol. 5. New York: Academic Press, 1972. Pp. 67–127.

NEISSER, U. Visual search. *Scientific American*, 1964, **210,** 94–102.

NEISSER, U. *Cognitive psychology*. New York: Appleton-Century-Crofts, 1967.

NORMAN, D. A. Memory while shadowing. *Quarterly Journal of Experimental Psychology*, 1969, **21,** 85–93.

NORMAN, D. A., & RUMELHART, D. E. A system for perception and memory. In D. A. Norman (Ed.) *Models of human memory*. New York: Academic Press, 1970. Pp 21–64.

PALMER, S. E., & ORNSTEIN, P. A. Role of rehearsal strategy in serial probed recall. *Journal of Experimental Psychology*, 1971, **88,** 60–66.

PETERSON, L. R. Short-term verbal memory and learning. *Psychological Review*, 1966, **73,** 193–207.

PETERSON, L. R., & JOHNSON, S. T. Some effects of minimizing articulation on short-term retention. *Journal of Verbal Learning and Verbal Behavior*, 1971, **10,** 346–354.

PETERSON, L. R., & KROENER, S. Dichotic stimulation and retention. *Journal of Experimental Psychology*, 1964, **68,** 125–130.

PHILLIPS, W. A., & BADDELEY, A. D. Reaction time and short-term visual memory. *Psychonomic Science*, 1971, **22,** 73–74.

POSNER, M. I. Short-term memory systems in human information processing. *Acta Psychologica*, 1967, **27,** 267–284.

POSNER, M. I. Abstraction and the process of recognition. In G. H. Bower and J. T. Spence (Eds.) *The psychology of learning and motivation: Advances in research and theory*, Vol. III. New York: McGraw-Hill, 1969, Pp. 152–179.

POSTMAN, L. Short-term memory and incidental learning. In A. W. Melton (Ed.) *Categories of human learning*. New York: Academic Press, 1964. Pp. 145–201.

ROSENBERG, S., & SCHILLER, W. J. Semantic coding and incidental sentence recall. *Journal of Experimental Psychology*, 1971, **90**, 345–346.

RUNDUS, D. Analysis of rehearsal processes in free recall. *Journal of Experimental Psychology*, 1971, **89**, 63–77.

SAVIN, H. B., & BEVER, T. G. The nonperceptual reality of the phoneme. *Journal of Verbal Learning and Verbal Behavior*, 1970, **9**, 295–302.

SCHULMAN, A. I. Recognition memory for targets from a scanned word list. *British Journal of Psychology*, 1971, **62**, 335–346.

SELFRIDGE, O. G., & NEISSER, U. Pattern recognition by machine. *Scientific American*, 1960, **203**, 60–68.

SHAFFER, W. O., & SHIFFRIN, R. M. Rehearsal and storage of visual information. *Journal of Experimental Psychology*, 1972, **92**, 292–296.

SHALLICE, T., & WARRINGTON, E. K. Independent functioning of verbal memory stores: A neuropsychological study. *Quarterly Journal of Experimental Psychology*, 1970, **22**, 261–273.

SHEPARD, R. N. Recognition memory for words, sentences, and pictures. *Journal of Verbal Learning and Verbal Behavior*, 1967, **6**, 156–163.

SHIFFRIN, R. M., & ATKINSON, R. C. Storage and retrieval processes in long-term memory. *Psychological Review*, 1967, **76**, 179–193.

SHULMAN, H. G. Encoding and retention of semantic and phonemic information in short-term memory. *Journal of Verbal Learning and Verbal Behavior*, 1970, **9**, 499–508.

SHULMAN, H. G. Similarity effects in short-term memory. *Psychological Bulletin*, 1971, **75**, 399–415.

SHULMAN, H. G. Semantic confusion errors in short-term memory. *Journal of Verbal Learning and Verbal Behavior*, 1972, **11**, 221–227.

SILVERSTEIN, C., & GLANZER, M. Concurrent task in free recall: Differential effects of LTS and STS. *Psychonomic Science*, 1971, **22**, 367–368.

SPERLING, G. Short-term memory, long-term memory, and scanning in the processing of visual information. In A. Young and D. B. Lindsley (Eds.) *Early experience and visual information processing in perceptual and reading disorders.* Washington: National Academy of Sciences, 1970. Pp. 198–215.

STOFF, M., & EAGLE, M. N. The relationship among reported strategies, presentation rate, and verbal ability and their effects on free recall learning. *Journal of Experimental Psychology*, 1971, **87**, 423–428.

SUTHERLAND, N. S. Outlines of a theory of visual pattern recognition in animals and man. *Proceedings of the Royal Society. Series B*, 1968, **171**, 297–317.

TREISMAN, A. Monitoring and storage of irrelevant messages in selective attention. *Journal of Verbal Learning and Verbal Behavior*, 1964, **3**, 449–459.

TRESSELT, M. E., & MAYZNER, M. S. A study of incidental learning. *Journal of Psychology*, 1960, **50**, 339–347.

TULVING, E. Subjective organization and effects of repetition in multi-trial free-recall learning. *Journal of Verbal Learning and Verbal Behavior*, 1966, **5**, 193–197.

TULVING, E., & MADIGAN, S. A. Memory and verbal learning. *Annual Review of Psychology*, 1970. **21**, 437–484.

TULVING, E., & PATTERSON, R. D. Functional units and retrieval processes in free recall. *Journal of Experimental Psychology*, 1968, **77**, 239–248.

TULVING, E., & PEARLSTONE, Z. Availability versus accessibility of information in memory for words. *Journal of Verbal Learning and Verbal Behavior*, 1966, **5**, 381–391.

TURVEY, M. T. Repetition and the preperceptual information store. *Journal of Experimental Psychology*, 1967, **74**, 289–293.

WARRINGTON, E. K. Neurological disorders of memory. *British Medical Bulletin*, 1971, **27** 243–247.

WATKINS, M. J. The characteristics and functions of primary memory. Unpublished Ph.D. thesis, University of London, 1972.

WAUGH, N. C., & NORMAN, D. A. Primary memory. *Psychological Review*, 1965, **72**, 89–104.

WICKER, F. W., & BERNSTEIN, A. L. Association value and orienting task in incidental and intentional paired-associate learning. *Journal of Experimental Psychology*, 1969, **81**, 308–311.

28

LEVELS OF PROCESSING VERSUS TRANSFER APPROPRIATE PROCESSING

C. Donald Morris, John D. Bransford and Jeffery J. Franks

Source: *Journal of Verbal Learning and Verbal Behavior*, 16 (1977): 519–533.

Levels of processing were manipulated as a function of acquisition task and type of recognition test in three experiments. Experiment 1 showed that semantic acquisition was superior to rhyme acquisition given a standard recognition test, whereas rhyme acquisition was superior to semantic acquisition given a rhyming recognition test. The former finding supports, while the latter finding contradicts, the levels of processing claim that depth of processing leads to stronger memory traces. Experiment 2 replicated these findings using both immediate and delayed recognition tests. Experiment 3 indicated that these effects were not dependent upon the number of times a rhyme sound was presented during acquisition. Results are interpreted in terms of an alternate framework involving transfer appropriate processing.

According to the levels of processing framework proposed by Craik and Lockhart (1972), the nature and duration of the memory trace is determined by the level or depth at which the input is processed. Inputs that receive only superficial analyses such as those prompted by nonsemantic orienting tasks are assumed to be more poorly retained than inputs subjected to deeper semantic analyses.

A large number of studies appear to support the levels of processing framework (e.g., Hyde & Jenkins, 1969; Till & Jenkins, 1973; Walsh & Jenkins, 1973). A somewhat smaller set of studies has pointed toward the need to further differentiate levels of processing within the semantic level of analysis (e.g., Craik & Tulving, 1975; Schulman, 1974; Klein & Saltz, 1976; Seamon & Murray, 1976) and to consider additional memory variables such as retrieval constraints, trace uniqueness, trace congruity, and so forth (e.g., Craik & Tulving, 1975; Moscovitch & Craik, 1976). To our knowledge, however, no theorists have explicitly addressed the question of what is meant by superficial or nonmeaningful processing in contrast to semantic processing. We shall argue that particular acquisition activities are never inherently "superficial" or "nonmeaningful." Instead, task meaningfulness must be defined relative to particular learning goals.

Consider a recent experiment conducted within the levels of processing framework. Seamon and Murray (1976) presented orienting instructions indicating that subjects should either attend to word meaning (Task A) or attend to the position of their lips during vocalization of each input (Task B). Results indicated that the deeper processing suggested by Task A produced better memory than did the superficial, nonmeaningful processing prompted by Task B. Seamon and Murray also manipulated the normative meaningfulness of input stimuli and found that meaningfulness facilitated recall only for acquisition Task A.

It is instructive to ask why attention to the position of one's lips during pronunciation constitutes a nonmeaningful or superficial level of processing. At first glance, the answer to such a question seems obvious. Subjects are not prompted to process the *meaning* of each word. However, is the failure to process the semantic meaning of inputs necessarily equivalent to performing a superficial or nonmeaningful task?

Assume that one wants to teach principles of speech perception and articulation to students. The present authors' experiences (as well as those of colleagues who have taught speech perception) suggest that an especially helpful teaching technique involves asking students to attend to the position of their lips and tongue while pronouncing words. Students usually find this to be an extremely *meaningful* exercise, despite the fact that they are not prompted to process the *semantic meaning* of the words used in the exercise. Indeed, the semantic meaning of the words presented is not necessarily a meaningful component of such an instructional exercise. Similarly, if one wants to teach students about rhyming, the semantic meaning of the words presented as illustrations is not necessarily a meaningful aspect of the task at hand.

Imagine that an instructor wishes to test the degree to which students learned from the above-mentioned classroom exercise. It would seem totally inappropriate to test students by asking them to identify the particular inputs (e.g., words) that were used during the learning exercises. The purpose of the speech perception and rhyme exercises is not to learn the particular inputs used as illustrations during instruction. Instead, the purpose is to learn sound–mouth and tongue relationships (for speech perception and articulation), to learn sound–sound relationships (for rhyming), and so forth. Such learning tasks are not necessarily shallow, superficial, or nonmeaningful. Do such tasks necessarily result in memory traces that are less adequate and durable than do other tasks which prompt subjects to process the semantic aspects of inputs? We suggest that the answer to this question has not yet been subjected to appropriate experimental test.

Investigators who have utilized the levels of processing framework have been equivalent to a speech perception or rhyme instructor who tests his student on the particular words used to exemplify the desired to-be-learned information. In a classroom situation, it seems clear that sophisticated students would strongly object to such a testing procedure. Clearly, the tests would not be designed to tap what was supposed to be learned. The levels of processing claim that less meaningful or more superficial analyses of inputs result in less durable memory traces is therefore questionable or at least highly ambiguous. It seems clear that one can test people inappropriately and therefore find evidence for "inadequate processing or learning" relative to that particular testing criterion. Will the superiority of deep, semantic processing persist irrespective of the test one employs? For example, assume that one group of subjects is asked to check for *es* in each word (Hyde & Jenkins, 1969), whereas a second group is prompted to process each word at a deeper, semantic level. Which group will be better and faster at estimating the number of acquisition stimuli that contained an "*e*?"

The present experiments are designed to begin an initial inquiry into the assumptions underlying the levels of processing framework. Their purpose is to explore the degree to which assumptions about the "goodness" of particular acquisition activities must be defined relative to particular learning goals (as well as to tests designed to be congruent with these goals). It is possible that so-called superficial or nonmeaningful tasks (e.g., rhyme acquisition) are inferior to semantic tasks irrespective of the testing situation. Alternatively, different modes or levels of processing may simply allow people to acquire different sorts of information, each of which may have the potential for being equally strong and durable (as revealed by appropriate testing situations). The present experiments provide an initial investigation of these possibilities.

Two incidental learning tasks were given to subjects to induce them to process verbal items at different levels. One task required subjects to judge the appropriateness of a target word within the context of a given sentence frame. The second task involved judging whether or not a target word rhymed with another word. The first task presumably tapped a semantic (deep) level of processing, whereas the second task induced subjects to process the words at a phonetic (a relatively more superficial) level. The levels of processing framework predicts that the semantic processing task should result in superior retention of items, relative to the phonetic processing task. But, as argued in the introduction, tests of this claim have generally used targets and foils that may be considered appropriate to and dependent upon semantic modes of processing. Thus, many of the results favoring the levels of processing claims may be due in large part to an inherent bias in the way in which memory was tested.

To provide a more adequate test of these claims it is necessary to consider not only the processing levels dictated by the acquisition tasks, but also the processing levels induced by the form of the memory test itself. Accordingly, the present experiments factorially varied the kind of acquisition task with the kind of memory test given to subjects. It was expected that these experimental manipulations would directly affect the levels at which subjects processed materials during acquisition and testing.

The basic paradigm of the present experiments is as follows: Subjects were given either a semantic or a phonetic orienting task. Half of the subjects in each experiment were given a recognition test in which targets were the *original* items presented during acquisition. The other half of the subjects received a recognition test in which targets were *rhymes* of the items presented originally. Thus, the level of processing for a set of items was varied not only at acquisition, but at the time of test as well.

Experiment 1

Experiment 1 was designed to investigate the possibility of an interaction between acquisition mode and type of memory test, given an immediate testing situation. It was hypothesized that a semantic level of processing during acquisition would indeed facilitate recognition performance relative to a rhyme-related level of processing, given a standard recognition test. This superiority was expected to be neutralized, and possibly reversed, however, when subjects were given a rhyming recognition test.

Method

Subjects

Thirty-two subjects from an introductory psychology class served in this experiment. Each subject was run individually.

Design

A 2 × 2 × 2 factorial design was utilized. There were two types of Acquisition Tasks, a Semantic orienting task and a Rhyme orienting task. These tasks induced deep and superficial levels of processing, respectively. Nested within this factor was a Congruency factor (see Craik & Tulving, 1975). Target words were either congruent or not with a particular context for both kinds of Acquisition Task. For example, targets were either meaningful or nonmeaningful within a particular sentence, or targets either rhymed or did not rhyme with the last word of the preceding sentence. The two levels of this factor are referred to as Yes and No, respectively. Both Acquisition Task and Congruency were varied within subjects. The third factor, Type of Test, was manipulated between subjects. Sixteen subjects were given a Standard recognition test in which target items were the *original* acquisition items. The other sixteen subjects were given a Rhyming recognition test in which targets were *rhymes* of the original items.

Materials and procedures

The experimental stimuli were 32 target words, embedded in sentences. These words were subsequently presented on a recognition test along with 32 foils. All targets and foils were common five-letter words, of either one or two syllables. Each word was chosen to meet the following constraints: (1) It bore little semantic or phonetic similarity to any other word on the list; and (2) at least one other word rhymed with it if it was a foil, or at least two other words rhymed with it if it was a target. (The reasoning for this last constraint is given below.)

During acquisition, the experimenter read aloud 32 sentences with one word (the target) missing from each. The word "BLANK" was said in place of the missing target word. Each sentence was followed by a 2-second pause, then the vocal presentation of the target word. There were four types of sentences, each with eight instances, and each representing a particular mode of acquisition. These acquisition modes corresponded to the four possible combinations of the within-subject factors: Semantic–Yes, Semantic–No, Rhyme–Yes, and Rhyme–No. Sentences requiring semantic processing of the targets were of the form "The _____ had a silver engine." Sentences inducing phonetic processing of the targets were of the form "_____ rhymes with legal." The target word was either a Yes or No. For example, given "The _____ had a silver engine," presentation of the target "TRAIN" would represent a Semantic–Yes acquisition mode, whereas presentation of the target "EAGLE" would represent a Semantic–No acquisition mode. Analogously, for a sentence such as "_____ rhymes with legal," presentation of targets such as "EAGLE" and "PEACH" represent Rhyme–Yes and Rhyme–No acquisition modes, respectively. Each subject received the same 32 target words. These words appeared in one of four different random orders and each target was presented equally often as an instance of each of the four acquisition modes. These last two considerations were both counterbalanced across subjects.

All sentences were short and constructed in such a way that subjects could easily decide if the target was meaningful or nonmeaningful, or a rhyme or nonrhyme. Subjects were simply to respond positively or negatively as to the appropriateness of each target given the immediately preceding sentence. Subjects were told that their responses were to serve as normative data for future experiments.

After receiving the 32 acquisition sentences, subjects were immediately given a recognition test consisting of 64 items, 32 targets and 32 foils in a random order. These words were read aloud by the experimenter at a rate of one word approximately every 5 seconds. Subjects responded on a binary yes–no scale and then responded on a 5-point scale rating their confidence of their recognition responses. For those subjects receiving the Standard recognition test, the to-be-remembered items were those they had received during acquisition. For those receiving a Rhyming recognition test, to-be-remembered items were words that rhymed with the original acquisition items. As mentioned before, all foils (e.g., "POUND") had at least one rhyme (e.g., "MOUND"). It was necessary, however, to choose targets (e.g., "EAGLE") that had at least two rhymes, one given in the acquisition sentences (e.g., "LEGAL") and one given in the recognition test (e.g., "REGAL").

Results

Table 1 presents a summary of the mean corrected recognition scores for each experimental condition. It was considered inappropriate to use uncorrected scores, since these would not take into account the response biases of individual subjects, that is, their inclinations to respond positively or negatively regardless of the acquisition mode of a particular item. In an attempt to remove at least part of this potential response bias, false positive responses were subtracted from the scores in each condition. The corrected scores are presented as proportions and were obtained in the following manner: Suppose a subject had correctly recognized six Semantic–Yes items and four Rhyme–Yes items but had also responded positively to eight of the 32 foils. The corrected scores would then be $(6/8) - (8/32) = 0.50$ and $(4/8) - (8/32) = 0.25$, respectively.

A survey of these means given that subjects received a Standard recognition test reveals that the Semantic acquisition mode was indeed superior to the Rhyme acquisition mode. This finding supports the levels of processing claim that greater depth of processing leads to improved memory traces (e.g., Craik & Tulving, 1975). An examination of the Rhyming recognition scores

Table 1 Mean corrected proportion scores as a function of type of recognition test and type of acquisition mode

Acquisition mode	Recognition test	
	Standard	Rhyming
Semantic–Yes	.844 (.155)[a]	.333 (.224)
Rhyme–Yes	.633 (.239)	.489 (.252)
Semantic–No	.859 (.163)	.325 (.236)
Rhyme–No	.524 (.271)	.184 (.166)

[a] Numbers in parentheses represent standard deviations.

suggests quite a different account, however. In this condition, memory performance was better when subjects had been given a Rhyme–Yes acquisition mode relative to a Semantic–Yes acquisition mode (although this did not hold for No acquisition sentences, see below). This latter effect is difficult to account for within the levels of processing framework.

A $2 \times 2 \times 2$ (Type of Test $\times$ Acquisition Task $\times$ Congruency) analysis of variance on the corrected proportion scores showed a significant main effect for Type of Test, $F(1, 30) = 39.09$, $p < .001$, indicating a general superiority of the Standard recognition test over the Rhyming recognition test; a significant main effect for Acquisition Task, $F(1, 30) = 21.31$, $p < .001$, indicating a general superiority of the Semantic acquisition mode over the Rhyme acquisition mode; and a significant Type of Test $\times$ Acquisition Task interaction, $F(1, 30) = 23.89$, $p < .001$, discussed more fully below. The analysis of variance also showed a significant Congruency effect, $F(1, 30) = 9.87$, $p < .004$, and a significant Acquisition Task $\times$ Congruency interaction, $F(1, 30) = 15.91$, $p < .001$. In general, targets embedded within congruent sentence frames were better remembered than those embedded in incongruent frames, replicating the findings of Craik and Tulving (1975). This effect was primarily attributable to the enhanced recognition of Rhyme–Yes over Rhyme–No scores.

The effect of primary interest in these scores is the observed interaction between Acquisition Task and Type of Test. This interaction was obtained in the analysis of variance with scores collapsed across the Yes–No acquisition dimensions. An examination of Table 1 indicates that the nature of this interaction varies substantially between the Yes and No conditions. Inspection of the upper half of Table 1 (for Yes acquisition conditions) reveals that, given a Standard recognition test, the Semantic acquisition mode was superior to the Rhyme acquisition mode, $.844 > .633$, $t(30) = 3.99$, $p < .001$. However, given that subjects received a Rhyming recognition test, the Rhyme acquisition mode provides superior recognition performance relative to the Semantic acquisition mode, $.489 > .333$, $t(30) = 2.95$, $p < .01$. If we now consider the lower half of Table 1 (for No acquisition conditions), it is evident that the Semantic acquisition mode was superior to the Rhyme acquisition mode for both types of recognition test, although the superiority was greater for the Standard test. Since there was no reversal here, as there was for Yes scores, no further statistical tests were considered necessary.

One reason for these results with No items may be the lack of integration of the target and its sentence frame for No acquisition sentences. This would lead to a decrement in performance, particularly for the Rhyme–No conditions. Craik and Tulving (1975), for instance, have noted that the role of congruency in encoding and retrieval operations needs further clarification. Its influence, particularly with other levels of processing factors, remains unclear at present.

A second reason why Rhyme–No conditions may have poor performance on the Rhyming test stems from the following consideration. Rhyme–No acquisition frames are of the form "_____ rhymes with ditch: LEGAL." Under these conditions LEGAL is assumed to be the target item and the rhyme transfer test assesses a subject's abilities to detect a rhyme word like REGAL. Although this procedure was utilized in the present studies in order to be congruent with previous investigations (e.g., Craik & Tulving, 1975; Moscovitch & Craik, 1976), there are certain reasons to doubt its adequacy. The focal point of a sentence like "_____ rhymes with ditch: LEGAL" may very well be "ditch" and not LEGAL. If subjects could somehow be instructed to understand that words rhyming with "ditch" were the target items for Rhyme–No sentences and were later tested with words like WITCH (rather than REGAL), performance might greatly improve on the Rhyming test, despite the lack of a sentence-target congruency effect. This possibility must await further research. In the meantime, it seems more appropriate to focus present analyses and discussions on the Yes items rather than the No items.

An analysis of the obtained confidence ratings provided no additional insights into the nature of the effects reported above.

Experiment 2

Experiment 2 was designed with two functions in mind. One function was to replicate the findings of Experiment 1. To this end, certain changes were made to provide greater reliability and power for the statistical tests of the phenomenon. The result to be replicated indicates that memory performance seems to be affected by processing level during acquisition task *and* by processing level during retention test. Given this finding, the levels of processing claim that semantic orienting tasks provide inherently stronger memory traces stands in need of qualification. The levels of processing framework also claims that semantic processing results in longer-lasting or more durable memory traces. Thus, the superiority of "semantic" traces over "rhyme" traces should increase, or at least remain constant, over time. The second function of Experiment 2 was to test this prediction, using the same basic paradigm as before. In this experiment, half the subjects received the recognition test immediately, as before, while the other half were tested after a 24-hour delay. Thus, it was hoped that more could be ascertained regarding the interaction between levels of processing at acquisition and test.

Method

Subjects

One hundred and fourteen subjects from an introductory psychology class served in this experiment. Subjects were run in 16 groups of six to eight persons each.

Design

The design was similar to that of Experiment 1 with the exception of an additional between-subjects factor, Time of Test. There were two levels of this factor, Immediate and Delayed. Thus, the design was now a $2 \times 2 \times 2 \times 2$ factorial design.

Materials and procedures

The materials were identical to those of Experiment 1 with the following exception: In Experiment 1 there were 16 distinct stimulus lists (four random orders × four acquisition modes per target), whereas the present experiment utilized only eight distinct stimulus lists (two random orders × four acquisition modes per target).

There were two procedural variations from Experiment 1: (1) Subjects could now respond "yes," "no," or "unsure" after each acquisition sentence, and (2) eight groups of subjects were tested immediately, whereas eight were tested after a 24-hour delay. To help insure the incidental nature of the task, subjects were told that they were to provide additional normative ratings on the following day and that the experiment concerned the reliability of such ratings over time.

Results

Table 2 presents a summary of mean corrected proportion scores for each experimental condition. A survey of these means reveals again that a Semantic acquisition mode is superior to a Rhyme acquisition mode when subjects were given a Standard recognition test. Thus, this finding replicates that found in Experiment 1 and supports the levels of processing claim. In addition, this superiority persists when subjects are tested after a 24-hour delay, although the absolute difference between Semantic and Rhyme acquisitions has diminished. When subjects are given a Rhyming recognition test,

Table 2 Mean corrected proportion scores as a function of type of test, time of test, and type of acquisition mode

	Immediate		Delayed	
Acquisition mode	Standard	Rhyming	Standard	Rhyming
Semantic–Yes	.757 (.169)[a]	.300 (.151)	.450 (.208)	.180 (.180)
Rhyme–Yes	.682 (.180)	.424 (.220)	.418 (.188)	.291 (.229)
Semantic–No	.699 (.206)	.299 (.176)	.387 (.209)	.238 (.221)
Rhyme–No	.528 (.192)	.272 (.251)	.249 (.171)	.166 (.218)

[a] Numbers in parentheses represent standard deviations.

a different pattern of results appears. As in Experiment 1, memory performance was better when subjects had been given a Rhyme–Yes acquisition rather than a Semantic–Yes acquisition. This effect holds not only for the Immediate condition (thus replicating the results of Experiment 1) but for the Delayed condition as well. It is interesting to note that the absolute difference between Semantic–Yes and Rhyme–Yes acquisitions remains fairly constant over the delay period. Note once again, however, that no reversal was found for the No scores. The Semantic–No condition was superior to the Rhyme–No condition for both the Standard and the Rhyming tests and for both the Immediate and the Delayed conditions.

A $2 \times 2 \times 2 \times 2$ analysis of variance (Type of Test $\times$ Acquisition Task $\times$ Congruency $\times$ Time of Test) on the corrected proportion scores showed significant main effects for Type of Test, $F(1, 110) = 86.51$, $p < .001$; Acquisition Task, $F(1, 110) = 5.37$, $p < .02$; Congruency, $F(1, 110) = 30.03$, $p < .001$; and Time of Test, $F(1, 110) = 54.18$, $p < .001$. These represent, in general, the superiority of Standard over Rhyming recognition tests, Semantic over Rhyme acquisition modes, Yes over No acquisition modes, and Immediate over Delayed tests, respectively. Significant interactions were found for Type of Test $\times$ Time of Test, $F(1, 110) = 11.88$, $p < .001$; Type of Test $\times$ Acquisition Task, $F(1, 110) = 21.24$, $p < .001$; and Congruency $\times$ Acquisition Task, $F(1, 110) = 16.71$, $p < .001$. The Type of Test $\times$ Time of Test interaction was due to a larger difference between the Standard and Rhyming recognition tests when tested immediately than when tested after a 24-hour delay. The Congruency $\times$ Acquisition Task interaction was primarily attributable to the relatively poor performance levels of the Rhyme–No acquisition mode relative to the other three acquisition modes. The Type of Test $\times$ Acquisition Task is described below.

For the reasons expressed in the discussion of the results of Experiment 1, it is difficult to interpret differences between Yes and No acquisition modes. Therefore, the critical Type of Test $\times$ Acquisition Task interaction was examined with respect to only the Yes scores. When subjects were given a Standard recognition test, Semantic acquisition was better than Rhyme acquisition for the Immediate test condition, $.757 > .682$, $t(110) = 1.66$, $p < .10$. Although this difference failed to reach conventional levels of significance for a two-tailed test, it was significant for a one-tailed test, $p < .05$. For the Delayed test condition, Semantic acquisition was also better than Rhyme acquisition, but again the advantage was not significant, $.450 > .418$, $t < 1.00$. Though these comparisons fail to suggest significant differences, the differences are in the direction predicted by the levels of processing claim. When subjects were given a Rhyming recognition test, Rhyme acquisition was significantly better than Semantic acquisition for both the Immediate and the Delayed tests, $.424 > .300$, $t(110) = 2.66$, $p < .01$ and $.290 > .180$, $t(110) = 2.38$, $p < .02$, respectively. Thus, the levels of processing claim that greater depth of processing results in stronger memory traces is, again, not supported.

The second claim, that depth of processing also provides more durable traces, is also questioned by the present data. The present authors had assumed that rhyme processing might yield extremely poor performance on a rhyme test after a 24-hour delay. In contrast semantic processing might well show much less decrement in performance on the delayed rhyme test. However, the three-way interaction among Time of Test, Type of Test, and Acquisition Task was not significant. Furthermore, an examination of the Yes scores in Table 2 reveals that the failure of the three-way interaction to reach significance was not due to a lack of statistical resolution. Instead, it appears that the results run in a direction opposite to that discussed above. For instance, given a Standard recognition test, the superiority of Semantic over Rhyme acquisition diminishes over time (.757 v .682 in the Immediate condition compared to .450 v .418 in the Delayed condition). This in itself is not surprising, but it offers an interesting contrast to the Rhyming recognition condition. In this condition, the superiority of Rhyme over Semantic acquisition diminishes to a lesser extent over time (.424 v .300 in the Immediate condition compared to .290 v .180 in the Delayed condition). A comparison of the differences between differences (.075 − .032 = .043 v .124 − .110 = .014, respectively) failed to reach statistical significance. Thus, these results question the assumption that semantic processing provides more durable memory traces.

Finally, there are two major questions regarding the recognition performance of Rhyme–Yes words. Examination of Tables 1 and 2 shows that Rhyme–Yes acquisition stimuli are better retained on Standard, rather than Rhyming, recognition tests. Although the present interest concerns the Acquisition Task × Type of Test interaction, these findings warrant further consideration. Two possibilities suggest themselves. One, the Standard recognition test is simply an easier test to perform. Two, and perhaps more importantly, items on the Standard recognition test contain both semantic and phonetic information relevant to correct identification of the target. Items on the Rhyming recognition test contain rhyme information which relates only to phonetically relevant information but not to semantic information. This possibility is currently being researched.

The second point to be considered involves an inherent procedural difference between Rhyme–Yes and Semantic–Yes conditions. In particular, the Rhyme–Yes condition includes two occurrences of items that rhyme with the Rhyming test target items (e.g., "_____ rhymes with legal: EAGLE"), whereas the Semantic–Yes condition includes only one occurrence of an item that rhymes with the Rhyming test target items (e.g., "A _____ has feathers: EAGLE"). Clearly, it takes two items to define a rhyme. However, it is possible that this procedural difference nevertheless represents a confound in the present design.

The procedural differences between semantic and rhyme modes of acquisition are important and in need of further consideration. For example,

Rhyme–Yes acquisition involves two sources of information that might be utilized in subsequent transfer situations (e.g., a Rhyming test); Semantic–Yes acquisition involves only one. One way to control for this difference is to present two sources of rhyme-related information for Semantic–Yes items as well. Thus, given a Rhyming recognition test, Semantic–Yes acquisition would not be at a disadvantage (in numerical terms) relative to Rhyme–Yes acquisition. Experiment 3 controls for this procedural factor in order to examine its role in determining previous results.

Experiment 3

Method

Subjects

Twenty-five subjects from an introductory psychology class served in this experiment. Subjects were tested in four groups of six or seven persons each.

Design

A 2 × 2 factorial design was utilized. The two factors were Acquisition Task and Congruency, as in Experiments 1 and 2. All subjects were given a Rhyming recognition test.

Materials and procedures

The materials were identical to those of Experiments 1 and 2 with the following exceptions: Only four distinct stimulus lists were used; the acquisition mode of each target was varied across these lists. A second change concerns the construction of the semantic encoding sentences. These sentences were altered so that four Semantic–Yes sentences and four Semantic–No sentences would have as their last word a rhyme of one of the eight Semantic–Yes acquisition target items. This rhyme word was not the Rhyming recognition test target nor did the rhyme word ever appear in the same sentence as the corresponding acquisition target. Consider the Semantic–Yes item EAGLE, which might appear in the following context "The _____ has feathers: EAGLE." Now, a rhyme of EAGLE, such as "regal," would appear at the end of another Semantic sentence frame. For example, subjects might hear "The _____ was very regal: LOCAL." The interval between presentation of a Semantic–Yes target (e.g., EAGLE) and its rhyme word (e.g., "regal") was variable.

The nature of the question under investigation concerns whether or not Rhyme–Yes items have an unfair advantage over Semantic–Yes items on a subsequent Rhyming recognition test. For this reason it was considered unnecessary to test subjects on a Standard recognition test. Therefore, Type of Test was not a factor in this experiment; all subjects received a Rhyming test.

Results

Table 3 presents a summary of the mean corrected proportion scores for each experimental condition. These results are in general agreement with those of Experiments 1 and 2. Of particular importance is the superiority of Rhyme–Yes acquisition over Semantic–Yes acquisition. This superiority holds even when Semantic–Yes items have a second presentation of the critical sound information during acquisition.

A 2 × 2 (Acquisition Task × Congruency) analysis of variance on the corrected proportion scores showed a significant main effect for Acquisition Task, $F(1, 24) = 6.09$, $p < .02$; a significant main effect for Congruency, $F(1, 24) = 13.10$, $p < .002$; and a significant Acquisition Task × Congruency interaction, $F(1, 24) = 10.84$, $p < .003$. These effects are generally attributable to the enhanced recognition for Rhyme–Yes items. The critical comparison of this experiment is between Rhyme–Yes and Semantic–Yes recognition scores. This comparison yields highly significant results, .446 > .303, respectively; $t(24) = 4.15$, $p < .001$. Thus, it appears that Rhyme–Yes acquisition is superior to Semantic–Yes acquisition when subjects are tested on Rhyming recognition. This effect persists even when Semantic–Yes items have had a second presentation within the acquisition list of the rhyme-related information relevant for a Rhyming test.

Overall summary and conclusions

The results of the present studies suggest a need to reconsider certain assumptions basic to the levels of processing framework. In particular, arguments that nonsemantic or shallow levels of processing are necessarily inferior to deeper levels of processing are questionable. To be sure, so-called

Table 3 Mean corrected proportion scores for rhyming recognition as a function of acquisition mode

Acquisition mode	Rhyming test
Semantic–Yes	.303 (.203)[a]
Rhyme–Yes	.446 (.187)
Semantic–No	.283 (.158)
Rhyme–No	.265 (.174)

[a] Numbers in parentheses represent standard deviations.

174

nonsemantic levels of processing may look inferior if subjects are asked to perform subsequent test tasks (e.g., reproducing the nominal stimuli) that are not directly related to what was learned during acquisition. In such cases, however, the reasons for the inferiority may be due to the inappropriateness of the relationship between acquisition and test rather than the inherent inferiority of the acquired memory traces. If one wants to know the number of words in a list that contains *es*, the number containing two syllables, and so forth, then "*e*-checking" or "syllable counting" would appear to be appropriate modes of processing. Similarly, if one wants to learn about rhyming information, it would seem beneficial to pay attention to the rhymes of words. In the present studies, acquisition manipulations that directed subjects to attend to the rhymes of inputs resulted in better performance on a rhyming test than did acquisition activities that prompted subjects to process the "semantic meaning" of inputs. Similar results were obtained following a 24-hour delay between acquisition and test and when number of potential rhyme items was controlled.

Results such as these suggest that it might be useful to replace the concept of "levels of processing" with one emphasizing "transfer appropriate processing." The latter concept emphasizes that the value of particular acquisition activities must be defined relative to particular goals and purposes. Furthermore, assumptions about the quality and durability of the resulting memory traces can only be determined relative to the appropriateness of the testing situation. The concept of transfer appropriate processing suggests that it is no longer beneficial to simply assume that the traces of certain items are less durable or adequate than others because those items were processed at a shallower level. The evidence that appears to support this latter assumption involves test situations that are not optimal for assessing what was actually learned.

The current assumptions about the potential durability of even superficial memory traces are congruent with results from other studies. For example, a number of researchers report data indicating that so-called superficial aspects of encoding activities (e.g., orthographic case, sound of voice, orientations of presented words or sentences) are retained for surprisingly long periods of times (see Arbuckle & Katz, 1976; Craik & Kirsner, 1974; Kirsner, 1973; Kolers, 1975, a, b; Kolers & Ostry, 1974). Note that these latter studies did not prompt subjects to orient solely to these superficial aspects at time of acquisition and then test them on memory for the particular inputs exemplifying these aspects. Instead, subjects apparently processed the inputs at a number of levels (including the semantic level). The data indicate that superficial as well as semantic information played a role in remembering, thereby indicating that the former information was in fact processed and must indeed be capable of being well retained.

One further aspect of the present data needs to be considered. In the present experiments, rhyme acquisition was superior to semantic acquisition for the rhyme test. Overall, however, the semantic acquisition–semantic test conditions resulted in better performance than the rhyme acquisition–rhyme test conditions. Do such results necessitate a concession to the levels of processing claim that superficial nonsemantic processing results in inherently less adequate and durable memory traces? In actuality, the present results suggest that so-called superficial aspects of "memory traces" were at least as durable as semantic traces (i.e., both were maintained over 24 hours). Nevertheless, in terms of absolute values, there is a superiority of semantic acquisition–semantic test over nonsemantic acquisition–nonsemantic test given both immediate and delayed tests. Do data such as these thereby require acceptance of the levels of processing approach?

The beginnings of an alternate conceptualization of data such as those noted above have been discussed by Jenkins (1974). He asks whether optimal memory might be most fruitfully viewed as being a function of (a) semantic processing or (b) skills possessed by the learner–rememberer. An implication of his discussion on skills is that semantic modes of processing may result in better memory for most college students, not because of any inherent advantages of semantic memory traces, but because college students are usually primed to utilize their semantic skills in an experimental setting. On the other hand, consider that an experienced poet or an expert in speech perception, linguistic dialects, and so forth may be as efficient at remembering certain types of auditory information (given appropriate testing situations) as she or he is at remembering semantically processed information. This approach suggests a need to formulate theoretical conceptualizations of memory that do not simply assume that certain types of memory traces are inherently inferior because of the "level" at which they were processed.

Following the lead of Jenkins (1974) let us assume that the adequacy and durability of memory traces are a function of whether or not a subject *has* and *uses* appropriate knowledge and skills to precisely comprehend (encode) each input and hence differentiate it from other potential inputs. In contrast to the levels of processing framework, let us further assume that there are no inherent differences in the nature of the memory traces resulting from semantic versus nonsemantic levels of processing. Instead the emphasis is on the activation of appropriate skills and knowledge structures that "set the stage" for knowing precisely how and *in what ways* certain inputs differ from other potential inputs (e.g., see Bransford & Franks, 1976). The importance of differentiation has been discussed elsewhere (e.g., Gibson, 1940; Saltz, 1971). We emphasize that *even semantic processing* may not facilitate remembering if it does not result in precise differentiation of the acquisition and test stimuli (e.g., see Bransford, McCarrell, Franks, & Nitsch, in press; Stein, in press). Furthermore, the term "semantic processing" is usually used in a very ambiguous way (see also Postman, 1975).

Note that the term "semantic processing" is not necessarily equivalent to meaningful processing and that "nonsemantic processing" is not necessarily equivalent to meaningless or superficial processing. For example, we have suggested that the linguistic semantic meanings of words presented during an exercise designed to teach speech articulation or rhyming are not necessarily meaningful components of the task. Similarly, the semantic meaning of the first and last words in a sentence like *Altitude precedes window* are not relevant for understanding the sentence. Instead, comprehension is enhanced by focusing on orthography and noting that "A" precedes "W" on an alphabetical scale (cf. Bransford, Nitsch, & Franks, 1976). Studies of comprehension (e.g., Bransford & Johnson, 1973; Bransford & McCarrell, 1975; Bransford & Franks, 1976; Bransford, Nitsch, & Franks, 1976) suggest a need to distinguish between the *semantic meaning* of inputs and their *understood meaning* (i.e., their significance). Indeed, perceptual artifacts, gestures, brush strokes, sounds, and so forth may or may not be *meaningful* to a person depending on whether or not an appropriate knowledge framework, or set of skills, is both available and activated at the time (e.g., see Bransford & McCarrell, 1975; Bransford, Nitsch, & Franks, 1976).

The preceding discussion suggests that even superficial aspects of inputs can be meaningful, depending on the knowledge possessed by subjects. In order to be well remembered, subjects also need to be able to use their past knowledge and skills to comprehend (encode) inputs in precise and unique ways. It seems useful to note that the current assumptions about the use of past knowledge structures to set the stage for more precisely comprehending (encoding) the unique aspects of particular inputs are different from assumptions about uniqueness that have appeared in the levels of processing literature. For example, a recent article by Moscovitch and Craik (1976) argues that uniqueness is somewhat important, but only in addition to assumptions about levels of processing.

The latter authors cite studies by Goldstein and Chance (1970) indicating that nonmeaningful visual patterns are poorly recognized even though each pattern is unique, as well as an experiment by Craik and Tulving (1975) indicating that recognition of case encoded words was not facilitated even though the number of such instances was reduced from 40 to four items.

From the present perspective, the Craik and Tulving (1975) experiment did not test what was actually learned. It would be more appropriate to test memory for orthographic case information than for the individual inputs illustrating such cases. Furthermore, the Goldstein and Chance (1970) study says nothing about the stage-setting role of past knowledge for helping one uniquely encode an input and hence precisely differentiate it from other inputs. Appropriate past knowledge permits one to know precisely how and in what ways particular inputs (plus acts of encoding them; e.g., see

Kolers & Ostry, 1974) differ from other aspects of one's knowledge. Without appropriate knowledge structures, one lacks precision with respect to differentiation (see especially Garner, 1974). For example, Indonesian words would be unique for most English speaking subjects, but the latter subjects would have few knowledge structures for uniquely differentiating each word from other things known (especially from one another). Precise memory for such "unique" inputs would therefore be quite poor.

Note, however, that inputs (e.g., words from another language, nonsense syllables, etc.) can always be differentiated from the rest of one's knowledge at *some* level. They are never totally meaningless. Subjects hearing a list of nonsense syllables could easily differentiate them from meaningful words, pictures of triangles, and so forth in a forced choice recognition experiment. Furthermore, such abilities to differentiate would probably persist over a relatively long period of time. The importance of focusing on levels at which people are asked to differentiate inputs from other things that they know is reflected in the large effects on recognition of the foil items. Even the memory traces of relatively non-meaningful unique items may seem quite durable if subjects are tested with foils that can be differentiated at the level of well-known, higher-order invariants that were perceived during acquisition. These more abstract, higher-order invariants seem to be more readily acquired and remembered than lower-level specifics, much as subjects in the Bransford and Franks (1971) experiments seem more apt to acquire higher-level semantic invariants than they are to acquire the precise acquisition inputs that were heard (see Bransford, McCarrell, Franks, & Nitsch, 1977). Arguments about "trace strength" or "durability" must therefore be defined relative to the levels of precision at which subjects are asked to, or able to, differentiate, as well as defined relative to the appropriateness of the test tasks.

In conclusion, it appears useful to summarize the differences between the present approach and the levels of processing framework, particularly since Craik and Tulving (1975) and Moscovitch and Craik (1976) (see also Lockhart, Craik, & Jacoby, 1975) have suggested modifications of the original formulation proposed by Craik and Lockhart (1972). In particular, these authors suggest that "spread of encoding" or "encoding elaboration" may also be important determinants of memory. At the same time, they maintain assumptions about inherent, qualitative differences among various processing levels or domains. For example, Craik and Tulving (1975) state:

> We assume that "depth" still gives a useful account of the major qualitative shifts in a word's encoding (from an analysis of physical features through phonemic features to semantic properties). Within one encoding domain, however, "spread" or "number of encoded features" may be better descriptions. (p. 34)

Assumptions of inherent, qualitative differences between nonsemantic and semantic levels of processing also seem to play important roles in theorizing about spread or elaboration of encoding. For example, Craik and Tulving (1975) state:

> It should be borne in mind that retention depends critically on the qualitative nature of the encoding operations performed—a minimal semantic analysis is more beneficial for memory than an elaborate structural analysis. (p. 48)

The present data suggest that evidence for this latter assumption is based on inadequate tests of what was learned, that is, a "structural" analysis of inputs was more beneficial than a "semantic" analysis for a subsequent rhyme test.

It seems clear that the two above-mentioned quotes from Craik and Tulving (1975) refer to the nature of the "traces" necessary for remembering the actual inputs (e.g., words) presented during acquisition. However, the levels of processing approach uses the term memory trace in an ambiguous manner. There are important differences between use of the term memory trace to refer to a trace of the nominal stimulus and the use of the term trace to refer to the result of a particular learning experience.

The major difference between the levels of processing and transfer appropriate processing frameworks involves their orientations toward the general problem of learning. In the current literature, the term "learning" is usually used synonymously with "learning a list of inputs," and the test is usually a test of memory for these inputs (e.g., see Craik & Tulving, 1975). The value of particular acquisition or learning activities is assessed in relation to the goal of remembering the acquisition inputs. However, even given the goal of remembering inputs, assumptions about the value of particular types of acquisition activities must be defined relative to the type of activities to be performed at the time of test. For example, acquisition processes optimal for recognition are not necessarily optimal for free recall or cued recall, and vice versa (e.g., see Tversky, 1973; Tulving & Thomson, 1973; Bransford, Nitsch, & Franks, 1976). Moreover, the transfer appropriate processing framework goes beyond measures of people's ability to remember the actual inputs presented during acquisition. The problem of learning is broader than this.

The present orientation assumes that learning involves learning from inputs as well as learning inputs (e.g., see Bransford & Franks, 1976; Bransford & Nitsch, in press; Hannigan, Note 1). For example, attention to the position of the lips and tongue can allow one to *learn from* a set of inputs presented as examples, but it will not necessarily allow one to learn (and hence remember) the exact inputs. Depending on what one desires people to learn (e.g., sound–mouth and tongue relationships; sound–sound relationships), processes optimal for learning may therefore be different from those optimal

179

for *remembering* the exact inputs presented during acquisition. Tasks designed to help people learn about speech sounds, word syllables, orthography, and so forth are not necessarily nonmeaningful, and nonsemantic levels of processing need not result in inherently inferior traces representing what was learned. In short, transfer appropriate processing may sometimes involve the superficial levels of analysis that are deemed less adequate by the levels of processing approach.

Note

This research was supported by Grant No. NEG-00-3-0026 from the National Institute of Education, awarded to the second and third authors. We gratefully acknowledge the assistance of Douglas Hintzman and an anonymous reviewer in providing especially helpful comments on an earlier draft of this paper. Reprints may be obtained from Donald Morris, Department of Psychology, Vanderbilt University, Nashville, Tennessee 37240.

Reference Note

1. HANNIGAN, M. L. *The effects of frameworks on sentence perception and memory.* Unpublished doctoral dissertation, Vanderbilt University, 1976.

References

ARBUCKLE, T. Y., & KATZ, W. A. Structure of memory traces following semantic and nonsemantic orientation tasks in incidental learning. *Journal of Experimental Psychology: Human Learning and Memory*, 1976, **2**, 362–369.

BRANSFORD, J. D., & FRANKS, J. J. The abstraction of linguistic ideas. *Cognitive Psychology*, 1971, **2**, 331–350.

BRANSFORD, J. D., & FRANKS, J. J. Toward a framework for understanding learning. In G. H. Bower (Ed.), *The psychology of learning and motivation.* New York: Academic Press, 1976.

BRANSFORD, J. D., & JOHNSON, M. K. Consideration of some problems of comprehension. In W. Chase (Ed.), *Visual information processing.* New York Academic Press, 1973.

BRANSFORD, J. D., & McCARRELL, N. S. A sketch of a cognitive approach to comprehension: Some thoughts about understanding what it means to comprehend. In W. Weimer & D. Palermo (Eds.), *Cognition and the symbolic processes.* Hillsdale, New Jersey: L. Erlbaum Associates, 1975.

BRANSFORD, J. D., McCARRELL, N. S. FRANKS, J. J., & NITSCH, K. E. Toward unexplaining memory. In R. E. Shaw & J. D. Bransford (Eds.), *Perceiving, acting and knowing: Toward an ecological psychology.* Hillsdale, New Jersey: L. Erlbaum Associates, 1977.

BRANSFORD, J. D., & NITSCH, K. E. Coming to understand things we could not previously understand. In J. F. Kavanagh & W. P. Strange (Eds.), *Implications of basic speech and language research for the schools and clinic* (working title). Cambridge, Massachusetts: MIT Press, in press.

BRANSFORD, J. D., NITSCH, K. E., & FRANKS, J. J. Schooling and the facilitation of knowing. In R. C. Anderson, R. J. Spiro, & W. E. Montague (Eds.), *Schooling and the acquisition of knowledge*. Hillsdale, New Jersey: L. Erlbaum Associates, 1976.

CRAIK, F. I. M., & KIRSNER, K. The effect of a speaker's voice on word recognition. *Quarterly Journal of Experimental Psychology*, 1974, **26**, 274–284.

CRAIK, F. I. M., & LOCKHART, R. S. Levels of processing: A framework for memory research. *Journal of Verbal Learning and Verbal Behavior*, 1972, **11**, 671–684.

CRAIK, F. I. M., & TULVING, E. Depth of processing and the retention of words in episodic memory. *Journal of Experimental Psychology: General*, 1975, **104**, 268–294.

GARNER, W. R. *The processing of information and structure*. Potomac, Maryland: L. Erlbaum Associates, 1974.

GIBSON, E. J. A systematic application of the concepts of generalization and differentiation to verbal learning. *Psychological Review*, 1940, **28**, 93–115.

GOLDSTEIN, A. G., & CHANCE, J. E. Visual recognition memory for complex configurations. *Perception and Psychophysics*, 1970, **9**, 237–241.

HYDE, T. S., & JENKINS, J. J. Differential effects of incidental tasks on the organization of recall of a list of highly associated words. *Journal of Experimental Psychology*, 1969, **82**, 472–481.

JENKINS, J. J. Can we have a theory of meaningful memory? In R. L. Solso (Ed.), *Theories in cognitive psychology: The Loyola Symposium*. Hillsdale, New Jersey: L. Erlbaum Associates, 1974.

KIRSNER, K. An analysis of the visual component in recognition memory for verbal stimuli. *Memory and Cognition*, 1973, **1**, 449–453.

KLEIN, K., & SALTZ, E. Specifying the mechanisms in a levels-of-processing approach to memory. *Journal of Experimental Psychology: Human Learning and Memory*, 1976, **2**, 671–679.

KOLERS, P. A. Specificity of operations in sentence recognition. *Cognitive Psychology*, 1975a, **7**, 289–306.

KOLERS, P. A. Memorial consequences of automatized encoding. *Journal of Experimental Psychology: Human Learning and Motivation*, 1975b, **1**, 689–701.

KOLERS, P. A., & OSTRY, D. Time course of loss of information regarding pattern-analysing operations. *Journal of Verbal Learning and Verbal Behavior*, 1974, **13**, 599–612.

LOCKHART, R. S., CRAIK, F. I. M., & JACOBY, L. L. Depth of processing, recognition and recall. In J. BROWN (Ed.), *Recognition and recall*. London: Wiley, 1975.

MOSCOVITCH, M., & CRAIK, F. I. M. Depth of processing, retrieval cues, and uniqueness of encoding as factors in recall. *Journal of Verbal Learning and Verbal Behavior*, 1976, **15**, 447–458.

POSTMAN, L. Verbal learning and memory. *Annual Review of Psychology*, 1975, **26**, 291–335.

SALTZ, E. *The cognitive bases of human learning*. Homewood, Illinois: The Dorsey Press, 1971.

SCHULMAN, A. I. Memory for words recently classified. *Memory and Cognition*, 1974, **2**, 47–52.

SEAMON, J. G., & MURRAY, P. Depth of processing in recall and recognition memory: Differential effects of stimulus meaningfulness and serial position. *Journal of Experimental Psychology: Human Learning and Memory*, 1976, **2**, 680–687.

STEIN, B. S. The effects of cue-target uniqueness on cued-recall performance. *Memory and Cognition*, in press.

TILL, R. E., & JENKINS, J. J. The effects of cued orienting tasks on the free recall of words. *Journal of Verbal Learning and Verbal Behavior*, 1973, **12**, 489–498.

TULVING, E., & THOMSON, D. M. Encoding specificity and retrieval processes in episodic memory. *Psychological Review*, 1973, **80**, 352–373.

TVERSKY, B. Encoding processes in recognition and recall. *Cognitive Psychology*, 1973, **5**, 275–287.

WALSH, D. A., & JENKINS, J. J. Effects of orienting tasks on free recall in incidental learning: "Difficulty," "effort," and "process" explanations. *Journal of Verbal Learning and Verbal Behavior*, 1973, **12**, 481–488.

29

BUILDING MEMORIES

Remembering and forgetting of verbal
experiences as predicted by brain activity

*Anthony D. Wagner, Daniel L. Schacter, Michael Rotte, Wilma
Koutstaal, Anat Maril, Anders M. Dale, Bruce R. Rosen and
Randy L. Buckner*

Source: *Science*, 281 (1998): 1188–1191.

A fundamental question about human memory is why some
experiences are remembered whereas others are forgotten. Brain
activation during word encoding was measured using blocked
and event-related functional magnetic resonance imaging to
examine how neural activation differs for subsequently remembered and subsequently forgotten experiences. Results revealed
that the ability to later remember a verbal experience is predicted by the magnitude of activation in left prefrontal and
temporal cortices during that experience. These findings provide direct evidence that left prefrontal and temporal regions
jointly promote memory formation for verbalizable events.

Memory encoding refers to the processes by which an experience is transformed into an enduring memory trace. Psychological studies have shown
that the memorability of an experience is influenced greatly by the cognitive
operations engaged during initial encoding of that experience, with semantic
processing leading to superior memorability relative to nonsemantic processing (*1*). Functional neuroimaging studies have implicated left prefrontal
cortex in verbal encoding: left prefrontal activation is greater during semantic relative to nonsemantic encoding (*2*), and left prefrontal participation
decreases and memorization is impaired when semantic encoding operations
are disrupted (*3*). These studies have all relied on blocked experimental
designs, where trials from each encoding condition are presented sequentially, inseparable from each other during the functional scan. While blocked

designs allow comparison between encoding conditions that yield, on average, higher or lower levels of subsequent recollection, they do not allow a direct trial-by-trial comparison between specific encoding trials that lead to subsequent remembering and those that lead to subsequent forgetting. Results from event-related potential (ERP) studies, which allow for trial-by-trial analysis, suggest that the neural signature during verbal encoding differs for subsequently remembered and subsequently forgotten experiences, with remembered experiences being associated with a greater positive-going response over frontal and parietal regions (4). However, ERP studies are characterized by limited spatial resolution. Thus, the precise functional neuroanatomic encoding differences that predict whether a particular verbal experience will be remembered or forgotten are currently unknown.

A second unanswered question concerns the exact roles of medial temporal structures in memory encoding. Lesion studies in humans and other species indicate that medial temporal regions are essential for the processing of experiences such that they can be remembered at a later time (5). However, modulated medial temporal activation has been notably absent in neuroimaging studies that systematically varied the nature of cognitive operations engaged during encoding (2). Rather, parahippocampal gyrus, a subcomponent of the medial temporal memory system, has been indirectly implicated in memory encoding because parahippocampal activation is greater during the processing of novel stimuli relative to familiar stimuli (6). These results raise the possibility that parahippocampal contributions to encoding may be restricted to novelty detection processes.

To address these issues, the neural correlates of incidental word encoding were examined in two whole-brain functional magnetic resonance imaging (fMRI) studies. One experiment used blocked-design procedures to investigate how systematic manipulation of the encoding task affects prefrontal and medial temporal activation, whereas the other used newly developed event-related procedures (7) that allow direct comparison between specific encoding trials that result in subsequent remembering and forgetting. In the blocked-design experiment, activation during performance of a semantic processing task (deciding if a word is abstract or concrete) was compared to that during a nonsemantic processing task (deciding if a word is printed in upper- or lowercase letters). Twelve normal, right-handed subjects were scanned while performing alternating task-blocks consisting of semantic processing, nonsemantic processing, and visual fixation (8, 9). The novelty of the words in the semantic and nonsemantic blocks was equivalent. Behaviorally, reaction times (RTs) were longer for semantic (873 ms) relative to nonsemantic (539 ms) decisions. Subsequent memory was superior following semantic (85% recognized) than following nonsemantic (47% recognized) processing (10).

Many brain regions demonstrated significantly greater activation during word processing relative to visual fixation (Fig. 1) (11). These activations

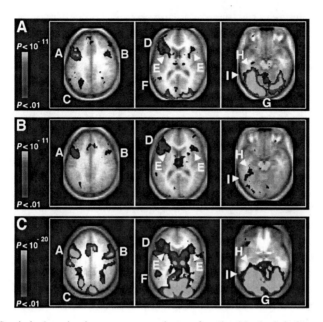

Figure 1 Statistical activation maps are shown for the blocked-design and event-related data. Images are transverse sections for the data averaged across subjects. The left hemisphere of the brain corresponds to the left side of the image. (**A**) In the blocked-design experiment, greater activation during word processing relative to fixation was noted in the posterior and dorsal extent of left inferior frontal gyrus (A: −34, 6, 34 and −43, 6, 31; BA 44/6), right inferior frontal gyrus (B: 37, 6, 34; BA 44/6), left lateral parietal cortex (C: −28, −68, 43; BA 7), anterior and ventral left inferior frontal gyrus (D: −46, 34, 15 and −43, 28, 12; BA 45/47), bilateral frontal operculum (E: left −31, 19, 12, and −40, 25, 3; right 34, 19, 6; BA 47), left middle temporal gyrus (F: −59, −43, 3; BA 21), bilateral visual cortex (G: BA 17/18/19), parahippocampal gyrus near fusiform gyrus (H: −31, −43, −18; BA 36/37/ 35), and fusiform gyrus (1: −37, −58, −15; BA 37). Other regions included the hippocampus (−37, −15, −15), supplementary motor area (0, 6, 62; BA 6), medial superior frontal gyrus (−3, 6, 50; BA 6), and right lateral cerebellum. (**B**) Regions demonstrating greater activation during semantic relative to nonsemantic processing included left frontal (A: −43, 9, 34 and −43, 13, 28; D: −40, 22, 21 and −40, 31, 12; E: −28, 22, 6), parahippocampal (H: −34, −40, −12), and fusiform (1: −43, −58, −9) cortices. (**C**) in the event-related study, comparison of word processing trials to fixation trials revealed many of the same regions noted in the blocked-design experiment. Complete listings of stereotaxic coordinates are available from the author upon request.

likely reflect processes associated with memory encoding and also more general processes associated with stimulus perception and response generation. To identify regions that demonstrate differential activation during encoding conditions that yield higher relative to lower subsequent memory, we directly compared the semantic and nonsemantic processing conditions. Regions demonstrating greater activation during semantic processing included several areas in left prefrontal cortex, as well as left parahippocampal and fusiform gyri (Fig. 1). Although these results indicate that temporal and prefrontal processes influence the encoding of verbal experiences, they do not directly specify the encoding differences that predict whether a specific experience will be later remembered or forgotten.

In a second experiment, event-related fMRI was used while participants performed a single incidental encoding task. The objective was to determine whether trial-by-trial differences in encoding activation predict subsequent memory for experiences even when the processing task was held constant. Thirteen normal, right-handed subjects underwent six fMRI scans, each consisting of word and fixation events presented in a continuous series of 120 rapidly intermixed trials (12). During word trials, subjects made a semantic decision ("abstract or concrete?"). Following the encoding scans, memory for the words was assessed by a recognition test. Subjects indicated whether they recognized each test word as studied, reporting their confidence (high or low) when they recognized the word (13). Behavioral results indicated that subjects discriminated between previously studied and unstudied words when responding with high confidence, but not when responding with low confidence (14, 15).

The fMRI data were analyzed by categorizing encoding trials based on whether the word was subsequently remembered or forgotten on the post-scan memory test. There were four trial types: high confidence hits, low confidence hits, misses, and fixation. Word processing relative to fixation resulted in greater activation in many brain regions, replicating most of the regions noted in the blocked-design study (Fig. 1). Importantly, the event-related design also permitted identification of regions that demonstrate differential activation during the encoding of words subsequently remembered and those subsequently forgotten. When comparing high confidence hits to misses, greater activation was noted in multiple left prefrontal regions (Fig. 2) and left parahippocampal and fusiform gyri (Fig. 3 (16, 17). This pattern was independently present and significant for these regions when comparing high confidence hits to misses within each of the word types (abstract or concrete). The subsequent memory effect was rather specific: other regions active during word processing relative to fixation failed to demonstrate greater activation during high confidence hits relative to misses (Fig. 3).

Our results specify how the neural signature during encoding differs for events subsequently remembered and events subsequently forgotten. When task demands were held constant across trials, similar regions were engaged during the encoding of both remembered and forgotten words. However, the magnitude of activation differed across remembered and forgotten experiences in anatomically specific brain regions. These effects cannot be attributed to differences in performance accuracy during encoding because accuracy was comparable for high confidence hits and misses. One possible interpretation

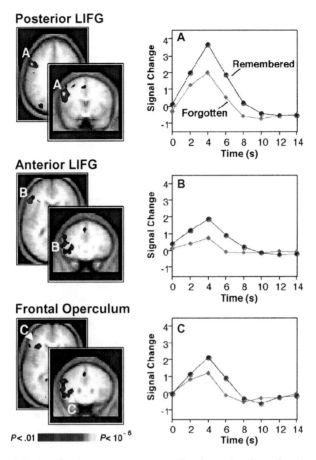

Figure 2 Statistical activation maps encompassing frontal regions that demonstrate a greater response during the encoding of words later remembered (high confidence hit trials) relative to words later forgotten (miss trials). Displayed at the left are transverse and coronal sections through the activation foci for the event-related data averaged across subjects. Greater activation was noted in the posterior and dorsal extent of left inferior frontal gyrus (LIFG) bordering precentral gyrus (A: −50, 9, 34; BA 44/6), the anterior and ventral extent of LIFG (B: −50, 25, 12; BA 45/47), and the left frontal operculum (C: −31, 22, 6; BA 47). Time courses were derived for each condition within a three-dimensional region surrounding the peak voxel and reflect raw mean signal changes. Regions were defined, using an automated algorithm that identified all contiguous voxels within 12 mm of the peak that reached the significance level.

187

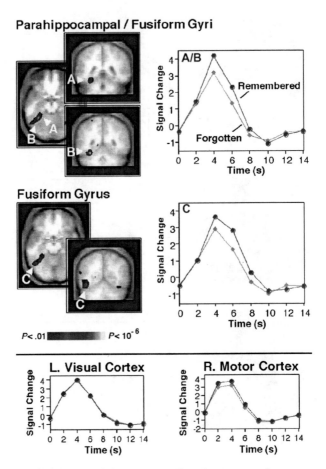

Figure 3 Activation maps and the corresponding time courses from temporal regions are shown for the trial comparison of remembered (greater response) to forgotten (lesser response) words. Temporal foci included a region (−31, −46, −12) that encompassed parahippocampal gyrus (A: BA 36/37/35) and the more medial extent of fusiform gyrus (B: BA 37), and a region that encompassed the lateral extent of fusiform gyrus and portions of inferior temporal gyrus (C: −43, −55, −9; BA 37). Other regions, including visual (L, left) and motor (R., right) cortices, did not show modulated activation across remembered and forgotten trials.

is that the present modulations reflect time-on-task or duty-cycle effects (*18*), such that subsequently remembered experiences are those that merely happened to be processed for a longer duration during learning. To examine the possible contribution of time-on-task, the event-related data were reanalyzed after matching the encoding RTs for high confidence hit and miss trials. Even when RTs were matched, left prefrontal and temporal regions still demonstrated significantly greater activation during the encoding of items subsequently remembered than during the encoding of items forgotten (*19*).

Our studies, together with previous results (*2*), suggest that what makes a verbal experience memorable partially depends on the extent to which left prefrontal and medial temporal regions are engaged during the experience. Although modulated parahippocampal activation has not been noted in many studies, our experiments demonstrate that left parahippocampal gyrus is more active during the encoding of verbal experiences that are later remembered relative to those later forgotten, even though these two classes of experiences were equally novel within the context of the experiment [see also (*20*)]. These results indicate that, although medial temporal regions are sensitive to stimulus novelty (*21*), the role of parahippocampal gyrus in memory encoding extends beyond novelty detection and encompasses more general encoding mechanisms. Parahippocampal gyrus is the principal neocortical input pathway to the hippocampal region (*22*), and thus it is suitably situated to play an important role in memory formation.

Parahippocampal and prefrontal regions may act interdependently to promote the encoding of event attributes important for conscious remembrance. Verbal experiences may be more memorable when semantic and phonological attributes of the experience are extensively processed via participation of left prefrontal regions (*2, 23*). Left prefrontal regions may serve to organize these attributes in working memory, with this information serving as input to parahippocampal gyrus and the medial temporal memory system (*24*). A specific experience may elicit the recruitment of these processes to a greater or lesser extent because of variable task demands, shifts in subjects' strategies, characteristics of target items, or attentional modulations. Regardless of the source of this variability, greater recruitment of left prefrontal and temporal processes will tend to produce more memorable verbal experiences.

References and Notes

1. F. I. M. Craik and R. S. Lockhart, *J. Verbal Learn. Verbal Behav.* **11**, 671 (1972).
2. S. E. Petersen, P. T. Fox, M. I. Posner, M. Mintun, M. E. Raichle, *Nature* **331**, 585 (1988); S. Kapur *et al.*, *Proc. Natl. Acad. Sci. U.S.A.* **91**, 2008 (1994); J. D. E. Gabrieli *et al.*, *Psychol, Sci.* **7**, 278 (1996). For reviews, see L. Nyberg, R. Cabeza, E. Tulving, *Psychonomic Bull. Rev.* **3**, 135 (1996); R. L Buckner and W. Koutstaal, *Proc. Natl. Acad. Sci. U.S.A.* **95**, 891 (1998).
3. P. C. Fletcher *et al.*, *Brain* **118**, 401 (1995); C. L. Grady *et al.*, *Science* **269**, 218 (1995).
4. T. E. Sanquist, J. W. Rohrbaugh, K. Syndulko, D. B. Lindsley, *Psychophysiology* **17**, 568 (1980); E. Hatgren and M. E. Smith, *Hum. Neurobiol.* **6**, 129 (1987); K. A. Paller, M. Kutas, A. R. Mayes, *Electroencephalogr. Clin. Neurophysiol,* **67**, 360 (1987); M. Fabiani and E. Donchin, *J. Exp. Psychol. Learn. Mem. Cogn.* **21**, 224 (1995).

5. W. B. Scoville and B. Milner, *J. Neurol. Neurosurg. Psychiatry* **20**, 11 (1957); L. R. Squire, *Psychol. Rev.* **99**, 195 (1992); N. J. Cohen and H. Eichenbaum, *Memory, Amnesia, and the Hippocampal System* (MIT Press, Cambridge, MA, 1993).
6. C. E. Stern *et al.*, *Proc. Natl. Acad. Sci. U.S.A.* **93**, 8660 (1996); E. Tulving, H. J. Markowitsch, F. I. M. Craik, R. Habib, S. Houle, *Cereb. Cortex* **6**, 71 (1996); J. D. E. Gabrieli, J. B. Brewer, J. E. Desmond, G. H. Glover, *Science* **276**, 264 (1997).
7. A. M. Dale and R. L. *Buckner, Hum. Brain Mapp.* **5**, 329 (1997); R. L. Buckner *et al.*, *Neuron* **20**, 285 (1998).
8. Informed consent was obtained from all subjects (seven men, five women, aged 18 to 29 years). Echo planar and conventional imaging was performed on a 1.5-T GE Signa scanner with an ANMR upgrade. Imaging procedures [see R. L. Buckner, W. Koutstaal. D. L. Schacter, A. D. Wagner, B. R. Rosen, *Neuroimage* **7**, 151 (1998)] included collection of structural images [radio frequency-spoiled GRASS (gradient-recalled acquisition in the steady state) sequence, 60-slice sagittal, 2.8-mm thickness] and echo planar functional images sensitive to blood-oxygen level-dependent contrast (118 sequential whole-brain acquisitions, 16 slices each, 3.125-mm in-plane resolution, 7-mm thickness, skip 1 mm; T_2*-weighted asymmetric spin-echo sequence: TR = 2 s, TE = 50 ms, 180° offset = −25 ms).
9. During each of four scans, blocks were ordered: non-semantic (40 s), fixation (24 s), semantic (40 s), fixation, nonsemantic, fixation, semantic. A brief (8 s) fixation block began each scan. During semantic and nonsemantic blocks, 20 words were visually presented: 10 abstract and 10 concrete nouns; half in uppercase and half in lowercase letters. Each word was presented for 1 s followed by 1 s of fixation between words. Subjects responded by left-handed key press. During fixation blocks, a cross-hair ("+") was presented for the entire duration.
10. Alpha was set to $P < 0.05$ for all behavioral analyses. Response latencies differed across tasks [$F(1, 11) = 89.97$]. Memory was assessed in the scanner 20 to 40 m later, using a yes-no recognition procedure (*8*). Subsequent memory differed across tasks [$F(1, 11) = 69.50$].
11. Functional runs were averaged within each subject, transformed into stereotaxic atlas space, and averaged across subjects (8). Activation maps were constructed using a nonparametric Kolmogorov-Smirnov statistic to compare (i) word processing (semantic and nonsemantic) to fixation and (ii) semantic to nonsemantic processing. Peak activations were identified by selecting local statistical activation maxima that were $P < 0.001$ within clusters of five contiguous significant voxels. These criteria minimize false positives, as verified using the local of control functional runs [E. Zarahn, G. K. Aguirre, M. D'Esposito, *Neuroimage* **5**, 179 (1997)].
12. Subjects were six men and seven women (aged 18 to 35 years). Three additional subjects were excluded because of excessively poor performance. Imaging procedures were similar to experiment one with the exception that imaging was performed using an echo planar T_2*-weighted gradient echo sequence (3.0-T, 128 images, TR = 2 s, TE = 30 ms, flip angle = 90°). During each scan, 40 abstract word trials, 40 concrete word trials, and 40 fixation trials were rapidly intermixed, with each trial lasting 2 s. For fixation trials, the fixation point remained on the screen for the entire 2 s. For word trials, the word was presented for 750 ms followed by 1250 ms of fixation. Abstract, concrete, and fixation trials were pseudo-randomly

intermixed with counterbalancing (each trial type followed every other trial type equally often).

13. Approximately 20 min later, subjects were administered a memory test consisting of 480 studied and 480 unstudied words. Words were presented individually with self-paced timing. Subjects responded "high confidence studied," "low confidence studied," or "new."

14. An item Type × Response interaction [$F(1, 12) = 22.97$] revealed that studied items were endorsed as "high confidence studied" more frequently than were unstudied items [52% and 7%, respectively, $F(1,12) = 57.04$], whereas studied and unstudied items were similarly endorsed as "low confidence studied" [24% and 20%, ($F < 1.0$)]. The low confidence response class likely reflects subject guessing and does not differentiate between encountered and novel stimuli.

15. Encoding task performance was analyzed based on whether the words were subsequently remembered with high confidence ("high confidence hits"), low confidence ("low confidence hits"), or were forgotten ("misses"). Accuracy during encoding was comparable for high confidence hits (88% correct), low confidence hits (88% correct), and misses (89% correct) ($F < 1.0$). Semantic decision RTs declined across trial types [$F(2,24) = 9.26$]; RTs were longer for high confidence hits (1000 ms) compared to low confidence hits (966 ms) [$F(1, 12) = 5.40$], which were in turn longer compared to misses (936 ms) [$F(1, 12) = 3.91$, $P < 0.06$].

16. The procedures for selective averaging and statistical map generation for rapidly intermixed trials are described elsewhere (7). Statistical activation maps were constructed based on the differences between trial types using a t-statistic (7). Fixation trial events were subtracted from the word trial events (collapsing across subsequent memory). Miss trial events and high confidence hit events were subtracted from each other, as were those for miss trial events and low confidence hit events. Clusters of five or more voxels exceeding a statistical threshold of $P < 0.001$ were considered significant foci of activation (7).

17. In addition, modest but significantly greater activation for high confidence hits relative to misses was noted in a more ventral extent of left inferior frontal gyrus [Brodmann's area (BA) 47: −34, 31, −3], left precentral gyrus (BA 6: −31, 0, 56), medial superior frontal gyrus (BA 8: −3, 28, 43), and left superior occipital gyrus (BA 19: −31, −77, 34). The superior occipital and medial superior frontal activations can be seen in Fig. 2. Two regions demonstrated less activation for high confidence hits relative to misses: precuneus (BA 31: 3, −43, 40) and left middle frontal gyrus (BA 9: −12, 31, 34). No regions demonstrated greater activation for low confidence hits relative to misses, which is in accord with the behavioral data indicating that these two trial types likely did not mnemonically differ.

18. M. D'Esposito et al., Neuroimage 6, 113 (1997). A similar interpretation may be applicable to the results from the blocked-design experiment. However, greater left prefrontal activation during semantic processing has been noted even when the nonsemantic processing task has a longer duty cycle [J. B. Demb et al., J. Neurosci, 15, 5870 (1995)].

19. RTs were matched as follows. First, the median RT across all trial types was determined for each subject. Trials with response latencies that fell below the median RT were selected and sorted based on subsequent memory. Selection of trials in this manner resulted in matched RTs for the high confidence hit (852 ms) and miss (839 ms) trial types [$F(1, 12) = 2.32$, $P > 0.15$)].

20. J. B. Brewer, Z. Zhao, J. E. Desmond, G. H. Glover, J. D. E. Gabrieli, *Science* **281**, 1185 (1998): G. Fernandez *et al., J. Neurosci,* **18**, 1841 (1998).
21. R. J. Dolan and P. C. Fletcher, *Nature* **388**, 582 (1997).
22. W. A. Suzuki and D. G. Amaral, *J. Comp. Neurol.* **350**, 497 (1994).
23. J. Jonides *et al., Nature* **363**, 623 (1993); J. A. Fiez *et al., J. Neurosci.* **16**, 808 (1996); R. L. Buckner. *Psychonomic Bull. Rev.* **3**, 149 (1996); A. D. Wagner, J. E. Desmond, J. B. Demb, G. H. Glover, J. D. E. Gabrieli, *J. Cogn. Neurosci.* **9**, 714 (1997).
24. M. Moscovitch, *J. Cogn. Neurosci,* **4**, 257 (1992).
25. Supported by grants from the National Institute on Aging (AG08441 and AG05778), the National Institute on Deafness and Other Communication Disorders (DC03245–02), the Human Frontiers Science Program, and the Deutsche Forschungsgemeinschaft (SFB426). We thank Y. and W. Jacobson and two anonymous referees for helpful comments on an earlier version of this manuscript, and C. Brenner and C. Racine for assistance with data collection.

Part 7

STORAGE

30

EXPERIMENTS ON REMEMBERING

(b) The method of repeated reproduction

Fredrick C. Bartlett

Source: Fredrick C. Bartlett, *Remembering: A Study in Experimental and Social Psychology*, Cambridge: Cambridge University Press, 1932, pp. 63–94.

1. Description of the method

The *Method of Repeated Reproduction* follows almost exactly the plan of investigation adopted by Philippe in his experiments *Sur les transformations de nos images mentales*,[1] except that the material used was different and the experiments themselves were continued for a much longer period. A subject was given a story, or an argumentative prose passage, or a simple drawing to study under prescribed conditions. He attempted a first reproduction usually after an interval of 15 minutes, and thereafter gave further reproductions at intervals of increasing length. By using this method I hoped to find something about the common types of change introduced by normal individuals into remembered material with increasing lapse of time. Obviously the nature of the experiment renders it rather hazardous to speculate as to the exact conditions of change, but it is fairly easy to keep a check on the progressive nature of such transformations as actually occur.

There is one difficulty which is particularly acute. I hoped to continue to get reproductions until the particular material concerned had reached a stereotyped form. If reproductions are effected frequently, however, the form tends to become fixed very rapidly, while if long intervals are allowed to elapse between successive reproductions the process of gradual transformation may go on almost indefinitely. Consequently, the results of the experiment as they are here described no doubt represent a section only of an incomplete process of transformation.

Further, it is certain that in the transformations of material which, for example, produce the popular legend, or which develop current rumours, social influences play a very great part. These cannot be fully studied by *The Method of Repeated Reproduction*, though they are present in varying degrees. The method needs in this respect to be supplemented by others, and as will be seen I made an attempt to develop in this direction later.[2]

The material used in *The Method of Repeated Reproduction* belonged to two groups, and was either (*a*) verbal, or (*b*) graphic. All verbal material was written by the subject at the time of recall, and all graphic material reproduced by drawings. In this chapter I shall not present any of the data gained from the use of the graphical material. Practically all of the points which they brought out were repeatedly illustrated in a yet more striking way, in methods to be described and discussed later, and will be more conveniently considered then.[3]

Moreover, it would be impossible to present more than a very small part of the data obtained from verbal material without prolonging the discussion to an intolerable length. I shall therefore confine all detailed illustrations to a study of some of the repeated reproductions of a single story, though I shall have in mind throughout a mass of corroborative detail which cannot be presented here.

2. The material used and the method of presenting results

I have selected for special consideration a story which was adapted from a translation by Dr Franz Boas[4] of a North American folk-tale. Several reasons prompted the use of this story.

First, the story as presented belonged to a level of culture and a social environment exceedingly different from those of my subjects. Hence it seemed likely to afford good material for persistent transformation. I had also in mind the general problem of what actually happens when a popular story travels about from one social group to another, and thought that possibly the use of this story might throw some light upon the general conditions of transformation under such circumstances. It may fairly be said that this hope was at least to some extent realised.

Secondly, the incidents described in some of the cases had no very manifest interconnexion, and I wished particularly to see how educated and rather sophisticated subjects would deal with this lack of obvious rational order.

Thirdly, the dramatic character of some of the events recorded seemed likely to arouse fairly vivid visual imagery in suitable subjects, and I thought perhaps further light might be thrown on some of the suggestions regarding the conditions and functions of imaging arising from the use of *The Method of Description*.

Fourthly, the conclusion of the story might easily be regarded as introducing a supernatural element, and I desired to see how this would be dealt with.

196

The original story was as follows:

The War of the Ghosts

One night two young men from Egulac went down to the river to hunt seals, and while they were there it became foggy and calm. Then they heard war-cries, and they thought: "Maybe this is a war-party". They escaped to the shore, and hid behind a log. Now canoes came up, and they heard the noise of paddles, and saw one canoe coming up to them. There were five men in the canoe, and they said:

"What do you think? We wish to take you along. We are going up the river to make war on the people".

One of the young men said: "I have no arrows".

"Arrows are in the canoe", they said.

"I will not go along. I might be killed. My relatives do not know where I have gone. But you", he said, turning to the other, "may go with them."

So one of the young men went, but the other returned home.

And the warriors went on up the river to a town on the other side of Kalama. The people came down to the water, and they began to fight, and many were killed. But presently the young man heard one of the warriors say: "Quick, let us go home: that Indian has been hit". Now he thought: "Oh, they are ghosts". He did not feel sick, but they said he had been shot.

So the canoes went back to Egulac, and the young man went ashore to his house, and made a fire. And he told everybody and said: "Behold I accompanied the ghosts, and we went to fight. Many of our fellows were killed, and many of those who attacked us were killed. They said I was hit, and I did not feel sick".

He told it all, and then he became quiet. When the sun rose he fell down. Something black came out of his mouth. His face became contorted. The people jumped up and cried.

He was dead.

Each subject read the story through to himself twice, at his normal reading rate. Except in the case which will be indicated later, the first reproduction was made 15 minutes after this reading. Other reproductions were effected at intervals as opportunity offered. No attempt was made to secure uniformity in the length of interval for all subjects; obviously equalising intervals of any length in no way equalises the effective conditions of reproduction in the case of different subjects. No subject knew the aim of the experiment. All who were interested in this were allowed to think that the test was merely one for accuracy of recall.

I shall analyse the results obtained in three ways:

197

First, a number of reproductions will be given in full, together with some comments;

Secondly, special details of interest in this particular story will be considered;

Thirdly, certain general or common tendencies in the successive remembering of the story will be stated and discussed more fully.

3. Some complete reproductions together with comments

(*a*) After an interval of 20 hours subject H produced the following first reproduction:

The War of the Ghosts

Two men from Edulac went fishing. While thus occupied by the river they heard a noise in the distance.

"It sounds like a cry", said one, and presently there appeared some men in canoes who invited them to join the party on their adventure. One of the young men refused to go, on the ground of family ties, but the other offered to go.

"But there are no arrows", he said.

"The arrows are in the boat", was the reply.

He thereupon took his place, while his friend returned home. The party paddled up the river to Kaloma, and began to land on the banks of the river. The enemy came rushing upon them, and some sharp fighting ensued. Presently some one was injured, and the cry was raised that the enemy were ghosts.

The party returned down the stream, and the young man arrived home feeling none the worse for his experience. The next morning at dawn he endeavoured to recount his adventures. While he was talking something black issued from his mouth. Suddenly he uttered a cry and fell down. His friends gathered round him.

But he was dead.

In general form (i) the story is considerably shortened, mainly by omissions; (ii) the phraseology becomes more modern, more 'journalistic', *e.g.* "refused, on the ground of family ties"; "sharp fighting ensued"; "feeling none the worse for his experience"; "endeavoured to recount his adventures"; "something black issued from his mouth"; (iii) the story has already become somewhat more coherent and consequential than in its original form.

In matter there are numerous omissions and some transformations. The more familiar "boat" once replaces "canoe"; hunting seals becomes merely "fishing"; Egulac becomes Edulac, while Kalama changes to Kaloma. The main point about the ghosts is entirely misunderstood. The two excuses made by the man who did not wish to join the war-party change places; that "he refused on the ground of family ties" becomes the only excuse explicitly offered.

Eight days later this subject remembered the story as follows:

The War of the Ghosts

Two young men from Edulac went fishing. While thus engaged they heard a noise in the distance. "That sounds like a war-cry", said one, "there is going to be some fighting." Presently there appeared some warriors who invited them to join an expedition up the river.

One of the young men excused himself on the ground of family ties. "I cannot come", he said, "as I might get killed." So he returned home. The other man, however, joined the party, and they proceeded on canoes up the river. While landing on the banks the enemy appeared and were running down to meet them. Soon someone was wounded, and the party discovered that they were fighting against ghosts. The young man and his companion returned to the boats, and went back to their homes.

The next morning at dawn he was describing his adventures to his friends, who had gathered round him. Suddenly something black issued from his mouth, and he fell down uttering a cry. His friends closed around him, but found that he was dead.

All the tendencies to change manifested in the first reproduction now seem to be more marked. The story has become still more concise, still more coherent. The proper name Kaloma has disappeared, and the lack of arrows, put into the second place a week earlier, has now dropped out completely. On the other hand a part of the other excuse: "I might get killed", now comes back into the story, though it found no place in the first version. It is perhaps odd that the friend, after having returned home, seems suddenly to come back into the story again when the young man is wounded. But this kind of confusion of connected incidents is a common characteristic of remembering.

(b) Subject N first dealt with the story in this way:

The Ghosts

There were two men on the banks of the river near Egulac. They heard the sound of paddles, and a canoe with five men in it appeared, who called to them, saying: "We are going to fight the people. Will you come with us?"

One of the two men answered, saying: "Our relations do not know where we are, and we have not got any arrows".

They answered: "There are arrows in the canoe".

So the man went, and they fought the people, and then he heard them saying: "An Indian is killed, let us return".

So he returned to Egulac, and told them he knew they were Ghosts.

He spoke to the people of Egulac, and told them that he had fought with the Ghosts, and many men were killed on both sides, and that he was wounded, but felt nothing. He lay down and became calmer, and in the night he was convulsed, and something black came out of his mouth.

The people said:

"He is dead".

Leaving aside smaller details, much the most interesting feature of this reproduction is the attempt made to deal with the ghosts. The subject volunteered an account of his procedure. "When I read the story", he said, "I thought that the main point was the reference to the Ghosts who went off to fight the people farther on. I then had images, in visual form, of a wide river, of trees on each side of it, and of men on the banks and in canoes. The second time I read through the story, I readily visualised the whole thing. The images of the last part were confused. The people left the wounded man, and went into the bush. Then I saw the man telling his tale to the villagers. He was pleased and proud because the Ghosts belonged to a higher class than he did himself. He was jumping about all the time. Then he went into convulsions, and a clot of blood came from his mouth. The people realised that he was dead and made a fuss about him.

"I wrote out the story mainly by following my own images. I had a vague feeling of the style. There was a sort of rhythm about it which I tried to imitate.

"I can't understand the contradiction about somebody being killed, and the man's being wounded, but feeling nothing.

"At first I thought there was something supernatural about the story. Then I saw that Ghosts must be a class, or a clan name. That made the whole thing more comprehensible."

In fact this subject has clearly missed the real point about the ghosts from the outset, although he makes them central in his version of the story. The reproduction is a beautiful illustration of a strong tendency to rationalise, common to all of my subjects. Whenever anything appeared incomprehensible, or "queer", it was either omitted or explained. Rather rarely this rationalisation was the effect of a conscious effort. More often it was effected apparently unwittingly, the subject transforming his original without suspecting what he was doing. Just as in all the other experimental series so far described, there may be prepotency of certain detail, without any explicit analysis. In this case, for example, the ghosts were the central part of the story. They alone remained in the title. They were always written with a capital initial letter—a true case of unwitting transformation which solved a special problem. Then came the specific explanation: "Ghosts" are a clan name; and the whole difficulty disappeared. This subject was extremely well satisfied with his version, just as the visualisers in the earlier experiments seemed to be contented with their work. The satisfaction persisted, and a fortnight later the "Ghosts" had become more prominent still. The story was remembered thus:

The Ghosts

There were two men on the banks of a river near the village of Etishu (?). They heard the sound of paddles coming from up-stream, and shortly a canoe appeared. The men in the canoe spoke, saying: "We are going to fight the people: will you come with us?"

One of the young men answered, saying: "Our relations do not know where we are; but my companion may go with you. Besides, we have no arrows".

So the young man went with them, and they fought the people, and many were killed on both sides. And then he heard shouting: "The Indian is wounded; let us return". And he heard the people say: "They are the Ghosts". He did not know he was wounded, and returned to Etishu (?). The people collected round him and bathed his wounds, and he said he had fought with the Ghosts. Then he became quiet. But in the night he was convulsed, and something black came out of his mouth.

And the people cried:

"He is dead".

By now the antagonists of the young man up the river are definitely made to say that the people he is helping are "the Ghosts" (*i.e.* members of the Ghost clan). The Indian becomes more of a hero and is a centre of interest at the end, when, for the first time, his wounds are "bathed". The Indian's ignorance of his wound, a point which had worried this subject a fortnight earlier, comes back into the main body of the story, but appears to be attributed to mere general excitement. In fact the supernatural element is practically entirely dropped out.

This ingenious rationalisation of the "Ghosts" was a clear instance of how potent may be a special interest in producing an unrealised distortion in remembered material. The subject was a keen student of Anthropology who, later, carried out much important field-work, particularly in regard to the topics of kinship names and clan systems. This subject also first dropped the "arrow" excuse to the second place, and later regarded it as probably an invention on his part. The reference to relatives persisted. Proper names again presented special difficulty.

(*c*) It is interesting to consider a case of rationalisation which was complete, and at the same time almost entirely unwitting. Subject L's first reproduction was:

War Ghost Story

Two young men from Egulac went out to hunt seals. They thought they heard war-cries, and a little later they heard the noise of the paddling of canoes. One of these canoes, in which there were five natives, came forward towards them. One of the natives shouted out: "Come with us: we are going to make war on some natives up the river". The two young men answered: "We have no arrows". "There are arrows in our canoes", came the reply. One of the young men then said: "My folk will not know where I have gone"; but, turning to the other, he said: "But you could go". So the one returned whilst the other joined the natives.

The party went up the river as far as a town opposite Kalama, where they got on land. The natives of that part came down to the river to meet them. There was some severe fighting, and many on both sides were slain. Then one of the natives that had made the expedition up the river shouted: "Let us return: the Indian has fallen". Then they endeavoured to persuade the young man to return, telling him that he was sick, but he did not feel as if he were. Then he thought he saw ghosts all round him.

When they returned, the young man told all his friends of what had happened. He described how many had been slain on both sides.

It was nearly dawn when the young man became very ill; and at sunrise a black substance rushed out of his mouth, and the natives said one to another: "He is dead".

This version shows the usual tendency towards increasing conventionalisation of language, a little increased dramatisation at the end, a few abbreviations, and the common difficulty about the ghosts. This last difficulty is here solved in a novel manner. Apart from these points the reproduction is on the whole accurate and full. Nearly four months later the subject tried to remember the story once more, and he dictated it to me as follows:

I have no idea of the title.

There were two men in a boat, sailing towards an island. When they approached the island, some natives came running towards them, and informed them that there was fighting going on on the island, and invited them to join. One said to the other: "You had better go. I cannot very well, because I have relatives expecting me, and they will not know what has become of me. But you have no one to expect you". So one accompanied the natives, but the other returned.

Here there is a part that I can't remember. What I don't know is how the man got to the fight. However, anyhow the man was in the midst of the fighting, and was wounded. The natives endeavoured to persuade the man to return, but he assured them that he had not been wounded.

I have an idea that his fighting won the admiration of the natives.

The wounded man ultimately fell unconscious. He was taken from the fighting by the natives.

Then, I think it is, the natives describe what happened, and they seem to have imagined seeing a ghost coming out of his mouth. Really it was a kind of materialisation of his breath. I know this *phrase* was not in the story, but that is the idea I have. Ultimately the man died at dawn the next day.

"First", said this subject, "my remembrance was in visual terms of a man approaching an island, and also of breath somehow materialising into a ghost. But perhaps this may belong to another story."

The two most incomprehensible parts of the original story, to all my subjects, were the ghosts and the final death of the Indian. In the first of these two reproductions the ghosts play a little and a very simple part: they are merely imagined by the Indian when he is wounded. But apparently they are not to be so simply disposed of, and in the later version, by a single stroke of condensation, and by a rationalisation which the subject certainly did not set himself consciously to carry through, both the difficulties are rendered manageable. This is only one of several versions in which the original "something black" became "escaping breath".

Once more, of the Indian's two excuses the one based on the probable anxiety of relatives gets increasing emphasis, and the other, in this case, disappears altogether. Title and proper names are forgotten.

The fact of rationalisation was illustrated in practically every reproduction or series of reproductions, but, as would be expected, the way in which it was effected varied greatly from case to case. For the particular form adopted is due directly to the functioning of individual special interests, as in the "Ghost clan" instance, or to some fact of personal experience, or to some peculiarity of individual attitude which determines the salience or potency of the details in the whole material dealt with.

Here is another version, for example, of *The War of the Ghosts*, as it was recalled by one subject six months after the original reading:

(No title was given.) Four men came down to the water. They were told to get into a boat and to take arms with them. They inquired "What arms?" and were answered "Arms for battle". When they came to the battle-field they heard a great noise and shouting, and a voice said: "The black man is dead". And he was brought to the place where they were, and laid on the ground. And he foamed at the mouth.

From this short version, all unusual terms, all proper names, all mention of a supernatural element have disappeared. But the most interesting point is the treatment of the troublesome "something black" which concludes the original story. "Black" was transferred to the man and so rendered perfectly natural, while "foamed at the mouth" is as much a rationalisation of the original statement as was the materialisation of the dying man's breath introduced by subject L. Why the one subject should use one phrase or notion and the other a different one is no doubt a matter of individual psychology; both served the same general rationalising tendency.

(*d*) Each illustration so far given shows a tendency to abbreviate and simplify both the story as a whole and also all the details that are reported. More rarely some incident was elaborated, usually with some dramatic flourish and at the expense of other incidents belonging to the story. A longer series of successive versions by subject P will illustrate this. The first reproduction was:

The War of the Ghosts

Two youths were standing by a river about to start seal-catching, when a boat appeared with five men in it. They were all armed for war.

The youths were at first frightened, but they were asked by the men to come and help them fight some enemies on the other bank. One youth said he could not come as his relations would be anxious about him; the other said he would go, and entered the boat.

*   *   *   *   *

In the evening he returned to his hut, and told his friends that he had been in a battle. A great many had been slain, and he had been wounded by an arrow; he had not felt any pain, he said. They told him that he must have been fighting in a battle of ghosts. Then he remembered that it had been queer and he was very excited.

In the morning, however, he became ill, and his friends gathered round; he fell down and his face became very pale. Then he writhed and shrieked and his friends were filled with terror. At last he became calm. Something hard and black came out of his mouth, and he lay contorted and dead.

The subject who produced this version is a painter. He definitely visualised the whole scene and drew for me a plan of his imagery on paper. The middle part of the story escaped him completely, but as will be seen, the final part was elaborated with increased dramatisation. "The story", he remarked, "first recalled a missionary story, and then took on a character of its own. It also vaguely recalled something about Egyptians who, I think, imagined that peoples' souls came out of their mouths when they died."

A fortnight later came the second attempt:

The War of the Ghosts

There were two young men who once went out in the afternoon to catch seals. They were about to begin when a boat appeared on the river and in it were five warriors. These looked so fierce that the men thought they were going to attack them. But they were reassured when they asked the youths to enter the boat and help them to fight some enemies.

The elder said he would not come because his relations might be anxious about him. But the other said he would go and went off.

* * * * *

He returned in the evening tired and excited, and he told his friends that he had been fighting in a great battle. "Many of us and many of the foe were slain", he said. "I was wounded, but did not feel sick."

Later in the evening he retired quietly to bed, after lighting a fire. The next morning, however, when the neighbours came to see him, he said that he must have been fighting in a battle of ghosts.

Then he fell down and writhed in agony. Something black jumped out of his mouth. All the neighbours held up their hands and shrieked with terror, and when they examined the youth they found that he was dead.

There are a few more omissions in this version, but both the beginning and the end of the story tend to become more elaborate, and more dramatic. The "fight" of the youths at the beginning is exaggerated, and it is now the "elder" of the two who says that he will not go. As usual the sole remaining alleged excuse is the anxiety of relatives. Direct speech is introduced at the end, and the "fire" of the original, having been omitted from the first version, returns to the story. As before, the subject pursued a definitely visualising method of recall.

A further month passed by, and the subject now remembered the story as follows:

The War of the Ghosts

Two youths went down to the river to fish for seals. They perceived, soon, coming down the river, a canoe with five warriors in it, and they were alarmed. But the warriors said: "We are friends. Come with us, for we are going to fight a battle".

The elder youth would not go, because he thought his relations would be anxious about him. The younger, however, went.

* * * * *

In the evening he returned from the battle, and he said that he had been wounded, but that he had felt no pain.

There had been a great fight and many had been slain on either side. He lit a fire and retired to rest in his hut. The next morning, when the neighbours came round to see how he was, they found him in a fever. And when he came out into the open at sunrise he fell down. The neighbours shrieked. He became livid and writhed upon the ground. Something black came out of his mouth, and he died. So the neighbours decided that he must have been to war with the ghosts.

Again the end part of the story gains additional detail. It is the neighbours who now decide, in a more or less reasonable fashion, that the young man must have been fighting with ghosts. In some respects, *e.g.* in the mention of sunrise, the version is nearer to the original form than those given earlier. "The whole of my imagery", he remarked, "has grown very dim. Details of the story seem mostly to have vanished. There was no difficulty in remembering as much as was written, but I have also disjointed ideas about the early part of the story, of *arrows* and a *rock*, which I cannot fit in. My memory seems to depend on visual images,[5] and it may really consist of them; and I can't set down any more."

Another two months elapsed, and the subject, at my request, remembered the story again, not having thought of it in the interval, he asserted. The "rock", already foreshadowed in his earlier comments, is now fitted into its setting, and is, in fact, put exactly into the place of the original "log".

The War of the Ghosts

Two youths went down to the river to hunt for seals. They were hiding behind a rock when a boat with some warriors in it came up to them. The warriors, however, said they were friends, and invited them to help them to fight an enemy over the river. The elder one said he could not go because his relations would be so anxious if he did not return home. So the younger one went with the warriors in the boat.

*   *   *   *   *

In the evening he returned and told his friends that he had been fighting in a great battle, and that many were slain on both sides.

After lighting a fire he retired to sleep. In the morning, when the sun rose, he fell ill, and his neighbours came to see him. He had told them that he had been wounded in the battle but had felt no pain then. But soon he became worse. He writhed and shrieked and fell to the ground dead. Something black came out of his mouth.

The neighbours said he must have been at war with the ghosts.

There is still some further elaboration in the early part of the story, but beyond that very little change. In its general form, and in several of the expressions used, the story seems now to be at least temporarily stereotyped. The ghosts have definitely taken up their position at the end of the narrative, and the whole thing has become more connected and coherent than at the beginning. With repetitions at fairly frequent intervals, as a rule the form of a story soon became fairly fixed, though some of the details suffered progressive change.

But what of the long interval? Two years and six months later, the subject not having seen or, according to his own statement, thought of the story in the meantime, he agreed to attempt a further reproduction and wrote:

> Some warriors went to wage war against the ghosts. They fought all day and one of their number was wounded.
> They returned home in the evening, bearing their sick comrade. As the day drew to a close, he became rapidly worse and the villagers came round him. At sunset he sighed: something black came out of his mouth. He was dead.

In bare outline the story remains. The ghosts, who seemed to have settled down at the end, now have moved up to the beginning of the narrative. All tendency to elaboration has disappeared, perhaps as a result of the almost complete disappearance of visualisation as the method of recall. "There was something", said the subject, "about a canoe, but I can't fit it in. I suppose it was his soul that came out of his mouth when he died." Thus it looks as though the rationalisation indicated in this subject's comment of nearly two years and nine months before, but never actually expressed in any of his reproductions, has yet somehow persisted. Now for the first time, in this series, the wounded man dies at sunset. This was a change several times introduced, probably unwittingly, in conformity with a common popular view that a man frequently dies as the sun goes down. The subject thought that there was certainly more to be said at the end, as if his earlier elaborations were still having some effect.

(*e*) The preceding reproductions may be compared with a short series obtained from a native of Northern India, subject R, who was on a very different educational plane from that of the rest of my subjects. He was a man of considerable intelligence, but ill-trained, from the point of view of an English University, and ill-adapted to the environment in which he was living. He was impressionable, imaginative, and, using the word in its ordinary conventional sense, nervous to a high degree. He first reproduced the story as follows:

Story

There were two young men, and they went on the river side. They heard war cries, and said: "There is a war of the ghosts". They had no arrows. They saw a canoe, and there were five men in it. They said: "The arrows are in the canoe". The war of the ghosts begins. Many were killed. There was one young man who was hit, but did not become sick. He heard that the Indian was wounded. He came back to his village in the canoe. In the morning he was sick, and his face contracted. Something black came out of his mouth, and they cried: "He was dead".

The subject appeared very excited. He said that he clearly visualised the whole scene, and that especially vivid were some Red Indians with feathers on their heads. The story is greatly abbreviated and is very jerky and inconsequential in style. "Ghosts" made a tremendous impression on this subject, and are introduced at the very beginning of the story, thought it may be that this is partly on account of the omission of the title.

A fortnight later the following version was obtained:

Story

There were two ghosts. They went on a river. There was a canoe on the river with five men in it. There occurred a war of ghosts. One of the ghosts asked: "Where are the arrows?" The other said: "In the canoe". They started the war and several were wounded, and some killed. One ghost was wounded but did not feel sick. He went back to the village in the canoe. The next morning he was sick and something black came out of his mouth, and they cried: "He is dead".

The ghosts appear to have strengthened their hold on the story during the interval, and have entirely displaced the two young men. If anything the narrative has become even less coherent.

After another month the subject tried again, and produced:

Story

There were ghosts. There took place a fight between them. One of them asked: "Where are the arrows?" The other said: "They are in the canoe". A good many of the combatants were wounded or killed. One of them was wounded, but did not feel sick. They carried him to his village some miles away by rowing in the canoe. The next day something black came out of his mouth and they cried: "He is dead".

The first part of the story has completely disappeared, and the whole is now entirely a matter of a fight between ghosts. The dominant detail seems to have suppressed or overmastered nearly all the rest. To the subject himself the tale seemed clear enough, but as compared with most of the preceding versions it appears very jerky and disconnected.

(*f*) Finally I will choose two of a number of long distance memories. They represent utterly different methods and processes. Each, in its own way, raises attractive problems.

The following version was obtained six and a half years after the original reading. The subject (W) had previously given only the one "immediate" reproduction. This offered the usual features: some abbreviation, a little modernisation of the phraseology and a comment, made at the end, after the reproduction, to the effect that the "something black" must have been the man's soul, after the "ancient Egyptian belief". At the end of six and a half years I unexpectedly met this man again and he volunteered to try to remember the story. He recalled it in steps, with some pondering and hesitation, but on the whole with surprising ease. I will give his version exactly as he wrote it:

1. Brothers.
2. Canoe.
3. Something black from mouth.
4. Totem.
5. One of the brothers died.
6. Cannot remember whether one slew the other or was helping the other.
7. Were going on journey, but why I cannot remember.
8. Party in war canoe.
9. Was the journey a pilgrimage for filial or religious reasons?
10. Am now *sure* it was a pilgrimage.
11. Purpose had something to do with totem.
12. Was it on a pilgrimage that they met a hostile party and one brother was slain?
13. I think there was some reference to a dark forest.
14. Two brothers were on a pilgrimage, having something to do with a totem, in a canoe, up a river flowing through a dark forest. While on their pilgrimage they met a hostile party of Indians in a war canoe. In the fight one brother was slain, and something black came from his mouth.
15. Am not confident about the way brother died. May have been something sacrificial in the manner of his death.
16. The cause of the journey had *both* something to do with a totem, and with filial piety.
17. The totem was the patron god of the family and so was connected with filial piety.

This is a brilliant example of obviously constructive remembering. The subject was very pleased and satisfied with the result of his effort, and indeed, considering the length of the interval involved, he is remarkably accurate and detailed. There is a good deal of invention, and it was precisely concerning his inventions that the subject was most pleased and most certain. The totem, the filial piety, the pilgrimage—these were what he regarded as his most brilliant re-captures, and he was almost equally sure of the dark forest, once it had come in. It looks very much as if the "ghost" element of the original, connected by this subject with Egyptian beliefs, and now apparently dropped out completely, is still somehow active, and helping to produce elaborations which take the forms of the totem, filial piety, a mysterious forest, and a sacrificial death. It will be noticed that the story as he constructed it is full of rationalisations and explanations, and most of the running comments of the subject concerned the interconnexion of the various events and were directed to making the whole narration appear as coherent as possible.

This constructive method, and its elaborate result, must now be compared with a very different case. The interval here was longer still, one of almost exactly ten years. The subject (C) read the story in the spring of 1917. In 1919 she unexpectedly saw me pass her on a bicycle and immediately afterwards found herself murmuring "Egulac", "Kalama". She then recognised me, and remembered reading the story, and that these names were a part of the story. In the summer of 1927 she agreed to try definitely to remember the tale. She wrote down at once "Egulac" and "Calama", but then stopped and said that she could do no more. Then she said that she had a visual image of a sandy bank and of two men going down a river in a boat. There, however, she stopped.

In both of these cases certain dominant detail remains, apparently, and is readily remembered. But in the one case these details are made a basis which the subject builds together, and upon which he constructs new detail, so that in the end he achieves a fairly complete structure. In the other case the dominant details remain relatively isolated. Almost certainly, with some encouragement, the second subject could have been induced to put her few details together and perhaps to amplify them. But I thought it best, for the purposes of these experiments, to try to influence the subjects' procedure as little as possible.

4. Certain particular points of interest in *The War of the Ghosts*

(a) A possible case of affective determination

Twenty subjects were given *The War of the Ghosts* in this experiment, seven being women and the rest men. If we take the two excuses given by the young men for not joining the war-party and see how they were dealt with, we find that the "we have no arrows" plea was omitted by half the subjects, either in their first reproduction or in subsequent versions. Of the ten subjects who continued to include the reference to arrows six were women. On the other hand, except in long-distance reproductions, only two subjects—one man and one woman—omitted the reference to relatives. Four men who gave the arrow excuse correctly on their first attempt relegated it to the second place and then omitted it from subsequent versions. *The Method of Description* has already shown that the positional factor, which gives an advantage in memory processes to material presented early in a series, can easily be disturbed. Nearly all the men who reproduced this story had been to the War or were faced with the probability that they would soon have to go, or thought that they ought to go. I think it not fanciful to say that this story reminded them of their situation, and in fact some of them admitted that it did. The reference to relatives had a personal application in most of the cases, and it is more than likely that it was this that made the reference a dominant detail in remembering. In all the later versions this excuse also disappeared. The anxiety about relatives, on which, if I am right, its preservation was based, was only a fleeting one, and with its passing the material which it had dealt with went too.

(b) "Sympathetic" weather

My next point may at first appear to be distinctly fantastic. Throughout the whole of these experiments, however, I had in mind the connexion between memory processes and the growth of all kinds of conventions and conventional modes of representation. Now an exceedingly common feature in popular fiction is what may be called "sympathetic weather"; storms blow up before the moment of tragedy, a peaceful sky presages a happy ending, and so on. I wondered how my subjects would deal, in the case of *The War of the Ghosts*, with the "calm and foggy night". Only eight ever reproduced it, and five of these speedily dropped it from their later versions. As a matter of fact, "sympathetic weather" seems to belong to a class of features which are very effective in setting up a sort of vague atmosphere of attitude, but do not provide outstanding detail, as a rule. Thus a subject who failed to record the weather in his first version said nevertheless: "I formed some sort of association, I do not know what, in connexion with the thick, still evening on the river. I think it recalled something I had been before, but I cannot exactly remember the circumstances". A fortnight later there appeared in his remembered version of the story: "The evening was misty down by the river, and for a time they were conscious only of their own presence". This seems to give us another case of the delayed appearance of material in a reproduction.

Even when the weather was recorded it was often given inaccurately. "Two Indians", said a subject, "went down to the marsh on the side of a lake in order to fish. However, the dampness of the air and the calmness of the sea were disadvantageous to their sport." In his second attempt he made the weather "calm" and the sea "hazy", and finally, much later, asserted: "the day was damp and misty". Another subject reported: "the night was cold and foggy"; and another: "while they were there darkness and mist gathered". Perhaps what is evoked in all such cases is, in fact, merely a 'weather scheme' which is consonant with a given mood, but no detailed weather characteristics.

(c) The order of events

If the suggestion made on the basis of the results from *The Method of Description* is right, the order of events in a story ought to be fairly well preserved in repeated reproduction. For it appeared probable that words are fit or apt material for dealing with order. And on the whole this was borne out very definitely in the present series of experiments, and the order of events was well preserved. But when any incident called out unusual interest, that incident tended to displace events which occurred earlier in the original version. As we have seen repeatedly, from the very beginning of this experimental work, salient features are a characteristic of practically every act of observation, however incapable of analysis both the act and its object may appear. Thus the two excuses of the young Indians were consistently transposed when one was not lost altogether. The ghosts, again and again, with greater emphasis as time elapsed, tended to be pushed up towards the beginning of the story. But the subject who was preoccupied with the mysterious death of the Indian, and to whom the ghosts, merely regarded as ghosts, were secondary, unwittingly let them drop down to the last place in the story. It also appeared as if the tendency to place striking units early was a special characteristic of the visualising subject; but the evidence on this point cannot yet be regarded as very definite.

(d) The reproduction of style

The style, rhythm or construction of a prose or verse narrative is perhaps in some ways analogous to the "rule of structure" of a regular figure. And as there are some people who are particularly sensitive to the latter, so in many cases the former may make an early and a lasting impression. Nearly all of my subjects who made any comments on *The War of the Ghosts* described it as "terse", "disjointed", "Biblical", "inconsequential", and so on. However, style seems to be one of those factors which are extremely readily responded to, but extremely rarely reproduced with any fidelity. Thus we may react to a narrative or an argument largely because of its formal character, may even remember it largely on this account, and yet the form may be singularly ineffective in shaping any subsequent reproduction. Completely satisfactory comprehension does not necessarily lead to complete fidelity of reproduction; the good auditor may be a bad mimic, the good reader a bad writer. Transformations of form and style are excessively likely to appear quickly. In this case it might happen that a subject, trying to retain the style of the original, as he thought, would merely use rather out-of-date or unusual phrases: the young man "drew in" towards the bank, taking refuge behind a "prone log"; the warriors, seeing many people, "accordingly touched in towards the bank of the river". One subject having produced an extremely matter-of-fact version, said: "I tried to reproduce the original story in all its terseness". Obviously, ability to respond to form does not of necessity carry with it ability to reproduce, or even to remember, form. Nevertheless, the form itself may well be an important factor in what makes remembering possible.

(e) The commonest omissions and transpositions

To work completely through the whole list of omissions and transpositions in the case of *The War of the Ghosts* would be a fruitlessly long and weary task. The commonest of these concerned (1) the title; (2) proper names; (3) definite numbers; (4) the precise significance of the "ghosts", and (5) canoes.

The title was speedily omitted by seven of the twenty subjects and transformed by ten of the others. Variants were: "The two young men of Egulack"; "War-Ghost story"; "The Ghosts"; "The story of the Ghosts", and so on. It would, I think, be a matter of some interest to try to discover how far titles of stories in general, headlines in newspapers, and, in fact, all such general initial labels influence perceiving and remembering. Some unpublished experiments, carried out in Cambridge by the late Prof. Bernard Muscio, suggested strongly that their importance is commonly greatly exaggerated, and my own results, for what they are worth, point in the same direction.

Sooner or later, the proper names dropped out of all the reproductions, with the single exception of the one in which they seemed, after ten years, to be the only readily accessible detail. As a rule, before they entirely disappeared, they suffered change. Egulac became Emlac, Eggulick, Edulac, Egulick; and Kalama became Kalamata, Kuluma, Karnac, to give only a few of the variations.

No subject retained for more than one reproduction the point about the ghosts as it was related in the original.

Every subject, at some point in the story, introduced "boats" for canoes. Some retained "canoes" as well. With the change to "boat", as a rule "paddling" was transformed into "rowing".

There were, of course, numerous other omissions from the various reproductions, and also a considerable number of inventions. In general character they were much the same as those which marked the course of *Serial Reproduction*, and may be better discussed in that connexion.

5. Some general points arising from the use of the method of repeated reproduction

Although all the illustrations given in the present chapter have, so far, been concerned with *The War of the Ghosts*, every one of the points raised could equally well have been illustrated from the repeated reproduction of other material. In all, I have used eight different stories, several descriptive and argumentative passages, and a considerable amount of graphic material. With some variations for the differing types of material, the general method of work and the main trend of the results were constant. Different subjects took part in the experiment and material was employed having a wide range of subject-matter and style, but this also, certain specifically individual points aside, made no essential difference. In attempting to discuss generally some of the wider conclusions which may be tentatively drawn at this stage, I shall have the whole of the work in mind.

(a) Persistence of 'form' in reproduction

The most general characteristic of the whole of this group of experiments was the persistence, for any given subject, of the 'form' of his first reproduction. With the single but probably significant exception of a few subjects of strongly visualising type, the great majority of the changes introduced into a story—save after a lapse of very long intervals indeed—were effected in the early stages of the experiment. In fact, response to a general scheme, form, order and arrangement of material seems to be dominant, both in initial reception and in subsequent remembering. The 'rule of structure' operated frequently in the perceiving experiments; the 'general outline' played a great part in the setting up of image responses; in the description of faces 'general impression' was extremely important, and here again, no sooner was a story presented than it was labelled, said to be of this or of that type, and in addition to possess a few outstanding details. The type gave the form of the story, and as a rule one or two striking details seemed to recur with as little change as the form itself. The other details were omitted, rearranged, or transformed—rearrangements and transformations being generally effected very rapidly, and omissions continuing for almost indefinite periods. However, although the general form, or scheme, or plan of a prose passage thus persisted with relatively little change, once the reproduction had been effected, as I have already shown, the actual style of the original was nearly always rapidly and unwittingly transformed.

This persistence of form was most of all marked in such instances as those of the well-known 'cumulative' type of story, and perhaps has something to do with the fact that stories of this type are more widely distributed than any others in the popular tales of various social groups. The two stories of this form of construction which I used were almost always greeted with the remark: "Yes, that's a story of the 'House that Jack Built' type".

The form, plan, type, or scheme of a story seems, in fact, for the ordinary, educated adult to be the most dominant and persistent factor in this kind of material. It ought to be possible experimentally to follow the development of the response to form, and to determine its relative importance in individuals of different ages and different intellectual status. Possibly, once the response to the form factor is established, its stability and effectiveness may be due to its possessing a marked affective character. This point, and also the study of the mechanisms by which transformations of detail are produced, are best pursued by a consideration of the parts played by the process of rationalisation in the course of repeated reproduction.

(b) The processes of rationalisation

There is a marked and well-known distinction, both in perceiving and in remembering, between direct reaction to what is literally present and reaction under the guidance of some tendency which gives to what is presented a setting and an explanation. The latter tendency is present to some extent in all perceiving and in all remembering, but may vary greatly in importance and in prominence from case to case. Sometimes, in these experiments, reasons were definitely and explicitly formulated and introduced into reproductions to account for material which had been presented without explanation. Sometimes, without any definite formulation of reasons, the material was so changed that it could be accepted by the observer without question and with satisfaction. The first process appears to be a special instance of the second. Both have the same general function in mental life, and I shall discuss both under the head of rationalisation.

In these experiments rationalisation was applied sometimes to the stories as a whole and sometimes to particular details. In the first case, the process expressed the need, felt by practically every educated observer, that a story should have a general setting. Hardly ever, at the outset, was there an attitude of simple acceptance. Every story presented had to be connected, certainly as a whole, and, if possible, as regards its details also, with something else. This is, of course, the factor which I have already called 'effort after meaning' coming again into play. It could be said that there is a constant effort to get the maximum possible of meaning into the material presented. So long as maximum of meaning is understood to imply an effort to find that connexion which puts a subject most at his ease in reference to a given story, the statement is true. The meaning, in this sense, however, may be of a very tenuous and undetermined nature, and apparently may even be mainly negative.

A very common remark made about the folk-stories used, for example, was: "That is not an English tale". Sometimes the narrative was rendered satisfactory by being called a "dream". "This", said one observer, "is very clearly a murder concealment dream." She proceeded to an interpretation along the lines of modern symbolism, and the story was, with no further trouble, comfortably accepted.

In fact, all incoming material, if it is to be accepted and dealt with in any manner, must be somehow labelled. A negative label is often enough. When an Englishman calls a tale "not English" he can at once proceed to accept odd, out of the way, and perhaps even inconsistent material, with very little resistance. How these labels are developed and in what ways they are taken over ready-made from society are matters of some interest, not out of the reach of experimental study.

The rationalisation which stops short at finding a label is interesting in two ways. Firstly, the process is emphatically not merely a question of relating the newly presented material to old acquirements of knowledge. Primarily, it depends upon the active bias, or special reaction tendencies, that are awakened in the observer by the new material, and it is these tendencies which then set the new into relation to the old. To speak as if what is accepted and given a place in mental life is always simply a question of what fits into already formed apperception systems is to miss the obvious point that the process of fitting is an active process, depending directly upon the pre-formed tendencies and bias which the subject brings to his task. The second point is that this process of rationalisation is only partially—it might be said only lazily—an intellectual process. No doubt the attempt, however little defined, to seek out the connexions of things is always to some degree intellectual. But here the effort stops when it produces an attitude best described as 'the attitude in which no further questions are asked'. The end state is primarily affective. Once reached, and it is generally reached very quickly, it recurs very readily, and it is this, more than anything else, which accounts for the persistent sameness of repeated reproduction.

The rationalisation which gives to material as a whole its appropriate frame is only a part of the total process. Details also must be dealt with, and every chain of reproductions illustrated how the rationalising process was applied to particular items.

The most direct method is to provide definite, stated links of connexion between parts of material which are *prima facie* disconnected. The current versions of most folk-stories appear jerky, perhaps incoherent in parts, and very badly strung together. This is because of their strong social setting, which makes it possible for narrators and hearers to take much for granted that is not expressed. If reproductions are obtained in a social community different from that in which the original version was developed, the subject, acting almost always unwittingly, supplies connecting links. In *The War of the Ghosts* events follow one another, but their connexion is not, as a rule, actually stated. The situation is like that which would confront the spectator of one of the earlier cinematograph films with the usual explanatory connecting tags omitted. The subjects, in the experiments, supplied the tags, but without realising what they were doing: "they (*i.e.* the young men) heard some canoes approaching them, *and so* hid . . ."; "one said he would not go *as* his relations did not know where he was"; "he heard the Indians cry: 'Let us go home, *as* the man of Egulack is wounded' "; "the young man did not feel sick (i.e. *wounded*), *but nevertheless* they proceeded home (*evidently the opposing forces were quite willing to stop fighting*)"; "when he got back the young man lit a fire (*probably to cook his breakfast*)"—all of these explanatory particles and phrases come from the version of one subject, and similar illustrations could be given in nearly all cases. The net result is that before long the story tends to be robbed of all its surprising, jerky and apparently inconsequential form, and reduced to an orderly narration. It is denuded of all the elements that left the reader puzzled and uneasy, or it has been given specific associative links which, in the original form, were assumed as immediately understood.

Suppose the very same observers, however, are presented with well-ordered argumentative passages, and are required to make repeated reproductions of these. It does not follow that the bonds of connexion which are now supplied will be retained and will reappear. They fulfil their function by making the material appear coherent. The form of whatever is presented may produce its effect, even though the elements of which the form is constructed are given but scanty notice. Any normal, educated observer strives after associative links, but whether the mode of connexion or the matter of such links, when they are supplied, is faithfully reproduced is another question altogether.

Rationalisation in regard to form found its main expression in the linking together of events within the stories; rationalisation as concerned with the details of material was usually carried out by connecting the given items with something outside the story and supplied by the observer himself. This is analogous to what I have called 'importation' in *The Method of Description*: it was of three main types.

First there was the process, in all instances witting during its early stages, but later producing unwitting transformations, by which presented material was connected with other matter outside the story, but having the same general nature. For example, in *The War of the Ghosts* the "something black" was frequently interpreted as a materialisation of the dying man's breath. Again, an instance telling how a raven's beak turned into a knife was accepted and persistently preserved by being treated as a symbol in a murder dream. To call these cases 'witting' is perhaps not strictly accurate. Usually there is some delay before the actual explanation is formulated, and in all such cases the material which is rationalised is first treated as symbolic. With repeated reproduction the symbolised materials or facts eventually replace completely that by which in the original they were symbolised. Perhaps, psychologically, all processes of symbolisation fall into place as subordinate to a wider process of rationalisation, and, in the complete process of symbolisation, the final stage is the obliteration of the symbol.[6]

The second process of rationalisation, as it here occurred, was unwitting from start to finish. The transformation of "something black" into "foamed at the mouth" was a case in point. So was the introduction of an "island" into *The War of the Ghosts* by several subjects. Probably the changing of an apparently irrelevant remark at the end of one of the tales: "And so the sparrow never got home", into: "And so the sparrow got home at last, and here ends my story" belonged to the same class. No symbolisation, in the proper sense of the word, was involved in this type of rationalisation. At no stage of the transformation had the material employed a double signification, so far, at any rate, as could be ascertained.

This is the type of rationalisation in which individual interests and peculiarities come most clearly into play. In the first type that part of the process which is witting tends to follow the lines of current belief, or of the modes of language expression which have been built into the general communication habits of a community. Thus it is likely to manifest the same development in different members of the same social group. In the third type, as I shall go on to show, although the process is unwitting, the results are extremely likely to display the same character throughout a given community. It is in the second type that individual bias and interest most directly determine the transformations effected.

For example, a long series of reproductions was obtained of a Provençal story which may be called *The Citizens and the Plague*. The last paragraph of this story in the original was:

> This city is like unto the world, for the world is filled with mad folk. Is not the greatest wisdom a man can have to love God and obey His will? But now this wisdom is lost, and covetousness and blindness have fallen like rain upon the earth. And if one man escapes this rain, his fellows account him mad. They have lost the wisdom of God, so they say that he is mad who has lost the wisdom of the world.

In a series of successive reproductions this moral was progressively elaborated and emphasised. The subject was all the time unwittingly satisfying a well-developed interest in moralising. His version remained extremely accurate, but the final paragraph was somewhat lengthened, as compared with the rest of the story, and was given a more definitely religious tone:

> This great city is like the world. For in the world are many people, and upon them at times come plagues from heaven, and none know how they come. For it is well that men should live simply, and love God, and do His will. But men turn aside and go about after wisdom

and the prizes of the world, nor pay heed to the high and simple life. And so it is that those few who seek to serve God and to live simply, as He desires, are despised by the rest, and being alone in their right thinking, are yet accounted mad by the madmen.

In this there is not much transformation, but considerable increase of emphasis. An original rationalising element in the story has been seized upon, and so developed that it plays a greater part in the whole. This development was directly the work of a marked individual interest, though the subject was utterly unaware at the time that the interest was coming into operation.

The third type of rationalisation is very closely related to the second. It is the case in which some particular, and maybe isolated detail, is transformed immediately into a more familiar character. Thus "canoe" rapidly became "boat"; "paddling" became "rowing"; a "peanut" became an "acorn"; a "bush-cat" became an ordinary "cat"; "Kashim" (a proper name for a shelter) became "cabin", and so on in a very large number of different cases.

Both the second and the third types of rationalisation are unwitting; neither results in the explicit provision of definite reasons, and both consist in changing the relatively unfamiliar into the relatively familiar. But the second is characteristically individual, so that an incident is likely to be transformed or developed differently as it is dealt with by different observers, while the third type is apt to exhibit the same results so long as the observers are drawn from the same social class or group. Changes of this type, which nearly all concern the names of common objects, or special phrases, or the like, may therefore be of particular importance when any attempt is being made to trace the line of passage of material from one social group to another.

The general function of rationalisation is in all the instances the same. It is to render material acceptable, understandable, comfortable, straightforward; to rob it of all puzzling elements. As such it is a powerful factor in all perceptual and in all reproductive processes. The forms it takes are often directly social in significance.

(c) The determination of outstanding detail

In all perceiving and remembering we have to take account both of a general setting and of outstanding detail. At first glance the problems set by the persistence of these appear to be different. Sometimes the setting seems to persist while the detail dwindles almost to nothing; or perhaps the setting vanishes, and only a few outstanding details are remembered. More commonly both remain to some degree.

In the determination of outstanding detail there are apparently four common groups of cases:

1. There is a strong presumption, most definitely increasing as the observer approximates to a true vocalising type, that words or phrases popular at the time of the experiment, in the group to which the observer belongs, will stand out prominently from their background, and be reproduced without change as to form, though possibly with change of position.

2. Any word, or combination of words, or any event which appears comic, is almost certain to be reproduced so long as the comic significance is retained. Nevertheless, the comic is extremely liable to change, for what appears comic varies within wide limits from person to person. Proper names, for example, which have a peculiar liability to produce laughter, are the more likely to reappear in proportion as they do this, but are at the same time excessively likely to be transformed.

3. Material which is a direct or an indirect stimulus to pre-formed interests is sure to reappear. Probably the affective tone accompanying the arousal of such interests is an important factor here. The affect is certainly not always pleasing. On the whole, the results indicate that, if the interesting material is pleasing, the change is in the direction of elaboration and development; if the affect is displeasing, distortions are most likely to occur. Persistence of material, in these cases, seems to be due rather to the interest or bias evoked than directly to the feeling itself. But the evidence of other methods ought to be called in at this point.

4. There is a puzzling class of material which appears striking by reason of its triviality. Much further analysis is doubtless called for in order to determine why and when material is treated as trivial. But when all has been said that may be, it remains that the trivial is in fact often striking, and that as such it is likely to be retained.

Most of these points can be more forcibly illustrated from the results of *The Method of Serial Reproduction*.[7]

(d) Inventions or importations

I have already discussed importation, or invention, in relation to *The Method of Description*. Little additional evidence can be gathered from the results of *The Method of Repeated Reproduction*, but what there is goes to confirm our earlier conclusions. Most of the importations concerned late stages in the reproductions, and they were often to be traced to a play of visual imagery. Two factors were important. First, the subject's attitude or point of view in relation to a particular story; and, secondly, the utilisation of any vividly presented material which seemed fit or appropriate to this point of view. In many cases of long-distance remembering, in particular, this attitude, or point of view, was by far the leading factor. Apparently in some way tied up with the attitude may go material belonging to very varied settings. If, at the time of reproduction, any of this material came vividly before the mind, as with the case of the particular and clear-cut visual image, it was apt to get incorporated in the story. This is how the "totem" came into *The War of the Ghosts*. The "pilgrimage", and "filial piety", each having a concrete visual symbol, had the same explanation. However, I must confess to some disappointment that this series of experiments should have given only scanty evidence of importation.

One thing did definitely emerge. Cumulative stories, of *The House that Jack Built* or *The Old Woman who Went to Market* type, definitely favoured invention. I shall illustrate this in dealing with the results of *The Method of Serial Reproduction*.[8]

(e) Delay in manifest change

I have already indicated that changes were sometimes foreshadowed before they were given a manifest place in the reproductions.[9]

For example, an observer who had completed one of his reproductions casually remarked: "I've a sort of feeling that there was something about a rock, but I can't fit it in". He gave the matter slight consideration and finally rejected the notion. Two months later, without a word of comment or of explanation, the rock took its place in the story. There was no rock in the original.

All the various transformations or importations that occurred in an observer's reproductions were apt to get connected together in the course of successive reproduction; and also, in a number of cases, tales reverted to their original form after an interval during which deviations from the original had occurred. Thus it appears that influences may be at work tending to settle the eventual form of material recalled which fail to find immediate expression.

Such delay—and we get numerous illustrations in everyday experience—raises difficult problems. For one thing, it seems to mean that when an attempt is being made to establish causal relations between psychical processes, direct temporal sequence may sometimes have comparatively little significance. We cannot look with certainty, for the leading conditions of a particular response, to other reactions immediately preceding the one which we are trying to explain.

A particular stimulus, or feature of a situation, gives rise to a tendency to respond in a specific manner. At first the tendency is held in check and produces slight or perhaps no manifest results. As time elapses, apparently the unexpressed tendency may gain strength, and so manifestly affect the response; or other tendencies simultaneously excited may lose strength, and in this way also a new manifest change of response may appear.

Can we understand how an unexpressed tendency may gain strength? There appears to be little real ground for holding, as some do, that the mere checking, suppression, or damming up of any tendency is able to add strength to that tendency. But perhaps we may hold that a weaker tendency may gain in strength by being associated with a stronger one. Many of the manifest changes, when they appeared, did so in close relation to other transformations which were actually made earlier in the series of reproductions. For example, one subject, in dealing with *The War of the Ghosts*, first said that the war-party were "heard to advance": three months later "they marched forward". He first made the only canoe mentioned the property of the young man who accompanied the party, and later described the warriors definitely as "a land force". In his later versions both young men were unwillingly forced upon the expedition, for they were both together hiding behind a log, a detail which made a marked impression upon this subject at the beginning of the experiment. In his first reproduction the Indian was "shot", later he was "struck by a bullet". Thereupon he "shouted: 'These are ghosts that we fight with' "; but at first he had not shouted this but only "thought" it. Very probably some of the delay in manifest change is due to the linking together of tendencies which are initially weak with others stronger than themselves. There is, however, no real evidence to show how, if at all, this takes place.

On the other hand, such transformations as that of the mention of a rock six weeks after the first reproduction of a story, and its definite introduction two months later, seems rather to be a case of the weakening of certain tendencies and the consequent relative strengthening of others. For the manifest change, when it appears, does not seem to be specifically connected with any preceding change. Whether, and in what precise sense, this view can be maintained, must depend upon definite experimental evidence as to the effect upon different, and particularly upon competing, tendencies of the mere lapse of time. For, on the face of it, there is little or no more reason for assuming that tendencies weaken with lapse of time than that they are strengthened by being merely denied immediate expression.

Finally, the whole notion of an unexpressed tendency, continuing for long periods to have the capacity of coming into operation, while to all outward appearance, and to inward observation also, it is wholly in abeyance, is not easy to understand. The notion seems to be demanded by many of the facts of mental life, but it clearly calls for a very critical consideration.

6. A summary of the main conclusions drawn from *The Method of Repeated Reproduction*

1. It again appears that accuracy of reproduction, in a literal sense, is the rare exception and not the rule.
2. In a chain of reproductions obtained from a single individual, the general form, or outline, is remarkably persistent, once the first version has been given.

3. At the same time, style, rhythm, precise mode of construction, while they are apt to be immediately reacted to, are very rarely faithfully reproduced.

4. With frequent reproduction the form and items of remembered detail very quickly become stereotyped and thereafter suffer little change.

5. With infrequent reproduction, omission of detail, simplification of events and structure, and transformation of items into more familiar detail, may go on almost indefinitely, or so long as unaided recall is possible.

6. At the same time, in long-distance remembering, elaboration becomes rather more common in some cases; and there may be increasing importation, or invention, aided, as in *The Method of Description*, by the use of visual images.

7. Long-distance remembering is of two types at least:

    (*a*) The general setting, as expressed mainly through the subject's attitude to the material, continues to function, as also does outstanding detail. The actual memory process is strongly and evidently constructive, and there is much use of inference.

    (*b*) All that appears to function are one or two isolated but striking details.

8. Detail is outstanding when it fits in with a subject's pre-formed interests and tendencies. It is then remembered, though often transformed, and it tends to take a progressively earlier place in successive reproductions.

9. There is some indication, as with *The Method of Description*, that, in some cases, the influence of affective attitude may be intensified with lapse of time.

10. In all successive remembering, rationalisation, the reduction of material to a form that can be readily and 'satisfyingly' dealt with is very prominent.

11. It is this process, itself often based upon an affective attitude, which gives the whole dealt with that specific ground, frame, or setting, without which it will not be persistently remembered.

12. Or, again, rationalisation may deal with details, explicitly linking them together and so rendering them apparently coherent, or linking given detail with other detail not actually present in the original setting.

13. In the latter case rationalisation has three main forms:

    (*a*) The given material is initially connected with something else—usually with some definitely formulated explanation—and treated as a symbol of that other material. Eventually it tends to be unwittingly replaced by that which it has symbolised.

    (*b*) The whole rationalising process is unwitting and involves no symbolisation. It then tends to possess characteristics peculiar to the work of the individual who effects it and due directly to his particular temperament and character.

(*c*) Names, phrases and events are immediately changed so that they appear in forms current within the social group to which the subject belongs.

14. There is evidence of delay in manifest change, transformations being foreshadowed weeks, or perhaps months, before they actually appear.

Notes

1 *Rev. Phil*, 1897, xlii, 481–93. My attention was drawn to Philippe's most interesting work by the late Prof. James Ward.
2 Cf. chs. vii and viii.
3 See ch. viii.
4 See *Ann. Rep. Bur. of Amer. Ethnol.* Bull. 26, pp. 184–5.
5 He means, of course, his memory processes in general. But though he says that his specific imagery in this case has become dim, the version does not appear much less detailed or definite than his earlier attempts.
6 Cf. F. C. Bartlett, "Symbolism in Folk Lore", *Seventh International Congress of Psychology*, Cambridge 1924, pp. 278–89.
7 See ch. vii.
8 See pp. 129–46.
9 See pp. 72–5.

31

A SPREADING-ACTIVATION
THEORY OF SEMANTIC
PROCESSING

Allan M. Collins and Elizabeth F. Loftus

Source: *Psychological Review*, 82 (1975): 407–428.

This paper presents a spreading-activation theory of human
semantic processing, which can be applied to a wide range of
recent experimental results. The theory is based on Quillian's
theory of semantic memory search and semantic preparation,
or priming. In conjunction with this, several of the misconceptions concerning Quillian's theory are discussed. A number of
additional assumptions are proposed for his theory in order to
apply it to recent experiments. The present paper shows how the
extended theory can account for results of several production
experiments by Loftus, Juola and Atkinson's multiple-category
experiment, Conrad's sentence-verification experiments, and
several categorization experiments on the effect of semantic
relatedness and typicality by Holyoak and Glass, Rips, Shoben,
and Smith, and Rosch. The paper also provides a critique of the
Smith, Shoben, and Rips model for categorization judgments.

Some years ago, Quillian[1] (1962, 1967) proposed a spreading-activation theory of human semantic processing that he tried to implement in computer
simulations of memory search (Quillian, 1966) and comprehension (Quillian,
1969). The theory viewed memory search as activation spreading from two or
more concept nodes in a semantic network until an intersection was found.
The effects of preparation (or priming) in semantic memory were also
explained in terms of spreading activation from the node of the primed concept. Rather than a theory to explain data, it was a theory designed to show
how to build human semantic structure and processing into a computer.

Since the theory was proposed, there have been a number of experiments
investigating retrieval and priming in semantic memory. In the present paper,

we attempt to show how an elaboration of Quillian's basic theory can account for many of the results. In the first section, we briefly review the original theory while trying to correct a number of the common misunderstandings concerning it. In the second section, we extend the theory in several respects, and in the third section show how the extended theory deals with some recent experimental findings. In the fourth section we compare the theory to the model of Smith, Shoben, and Rips (1974).

Quillian's theory of semantic memory

The fact that Quillian's theory was developed as a program for a digital computer imposed certain constraints on the theory, which Quillian felt were psychologically unrealistic. We will recount the theory as he proposed it, and then elaborate the theory in psychological terms. The theory made a number of assumptions about structure and processing in human semantic memory. A brief discussion of these assumptions follows.

People's concepts contain indefinitely large amounts of information. Quillian used the example of a machine. If one asks people to tell everything they know about machines, they will start off giving obvious properties, for example, that machines are man-made and have moving parts. But soon people run out of obvious facts and begin giving facts that are less and less relevant, for example, that a typewriter is a machine or even that the keys on the IBM electric typewriters select the position of a ball that strikes the ribbon against the paper. The amount of information a person can generate about any concept in this way seems unlimited.

In these terms concepts correspond to particular senses of words or phrases. For example, not only is the noun "machine" a concept, but the verb "to machine" is a concept; the "particular old car I own" is a concept; the notion of "driving a car" is a concept; even the notion of "what to do if you see a red light" has to be a concept. Thus, people must have a very large number of concepts, and concepts must have very complicated structures.

A concept can be represented as a node in a network, with properties of the concept represented as labeled relational links from the node to other concept nodes. These links are pointers, and usually go in both directions between two concepts. Links can have different *criterialities*, which are numbers indicating how essential each link is to the meaning of the concept. The criterialities on any pair of links between two concepts can be different; for example, it might be highly criterial for the concept of a typewriter that it is a machine, and not very criterial for the concept of machine that one kind is a typewriter. From each of the nodes linked to a given node, there will be links to other concept nodes and from each of these in turn to still others. In Quillian's theory, the full meaning of any concept is the whole network as entered from the concept node.

226

The links are not simply undifferentiated links, but must be complicated enough to represent any relation between two concepts. In the original theory, Quillian proposed five different kinds of links: (a) superordinate ("isa") and subordinate links, (b) modifier links, (c) disjunctive sets of links, (d) conjunctive sets of links, and (e) a residual class of links, which allowed the specification of any relationship where the relationship (usually a verb relationship) itself was a concept. These different kinds of links could be nested or embedded to any degree of depth, so that the format was designed to be flexible enough to express anything, however vague or specific, that can be expressed in natural language.

The search in memory between concepts involves tracing out in parallel (simulated in the computer by a breadth-first search) along the links from the node of each concept specified by the input words. The words might be part of a sentence or stimuli in an experimental task. The spread of activation constantly expands, first to all the nodes linked to the first node, then to all the nodes linked to each of these nodes, and so on. At each node reached in this process, an activation tag is left that specifies the starting node and the immediate predecessor. When a tag from another starting node is encountered, an *intersection* between the two nodes has been found.[2] By following the tags back to both starting nodes, the *path* that led to the intersection can be reconstructed.

When an intersection has been found, it is necessary to *evaluate* the path to decide if it satisfies the constraints imposed by syntax and context. The complicated kinds of decision rules that are invoked for comprehension of sentences in this evaluation phase are described in Quillian (1969). For categorization tasks these rules are described by Collins and Quillian (1972b) and in the next section of this paper. As an example, in a phrase such as "the fall leaves," a path found between the concept "to fall" and the concept "tree leaf" would be rejected as a wrong interpretation, because syntax requires a participal form of "fall" to fit that interpretation. If a path found is rejected, other paths are considered in the order in which they are found.

Priming (or preparation) involves the same tracing process that was described for memory search. When a concept is primed, activation tags are spread by tracing an expanding set of links in the network out to some unspecified depth. When another concept is subsequently presented, it has to make contact with one of the tags left earlier to find an intersection. One of the non-obvious implications of this view of priming is that links as well as nodes will be primed. This is because Quillian treated links themselves as concepts (see above). Thus priming a node such as "red" will prime the links involving the relation "color" throughout the network. This provides a very powerful context mechanism.

Common misinterpretations of Quillian's theory

There is a rich variety of misinterpretations of Quillian's theory, many of them deriving from Collins's (Collins & Quillian, 1969, 1970a, 1970b) simplifications of the theory. The problem arose because Collins and Quillian were investigating specific aspects of the theory and only described enough of the theory to motivate a particular experiment. In turn experiments made interpretations of these simplified versions, which did not fit with the theory as described elsewhere (Bell & Quillian, 1971; Quillian, 1966, 1969).

Perhaps the most prevalent misinterpretation of Quillian's theory concerns the idea of cognitive economy (Anderson & Bower, 1973; Conrad, 1972). In this regard, it is important to distinguish the strong theory of cognitive economy, which Conrad takes issue with in her attack on Collins and Quillian (1969), and the weak theory of cognitive economy, which Collins and Quillian were testing (though they did not spell it out clearly enough). As Conrad (1972) states, she rejects the "hypothesis that all properties are stored only once in memory and must be retrieved through a series of inferences for all words except those that they most directly define" (p. 153). This is a statement of the strong theory of cognitive economy. Undoubtedly the Collins and Quillian (1969) paper gave rise to this notion, but the authors cautioned against making that interpretation of the theory. As they said, "people surely store certain properties at more than one level in the hierarchy" (p. 242), and they cited the maple leaf as an example of this general rule.

The strong theory requires erasing information whenever it applies at a more general level. If a person learns a robin can fly and then later that birds fly, the strong theory implies that "flying" must be erased from "robin." The weak theory of cognitive economy merely assumes that every time one learns that X is a bird, one does not at that time store all the properties of birds with X in memory. Thus, an inference will be necessary to decide that X can fly, unless one encounters this fact directly. Hence, Collins and Quillian, in testing the weak theory of cognitive economy, picked instances where people were not likely to have encountered the general property with the specific instance (e.g., "A wren can fly"). The point of the experiment was to test whether it was possible to measure inference time, when the weak theory of cognitive economy implies that an inference is likely to be necessary for most subjects.

Another assumption sometimes made about Quillian's theory is that all links are equal (Anderson & McGaw, 1973; Rips, Shoben, & Smith, 1973; Wilkins, Note 1). In Quillian's original theory, there were criteriality tags on links, as we described earlier. In Collins and Quillian (1969, 1972b) links were assumed to have differential accessibility (i.e., strength or travel time). The accessibility of a property depends on how often a person thinks about or uses a property of a concept. Whether criteriality and accessibility are treated as the same or different is a complex issue, but network models allow them to be treated either way. Thus for example, even though "lungs," "hands," and "warts" are all linked directly to the concept "human," these links need not be in any sense equal. The same is true for the links between "bird" and its exemplars, such as "robin," "chicken," or "penguin." Rips et al. (1973) suggest that intermediate nodes are necessary for a network model to explain the reaction time differences they find in categorizing different birds. This makes the mistaken assumption that all links are equally criterial or accessible in any network model. It turns out, however, that differences in links are crucial to many different aspects of human semantic processing as Carbonell and Collins (1973) point out in their discussion of importance (or criteriality) tags.

A related implication of the Rips et al. (1973) paper and also a more recent paper of Smith et al. (1974) is that feature models can account for data that network models cannot. A feature model posits that a concept consists of a set of values on a large number of semantic dimensions (e.g., animateness, color, etc.). What is strange about this argument is that network models were developed as a method of representing features in a computer. Any process that can be represented in a feature model is representable in a network model; in particular, the Smith et al. model itself could be implemented in a semantic network (Hollan, 1975). In fact, network models are probably *more* powerful than feature models, because it is not obvious how to handle inferential processing or embedding in feature models.

Smith et al. (1974) argued in favor of feature models because their data for comparison of concepts seemed to fit a feature comparison process. What should be emphasized about Quillian's theory is that the parallel search would inevitably lead to just such a feature comparison process, though the process would take place over a period of time as different connections are found. One way that Quillian's theory is different from the Smith et al. models is that superordinate connections, if they exist, would also be found and evaluated. The distinction between these two theories is so crucial that we will discuss it at length in conjunction with the spreading activation theory's explanation of the Rips et al. (1973) results.

Another common misconception of Quillian's theory shows up in Juola and Atkinson's (1971) work on categorization judgments. In a categorization task, response time is measured for a subject to decide whether or not a particular instance (e.g., "car") is a member of one or more categories (e.g., "flower" or "vehicle"). Juola and Atkinson assume that in Quillian's theory the memory search to make a categorization judgment proceeds from the instance to the category. In fact, the wording in Collins and Quillian (1969) mistakenly gives that impression. But Quillian's theory (1966, 1969) assumes the search proceeds from both the instance and category in parallel. However, if one or the other is presented first, this gives the search from that node a head start, which is the notion of priming. Juola and Atkinson's experiment involves priming in a complicated way, which we will discuss below.

Anderson and Bower (1973) reject a Quillian-like model of a parallel search, while acknowledging that their data are compatible with "a parallel model whose search rate is slower in proportion to the number of paths that must be searched" (p. 371). Anderson and Bower's argument implies wrongly that Quillian has made the independence assumption for his parallel search. An independent parallel search is like a race where the speed of each runner is independent of the other runners. This is a common assumption in psychology, because it makes it possible to assign an upper bound to reaction time (see Sternberg, 1966). But there is no difficulty for Quillian's theory if the parallel search rate depends on the number of paths searched. Hence, Anderson and Bower's data are perfectly compatible with Quillian's parallel search.

The above discussion, then, shows what Quillian's theory is *not*, or at least some of what it is not. Several other misconceptions are discussed in Collins and Quillian (1972b), in particular the notion that Quillian's theory of memory is rigidly hierarchical, which Anderson and Bower (1973, p. 379) still believe, and Schaeffer and Wallace's (1970) argument that Quillian's theory predicts it will always take less time to compare concepts that are close together in the semantic network. We will return to some of these same papers below, in order to describe how the extended version of Quillian's theory accounts for some of the results these experimenters have used to reject Quillian's theory.

The extended theory

In order to deal with the specific experimental results that have appeared in recent years, several more processing and structural assumptions must be added to the basic Quillian theory. These do not bend the theory, but merely elaborate it in such a way that it can be applied to the kinds of experiments on semantic memory that have been performed recently. The elaboration may itself be wrong, so our mistakes should not be held against Quillian's theory.

Local processing assumptions

There are four local processing assumptions in the extended theory. These four assumptions transform the theory from computer terms to quasi-neurological terms, a la Pavlov. But all the assumptions of the original theory should be preserved despite the transformation, except that activation tags are to be considered as source-specific activation (i.e., activation that is traceable to its node of origin).

1. When a concept is processed (or stimulated), activation spreads out along the paths of the network in a decreasing gradient. The decrease is

inversely proportional to the accessibility or strength of the links in the path. Thus, activation is like a signal from a source that is attenuated as it travels outward.

2. The longer a concept is continuously processed (either by reading, hearing, or rehearsing it), the longer activation is released from the node of the concept at a fixed rate. Only one concept can be actively processed at a time, which is a limitation imposed by the serial nature of the human central process (Collins & Quillian, 1972b). This means that activation can only start out at one node at a time. But it continues in parallel from other nodes that are encountered as it spreads out from the node of origin.

3. Activation decreases over time and/or intervening activity. This is a noncommittal assumption that activation goes away gradually by some mechanism. Assumptions 2 and 3 impose a limitation on the amount of activation that can be allocated in priming more than one concept, because the more concepts that are primed, the less each will be primed.

4. With the assumption that activation is a variable quantity, the notion of intersection requires a threshold for firing. The assumption is that activation from different sources summates and that when the summation at the point of intersection reaches threshold, the path in the network producing the intersection will be evaluated.

Global assumptions about memory structure and processing

There are three assumptions in the extended theory concerned with the global structure of memory and its processing. These are generalizations of Loftus's (Note 2) arguments that semantic memory is organized primarily into noun categories and that there is a "dictionary" (or lexical memory) separate from the conceptual network.

5. The conceptual (semantic) network is organized along the lines of semantic similarity. The more properties two concepts have in common, the more links there are between the two nodes via these properties and the more closely related are the concepts. This means that different vehicles or different colors will all be highly interlinked through their common properties. This also implies that red things (e.g., fire engines, cherries, sunsets, and roses) are *not* closely interlinked, despite the one property they have in common. In these terms semantic relatedness is based on an aggregate of the interconnections between two concepts.[3]

Figure 1 illustrates this aggregate notion of concept relatedness for a hypothetical human memory. (It is the kind of diagram that the scaling techniques of Rips et al., 1973, would produce.) In the figure the various vehicles are shown as closely related, because of the numerous individual connections that are assumed to exist between them. Conversely, the concepts associated with "red" are shown as less related, because of the presumed paucity of inter-connections between them.

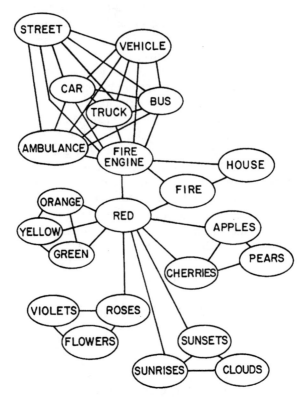

Figure 1 A schematic representation of concept relatedness in a stereotypical fragment of human memory (where a shorter line represents greater relatedness).

From the assumption that memory is organized according to semantic similarity, together with earlier assumptions, it follows that if "vehicle" is primed, activation at any type of vehicle will accumulate from many neighboring nodes. That is to say, to the degree that "fire engine" is primed by "vehicle," it will in turn prime "ambulance," "truck," "bus," etc., and each of these in turn will prime the others. On the other hand, if "red" is primed, the activation that spreads to "fire engine" will not prime "cherries," "roses," or "sunsets" to any great extent, because there are so few connections between these concepts. Instead, "fire engine" will tend to prime other vehicles, and "cherries" to prime other fruits. Hence, the same amount of activation will be diffused among a greater number of concepts.

6. The names of concepts are stored in a lexical network (or dictionary) that is organized along lines of phonemic (and to some degree orthographic) similarity. The links from each node in the lexical network are the phonemic properties of the name, specified with respect to their position in the word. The properties stored about names are assumed to be the properties that

Brown and McNeill (1966) found people could identify about words on the "tip of their tongue." Each name node in the lexical network is connected to one or more concept nodes in the semantic network.

7. Loftus's (Note 2) data lead to the further assumption that a person can control whether he primes the lexical network, the semantic network, or both. For example, a person can control whether to prime (a) words in the lexical network that sound like "bird," (b) concepts in the semantic network related to "bird," or (c) words in the lexical network corresponding to the concepts in (b). This control over priming can be thought of in terms of summation of diffuse activation for an entire network (perhaps in a particular part of the brain) and source-specific activation released from a particular node. Thus, (a) would derive from activation of the lexical network together with the word "bird," (b) would derive from activation of the semantic network together with the concept "bird," and (c) would derive from activation of both networks together with the concept "bird."

Assumptions about semantic matching process

There are a number of assumptions about the decision process for evaluating whether or not two concepts match semantically. This is a fundamental process that occurs in many aspects of language processing, such as matching referents, assigning cases, and answering questions (Collins & Quillian, 1972b; Collins, Warnock, Aiello, & Miller, 1975). Categorization tasks, which ask "Is X a Y?" (where X and Y are concepts), directly investigate this process. The decision process described here is a more explicit and somewhat revised version of the process postulated by Collins and Quillian (1972b), with additions to encompass the results of Holyoak and Glass (1975).

8. In order to decide whether or not a concept matches another concept, enough evidence must be collected to exceed either a positive or a negative criterion. The evidence consists of various kinds of intersections that are found during the memory search. Evidence from different paths in memory sum together. Positive and negative evidence act to cancel each other out, as shown by dialogue excerpts in Carbonell and Collins (1973). Failure to reach either criterion before running out of relevant evidence leads to a "don't know" response (Collins et al., 1975). This process is essentially the Bayesian decision model that is common in the reaction time literature (see, for example, Fitts, 1966; Stone, 1960).

There are a number of different kinds of paths between the two concepts that constitute positive or negative evidence. Any of these types of evidence might contribute to a particular decision. The different types are listed in Table 1 and described below in Assumptions 9–13.

9. If the memory search finds that there is a superordinate (or a negative superordinate) connection from X to Y, that fact alone can push the decision

Table 1 Types of paths found in memory that constitute positive or negative evidence

Positive evidence	Negative evidence
Superordinate connection	Negative superordinate connection
Property comparison, matching property	Property comparison, distinguishing property
Wittgenstein strategy, matching property	Wittgenstein strategy, distinguishing property
	Mutually exclusive subordinates
	Counterexamples

over the positive (or negative) criterion. Superordinate links act like highly criterial property links (see below). For example, it is conclusive positive evidence that a mallard is a bird, if superordinate links are found between "mallard" and "duck" and between "duck" and "bird." Similarly, if a negative superordinate link is found between "bat" and "bird," it is conclusive evidence that a bat is not a bird.

10. If the memory search finds properties on which X and Y match (i.e., common properties), this is positive evidence proportional to the criteriality of the property for Y. If the memory search finds properties on which X and Y mismatch (i.e., distinguishing properties), this is negative evidence proportional to the criteriality of the property for Y. There is an asymmetry in the weighing of positive and negative evidence in a property comparison, because a mismatch on just one fairly criterial property can lead to a negative decision, whereas most of the highly criterial properties must match in order to reach a positive decision (Collins & Quillian, 1972b).

It is important to note that property comparisons and superordinate connections sum together in reaching either criterion as the memory search finds them. Thus, distinguishing properties make it harder to reach the positive criterion when there is a superordinate connection and therefore slow down the process.

As an example of property comparison, suppose there is no superordinate connection in a particular person's memory between "mink" and "farm animal" and between "cat" and "farm animal." Then the decision as to whether minks or cats are farm animals might be based on a comparison of the properties of minks or cats on one hand, and farm animals on the other. The most criterial properties of farm animals are presumably being animate and being kept on farms, but other less criterial properties include being domesticated, being raised for some purpose, or being kept in barns or outside. How a particular person would weigh the various properties of minks and cats to decide whether they are farm animals would vary from person to person (our intuition is that minks are farm animals and cats are not, even though both have the two most criterial properties of farm animals—what Smith et al., 1974, called defining properties). This decision strategy is similar to that proposed by Smith et al., as we will discuss later.

11. The Wittgenstein strategy is a variant of the property comparison strategy. It is postulated on the basis of Wittgenstein's (1953) observation that to decide whether something is a game (for example, frisbee), a person compares it to similar instances that are known to be games. Our assumption is that if any properties of X are found that match properties of another instance whose superordinate is Y, these constitute positive evidence. Similarly, any distinguishing properties constitute negative evidence. In the Wittgenstein strategy, unlike the property comparison strategy, matching properties count just as much toward a positive decision as distinguishing properties count toward a negative decision.

To illustrate the Wittgenstein strategy, Collins and Quillian (1972b) pointed out that in deciding whether a stagecoach is a vehicle, it might be compared to a car. The many properties that a stagecoach has in common with a car constitute strong positive evidence that a stagecoach is a vehicle. But notice that a stagecoach does not have a motor, which is highly criterial for being a car. Though this is strong evidence that a stagecoach is not a car, it is only weak evidence that it is not a vehicle. This illustrates how the same evidence is weighed differently in the property comparison strategy and the Wittgenstein strategy. The final decision that a stagecoach is a vehicle might depend both on matching properties between a stagecoach and vehicles in general (conveyance, motion, etc.) and matching properties between a stagecoach and particular vehicles like a car (seats, doors, etc.). Thus the property comparison strategy and the Wittgenstein strategy might combine to determine a person's response.

12. The mutually exclusive subordinates strategy was necessary for programming a computer to answer questions (Collins et al., 1975). Holyoak and Glass (1975) argue that this strategy accounts for some of their reaction time data (they call it a contradiction). The assumption is that if two concepts have a common superordinate with mutually exclusive links into the common superordinate, then this constitutes strong negative evidence, almost comparable to a negative superordinate link.

For example, if the question is whether a mallard is an eagle, the fact that a mallard is a duck and ducks and eagles are mutually exclusive kinds of birds is rather conclusive evidence that a mallard is not an eagle. Though Holyoak and Glass (1975) do not mention it, the mutually exclusive restriction is necessary. For example, the fact that Mike Mansfield is a politician does not exclude him from being a lawyer. Although "politician" and "lawyer" are both occupational roles, they are not mutually exclusive and in fact most politicians are lawyers. But lacking specific information to the contrary, people may make a default assumption of mutual exclusivity when two concepts have a common superordinate.

13. Counterexamples also can be used as negative evidence. This strategy derives from Holyoak and Glass (1975), who argue that statements of the kind "All birds are canaries" are disconfirmed by finding a counterexample, such as "robin." If the question is of the form "Is X a Y?" and there is a superordinate link from Y to X, then finding a counterexample involves finding a Z that also has X as superordinate and is mutually exclusive from Y. This is conclusive evidence that X is not always a Y.

Holyoak and Glass (1975) discuss counterexamples in the context of the universal quantifier "all," but the same process would occur for a question of the kind "Is a marsupial a kangaroo?" In such a case, retrieving a counterexample (such as a wallaby) can be used to determine that kangaroos are a subset of marsupials and not equivalent (e.g., "automobiles" and "cars" are equivalent concepts).

Though these five kinds of evidence (Assumptions 9–13) are the only ones we have postulated for the semantic matching process seen in categorization tasks, there may be other kinds of evidence of this sort. We should stress that there are many other kinds of evidence people use for answering more complicated questions (Collins et al., 1975). It is beyond the scope of this paper, however, to consider all the different ways people use evidence to make semantic decisions.

Recent experiments

In this section, we discuss how the theory deals with some different kinds of recent experiments. The four types of studies to which we apply the theory are (a) several production experiments by Loftus (Freedman & Loftus, 1971; Loftus, 1973a, 1973b, Note 2); (b) Juola and Atkinson's (1971) multiple-category experiment; (c) the Conrad (1972) sentence-verification experiment; and (d) several categorization experiments on the effects of semantic relatedness and typicality (Holyoak & Glass, 1975; Rips et al., 1973; Rosch, 1973; Smith et al., 1974). We intend to deal with the major kinds of available findings to which the Quillian theory has not yet been applied. Our objective is to show how a spreading-activation theory can handle these results, not to consider all the possible alternative explanations of the experiments.

Production experiments of Loftus

There are several Loftus experiments we want to discuss in terms of the spreading-activation theory. The first of these is an experiment by Freedman and Loftus (1971), in which subjects had to produce an instance of a category that began with a given letter or was characterized by a given adjective. For example, subjects might be asked to name a fruit that begins with the letter *A* or a fruit that is red. On some trials the category was shown first and on some trials second. Hence, this was a priming experiment in that one concept was activated before the other. Reaction time was measured from the onset of the second stimulus.

Our concern is with the finding that subjects were faster when the category (e.g., "fruit") was given first than when either the letter or the adjective was given first. This basic result was later replicated even for cases in which the instance named was a more frequent associate to the adjective than to the category noun (e.g., "lemon" is a closer associate of "sour" than of "fruit").

The explanation in terms of the theory is as follows: When a noun, such as "fruit," is presented first, the activation spreads to nodes connected to "fruit," among which are instances such as "apple," "pear," "peach," "orange," and "lemon." But these concepts are all highly interlinked with each other (though some, such as "orange" and "lemon," are more closely interlinked than others). Thus, the total amount of activation is spread among a relatively small number of closely interlinked concepts (see Assumption 5). However, when an adjective or letter is presented first, say "red" or "A," the activation spreads to a much wider set of concepts, which are not particularly interlinked with each other. Thus, the large variety of different things that are red or that start with the letter A will receive relatively little priming when the adjective or letter are given first. Because priming the noun leads to a greater accumulation of activation on the instances, these are closer to their threshold for firing, so that it takes less stimulation, and hence less time, to trigger an intersection when the second stimulus is presented.

Freedman and Loftus (1971) explained their finding in terms of entering the category when a noun is presented and entering a cluster within the category when the adjective or letter is presented. Thus if the noun is presented first, the subject can enter the category immediately and need only choose the correct cluster when the adjective or letter is presented. But if the adjective or letter is presented first, the subject must wait until the category is presented, because the cluster is specific to that category. (However, Loftus, Note 2, has revised this explanation for the letter stimulus in her dictionary-network model.)

The Freedman and Loftus explanation is not altogether different from the explanation offered here, though our theory is less rigidly hierarchical. The rigid hierarchy gets into trouble with errors such as one we encountered where a subject produced "Ben Franklin," given the stimulus pair "president" and "F," although he later recognized his mistake. In an activation theory, "Franklin" is a very likely intersection starting at "president" and "F," because he is so closely linked with the concept, "president," and some of its foremost instances, such as "Washington." Such a wrong intersection was likely in this case because the correct answer (prior to Ford) was "Fillmore," who is rather inaccessible and unlikely to be found quickly enough to preclude finding "Franklin." Once such an intersection is found, it is only by evaluating the connection between "president" and "Franklin," that it can be rejected (see Assumptions 8–13). It is a general problem of category-search models that they cannot deal with such errors.

Perhaps the major advantage of the spreading-activation theory over the Freedman and Loftus (1971) explanation is in tying their result to a parallel result in a quite different experiment by Loftus (1973b). In a categorization experiment, Loftus found that the direction of the association between the category and the instance determined whether subjects were faster when given the category first or the instance first. In the experiment she used four kinds of category-instance pairs: (a) pairs where both the category and instance evoked the other with high frequency (e.g., "tree–oak"); (b) pairs where the category evoked the instance with high frequency, but the instance evoked the category with low frequency (e.g., "seafood–shrimp"); (c) pairs where the category evoked the instance with low frequency, but the instance evoked the category with high frequency (e.g., "insect–butterfly"); and (d) pairs where both the category and instance evoked the other with low frequency (e.g., "cloth–orlon"). When the category was presented before the instance, reaction time for Conditions (a) and (b) was approximately equal and significantly faster than for Conditions (c) and (d). However, when the instance was presented first, reaction time for Conditions (a) and (c) was approximately equal and significantly faster than for Conditions (b) and (d). That is to say, subjects are fast when the category is presented first, if the category evokes the instance with high frequency, and subjects are fast when the instance is presented first, if the instance evokes the category with high frequency. The spreading-activation theory explains the pattern of reaction times in the following way, assuming that production frequency is a measure of the strength or accessibility of the path from one concept to another. When the first concept (i.e., the one presented first) evokes the second with a relatively high frequency, this means that more activation spreads to the second, and it takes less time to reach the threshold for an intersection. Thus, the amount the first concept primes the second concept determines the reaction time.

By comparing this experiment with the Freedman and Loftus (1971) study, it can be seen that the two results are exactly parallel. Based on our structural assumptions, "fruit" primes "apple" more than "red" or the letter "A" primes "apple" in the Freedman and Loftus study. Hence, the shorter reaction time occurs when "fruit" or "A" is presented first. Similarly in the Loftus (1973b) study, when the category primes the instance most highly, the shortest reaction times occur when the category is presented first. But when the instance primes the category most highly, the shortest reaction times occur when the instance is presented first. A spreading-activation explanation is quite compelling to account for the Loftus (1973b) results, and the theory offered here encompasses the order effect in both the Loftus study and the earlier Freedman and Loftus experiment within a single framework.

Recently Loftus (Note 2) has found two different ways in which presenting a letter acts differently from presenting an adjective, in variations of the

Freedman and Loftus paradigm. This has led her to the development of a dictionary-network model, which we will translate into spreading-activation terms. The first difference between presenting a letter and an adjective appeared when Grober and Loftus (1974) compared reaction time in two conditions: one where noun-adjective (e.g., "fruit–red") and noun–letter (e.g., "fruit–A") trials were randomly intermixed, and one where noun–adjective and noun–letter trials were separated into blocks. In all cases the noun preceded the adjective or letter. The results of this experiment are shown in Figure 2. It is clear that when the subject knows a letter is coming, he can prepare for it. But in the mixed condition, the subject apparently prepares for either kind of trial the same way he prepares for an adjective trial, since adjective trials take the same amount of time in either case. The theory's description of semantic processing on the adjective trials is the same as that given earlier for the Freedman and Loftus (1971) experiment, with the amendment that only the semantic network and not the lexical network would be diffusely primed before the adjective is presented. When an intersection is found in the semantic network, then the subject must retrieve the name from the lexical network.

Loftus (Note 2) described what must happen on noun-letter trials in the blocked condition as follows:

> The first step of the process is entering the category. The next step is a quasi-parallel simultaneous search towards the Dictionary. That is to say, the subject traces some number of pathways leading from

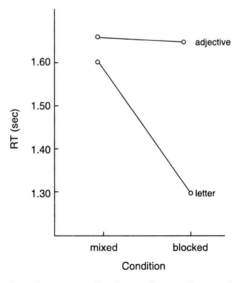

Figure 2 Reaction time for noun-adjective and noun-letter stimuli in mixed and blocked conditions (from Loftus, Note 2).

category instances to the Dictionary representations of those instances. This step can be started during the interval between the presentation of the category name and the restricting letter *if* the subject knows a letter is coming. (p. 13)

This is essentially the spreading-activation explanation, if the dictionary is taken to be a lexical network. Rather than saying that "the subject traces some number of pathways," which suggests a conscious tracing process, the present theory would say that activation spreads along some number of pathways, because the subject has activated the lexical network in addition to the semantic network (see Assumption 7). Hence, in the present explanation, the subject's control is reduced to diffusely activating whole networks rather than specific pathways (in addition to the specific nodes activated by the stimuli in the experiment). The difference in the results for the noun–letter trials in the two conditions then depends on whether the subject primes both networks (as in the blocked condition) or only the semantic network (as in the mixed condition). The reason he only activates the semantic network in the mixed condition may be either because of a principle of least effort (hence he could speed up his reaction time if he tried) or because there is less activation available to the semantic network if both are primed (hence he will be slower on noun–adjective trials if he primes both).

As can be seen in Figure 2, the subject is much slower on noun–adjective trials than on noun–letter trials in the blocked condition. This is accounted for by the fact that an intersection on a noun–adjective trial occurs in the semantic network and requires the further step of retrieving the corresponding name in the lexical network. On the other hand, the intersection on a noun–letter trial occurs at the name in the lexical network. Therefore, the name does not then need to be retrieved.

The second result that shows up the difference between adjectives and letters was predicted by Loftus from the dictionary-network model. In this experiment (Loftus & Cole, 1974) subjects saw three stimuli, ordered either noun, adjective, letter or noun, letter, adjective. For example, the three stimuli might be "animal," "small," and "M," for which an appropriate response is "mouse." The prediction was that the subject should be faster when the adjective is presented before the letter, and this was the result found. The reasoning is as follows: When the adjective appears before the letter, activation will spread from a small set of instances in the semantic network to the lexical network where the intersection occurs, since the letter can be expected just as in the blocked condition. When the letter is presented before the adjective, activation will spread from a small set of instances in the lexical network back to the semantic network where an intersection with the adjective will occur. Then the subject must return again to the lexical network to retrieve the name, so there is an extra transit necessary in this condition.

Loftus has also run a series of experiments in which subjects were asked to produce a member of a category and a short time later asked to produce a different member of that category (Loftus, 1973a; Loftus, Senders, & Turkletaub, 1974; Loftus & Loftus, 1974). This was accomplished by showing a category–letter pair (e.g., "fruit–P"), which asked the subject for an appropriate instance, then following 0, 1, or 2 intervening items, showing the same category paired with a different letter (e.g., "fruit–A"), which asked for a different instance. The general finding is that reaction time for the second instance is shorter than reaction time for the first instance and increases monotonically with the number of intervening items. For example, in Loftus (1973a) a subject's baseline time to name a fruit beginning with the letter "P" was 1.52 sec. However, it took him 1.22 sec to produce the same response if he had named a different fruit on the previous trial and 1.29 sec to produce the response if he had named a different fruit two trials back.

The spreading-activation theory predicts these results by assuming that when an item is processed, other items are activated to the extent that they are closely related to that item. That is, retrieving one category member produces a spread of activation to other category members, facilitating their later retrieval. The assumption (Assumption 3) that activation decreases over time or trials predicts the lag effect.

Meyer and Schvaneveldt (Meyer, 1973; Meyer & Schvaneveldt, 1971; Schvaneveldt & Meyer, 1973; Meyer, Schvaneveldt, & Ruddy, Note 3) have also shown that the time to retrieve information from memory is faster if related information has been accessed a short time previously. Their paradigm is somewhat different. Subjects were required to classify letter strings as words or nonwords. The general finding was that the response time to classify a letter string as a word is faster if the subject has just classified a semantically similar word as opposed to a semantically dissimilar word. Thus, for example, the time it takes to classify "butter" as a word is faster if "butter" is preceded by "bread" than if it is preceded by "nurse." Their results have led Meyer and Schvaneveldt to an explanation in terms of spreading activation and illustrate the widely different paradigms that such a theory can encompass.

Juola and Atkinson's study with multiple categories

An increase in reaction time with multiple categories has been found by Juola and Atkinson (1971) in a task where subjects had to decide whether a stimulus word belonged to one of a variable number (1–4) of pre-specified (target) categories. They compared this task with one where subjects decided if the stimulus word was the same as one of a variable number (1–4) of target words. Their experiment was designed to distinguish between two kinds of models, one they attribute to Landauer and Freedman (1968) and one they attribute to Collins and Quillian (1970a). In most respects, their results fit the model they derived from Landauer and Freedman, but since the spreading-activation theory provides an alternative explanation for their results, we want to compare their two models with our theory.

The model Juola and Atkinson (1971) derived from Landauer and Freedman (1968) is very similar to what Landauer and Meyer (1972) call the "category-search model." It assumes that the subject searches through instances of the categories in memory seeking a match for the stimulus word. Such a model predicts that as the number of categories or words in the memory set increases, reaction time for the category-matching task should increase at a greater slope than reaction time for the word-matching task. This is because each additional target category adds more instances that must be searched, whereas each additional target word only adds one, the word itself. This result was essentially what Juola and Atkinson found.

The model they ascribed to Collins and Quillian (1970a) assumed that subjects perform the category-matching task by retrieving their stored category for the stimulus word and comparing this to the given categories to see if it matches one of them. This model would predict that the slope for the two tasks should be about the same, and the intercept for the category-matching task should be greater than for the word-matching task. Their results clearly reject this model. Although attributed to Collins and Quillian, this model is quite different from Quillian's theory, because the semantic search in Quillian's (1966) theory is assumed to spread in parallel from both categories and instances. When the categories are given first, as in Juola and Atkinson's experiment, then activation would spread out from the categories before the instance even appeared.

In order to explain our interpretation of Juola and Atkinson's results, it is necessary to describe their procedure in more detail. They chose 10 large categories and 12 common instances from each category as stimuli. This makes a total of 120 instances in all. In the word-matching task, they presented from 1 to 4 of the 120 instances as targets on each trial. In the category-matching task, they presented from 1 to 4 of the 10 categories as targets on each trial. In both cases the negative stimuli were chosen from the same set of 120 instances. In the word-matching task, then, the discrimination necessary to categorize the stimulus was between one of the target words or a word that had not occurred as a target for a large number of trials (on the average about 24 trials earlier). In the category-matching task, however, the discrimination was between a word in one of the target categories and a word in one of the categories from a recent trial (on the average about 2 trials earlier). The discrimination, therefore, was rather easy in the word-matching task and quite difficult in the category-matching task.

What we think must be happening in the task is that the discrimination between positive and negative responses is made (at least partly) on the basis of activation level. In the category-matching task, as the number of categories increases, the amount of activation allocated to each category decreases (see Assumptions 2 and 3). Furthermore, activation will be left over from previous trials on the categories corresponding to negative instances, though it will have partly decayed (Assumption 3). For example, suppose "tree" was a target category on a particular trial and "body part" was not, but "body part" was a target on a previous trial. Then "tree" will have a higher activation level than "body part," but the difference will not be very large because "body part" was presented so recently. If a positive instance such as "oak" is presented, it will intersect with "tree"; if a negative instance such as "arm" is presented, it will intersect with "body part." The less activation on "tree," which depends on how many other targets there are, the harder it is to discriminate that it is in fact a target or that "body part" is not a target. The more difficult the discrimination is, the longer it takes to make, and thus there will be a fairly large effect of the size of the target set on reaction time.

In the word-matching task, however, the difference in activation level as the number of targets is varied will not be so critical a factor. This is because the absolute difference between the activation level of targets and nontargets is so much greater in the word-matching task, given Juola and Atkinson's experimental procedure. That is to say, each nontarget was presented as a target so many trials previously (approximately 24) that the activation level for a nontarget would have decayed (Assumption 3) to a very low activation level as compared to any target. Hence, the large absolute difference in activation levels between targets and non-targets makes the differences due to target-set size relatively unimportant.

In conclusion, the spreading-activation theory's explanation of Juola and Atkinson's (1971) results is that the effect of differences in activation level due to target-set size matter more when the discrimination is difficult and matter less when the discrimination is easier. Furthermore, as Juola and Atkinson point out, there are two aspects of their data (namely, the fact that the data for positive responses are not linear, and the marked recency effects in the serial position curves) that fit much better with a parallel model, such as spreading-activation theory, than they do with a serial model, such as the one they derive from Landauer and Freedman (1968).

There are two implications of this view that could be tested fairly easily. One is that reaction time to decide that an instance such as "arm" is a negative instance will depend on the recency with which "body part" was presented as a target category. The more recent its presentation, the longer it will take to say "no." A more global implication is simply that the slope of the curve with respect to target size depends on those factors that affect the difficulty of discrimination, such as the recency with which negative instances occurred as targets (and probably as nontargets as well). This has important implications for the memory-search literature as a whole.

Conrad's study

Using a true–false reaction time technique for sentences (e.g., the task is to decide whether "A salmon can eat" is true or false), Conrad (1972) found results which she interpreted as contradictory to Quillian's (1966, 1969) theory of semantic processing. In fact, the results of her study are quite close to what Quillian's theory would predict given Conrad's methodology.

In her first experiment, which was like the Collins and Quillian (1969) study, Conrad selected 2-level and 3-level hierarchies from the common culture (e.g. salmon→fish→animal) and properties associated with the objects at different levels. Then she constructed sentences with instances, such as "salmon," from the lowest level and properties from all three levels. The results Collins and Quillian found were that reaction time increased as the property was farther removed from the instance in the hierarchy. The reason for the increases in reaction time according to spreading-activation theory is that as the instance and property are farther apart in the hierarchy, it takes activation longer to spread between them and to trigger an intersection (and perhaps to evaluate the path found as well).

Unlike Collins and Quillian (1969), Conrad (1972) broke down the properties in her sentences into three groups on the basis of the frequency (high, medium, low) with which people generated each property, given the different objects in the hierarchies. Another difference from Collins and Quillian's study is that she collected data over 5 days by repeating all the sentences each day.

The results of her first experiment were generally in the same direction as the increases in reaction time that Collins and Quillian found when the property was farther removed from the instance in the hierarchy. There was one reversal in her data out of nine comparisons, and this occurred for the high-frequency properties, where it was not unexpected given the weak theory of cognitive economy (as we will argue below). However, the increases she found were much smaller on the average than those of Collins and Quillian. The weak theory of cognitive economy predicts that people store a property with whatever instance it is linked to in a sentence, so Conrad's repetition of sentences over 5 days should lead to the smaller reaction time increases she found. This is because an inference necessary on the first day would be less likely on the second day, and so on. Conrad, in fact, reports a large Level × Day interaction.

In general, Conrad found that the higher the frequency of the property, the smaller the increases between levels. Given the weak theory of cognitive economy, we would expect that high-frequency properties are more likely to be stored at several levels in the hierarchy, because they are more likely to be encountered in contexts involving specific instances. For example, "leaves" are more likely to be stored as a property with particular types of trees (such as "maple" and "oak") than is "bark," because leaves are a higher frequency property. Thus, the effect of property frequency found by Conrad is consistent with the weak theory.

Conrad (1972) argued that Collins and Quillian's (1969) results could be explained by a confounding of property level and property frequency. Her argument was that the sentences Collins and Quillian used may have been based on high-frequency properties for Level 1 sentences (e.g., "A salmon is pink"), moderate-frequency properties for Level 2 sentences (e.g., "A salmon has fins"), and low-frequency properties for Level 3 sentences (e.g., "A salmon can eat"). To support her argument, she showed that if one plots her reaction time data in the above way, one obtains approximately the same slope as Collins and Quillian did, whereas if one plots the slope for low-, medium-, or high-frequency properties separately, one obtains much smaller slopes.

However, there are two weaknesses in Conrad's argument. First, she did not use her frequency data to evaluate systematically the frequency of the properties in Collins and Quillian's sentences, so her conjecture about such a confounding had no empirical basis. Collins and Quillian (1969) did obtain subject ratings of importance of the property for the relevant level concept, which should correlate with Conrad's frequency measure. These ratings averaged 1.90 for Level 1 sentences, 1.92 for Level 2 sentences, and 2.16 for Level 3 sentences (based on a 5-point scale, where 1 = very important and 5 = not important). These are small differences and certainly do not support the notion that the slope between Level 1 and Level 2 sentences was due to the confounding Conrad hypothesized. The difference between Level 3 sentences and the others may have contributed to the greater slope that Collins and Quillian found, but even that is doubtful. For those subjects who had sentences with all 3 levels, the slope was actually larger (approximately 100 msec rather than 75 msec), but this was offset by a group of subjects who were slower overall and saw only Level 1 and 2 sentences. So the latter group acted to cancel out any exaggeration of the slope due to the lower importance of Level 3 properties.

Second, the comparison Conrad (1972) made in plotting her data against Collins and Quillian's data compared data based on five responses to the same sentence with data based on one response to a sentence. As indicated above, the weak theory of cognitive economy predicts that repetition of a sentence makes an inference less likely and should reduce the slopes in the way Conrad found. A fairer comparison would be between her data on the first day and Collins and Quillian's data. But even that comparison has the problem that she may well have included sentences of the kind, "A maple has leaves," where the property is a general property of trees, but where most people would store it as a property of maples as well. This suggests that the fairest comparison is between Collins and Quillian's data and her data on the first day for low-frequency properties, where the properties were least likely to be stored at more than one level. But we cannot make this comparison because she did not break down her data by days. In conclusion, the differences between the two experiments and the fact that the only relevant data do not particularly support the conjecture about a confounding of property level and property frequency make Conrad's argument rather tenuous.

It was Conrad's second experiment that appears more damaging to Quillian's theory, but here she made a crucial methodological change. She presented the object 1 sec before the property, and this turned the experiment into a priming study. In the study she presented properties true of the highest level nodes, together with objects (e.g., "salmon," "fish," or "animal") at different levels in the hierarchy. Therefore, she predicted from Quillian's theory that the lower level objects, such as "salmon," would take longer to confirm, since it would take activation longer to spread between lower level objects and higher level properties. But by presenting the object 1 sec before the property and by using only high-level properties, she made it possible for her subjects to prepare during the interval by priming the object's superordinates. For example, if a subject saw "salmon," his best strategy was to retrieve the superordinates, "fish" and "animal," because the property to appear would be a high-level property, such as "eating." In these circumstances, there is little reason to expect systematic differences between objects such as "salmon," "fish," and "animal." Thus, this particular experiment had real methodological problems as a test of Quillian's theory, and it is weaker evidence *against* spreading-activation theory than her first experiment is evidence *for* the theory.

Effects of typicality and semantic relatedness in categorization tasks

In recent experiments, Rips et al. (1973), Rosch (1973), and Smith et al. (1974) have shown that reaction time in a categorization task corresponds very closely to ratings of how typical the instance is of the category. For example, robins and sparrows are considered typical birds whereas chickens and geese are not. The effect of typicality on reaction time is quite large even when frequency of the particular instances in the language is controlled. Like Smith et al., we would argue that the typicality effect is one more manifestation of the fact that semantic similarity speeds up positive decisions and slows down negative decisions. Such an effect has been found repeatedly (Collins & Quillian, 1969, 1970a, 1972b; Schaeffer & Wallace, 1969, 1970; Wilkins, 1971). While Landauer and Meyer (1972) argued that the evidence for similarity effect at that time was either questionable or artifactual, the evidence now seems so overwhelming that any viable theory must account for them. They are very damaging to the category-search model.

There are two reasons why spreading-activation theory predicts that atypical instances will take longer to categorize than typical instances. The most important reason derives from the way evidence is aggregated (see Assumptions 8–13). Because different connections that are found are combined as evidence, distinguishing properties can slow down a positive decision based on a superordinate connection or on matching properties. For example, the decision that a chicken is a bird (i.e., an atypical instance) might be made on the basis of a superordinate connection from "chicken" to "bird," which people learn because chickens are frequently referred to as birds. But the fact that people eat chickens, that they are raised on farms, and that they are rather large are all properties that distinguish chickens from most birds. If these distinguishing properties are found during the memory search, as some are likely to be, they act to slow down the positive decision, because they are negative evidence. Similarly, matching properties can slow down a negative decision. For example, the decision that a goose is not a duck might be made on the basis of the difference in their necks (a distinguishing property) or simply because they are stored as mutually exclusive kinds of birds (see Assumption 12), but the matching properties that are found (e.g., their affinity to ponds, their webbed feet, their large size) will slow down the decision that they are different. The argument here is similar to that of Smith et al. (1974), which we will discuss in comparing the two theories.

The second reason for the typicality effects relates to those cases where a superordinate connection is found. As we indicated earlier, superordinate links differ in accessibility (or strength), and accessibility depends on use. If a person frequently uses the link that a robin is a bird, and less frequently uses the link that a chicken is a bird (assuming approximately equal frequency for chickens and robins), then the accessibility of "bird" from "robin" will be greater than from "chicken." Because of this, accessibility will be highly correlated with typicality ratings. All the factors acting to make a chicken or a goose an atypical bird in the real world will also act to make the use of the superordinate link in a person's mind from "chicken" or "goose" to "bird" infrequent. It is because they are atypical that the superordinate link is weak, and this will also act to slow down reaction time in making categorization judgments about atypical instances.

The way evidence is aggregated in the theory also explains the common finding (Collins & Quillian, 1970a, 1972b; Holyoak & Glass, 1975; Rips et al., 1974) that people are fast to decide that semantically unrelated concepts are different (e.g., that a book is not a dog). In comparing such concepts, there are not likely to be any superordinate connections, and almost all property connections will involve distinguishing rather than matching properties. Therefore, almost all the connections found will constitute negative evidence, and subjects will be quite fast to reach the negative criterion in such cases. This too is similar to the explanation in the Smith et al (1974) model.

Recently, Holyoak and Glass (1975) have isolated two different cases where semantic relatedness or typicality does not produce the usual effect on reaction time for negative judgments. One case arises when the decision depends on what they call a contradiction and what we have called mutually exclusive subordinates. The other case arises when the decision depends on a counterexample.

In the first case, Holyoak and Glass found that people are faster to reject sentences such as "All fruits are vegetables" or "Some chairs are tables" than sentences such as "All fruits are flowers" or "Some chairs are beds." In these four sentences the two nouns are mutually exclusive subordinates. The difference between the sentences is that "vegetables" and "tables" are generated with high frequency, while "flowers" and "beds" are generated with low frequency, when subjects are given the frame "All fruits are . . ." or "Some chairs are . . ." and asked to produce a false sentence. This difference is in the opposite direction of the usual finding that negative judgments are slower when the two concepts are more closely related semantically. The explanation for this reversal according to the theory (and to Holyoak and Glass) is that people make these decisions not on the basis of distinguishing properties (though some might be considered), but because they are stored as mutually exclusive subordinates (Assumption 12). Generation frequency in this case is a measure of the strength of the connection between the two concepts and therefore of how long it will take to find the contradiction between the two mutually exclusive concepts.

The second finding of Holyoak and Glass (1975) involves sentences where people reject the sentence by finding a counterexample (Assumption 13). For example, "All animals are birds," can be rejected by finding another kind of animal, such as a mammal. In this case Holyoak and Glass varied the production frequency of the predicate noun (e.g., "birds") independently of the production frequency of the counterexample (e.g., "mammals"). Their finding was that reaction time depended not on the production frequency of the predicate noun (which is a measure of the semantic relatedness of the concepts in the sentence) but on the frequency of producing a counterexample. Here again where a decision strategy that is not based on distinguishing properties is appropriate, the reaction time data do not depend on the semantic relatedness of the two concepts.

The importance of these two findings by Holyoak and Glass (1975), in our view, is that they demonstrate that different kinds of evidence can be involved in making categorization judgments. This suggests that approaches such as that of Meyer (1970) and Smith et al. (1974), which try to formulate a single strategy for making such judgments, will inevitably fail.

Relation of the theory to the model of Smith, Shoben, and Rips

Quillian's (1966, 1969) theory was a forerunner of a number of global theories of semantic processing based on network representations, in particular those of Anderson and Bower (1973), Norman and Rumelhart (1975), and

Schank (1972). These theorists have made important advances on the Quillian theory (especially in the representation of acts and causes) which in no way contradict the basic thrust of Quillian's theory. There are some differences between these theories and Quillian's, but the basic intent of this paper is to deal with those aspects of semantic processing where the model of Smith et al. (1974) is the major competitor to Quillian's theory.

Unlike the various network models, the model of Smith et al. represents concepts as bundles of semantic features. Their model has the virtues of being quite clear and explicit, and it agrees quite well with the reaction time data for categorization judgments, except for the Holyoak and Glass (1975) results. Because it is such an initially compelling model, we want to emphasize how it differs from spreading-activation theory and point out what we think are its inherent difficulties.

In the model of Smith et al. (1974), the meaning of a concept is assumed to be represented by semantic features of two kinds: defining features and characteristic features. Defining features are those that an instance must have to be a member of the concept, and the model assumes that features can be more or less defining. Characteristic features are those that are commonly associated with the concept, but are not necessary for concept membership. For example, "wings" might be a defining feature of "birds" and "flying" a characteristic feature, since all birds have wings but not all fly. In a categorization task, the model assumes that the two concepts are first compared in Stage 1 with respect to all their features, both characteristic and defining. If the match is above a positive criterion, the subject answers "yes"; if it is below a negative criterion, the subject answers "no"; and if it is in-between, the subject makes a second comparison in Stage 2 based on just the defining features. If the instance has all the defining features of the category, the subject says "yes" and otherwise says "no." If the subject can decide in Stage 1, his reaction time will be faster than if he decides in Stage 2.

There are several minor differences between the model of Smith et al. (1974) and the spreading-activation theory that could be minimized by slightly changing their model. The difference in wording between comparing features in their model and finding links between properties in our theory is really a nondifference. But the distinction between defining and characteristic features has the inherent difficulty, pointed out through the ages, that there is no feature that is absolutely necessary for any category.[4] For example, if one removes the wings from a bird, it does not stop being a bird. Furthermore, we doubt if people can make consistent decisions as to whether a feature is defining or characteristic, either from time to time or from one person to another. Smith et al. recognized that features are more or less defining (or criterial), but they were forced into making the artificial distinction between defining and characteristic in order to have a two-stage model. Still, the model could be revised to work without the two stages and make essentially the same reaction time predictions.

The revision is as follows: If features are compared over time, as in Quillian's (1966) theory, then as the process goes on longer, more features will be compared (assuming features have different accessibilities). The comparison process can have a positive criterion and a negative criterion just as before, and features can be weighted by their criteriality. If the match at any point in time is above the positive criterion, the subject says "yes"; if the match falls below the negative criterion, the subject says "no"; and otherwise he goes on comparing features. Finally, if he is running out of relevant information, he says "I don't know." This is simply the Bayesian decision model described in Assumption 9 of the extended theory, where the evidence consists of matching and mismatching features as in the property comparison of Assumption 11.

Thus, we agree that a decision process similar to the one that Smith et al. (1974) postulate does occur for *some* categorization decisions. But there is a fundamental disagreement, because they argue that *all* categorizations judgments are made by comparing features of the instance and category, whereas we argue that people use whatever evidence they find, including superordinate links.

Because they exclude the use of superordinate links, the model of Smith et al. has several inherent difficulties. The most obvious is the assumption that even when people have superordinate information stored, they do not use it. While most people may not have learned some superordinate relations (e.g., that a beaver is a mammal, or a sled is a vehicle), there are many they have learned (e.g., that a wren is a bird, and a beaver is an animal). Why would they not use such information if it is stored? How in fact can they avoid using it? It is an unlikely model which postulates that people use information that is less relevant to make a decision, instead of information that is more relevant.

Another obvious difficulty with the Smith et al. (1974) model is that people seldom know the defining properties of concepts. For example, consider whether a whale is a mammal, a sponge is an animal, a bat is a bird, or a wren is a sparrow. In the Smith et al. model, these difficult (and slow) decisions would be made in Stage 2 on the basis of defining properties. But people generally have no idea what the defining properties of a mammal, an animal, a bird, or a sparrow are. Even if they know that one of the most criterial properties for being a mammal is that it bears its young alive, it seems highly unlikely that they know whether whales (or beavers for that matter) bear their young alive. Neither of the authors has any idea what properties of a sponge make it an animal, but if asked in an experiment whether a sponge was an animal, we would answer "yes," and we would be comparatively slow about it. The reason we would answer "yes" is simply that we were told at one time that a sponge is an animal. We were also told that a bat is not a bird, and if we had not been told, we fear we might have responded "yes" if asked whether a bat is a bird in a categorization experiment. The decision that a wren is not a sparrow would be made because they are mutually exclusive kinds of birds (See assumption 12). They are both small song-birds, and it is hard to believe that many people know what the defining features of a sparrow are that a wren does not have. The fact that there are cases where people must use superordinate information to make correct categorization judgments makes it unlikely that they do not use such information in other cases where they could make the decision simply by matching features or properties. This is one of the strongest arguments for a hybrid theory.

We would like to close this section by raising the question of why one should adopt such a complicated theory when the Smith et al. (1974) model is simpler and predicts the reaction time data quite well. We have tried to stress the inherent difficulties that their model has in ignoring superordinate information and in relying on defining properties. Experimental tests can probably be devised that will show up those difficulties. We will suggest one such test, but first we might point out that the results of the Loftus (1973b) categorization experiment described earlier do not fit the Smith et al. model very well. If a person is merely comparing features between the instance and the category, then it should not matter whether the instance or category is presented first. It is the asymmetry in the superordinate connections that predicts the asymmetry Loftus found in reaction time, and it is hard to imagine how one could have an asymmetry of that kind in comparing features of two concepts.

One experiment that might show difficulties with the Smith et al. (1974) model is a categorization task. The categories and instances used are based on their multidimensional scaling of birds and animals on the one hand, and mammals and animals on the other. As both Collins and Quillian (Note 4) and Rips et al. (1973) report, subjects are faster at deciding that bird names are in the category "bird" than in the category "animal," whereas they are slower at deciding that mammal names are in the category "mammal" than in the category "animal." Collins and Quillian argue that this is the way people learn the superordinates: that pigeons are birds and lions are animals. Smith et al. argue that it is based on shared features, and they show by their scaling solution that most birds are closer to "bird" than to "animal," and most mammals are closer to "animal" than to "mammal." But there are several bird names that are closer to "animal" than to "bird" (in particular, "goose," "chicken," and "duck"; "pigeon" is equidistant), and there are several mammal names that are closer to "mammal" than "animal" (in particular, "deer," "bear," and "lion"; "horse" is equidistant). We would predict that even for those instances the above pattern would hold, whereas a pure feature-matching theory, such as the Smith et al. model, makes the opposite prediction. So this is a possible test of the two theories. There are undoubtedly many other tests.

Finally, we want to explain why we have been led to such a complicated theory. In trying to write computer programs that answer different types of questions, it becomes apparent that any decision procedure that gives correct answers must be flexible enough to deal with many different configurations of knowledge in memory. This is because people have incomplete knowledge about the world (see Collins et al., 1975), and they often do not have stored particular superordinate links or criterial properties. Any realistic data base for a computer system will have this same kind of incomplete knowledge. Therefore, perhaps our strongest criticism of the Smith et al. (1974) model is that it breaks down when people lack knowledge about defining features.

While at one level this is a complicated theory, at another level it is a simpler theory than the Smith et al. model. By viewing superordinate links as highly criterial properties, the theory becomes a simple Bayesian model. It is only in specifying the particular configurations of knowledge that constitute positive or negative evidence for the Bayesian process that the theory becomes complicated. The difference between the two theories is that the Smith et al. model allows only one kind of evidence (matching or mismatching features), whereas the theory presented here allows other kinds of evidence as well. Thus the theory encompasses a revised version of the Smith et al. model as a special case of a more general procedure.

Conclusion

We have extended Quillian's spreading-activation theory of semantic processing in order to deal with a number of experiments that have been performed on semantic memory in recent years. The result is a fairly complicated theory with enough generality to apply to results from many different experimental paradigms. The theory can also be considered as a prescription for building human semantic processing in a computer, though at that level many details are omitted about decision strategies for different judgments that arise in language processing (see Carbonell & Collins, 1973; Collins et al., 1975; Quillian, 1969). We would argue that the adequacy of a psychological theory should no longer be measured solely by its ability to predict experimental data. It is also important that a theory be sufficiently powerful to produce the behavior that it purports to explain.

Notes

This research was supported by the National Institute of Education, U.S. Department of Health, Education, and Welfare, Project 1–0420, under Contract OEC-1-71-0100(508) with Bolt Beranek and Newman Inc. Revision of the paper was supported by a grant from the John Simon Guggenheim Memorial Foundation to the first author. We would like to thank Stephen Woods, Colin MacLeod, Mark L. Miller, and the reviewers for their comments on previous drafts of this paper.

1 Quillian's theory of priming appeared in the unpublished version of the 1967 paper (i.e., CIP Paper No. 79, Carnegie Institute of Technology, 1965).

2 There can be intersections with more than two starting nodes, but we have limited our discussion in this paper to the case of two nodes (as did Quillian, 1966, initially). The basic assumptions in Quillian's theory and our elaboration can apply to intersections with more than two starting nodes, but this leads to complications in the evaluation of intersections. Some of these were discussed by Quillian (1969) in regard to comprehension, but for the experiments considered in this paper, only the case of two starting nodes needs to be considered.

3 Semantic relatedness is a slightly different notion from semantic distance, though the two terms are sometimes used interchangeably. Semantic distance is the distance along the shortest path, and semantic relatedness (or similarity) is an aggregate of all the paths. Two concepts may be close in distance, say by a path through "red," and still not be closely related because that is the only path. Our use of *close* to refer to both relationships is admittedly confusing. In this paper we shall use close to refer to relatedness or similarity, though in some tasks (Quillian, 1966) it is only distance that matters.

4 There is for living things a biologists' taxonomy, which categorizes objects using properties that are not always those most apparent to the layman. Thus, there are arbitrary, technical definitions that are different from the layman's ill-defined concepts, but this is not true in most domains. There is no technical definition of a game, a vehicle, or a country that is generally accepted.

Reference notes

1. Wilkins, A. J. *Categories and the internal lexicon.* Paper presented at the meeting of the Experimental Psychology Society, Oxford, England, 1972.
2. Loftus, E. F. *How to catch a zebra in semantic memory.* Paper presented at the Minnesota Conference on Cognition, Knowledge, and Adaptation, Minneapolis, 1973.
3. Meyer, D. E., Schvaneveldt, R. W., & Ruddy, M. G. *Activation of lexical memory.* Paper presented at the meeting of the Psychonomic Society, St. Louis, 1972.
4. Collins, A. M., & Quillian, M. R. *Categories and subcategories in semantic memory.* Paper presented at the meeting of the Psychonomic Society, St. Louis, 1971.

References

Anderson, J. R., & Bower, G. H. *Human associative memory.* Washington, D.C.: V. H. Winston, 1973.

Anderson, R. C., & McGaw, B. On the representation of meanings of general terms. *Journal of Experimental Psychology*, 1973, *101*, 301–306.

Bell, A., & Quillian, M. R. Capturing concepts in a semantic net. In E. L. Jacks (Ed.), *Associative information techniques.* New York: American Elsevier, 1971.

Brown, R. W., & McNeill, D. The "tip of the tongue" phenomenon. *Journal of Verbal Learning and Verbal Behavior*, 1966, *6*, 325–337.

Carbonell, J. R., & Collins, A. M. Natural semantics in artificial intelligence. *Proceedings of the Third International Joint Conference on Artificial Intelligence*, 1973, 344–351.

Collins, A. M., & Quillian, M. R. Retrieval time from semantic memory. *Journal of Verbal Learning and Verbal Behavior*, 1969, *8*, 240–248.

Collins, A. M., & Quillian, M. R. Does category size affect categorization time? *Journal of Verbal Learning and Verbal Behavior*, 1970, *9*, 432–438. (a)

Collins, A. M., & Quillian, M. R. Facilitating retrieval from semantic memory: The effect of repeating part of an inference. *Acta Psychologica*, 1970, *33*, 304–314. (b)

Collins, A. M., & Quillian, M. R. Experiments on semantic memory and language comprehension. In L. W. Gregg (Ed.), *Cognition in learning and memory*. New York: Wiley, 1972. (a)

Collins, A. M., & Quillian, M. R. How to make a language user. In E. Tulving & W. Donaldson (Eds.), *Organization of memory*. New York: Academic Press, 1972. (b)

Collins, A., Warnock, E. H., Aiello, N., & Miller, M. L. Reasoning from incomplete knowledge. In D. G. Bobrow & A. Collins (Eds.), *Representation and understanding: Studies in cognitive science*. New York: Academic Press, 1975.

Conrad, C. Cognitive economy in semantic memory. *Journal of Experimental Psychology*, 1972, *92*, 149–154.

Fitts, P. M. Cognitive aspects of information processing: III. Set for speed versus accuracy. *Journal of Experimental Psychology*, 1966, *71*, 849–857.

Freedman, J. L., & Loftus, E. F. Retrieval of words from long-term memory. *Journal of Verbal Learning and Verbal Behavior*, 1971, *10*, 107–115.

Grober, E., & Loftus, E. F. Semantic memory: Searching for attributes versus searching for names. *Memory & Cognition*, 1974, *2*, 413–416.

Hollan, J. D. Features and semantic memory: Set-theoretic or network model? *Psychological Review*, 1975, *82*, 154–155.

Holyoak, K. J., & Glass, A. L. The role of contradictions and counterexamples in the rejection of false sentences. *Journal of Verbal Learning and Verbal Behavior*, 1975, *14*, 215–239.

Juola, J. F., & Atkinson, R. C. Memory scanning for words versus categories. *Journal of Verbal Learning and Verbal Behavior*, 1971, *10*, 522–527.

Landauer, T. K., & Freedman, J. L. Information retrieval from long-term memory: Category size and recognition time. *Journal of Verbal Learning and Verbal Behavior*, 1968, *7*, 291–295.

Landauer, T. K., & Meyer, D. E. Category size and semantic memory retrieval. *Journal of Verbal Learning and Verbal Behavior*, 1972, *11*, 539–549.

Loftus, E. F. Activation of semantic memory. *American Journal of Psychology*, 1973, *86*, 331–337. (a)

Loftus, E. F. Category dominance, instance dominance, and categorization time. *Journal of Experimental Psychology*, 1973, *97*, 70–74, (b)

Loftus, E. F., & Cole, W. Retrieving attribute and name information from semantic memory. *Journal of Experimental Psychology*, 1974, *102*, 1116–1122.

Loftus, E. F., Senders, J. W., & Turkletaub, S. Retrieval of phonetically similar and dissimilar category members. *American Journal of Psychology*, 1974, *87*, 57–64.

Loftus, G. R., & Loftus, E. F. The influence of one memory retrieval on a subsequent memory retrieval. *Memory & Cognition*, 1974, *2*, 467–471.

Meyer, D. E. On the representation and retrieval of stored semantic information. *Cognitive Psychology*, 1970, *1*, 242–300.

Meyer, D. E. Correlated operations in searching stored semantic categories. *Journal of Experimental Psychology*, 1973, *99*, 124–133.

Meyer, D. E., & Schvaneveldt, R. W. Facilitation in recognizing pairs of words: Evidence of a dependence between retrieval operations. *Journal of Experimental Psychology*, 1971, *90*, 227–234.

Norman, D. A., & Rumelhart, D. E. *Explorations in cognition*. San Francisco: W. H. Freeman, 1975.

Quillian, M. R. A revised design for an understanding machine. *Mechanical Translation*, 1962, *7*, 17–29.

Quillian, M. R. *Semantic memory*. Unpublished doctoral dissertation, Carnegie Institute of Technology, 1966. (Reprinted in part in M. Minsky [Ed.], *Semantic information processing*. Cambridge, Mass.: M.I.T. Press, 1968.)

Quillian, M. R. Word concepts: A theory and simulation of some basic semantic capabilities. *Behavioral Science*, 1967, *12*, 410–430.

Quillian, M. R. The Teachable Language Comprehender: A simulation program and theory of language. *Communications of the ACM*, 1969, *12*, 459–476.

Rips, L. J., Shoben, E. J., & Smith, E. E. Semantic distance and the verification of semantic relations. *Journal of Verbal Learning and Verbal Behavior*, 1973, *12*, 1–20.

Rosch, E. On the internal structure of perceptual and semantic categories. In T. E. Moore (Ed.), *Cognitive development and acquisition of language*. New York: Academic Press, 1973.

Schaeffer, B., & Wallace, R. Semantic similarity and the comparison of word meanings. *Journal of Experimental Psychology*, 1969, *82*, 343–346.

Schaeffer, B., & Wallace, R. The comparison of word meanings. *Journal of Experimental Psychology*, 1970, *86*, 144–152.

Schank, R. C. Conceptual dependency: A theory of natural language understanding. *Cognitive Psychology*, 1972, *3*, 552–631.

Schvaneveldt, R. W., & Meyer, D. E. Retrieval and comparison processes in semantic memory. In S. Kornblum (Ed.), *Attention and performance IV*. New York: Academic Press, 1973.

Smith, E. E., Shoben, E. J., & Rips, L. J. Comparison processes in semantic memory. *Psychological Review*, 1974, *81*, 214–241.

Sternberg, S. High-speed scanning in human memory. *Science*, 1966, *153*, 652–654.

Stone, M. Models of choice-reaction time. *Psychometrika*, 1960, *25*, 251–260.

Wilkins, A. J. Conjoint frequency, category size, and categorization time. *Journal of Verbal Learning and Verbal Behavior*, 1971, *10*, 382–385.

Wittgenstein, L. *Philosophical investigations* (G. E. M. Anscombe, trans.). Oxford: Blackwell, 1953.

32

DISTRIBUTED MEMORY AND THE REPRESENTATION OF GENERAL AND SPECIFIC INFORMATION

James L. McClelland and David E. Rumelhart

Source: *Journal of Experimental Psychology: General*, 114 (1985): 159–188.

We describe a distributed model of information processing and memory and apply it to the representation of general and specific information. The model consists of a large number of simple processing elements which send excitatory and inhibitory signals to each other via modifiable connections. Information processing is thought of as the process whereby patterns of activation are formed over the units in the model through their excitatory and inhibitory interactions. The memory trace of a processing event is the change or increment to the strengths of the interconnections that results from the processing event. The traces of separate events are superimposed on each other in the values of the connection strengths that result from the entire set of traces stored in the memory. The model is applied to a number of findings related to the question of whether we store abstract representations or an enumeration of specific experiences in memory. The model simulates the results of a number of important experiments which have been taken as evidence for the enumeration of specific experiences. At the same time, it shows how the functional equivalent of abstract representations—prototypes, logogens, and even rules—can emerge from the superposition of traces of specific experiences, when the conditions are right for this to happen. In essence, the model captures the structure present in a set of input patterns; thus, it behaves as though it had learned prototypes or rules, to the extent that the structure of the environment it has learned about can be captured by describing it in terms of these abstractions.

In the late 1960s and early 1970s a number of experimenters, using a variety of different tasks, demonstrated that subjects could learn through experience with exemplars of a category to respond better—more accurately, or more rapidly—to the prototype than to any of the particular exemplars. The seminal demonstration of this basic point comes from the work of Posner and Keele (1968, 1970). Using a categorization task, they found that there were some conditions in which subjects categorized the prototype of a category more accurately than the particular exemplars of the category that they had previously seen. This work, and many other related experiments, supported the development of the view that memory by its basic nature somehow abstracts the central tendency of a set of disparate experiences, and gives relatively little weight to the specific experiences that gave rise to these abstractions.

Recently, however, some have come to question this "abstractive" point of view, for two reasons. First, specific events and experiences clearly play a prominent role in memory and learning. Experimental demonstrations of the importance of specific stimulus events even in tasks which have been thought to involve abstraction of a concept or rule are now legion. Responses in categorization tasks (Brooks, 1978; Medin & Shaffer, 1978), perceptual identification tasks (Jacoby, 1983a, 1983b; Whittlesea, 1983), and pronunciation tasks (Glushko, 1979) all seem to be quite sensitive to the congruity between particular training stimuli and particular test stimuli, in ways which most abstraction models would not expect.

At the same time, a number of models have been proposed in which behavior which has often been characterized as *rule-based* or *concept-based* is attributed to a process that makes use of stored traces of specific events or specific exemplars of the concepts or rules. According to this class of models, the apparently rule-based or concept-based behavior emerges from what might be called a conspiracy of individual memory traces or from a sampling of one from the set of such traces. Models of this class include the Medin and Shaffer (1978) context model, Hintzman's (1983) multiple trace model, and Whittlesea's (1983) episode model. This trend is also exemplified by our interactive activation model of word perception (McClelland & Rumelhart, 1981; Rumelhart & McClelland, 1981, 1982), and an extension of the interactive activation model to generalization from exemplars (McClelland, 1981).

One feature of some of these exemplar-based models troubles us. Many of them are internally inconsistent with respect to the issue of abstraction. Thus, though our word perception model assumes that linguistic rules emerge from a conspiracy of partial activations of detectors for particular words, thereby eliminating the need for abstraction of rules, the assumption that there is a single detector for each word implicitly assumes that there is an abstraction process that lumps each occurrence of the same word into the same single detector unit. Thus, the model has its abstraction and creates it too, though at slightly different levels.

One logically coherent response to this inconsistency is to simply say that each word or other representational object is itself a conspiracy of the entire ensemble of memory traces of the different individual experiences we have had with that unit. We will call this view the *enumeration of specific experiences* view. It is exemplified most clearly by Jacoby (1983a, 1983b), Hintzman (1983), and Whittlesea (1983).

As the papers just mentioned demonstrate, enumeration of specific experiences can work quite well as an account of quite a number of empirical findings. However, there still seems to be one drawback. Such models seem to require an unlimited amount of storage capacity, as well as mechanisms for searching an almost unlimited mass of data. This is especially true when we consider that the primitives out of which we normally assume one experience is built are themselves abstractions. For example, a word is a sequence of letters, or a sentence is a sequence of words. Are we to believe that all of these abstractions are mere notational conveniences for the theorist, and that every event is stored as an extremely rich (obviously structured) representation of the event, with no abstraction?

In this article, we consider an alternative conceptualization: a distributed, superpositional approach to memory. This view is similar to the separate enumeration of experiences view in some respects, but not in all. On both views, memory consists of traces resulting from specific experiences; and on both views, generalizations emerge from the superposition of these specific memory traces. Our model differs, though, from the enumeration of specific experiences in assuming that the superposition of traces occurs at the time of storage. We do not keep each trace in a separate place, but rather we superimpose them so that what the memory contains is a composite.

Our theme will be to show that distributed models provide a way to resolve the abstraction-representation of specifics dilemma. With a distributed model, the superposition of traces automatically results in abstraction though it can still preserve to some extent the idiosyncrasies of specific events and experiences, or of specific recurring subclasses of events and experiences.

We will begin by introducing a specific version of a distributed model of memory. We will show how it works and describe some of its basic properties. We will show how our model can account for several recent findings (Salasoo, Shiffrin, & Feustel, 1985; Whittlesea, 1983), on the effects of specific experiences on later performance, and the conditions under which functional equivalents of abstract representations such as prototypes or logogens emerge. The discussion considers generalizations of the approach to the semantic-episodic distinction and the acquisition of linguistic rule systems, and considers reasons for preferring a distributed-superpositional memory over other models.

Previous, related models

Before we get down to work, some important credits are in order. Our distributed model draws heavily from the work of Anderson (e.g., 1977, 1983; Anderson, Silverstein, Ritz, & Jones, 1977; Knapp & Anderson, 1984) and Hinton (1981a). We have adopted and synthesized what we found to be the most useful aspects of their distinct but related models, preserving (we hope) the basic spirit of both. We view our model as an exemplar of a class of existing models whose exploration Hinton, Anderson, Kohonen (e.g., Kohonen, 1977; Kohonen, Oja, & Lehtio, 1981), and others have pioneered. A useful review of prior work in this area can be obtained from Anderson and Hinton (1981) and other articles in the volume edited by Hinton and Anderson (1981). Some points similar to some of these we will be making have recently been covered in the papers of Murdock (1982) and Eich (1982), though the distributed representations we use are different in important ways from the representations used by these other authors.

Our distributed model is not a complete theory of human information processing and memory. It is a model of the internal structure of some components of information processing, in particular those concerned with the retrieval and use of prior experience. The model does not specify in and of itself how these acts of retrieval and use are planned, sequenced, and organized into coherent patterns of behavior.

A distributed model of memory

General properties

Our model adheres to the following general assumptions, some of which are shared with several other distributed models of processing and memory.

Simple, highly interconnected units

The processing system consists of a collection of simple processing units, each interconnected with many other units. The units take on activation values, and communicate with other units by sending signals modulated by weights associated with the connections between the units. Sometimes, we may think of the units as corresponding to particular representational primitives, but they need not. For example, even what we might consider to be a primitive feature of something, like having a particular color, might be a pattern of activation over a collection of units.

Modular structure

We assume that the units are organized into modules. Each module receives inputs from other modules, the units within the module are richly interconnected with each other, and they send outputs to other modules. Figure 1 illustrates the internal structure of a very simple module, and Figure 2 illustrates some hypothetical interconnections between a number of modules. Both figures grossly underrepresent our view of the number of units per module and the number of modules. We would imagine that there would be thousands to millions of units per module and many hundreds or perhaps many thousands of partially redundant modules in anything close to a complete memory system.

The state of each module represents a synthesis of the states of all of the modules it receives inputs from. Some of the inputs will be from relatively more sensory modules, closer to the sensory end-organs of one modality or another. Others will come from relatively more abstract modules, which

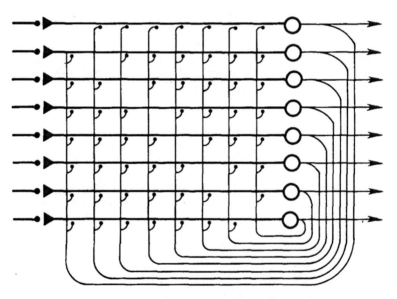

Figure 1 A simple information processing module, consisting of a small ensemble of eight processing units. [Each unit receives inputs from other modules (indicated by the single input impinging on the input line of the node from the left; this can stand for a number of converging input signals from several nodes outside the module) and sends outputs to other modules (indicated by the output line proceeding to the right from each unit). Each unit also has a modifiable connection to all the other units in the same module, as indicated by the branches of the output lines that loop back onto the input lines leading into each unit. All connections, which may be positive or negative, are represented by dots.]

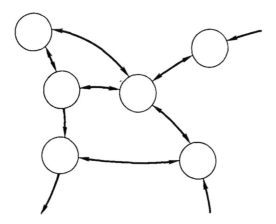

Figure 2 An illustrative diagram showing several modules and interconnections among them. (Arrows between modules simply indicate that some of the nodes in one module send inputs to some of the nodes in the other. The exact number and organization of modules is of course unknown; the figure is simply intended to be suggestive.)

themselves receive inputs from and send outputs to other modules placed at the abstract end of several different modalities. Thus, each module combines a number of different sources of information.

Mental state as pattern of activation

In a distributed memory system, a mental state is a pattern of activation over the units in some subset of the modules. The patterns in the different modules capture different aspects of the content of the mental states in a partially overlapping fashion. Alternative mental states are simply alternative patterns of activation over the modules. Information processing is the process of evolution in time of mental states.

Units play specific roles within patterns

A pattern of activation only counts as the same as another if the same units are involved. The reason for this is that the knowledge built into the system for recreating the patterns is built into the set of interconnections among the units, as we will explain later. For a pattern to access the right knowledge it must arise on the appropriate units. In this sense, the units play specific roles in the patterns. Obviously, a system of this sort is useless without sophisticated perceptual processing mechanisms at the interface between memory and the outside world, so that similar input patterns arising at different locations in the world can be mapped into the same set of units internally. Such mechanisms are outside the scope of this article (but see Hinton, 1981b; McClelland, 1985).

Memory traces as changes in the weights

Patterns of activation come and go, leaving traces behind when they have passed. What are the traces? They are changes in the strengths or *weights* of the connections between the units in the modules.

This view of the nature of the memory trace clearly sets these kinds of models apart from traditional models of memory in which some copy of the "active" pattern is generally thought of as being stored directly. Instead of this, what is actually stored in our model is changes in the connection strengths. These changes are derived from the presented pattern, and are arranged in such a way that, when a part of a known pattern is presented for processing, the interconnection strengths cause the rest of the pattern to be reinstated. Thus, although the memory trace is not a copy of the learned pattern, it is something from which a replica of that pattern can be recreated. As we already said, each memory trace is distributed over many different connections, and each connection participates in many different memory traces. The traces of different mental states are therefore superimposed in the same set of weights. Surprisingly enough, as we will see in several examples, the connections between the units in a single module can store the information needed to complete many different familiar patterns.

Retrieval as reinstatement of prior pattern of activation

Retrieval amounts to partial reinstatement of a mental state, using a cue which is a fragment of the original state. For any given module, we can see the cues as originating from outside of it. Some cues could arise ultimately from sensory input. Others would arise from the results of previous retrieval operations fed back to the memory system under the control of a search or retrieval plan. It would be premature to speculate on how such schemes would be implemented in this kind of a model, but it is clear that they must exist.

Detailed assumptions

In the rest of our presentation, we will be focusing on operations that take place within a single module. This obviously oversimplifies the behavior of a complete memory system because the modules are assumed to be in continuous interaction. The simplification is justified, however, in that it allows us to focus on some of the basic properties of distributed memory that are visible even without these interactions with other modules.

Let us look, therefore, at the internal structure of one very simple module, as shown in Figure 1. Again, our image is that in a real system there would be much larger numbers of units. We have restricted our analysis to small numbers simply to illustrate basic principles as clearly as possible; this also helps to keep the running time of simulations in bounds.

Activation values

The units take on activation values which range from −1 to +1. Zero represents in this case a neutral resting value, toward which the activations of the units tend to decay.

Inputs, outputs, and internal connections

Each unit receives input from other modules and sends output to other modules. For the present, we assume that the inputs from other modules occur at connections whose weights are fixed. In the simulations, we treat the input from outside the module as a fixed pattern, ignoring (for simplicity) the fact that the input pattern evolves in time and might be affected by feedback from the module under study. Although the input to each unit might arise from a combination of sources in other modules, we can lump the external input to each unit into a single real valued number representing the combined effects of all components of the external input. In addition to extra-modular connections, each unit is connected to all other units in the module via a weighted connection. The weights on these connections are modifiable, as described later. The weights can take on any real values, positive, negative, or 0. There is no connection from a unit onto itself.

The processing cycle

Processing within a module takes place as follows. Time is divided into discrete ticks. An input pattern is presented at some point in time over some or all of the input lines to the module and is then left on for several ticks, until the pattern of activation it produces settles down and stops changing.

Each tick is divided into two phases. In the first phase, each unit determines its net input, based on the external input to the unit and activations of all of the units at the end of the preceding tick modulated by the weight coefficients which determine the strength and direction of each unit's effect on every other.

For mathematical precision, consider two units in our module, and call one of them unit i, and the other unit j. The input to unit i from unit j, written i_{ij} is just

$$i_{ij} = a_j w_{ij},$$

where a_j is the activation of unit j, and w_{ij} is the weight constant modulating the effect of unit j on unit i. The total input to unit i from all other units internal to the module, i_i, is then just the sum of all of these separate inputs:

$$i_i = \sum_j i_{ij}.$$

Here, j ranges over all units in the module other than i. This sum is then added to the *external* input to the unit, arising from outside the module, to obtain the net input to unit i, n_i:

$$n_i = i_i + e_i,$$

where e_i is just the lumped external input to unit i.

In the second phase, the activations of the units are updated. If the net input is positive, the activation of the unit is incremented by an amount proportional to the distance left to the ceiling activation level of $+1.0$. If the net input is negative, the activation is decremented by an amount proportional to the distance left to the floor activation level of -1.0. There is also a decay factor which tends to pull the activation of the unit back toward the resting level of 0.

Mathematically, we can express these assumptions as follows: For unit i, if $n_i > 0$,

$$\dot{a}_i = En_i(1 - a_i) - Da_i.$$

If $n_i \le 0$,

$$\dot{a}_i = En_i[a_i - (-1)] - Da_i.$$

In these equations, E and D are global parameters which apply to all units, and set the rates of excitation and decay, respectively. The term a_i is the activation of unit i at the end of the previous cycle, and $\dot{a}_i$ is the change in a_i; that is, it is the amount added to (or, if negative, subtracted from) the old value a_i to determine its new value for the next cycle.

Given a fixed set of inputs to a particular unit, its activation level will be driven up or down in response until the activation reaches the point where the incremental effects of the input are balanced by the decay. In practice, of course, the situation is complicated by the fact that as each units' activation is changing it alters the input to the others. Thus, it is necessary to run the simulation to see how the system will behave for any given set of inputs and any given set of weights. In all the simulations reported here, the model is allowed to run for 50 cycles, which is considerably more than enough for it to achieve a stable pattern of activation over all the units.

Memory traces

The memory trace of a particular pattern of activation is a set of changes in the entire set of weights in the module. We call the whole set of changes an *increment* to the weights. After a stable pattern of activation is achieved, weight adjustment takes place. This is thought of as occurring simultaneously for all of the connections in the module.

The Delta rule

The rule that determines the size and direction (up or down) of the change at each connection is the crux of the model. The idea is often difficult to grasp on first reading, but once it is understood it seems very simple, and it directly captures the goal of facilitating the completion of the pattern, given some part of the pattern as a retrieval or completion cue.

To allow each part of a pattern to reconstruct the rest of the pattern, we simply want to set up the internal connections among the units in the module so that when part of the pattern is presented, activating some of the units in the module, the internal connections will lead the active units to tend to reproduce the rest. To do this, we want to make the internal input to each unit have the same effect on the unit that the external input has on the unit. That is, given a particular pattern to be stored, we want to find a set of connections such that the internal input to each unit from all of the other units matches the external input to that unit. The connection change procedure we will describe has the effect of moving the weights of all the connections in the direction of achieving this goal.

The first step in weight adjustment is to see how well the module is already doing. If the network is already matching the external input to each unit with the internal input from the other units, the weights do not need to be changed. To get an index of how well the network is already doing at matching its excitatory input, we assume that each unit i computes the difference Δ_i between its external input and the net internal input to the unit from the other units in the module:

$$\Delta_i = e_i - i_i.$$

In determining the activation value of the unit, we added the external input together with the internal input. Now, in adjusting the weights, we are taking the difference between these two terms. This implies that the unit must be able to aggregate all inputs for purposes of determining its activation, but it must be able to distinguish between external and internal inputs for purposes of adjusting its weights.

Let us consider the term Δ_i for a moment. If it is positive, the internal input is not activating the unit enough to match the external input to the unit. If negative, it is activating the unit too much. If zero, everything is fine and we do not want to change anything. Thus, Δ_i determines the magnitude and direction of the overall change that needs to be made in the internal input to unit i. To achieve this overall effect, the individual weights are then adjusted according to the following formula:

$$\dot{w}_{ij} = S\Delta_i a_j.$$

The parameter S is just a global strength parameter which regulates the overall magnitude of the adjustments of the weights; $\dot{w}_{ij}$ is the change in the weight to i from j.

We call this weight modification rule the *delta rule*. It has all the intended consequences; that is, it tends to drive the weights in the direction of the right values to make the internal inputs to a unit match the external inputs. For example, consider the case in which Δ_i is positive and a_j is positive. In this case, the value of Δ_i tells us that unit i is not receiving enough excitatory input, and the value of a_j tells us that unit j has positive activation. In this case, the delta rule will increase the weight from j to i. The result will be that the next time unit j has a positive activation, its excitatory effect on unit i will be increased, thereby reducing Δ_i.

Similar reasoning applies to cases where Δ_i is negative, a_j is negative, or both are negative. Of course, when either Δ_i or a_j is 0, w_{ij} is not changed. In the first case, there is no error to compensate for; in the second case, a change in the weight will have no effect the next time unit j has the same activation value.

What the delta rule can and cannot do

The delta rule is a continuous variant of the perceptron convergence procedure (Rosenblatt, 1962), and has been independently invented many times (see Sutton & Barto, 1981, for a discussion). Its popularity is based on the fact that it is an error-correcting rule, unlike the Hebb rule used until recently by Anderson (1977; Anderson et al., 1977). A number of interesting theorems have been proven about this rule (Kohonen, 1977; Stone, 1985). Basically, the important result is that, for a set of patterns which we present repeatedly to a module, if there is a set of weights which will allow the system to reduce Δ to 0 for each unit in each pattern, this rule will find it through repeated exposure to all of the members of the set of patterns.

It is important to note that the existence of a set of weights that will allow Δ to be reduced to 0 is not guaranteed, but depends on the structure inherent in the set of patterns which the model is given to learn. To be perfectly learnable by our model, the patterns must conform to the following *linear predictability constraint:*

> Over the entire set of patterns, the external input to each unit must be predictable from a linear combination of the activations of every other unit.

This is an important constraint, for there are many sets of patterns that violate it. However, it is necessary to distinguish between the patterns used inside the model, and the stimulus patterns to which human observers might be exposed in experiments, as described by psychologists. For our model to work, it is important for patterns to be assigned to stimuli in a way that will allow them to be learned.

A crucial issue, then, is the exact manner in which the stimulus patterns are encoded. As a rule of thumb, an encoding which treats each dimension or aspect of a stimulus separately is unlikely to be sufficient; what is required is a *context sensitive* encoding, such that the representation of each aspect is colored by the other aspects. For a full discussion of this issue, see Hinton, McClelland, and Rumelhart (in press).

Decay in the increments to the weights

We assume that each trace or increment undergoes a decay process though the rate of decay of the increments is assumed to be much slower than the rate of decay of patterns of activation. Following a number of theorists (e.g., Wickelgren, 1979), we imagine that traces at first decay rapidly, but then the remaining portion becomes more and more resistant to further decay. Whether it ever reaches a point where it is no longer decaying at all we do not know. The basic effect of this assumption is that individual inputs exert large short-term effects on the weights, but after they decay the residual effect is considerably smaller. The fact that each increment has its own temporal history increases the complexity of computer simulations enormously. In all of the particular cases to be examined, we will therefore specify simplified assumptions to keep the simulations tractable.

Illustrative examples

In this section, we describe a few illustrative examples to give the reader a feel for how we use the model, and to illustrate key aspects of its behavior.

Storage and retrieval of several patterns in a single memory module

First, we consider the storage and retrieval of two patterns in a single module of 8 units. Our basic aim is to show how several distinct patterns of activation can all be stored in the same set of weights, by what Lashley (1950) called a kind of algebraic summation, and not interfere with each other.

Before the first presentation of either pattern, we start out with all the weights set to 0. The first pattern is given at the top of Table 1. It is an arrangement of +1 and −1 inputs to the eight units in the module. (In Table 1, the 1s are suppressed in the inputs for clarity). When we present the first pattern to this module, the resulting activation values simply reflect the effects of the inputs themselves because none of the units are yet influencing any of the others.

Then, we teach the module this pattern by presenting it to the module 10 times. Each time, after the pattern of activation has had plenty of time to settle down, we adjust the weights. The next time we present the complete pattern after the 10 learning trials, the module's response is enhanced, compared with the earlier situation. That is, the activation values are increased in magnitude, owing to the combined effects of the external and internal inputs to each of the units. If we present an incomplete part of the pattern, the module can complete it; if we distort the pattern, the module tends to drive the activation back in the direction it thinks it ought to have. Of course, the magnitudes of these effects depend on parameters; but the basic nature of the effects is independent of these details.

Figure 3 shows the weights our learning procedure has assigned. Actual numerical values have been suppressed to emphasize the basic pattern of excitatory and inhibitory influences. In this example, all the numerical values

Table 1 Behavior of an 8-unit distributed memory module

Case	Input or response for each unit							
Pattern 1								
The Pattern:	+	−	+	−	+	+	−	−
Response to Pattern before learning	+.5	−.5	+.5	−.5	+.5	+.5	−.5	−.5
Response to Pattern after 10 learning trials	+.7	−.7	+.7	−.7	+.7	+.7	−.7	−.7
Test Input (Incomplete version of Pattern)	+	−	+	−				
Response	+.6	−.6	+.6	−.6	+.4	+.4	−.4	−.4
Test Input (Distortion of Pattern)	+	−	+	−	+	+	−	+*
Response	+.6	−.6	+.6	−.6	+.6	+.6	−.6	+.1
Pattern 2								
The Pattern:	+	+	−	−	−	+	−	+
Response to Pattern with weights learned for Pattern 1	+.5	+.5	−.5	−.5	−.5	+.5	−.5	+.5
Response to Pattern after 10 learning trials	+.7	+.7	−.7	−.7	−.7	+.7	−.7	+.7
Retest of response to Pattern 1	+.7	−.7	+.7	−.7	+.7	+.7	−.7	−.7

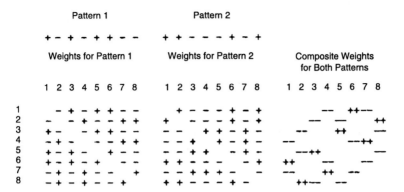

Figure 3 Weights acquired in learning Pattern 1 and Pattern 2 separately, and the composite weights resulting from learning both. (The weight in a given cell reflects the strength of the connection from the corresponding column unit to the corresponding row unit. Only the sign and relative magnitude of the weights are indicated. A blank indicates a weight of 0; + and – signify positive and negative, with a double symbol, ++ or ––, representing a value twice as large as a single symbol, + or –.

are identical. The pattern of + and – signs simply gives the pattern of pairwise correlations of the elements. This is as it should be to allow pattern enhancement, completion, and noise elimination. Units which have the same activation in the pattern have positive weights, so that when one is activated it will tend to activate the other, and when one is inhibited it will tend to inhibit the other. Units which have different activations in the pattern have negative weights, so that when one is activated it will inhibit the other and vice versa.

What happens when we present a new pattern, dissimilar to the first? This is illustrated in the lower portion of Table 1. At first, the network responds to it just as though it knew nothing at all: The activations simply reflect the direct effects of the input, as they would in a module with all 0 weights. The reason is simply that the effects of the weights already in the network cancel each other out. This is a result of the fact that the two patterns are maximally dissimilar from each other. If the patterns had been more similar, there would not have been this complete cancellation of effects.

Now we learn the new pattern, presenting it 10 times and adjusting the weights each time. The resulting weights (Figure 3) represent the sum of the weights for Patterns 1 and 2. The response to the new pattern is enhanced, as shown in Table 1. The response to the old, previously learned pattern is not affected. The module will now show enhancement, completion, and noise elimination for both patterns though these properties are not illustrated in Table 1.

Thus, we see that more than one pattern can coexist in the same set of weights. There is an effect of storing multiple patterns, of course. When only one pattern is stored, the whole pattern (or at least, a pale copy of it) can be retrieved by driving the activation of any single unit in the appropriate direction. As more patterns are stored, larger subpatterns are generally needed to specify the pattern to be retrieved uniquely.

Learning a prototype from exemplars

In the preceeding section, we considered the learning of particular patterns and showed that the delta rule was capable of learning multiple patterns, in the same set of connections. In this section, we consider what happens when distributed models using the delta rule are presented with an ensemble of patterns that have some common structure. The examples described in this section illustrate how the delta rule can be used to extract the structure from an ensemble of inputs, and throw away random variability.

Let us consider the following hypothetical situation. A little boy sees many different dogs, each only once, and each with a different name. All the dogs are a little different from each other, but in general there is a pattern which represents the typical dog: each one is just a different distortion of this prototype. (We are not claiming that the dogs in the world have no more structure than this; we make this assumption for purposes of illustration only.) For now we will assume that the names of the dogs are all completely different. Given this experience, we would expect that the boy would learn the prototype of the category, even without ever seeing any particular dog which matches the prototype directly (Posner & Keele, 1968, 1970; Anderson, 1977, applies an earlier version of a distributed model to this case). That is, the prototype will seem as familiar as any of the exemplars, and he will be able to complete the pattern corresponding to the prototype from any part of it. He will not, however, be very likely to remember the names of each of the individual dogs though he may remember the most recent ones.

We model this situation with a module consisting of 24 units. We assume that the presentation of a dog produces a visual pattern of activation over 16 of the units in the hypothetical module (the 9th through 24th, counting from left to right). The name of the dog produces a pattern of activation over the other 8 units (Units 1 to 8, counting from left to right).

Each visual pattern, by assumption, is a distortion of a single prototype. The prototype used for the simulation simply had a random series of +1 and −1 values. Each distortion of the prototype was made by probabilistically flipping the sign of randomly selected elements of the prototype pattern. For each new distorted pattern, each element has an independent chance of being flipped, with a probability of .2. Each name pattern was simply a random sequence of +1s and −1s for the eight name units. Each encounter with a new dog is modeled as a presentation of a new name pattern with a new distortion of the prototype visual pattern. Fifty different trials were run, each with a new name pattern-visual pattern pair.

For each presentation, the pattern of activation is allowed to stabilize, and then the weights are adjusted as before. The increment to the weights is then allowed to decay considerably before the next input is presented. For simplicity, we assume that before the next pattern is presented, the last increment decays to a fixed small proportion of its initial value, and thereafter undergoes no further decay.

What does the module learn? The module acquires a set of weights which is continually buffeted about by the latest dog exemplar, but which captures the prototype dog quite well. Waiting for the last increment to decay to the fixed residual yields the weights shown in Figure 4.

These weights capture the correlations among the values in the prototype dog pattern quite well. The lack of exact uniformity is due to the more recent distortions presented, whose effects have not been corrected by subsequent distortions. This is one way in which the model gives priority to specific exemplars, especially recent ones. The effects of recent exemplars are particularly strong, of course, before they have had a chance to decay. The module can complete the prototype quite well, and it will respond more strongly to the prototype than to any distortion of it. It has, however, learned

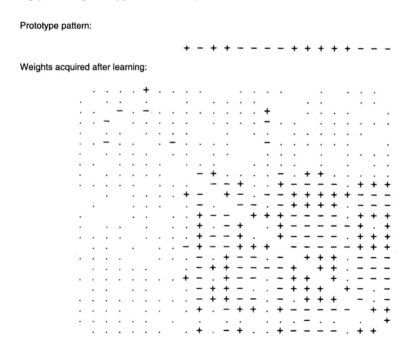

Prototype pattern:

Weights acquired after learning:

Figure 4 Weights acquired in learning from distorted exemplars of a prototype. (The prototype pattern is shown above the weight matrix. Blank entries correspond to weights with absolute values less than .01; dots correspond to absolute values less than .06; pluses or minuses are used for weights with larger absolute values.)

no particular relation between this prototype and any name pattern, because a totally different random association was presented on each trial. If the pattern of activation on the name units had been the same in every case (say, each dog was just called *dog*), or even in just a reasonable fraction of the cases, then the module would have been able to retrieve this shared name pattern from the prototype of the visual pattern and the prototype pattern from the name.

Multiple, nonorthogonal prototypes

In the preceeding simulation we have seen how the distributed model acts as a sort of signal averager, finding the central tendency of a set of related patterns. In and of itself this is an important property of the model, but the importance of this property increases when we realize that the model can average several different patterns in the same composite memory trace. Thus, several different prototypes can be stored in the same set of weights. This is important, because it means that the model does not fall into the trap of needing to decide which category to put a pattern in before knowing which prototype to average it with. The acquisition of the different prototypes proceeds without any sort of explicit categorization. If the patterns are sufficiently dissimilar, there is no interference among them at all. Increasing similarity leads to increased confusability during learning, but eventually the delta rule finds a set of connection strengths that minimizes the confusability of similar patterns.

To illustrate these points, we created a simulation analog of the following hypothetical situation. Let us say that our little boy sees, in the course of his daily experience, different dogs, different cats, and different bagels. First, let's consider the case in which each experience with a dog, a cat, or a bagel is accompanied by someone saying *dog, cat,* or *bagel*, as appropriate.

The simulation analog of this situation involved forming three *visual* prototype patterns of 16 elements, two of them (the one for dog and the one for cat) somewhat similar to each other ($r = .5$), and the third (for the bagel) orthogonal to both of the other two. Paired with each visual pattern was a name pattern of eight elements. Each name pattern was orthogonal to both of the others. Thus, the prototype visual pattern for cat and the prototype visual pattern for dog were similar to each other, but their names were not related.

Stimulus presentations involved presentations of distorted exemplars of the name–visual pattern pairs to a module of 24 elements like the one used in the previous simulation. This time, both the name pattern and the visual pattern were distorted, with each element having its sign flipped with an independent probability of .1 on each presentation. Fifty different distortions of each name–visual pattern pair were presented in groups of three consisting of one distortion of the dog pair, one distortion of the cat pair, and one distortion of the bagel pair. Weight adjustment occurred after each presentation, with decay to a fixed residual before each new presentation.

At the end of training, the module was tested by presenting each name pattern and observing the resulting pattern of activation over the visual nodes, and by presenting each visual pattern and observing the pattern of activation over the name nodes. The results are shown in Table 2. In each case, the model reproduces the correct completion for the probe, and there is no apparent contamination of the cat pattern by the dog pattern, even though the visual patterns are similar to each other.

In general, pattern completion is a matter of degree. One useful measure of pattern completion is the dot product of the pattern of activation over the units with the pattern of external inputs to the units. Because we treat the external inputs as +1s and −1s, and because the activation of each node can only range from +1 to −1, the largest possible value the dot product can have is 1.0. We will use this measure explicitly later when considering some simulations of experimental results. For getting an impression of the degree of pattern reinstatement in the present cases, it is sufficient to note that when the sign of all of the elements is correct, as it is in all of the completions in Table 2, the average magnitude of the activations of the units corresponds to the dot product.

In a case like the present one, in which some of the patterns known to the model are correlated, the values of the connection strengths that the model produces do not necessarily have a simple interpretation. Though their sign

Table 2 Results of tests after learning the dog, cat, and bagel patterns

	Input or response for each unit	
Case	Name units	Visual pattern units
Pattern for dog prototype	+ − + − + − + −	+ − + + − − − − + + + + + − − −
Response to dog name		+3 −4 +4 +4 −4 −4 −4 −4 +4 +4 +4 +4 +3 +4 −4 −4 −3
Response to dog visual pattern	+5 −4 +4 −5 +5 −4 +4 −4	
Pattern for cat prototype	+ + − − + + − −	+ − + + − − − − + − + − + + − +
Response to cat name		+4 −3 +4 +4 −4 −3 −3 −4 +4 −4 +4 −4 +4 +4 −4 +4
Response to cat visual pattern	+5 +4 −4 −5 +4 +4 −4 −4	
Pattern for bagel prototype	+ − − + + − − +	+ + − + − + + − + − + − − + + + + −
Response to bagal name		+3 +4 −4 +4 −4 +4 +4 −4 +4 −4 −4 +4 +3 +4 +4 −4
Response to bagel visual pattern	+4 −4 −4 +4 +4 −4 −4 +4	

Note. Decimal points have been suppressed for clarity; thus, an entry of +4 represents an activation value of +.4.

always corresponds to the sign of the correlation between the activations of the two units, their magnitude is not a simple reflection of the magnitude of their correlation, but is influenced by the degree to which the model is relying on this particular correlation to predict the activation of one node from the others. Thus, in a case where two nodes (call them i and j) are perfectly correlated, the strength of the connection from i to j will depend on the number of other nodes whose activations are correlated with j. If i is the only node correlated with j, it will have to do all the work of predicting j, so the weight will be very strong; on the other hand, if many nodes besides i are correlated with j, then the work of predicting j will be spread around, and the weight between i and j will be considerably smaller. The weight matrix acquired as a result of learning the dog, cat, and bagel patterns (Figure 5) reflects these effects. For example, across the set of three prototypes, Units 1 and 5 are perfectly correlated, as are Units 2 and 6. Yet the connection from 2 to 5 is stronger than the connection from 1 to 4 (these connections are *d in Figure 5). The reason for the difference is that 2 is one of only three units which correlate perfectly with 5, whereas Unit 1 is one of seven units which correlate perfectly with 4. (In Figure 5, the weights do not reflect these contrasts perfectly in every case, because the noise introduced into the learning happens by chance to alter some of the correlations present in the prototype patterns. Averaged over time, though, the weights will conform to their expected values.)

Thus far we have seen that several prototypes, not necessarily orthogonal, can be stored in the same module without difficulty. It is true, though we do not illustrate it, that the model has more trouble with the cat and dog visual patterns earlier on in training, before learning has essentially reached asymptotic levels as it has by the end of 50 cycles through the full set of patterns. And, of course, even at the end of learning, if we present as a probe a part of the visual pattern, if it does not differentiate between the dog and the cat, the model will produce a blended response. Both these aspects of the model seem generally consistent with what we should expect from human subjects.

Category learning without labels

An important further fact about the model is that it can learn several different visual patterns, even without the benefit of distinct identifying name patterns during learning. To demonstrate this we repeated the previous simulation, simply replacing the name patterns with 0s. The model still learns about the internal structure of the visual patterns, so that, after 50 cycles through the stimuli, any unique subpart of any one of the patterns is sufficient to reinstate to the rest of the corresponding pattern correctly. This aspect of the model's behavior is illustrated in Table 3. Thus, we have a model that can, in effect, acquire a number of distinct categories, simply through a process of incrementing connection strengths in response to each

Prototypes:

```
Dog:    + - + - + - + -    + - + + - - - - + + + + + - - -
Cat:    + + - - + + - -    + - + + - - - - + - + - + + - +
Bagel:  + - - + + - - +    + + - + - + + - + - - + + + + -
```

Weights:

```
   -1 -1    +2*-1    -1   +3      +5 -2 -1    -3 +2 -1        +2        -1
            -2    -1 +4*       +1 -1        -1 -1 +1 -1 -1    -3 -1    -3 +3
   -1 -2    -1      +5          +1    +1 -1 -1    -1 +4    +1      -5    -1
            -1    -1    -1 +2   -1 +3 -3       +2 +3      -1 -2    -1 +1 +3
   +3 -1 -1          +1       -1    +3 -3      -2 +2      +1 +3 +1 -1 -1
   -1 +5 -3         -2       -1 -1    -1      -1      -1 -2 +1 -5 -1 +2 -1 +5
   -1    +3 -1 -1 -2         +1       -1    +1      +4      -1 -2
   -1 -1 -1 +2        -1    -1 +3 -2 -1    +3 +3    -1 -1 -3 +1 -1 +3 +3


   +3   -1 -1 +2 -1 -1         +3 -2      -3 +2    +1      +3 +1      -1
   -1 -1 -1 +3   -1   +3      -3 -1    +3 +3 +1 -1 -2 -2 +1 -1      +2
   +1 +1 +1 -3      -2    +1 -3     -1 -3 -3      +1 +3 -1    -1 -2 +2
   +2 -1 -1 -1 +3   -1      +3 -1 +1    -2 -1    -2 +2 -1      +2 +1 -1
   -2 +1 +1    -2 +1 +1 +1   -3      -3      +1 +2 -3      -1 -2 -1 +1
   -1    +2 -1       +2   -1 +2 -2    +1    +2 +1 -1    -3    -1    +2
   -1 -1 -1 +2    -1 +2      +2 -3      +3.    +1      -3    -1  +3
   -2 +1 +1 +1 -3    +1 +1   -2 +1 -1 -3 +3      -2 +1 -1 -1 -3 -1 +1
   +3    -1    +2    -1      +2      +3 -3      -3    -1 +1    +3 +1 -1 -1
         +5 -1 -1 -1 +4 -1         +1    -3 +1      +1    -1 -5 -1 -1
   +1      -2    +1 +1 -3   +1 -2 +2 +1 -1 -3 -3 -1    +1    -2      -3 +1
   +1 -5 +2 +1 +1 -5 +3         -2 +1 -1 +1      +1 +1 -2    +1 -2 +1 -3
   +2 -1 -1    +3 -1      +2    +1 +2 -2      -3 +2    +1
   +3 -4 +1    +3 -4 +1   +1    -1      +1 +1    +1 -5 -1 -3      +1 +2
         +2 -1    -1      -1 +2 -3      +2 +2      -1 -3    +1
   -1 +3 -2 -1 -1 +5 -3      -1 +3    +1 -1      -1    +1 -2    +3 -1
```

Figure 5 Weights acquired in learning the three prototype patterns shown. (Blanks in the matrix of weights correspond to weights with absolute values less than or equal to .05. Otherwise the actual value of the weight is about .05 times the value shown; thus +5 stands for a weight of +.25. The gap in the horizontal and vertical dimensions is used to separate the name field from the visual pattern field.)

new stimulus presentation. Noise, in the form of distortions in the patterns, is filtered out. The model does not require a name or other guide to distinguish the patterns belonging to different categories.

Coexistence of the prototype and repeated exemplars

One aspect of our discussion up to this point may have been slightly misleading. We may have given the impression that the model is simply a prototype extraction device. It is more than this, however; it is a device that captures

Table 3 Results of tests after learning the dog, cat, and bagel patterns without names

Case	Input or response for each visual unit	
Dog visual pattern	+ − + + − − − −	+ + + + + − − −
Probe		+ + + +
Response	+3 −3 +3 +3 −3 −4 −3 −3	+6 +5 +6 +5 +3 −2 −3 −2
Cat visual pattern	+ − + + − − − −	+ − + − + + − +
Probe		+ − + −
Response	+3 −3 +3 +3 −3 −3 −3 −3	+6 −5 +6 −5 +3 +2 −3 +2
Bagel visual pattern	+ + − + − + + −	+ − − + + + + −
Probe		+ − − +
Response	+2 +3 −4 +3 −3 +3 +3 −3	+6 −6 −6 +6 +3 +3 +3 −3

whatever structure is present in a set of patterns. When the set of patterns has a prototype structure, the model will act as though it is extracting prototypes; but when it has a different structure, the model will do its best to accommodate this as well. For example, the model permits the coexistence of representations of prototypes with representations of particular, repeated exemplars.

Consider the following situation. Let us say that our little boy knows a dog next door named Rover and a dog at his grandma's house named Fido. And let's say that the little boy goes to the park from time to time and sees dogs, each of which his father tells him is a dog.

The simulation-analog of this involved three different eight-element name patterns, one for Rover, one for Fido, and one for Dog. The visual pattern for Rover was a particular randomly generated distortion of the dog prototype pattern, as was the visual pattern for Fido. For the dogs seen in the park, each one was simply a new random distortion of the prototype. The probability of flipping the sign of each element was again .2. The learning regime was otherwise the same as in the dog–cat–bagel example.

At the end of 50 learning cycles, the model was able to retrieve the visual pattern corresponding to either repeated exemplar (see Table 4) given the associated name as input. When given the Dog name pattern as input, it retrieves the prototype visual pattern for dog. It can also retrieve the appropriate name from each of the three visual patterns. This is true, even though the visual pattern for Rover differs from the visual pattern for dog by only a single element. Because of the special importance of this particular element, the weights from this element to the units that distinguish Rover's name pattern from the prototype name pattern are quite strong. Given part of a visual pattern, the model will complete it; if the part corresponds to the prototype, then that is what is completed, but if it corresponds to one of the repeated exemplars, that exemplar is completed. The model, then, knows both the prototype and the repeated exemplars quite well. Several other sets of prototypes and their repeated exemplars could also be stored in the same

Table 4 Results of tests with prototype and specific exemplar patterns

	Input or response for each unit	
Case	Name units	Visual pattern units
Pattern for dog prototype	+ − + − + − + −	+ − + + − − − − + + + + + − − −
Response to prototype name		+4 −5 +3 +3 −4 −3 −3 −3 +3 +3 +4 +3 +4 −3 −4 −4
Response to prototype visual pattern	+5 −4 +4 −4 +5 −4 +4 −4	
Pattern for "Fido" exemplar	+ − − − + − − −	+ − (−) + − − − − + + + + + (+) − −
Response to Fido name		+4 −4 −4 +4 −4 −4 −4 −4 +4 +4 +4 +4 +4 +4 −4 −4
Response to Fido visual pattern	+5 −5 −3 −5 +4 −5 −3 −5	
Pattern for "Rover" exemplar	+ − − + + + − +	+ (+) + + − − − − + + + + + − − −
Response to Rover name		+4 +5 +4 +4 −4 −4 −4 −4 +4 +4 +4 +4 +4 −4 −4 −4
Response to Rover visual pattern	+4 −4 −2 +4 +4 +4 −2 +4	

module, as long as its capacity is not exceeded; given large numbers of units per module, a lot of different patterns can be stored.

Let us summarize the observations we have made in these several illustrative simulations. First, our distributed model is capable of storing not just one but a number of different patterns. It can pull the central tendency of a number of different patterns out of the noisy inputs; it can create the functional equivalent of perceptual categories with or without the benefit of labels; and it can allow representations of repeated exemplars to coexist with the representation of the prototype of the categories they exemplify in the same composite memory trace. The model is not simply a categorizer or a prototyping device; rather, it captures the structure inherent in a set of patterns, whether it be characterizable by description in terms of prototypes or not.

The ability to retrieve accurate completions of similar patterns is a property of the model which depends on the use of the delta learning rule. This allows both the storage of different prototypes that are not completely orthogonal and the coexistence of prototype representations and repeated exemplars.

Simulations of experimental results

Up to this point, we have discussed our distributed model in general terms and have outlined how it can accommodate both abstraction and representation of specific information in the same network. We will now consider, in the next two sections, how well the model does in accounting for some recent evidence about the details of the influence of specific experiences on performance.

Repetition and familiarity effects

When we perceive an item—say a word, for example—this experience has effects on our later performance. If the word is presented again, within a reasonable interval of time, the prior presentation makes it possible for us to recognize the word more quickly, or from a briefer presentation.

Traditionally, this effect has been interpreted in terms of units that represent the presented items in memory. In the case of word perception, these units are called *word detectors* or *logogens*, and a model of repetition effects for words has been constructed around the logogen concept (Morton, 1979). The idea is that the threshold for the logogen is reduced every time it *fires* (that is, every time the word is recognized), thereby making it easier to fire the logogen at a later time. There is supposed to be a decay of this priming effect, with time, so that eventually the effect of the first presentation wears off.

This traditional interpretation has come under serious question of late, for a number of reasons. Perhaps paramount among the reasons is the fact that the exact relation between the specific context in which the priming event occurs and the context in which the test event occurs makes a huge difference (Jacoby, 1983a, 1983b). Generally speaking, nearly any change in the stimulus—from spoken to printed, from male speaker to female speaker, and so forth—tends to reduce the magnitude of the priming effect.

These facts might easily be taken to support the enumeration of specific experiences view, in which the logogen is replaced by the entire ensemble of experiences with the word, with each experience capturing aspects of the specific context in which it occurred. Such a view has been championed most strongly by Jacoby (1983a, 1983b).

Our distributed model offers an alternative interpretation. We see the traces laid down by the processing of each input as contributing to the composite, superimposed memory representation. Each time a stimulus is processed, it gives rise to a slightly different memory trace: either because the item itself is different or because it occurs in a different context that conditions its representation. The logogen is replaced by the set of specific traces, but the traces are not kept separate. Each trace contributes to the composite, but the characteristics of particular experiences tend nevertheless to be preserved, at least until they are overridden by cancelling characteristics of other traces. And the traces of one stimulus pattern can coexist with the traces of other stimuli, within the same composite memory trace.

It should be noted that we are not faulting either the logogen model or models based on the enumeration of specific experiences for their physiological implausibility here, because these models are generally not stated in physiological terms, and their authors might reasonably argue that nothing in their models precludes distributed storage at a physiological level. What we are suggesting is that a model which proposes explicitly distributed, superpositional storage can account for the kinds of findings that logogen models have been proposed to account for, as well as other findings which strain the utility of the concept of the logogen as a psychological construct. In the discussion section we will consider ways in which our distributed model differs from enumeration models as well.

To illustrate the distributed model's account of repetition priming effects, we carried out the following simulation experiment. We made up a set of eight random vectors, each 24 elements long, each one to be thought of as the prototype of a different recurring stimulus pattern. Through a series of 10 training cycles using the set of eight vectors, we constructed a composite memory trace. During training, the model did not actually see the proto-types, however. On each training presentation it saw a new random distor-tion of one of the eight prototypes. In each of the distortions, each of the 24 elements had its value flipped with a probability of .1. Weights were adjusted after every presentation, and then allowed to decay to a fixed residual before the presentation of the next pattern.

The composite memory trace formed as a result of the experience just described plays the same role in our model that the set of logogens or detectors play in a model like Morton's or, indeed, the interactive activation model of word preception. That is, the trace contains information which allows the model to enhance perception of familiar patterns, relative to unfamiliar ones. We demonstrate this by comparing the activations resulting from the processing of subsequent presentations of new distortions of our eight familiar patterns with other random patterns with which the model is not familiar. The pattern of activation that is the model's response to the input is stronger, and grows to a particular level more quickly, if the stimulus is a new distortion of an old pattern than if it is a new pattern. We already observed this general enhanced response to exact repetitions of familiar patterns in our first example (see Table 1). Figure 6 illustrates that the effect also applies to new distortions of old patterns, as compared with new pat-terns, and illustrates how the activation process proceeds over successive time cycles of processing.

Pattern activation and response strength

The measure of activation shown in the Figure 6 is the dot product of the pattern of activation over the units of the module times the stimulus pattern itself, normalized for the number n of elements in the pattern: For the pat-tern j we call this expression a_j. The expression a_j represents the degree to which the actual pattern of activation on the units captures the input pattern.

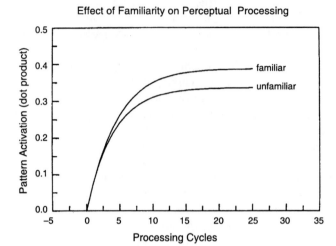

Figure 6 Growth of the pattern of activation for new distortions of familiar and unfamiliar patterns. (The measure of the strength of the pattern of activation is the dot product of the response pattern with the input vector. See text for an explanation.)

It is an approximate analog to the activation of an individual unit in models which allocate a single unit to each whole pattern.

To relate these pattern activations to response probabilities, we must assume that mechanisms exist for translating patterns of activation into overt responses measurable by an experimenter. We will assume that these mechanisms obey the principles stated by McClelland and Rumelhart (1981) in the interactive activation model of word perception, simply replacing the activations of particular units with the a measure of pattern activation.

In the interactive activation model, the probability of choosing the response appropriate to a particular unit was based on an exponential transform of a time average of the activation of the unit. This quantity, called the *strength* of the particular response, was divided by the total strength of all alternatives (including itself) to find the response probability (Luce, 1963). One complication arises because of the fact that it is not in general possible to specify exactly what the set of alternative responses might be for the denominator. For this reason, the strengths of other responses are represented by a constant C (which stands for the competition). Thus, the expression for probability of choosing the response appropriate to pattern j is just $p(r_j) = e^{k\bar{a}_j}/(C + e^{k\bar{a}_j})$, where $\bar{a}_j$ represents the time average of a_j, and k is a scaling constant.

These assumptions finesse an important issue, namely the mechanism by which a pattern of activation give rise to a particular response. A detailed discussion of this issue will appear in Rumelhart and McClelland (in press).

For now, we wish only to capture basic properties any actual response selection mechanism must have: It must be sensitive to the input pattern, and it must approximate other basic aspects of response selection behavior captured by the Luce (1963) choice model.

Effects of experimental variables on time-accuracy curves

Applying the assumptions just described, we can calculate probability of correct response as a function of processing cycles for familiar and unfamiliar patterns. The result, for a particular choice of scaling parameters, is shown in Figure 7. If we assume performance in a perceptual identification task is based on the height of the curve at the point where processing is cut off by masking (McClelland & Rumelhart, 1981), then familiarity would lead to greater accuracy of perceptual identification at a given exposure duration. In a reaction time task, if the response is emitted when its probability reaches a particular threshold activation value (McClelland, 1979), then familiarity would lead to speeded responses. Thus, the model is consistent with the ubiquitous influence of familiarity both on response accuracy and speed, in spite of the fact that it has no detectors for familiar stimuli.

But what about priming and the role of congruity between the prime event and the test event? To examine this issue, we carried out a second experiment. Following learning of eight patterns as in the previous experiment, new distortions of half of the random vectors previously learned by the model were presented as primes. For each of these primes, the pattern of activation was

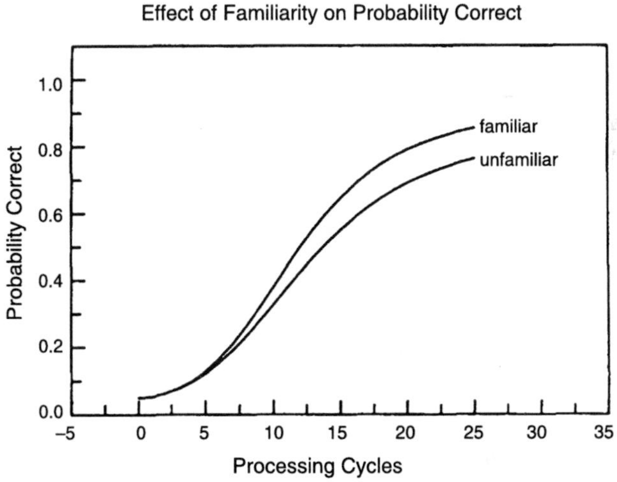

Figure 7 Simulated growth of response accuracy over the units in a 24-unit module, as a function of processing cycles, for new distortions of previously learned patterns compared with new distortions of patterns not previously learned.

allowed to stabilize, and changes in the strengths of the connections in the model were then made. We then tested the model's response to (a) the same four distortions; (b) four new distortions of the same patterns; and (c) distortions of the four previously learned patterns that had not been presented as primes. There was no decay in the weights over the course of the priming experiment; if decay had been included, its main effect would have been to reduce the magnitude of the priming effects.

The results of the experiment are shown in Figure 8. The response of the model is greatest for the patterns preceded by identical primes, intermediate for patterns preceded by similar primes, and weakest for patterns not preceded by any related prime.

Our model, then, appears to provide an account, not only for the basic existence of priming effects, but also for the graded nature of priming effects as a function of congruity between prime event and test event. It avoids the problem of multiplication of context-specific detectors which logogen theories fall prey to, while at the same time avoiding enumeration of specific experiences. Congruity effects are captured in the composite memory trace.

The model also has another advantage over the logogen view. It accounts for repetition priming effects for unfamiliar as well as familiar stimuli. When a pattern is presented for the first time, a trace is produced just as it would be for stimuli that had previously been presented. The result is that, on a second presentation of the same pattern, or a new distortion of it, processing is facilitated. The functional equivalent of a logogen begins to be established from the very first presentation.

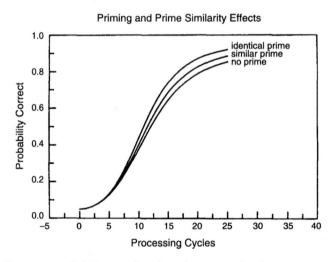

Figure 8 Response probability as a function of exposure time for patterns preceded by identical primes, similar primes, or no related prime.

To illustrate the repetition priming of unfamiliar patterns and to compare the results with the repetition priming we have already observed for familiar patterns, we carried out a third experiment. This time, after learning eight patterns as before, a priming session was run in which new distortions of four of the familiar patterns and distortions of four new patterns were presented. Then, in the test phase, 16 stimuli were presented: New distortions of the primed, familiar patterns; new distortions of the unprimed, familiar patterns; new distortions of the primed, previously unfamiliar patterns; and finally, new distortions of four patterns that were neither primed nor familiar. The results are shown in Figure 9. What we find is that long-term familiarity and recent priming have approximately additive effects on the asymptotes of the time-accuracy curves. The time to reach any given activation level shows a mild interaction, with priming having slightly more of an effect for unfamiliar than for familiar stimuli.

These results are consistent with the bulk of the findings concerning the effects of preexperimental familiarity and repetition in the recent series of experiments by Feustel, Shiffrin, and Salasoo (1983) and Salasoo et al. (1985). They found that preexperimental familiarity of an item (word vs. nonword) and prior exposure had this very kind of interactive effect on exposure time required for accurate identification of all the letters of a string, at least when words and nonwords were mixed together in the same lists of materials.

A further aspect of the results reported by Salasoo, Shiffrin, and Feustel is also consistent with our approach. In one of their experiments, they examined threshold for accurate identification as a function of number of

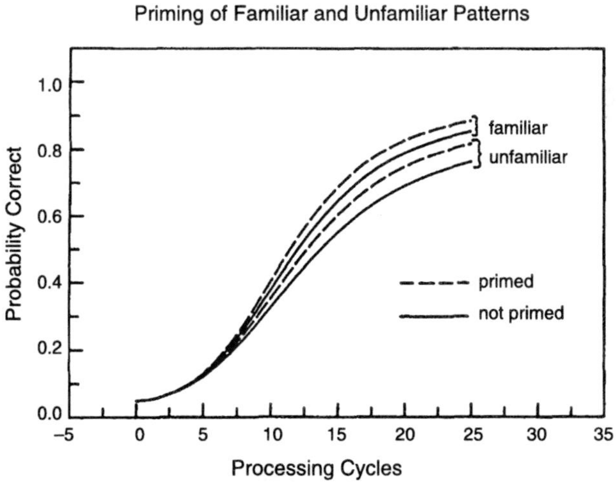

Figure 9 Response to new distortions of primed, familiar patterns, unprimed, familiar patterns, primed, unfamiliar patterns, and unprimed, unfamiliar patterns.

283

prior presentations, for both words and pseudowords. Although thresholds were initially elevated for pseudowords, relative to words, there was a rather rapid convergence of the thresholds over repeated presentations, with the point of convergence coming at about the same place on the curve for two different versions of their perceptual identification task. (Salasoo et al., 1985, Figure 7.) Our model, likewise, shows this kind of convergence effect, as illustrated in Figure 10.

The Feustel et al. (1983) and Salasoo et al. (1985) experiments provide very rich and detailed data that go beyond the points we have extracted from them here. We do not claim to have provided a detailed account of all aspects of their data. However, we simply wish to note that the general form of their basic findings is consistent with a model of the distributed type. In particular, we see no reason to assume that the process by which unfamiliar patterns become familiar involves the formation of an abstract, logogenlike unit separate from the episodic traces responsible for repetition priming effects.

There is one finding by Salasoo et al. (1985) that appears to support the view that there is some special process of unit formation that is distinct from the priming of old units. This is the fact that after a year between training and testing, performance with pseudowords used during training is indistinguishable from performance with words, but performance with words used during training shows no residual benefit compared with words not previously used. The data certainly support the view that training experience made the pseudowords into lasting perceptual units, at the same time that is produced transitory priming of existing units. We have not attempted to account for this finding in detail, but we doubt that it is inconsistent with

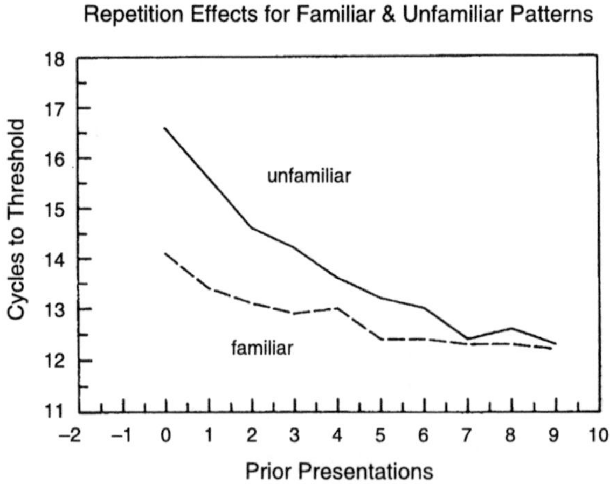

Figure 10 Time to reach a fixed-accuracy criterion (60% correct) for previously familiar and unfamiliar patterns, as a function of repetitions.

a distributed model. In support of this, we offer one reason why repetition effects might seem to persist longer for pseudowords rather than for words in the Salasoo et al. experiment. For pseudowords, a strong association would be built up between the item and the learning context during initial training. Such associations would be formed for words, but because these stimuli have been experienced many times before and have already been well learned, smaller increments in connection strength are formed for these stimuli during training, and thus the strength of the association between the item and the learning context would be less. If this view is correct, we would expect to see a disadvantage for pseudowords relative to words if the testing were carried out in a situation which did not reinstate the mental state associated with the original learning experience, because for these stimuli much of what was learned would be tied to the specific learning context: such a prediction would appear to differentiate our account from any view which postulated the formation of an abstract, context-independent logogen as the basis for the absence of a pseudoword decrement effect.

Representation of general and specific information

In the previous section, we cast our distributed model as an alternative to the view that familiar patterns are represented in memory either by separate detectors or by an enumeration of specific experiences. In this section, we show that the model provides alternatives to both abstraction and enumeration models of learning from exemplars of prototypes.

Abstraction models were originally motivated by the finding that subjects occasionally appeared to have learned better how to categorize the prototype of a set of distorted exemplars than the specific exemplars they experienced during learning (Posner & Keele, 1968). However, pure abstraction models have never fared very well, because there is nearly always evidence of some superiority of the particular training stimuli over other stimuli equally far removed from the prototype. A favored model, then, is one in which there is both abstraction and memory for particular training stimuli.

Recently, proponents of models involving only enumeration of specific experiences have noted that such models can account for the basic fact that abstraction models are primarily designed to account for—enhanced response to the prototype, relative to particular previously seen exemplars, under some conditions—as well as failures to obtain such effects under other conditions (Hintzman, 1983; Medin & Shaffer, 1978). In evaluating distributed models, it is important to see if they can do as well. Anderson (1977) has made important steps in this direction, and Knapp and Anderson (1984) have shown how their distributed model can account for many of the details of the Posner–Keele experiments. Recently, however, two sets of findings have been put forward which appear to strongly favor the enumeration of specific experiences view, at least relative to pure abstraction models. It is important, therefore, to see how well our distributed model can do in accounting for these kinds of effects.

The first set of findings comes from a set of studies by Whittlesea (1983). In a large number of studies, Whittlesea demonstrated a role for specific exemplars in guiding performance on a perceptual identification task. We wanted to see whether our model would demonstrate a similar sensitivity to specific exemplars. We also wanted to see whether our model would account for the conditions under which such effects are not obtained.

Whittlesea used letter strings as stimuli. The learning experiences subjects received involved simply looking at the stimuli one at a time on a visual display and writing down the sequence of letters presented. Subjects were subsequently tested for the effect of this training on their ability to identify letter strings bearing various relations to the training stimuli and to the prototypes from which the training stimuli were derived. The test was a perceptual identification task; the subject was simply required to try to identify the letters from a brief flash.

The stimuli Whittlesea used were all distortions of one of two prototype letter strings. Table 5 illustrates the essential properties of the sets of training and test stimuli he used. The stimuli in Set Ia were each one step away from the prototype. The Ib items were also one step from the prototype and one step from one of the Ia distortions. The Set IIa stimuli were each two steps from the prototype, and one step from a particular Ia distortion. The Set IIb items were also two steps from the prototype, and each was one step from one of the IIa distortions. The Set IIc distortions were two steps from the prototype also, and each was two steps from the closest IIa distortion. Over the set of five IIc distortions, the A and B subpatterns each occurred once in each position, as they did in the case of the IIa distortions. The distortions in Set III were three steps from the prototype, and one step from the closest member of Set IIa. The distortions in Set V were each five steps from the prototype.

Table 5 Schematic description of stimulus sets used in simulations of Whittlesea's experiments

	Stimulus set						
Prototype	Ia	Ib	IIa	IIb	IIc	III	V
PPPPP	APPPP	BPPPP	ABPPP	ACPPP	APCPP	ABCPP	CCCCC
	PAPPP	PBPPP	PABPP	PACPP	PAPCP	PABCP	CBCBC
	PPAPP	PPBPP	PPABP	PPACP	PPAPC	PPABC	BCACB
	PPPAP	PPPBP	PPPAB	PPPAC	CPPAP	CPPAB	ABCBA
	PPPPA	PPPPB	BPPPA	CPPPA	PCPPA	BCPPA	CACAC

Note. The actual stimuli used can be filled in by replacing P with +—+; A with ++—; B with +—+; and C with ++++. The model is not sensitive to the fact the same subpattern was used in each of the five slots.

Whittlesea ran seven experiments using different combinations of training and test stimuli. We carried out simulation analogs of all of these experiments, plus one additional experiment that Whittlesea did not run. The main difference between the simulation experiments and Whittlesea's actual experiments was that he used two different prototypes in each experiment, whereas we only used one.

The simulation used a simple 20-unit module. The set of 20 units was divided into five submodules, one for each letter in Whittlesea's letter strings. The prototype pattern and the different distortions used can be derived from the information provided in Table 5.

Each simulation experiment began with null connections between the units. The training phase involved presenting the set or sets of training stimuli analogous to those Whittlesea used, for the same number of presentations. To avoid idiosyncratic effects of particular orders of training stimuli, each experiment was run six times, each with a different random order of training stimuli. On each trial, activations were allowed to settle down through 50 processing cycles, and then connection strengths were adjusted. There was no decay of the increments to the weights over the course of an experiment.

In the test phase, the model was tested with the sets of test items analogous to the sets Whittlesea used. As a precaution against effects of prior test items on performance, we simply turned off the adjustment of weights during the test phase.

A summary of the training and test stimuli used in each of the experiments, of Whittlesea's findings, and of the simulation results are shown in Table 6. The numbers represent relative amounts of enhancement in performance as a result of the training experience, relative to a pretest baseline. For Whittlesea's data, this is the per letter increase in letter identification probability between a pre- and posttest. For the simulation, it is the increase in the size of the dot product for a pretest with null weights and a posttest after training. For comparability to the data, the dot product difference scores have been doubled. This is simply a scaling operation to facilitate qualitative comparison of experimental and simulation results.

A comparison of the experimental and simulation results shows that wherever there is a within-experiment difference in Whittlesea's data, the simulation produced a difference in the same direction. (Between experiment comparisons are not considered because of subject and material differences which renders such differences unreliable.) The next several paragraphs review some of the major findings in detail.

Some of the comparisons bring out the importance of congruity between particular test and training experiences. Experiments 1, 2, and 3 show that when distance of test stimuli from the prototype is controlled, similarity to particular training exemplars makes a difference both for the human subject and in the model. In Experiment 1, the relevant contrast was between Ia and

Table 6 Summary of perceptual identification experiments with experimental and simulation results

Whittlesea's experiment	Training stimulus set(s)	Test stimulus sets	Experimental results	Simulation results
1	Ia	Ia	.27	.24
		Ib	.16	.15
		V	.03	−.05
2	IIa	IIa	.30	.29
		IIc	.15	.12
		V	.03	−.08
3	IIa	IIa	.21	.29
		IIb	.16	.14
		IIc	.10	.12
4	IIa	P	−	.24
		Ia	.19	.21
		IIa	.23	.29
		III	.15	.15
4′	Ia	P	−	.28
		Ia	−	.24
		IIa	−	.12
5	IIa, b, c	P	−	.25
		Ia	.16	.21
		IIa	.16	.18
		III	.10	.09
6	III	Ia	.16	.14
		IIa	.16	.19
		III	.19	.30
7	IIa	IIa	.24	.29
		IIc	.13	.12
		III	.17	.15

Ib items. In Experiment 2, it was between IIa and IIc items. Experiment 3 shows that the subjects and the model both show a gradient in performance with increasing distance of the test items from the nearest old exemplar.

Experiments 4, 4′, and 5 examine the status of the prototype and other test stimuli closer to the prototype than any stimuli actually shown during training. In Experiment 4, the training stimuli were fairly far away from the prototype, and there were only five different training stimuli (the members of the IIa set). In this case, controlling for distance from the nearest training stimuli, test stimuli closer to the prototype showed more enhancement than those farther away (Ia vs. III comparison). However, the actual training stimuli nevertheless had an advantage over both other sets of test stimuli, including those that were closer to the prototype than the training stimuli themselves (IIa vs. Ia comparison).

In Experiment 4′ (not run by Whittlesea) the same number of training stimuli were used as in Experiment 4, but these were closer to the prototype.

The result is that the simulation shows an advantage for the prototype over the old exemplars. The specific training stimuli used even in this experiment do influence performance, however, as Whittlesea's first experiment (which used the same training set) shows (Ia–Ib contrast). This effect holds both for the subjects and for the simulation. The pattern of results is similar to the findings of Posner and Keele (1968), in the condition where subjects learned six exemplars which were rather close to the prototype. In this condition, their subjects' categorization performance was most accurate for the prototype, but more accurate for old than for new distortions, just as in this simulation experiment.

In Experiment 5, Whittlesea demonstrated that a slight advantage for stimuli closer to the prototype than the training stimuli would emerge, even with high-level distortions, when a large number of different distortions were used once each in training, instead of a smaller number of distortions presented three times each. The effect was rather small in Whittlesea's case (falling in the third decimal place in the per letter enhancement effect measure) but other experiments have produced similar results, and so does the simulation. In fact, because the prototype was tested in the simulation, we were able to demonstrate a monotonic drop in performance with distance from the prototype in this experiment.

Experiments 6 and 7 examine in different ways the relative influence of similarity to the prototype and similarity to the set of training exemplars, using small numbers of training exemplars rather far from the prototype. Both in the data and in the model, similarity to particular training stimuli is more important than similarity to the prototype, given the sets of training stimuli used in these experiments.

Taken together with other findings, Whittlesea's results show clearly that similarity of test items to particular stored exemplars is of paramount importance in predicting perceptual performance. Other experiments show the relevance of these same factors in other tasks, such as recognition memory, classification learning, and so forth. It is interesting to note that performance does not honor the specific exemplars so strongly when the training items are closer to the prototype. Under such conditions, performance is superior on the prototype or stimuli closer to the prototype than the training stimuli. Even when the training stimuli are rather distant from the prototype, they produce a benefit for stimuli closer to the prototype, if there are a large number of distinct training stimuli each shown only once. Thus, the dominance of specific training experiences is honored only when the training experiences are few and far between. Otherwise, an apparent advantage for the prototype, though with some residual benefit for particular training stimuli, is the result.

The congruity of the results of these simulations with experimental findings underscores the applicability of distributed models to the question of the nature of the representation of general and specific information. In fact, we were somewhat surprised by the ability of the model to account for Whittlesea's results, given the fact that we did not rely on context-sensitive encoding of the letter string stimuli. That is, the distributed representation we assigned to each letter was independent of the other letters in the string. However, a context sensitive encoding would prove necessary to capture a large ensemble of stimuli.

Whether a context-sensitive encoding would produce the same or slightly different results depends on the exact encoding. The exact degree of overlap of the patterns of activation produced by different distortions of the same prototype determines the extent to which the model will tend to favor the prototype relative to particular old exemplars. The degree of overlap, in turn, depends on the specific assumptions made about the encoding of the stimuli. However, the general form of the results of the simulation would be unchanged: When all the distortions are close to the prototype, or when there is a very large number of different distortions, the central tendency will produce the strongest response; but when the distortions are fewer, and farther from the prototype, the training exemplars themselves will produce the strongest activations. What the encoding would effect is the similarity metric.

In this regard, it is worth mentioning another finding that appears to challenge our distributed account of what is learned through repeated experiences with exemplars. This is the finding of Medin and Schwanenflugel (1981). Their experiment compared ease of learning of two different sets of stimuli in a categorization task. One set of stimuli could be categorized by a linear combination of weights assigned to particular values on each of four dimensions considered independently. The other set of stimuli could not be categorized in this way; and yet, the experiment clearly demonstrated that linear separability was not necessary for categorization learning. In one experiment, linearly separable stimuli were less easily learned than a set of stimuli that were not linearly separable but had a higher degree of intraexemplar similarity within categories.

At first glance, it may seem that Medin and Schwanenflugel's experiment is devastating to our distributed approach, because our distributed model can only learn linear combinations of weights. However, whether a linear combination of weights can suffice in the Medin and Schwanenflugel experiments depends on how patterns of activation are assigned to stimuli. If each stimulus dimension is encoded separately in the representation of the stimulus, then the Medin and Schwanenflugel stimuli cannot be learned by our model. But if each stimulus dimension is encoded in a context sensitive way, then the patterns of activation associated with the different stimuli become linearly separable again.

One way of achieving context sensitivity is via separate enumeration of traces. But it is well known that there are other ways as well. Several different kinds of context-sensitive encodings which do not require separate enumeration of traces, or the allocation of separate nodes to individual experiences are considered in Hinton (1981a), Hinton, McClelland, and Rumelhart (in press), and Rumelhart and McClelland (in press).

It should be noted that the motivation for context-sensitive encoding in the use of distributed representations is captured by but by no means limited to the kinds of observations reported in the experiment by Medin and Schwanenflugel. The trouble is that the assignment of particular context-sensitive encodings to stimuli is at present rather ad hoc: There are too many different possible ways it can be done to know which way is right. What is needed is a principled way of assigning distributed representations to patterns of activation. The problem is a severe one, but really it is no different from the problem that all models face, concerning the assignment of representations to stimuli. What we can say for sure at this point is that context-sensitive encoding is necessary, for distributed models or for any other kind.

Discussion

Until very recently, the exploration of distributed models was restricted to a few workers, mostly coming from fields other than cognitive psychology. Although in some cases, particularly in the work of Anderson (1977; Anderson et al., 1977; Knapp & Anderson, 1984), some implications of these models for our understanding of memory and learning have been pointed out, they have only begun to be applied by researchers primarily concerned with understanding cognitive processes per se. The present article, along with those of Murdock (1982) and Eich (1982), represents what we hope will be the beginning of a more serious examination of these kinds of models by cognitive psychologists. For they provide, we believe, important alternatives to traditional conceptions of representation and memory.

We have tried to illustrate this point here by showing how the distributed approach circumvents the dilemma of specific trace models. Distributed memories abstract even while they preserve the details of recent, or frequently repeated, experiences. Abstraction and preservation of information about specific stimuli are simply different reflections of the operation of the same basic learning mechanism.

The basic points we have been making can of course be generalized in several different directions. Here we will mention two: The relation between episodic and semantic memory (Tulving, 1972) and the representations underlying the use of language.

With regard to episodic and semantic memory, our distributed model leads naturally to the suggestion that semantic memory may be just the residue of the superposition of episodic traces. Consider, for example, representation of a proposition encountered in several different contexts, and assume for the moment that the context and content are represented in separate parts of the same module. Over repeated experience with the same proposition in different contexts, the proposition will remain in the interconnections of the units in the proposition submodule, but the particular associations to particular contexts will wash out. However, material that is only encountered in one particular context will tend to be somewhat contextually bound. So we may not be able to retrieve what we learn in one context when we need it in other situations. Other authors (e.g., Anderson & Ross, 1980) have recently argued against a distinction between episodic and semantic memory, pointing out interactions between traditionally episodic and semantic memory tasks. Such findings are generally consistent with the view we have taken here.

Distributed models also influence our thinking about how human behavior might come to exhibit the kind of regularity that often leads linguists to postulate systems of rules. We have recently developed a distributed model of a system that can learn the past tense system of English, given as inputs pairs of patterns, corresponding to the phonological structure of the present and past tense forms of actual English verbs (Rumelhart & McClelland, in press). Given plausible assumptions about the learning experiences to which a child is exposed, the model provides a fairly accurate account of the time course of acquisition of the past tense (Brown, 1973; Ervin, 1964; Kuczaj, 1977).

In general distributed models appear to provide alternatives to a variety of different kinds of models that postulate abstract, summary representations such as prototypes, logogens, semantic memory representations, or even linguistic rules.

Why prefer a distributed model?

The fact that distributed models provide alternatives to other sorts of accounts is important, but the fact that they are sometimes linked rather closely to the physiology often makes them seem irrelevant to the basic enterprise of cognitive psychology. It may be conceded that distributed models describe the *physiological substrate* of memory better than other models, but why should we assume that they help us to characterize human information processing at a more abstract level of description? There are two parts to the answer to this question. First, though distributed models may be approximated by other models, on close inspection they differ from them in ways that should have testable consequences. If tests of these consequences turn out to favor distributed models—and there are indications that in certain cases they will—it would seem plausible to argue that distributed models provide an importantly different description of cognition, even if it does take the phenomena somewhat closer to the physiological level of analysis. Second, distributed models alter our thinking about a number of aspects of cognition at the same time. They give us a whole new constellation of assumptions about the structure of cognitive processes. They can change the way we think about the learning process, for example, and can even help shed some light on why and how human behavior comes to be as regular (as bound by rules and concepts) as it seems to be. In this section we consider these two points in turn.

A different level, or a different description?

Are distributed models at a different level of analysis than cognitive models, or do they provide a different description of cognition? We think the answer is some of both. Here we focus primarily on underscoring the differences between distributed and other models.

Consider, first, the class of models which state that concepts are represented by prototypes. Distributed models approximate prototype models, and under some conditions their predictions converge, but under other conditions their predictions diverge. In particular, distributed models account both for conditions under which the prototype dominates and conditions under which particular exemplars dominate performance. Thus, they clearly have an advantage over such models, and should be preferred as accounts of empirical phenomena.

Perhaps distributed models are to be preferred over some cognitive level models, but one might argue that they are not to be preferred to the correct cognitive level model. For example, in most of the simulations discussed in this article, the predictions of enumeration models are not different from the predictions of our distributed model. Perhaps we should see our distributed model as representing a physiologically plausible implementation of enumeration models.

Even here, there are differences, however. Though both models superimpose traces of different experiences, distributed models do so at the time of storage, while enumeration models do so at the time of retrieval. But there is no evidence to support the separate storage assumption of enumeration models. Indeed, most such models assume that performance is always based on a superimposition of the specific experiences. Now, our distributed model could be rejected if convincing evidence of separate storage could be provided, for example, by some kind of experiment in which a way was found to separate the effects of different memory experiences. But the trend in a number of recent approaches to memory has been to emphasize the ubiquity of interactions between memory traces. Distributed models are essentially constructed around the assumption that memory traces interact by virtue of the nature of the manner in which they are stored, and they provide an explanation for these interactions. Enumeration models, on the other hand, simply assume interactions occur and postulate separate storage without providing any evidence that storage is in fact separate.

There is another difference between our distributed model and the enumeration models, at least existing ones. Our distributed model assumes that learning is an *error-correcting* process, whereas enumeration models do not. This difference leads to empirical consequences which put great strain on existing enumeration models. In existing enumeration models, what is stored in memory is simply a copy of features of the stimulus event, independent of the prior knowledge already stored in the memory system. But there are a number of indications that what is learned depends on the current state of knowledge. For example, the fact that learning is better after distributed practice appears to suggest that more learning occurs on later learning trials, if subjects have had a chance to forget what they learned on the first trial. We would expect such effects to occur in an error-correcting model such as ours.

The main point of the foregoing discussion has been to emphasize that our distributed model is not simply a plausible physiological implementation of existing models of cognitive processes. Rather, the model is an alternative to most, if not all, existing models, as we have tried to emphasize by pointing out differences between our distributed model and other models which have been proposed. Of course this does not mean that our distributed model will not turn out to be an exact notational variant of some particular other model. What it does mean is that our distributed model must be treated as an alternative to—rather than simply an implementation of—existing models of learning and memory.

Interdependence of theoretical assumptions

There is another reason for taking distributed models seriously as psychological models. Even in cases where our distributed model may not be testably distinct from existing models, it does provide an entire constellation of assumptions which go together as a package. In this regard, it is interesting to contrast a distributed model with a model such as John Anderson's ACT* model (J. R. Anderson, 1983). One difference between the models is that in ACT* it is productions rather than connection strengths that serve as the basis of learning and memory. This difference leads to other differences: in our model, learning occurs through connection strength modulation, whereas in ACT* learning occurs through the creation, differentiation, and generalization of productions. At a process level the models look very different, whether or not they make different empirical predictions. Learning in our distributed model is an automatic consequence of processing based on information locally available to each unit whose connections are changing; in ACT*, learning requires an overseer that detects cases in which a production has been misapplied, or in which two productions with similar conditions both fit the same input, to trigger the differentiation and generalization processes as appropriate.

Similar contrasts exist between our distributed model and other models; in general, our model differs from most abstractive models (that is, those that postulate the formation of abstract rules or other abstract representations) in doing away with complex acquisition mechanisms in favor of a very simple connection strength modulation scheme. Indeed, to us, much of the appeal of distributed models is that they do not already have to be intelligent in order to learn, like some models do. Doubtless, sophisticated hypothesis testing models of learning such as those which have grown out of the early concept identification work of Bruner, Goodnow, and Austin (1956) or out of the artificial intelligence learning tradition established by Winston (1975) have their place, but for many phenomena, particularly those that do not seem to require explicit hypothesis formation and testing, the kind of learning mechanism incorporated in our distributed model may be more appropriate.

Two final reasons for preferring a distributed representation are that it leads us to understand some of the reasons why human behavior tends to exhibit such strong regularities. Some of the regularity is due to the structure of the world, of course, but much of it is a result of the way in which our cultures structure it; certainly the regularity of languages is a fact about the way humans communicate that psychological theory can be asked to explain. Distributed models provide some insight both into why it is beneficial for behavior to be regular, and how it comes to be that way.

It is beneficial for behavior to be regular, because regularity allows us to economize on the size of the networks that must be devoted to processing in a particular environment. If all experiences were completely random and unrelated to each other, a distributed model would buy us very little—in fact it would cost us a bit—relative to separate enumeration of experiences. An illuminating analysis of this situation is given by Willshaw (1981). Where a distributed model pays off, though, is in the fact that it can capture generalizations economically, given that there are generalizations. Enumeration models lack this feature. There are of course limits on how much can be stored in a distributed memory system, but the fact that it can abstract extends those limits far beyond the capacity of any system relying on the separate enumeration of experiences, whenever abstraction is warranted by the ensemble of inputs.

We have just explained how distributed models can help us understand why it is a good thing for behavior to exhibit regularity, but we have not yet indicated how they help us understand how it comes to be regular. But it is easy to see how distributed models tend to impose regularity. When a new pattern is presented, the model will impose regularity by dealing with it as it has learned to deal with similar patterns in the past; the model automatically generalizes. In our analysis of past tense learning (Rumelhart & McClelland, in press), it is just this property of distributed models which leads them to produce the kinds of over-regularizations we see in language development;

the same property, operating in all of the members of a culture at the same time, will tend to produce regularizations in the entire language.

Conclusion

The distributed approach is in its infancy, and we do not wish to convey the impression that we have solved all the problems of learning and memory simply by invoking it. Considerable effort is needed on several fronts. We will mention four that seem of paramount importance: (a) Distributed models must be integrated with models of the overall organization of information processing, and their relation to models of extended retrieval processes and other temporally extended mental activities must be made clear. (b) Models must be formulated which adequately capture the structural relations of the components of complex stimuli. Existing models do not do this in a sufficiently flexible and open-ended way to capture arbitrarily complex propositional structures. (c) Ways must be found to take the assignment of patterns of activation to stimuli out of the hands of the modeler, and place them in the structure of the model itself. (d) Further analysis is required to determine which of the assumptions of our particular distributed model are essential and which are unimportant details. The second and third of these problems are under intensive study. Some developments along these lines are reported in a number of recent papers (Ackley, Hinton, & Sejnowski, 1985; McClelland, 1985; Rumelhart & Zipser, 1985).

Although much remains to be done, we hope we have demonstrated that distributed models provide distinct, conceptually attractive alternatives to models involving the explicit formation of abstractions or the enumeration of specific experiences. Just how far distributed models can take us toward an understanding of learning and memory remains to be seen.

Notes

Preparation of this article was supported in part by a grant from the Systems Development Foundation and in part by a National Science Foundation Grant BNS-79-24062. The first author is a recipient of a Career Development Award from the National Institute of Mental Health (5-K01-MH00385).

This article was originally presented at a conference organized by Lee Brooks and Larry Jacoby on "The Priority of the Specific." We would like to thank the organizers, as well as several of the participants, particularly Doug Medin and Rich Shiffrin, for stimulating discussion and for empirical input to the development of this article.

References

Ackley, D., Hinton, G. E., & Sejnowski, T. J. (1985). Boltzmann machines: Constraint satisfaction networks that learn. *Cognitive Science, 9*, 147–169.

Anderson, J. A. (1977). Neural models with cognitive implications. In D. LaBerge & S. J. Samuels (Eds.), *Basic processes in reading: Perception and comprehension.* Hillsdale, NJ: Erlbaum.

Anderson, J. A. (1983). Cognitive and psychological computation with neural models. *IEEE Transactions on Systems, Man, and Cybernetics, SMC-13,* 799–815.

Anderson, J. A., & Hinton, G. E. (1981). Models of information processing in the brain. In G. E. Hinton & J. A. Anderson (Eds.), *Parallel models of associative memory.* Hillsdale, NJ: Erlbaum.

Anderson, J. A., Silverstein, J. W., Ritz, S. A., & Jones, R. S. (1977). Distinctive features, categorical perception, and probability learning: Some applications of a neural model. *Psychological Review, 84,* 413–451.

Anderson, J. R. (1983). *The architecture of cognition.* Cambridge, MA: Harvard.

Anderson, J. R., & Ross, B. H. (1980). Evidence against a semantic-episodic distinction. *Journal of Experimental Psychology: Human Learning and Memory, 6,* 441–465.

Brooks, L. R. (1978). Nonanalytic concept formation and memory for instances. In E. Rosch & B. B. Lloyd (Eds.), *Cognition and categorization.* Hillsdale, NJ: Erlbaum.

Brown, R. (1973). *A first language.* Cambridge, MA: Harvard University Press.

Bruner, J. S., Goodnow, J. J., & Austin, G. A. (1956). *A study of thinking.* New York: Wiley.

Eich, J. M. (1982). A composite holgraphic associative retrieval model. *Psychological Review, 89,* 627–661.

Ervin, S. (1964). Imitation and structural change in children's language. In E. Lenneberg (Ed.), *New directions in the study of language.* Cambridge, MA: MIT Press.

Feustel, T. C., Shiffrin, R. M., & Salasoo, A. (1983). Episodic and lexical contributions to the repetition effect in word identification. *Journal of Experimental Psychology: General, 112,* 309–346.

Glushko, R. J. (1979). The organization and activation of orthographic knowledge in reading aloud. *Journal of Experimental Psychology: Human Perception and Performance, 5,* 674–691.

Hinton, G. E. (1981a). Implementing semantic networks in parallel hardware. In G. E. Hinton & J. A. Anderson (Eds.), *Parallel models of associative memory.* Hillsdale, NJ: Erlbaum.

Hinton, G. E. (1981b). A parallel computation that assigns canonical object-based frames of reference. *Proceedings of the Seventh International Joint Conference in Artificial Intelligence* (pp. 683–685). Vancouver, British Columbia, Canada.

Hinton, G. E., & Anderson, J. A. (Eds.). (1981). *Parallel models of associative memory.* Hillsdale, NJ: Erlbaum.

Hinton, G. E., McClelland, J. L., & Rumelhart, D. E. (in press). Distributed representations. In D. E. Rumelhart & J. L. McCelland (Eds.), *Parallel distributed processing: Explorations in the microstructure of cognition. Volume I: Foundations.* Cambridge, MA; Bradford Books.

Hintzman, D. (1983). *Schema abstraction in a multiple trace memory model.* Paper presented at conference on "The priority of the specific." Elora, Ontario, Canada.

Jacoby, L. L. (1983a). Perceptual enhancement: Persistent effects of an experience. *Journal of Experimental Psychology: Learning, Memory, and Cognition, 9,* 21–38.

Jacoby, L. L. (1983b). Remembering the data: Analyzing interaction processes in reading. *Journal of Verbal Learning and Verbal Behavior, 22,* 485–508.

Knapp, A., & Anderson, J. A. (1984). A signal averaging model for concept formation. *Journal of Experimental Psychology: Learning, Memory, and Cognition, 10,* 616–637.

Kohonen, T. (1977). *Associative memory: A system-theoretical approach.* Berlin: Springer-Verlag.

Kohonen, T., Oja, E., & Lehtio, P. (1981). Storage and processing of information in distributed associative memory systems. In G. E. Hinton & J. A. Anderson (Eds.), *Parallel models of associative memory.* Hillsdale, NJ: Erlbaum.

Kuczaj, S. A., II. (1977). The acquisition of regular and irregular past tense forms. *Journal of Verbal Learning and Verbal Behavior, 16,* 589–600.

Lashley, K. S. (1950). In search of the engram. *Society for Experimental Biology Symposium No. 4: Physiological Mechanisms in Animal Behavior* (pp. 478–505). London: Cambridge University Press.

Luce, R. D. (1963). Detection and recognition. In R. D. Luce, R. R. Bush, & E. Galanter (Eds.), *Handbook of Mathematical Psychology: Vol. I.* New York: Wiley.

McClelland, J. L. (1979). On the time-relations of mental processes: An examination of systems of processes in cascade. *Psychological Review, 86,* 287–330.

McClelland, J. L. (1981). Retrieving general and specific information from stored knowledge of specifics. *Proceedings of the Third Annual Meeting of the Cognitive Science Society* (pp. 170–172). Berkeley, CA.

McClelland, J. L. (1985). Putting knowledge in its place: A framework for programming parallel processing structures on the fly. *Cognitive Science, 9,* 113–146.

McClelland, J. L., & Rumelhart, D. E. (1981). An interactive activation model of the effect of context in perception, Part I. An account of basic findings. *Psychological Review, 88,* 375–407.

Medin, D., & Schwanenflugel, P. J. (1981). Linear separability in classification learning. *Journal of Experimental Psychology: Human Learning and Memory, 7,* 355–368.

Medin, D. L., & Shaffer, M. M. (1978). Context theory of classification learning. *Psychological Review, 85,* 207–238.

Morton, J. (1979). Facilitation in word recognition: Experiments causing change in the logogen model. In P. A. Kohlers, M. E. Wrolstal, & H. Bouma (Eds.), *Processing visible language I.* New York: Plenum.

Murdock, B. B. (1982). A theory for the storage and retrieval of item and associative information. *Psychological Review, 89,* 609–626.

Posner, M. I., & Keele, S. W. (1968). On genesis of abstract ideas. *Journal of Experimental Psychology, 77,* 353–363.

Posner, M. I., & Keele, S. W. (1970). Retention of abstract ideas. *Journal of Experimental Psychology, 83,* 304–308.

Rosenblatt, F. (1962). *Principles of neurodynamics.* Washington, DC: Spartan.

Rumelhart, D. E., & McClelland, J. L. (1981). Interactive processing through spreading activation. In A. M. Lesgold & C. A. Perfetti (Eds.), *Interactive Processes in Reading.* Hillsdale, NJ: Erlbaum.

Rumelhart, D. E., & McClelland, J. L. (1982). An interactive activation model of the effect of context in perception Part II. The contextual enhancement effect and some tests and extensions of the model. *Psychological Review, 89,* 60–94.

Rumelhart, D. E., & McClelland, J. L. (in press). On learning the past tenses of English verbs. In J. L. McClelland & D. E. Rumelhart (Eds.), *Parallel distributed processing: Explorations in the microstructure of cognition. Volume II: Applications.* Cambridge, MA: Bradford Books.

Rumelhart, D. E., & Zipser, D. (1985). Competitive learning. *Cognitive Science, 9,* 75–112.

Salasoo, A., Shiffrin, R. M., & Feustel, T. C. (1985). Building permanent memory codes: Codification and repetition effects in word identification. *Journal of Experimental Psychology: General, 114,* 50–77.

Stone, G. (1985). *An analysis of the delta rule.* Manuscript in preparation.

Sutton, R. S., & Barto, A. G. (1981). Toward a modern theory of adaptive networks: Expectation and prediction. *Psychological Review, 88,* 135–170.

Tulving, E. (1972). Episodic and semantic memory. In E. Tulving & W. Donaldson (Eds.), *Organization of Memory.* New York: Academic Press.

Whittlesea, B. W. A. (1983). *Representation and generalization of concepts: The abstractive and episodic perspectives evaluated.* Unpublished doctoral dissertation, MacMaster University.

Wickelgren, W. A. (1979). Chunking and consolidation: A theoretical synthesis of semantic networks, configuring in conditioning, S-R versus cognitive learning, normal forgetting, the amnesic syndrome, and the hippocampal arousal system. *Psychological Review, 86,* 44–60.

Willshaw, D. (1981). Holography, associative memory, and inductive generalization. In G. E. Hinton & J. A. Anderson (Eds.), *Parallel models of associative memory.* Hillsdale, NJ: Erlbaum.

Winston, P. H. (1975). Learning structural descriptions from examples. In P. H. Winston (Ed.), *The psychology of computer vision.* Cambridge, MA: Harvard.

33

LIMITATIONS OF EXEMPLAR-BASED GENERALIZATION AND THE ABSTRACTION OF CATEGORICAL INFORMATION

Donald Homa, Sharon Sterling and Lawrence Trepel

Source: *Journal of Experimental Psychology: Human Learning and Memory*, 7 (1981): 418–439.

An evaluation of exemplar-based models of generalization was provided for ill-defined categories in a category abstraction paradigm. Subjects initially classified 35 high-level distortions into three categories, defined by 5, 10, and 20 different patterns, followed by a transfer test administered immediately and after 1 wk. The transfer patterns included old, new, prototype, and unrelated exemplars, of which the new patterns were at one of five levels of similarity to a particular training (old) stimulus. In both experiments, increases in category size and old–new similarity facilitated transfer performance. However, the effectiveness of old–new similarity was strongly attenuated by increases in category size and delay of the transfer test. It was concluded that examplar-based generalization may be effective only under conditions of minimal category experience and immediacy of test; with continued category experience, performance on the prototype determines classification accuracy.

Categories are said to be ill defined (Neisser, 1967) when it is not obvious what dimensions characterize a category, and the variety among the potential members of a category is essentially infinite. Examples of ill-defined categories are quite diverse and would include the natural categories, musical style, hand-written letter *A*s, and the class of sound patterns associated with a specific spoken word.

How the human organism learns ill-defined categories, and how this knowledge is transferred to novel situations, has been a topic of considerable attention over the past 10 years. Posner and Keele (1968, 1970) argued that a prototype or central tendency is abstracted during the classification of distorted but related patterns. In their experiments, the subject initially sorted dot-pattern stimuli into a number of categories, with each category represented by a different reference pattern (objective prototype). Classification of old, new, and prototype patterns on a transfer test, administered immediately and again after a delay of 1 week, revealed that significant forgetting occurred for the old training stimuli. However, classification of the objective prototype was unaffected by this delay period. As a consequence, Posner and Keele (1970) argued that the objective prototype could not have been classified on the transfer test via generalization to the old, stored patterns, since any performance decrement on the old patterns should have been accompanied by a similar decrement for the prototype. Rather, they proposed that the subject abstracted the prototype during the classification phase and that the prototype was simply resistent to decay. The stability of prototypical performance, within the context of a deterioration for the old patterns, has now been obtained in numerous experiments (Homa, Cross, Cornell, Goldman, & Schwartz, 1973; Homa & Vosburgh, 1976; Strange, Kenney, Kessel, & Jenkins, 1970), in which delays varied from 4 days to 10 weeks.

These results do not suggest, however, that old information is unavailable or lost completely from storage. In fact, most experiments have found that performance on the old patterns is superior to performance on the new instances, even after lengthy time delays. For example, in the experiment by Homa and Vosburgh (1976), performance accuracy on the old learning stimuli exceeded that of the new patterns at the same level of distortion by 10% to 20% after 10 weeks. As a consequence, it seems likely that specific information, as well as information about the central tendency of the category, remains in memory. However, transfer to novel stimuli is thought to be accomplished primarily via generalization to the abstracted prototype, especially after lengthy time delays. Support for this view has also been based on transfer performance; with variable time delays, transfer performance for novel patterns is also unaffected, although some deterioration may occur for high-level distortions of a category (Homa & Vosburgh, 1976).

Recently, an alternative view of category learning has been proposed that is based on generalization to the stored exemplars (Brooks, 1978; Medin & Schaffer, 1978). According to this view, classification of a novel stimulus is determined by its similarity to the stored exemplars. The differential retention that is typically found for old and new stimuli (e.g., Posner & Keele, 1970) is accounted for, according to one version of exemplar theory (Medin & Schaffer, 1978), by alterations of the dimensional weights that characterize the stimuli. Although this prediction has not received empirical confirmation, Hintzman and Ludlam (1980) were able to simulate the differential forgetting of prototype and old exemplars with a computer model that used the stored exemplars as the sole basis for generalization. Here, forgetting of stimulus properties occurred in an all-or-none manner, and only a single exemplar was retrieved from each category at the time of transfer. Nonetheless, a number of procedural differences exist between these experiments and those which have used artificial categories: (a) The categories used by Brooks (1978) and Medin and Schaffer (1978) were not ill defined; (b) category experience is usually minimal, in that as few as three to six stimuli may define a category in the learning phase; and (c) learning variables known to shape generalization gradients in the category abstraction paradigm (e.g., category size, stimulus distortion, and category similarity) were not manipulated in these experiments.

For example, in the experiments by Medin and Schaffer (1978), the stimulus consisted of forms that varied along four binary-valued dimensions (such as red–green; triangle–circle), only two categories were learned,[1] and as few as three patterns may have represented each category. Each of these characteristics may be contrasted with research that has used ill-defined stimuli (e.g., Homa, 1978); the stimuli are typically statistically distorted forms, where the potential size of the population is essentially infinite, the dimensions underlying each category are obscure, numerous categories may be learned, and as many as 30 different patterns may represent a category during learning. As a result of these differences in stimulus composition, it makes sense to manipulate stimulus variables when ill-defined categories are investigated, whereas variable manipulations are largely precluded when well-defined stimuli are used. For example, the size of the stimulus population in the Medin and Schaffer (1978) study was 16, a number that is further reduced by using more than one category and by using different stimuli in the learning and transfer phases. Given these constraints, manipulations of variables like category size in the learning phase become virtually impossible.[2]

The importance of learning variables on category abstraction when ill-defined categories are used has been inferred from the effect of variable manipulations during learning on subsequent transfer to novel patterns. For example, when the number of patterns that defines a category in learning is increased, later transfer to novel patterns on an immediate (Homa, 1978; Homa et al., 1973; Homa & Vosburgh, 1976) and delayed (Homa et al., 1973; Homa & Vosburgh, 1976) test is enhanced. Furthermore, when the number of categories discriminated during learning is increased (Homa & Chambliss, 1975) or when the within-category stimulus variance is increased for categories defined by numerous exemplars (Homa & Vosburgh, 1976), generalization to new patterns is improved. In these studies, it has been argued that the abstracted prototype evolves with or is modified by exemplar experience, in which the aforementioned learning variables play a critical role in shaping the subject's knowledge of a category and its breadth.

A second reason for considering the role of learning variables on category abstraction is that they are an inevitable by-product of most naturally occurring learning situations. For example, the human organism most likely acquires information about concepts by exemplar experience. Not only are the examples of most naturally occurring categories likely to span a wide range of variation, but the sheer number of exemplars of a category is countless. As such, evaluations of categorization models that are based on as few as three examples of a category (e.g., Medin & Schaffer, 1978) may be misleading. Nonetheless, exemplar-based models of classification have not been directly evaluated in a category abstraction paradigm, in which the categories are ill defined.

In the present study, the effectiveness of old–new similarity on subsequent transfer to novel stimuli was determined for five levels of similarity. Thus, each new pattern presented on the transfer test had a specific similarity relationship to a given old training stimulus. Otherwise, each new pattern was a high-level distortion of the category prototype and, therefore, roughly equidistant from the prototype. In addition, old–new similarity was evaluated in the context of two variables known to influence subsequent generalization performance: category size and the time of the transfer test.

Predictions of exemplar and prototype models

In general, exemplar-based models of classification predict that performance on a transfer test will be heavily influenced by the degree of similarity of a new pattern to a particular old stimulus. Three different versions of exemplar-based generalization were considered in the present study, a single member (SM) model, a fixed set (FS) model, and a complete set (CS) model. These models differ only in the number of stored exemplars retrieved in response to the presentation of a test stimulus at the time of transfer. According to the SM model, the stored member that is most similar to the presented stimulus is retrieved from each category, and classification occurs to that category that results in the best similarity match (Hintzman & Ludlam, 1980). In the FS and CS models, the subject retrieves either a fixed number of stored members from each category or the entire set of stored patterns, respectively, at the time of classification. For example, if three categories were each defined by 20 different exemplars, then the number of patterns retrieved per category would be 1, N, and 20 for the SM, FM, and CS models, respectively, where N is some number between 1 and 20. Whereas the CS model is similar to the context model of Medin and Schaffer (1978), there has been little investigation of examplar-based models involving the retrieval of a fixed set of stored patterns (Reed, 1972, is an exception). The major motivation for considering the FS model is based on results that suggest that only a portion of the original category members are available at the conclusion of learning (Omohundro 1981; Homa, Omohundro, & Courter, Note 1). For both the SM and FS models, it is assumed that the stored exemplar most similar to the transfer stimulus is always included in the retrieved set of exemplars.

To clarify the predictions of these models for the present study, let x be the similarity between a test probe and the closest same-category member that is stored, let s_w be the average within-category similarity to the remaining members of the category, and let s_b be the average between-category similarity of the test probe to members of alternative categories. Then the classification algorithm for the CS exemplar model (Medin & Schaffer, 1978) appropriate to the present study would be

$$E_{a,i} = (x + (n_a - 1)s_w)/(x + (n_a - 1)s_w + n_b s_b), \tag{1}$$

where $E_{a,i}$ = evidence favoring classification of Pattern i into Category A, n_a is the number of patterns stored in Category A, and n_b is the number of patterns stored in alternative categories.

For the SM exemplar model, Equation 1 reduces to

$$E_{a,i} = x/(x + (M - 1)s_b), \tag{2}$$

whereas for the FS exemplar model, Equation 1 can be rewritten as

$$E_{a,i} = (x = (N - 1)s_w)/(x + (N - 1)s_w + (M - 1)Ns_b), \tag{3}$$

where M = number of categories learned, and N = number of stored exemplars retrieved per category at the time of classification.

If we assume that only the similarity between the test probe and the closest within-category member is varied (i.e., x is varied), and that the average within- and between-category similarity is held roughly constant for the remaining patterns, then classification accuracy ($E_{a,i}$) for all three exemplar models should be a monotonically increasing function of old–new similarity. These models do make one differential prediction, however. Both the SM (Equation 2) and FS (Equation 3) exemplar models predict that old–new similarity and the size of the category should be additive. That is, the effect of the similarity between the test probe and its closest stored member on classification performance should not interact with the number of patterns that originally defined the category in learning. In contrast, the CS (Equation 1) exemplar model can predict an interaction between old–new similarity and category size, because the *relative* contribution of specific old–new similarity on classification is diminished by increases in category size.[3]

The predictions of a prototype model on classification vary depending upon how the prototype is characterized and whether information other than the central tendency is stored. In most classificatory problems, three potential sources of information can be identified: (a) the central tendency or abstracted prototype for that category; (b) specific information about the exemplars that defined the category during learning; and (c) the boundary or breadth of the category. If only the prototype is stored following the learning phase, then classification of new patterns should be determined primarily by the similarity of the test patterns to the prototype; that is, classification should be monotonically related to the distortion level of the test pattern. Since all transfer patterns in the present study were high-level distortions a pure prototype model would predict that all new patterns would be classified equally well and independently of old–new similarity.

According to a mixed model, all three sources of information (prototype, specific exemplar information, and category breadth) may be available at the time of transfer, but their availability is modulated by the amount and degree of exemplar experience provided during learning. If few patterns represented a category during learning, the subject's representation for that category may consist primarily of information about the specific exemplars. As the degree of exemplar experience is increased, the representation of the category is increasingly dominated by information about the central tendency and the breadth for that category. The role of specific exemplar information is further reduced by time delays between original learning and test. The major predictions of a mixed prototype model in the present study are that old–new similarity should be an effective variable primarily when the category size is small and the transfer test is given immediately. For categories defined by increasing numbers of exemplars, the importance of old–new similarity should be diminished, especially on a delayed test. In effect, a mixed prototype model predicts an interaction between old–new similarity and time of test. Finally, a mixed prototype model predicts that accurate classification of the objective prototype, relative to other novel patterns, should be a function of variable manipulations that affect category abstraction. In particular, defining a category by few high-level distortions may result in minimal abstraction. As a consequence, the objective prototype may be classified more poorly than new patterns that are highly similar to old patterns. However, classification of the objective prototype should exceed that of novel stimuli when category size is large and the test is delayed, regardless of old–new similarity.

Mixed prototype versus complete set exemplar model

Given that the SM and FS exemplar models predict that old–new similarity and category size should be additive, whereas the CS exemplar model and the mixed prototype model both predict an interaction between these two variables, it may be asked whether the latter two models can be distinguished. In the present study, support for the CS exemplar model would be obtained if the derived values of x (Equation 1) were lawfully related to objective old–new similarity and independent of category size. If the derived values of x were found to be independent of objective old–new similarity and/or interacted with category size, then it would follow that factors other than objective old–new similarity were responsible for classification accuracy. A similar conclusion would result if the derived values of x approached 0.00. In this case, the contribution of specific old–new similarity to classification would be negligible. In summary, the CS exemplar model would be strongly supported if classification performance were shown to be an interactive function of old–new similarity and category size, even though the derived values of x were systematically related to old–new similarity and independent of category size. The mixed prototype model would be supported if significant interactions between old–new similarity and category size and between old–new similarity and time of test were obtained for the classification data, and the derived values of x were independent of objective old–new similarity.

Two additional controls were introduced to maximize the likelihood that exemplar generalization might occur; the transfer test was administered only following errorless classification of the learning stimuli, thus insuring that the transfer patterns were well learned, and all transfer patterns were high-level distortions (Posner, Goldsmith, & Welton, 1967) of a category prototype. The latter control guaranteed the occurrence of transfer patterns that were markedly more similar to a learning pattern than to the prototype.

Experiment 1

In Experiment 1, the transfer phase followed a criterial classification phase in which categories were represented by 5, 10, and 20 different high-level distortions of a prototype. High-level distortions share little obvious physical similarity to each other (Homa, Rhoads, & Chambliss, 1979). In terms of physical distortion, the high-level distortion stands roughly midway between the category prototype and unrelated patterns (Posner et al., 1967).

On the transfer test, administered both immediately after learning and after a week's delay, the subject again classified—without feedback—old, new, prototypical, and unrelated stimuli. Of major interest was the similarity relationship between the old and new stimuli on the transfer test. Each new stimulus had a manipulated similarity (distance) relationship to one of the original learning stimuli. Specifically, 20% of all new patterns were minimal distortions of a particular learning stimulus, having an average distance from an old pattern of 1.00 Euclidean unit/dot. The remaining new patterns were either 2.00 units/dot (20%), 3.00 units/dot (20%), 4.00 units/dot (20%), or 5.00 units/dot (20%) from a particular old stimulus. All new patterns, regardless of the old–new similarity relationship, were high-level distortions of a prototype. That is, all new patterns were, on the average, about 4.60 units/dot from the prototype. Thus, all new patterns on the transfer test were closer or more similar to a particular old training stimulus than to the category prototype, except for those new patterns which were 5.00 units/dot from an old pattern. Figure 1 shows an example of a prototypical form, a particular old stimulus, and five new transfer stimuli, each at a different level of old–new similarity from the old stimulus.

Two comments regarding the construction of the new stimuli on the transfer test should be mentioned. First, each vertex of an old pattern was displaced by an *equal* amount in the construction of a new pattern at a particular old–new similarity level. In effect, the distortion of a new pattern from a particular old stimulus was uniformly applied to each vertex. Second, each new pattern was always closer to its designated old pattern than to any other training stimulus, even when the old–new similarity value was 5.00 units/dot (a high-level distortion of an old pattern). The sampling distribution for distances between pairs of high-level distortions typically varies from about 5.00 to 9.00 units/dot (Homa, 1978). To verify this for the stimuli employed in the present study, the average distance moved per dot was computed for all old/new patterns for each prototype; a subset of the old–new similarity matrix is shown in Table 1. For example, Transfer Pattern 1 was a new pattern that was 5.0 units/dot from the prototype, 2.0 units/dot from its designated old pattern (Pattern 11), and 6.0–8.9 units/dot from the remaining 19 old patterns. Similarly, Transfer Pattern 4 was a new pattern that was 5.1 units/dot from the same prototype, 5.0 units/dot from its designated old pattern (Pattern 14), and 5.3–8.6 units/dot from the remaining patterns.

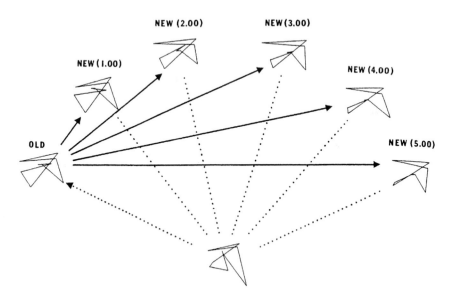

Figure 1 Example of a prototypical form, a high-level training (old) distortion, and five transfer (new) patterns. (The five transfer patterns are equidistant from the prototype and at one of five distances from the old pattern.)

Table 1 Mean interpoint distances between 10 new and 20 old patterns for one category

New pattern	P	Old (training) patterns																			
		1	2	3	4	5	6	7	8	9	10	11	12	13	14	15	16	17	18	19	20
1	5.0	8.1	8.3	8.9	8.3	7.5	6.0	7.4	7.2	6.2	6.0	*2.0*	6.8	8.2	6.0	7.5	8.4	6.9	6.7	7.2	7.8
2	4.8	6.0	6.7	7.3	7.6	7.0	4.4	6.6	6.6	6.3	6.8	6.5	*3.0*	7.3	5.8	7.9	7.0	5.6	7.6	8.1	7.4
3	5.3	7.7	7.4	8.9	6.1	7.4	6.2	8.0	5.7	6.8	6.5	6.5	7.7	*4.0*	7.1	7.2	6.3	6.7	7.9	5.5	8.4
4	5.1	8.5	7.1	8.6	8.4	7.4	5.3	6.2	6.2	6.2	5.8	5.8	6.9	7.1	*5.0*	8.3	8.0	7.2	7.3	7.3	8.0
5	4.8	6.5	7.6	7.6	4.8	7.7	7.5	7.4	7.4	7.1	6.8	6.3	7.2	7.0	7.3	*1.0*	7.1	6.8	7.6	7.3	7.7
6	5.2	6.9	7.1	7.8	7.1	7.4	5.0	7.4	6.1	5.5	7.2	7.6	6.4	6.4	7.7	7.9	*2.0*	7.6	8.5	6.9	8.1
7	5.2	6.2	6.9	7.8	7.2	8.5	4.6	7.6	5.9	7.1	6.4	6.4	5.2	6.7	6.1	7.1	7.1	*3.0*	7.8	8.5	8.2
8	5.0	7.4	6.6	8.0	7.6	5.9	6.3	5.4	7.2	6.7	6.7	6.0	6.6	7.7	6.4	7.5	8.7	8.7	*4.0*	6.5	7.7
9	5.2	8.3	7.2	9.4	6.0	7.6	6.0	7.0	6.7	6.8	6.9	6.0	7.8	6.6	7.2	6.4	6.9	7.9	7.8	*5.0*	7.7
10	5.1	7.6	6.6	7.4	7.0	6.9	8.1	8.4	5.7	7.3	6.8	6.7	6.8	7.1	5.5	7.5	7.7	7.0	7.3	7.2	*1.0*

Note. P = prototype. Italicized values refer to manipulated levels of old–new similarity.

Method

Subjects

A total of 24 Arizona State University undergraduates served as subjects. Two subjects were replaced, due to abnormally high error rates on the transfer test.

Materials and apparatus

Members of three form categories (P2, P3, P4) served as stimuli. Construction of these forms has been described previously (Homa, 1978). Briefly, a form category is created by first generating a random nine-dot pattern, and then connecting the dots with lines. This pattern is arbitrarily designated as a prototype. Different members of this category are then generated by statistically moving each of the dots of the prototype. Generally, patterns that are high-level distortions share little obvious similarity to the prototype, and low-level distortions appear very similar to the prototype. The dots of each pattern occupy locations within a 50×50 unit grid. For high-level distortions, each dot is displaced, on the average, about 4.6 units from each corresponding dot of the prototype. Thus, the topography of a category can be thought of as a hypersphere with the prototype located in the center and the high-level distortions on the surface of the sphere. The radius of the sphere would be equal to 4.6 units, and the average chord distance between any two high-level distortions on this sphere would be about 7.5 units. The new transfer stimuli would also reside on the surface of the sphere, but would have chord distances to a particular old pattern of 1.0–5.0 units.

Unlike previous studies that manipulated the degree of distortion of a pattern to the prototype, the present study systematically varied the degree of distortion of a new pattern to a particular old pattern. Each dot of a new pattern was displaced exactly 1.0, 2.0, 3.0, 4.0, or 5.0 units from the dots in a particular old pattern. The degree of distortion of the new pattern was then computed relative to the prototype; if the degree of distortion from the prototype was either too large or too small, the direction (but not the magnitude) of the dot movement of the new pattern was adjusted until the new pattern was both a high-level distortion of the prototype and at its proper distance from an old pattern.

The basic stimulus pool consisted of 228 patterns. Of these, 71 belonged to each of three different prototype categories, and 15 functioned as foils in the transfer phase; these latter 15 stimuli were essentially random patterns that were statistically unrelated to the three prototype categories.[4] For a given category, the 71 patterns consisted of the category prototype, 20 training patterns (old), and 50 high-level transfer patterns (new). These patterns were drawn by a Cal-Comp plotter and affixed to 6×9 in. cards. During the learning and transfer phase, each stimulus was hand held by the experimenter, with the subject viewing the stimulus from across a small table.

Procedure

The subject was told that a series of patterns would be shown in which the task was to determine which patterns belonged to the same category. The subject was instructed to classify the forms into three groups, called A, B, and C, and told not to expect an equal number of patterns in each group. Stimuli were presented one at a time, and learning was self-paced. Each response was followed by correct feedback ("no, that is a B pattern"), and learning was ended after two consecutive errorless trials. Each trial contained 35 different stimuli, 5 belonging to one category, 10 to another, and 20 to the third. Four different random orders of the 35 learning stimuli were used to present the stimuli.

The transfer phase began immediately after completion of the learning phase. Each subject was tested twice, once immediately and once after a delay of 1 wk. A total of 111 transfer stimuli were presented, 15 belonging to none of the three learned categories (foils), and 32 from each of the three learned categories. The 32 stimuli that belonged to each learned category consisted of 2 copies of the category prototype, 5 old (learning) patterns, and 25 new patterns. The 25 new patterns were distributed evenly across five levels of old/new similarity; that is, 5 patterns were 1.00 unit/dot from a particular old pattern, 5 were 2.00 units/dot from another old pattern, and so on. The 111 transfer patterns were presented in one of three different random orders, and no feedback was provided. Prior to the transfer task, the subject was told, in part: "A small percentage of patterns belong, in fact, to none of the three categories. If you feel that a given pattern doesn't belong to one of the three categories—and about 10% will not—then assign that pattern to a 'junk' category." The subject was also told to assign a confidence value to each classification, 1 indicating little confidence in their assignment, 2 indicating that they were somewhat confident, and 3 indicating that they were very confident of their choice. Finally, each subject was told that, unlike the learning phase, each category would be represented by the same number of patterns.

Design

The major variables of category size (5, 10, 20), time of test (immediate, 1 wk. delay), stimulus type (prototype, old, new, random), and old–new similarity (1.0–5.0 units/dot) were manipulated in a within-subject design. A Greco-Latin square was used to assign stimuli to the factors of category size, prototype representing each category (P2, P3, P4), and name assigned the category during learning (A, B, C). A total of eight subjects were randomly

310

assigned to each row of the resulting square. As a consequence, each category size was represented equally often by each prototype and each category name.

Results

Original learning

The mean number of trials to reach criterion was 16.96, with about 80% of the subjects requiring 12–21 trials. The trial of last error for any pattern belonging to categories represented by 5, 10, and 20 patterns was 12.75, 13.92, and 13.29, respectively ($p > .05$). Thus, speed of learning was not different for categories represented by different numbers of patterns.

Transfer performance

As expected, overall performance systematically improved with increases in category size; for 5-, 10-, and 20-instance categories, accuracy of classification was .678, .753, and .853, respectively, $F(2, 46) = 16.73$ ($MS_e = 1,160$), $p < .001$.[5] The facilitative effect of increasing category size was especially pronounced for the prototype stimulus, with an accuracy difference of 40% for categories defined by 5 and 20 instances; the magnitude of this facilitation for new and old patterns was about 17% and 7%, respectively. As might be expected, the Category Size × Stimulus type interaction was highly significant, $F(4, 92) = 7.83$ ($MS_e = 592$), $p < .001$.

The main effect of stimulus type (old, new, prototype) was highly significant, $F(2, 46) = 19.04$ ($MS_e = 559$), with old stimuli (.885) classified significantly better than new (.740) or prototypical (.732) stimuli. Although the main effect of delay was not significant ($F < 1$), the interaction between stimulus type and delay was significant, $F(2, 46) = 5.20$ ($MS_e = 188$), $p < .01$. The latter interaction was due to the fact that classification accuracy for old stimuli slightly deteriorated across the week delay (.906 vs. .864), whereas performance on the new (.732 vs. .747) and prototype (.701 vs. .764) stimuli actually improved somewhat on the delayed test.

In summary, the initial analysis confirmed the importance of category size on subsequent transfer, both immediately and after a delay of 1 wk. This analysis, however, does not address the issue of whether classification accuracy of new stimuli on the transfer test was influenced by old–new similarity. Figure 2 shows the mean classification accuracy of new transfer patterns as a function of their distances from old training stimuli (1.0–5.0 units/dot) for each category size and time of test. Also shown is the performance on the old and prototype stimuli. It should be noted that the prototype is, on the average, about 4.6 units/dot from old patterns. If the prototype were treated as simply a new pattern, then it should be classified no better than the most

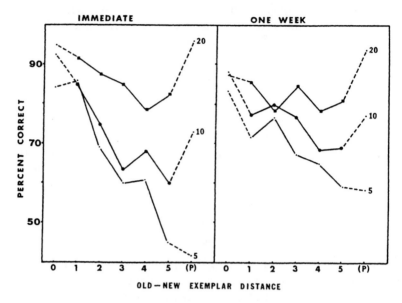

Figure 2 Mean classification accuracy of new stimuli on the transfer test, as a function of old–new similarity, category size, and time of test, Experiment 1.

distant of the new patterns from an old stimulus (new patterns with old–new similarity of 5.0 units/dot).

An analysis based on old–new similarity (1.0–5.0 units/dot) for new stimuli was performed, with the variables of category size and time of test. As before, performance on the new patterns increased with an increase in category size, $F(2, 46) = 11.76$ ($MS_e = 3.89$), $p < .01$. The main effect of old–new similarity on classification of new patterns was highly significant, $F(4, 92) = 15.11$ ($MS_e = 1.04$), $p < .01$. The effectiveness of old–new similarity on transfer may be defined by the difference in classification accuracy for patterns that are 1.0 unit/dot versus those that are 5.0 units/dot from an old pattern. In general, the effectiveness of old–new similarity was diminished by both increasing category size and delay of the transfer test; for example, for the 5-instance category and an immediate test, the effectiveness of old–new similarity was 41%; for the 20-instance category on a delayed test, this value dropped to 7%. The interaction between old–new similarity and time of test was highly significant, $F(4, 92) = 8.64$ ($MS_e = 0.46$), $p < .01$, as was the Category Size × Old–New Similarity interaction, $F(8, 184) = 2.80$ ($MS_e = .77$), $p < .01$. In general, an increase of about 10% across the old–new similarity variable is necessary for statistical significance. Thus, the 6.7% difference due to old–new similarity for the 20-instance category on a delayed test was not significant, $F(4, 92) = 1.31$ ($MS_e = 0.59$), $p > .20$.

Figure 2 also reveals an interesting relationship between category size and old–new similarity on prototype classification. For the category defined by 5 exemplars, the prototype was classified more poorly than any type of new stimulus. In contrast, the prototype was classified better than any new pattern when the category was defined by 20 instances. For the category defined by 10 instances, the prototype was classified better than all new instances except for those that were very close to a particular old pattern. The importance of these results for exemplar-based versus prototype-based models of classification is discussed later.

Confidence ratings

Following the classification of each stimulus on the transfer test, the subjects were required to indicate how confident they were of their choice, with 1 = very uncertain, 2 = moderately confident, and 3 = very confident. Figure 3 shows the mean confidence ratings for correctly classified patterns, as a function of stimulus type, category size, and time of test. In addition, the mean confidence ratings for unrelated patterns that were erroneously classified into the learned categories are shown.

For the most part, the confidence ratings tended to mirror the classification performance. For example, the highest confidence ratings were obtained for the old stimuli, changes in confidence across category size were greatest

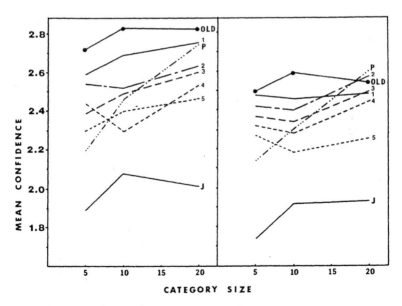

Figure 3 Mean confidence ratings for correctly classified patterns, as a function of stimulus type, old–new similarity, category size, and time of test, Experiment 1.

for the prototype stimulus, and, overall, confidence ratings were reduced on the delayed test. Whereas the effect of old–new similarity was nicely ordered on an immediate test, it was less so on the delayed test, especially for the 20-instance category. For example, the ratings for the 20-instance patterns on the delayed test varied within a narrow range (2.25–2.60), with the highest ratings obtained for the prototype, and followed, in order, by the new–2 (new patterns with an old–new similarity of 2.0 units/dot), old, new–3, new–1, new–4, and new–5. This may be contrasted with the more orderly effect of old–new similarity on confidence for patterns in the 5- and 10-instance categories. Finally, the unrelated patterns were consistently accorded the lowest confidence ratings, independent of category size and time of test. Thus, whenever a new stimulus was properly assigned to its category, its associated confidence value far exceeded the confidence of an unrelated pattern that was assigned to the same category.

Classification of unrelated patterns

The likelihood that unrelated patterns were correctly assigned to the junk category was .461 on an immediate test and .442 on the delayed test. Unrelated patterns were erroneously classified into the 5-, 10-, and 20-instance categories with probabilities of .097, .167, and .275, respectively, on the immediate test; on the delayed test, these values were .117, .172, and .269, respectively. If the classification of unrelated patterns into the learned categories is viewed as a form of response bias (false alarm), then clearly a bias existed for those categories originally defined by more exemplars. However, corrections for bias, such as high-threshold models (Green & Swets, 1966), only reduce the magnitude of the category size effect, and leave untouched the interaction of old–new similarity with category size. For example, the corrected values for new instances belonging to the 5-, 10-, and 20-instance categories were $p' = .620$, .666, and .772, respectively; the corresponding values for the prototypes were .440, .699, and .929, respectively.

There is some question, however, whether the classification tendencies of unrelated patterns should be used as an index of bias. First, the confidence ratings (Figure 3) indicate that the assignment of new and unrelated patterns that are sorted into the same category are clearly discriminated. Had subjects simply assigned more patterns into the larger categories on the transfer test, then it is unclear why the confidence ratings for correct assignments should markedly exceed the confidence ratings for erroneous assignments of unrelated patterns into the same category. Second, the correlation between hits and false alarms was computed for the 10- and 20-instance categories on both the immediate and delayed tests.[6] Contrary to what might be expected from a guessing interpretation, these correlations tended to be low and nonsignificant; for the 10-instance categories, these correlations were .33

(immediate) and .03 (delayed); for the 20-instance category, these values were .09 (immediate) and .42 (delayed), respectively. A complete summary of response tendencies for all stimulus types (old, new, prototype, unrelated) as a function of category size and time of test is shown in the left-hand panels of Table 2; the overall category response percentages are given on the bottom row. The implication of these response tendencies is discussed more fully in the general discussion.

Discussion

The results of Experiment 1 demonstrated that old–new similarity is an important factor influencing subsequent transfer, but that its influence is substantially diminished by increases in category size and a delay of the transfer test. Thus, the improved transfer performance obtained for the larger categories was associated with a diminished influence of old–new similarity. This result was obtained for both the accuracy data and the confidence ratings.

Nonetheless, one aspect of the procedure in Experiment 1 produced some bothersome concerns. A number of subjects reported at the conclusion of the study that the lengthy learning session (which sometimes lasted 1½–2 hr.) left them mentally exhausted by the time they participated in the immediate transfer test. If true, performance on the immediate transfer test may have underestimated the subject's knowledge about the acquired categories. The slight improvement on the delayed transfer test is consistent with this concern.

Experiment 2 was essentially a replication of Experiment 1, but a between-subject design was used to assess the effect of immediate and delayed transfer performance. In addition, the learning phase was slightly modified for those subjects in the immediate condition. On the first day, these subjects were brought to learning criterion. On the following day, these subjects were brought back to criterion and then administered the (immediate) transfer test. It was hoped that this procedural modification for the immediate subjects would provide an index of immediate transfer performance that was uncontaminated by fatigue.

Experiment 2

Method

Subjects

A total of 48 Arizona State University undergraduates served as subjects, half in an immediate transfer condition and half in a 1-wk.-delay condition.

Table 2 Summary of response tendencies

		Category response															
		Experiment 1								Experiment 2							
		Immediate				Week delay				Immediate				Week delay			
Category membership	Stimulus type	5	10	20	None	5	10	20	None	5	10	20	None	5	10	20	None
5	Old	*.842*	.033	.042	.083	*.833*	.058	.058	.050	*.975*	.008	.017	.000	*.808*	.067	.100	.025
	New	*.642*	.065	.108	.185	*.680*	.085	.097	.138	*.782*	.038	.075	.105	*.635*	.130	.167	.068
	Prototype	*.417*	.083	.271	.229	*.583*	.146	.062	.208	*.625*	.104	.167	.104	*.521*	.208	.146	.125
10	Old	.008	*.925*	.050	.017	.017	*.883*	.075	.025	.008	*.900*	.058	.033	.042	*.850*	.108	.000
	New	.030	*.703*	.100	.167	.040	*.743*	.112	.104	.028	*.787*	.107	.078	.050	*.757*	.138	.055
	Prototype	.000	*.729*	.167	.104	.000	*.771*	.104	.125	.021	*.917*	.000	.062	.062	*.729*	.188	.021
20	Old	.000	.008	*.950*	.042	.008	.042	*.875*	.075	.000	.042	*.942*	.017	.025	.083	*.850*	.042
	New	.008	.037	*.850*	.105	.023	.037	*.817*	.123	.018	.057	*.842*	.083	.053	.083	*.770*	.093
	Prototype	.000	.042	*.958*	.000	.000	.042	*.938*	.021	.000	.000	*.938*	.062	.000	.042	*.958*	.000
None	Unrelated	.097	.167	.275	*.461*	.117	.172	.269	*.442*	.083	.192	.292	*.433*	.142	.192	.328	*.339*
	Total	.212	.263	.348	.178	.232	.280	.333	.159	.254	.286	.336	.125	.235	.307	.357	.100

Note. Italicized values signify correct category responses.

Procedure

The procedure was identical to that used in Experiment 1, except that subjects in the immediate test condition received their learning and transfer tests on consecutive days. Specifically, all subjects in the immediate condition classified patterns to a criterion of two consecutive errorless trials on the first day, and were then dismissed with instructions to return the following day. On the following day, each subject again classified patterns to two consecutive errorless trials and then received the transfer test. With a few exceptions, most subjects received the minimum number of trials on the second day.

Design

A mixed design was used, with the variables of category size (5, 10, 20), stimulus type (prototype, old, new, random), and old–new similarity (1.0–5.0 units/dot) manipulated as within-subject variables, and time of the transfer test (immediate, 1-wk. delay) as a between-subject variable.

Results

Original learning

The mean number of trials to reach criterion was 14.33 for the immediate subjects and 13.04 for the delay subjects ($p > .05$). The trials of last error for categories represented by 5, 10, and 20 patterns were 9.54, 11.38, and 10.00, respectively, for the immediate subjects; for the delay subjects, the corresponding values were 8.96, 10.61, and 8.48, respectively. The apparent tendency for the intermediate-size category to be learned more slowly was significant, $F(2, 46) = 11.98$ ($MS_e = 4.14$), $p < .05$. Neither the effect of delay nor the Delay × Category Size interaction was significant.

Transfer performance

As was the case in Experiment 1, the main effects of category size, $F(2, 92) = 16.33$ ($MS_e = 568$), and stimulus type, $F(2, 92) = 12.87$ ($MS_e = 512$), were highly significant, as was the Category Size × Stimulus Type interaction, $F(4, 184) = 13.04$ ($MS_e = 363$), all $ps < .001$. Performance systematically improved with increases in category size (.729, .792, .829), with overall accuracy on the old patterns (.888) exceeding that of the new (.762) or prototype (.781) stimuli. The effect of increasing category size resulted in a 38% improvement for the prototype stimulus, 10% for new patterns, and 0% for the old stimuli. Contrary to the results of Experiment 1, performance on an immediate test (.826) exceeded that on the delayed test (.740), $F(1, 46) = 8.96$ ($MS_e = 1019$),

317

$p < .01$. The size of the decrement was largest for items belonging to the 5-instance category (10%—16%) and smallest for the new and prototype stimuli belonging to the 20-instance category (0%–7%).

The mean classification accuracy of new transfer patterns at each level of distance from an old training stimulus (1.0–5.0 units/dot) is shown in Figure 4, as a function of category size and time of test. Also shown is the performance on the old and prototype stimuli.

An analysis of variance was performed on the new stimuli only, for the variables of old–new similarity, category size, and time of test. The main effects of category size and old–new similarity were highly significant, $F(2, 92) = 5.61$ ($MS_e = 2.71$), and $F(4, 184) = 38.52$ ($MS_e = 0.72$), respectively, both $ps < .01$. The effect of category size on subsequent transfer was minimal when the old–new similarity was high. However, as the old–new similarity decreased, the facilitative effect of increased category size became more pronounced. For example, the mean classification accuracy of new patterns that were minimal distortions of an old pattern (new-1) was .850 for the 5-instance category and .871 for the 20-instance category. When new patterns were substantial distortions of an old stimulus, the effects of category size were substantial. For example, for new-4 patterns, the classification accuracy was .662 and .796 for the 5- and 20-instance categories, respectively; for new-5 patterns, the corresponding values were .492 and .716. As expected, the Category Size × Old–New Similarity interaction was significant, $F(8, 368) = 4.18$ ($MS_e = .67$), $p < .01$.

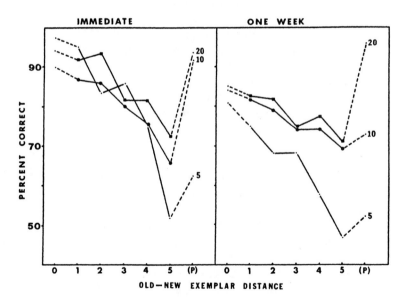

Figure 4 Mean classification accuracy on new stimuli on the transfer test, as a function of old–new similarity, category size, and time of test, Experiment 2.

Overall, classification accuracy for the new patterns decreased by 8.4% across the week delay, $F(1, 46) = 8.41$ ($MS_e = 3.77$), $p < .01$. The transfer decrement was greater for patterns belonging to the 5-instance category (15.0%) than either the 10- or 20-instance categories (3.0% and 7.9%, respectively). The transfer decrement across the week delay also tended to be reduced by increases in old–new dissimilarity; for the new–1, new–2, new–3, new–4, and new–5 patterns, the magnitude of this decrement was 10.7%, 10.3%, 11.6%, 8.6%, and 1.9%, respectively. However, the interaction between old–new similarity and time of the transfer test fell just short of significance, $F(4, 184) = 2.36$ ($MS_e = 0.72$), $.05 < p < .10$.

Finally, performance on the prototype mirrored the results obtained in Experiment 1. Specifically, (a) classification accuracy for the prototype was markedly enhanced by increases in category size, the magnitude of this facilitation being 31% on the immediate test and 41% on the delayed test; and (b) the prototype was classified more poorly than most new patterns when the category was defined by only 5 patterns; when the category was defined by 20 exemplars, the prototype was classified more accurately than any new pattern.

Confidence ratings

Figure 5 shows the mean confidence ratings for correctly classified patterns, as a function of stimulus type, category size, and time of test. As was the case in Experiment 1, the mean confidence ratings were nicely ordered according to old–new similarity for patterns belonging to the 5- and 10-instance categories on an immediate test, with the old stimuli receiving the highest ratings and the prototype receiving the lowest ratings for the 5-instance category. This systematic ordering becomes somewhat muddled for the 20-instance category on the immediate test, and for both the 10- and 20-instance category on the delayed test. The mean confidence ratings for the prototype belonging to the 20-instance category exceeded the mean confidence for the old patterns and all new patterns on the delayed test. Unrelated patterns, when (erroneously) classified into the learned categories, were clearly the recipient of the lowest confidence ratings. Unlike the results of Experiment 1, the mean confidence ratings were reduced for all stimulus types on the delayed test, with the old patterns and new–1 and new–2 patterns showing the greatest decrement.

Classification of unrelated patterns

The likelihood that unrelated patterns were correctly assigned to the junk category was .433 on the immediate test and .339 on the delayed test. Unrelated patterns were erroneously classified into the 5-, 10-, and 20-instance categories with probabilities of .083, .192, and .292, respectively, on

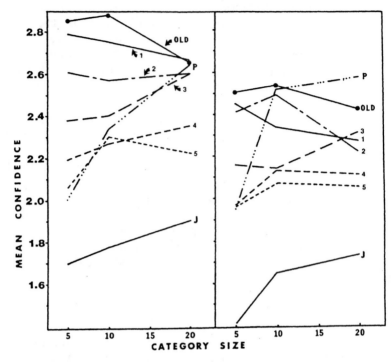

Figure 5 Mean confidence ratings for correctly classified patterns, as a function of stimulus type, old–new similarity, category size, and time of test, Experiment 2.

the immediate test; on the delayed test, these values were .142, .192, and .328, respectively.

The correlation between false alarms and hits for the 10-instance category was −.13 (immediate) and +.16 (delay); for the 20-instance category, these correlations were +.12 (immediate) and −.02 (delay). None of these correlations approached significance. A summary of response tendencies for all stimulus types, as a function of category size and time of test, is shown in the right-hand panels of Table 2.

General discussion

Two major results emerged from the present study: (a) Increases in the number of exemplars that represented a category in the learning phase resulted in a marked improvement in the classification of novel patterns belonging to that category on a later transfer test; and (b) the likelihood that a novel pattern was categorized by its similarity to an old pattern was increasingly attenuated by increases in category size and delay of the transfer test. The former result has been obtained repeatedly (e.g., Homa, 1978) and is consistent with the view that the mental representation of a category evolves with increasing exemplar experience. The latter result is germane to the issue of what determines generalization in a categorization task. As noted previously, exemplar-based models of generalization that posit the retrieval of a single most similar exemplar (Hintzman & Ludlam, 1980) or a fixed number of exemplars at the time of classification must predict that classification is an additive function of old–new similarity and category size. Since these variables strongly interacted in both experiments, exemplar models of this type are inadequate to account for the present results. Prototype models that assume that only the central tendency is stored can also be rejected as explanations for the present results, at least when categories are defined by relatively few exemplars, since objective old–new similarity was a significant determinant of classification. Only the mixed prototype model and the complete set exemplar model seem potentially compatible with the present results, since both models can predict an interaction between category size and old–new similarity.

The suitability of these two models was further assessed by noting the nature of the quantitative fit of Equation 1 to the observed classification data. According to Medin and Schaffer (1978), x varies from .00 to 1.00 and represents the similarity contribution to classification of an old pattern to a transfer pattern. At issue is whether the similarity contribution to classification of specific old–new similarity is independent of category size and time of test (complete set exemplar model) or whether the contribution of specific old–new similarity is diminished by increases in category size and length of time between acquisition and transfer (mixed prototype model). In one case, the x values were derived separately for each category size at each level of objective old–new similarity such that a perfect fit of the classification data resulted. In another case, a best fit of the classification data was computed for a set of x values common to category size. The concern was whether the goodness of fit seemed adequate to account for the present results, and whether the magnitude of the observed category size effect was accounted for by Equation 1.

For the first case, three different sets of derived x values were determined, each under slightly different assumptions: For Condition 1, assume $x_0 = 1.00$, $S_w = .01$, and S_b is estimated separately for each category size and time of test; for Condition 2, assume $x_5 = .05$, $S_w = .01$, and S_b is estimated separately for each category size and time of test; and for Condition 3, assume $S_w = .01$, and hold S_b constant across category size and time of test, with x unbounded. Here, x_0 represents the similarity contribution to classification of an old pattern presented at transfer to its stored representation, and x_1, . . ., x_5 represent the estimated contributions to classification for new patterns that objectively differed by 1.00 unit/dot, . . ., 5.00 units/dot, respectively, from a stored old pattern. In Condition 1, the x values are derived under the assumption that an old pattern on a transfer test has a similarity value of 1.00 with its stored representation. The value of S_w is set equal to .01 for all category sizes and times of test for two reasons. First, $S_w = .01$ is about the maximum value that is permissible for all category sizes and times of test, given that x must vary between .00 and 1.00. Second, the objective distance of new patterns to all training patterns (except for the old pattern that was at a manipulated distance to a new pattern) was roughly equal for each category size. By estimating S_b separately for each category size and time of test, it was possible to derive values of x that perfectly predicted the classification data. In Condition 2, the x values are derived under the assumption that the most distant of the manipulated levels of old–new objective similarity (old–new = 5.00 units/dot) results in a low value of x that is constant across category size and time of test. The assumed value of x_5 still exceeds that for S_w (.05 vs. .01). Thus, the contribution to classification of the most extreme level of manipulated old–new similarity is still greater than that of two arbitrarily selected patterns within the same category. This assumption is consistent with the fact that the objective interpattern distance for two arbitrary patterns within the same category is greater (7.50 units/dot) than for patterns at the most extreme level of old–new similarity (see Table 1). In Condition 3, a single value of S_w and S_b is selected for all category sizes and times of test, and x is allowed to assume whatever value is needed to fit the classification data (including negative values).

The estimated values for x under these three conditions are shown in Table 3, as a function of category size, time of test, and objective old–new similarity. The derived x values shown in Table 3 represent only a sample of the conditions that have been explored. The classification data for Experiment 1 are used for Conditions 1 and 2; the classification data for Experiment 2 are used for Condition 3.

For all three conditions, the derived x values interact with category size and tend to become uniform across objective old–new similarity on the delayed test. In all cases, the greatest values of x are obtained for the 5-instance category, and the smallest values are generally associated with the 20-instance category.[7] It should be noted that Condition 1 effectively pegs the x values at the most similar of the manipulated levels of similarity ($x_o = 1.00$), whereas Condition 2 pegs the x values at the most dissimilar level of old–new similarity ($x_5 = .05$). There exists a family of curves relating x to old–new similarity for the variables of category size and time of test that are intermediate to Conditions 1 and 2. None of these functions would alter the fact that the derived values of x are an interactive function of category size and time of test. In Condition 3, the estimated x values are shown when S_b has been set equal to .002. However, no value of S_b would alter the basic patterning of results; the values of x again interact with category size and, on the delayed test, become relatively uniform across old–new similarity. Taken at face value, these results indicate that the contribution of specific

Table 3 Estimated values of x as a function of old-new similarity, category size (5, 10, 20), and time of test, under three different sets of assumptions (1, 2, 3)

| | Values of x | | | | | | | | |
| | 1 ($x_o = 1.00$) | | | 2 ($x_s = .05$) | | | 3 (x unbounded) | | |
Objective similarity	5	10	20	5	10	20	5	10	20
Immediate									
Old–new									
1.0	1.18	.40	.51	.64	.43	.37	1.10	.24	.14
2.0	.40	.17	.25	.21	.19	.17	.26	.21	.23
3.0	.24	.06	.17	.12	.07	.10	.32	.11	−.06
4.0	.28	.10	.04	.14	.11	−.01	.14	.06	−.06
5.0	.12	.04	.11	.05	.05	.05	.02	.01	−.11
Old–Prototype	.03	.02	.07	.02	.02	.06	.02	.06	.02
Delayed									
Old–New									
1.0	.49	.41	.83	.12	.12	.15	.14	.13	−.05
2.0	.65	.49	.42	.17	.16	.02	.09	.10	−.06
3.0	.40	.39	.77	.09	.12	.13	.09	.05	−.10
4.0	.35	.22	.42	.08	.04	.02	.04	.05	−.09
5.0	.26	.24	.52	.05	.05	.05	.01	.02	−.12
Old–Prototype	.06	.05	.13	.02	.02	.04	.01	.01	.03
S_w	.0100	.0100	.0100	.0100	.0100	.0100	.0100	.0100	.0100
S_b: immed.	.0066	.0035	.0042	.0037	.0037	.0034	.0020	.0020	.0020
S_b: delay	.0070	.0058	.0113	.0021	.0025	.0038	.0020	.0020	.0020

Note. S_w = average within-category similarity; S_b = average between-category similarity.

old–new similarity is diminished by the variables of category size and time of test.

Still, it may be argued that the parameter space in the present study is not sufficiently sharp to warrant conclusions regarding the derived x values. To assess this possibility, a best fit of the classification data was computed with x values common to category size.[8] Table 4 shows the results of a best fit to the data of Experiment 1, immediate test. Generally, the complete set exemplar model provides a reasonable fit to the observed data, predicting a strong effect of objective old–new similarity for the 5-instance category and a diminished effect of old–new similarity for the 20-instance category. The major shortcomings of the best fit are shown in Table 5, which summarizes the predicted and observed category size effects for this set of data. Here, the category size effect is computed separately for old, new, and prototype patterns and reflects the difference in classification accuracy for the 5-instance and 20-instance categories. As indicated in Table 5, the predicted benefits of category size for old

Table 4 Best fit of classification performance for experiment 1, immediate test

| Estimated value of x | Category size | | | | | |
| | 5 | | 10 | | 20 | |
	Predicted	Observed	Predicted	Observed	Predicted	Observed
$x_0 = 1.00$	.874	.842	.897	.925	.941	.950
$x_1 = .72$	.835	.858	.866	.850	.924	.917
$x_2 = .30$	.694	.692	.757	.750	.867	.875
$x_3 = .17$	.583	.600	.675	.633	.828	.850
$x_4 = .16$	.571	.608	.667	.683	.824	.783
$x_5 = .10$	.483	.450	.603	.600	.795	.825
$x_p = .03$	.500	.417	.706	.729	.889	.958

Table 5 Predicted and observed category size effects

Stimulus type	Predicted	Observed	Error
Old	.067	.108	−.041
New	.223	.316	−.093
Prototype	.389	.541	−.152

patterns (.067) are somewhat less than observed (.108). More bothersome, however, is the fact that the predicted category size effect is substantially smaller than observed for new and, especially, for prototype patterns. In fact, when best fits are computed separately for each of the four data sets (Experiment 1, immediate and delayed test; Experiment 2, immediate and delayed test), a similar outcome is obtained: In each case, the predicted magnitude of the category size effect is smaller than observed for new and prototype patterns, whereas the predicted category size effect is usually overestimated for the old patterns (Experiment 1, immediate test, is the lone exception).[9]

The consistency between the two quantitative approaches can now be appreciated. For the data to be perfectly predicted (Table 3), it is necessary to have x values interact with category size and time of test; when a common set of x values are selected that produce a best fit to the classification data (Table 4), the magnitude of the predicted category size effect is, for new and prototype patterns, consistently underestimated. These two outcomes can only be realized by assuming that the contribution to classification of specific old–new similarity is increasingly diminished by increases in category size and delay of test.

The overestimation of the category size effect for old patterns by Equation 1 deserves comment. In abstraction research, the transfer performance of old patterns is usually invariant across category size; that is, the category size effect is typically of small magnitude or absent totally (e.g., Homa et al., 1973; Homa & Hibbs, 1978). This outcome is hardly surprising, since transfer is assessed only following errorless classification in the learning phase. In the present study, which also used an errorless learning criterion, the magnitude of the observed category size effect for old patterns was .108 and .042 in Experiment 1, immediate and delayed test, respectively; in Experiment 2, these values were −.033 and +.042. Thus, with the exception of performance in Experiment 1, immediate test, the observed magnitude of the category size effect was quite small, averaging less than a 2% facilitation. In contrast, the predicted magnitude of the category size effect by Equation 1 was sizable, averaging 8.5%, with a range of 6.7% to 10.9% for the four data sets. The predicted category size effect arises because the denominator of Equation 1 cumulates dissimilarities from the contrasting categories; the larger the size of the contrasting categories, the poorer the predicted performance on old patterns from the smallest category will be. In fact, for the best fitting parameters in the present study, an upper bound of 87% is predicted for old patterns belonging to the smallest category. This upper limit was substantially exceeded in Experiment 2, immediate test (observed = .975; predicted = .874), resulting in the category size effect being overestimated by 10%.

Since the complete set exemplar model has no assumptions to distinguish the classification of old and new patterns, a category size effect is predicted for both stimulus types. As a consequence, it seems inevitable that the category size effect for old patterns will be overestimated by Equation 1 whenever an errorless learning criterion is adopted, especially when the categories are also defined by numerous exemplars. It is not clear that Equation 1 could be modified to rectify this problem. For example, the magnitude of error for old patterns could be reduced by simply assuming that a near-equal number of patterns is stored for each category, regardless of how many patterns actually defined each category. Generally, this would reduce the predicted magnitude of the category size effect for old patterns to be more in line with the obtained values. However, modifications of this type would only further increase the error for new and prototype patterns; that is, the predicted category size effect for these patterns would also be reduced, thereby underestimating the category size effect by an even greater amount. Alternatively, Equation 1 could be modified to include a familiarity or strength parameter for old patterns that would be at asymptote immediately and decay thereafter. By setting the strength parameter equal for all category sizes at the conclusion of learning, predicted differences across category size for old patterns would be reduced. However, assumptions of this type would violate the spirit of current versions of exemplar theory that assumes that the same mechanism mediates classification of old and new patterns (Medin & Schaffer, 1978). Regardless, even this modification would leave untouched the underestimation of the category size effect for new and prototype patterns.

In sum, the results of the present study are more compatible with a mixed prototype model. There are two major shortcomings of an exemplar-based model of generalization such as is expressed in Equation 1; the model *under-estimates* the observed category size effect for the category prototype and, to a lesser extent, new patterns, and it generally *overestimates* the observed category size effect for old patterns. The patterning of results shown in Table 3 suggests that transfer to specific, stored exemplars may be most likely when the category is represented by a small number of exemplars, an immediate test is administered, and the similarity between a novel stimulus and a stored exemplar is high. However, exemplar-based generalization is increasingly unlikely once exemplar experience becomes substantial and a delayed test is used. Previous support for exemplar-based generalization was obtained under conditions of minimal exemplar experience and an immediate transfer test (Medin & Schaffer, 1978). A reasonable hypothesis is that a concept, in its early stage of development, is represented primarily by a small number of exemplars. With continued learning, however, the concept becomes increasingly represented by the central tendency (abstracted prototype) and the breadth of that concept. Consistent with this view is the fact that variable manipulations that enhanced the classification of the prototype were also associated with a diminished importance of old–new similarity on classification. One obvious implication of the present results is that the importance of exemplar similarity on generalization may asymptote to zero as category experience continues to increase.

The theoretical importance of increased exemplar experience on transfer for classification models cannot be stressed enough. The human organism encounters an essentially limitless array of examples that belong to biological, invented, and esthetic categories. It has even been proposed that the beginning scientist is able to appreciate the abstract concepts and paradigmatic rules of a profession only after repeated laboratory demonstrations (Kuhn, 1970), that is, by numerous, concrete examples. The suggestion here is that the nature of categorical information that guides generalization behavior (specific exemplars or an abstracted prototype) interacts with the amount of exemplar experience relevant to a category.

A number of secondary results are of interest. First, the category prototype need not be classified any better than other new instances, especially when category experience is minimal and only high-level distortions represent a category. In both Experiments 1 and 2, the objective prototype was classified more poorly than most new stimuli when the category size for that category was small (e.g., 5 exemplars). The advantaged position of the prototype on the transfer test was realized only when the category was defined by numerous exemplars. Second, confidence ratings provided a good mirror of classification accuracy. For example, confidence ratings declined across the delay, especially for old stimuli and new patterns that shared a high degree of similarity to the old stimuli. The mean confidence ratings tended to be more stable for the prototype and new patterns that shared a minimal similarity to the old patterns. Third, the overall performance on the transfer test was influenced by the type of experimental design used (within- vs. between-subject). Specifically, less forgetting was obtained when a within-subject design was used (Experiment 1), a result inconsistent with earlier findings in category abstraction (Strange et al., 1970), which had found no retention differences. The source of this discrepancy is unclear, although the present study would seem to be a more difficult task (35 high-level distortions had to be classified in the learning phase vs. 12 distortions in the experiment by Strange et al.).

Two other issues warrant discussion. First, exemplar-based generalization was assessed in the present study by the manipulation of *objective* similarity between old and new patterns. Is it possible that the *subjective* similarity between old and new exemplars determined transfer performance, even for the largest categories in which objective similarity played a negligible role? Second, why did increased exemplar experience in the learning phase result in a greater tendency to classify unrelated patterns into the category on the transfer test? With regard to the first issue, the present study cannot directly address the nature of the internal representation of the category members. Nonetheless, the objective similarity between old and new stimuli was an important predictor of transfer performance, but primarily when the category size was small. If the subject stored intact patterns but the encoded representation failed to preserve the objective old–new similarity, then the objective manipulation of old–new similarity should have been ineffective for all category sizes at each delay. Since this was not the case, exemplar-based models of classification would have to explain why an effective manipulation of objective old–new similarity interacted with category experience and time of test.

The question of why overgeneralization appears to occur for those categories that show the greatest levels of abstraction is unclear. A simple explanation is that the subject simply increases his willingness to classify patterns into that category originally defined by the most patterns in learning (a bias explanation). An alternative explanation is that increased levels of abstraction produce, as an initial by-product, a categorical breadth that is overly extended. An explanation for overgeneralization that is based solely on bias seems unlikely for a number of reasons. First, a bias explanation would predict that a subject's hit and false alarm rate should be positively correlated. However, the correlation between hits (correct assignments of new patterns) and false alarms (erroneous classifications of unrelated patterns into the learned categories) was low and nonsignificant in the present study. In effect, a subject who gave evidence of strong abstraction tendencies by sorting nearly all the new patterns into the appropriate category was as likely to sort few unrelated patterns into that category as many. Second, subjects clearly discriminated between the new and unrelated patterns that were classified together into the same category, as judged from the confidence ratings. If transfer performance were corrected by including only those new patterns that were correctly classified and that exceeded the confidence value for unrelated patterns sorted into that category, then the magnitude of the category size effect would be virtually unchanged. What is most puzzling is the fact that a subject who clearly discriminates new from unrelated patterns will nonetheless sort both stimulus types into the same category. A partial answer is that some subjects view the unrelated patterns as extreme distortions of the category, that is, make an overgeneralization based on the information contained in the pattern rather than a criterion shift.

Two results from previous research also argue against a bias interpretation: (a) It is not unusual to obtain a category size effect when differential bias is absent (e.g., Homa, 1978, Experiment 2; Homa & Hibbs, 1978; Omohundro, 1981); and (b) the magnitude of the category size effect on subsequent transfer is unaffected by either explicit (Homa & Field, Note 2) or implicit (Omohundro & Homa, 1981) manipulations of a supposed criterion. In sum, the evidence suggests that manipulations that enhance the degree of abstraction for a category may also result in a representation that is overly extended. It may well be the case that only manipulations that emphasize category discriminability (e.g., training on numerous rather than few categories, Homa & Chambliss, 1975) can effectively counteract tendencies toward overgeneralization.

Notes

This research was supported by National Institute of Mental Health Grant 5 R01 MH28270.

The authors would like to thank Julie Omohundro and Harold Makoany for their comments on an earlier draft of this manuscript. Portions of this study were presented to the Western Psychological Association, San Diego, April 1979.

1 An interpretative problem with the experiments by Medin and Schaffer (1978) is that subjects were not taken to an errorless learning criterion before the transfer test was given; in Experiments 2–4, more than 50% of the subjects failed to reach criterion. As a consequence, it is questionable whether generalization to old patterns can be properly evaluated, given that there is no assurance that the old patterns were stored in memory.

2 These same concerns may be registered about the computer simulation by Hintzman and Ludlam (1980), who held constant the number (two) and similarity (unknown) of categories during learning, the degree of pattern distortion during learning and transfer (low), and so on. It would be worthwhile to know whether the results simulated in their study are specific to the conditions explored, or whether their model can be extended to other situations as well, such as the use of two or more categories, or variable levels of pattern distortion in learning and transfer. Also, stable classification of the category prototype has been obtained under conditions in which a default or "none" category is available at the time of transfer (e.g., Hartley & Homa, 1981; Homa & Hibbs, 1978). Had a default category been available in the Hintzman and Ludlam simulation, it is less clear whether stable performance would

have been obtained for the new and prototype stimuli. Specifically, since all stored items underwent progressive deterioration in the simulation, it seems inevitable that an increasing percentage of old, new, and prototype stimuli would be assigned to the default category. Finally, the simulation was conducted on well-defined patterns in which the total pool of acceptable properties were specified at the outset. From introspective reports, as well as recent pilot work of ours, it is likely that the number and quality of features are not constant for ill-defined categories, but may change with the level of learning (a point also noted by Fisher, 1916, and Hull, 1920). If it could be demonstrated that the patterning of results obtained by Hintzman and Ludlam is robust across these conditions, then obviously examplar-based and prototype-based models of classification cannot be distinguished by the differential forgetting of prototype and old examplars.

3 Equation 1 is a general form for a class of exemplar models. However, it should be noted that the similarity between two patterns in the context model (Medin & Schaffer, 1978) is determined in a multiplicative manner for the component dimensions. As such, two stimuli that are highly similar along all dimensions but one could be viewed as quite dissimilar if that disparate dimension was both salient and psychologically discriminating to the subject. In the present study, any two high-level distortions (except for the manipulated transfer pattern and its stored counterpart) should be viewed as quite dissimilar, since the average distance moved per dot between two high-level patterns is quite large. More critically, the likelihood is near certainty that at least one of the corresponding points in the two high-level patterns will be sufficiently separated to reach values obtained by randomly related patterns.

4 It is not obvious how one should measure the distance between two patterns from different categories, since corresponding points in two patterns from different categories cannot be determined. If the correspondence is made randomly, then the average Euclidean distance moved per point is about 15.00 for patterns from different categories. If corresponding points are defined in terms of a best fit, then this distance can be reduced to about 10.00 units/point. This is achieved by computing the average distance for all pattern rotations and defining the best fit as the rotation that minimizes point separation. To date, we have not found that this value (10.00 units/dot) is further reducible. Still, this minimum value is not substantially greater than that obtained between two high-level distortions from the same category (about 7.50 units/dot). Regardless, it seems likely that the objective representation of the categorical space is composed of nonoverlapping spheres, with the distance between spheres (categories) still undetermined.

5 Since the opportunities of an error differed for the old (5), new (25), and prototype (2) stimuli, errors were manipulated by 20, 4, and 50, respectively, prior to the analysis. This had the effect of equating error opportunities for the different stimulus types, and produced a slightly more conservative test.

6 Correlations were confined to the 10- and 20-instance categories, because only these categories exhibited a reasonable range of false alarm values. Although the correlation between hits and false alarms was also low for the 5-instance category, the truncated false alarm range precluded an adequate test.

7 The single exception occurs in Condition 1 on the delayed test, where the x values for the 20-instance category are quite large. This outcome was produced by the unusually large value of S_b (.0113) that was needed to fit the classification data. In fact, S_b (the similarity between patterns in different categories) has a slightly larger value than S_w (the similarity between patterns in the same category).

8 Best fits were computed separately for each of the four data sets and involved the estimation of 8 parameters (S_w, S_b, x_o, . . ., x_5 and x_p) to 21 data points (3 Category

Sizes × 7 Transfer Items: old, prototype, and 5 levels of new). The only restrictions were that the x values be bounded between .00 and 1.00, and that the estimated x values decrease with increases in objective old–new similarity.

9 Ideally, the parameter values resulting from a best fit to data will be theoretically meaningful. If one were to accept Equation 1 as appropriate to the present study, then the resulting parameter values describe a complex, if not peculiar, set of influences that determined classification performance. For both experiments, the value of S_b increased on the delayed test, suggesting that between-category discriminability was worsened by a week's delay. However, the best-fitting values of x_1–x_5 interacted with time of test, with the result that the x values for moderate and extreme levels of objective old–new similarity were considerably larger on the delayed test. For example, in Experiment 1, immediate test, the values of x_1–x_5 were .72, .30, .17, .16, and .10, respectively. On the delayed test, the corresponding values were .57, .56, .50, .34, and .33. A similar result, in which x values again interacted with time of test, was obtained in Experiment 2. On the one hand, we would have to explain why the x values associated with minimal old–new differences declined on the delayed test, whereas the x values for the largest old–new differences increased. On the other hand, we would have to explain why the generally elevated x values on the delayed test occurred, given that the *degree* of specific old–new similarity was considerably less important on the delayed test; that is, the x values are near asymptote across objective old–new similarity. Given the occurrence of these events within the context of a general deterioration of between-category discriminability, it is as if the entire categorical space were decaying to an unlearned state, and all new patterns were located equidistant from their designated old patterns.

Reference notes

1. Homa, D., Omohundro, J., & Courter, S. *Perception of abstracted form.* Paper presented to the Rocky Mountain Psychological Association, Albuquerque, N.M., May 1977.
2. Homa, D., & Field, D. *Breadth and bias in category abstraction.* Paper presented to the Psychonomic Society, St. Louis, Mo., November 1980.

References

Brooks, L. Nonanalytic concept formation and memory for instances. In E. Rosch & B. B. Lloyd (Eds.), *Cognition and categorization.* Hillsdale, N.J.: Erlbaum, 1978.

Fisher, S. C. The process of generalizing abstraction; and its product, the general concept. *Psychological Monographs*, 1916, *21*(2, Whole No. 90).

Green, D. M., & Swets, J. A. *Signal detection theory and psychophysics.* New York: Wiley, 1966.

Hartley, J., & Homa, D. Abstraction of stylistic concepts. *Journal of Experimental Psychology: Human Learning and Memory*, 1981, 7, 33–46.

Hintzman, D. L., & Ludlam, G. Differential forgetting of prototypes and old instances: Simulation by an exemplar-based classification model. *Memory & Cognition*, 1980, *8*, 378–382.

Homa, D. Abstraction of ill-defined form. *Journal of Experimental Psychology: Human Learning and Memory*, 1978, *4*, 407–416.

Homa, D., & Chambliss, D. The relative contributions of common and distinctive information on the abstraction from ill-defined categories. *Journal of Experimental Psychology: Human Learning and Memory*, 1975, *1*, 351–359.

Homa, D., Cross, J., Cornell, D., Goldman, D., & Schwartz, S. Prototype abstraction and classification of new instances as a function of number of instances defining the prototype. *Journal of Experimental Psychology*, 1973, *101*, 116–122.

Homa, D., & Hibbs, B. Prototype abstraction and the rejection of extraneous patterns. *Bulletin of the Psychonomic Society*, 1978, *11*, 1–4.

Homa, D., Rhoads, D., & Chambliss, D. The evolution of conceptual structure. *Journal of Experimental Psychology: Human Learning and Memory*, 1979, *5*, 11–23.

Homa, D., & Vosburgh, R. Category breadth and the abstraction of prototypical information. *Journal of Experimental Psychology: Human Learning and Memory*, 1976, *2*, 322–330.

Hull, C. L. Quantitative aspects of the evolution of concepts. *Psychological Monographs*, 1920, *28*(1, Whole No. 123).

Kuhn, T. S. *The structure of scientific revolutions* (2nd ed.). Chicago: University of Chicago Press, 1970.

Medin, D. L., & Schaffer, M. M. Context theory of classification learning. *Psychological Review*, 1978, *85*, 207–238.

Neisser, U. *Cognitive psychology*. New York: Appleton-Century-Crofts, 1967.

Omohundro, J. Recognition vs. classification of ill-defined category exemplars. *Memory & Cognition*, 1981, *9*, 324–331.

Omohundro, J., & Homa, D. Search for abstracted information. *American Journal of Psychology*, 1981, *94*, 267–290.

Posner, M. I., Goldsmith, R., & Welton, K. E., Jr. Perceived distance and the classification of distorted patterns. *Journal of Experimental Psychology*, 1967, *73*, 28–38.

Posner, M. I., & Keele, S. W. On the genesis of abstract ideas. *Journal of Experimental Psychology*, 1968, *77*, 353–363.

Posner, M. I., & Keele, S. W. Retention of abstract ideas. *Journal of Experimental Psychology*, 1970, *83*, 304–308.

Reed, S. K. Pattern recognition and categorization. *Cognitive Psychology*, 1972, *3*, 382–407.

Strange, W., Kenney, T., Kessel, F. S., & Jenkins, J. J. Abstraction over time of prototypes from distortions of random dot patterns: A replication. *Journal of Experimental Psychology*, 1970, *83*, 508–510.

34

CONTEXT-INDEPENDENT AND CONTEXT-DEPENDENT INFORMATION IN CONCEPTS

Lawrence W. Barsalou

Source: *Memory & Cognition*, 10(1) (1982): 82–93.

It is proposed that concepts contain two types of properties. Context-independent properties are activated by the word for a concept on all occasions. The activation of these properties is unaffected by contextual relevance. Context-dependent properties are not activated by the respective word independent of context. Rather, these properties are activated only by relevant contexts in which the word appears. Context-independent properties form the core meanings of words, whereas context-dependent properties are a source of semantic encoding variability. This proposal lies between two opposing theories of meaning, one that argues all properties of a concept are active on all occasions and another that argues the active properties are completely determined by context. The existence of context-independent and context-dependent properties is demonstrated in two experimental settings: the property-verification task and judgments of similarity. The relevance of these property types to cross-classification, problem solving, metaphor and sentence comprehension, and the semantic-episodic distinction is discussed.

Some properties in a concept seem to come to mind on all occasions. The word "skunk" usually makes people think of the property "unpleasant smell," and "rattlesnake" usually makes people think of "poisonous." In contrast, other properties in a concept rarely seem to come to mind, and when they do, it is only in relevant contexts. For example, "basketball" rarely makes people think of "floats." However, the sentence frame "Chris used X as a life preserver when the boat sank" would probably bring "floats" to mind for "basketball" when "X" is "basketball." In this paper, I propose there are two important types of properties associated with concepts: context-independent (CI) properties and context-dependent (CD) properties. CI properties are activated by the word for a concept on all occasions (e.g., "unpleasant smell" for "skunk"). CD properties are rarely if ever activated by the word for a concept and are only activated by relevant contexts in which the word appears (e.g., "floats" for "basketball").

CI properties form the core meanings of words. This is because they are activated by the respective word on all occasions, independent of contextual relevance. Barsalou and Bower (Note 1) have proposed that properties become automatically activated by a word after being frequently associated with it during processing. Frequent pairings of a word and a property cause an automatized relation between them to be established in memory (also see Shiffrin & Schneider, 1977). Barsalou and Bower (Note 1) showed that two types of properties are likely to be frequently active during the processing of a word. First, properties having high diagnosticity may often be active, since they are useful for distinguishing instances of a concept from instances of other concepts. "Gills" becomes CI for "fish" because all fish have gills and no other things do. The second type of property likely to be frequently active during the processing of a word includes properties relevant to how people typically interact with instances of the respective concept. "Edible" becomes CI for "apples" because it is central to how people typically interact with them. As shown by "edible" in relation to "apple," properties frequently relevant to human interaction can become CI even if they have low diagnosticity (i.e., "edible" is true of many other things).

CD properties are a source of semantic encoding variability. CD properties may be represented in concepts, but they are not usually activated by encoding the respective words. Rather, these properties are activated only by relevant encoding contexts in which a word appears. Semantic encoding variability is the result of different encoding contexts of a word activating different subsets of CD properties in the respective concept. This phenomenon has frequently been observed empirically (e.g., R.C. Anderson & Ortony, 1975; R.C. Anderson, Pichert, Goetz, Schallert, Stevens, & Trollip, 1976; Barclay, Bransford, Franks, McCarrell, & Nitsch, 1974; Tulving & Thompson, 1973) and has been incorporated theoretically by Bower (1972) and Estes (1955, 1959). Barsalou and Bower (Note 1) suggest that CD properties are typically inactive because they have rarely, if ever, been processed simultaneously with their respective words. Hence, the associations between these properties and their respective words are weak or non-existent. When such associations do not exist, various inference processes may be required to compute them. People may not have stored the fact that "fits in a suitcase" is a property of "flashlight," but they can certainly infer it. If a CD property comes to be frequently processed with a word, the property may change status and become CI. Although "wears horseshoes" may be CD for "horse" for people who are rarely around horses, it could become CI for someone during the course of learning to be a horseshoer.

Some properties are probably neither CI nor CD. These may sometimes be activated by a word, although not on all occasions, and may sometimes be activated by context. Such properties may occasionally be activated by a word because of random fluctuations in the amount of activation the property receives. On other occasions, however, these properties may be activated by relevant contexts. The senses of ambiguous words can similarly not be classified as strictly CI or CD. This is because they often come to mind without context, but they are also influenced by sentence contexts in which they occur (Swinney, 1979; Tanenhaus, Leiman, & Seidenberg, 1979). Nevertheless, the senses of ambiguous words can be viewed as concepts that contain CI and CD properties. Once an ambiguous word is disambiguated in context, the distinction between CI and CD properties becomes applicable to the concept converged upon. Consider "bear" in the sentence "The bear caught pneumonia." "Bear" and the sentence frame both converge on the mammalian sense of "bear." However, some of the properties activated for this sense are CI (e.g., "is furry," "can be dangerous") and some are CD (e.g., "can be sick," "has lungs"). Beyond acknowledging their existence, I will not further consider properties and word senses that are neither CI nor CD. Rather, the purposes of this paper are (1) to demonstrate the existence of CI and CD properties in concepts and (2) to consider the roles these property types play in various cognitive phenomena.

This paper addresses a particular aspect regarding the structure of concepts, namely, the accessibility of properties. Two theories of meaning take more extreme views on this aspect. Traditional views of semantics (e.g., Katz & Postal, 1964) assume that the meaning of a word contains a fixed set of semantic features applicable on all occasions on which the word is used. It appears that semantic memory models usually make a similar assumption (e.g., Glass & Holyoak, 1975; McCloskey & Glucksberg, 1979; Smith, Shoben, & Rips, 1974). In the terms of this paper, this approach argues that all of a concept's properties are CI. An opposing and more radical view of semantics (e.g., Olson, 1970) argues that the meaning of a word completely depends on the context in which the word is used. Specifically, the meaning of a word in a given context is a function of the distinctions it is supposed to convey in that context. According to this view, there may be no overlap between uses of the same word across contexts. Psychologists who have observed contextual effects on encoding have often reached a similar conclusion (e.g., Jacoby, Craik, & Begg, 1979). In the terms of this paper, this approach argues that all of a concept's properties are CD. The proposal that some of a concept's properties are CI and others are CD lies between these two theories of meaning. Consequently, evidence for the existence of CI and CD properties in concepts would have implications for theories of natural language semantics.[1]

The definitions of CI and CD properties lead to several empirical predictions. First, in a given context, all CI properties should be available and irrelevant CD properties should not. This is because CI properties are always activated by their respective words, whereas irrelevant CD properties remain inactive due to lack of contextual activation. The second prediction follows from the definition of CI properties. Since CI properties are always activated by the respective words on all occasions, they should be unaffected by contextual relevance: A CI property should be just as available in an irrelevant context as in a relevant context. This assumes that the activation of a CI property by a word maximally activates that property. The third prediction follows from the definition of CD properties. Since CD properties depend on relevant contexts for activation, they should be available in working memory for processing when the context is relevant and unavailable when the context is irrelevant. The alternative hypotheses are (1) all the properties in a concept are activated by the respective word on all occasions and (2) all the properties active in a concept are determined by context.

These hypotheses and their alternatives are contrasted in the two experiments that follow. The first experiment tests these predictions in the property-verification task. The second experiment tests these predictions in judgments of similarity. Evidence from other current work is also brought to bear on these issues. Finally, the relevance of CI and CD properties to cross-classification, problem solving, metaphor and sentence comprehension, and the semantic-episodic distinction is discussed.

Experiment 1

A version of the property-verification task was used to test the predictions following from the definitions of CI and CD properties. On each trial, subjects read a sentence containing an underlined subject noun. Several seconds later, the label for a property was presented, and subjects indicated whether or not the subject noun in the preceding sentence possessed the property.

The logic of the experiment is as follows. If the property for a trial is CI information of the subject noun, then verification time should not vary across sentence contexts. In particular, verification time should be no less when the sentence context is related to the property than when the sentence context is unrelated. This is because the property, being CI, is always activated by the subject noun itself and therefore is not dependent on context for activation. However, if the property for a trial is CD information of the subject noun, then verification time should depend on context. Specifically, verification time should be much less when the sentence context is related to the property than when the sentence context is unrelated. This is because the property, being CD, is not activated by the subject noun and therefore is dependent on context for activation. If the difference between related and unrelated contexts for CD properties is substantial (i.e., on the order of several hundred milliseconds), this would suggest that CD properties are, in fact, inactive in irrelevant contexts.

Method

Procedure

Subjects looked into a modified Siliconix tachistoscope and rested their forefingers on two response buttons 7 cm apart. When prepared for a trial, subjects pressed the "start" button (positioned colinearly and midway between the two response buttons) with the same finger used to press the "true" button. After a 500-msec interval, a context sentence appeared in the top field of the tachistoscope. All sentences began with "The," followed by an underlined subject noun and a predication of the subject noun. Subjects were instructed to fully comprehend the sentence and to read it out loud. The context sentence was removed after 6 sec, and a property label immediately appeared in the bottom field; subjects did not read the label aloud. If the subject noun in the context sentence possessed the property, subjects pressed the "true" response button; otherwise, they pressed the "false" response button. For each trial, time was measured from the onset of the property to the point at which a response was detected. Subjects were instructed to respond as quickly as possible, but to avoid making errors.

Subjects received 24 practice trials and 60 test trials. There was a short break between the practice and test trials. Subjects could take a break anytime during the test trials, but they rarely did. Following the last test trial, subjects were asked a series of questions concerning their strategies.

Subjects and materials

The subjects were 19 Stanford students participating for pay or course credit. One subject's data were not used because of an error rate exceeding 15% (the average error rate for the remaining subjects was 2.8%). The materials consisted of context sentences and properties, related as discussed next. Examples of the materials are shown in Table 1.

Trues

Thirty properties were chosen for the "true" trials; 15 were randomly assigned to the CI condition and 15 to the CD condition. The average number of syllables per property did not vary between conditions [4.06 and 4.13 for the CI and CD properties, respectively; $t(28) = .14$, $p > .30$]. For each CI property, three context sentences were constructed. Two of these contained the same subject noun, which was highly related to the property; the predicate for one of these sentences was related to the property (the

Table 1 Examples of materials used in Experiment 1

Property	Context	Item
		Context-Independent "True" Items
	Unrelated	The *skunk* was under a large willow.
Has a smell	Related	The *skunk* stunk up the entire neighborhood.
	Control	The *fire* was easily visible through the trees.
	Unrelated	The *bank* had been built ten years ago.
Can contain money	Related	The *bank* was robbed by three bandits.
	Control	The *jar* was an old antique.
		Context-Dependent "True" Items
	Unrelated	The *roof* had been renovated prior to the rainy season.
Can be walked upon	Related	The *roof* creaked under the weight of the repairman.
	Control	The *tightrope* was high off the ground.
	Unrelated	The *hospital* was internationally famous for its progressive techniques.
Where cooking can occur	Related	The *hospital* was quiet when dinner was served.
	Control	The *kitchen* had been repainted over the holidays.
		"False" Items
Has gills		The *cheese* was growing moldy in the refrigerator.
Can be tied in a knot		The *refrigerator* was set to a low temperature to cool the beer.

related-context sentence), and the predicate for the other was unrelated (the unrelated-context sentence). Degree of relatedness was determined by the ratings of an independent group of subjects, as reported later.) The remaining context sentence contained a subject noun, weakly related to the property, and an unrelated predicate; this sentence served as a control sentence (to be explained in a moment).

Similarly, for each of the 15 CD properties, three context sentences were constructed. Two of these contained the same subject noun, which was weakly related to the property; the predicate for one of these sentences was related to the property (the related-context sentence), and the predicate for the other was unrelated (the unrelated-context sentence). The remaining sentence (the control sentence) contained a subject noun, highly related to the property, and an unrelated predicate.

A control sentence in the CI condition (having a weakly related subject noun and an unrelated predicate) served as a contrast to verify that the other two context sentences for the property had a subject noun highly related to the property. The time to verify the unrelated-context sentence (having a highly related subject noun and an unrelated predicate) should be less than that for the control sentence. Similarly, a control sentence in the CD condition (having a highly related subject noun and an unrelated predicate) served as a contrast to verify that the other two context sentences for the property had a subject noun weakly related to the property. The time to verify the unrelated context sentence (having a weakly related subject noun and an unrelated predicate) should be longer than that for the control sentence.

Ratings were obtained to confirm the assumed relations between the subject nouns and properties, and between the predicates and properties. Of primary importance is that context be manipulated equally for the CI and CD conditions. This insures that an effect of context on CD subject nouns but not on CI subject nouns for the latency data cannot be attributed to CD materials having more relatedness for related predicates or less relatedness for unrelated predicates than the CI materials. Four judges rated the 60 subject nouns first (30 for the control and 30 for the noncontrol sentences) and the 90 predicates second (3 for each property). Subjects read either a subject noun or a predicate on one side of an index card and then flipped the card to read the property. Subjects rated how much the subject noun or predicate made them think of the property. Subjects used a scale from 1 to 7, on which 1 meant the property did not come to mind at all and 7 meant the property immediately came to mind. Within each group, the cards were randomly ordered for each subject.

An ANOVA was performed on the ratings for the subject nouns. The two factors of interest were condition (i.e., CI vs. CD) and relatedness (i.e., weakly vs. highly related). Note that for the CI materials, the nouns in the related- and unrelated-context sentences were supposed to be highly related and the nouns in the control sentences were supposed to be weakly related to their respective properties. For the CD materials, the nouns in the related- and unrelated-context sentences were supposed to be weakly related and the nouns in the control sentences were supposed to be highly related to their respective properties. The mean ratings from this analysis are shown in Table 2. There was no effect of CI/CD [$F(1,3) = 1.74$, $p > .25$], there was an effect

Table 2 Average association-to-property ratings for Experiment 1 materials

	A Priori Relatedness to Property				
	Subject Nouns		Predicates		
Condition	Noncontrol*	Control	Control**	Unrelated	Related
Context-Independent	6.80	3.30	3.00	3.10	6.60
Context-Dependent	3.18	6.72	3.22	2.68	6.25

* These are the subject nouns for the unrelated and related context sentences.
** Unrelated.

of relatedness [$F(1,3) = 204.54$, $p < .001$], and there was no interaction between these two factors ($F < 1$). Thus the assumed difference in relatedness was substantial and equivalent for the CI and CD materials. A similar ANOVA was performed for the predicates. Again, there was no effect of CI/CD [$F(1,3) = 1.71$, $p > .25$] and no interaction of this factor with relatedness [$F(1,6) = 1.19$, $p > .25$]. The predicates for the control and unrelated-context sentences did not differ in relatedness ($F < 1$). However, the predicates for the related-context sentences were higher in relatedness than those for the unrelated-context sentences [$F(1,6) = 89.97$, $p < .001$] and those for the control sentences [$F(1,6) = 79.28$, $p < .001$]. Thus the assumed difference in relatedness was again substantial and equivalent for the CI and CD materials. Crucial to the interpretation of the latency results are the findings that (1) the related predicates for the CD materials were not higher in relatedness than those for the CI materials ($F < 1$) and (2) the unrelated predicates for the CD materials were not lower in relatedness than those for the CI materials ($F < 1$).

Falses

Thirty context sentence/property pairs were constructed, each context sentence having a subject noun that clearly did not possess the property. The context sentences and properties used were similar in nature to those for the "true" materials. Five of the 30 "true" context sentences presented to a subject (as discussed in the Design section) contained a subject noun and a predicate both highly related to the same property (i.e., the CI related-context sentences). Therefore, 5 of the 30 "false" context sentences also contained a subject noun and a predicate both highly related to some property; however, this was not the property actually tested (i.e., for the "false" items, the subject noun could not possess the property). Creating some "false" items in this manner made it impossible for subjects to discriminate the "true" from the "false" items on the basis of subject-predicate-property relations.

Practice items

Twenty-four context sentence/property pairs were constructed; half were true and half were false. These items were similar in nature to the "true" and "false" test items. Also, the distribution of item types was similar to that found in the set of test items.

Design

Three lists were constructed. Each contained the same 30 context sentence/property pairs for the "false" items and the same 30 properties for the "true" items. The lists differed only with respect to the context sentences for the "true" properties, as discussed next.

The 15 CI properties for the "true" items were randomly divided into three groups of five properties each; the 15 CD properties were also randomly divided into three groups of five properties each. The 30 "true" context sentences in a given list consisted of (1) the control sentences from one CI group and one CD group, (2) the unrelated-context sentences from a second CI group and a second CD group, and (3) the related-context sentences from the remaining CI group and the remaining CD group. Each of the three context sentence types for each property group was instantiated in one and only one of the lists. This rotation of context sentence type through property group and list was done as randomly as possible, given the necessary constraints of a Latin square.

The 24 practice items were presented in the same random order to all subjects. The 60 test items were presented to each subject in a different, computer-generated, random order. Half the subjects used their right forefingers to press the "start" and "true" buttons and their left forefingers to press the "false" button; the other subjects had the inverse assignment. Subjects were assigned randomly to one of the six lists by hand assignment cells of the design, three subjects per cell.

Results

Latencies for the correct true trials were analyzed as follows. Averages were computed separately across subjects and across items (i.e., properties). For each subject, the average latency was determined for each of the six subject relation by predicate relation conditions. For each property in the CI and CD conditions, the average latency was determined for each of the three predicate relations. The results for the subject averages are shown in Table 3. Separate subject relation by predicate relation ANOVAs were performed on the subject averages and item averages. The results of both analyses were combined to compute min F' planned comparisons of interest (H. H. Clark, 1973).

Table 3 Average latencies and error rates per subject for correct true trials (Experiment 1)

| | Predicate Relation | | | | | |
| | Control (Unrelated) | | Unrelated | | Related | |
Condition	L	% E	L	% E	L	% E
Context-Independent	1335	11	1113	0	1145	3
Context-Dependent	1098	1	1404	11	1259	3

Note: L = average latency; %E = error rate.

For the CI items, the control sentences led to longer latencies than the unrelated-context sentences [min $F'(1,89) = 15.80$, $p < .001$]. For the CD items, the control sentences led to shorter latencies than the unrelated-context sentences [min $F'(1,90) = 24.80$, $p < .001$]. These two results show that (1) the subject nouns in the CI noncontrol sentences were in fact highly related to their respective CI properties, and (2) the subject nouns in the CD noncontrol sentences were in fact weakly related to their respective properties.[2]

The remaining results pertain only to the noncontrol sentences. For the CI items, there was no difference between related- and unrelated-context sentences (min $F' < 1$; the subject's F and item's F were also less than 1). For the CD items, related-context sentences led to shorter latencies than unrelated-context sentences [min $F'(1,90) = 5.97$, $p < .025$]. For the unrelated-context sentences, the latencies were less for the CI items than for the CD items [min $F'(1,90) = 22.13$, $p < .001$]. For the related-context sentences, there was a marginal difference between the CI and CD items [min $F'(1,89) = 3.16$, $.10 > p > .05$]; however, the subject's F was significant [$F(1,34) = 9.66$, $p < .01$], as was the item's F [$F(1,56) = 4.70$, $p < .05$]. There was a significant Subject Relation by Predicate Relation interaction for the noncontrol sentences [min $F'(1,90) = 4.19$, $p < .05$].

These data indicate that context had no effect on the CI items but had an effect on the CD items. More specifically, related contexts did not increase the priming of properties when the subject noun was highly related to the target property. However, related contexts did increase the priming of properties when the subject noun was weakly related to the property. It is not clear whether the facilitation caused by related contexts for the CD subject nouns was equivalent to the facilitation caused by the CI subject nouns themselves.

Mean latency for the correct "true" trials was 1,226 msec, and for the correct "false" trials, it was 1,253 msec. The average "true" latency for 13 of the 18 subjects was less than the average "false" latency. The average error rate per subject for all 60 test trials was 2.8%. The average error rate per subject for the 30 "true" trials was 5%, and for the 30 "false" trials, it was .6%. The average error rates per subject for the six subject relation by predicate relation cells of the design are shown in Table 3. These data, in conjunction with the latencies, indicate there was no speed-accuracy tradeoff. Notably, the most errors occurred for sentences having weakly related subject nouns and unrelated contexts. When questioned at the end of the experiment about errors on these sentences, subjects said they believed the correct response was "true" in all cases. They also indicated they had realized this almost immediately after responding "false." This suggests that CD properties in irrelevant contexts are normally inactive and that errors for these sentences occur when subjects decide to respond prior to this information's becoming active.

341

During the postexperimental interviews, most subjects reported not trying to guess properties before their presentation. The most common strategy involved focusing attention on the subject noun and forgetting the predicate while waiting for the property. All subjects reported either rehearsing the subject noun or focusing on it during the waiting period. Several subjects said they imaged referents of the subject nouns; several said they rehearsed the subject nouns once and then focused on them until presentation of the property. All but one subject reported that the psychological status of the predicate was either peripheral or gone from consciousness. Some subjects indicated that trying to maintain the predicate interfered with the task. In general, subjects appeared to be focusing only on the subject noun, believing this would maximize their ability to perform the verification task. Interestingly, the predicates still had an effect, as shown by the results for the CD properties.

Discussion

These data are consistent with the distinction between CI and CD properties. Some properties are CI because their verification is unaffected by contextual relevance. Others are CD because their verifications are faster in relevant contexts than in irrelevant contexts (a facilitation of 145 msec in this experiment). These data suggest that CD properties are not activated in irrelevant contexts. Specifically, properties weakly related to subject nouns were verified 237 and 291 msec more slowly than properties highly related to subject nouns for control and unrelated sentences, respectively. It seems unlikely that differences of this size could occur if the weakly related properties were activated by their respective words. Rather, these differences may largely reflect the time it takes to activate these properties.

These results provide a functional account of property availability: Highly accessible properties of a concept are available independent of context, whereas less accessible ones are available only in relevant contexts. Conrad (1978) has also found results consistent with this account. Her task employed interference in a color-naming task as the dependent variable. On each trial, subjects read a sentence and reported the ink color of a subsequent word. For "true" trials, the word in colored ink was either a highly related or weakly related property of the last word in the sentence. This factor was crossed with whether or not the sentence context made the property in colored ink relevant to the last word in the sentence. The results were analogous to those in this experiment. The amount of interference for the highly related properties was independent of contextual relevance. For the weakly related properties, however, interference occurred only when the context made the critical property relevant to the final sentence word.

Tabossi and Johnson-Laird (1980) also found results similar to those reported here. In a property-verification task, in which only predicate relatedness was systematically varied, subjects were faster to verify properties in relevant than in irrelevant contexts. This indicates that some of the properties must have been CD. If they had all been CI, this effect would not have occurred, given the results of the current experiment and those of Conrad (1978). Besides using contexts that primed the target property and contexts that primed no property of the target noun, Tabossi and Johnson-Laird also used contexts that primed a property of the target noun other than the target property. This third type of context led to the longest verification times. But since strength of association between the target noun and the target property was not controlled, it is not clear whether this interference effect occurred for CI properties, CD properties, or both. Nevertheless, this effect further constrains a functional account of property availability: Contexts can inhibit the activation of properties, although this may not be true of all properties.

In the current experiment and in Tabossi and Johnson-Laird's (1980) Experiment 2, the context sentences were presented 6 sec before the target properties (Conrad, 1978, did not report the details of her procedure). These experiments, therefore, are not informative at any level more specific than a functional one. This is because both automatic and conscious priming effects have been shown to occur well within 2 sec (Neely, 1977; Posner & Snyder, 1975; Swinney, 1979; Tanenhaus et al., 1979). However, Posner and Snyder's (1975) theory of attention may be an interesting way to think about property availability. They propose two types of attentional processes: (1) unconscious, automatic processes that are the result of past learning, and (2) conscious processes that are subject to capacity limitations. Although both types cause priming, conscious processes do so more slowly and interfere with other processing. Viewing property availability in this framework, the perception of a word may automatically activate its CI properties. In contrast, conscious attention may be responsible for activating relevant CD properties and for keeping both types of property active via rehearsal. (It is also possible that some CD properties are automatically activated.) Finally, focusing conscious attention away from automatically activated properties may eventually inhibit their verification.

This information processing account of property availability is consistent with the results reported here and with those of Conrad (1978): CI properties are always available because they are automatically activated by their respective words and are kept active by conscious rehearsal; CD properties are available only in irrelevant contexts because they are either automatically or consciously activated via contexts and are kept active by conscious rehearsal. This account also explains the Tabossi and Johnson-Laird (1980) interference effect: The verification of an automatically activated property may be inhibited if context focuses attention away from it.

Priming in this experiment appears at first glance to be nonadditive (cf. Foss, Cirilo, & Blank, 1979). For the CI properties, priming from the word and from the context did not add, since CI related-context sentences did not lead to faster verifications than CI unrelated-context sentences (i.e., there was no additional priming from the contexts). But in the Posner and Snyder (1975) framework, this pattern could well be additive. CI properties may receive their initial activation from encoding their respective words, this automatic activation dissipating within a few hundred milliseconds. But once these properties become active, they may receive conscious attention, which increases as automatic activation decreases. The activation of CI properties may therefore be additive in the sense that different processes are responsible for maintaining a high level of activation.

Finally, it is necessary to comment on the activation of CD properties. Functionally speaking, these properties are available in relevant but not in irrelevant contexts. But trying to explain this in information processing terms quickly becomes complex. CD properties may become available in two ways. First, they may actually be stored in a concept and be activated by contexts containing similar or associated information. Certain noun-property relations in this experiment appear to have been of this type (e.g., "snake–can be a pet"; "fingers–can be used for eating"; "frog–can be eaten"). Just how contexts activate these properties is a topic worthy of future interest. The second way CD properties can become available is via inference. Certain CD properties may not be stored in a concept but may be computed with various inference procedures (e.g., cognitive economy; Collins & Quillian, 1969; Conrad, 1972). Certain noun-property relations in this experiment may have been of the inference type for certain subjects (e.g., "basketball–can float"; "pencil–can pierce something"; "zebra–has ears"). The range and nature of these inference processes are other topics worthy of future interest. In particular, they appear to present a problem for theories of semantics, which usually try to characterize word meanings with finite sets of properties.

Experiment 2

A much different task was used in this experiment to further demonstrate the distinction between CI and CD information. Subjects judged the similarity of instance pairs drawn from various categories (e.g., "desk–sofa" from "furniture"). Two types of categories, common and ad hoc, were used. Common categories are highly conventional categories, such as those studied by Rosch, Smith, and their colleagues (e.g., Rips, Shoben, & Smith, 1973; Rosch, 1975; Rosch & Mervis, 1975; Rosch, Mervis, Gray, Johnson, & Boyes-Braem, 1976; Smith et al., 1974). Examples of these categories are "birds," "furniture," and "vegetables." In contrast, ad hoc categories are highly unusual categories that are rarely, if ever, used (Barsalou, Note 2). As a result, they are not well established in memory. Examples of these categories are "things that have a smell," "things that float," and "things that can be thrown."

Half the subjects received the category name prior to judging the similarity of each pair (the context condition); the remaining subjects did not receive the category names (the no-context condition). The predictions for this experiment are derived from Barsalou's (Note 2) finding that the properties shared by common category instances are usually CI, whereas the properties shared by ad hoc category instances may often be CD. For example, it is fairly obvious that carrots and broccoli share properties common to vegetables. However, it is not obvious that basketballs and logs share properties common to things that float. It follows that the similarity of pairs from ad hoc categories should be greater when these pairs are preceded by their category names than when they are not. This is because the category names activate shared properties that are normally inactive. Thus, there should be more common properties active in the context than in the no-context condition for ad hoc categories. In contrast, the similarity of pairs from common categories should not be increased by the addition of category names. This is because the shared properties are equally active with and without context. Combining the different patterns for ad hoc and common categories, the central prediction for this experiment is that there should be a Context by Category Type interaction. The difference in similarity between pairs from common and ad hoc categories should be less with context than without.

One other prediction for this experiment also follows from Barsalou (Note 2). The similarities should generally be greater for common than for ad hoc categories. This is because common categories are some of the categories having the highest intraclass similarity, whereas the exemplars of ad hoc categories often have much less in common. This effect is not relevant to the purpose of the experiment, but it is expected to occur.

Method

Materials and design

Twenty common categories were selected from Battig and Montague (1969) and Rosch (1975). These categories intuitively appeared to be well-known and often used. Twenty ad hoc categories were selected that appeared to be atypical and infrequently used. Two instances were chosen from each category. The common category instances were selected such that the category properties shared by these instances appeared to be CI. The ad hoc category instances were selected such that the category properties shared by these instances appeared to be CD. Examples of the materials are shown in Table 4.

Eight judges verified that the CI properties were indeed more accessible for the common category instances than the CD properties were for the ad hoc category instances. The judges read the name of an instance on one side of an index card and then read the category name on the other side. They rated

345

Table 4 Examples of materials used in Experiment 2

Category	Pair
Common Categories	
birds	robin-eagle
furniture	sofa-desk
kitchen utensils	cup-plate
beverages	coffee-milk
Ad Hoc Categories	
plunder taken by conquerors	slaves-jewelry
possible gifts	record album-necklace
taken on camping trips	flashlight-rope
can be a pet	raccoon-snake

how much reading the instance name brought to mind the properties associated with the category name. The judges used a scale from 1 to 7, on which 1 meant the properties did not come to mind at all and 7 meant the properties immediately came to mind. Each judge rated only one instance per pair, to avoid priming effects between instances. So, four judges rated each instance, and each judge rated 20 common category instances and 20 ad hoc category instances. The 40 cards were randomly ordered for each judge. The mean accessibility rating for common category instances was 5.52, and for ad hoc category instances, it was 2.32 [$F(1,6) = 164.39$, $p < .001$]. This indicates that there was a substantial difference in property accessibility between the common and ad hoc category materials.

Two versions of the pairs were constructed. In each version, the 40 pairs were randomly ordered, as were the two words in each pair. The pairs were typed onto two pages, 20 per page. In the context condition, the category name appeared to the left of each pair; in the no-context condition, the pairs appeared in isolation. Thus, there were four lists: two versions of the context list and two versions of the no-context list. To the right of each pair appeared the integers from 1 to 9. At the top of the page, above this block of response scales, appeared labels for the scale. Above 1 appeared "not similar at all," above 9 appeared "very similar," and above the remaining integers appeared "increasing similarity."

Subjects and procedure

The subjects were 28 Stanford students participating to earn course credit. Fourteen subjects were randomly assigned to the context condition and 14 to the no-context condition. Within each of these groups, half the subjects received each version of the list. Subjects were asked to think of the thing to which each word in a pair referred. They were then to judge the similarity of these two referents. Subjects were told about the scale and asked to circle one of the numbers for each pair to indicate their judgment. Subjects in the context condition were told that each pair was preceded by the name of a category to which the words in the pair belonged.

Results

The reliability of the mean ratings for the pairs was computed using the intraclass correlation for averages (Guilford & Fruchter, 1973). The reliability of the mean ratings was .96 for the no-context condition and .88 for the context condition.

A four-way ANOVA, context by category type by categories by subjects, was performed on the data. Since categories and subjects were both random factors, it was necessary to compute quasi-F's (H. H. Clark, 1973; Winer, 1971). The relevant means from this analysis are shown in Table 5. There was no main effect of context ($F' < 1$). However, there was a main effect of category type [$F'(1,62) = 52.80$, $p < .001$], common categories exhibiting more similarity than ad hoc categories, as predicted. Most important, there was a Context by Category Type interaction [$F'(1,48) = 12.50$, $p < .001$]. The difference between common and ad hoc categories was less with context than without, as predicted by the definitions of CI and CD properties. Planned comparisons were computed by performing separate ANOVAs on only the relevant data. For the ad hoc categories, the similarities were higher with context than without [$F'(1,35) = 8.31$, $p < .01$]. In contrast, the context manipulation had no effect on the similarity of common category pairs ($F' < 1$).

Discussion

The presence of context reduced the difference in similarity between common and ad hoc categories by one-half. Without context, the difference was 3.21, whereas with context, the difference was 1.61. This is further support for the existence of CI and CD information. The category properties shared by ad hoc category instances were CD, since the similarity of these pairs was greater with relevant context than without. Relevant context was necessary

Table 5 Effects of context and category type on average similarity (Experiment 2)

Conditions	Category Type	
	Ad hoc	Common
Context	3.67	5.28
No Context	2.52	5.73

to activate shared properties not activated by the words themselves. In contrast, the category properties shared by common category instances were CI, since the similarity of these pairs did not change across context. Relevant context was not required to activate shared properties activated by the words themselves.

Again, these results only provide support for a functional account of property availability: Some properties of a concept are available independent of context, since they are activated by the respective word, whereas others become available only in relevant contexts. Since subjects had as much time as they needed to perform their judgments, it was not possible to observe the time course of property activation. For this reason, it is not possible to test explanations based on the concepts of automatic and conscious attentional processes. However, the application of the Posner and Snyder (1975) framework to property availability, as discussed for Experiment 1, also makes sense in the context of the current experiment.

General discussion

These experiments demonstrate the existence of CI and CD properties. CI properties were shown to be activated by their respective words independently of context. In Experiment 1, the verification of CI properties was unaffected by the relevance of sentence frames. In Experiment 2, the similarity of two concepts was not increased when a context relevant to shared CI properties was presented. In contrast, CD properties were shown not to be activated by their respective words, but only by relevant contexts in which the words appeared. In Experiment 1, the verification of CD properties was faster in relevant than in irrelevant contexts. In Experiment 2, the similarity of two concepts increased when a relevant context activated shared CD properties.

These findings have implications for theories of natural language semantics and for semantic memory models. Given the existence of CD properties, the meaning of a word is not a fixed set of properties that is activated as a whole every time the respective word is encoded. Rather, the meaning of a word also contains weakly associated and inferable properties that are inactive in irrelevant contexts and active in relevant contexts. Given the existence of CI properties, the meaning of a word is not completely determined by context. Rather, certain properties appear to be automatically activated by a word independently of context. These findings indicate that accounts of natural language semantics should include assumptions regarding (1) the accessibility of semantic properties and (2) the impact of context on the accessibility of these properties.

The remainder of this paper addresses the roles of CI and CD properties in the following cognitive phenomena: cross-classification, problem solving, metaphor, and sentence comprehension. Also discussed are implications for the semantic-episodic distinction.

Cross-classification

Any concept is potentially cross-classifiable into an indefinitely large number of categories (see Barsalou, Note 2). For example, "chair" belongs to "furniture," "gifts," "things to sell at a garage sale," "things that can be used to hold a door open," and so on. Some of the classifications of a concept may be explicitly represented in memory (e.g., a robin is a bird) such that they can be directly accessed from the word for the concept. Many cross-classifications, however, may be implicit, in that they are not prestored but are computed by various inference processes when necessary (cf. Camp, Lachman, & Lachman, 1980). For example, there could be a process that takes any property, X, associated with a concept and infers that instances of the concept belong to the category of things that exhibit X. "Bear" can be cross-classified into things that have fur because fur is associated with bears.

Barsalou (Note 2) proposed a model of how implicit cross-classifications are computed. The model's first assumption is that for each possible classification, there is a set of criterial properties (coupled with a decision rule) used to discriminate category instances. The model's second assumption is that the properties active for a concept on a given occasion are a subset of the properties in that concept, this subset containing CI and CD properties. It follows that the implicit cross-classifications of a concept computable in a given context are those whose criterial properties are contained in the concept's active subset. Consequently, cross-classifications based on CI properties should be possible on any occasion. The category "things that are round" should be computable on all occasions for "basketball" if "round" is CI for "basketball." Cross-classifications based on CD properties should similarly be possible on occasions when these properties are active, but they should not be possible when these properties are inactive. "Things that float" should only be computable for "basketball" if a relevant context (e.g., a need for a life preserver) activates "floats" in the concept for "basketball." Barsalou (Note 2) reports data consistent with this view of cross-classification.

Problem solving

The account of cross-classification just discussed bears upon functional fixedness in problem solving (Duncker, 1945). Functional fixedness is the phenomenon of an object's typical function preventing insight into other, less typical functions that might be more useful in a particular situation. In one problem, subjects are presented several objects and asked to use them to support a board (Duncker, 1945). Crucial to solving this problem is using a pair of pliers as a support. But since "can provide support" is not a salient function of pliers, subjects often have difficulty solving the problem. In many such cases, the salient function may be CI, whereas the less salient function may be CD. Perception of the less salient cross-classification may depend on attending to the critical object in the appropriate mental context such that the CD-based classification can be inferred. For example, the CI properties in the concept for things that could support the board might activate relevant CD properties in the representation of pliers if these two concepts were simultaneously active in memory. These CD properties could then be used to infer that "pliers" belongs to "things that could support the board."

Finding a solution to this problem may be delayed because subjects are misled by the CI properties of the critical object. For example, "to grasp something" is probably CI for "pliers." Once this property is automatically activated, subjects may rule out pliers as a possible support. Consequently, the object is not attended to in the context necessary for activating the relevant properties. When subjects get desperate, this initial classification may be discarded such that the object is more carefully scrutinized and properly classified. In support of this, Duncker (1945) and Glucksberg and Danks (1968) have found that it takes longer to solve a problem when attention is drawn to the interfering CI properties. Duncker (1945) distracted subjects by having them use the pliers to grasp something before solving the problem. Glucksberg and Danks (1968) either mentioned the word for the critical object or labeled the object with a nonsense syllable. Mentioning the word delayed solutions, presumably because hearing the word automatically activated interfering CI properties.

Sometimes the activation of CI properties may facilitate finding a solution. In the candle problem, subjects are given a candle, some matches, and a box of tacks; their task is to attach the candle to the wall and light it (Duncker, 1945). Usually it takes subjects a while to cross-classify the box as something that could contain the candle. However, Glucksberg and Weisberg (1966) found that having the experimenter label the box as "box" resulted in faster solutions than when the box of tacks was simply labeled "tacks." They argued that using "box" drew attention to an object that was otherwise obscured by what it contained. However, another factor may be involved as well. Assuming that "contains things" is CI for "box," it follows that this property should become available when subjects hear the experimenter say "box." Having this property available should then facilitate cross-classifying the box as something that could contain the candle.

Metaphor and sentence comprehension

Ortony (1979) has proposed that metaphoricity depends on a particular type of salience imbalance. Specifically, the property brought to mind by a metaphor should have low salience for the subject and high salience for the referent of the metaphor. For "sermons are sleeping pills," the property "induces drowsiness or sleep" has low salience for "sermons," but high salience for "sleeping pills."

In many metaphors, the shared property may be CD in the subject and CI in the referent. In these cases, the CI property in the referent may automatically activate the corresponding CD property in the subject (see Glucksberg, Dial, & Bookin, Note 3). That is, the referent serves as context for the subject, activating relevant CD properties. It follows from Ortony's (1979) analysis that the best metaphors should be those in which the shared property is CD in the subject and CI in the referent. This is because these are the cases in which salience imbalance is maximized. Metaphors in which the shared property is not CD in the subject should not appear as metaphorical, since the property may come to mind for the subject outside the context of the referent.

In general, the mechanism of CI properties in one word activating CD properties in other words may be central to sentence comprehension. As shown in Experiment 1, the predicate in a sentence can bring to mind properties of the subject (e.g., the predicate in "The rag was used to start the fire" brings to mind "is flammable" for "rag"). There appear to be many other ways in which CI properties of one sentence word activate CD properties of another sentence word. For example, CI properties can bring to mind the appropriate senses of ambiguous words.[3] This occurs from direct objects to verbs. For "John ate X," the instantiation of X determines the sense of "eat" that comes to mind (e.g., consider X = soup, a sandwich, a steak, and so on). Similarly, the CI properties of a noun serve to disambiguate modifiers. For "the broken X," the instantiation of X determines the sense of "broken" that comes to mind (e.g., consider X = bowl, truck, plan, and so on). Similarly, the CI properties of an object in a prepositional phrase determine the sense of the preposition that comes to mind. For "on the X," the instantiation of X determines the sense of "on" that comes to mind [e.g., consider X = table, television, roof (where the subject is a person vs. a fly), and so on]. In general, converging on the intended meaning of a sentence may often involve selecting the properties associated with individual words that result in the most coordinated interpretation. This selection mechanism can be characterized, at least to some extent, as the activation of relevant CD properties in some words by CI properties in other words. This mechanism serves to minimize the number of words necessary for communicating all possible intended meanings. This is because it allows words to be used in many different ways, rather than requiring a different word for every possible meaning.

The semantic-episodic distinction

Tulving (1972) proposed a distinction between episodic and semantic memories. Episodic memories represent autobiographical experiences, that is, events coded by space and time. In contrast, semantic memories represent our knowledge of the world and the meanings of words.[4] Although most investigators have not argued for physically separate memories in the brain, many have agreed that there may be different representations and processes associated with each memory type. Recently, this view has come under attack. J. R. Anderson and Ross (1980) and McKoon and Ratcliff (1979) have argued that episodic and semantic memories may be similarly represented and subject to the same processes. Barsalou and Bower (Note 1) further argue that the CI-CD distinction is problematic for the semantic-episodic distinction. If CI properties are automatized, and if practice results in automaticity, then particular processing episodes determine the accessibility of semantic memories. Similarly, CD properties are CD because there have not been many episodes in which the property and the respective word were simultaneously processed. Since the availability of semantic information depends directly on episodic information, it is not clear that two types of memories are needed when one would probably be sufficient.

Barsalou and Bower (Note 1) discuss specific ways in which particular processing episodes may affect the psychology of lexical semantics. To start with, a word can refer to different kinds of instances. "Car" can refer to cars with or without air conditioning. Consequently, the accessibility of "air conditioning" should depend on the type of car someone is used to. In general, properties of a concept not typically found for familiar referents may become CD through disuse. In contrast, properties typically encountered are more likely to become CI. Analogously, particular uses of an object may vary in accessibility. Someone who has just been to a circus may be more likely to categorize "chair" as something to fight lions with. In general, encoding a particular episode in which an object is put to atypical use may make that use more accessible, at least temporarily.

It should be pointed out that CI properties are not necessarily more semantic than CD properties. Episodes can be CI (e.g., "doberman pincher" may always activate a particular, well rehearsed episode of being bitten by one of these dogs), and semantic properties can be CD (e.g., properties that are usually irrelevant for an object, such as "floats" for "basketball"). The primary difference between CI and CD information is simply the means by which they are activated: CI information is activated by the word for a concept, whereas CD information is activated by relevant contexts in which the word is encoded. As suggested by Barsalou and Bower (Note 1), this difference in accessibility is a function of the frequency and recency of processing episodes, regardless of whether the information is an episode, a semantic feature, an affect, or some other type of information.

Finally, E. V. Clark and H.H. Clark (1979) have shown that certain innovative uses of words can result in new meanings for those words. Computing these novel meanings often requires retrieving a particular episode. Consider their example of "teapotting." Suppose someone named Max has a strange habit of rubbing a teapot on the backs of people's legs. Imagine that two people had seen Max do this before, and one of them said, "Max is in trouble, he just teapotted a policeman." The listener would compute the meaning of "teapotted" by retrieving the relevant episodes, even though he or she has never heard the word used that way. Clearly, this example illustrates the necessity of using episodic information to arrive at the speaker's intended meaning. There is no linguistic rule that could generate the exact meaning intended by the speaker in this situation. Instead, the specifics of the meaning are derived from the structure of the relevant episodes. With recurrent uses of "teapot" in this manner, however, the new meaning could eventually be abstracted away from the particulars of episodes and become CI. Thus, particular processing episodes not only enable comprehension of certain linguistic innovations but are also responsible for the respective word senses' becoming well established in memory. In general, changes in word meanings over time may often be the result of changes in the accessibility of CI and CD properties.

Notes

This research was supported by Grant MH 13950 from the National Institute of Mental Health to Gordon H. Bower and by a National Science Foundation graduate fellowship to the author. I am grateful to Gordon Bower for supporting this research and to Kathleen Hemenway, Brian Ross, Ronald Finke, Michael McCloskey, and an anonymous reviewer for excellent comments on earlier drafts.

1 It should be pointed out that this proposal regarding the existence of CI and CD properties is not a theory of meaning. It simply addresses one aspect of concepts, namely, the accessibility of properties.
2 The CI control and CD unrelated-context items both have weakly related subject relations and unrelated predicate relations; analogously, the CD control and CI unrelated-context items both have highly related subject relations and unrelated predicate relations. It is not possible, however, to pool the latencies within these two sets of items, since this would make comparisons between unrelated- and related-context items impossible. The proper way to compare related and unrelated contexts is to observe latencies for the same properties under different context conditions. Pooling violates this design, since latencies for the control properties would be included in the unrelated-context conditions but not in the related-context conditions.
3 As discussed earlier, these senses may not be strictly CD. Even though context is required to converge on a particular sense, many may easily come to mind in no context (Swinney, 1979; Tanenhaus et al., 1979). Consequently, the primary senses of an ambiguous word may lie in the middle ground between CI and CD properties. These senses are CD in the weaker sense that they are attenuated or strengthened by context once their linguistic form has automatically activated them.
4 This use of "semantic" is nonstandard, since "semantics" is typically used to refer only to the meanings of words.

Reference notes

1. Barsalou, L. W., & Bower, G. H. *A priori determinants of a concept's highly accessible information.* Paper presented at the annual meeting of the American Psychological Association, Montreal, September 1980.
2. Barsalou, L. W. *Ad hoc categories and cross-classification.* Unpublished manuscript, 1981.
3. Glucksberg, S., Dial, P. G., & Bookin, H. B. *On understanding nonliteral speech: Can people ignore metaphors?* Manuscript in preparation, 1980.

References

ANDERSON, J. R., & Ross, B. H. Evidence against the semantic-episodic distinction. *Journal of Experimental Psychology: Human Learning and Memory*, 1980, **6**, 441–466.

ANDERSON, R. C., & ORTONY, A. On putting apples into bottles—A problem of polysemy. *Cognitive Psychology*, 1975, **7**, 167–180.

ANDERSON, R. C., PICHERT, J. W., GOETZ, E. T., SCHALLERT, D. L., STEVENS, K. V., & TROLLIP, S. R. Instantiation of general terms. *Journal of Verbal Learning and Verbal Behavior*, 1976, **15**, 667–679.

BARCLAY, J. R., BRANSFORD, J. D., FRANKS, J. J., McCARRELL, N. S., & NITSCH, K. Comprehension and semantic flexibility. *Journal of Verbal Learning and Verbal Behavior*, 1974, **13**, 471–481.

BATTIG, W. F., & MONTAGUE, W. E. Category norms for verbal items in 56 categories: A replication and extension of the Connecticut category norms. *Journal of Experimental Psychology*, 1969, **80**(Whole No. 3, Pt. 2).

BOWER, G. H. Stimulus-sampling theory of encoding variability. In A. W. Melton & E. Martin (Eds.), *Coding processes in human memory*. Washington, D.C: Winston, 1972.

CAMP, C. J., LACHMAN, J. L., & LACHMAN, R. Evidence for direct-access and inferential retrieval in question-answering. *Journal of Verbal Learning and Verbal Behavior*, 1980, **19**, 583–596.

CLARK, E. V., & CLARK, H. H. When nouns surface as verbs. *Language*, 1979, **55**, 767–811.

CLARK, H. H. The language-as-fixed-effect fallacy: A critique of language statistics in psychological research. *Journal of Verbal Learning and Verbal Behavior*, 1973, **12**, 335–359.

COLLINS, A. M., & QUILLIAN, M. R. Retrieval time from semantic memory. *Journal of Verbal Learning and Verbal Behavior*, 1969, **8**, 240–247.

CONRAD, C. Cognitive economy in semantic memory. *Journal of Experimental Psychology*, 1972, **92**, 149–154.

CONRAD, C. Some factors involved in the recognition of words. In J. W. Cotton & R. L. Klatzky (Eds.), *Semantic factors in cognition*. Hillsdale, N.J: Erlbaum, 1978.

DUNCKER, K. On problem solving. *Psychological Monographs*, 1945, **58**(Whole No. 270).

ESTES, W. K. Statistical theory of spontaneous recovery and regression. *Psychological Review*, 1955, **62**, 145–154.

ESTES, W. K. The statistical approach to learning theory. In S. Koch (Ed.), *Psychology: A study of a science* (Vol. 2). New York: McGraw-Hill, 1959.

FOSS, D. J., CIRILO, R. K., & BLANK, M. A. Semantic facilitation and lexical access during sentence processing: An investigation of individual differences. *Memory & Cognition*, 1979, **7**, 346–353.

GLASS, A. L., & HOLYOAK, K. J. Alternative conceptions of semantic memory. *Cognition*, 1975, **3**, 313–339.

GLUCKSBERG, S., & DANKS, J. Effects of discriminative labels and of nonsense labels upon availability of novel function. *Journal of Verbal Learning and Verbal Behavior*, 1968, **7**, 72–76.

GLUCKSBERG, S., & WEISBERG, R. W. Verbal behavior and problem solving: Some effects of labeling in a functional fixedness problem. *Journal of Experimental Psychology*, 1966, **71**, 659–664.

GUILFORD, J. P., & FRUCHTER, B. *Fundamental statistics in psychology and education.* New York: McGraw-Hill, 1973.

JACOBY, L. L., CRAIK, F. I. M., & BEGG, I. Effects of decision difficulty on recognition and recall. *Journal of Verbal Learning and Verbal Behavior*, 1979, **18**, 585–600.

KATZ, J. J., & POSTAL, P. *An integrated theory of linguistic descriptions.* Cambridge, Mass: M.I.T. Press, 1964.

MCCLOSKEY, M., & GLUCKSBERG, S. Decision process in verifying category membership statements: Implications for models of semantic memory. *Cognitive Psychology*, 1979, **11**, 1–37.

MCKOON, G., & RATCLIFF, R. Priming in episodic and semantic memory. *Journal of Verbal Learning and Verbal Behavior*, 1979, **18**, 463–480.

NEELY, J. H. Semantic priming and retrieval from lexical memory: Roles of inhibitionless spreading activation and limited-capacity attention. *Journal of Experimental Psychology: General*, 1977, **106**, 226–254.

OLSON, D. R. Language and thought: Aspects of a cognitive theory of semantics. *Psychological Review*, 1970, **77**, 257–273.

ORTONY, A. Beyond literal similarity. *Psychological Review*, 1979, **86**, 161–180.

POSNER, M. I., & SNYDER, C. R. R. Attention and cognitive control. In R. L. Solso (Ed.), *Information processing and cognition: The Loyola symposium.* Hillsdale, N.J: Erlbaum, 1975.

RIPS, L. J., SHOBEN, E. J., & SMITH, E. E. Semantic distance and the verification of semantic relations. *Journal of Verbal Learning and Verbal Behavior*, 1973, **12**, 1–20.

ROSCH, E. H. Cognitive representations of semantic categories. *Journal of Experimental Psychology: General*, 1975, **104**, 192–233.

ROSCH, E. H., & MERVIS, C. B. Family resemblances: Studies in the internal structure of categories. *Cognitive Psychology*, 1975, **7**, 573–605.

ROSCH, E. H., MERVIS, C. B., GRAY, W. D., JOHNSON, D. M., & BOYES-BRAEM, P. Basic objects in natural categories. *Cognitive Psychology*, 1976, **8**, 382–439.

SHIFFRIN, R. M., & SCHNEIDER, W. Controlled and automatic human information processing: II. Perceptual learning, automatic attending, and a general theory. *Psychological Review*, 1977, **84**, 127–190.

SMITH, E. E., SHOBEN, E. J., & RIPS, L. J. Structure and process in semantic memory: A featural model for semantic decisions. *Psychological Review*, 1974, **81**, 214–241.

SWINNEY, D. A. Lexical access during sentence comprehension: (Re)Consideration of context effects. *Journal of Verbal Learning and Verbal Behavior*, 1979, **18**, 645–659.

TANENHAUS, M. K., LEIMAN, J. M., & SEIDENBERG, M. S. Evidence for multiple stages in the processing of ambiguous words in syntactic contexts. *Journal of Verbal Learning and Verbal Behavior*, 1979, **18**, 427–440.

TABOSSI, P., & JOHNSON-LAIRD, P. N. Linguistic context and the priming of semantic information. *Quarterly Journal of Experimental Psychology*, 1980, **32**, 595–603.

TULVING, E. Episodic and semantic memory. In E. Tulving & W. Donaldson (Eds.), *Organization and memory*. New York: Academic Press, 1972.

TULVING, E., & THOMPSON, D. M. Encoding specificity and retrieval processes in episodic memory. *Psychological Review*, 1973, **80**, 352–373.

WINER, B. J. *Statistical principles in experimental design*. New York: McGraw-Hill, 1971.

Part 8

RETRIEVAL

35

FACILITATION IN RECOGNIZING PAIRS OF WORDS

Evidence of a dependence between retrieval operations[1]

David E. Meyer and Roger W. Schvaneveldt

Source: *Journal of Experimental Psychology*, 90 (1971): 227–234.

Two experiments are reported in which Ss were presented two strings of letters simultaneously, with one string displayed visually above the other. In Exp. I, Ss responded "yes" if both strings were words, otherwise responding "no." In Exp. II, Ss responded "same" if the two strings were either both words or both nonwords, otherwise responding "different." "Yes" responses and "same" responses were faster for pairs of commonly associated words than for pairs of unassociated words. "Same" responses were slowest for pairs of nonwords. "No" responses were faster when the top string in the display was a nonword, whereas "different" responses were faster when the top string was a word. The results of both experiments support a retrieval model involving a dependence between separate successive decisions about whether each of the two strings is a word. Possible mechanisms that underlie this dependence are discussed.

Several investigators recently have studied how Ss decide that a string of letters is a word (Landauer & Freedman, 1968; Meyer & Ellis, 1970; Rubenstein, Garfield, & Millikan, 1970). They typically have presented a single string on a trial, measuring reaction time (RT) of the *lexical decision* as a function of the string's meaning, familiarity, etc. In one such experiment, RT varied inversely with word frequency (Rubenstein et al., 1970). When word frequency was controlled, lexical decisions were faster for homographs (i.e., words having two or more meanings) than for nonhomographs. To explain these results, Rubenstein et al. proposed that word frequency affects the order of examining stored words in long-term memory and that more replicas of homographs than of nonhomographs are stored in long-term memory.

In another experiment, Meyer and Ellis (1970) measured both the time taken to decide that a string of letters (e.g., HOUSE) is a word and the time taken to decide that it belongs to a prespecified semantic category. When the category was relatively small (e.g., BUILDINGS), the latter type of *semantic decision* was significantly faster than the former lexical decision. However, when the category was relatively large (e.g., STRUCTURES), the semantic decision was slightly slower than the lexical decision. To explain these and other results, Meyer and Ellis suggested that the semantic decision may have involved searching through stored words in the semantic category and that the lexical decision did *not* entail a search of this kind among the set of all words in memory.

The present paper provides further data about the effect of meaning on lexical decisions. To deal with this problem, we have extended the lexical-decision task by simultaneously presenting two strings of letters for *S* to judge. The stimulus may involve either a pair of words, a pair of nonwords, or a word and a nonword. In one task, *S* is instructed to respond "yes" if both strings are words, and otherwise to respond "no." In a second task, the instructions require *S* to respond "same" if the two strings are either both words or both nonwords, and otherwise to respond "different." In each task, RT for pairs of words is measured as a function of the associative relation between the two words.

The two tasks together are designed to give information about the nature and the invariance of underlying retrieval operations. One of their advantages is that the relation between words can be varied while keeping the overt response constant. We reasoned that the response might involve separate, successive decisions about each of the two words. By varying the degree of association between the words, we then hoped it would be possible to test for a dependence between memory-accessing components of the two decisions. Experiment I reports the results of such variation in the context of the yes–no task.

Experiment I

Method

Subjects

The *S*s were 12 high school students who served as paid volunteers.

Stimuli

The following test stimuli were used: 48 pairs of associated words, e.g., BREAD-BUTTER and NURSE-DOCTOR, selected from the Connecticut Free Associational

Norms (Bousfield, Cohen, & Whitmarsh, 1961); 48 pairs of unassociated words, e.g., BREAD-DOCTOR and NURSE-BUTTER, formed by randomly interchanging the response terms between the 48 pairs of associated words so that there were no obvious associations within the resulting pairs; 48 pairs of nonwords; and 96 pairs involving a word and a nonword. Within each pair of associated words, the second member was either the first or second most frequent free associate given in response to the first member. Within each pair of unassociated words, the second member was never the first or second most frequent free associate of the first member. The median length of strings in the pairs of associated words and pairs of unassociated words was 5 letters and ranged from 3 to 7 letters; the median word frequency was 59 per million, and ranged from 1,747 to less than 1 per million (Kucera & Francis, 1967). A separate set of 96 words was used for the pairs involving a word and a nonword. These words were similar to the associated words in terms of frequency, length, and semantic classification. Nonwords were constructed from common words, e.g., MARK, replacing at least one letter with another letter. Vowels were used to replace vowels, and consonants were used to replace consonants. The resulting strings of letters, e.g., MARB, were pronounceable and were equal in average length to the words paired with them. A majority of the nonwords differed by only a single letter from some English word, and the differences were not systematically associated with any one letter position.

In addition to the test stimuli, 24 pairs of words, 8 pairs of nonwords, and 16 pairs involving a word and a nonword were constructed as practice stimuli. Degree of association was not varied systematically among the pairs of practice words.

Apparatus

The stimuli were generated on a Stromberg Carlson SC4060 graphics system, photographed on 16-mm. movie film and presented on a rear-projection screen by a Perceptual Development Laboratories' Mark III Perceptoscope. The Ss responded via a panel having finger keys for the right and left hands. Reaction time was measured to the nearest millisecond by counting the cycles of a 1,000-Hz. oscillator.

Procedure and design

The Ss were run individually during one session involving a series of discrete RT trials. The S was seated in front of the darkened screen throughout the session. At the beginning of each trial, the word READY was presented briefly as a warning signal on the screen. A small fixation box, which subtended approximate visual angles of 3°40′ horizontally and 1°50′ vertically, then appeared during a 1-sec. foreperiod. Following the foreperiod, the stimulus

361

was displayed horizontally in (white) capital letters in the middle of the box, with one string of letters centered above the other. If both strings were words, *S* pressed a key labeled "yes" with his right index finger, otherwise pressing a "no" key with the left index finger. Reaction time was measured from stimulus-onset to the response, which terminated the stimulus display. During an approximate 2-sec. interval when the screen was blank after each trial, *S* was informed of whether his response had been correct.

The session lasted about 45 min. and included a short instruction period and two blocks of 24 practice trials, followed by four blocks of 24 test trials. After each block, *S* was informed of his mean RT and total number of errors for the block, while he rested for about 2 min. This feedback was intended to encourage fast and accurate responses. To further motivate good performance, *S* was given $3 at the start of the session and then penalized 1¢ for each .1 sec. in mean RT on each trial block, and 3¢ for each error. Whatever money remained at the end of the session served as *S*'s payment for the experiment.

The entire set of practice stimuli was presented during the two practice trial blocks. During the test trial blocks, each *S* was shown 16 pairs of non-words, 32 pairs involving a word and a nonword, 24 pairs of associated words, and 24 pairs of unassociated words from the total set of test stimuli. Half of the practice trials and test trials therefore required "yes" responses. Presentation of the test stimuli was balanced, so that each individual stimulus of a given type was presented equally often across *S*s; e.g., each pair of associated words was presented a total of six times across *S*s, while each pair of nonwords was presented a total of four times. No *S* saw any string of letters more than once. In displaying both the pairs of associated words and the pairs of unassociated words, the top string (e.g., BREAD) was always a stimulus term from the norms of Bousfield et al. (1961), while the bottom string (e.g. BUTTER) was always a response term. For the stimuli containing at least one nonword, each string was assigned equally often across *S*s to the top and bottom display positions. There were thus five types of stimuli, which are listed in Table 1 together with their relative frequencies of occurrence. Relative frequencies of these types were balanced within trial blocks to equal their relative frequencies in the total set of test stimuli. The above set of constraints on stimulus presentation was used to construct six lists of 96 test stimuli each. Subject to these constraints, two random orders of stimulus presentation were obtained for each list. Each *S* was then randomly assigned one of the lists presented in one of the orders, so that each list in each order was used for exactly one *S*.

Results and discussion

Reaction time and error data from the test trials were subjected to *S*s × Treatments analyses of variance (Winer, 1962). Prior to analysis, an arc-sine

362

Table 1 Mean reaction times (RTs) of correct responses and mean percent errors in the yes–no task

Type of stimulus pair		Correct response	Proportion of trials	Mean RT (msec.)	Mean % errors
Top string	Bottom string				
word	associated word	yes	.25	855	6.3
word	unassociated word	yes	.25	940	8.7
word	nonword	no	.167	1,087	27.6
nonword	word	no	.167	904	7.8
nonword	nonword	no	.167	884	2.6

transformation was applied to each *S*'s error rates. The reported standard errors and *F* ratios were computed using error terms derived from the *S*s × Treatments interactions.

Table 1 summarizes mean RTs of correct responses and mean percent errors averaged over *S*s. "Yes" responses averaged 85 ± 19 msec. faster for pairs of associated words than for pairs of unassociated words, $F(1, 11) = 20.6$, $p < .001$. "No" responses to pairs involving a word and a nonword averaged 183 ± 14 msec. faster when the nonword was displayed above the word, $F(1, 11) = 171.7$, $p < .001$. "No" responses for pairs of nonwords were not significantly faster (20 ± 14 msec.) than "no" responses for pairs where a nonword was displayed above a word, $F(1, 11) = 2.0$, $p > .10$.

The error rates for pairs of unassociated words versus pairs of associated words did not differ significantly, $F(1, 11) = 2.1$, $p > .10$. The error rate for pairs involving a word and a nonword was significantly greater when the word was displayed above the nonword, $F(1, 11) = 18.9$, $p < .005$. The error rate for pairs of nonwords was significantly less than that for pairs where a nonword was displayed above a word, $F(1, 11) = 5.5$, $p < 0.05$.

Error rates were relatively low except for pairs where a word was displayed above a nonword. A possible reason for this exception is considered in later discussion. The pattern of errors suggests that a speed-accuracy trade-off did not cause the observed differences in mean RTs; i.e., mean error rates tended to correlate positively with mean RTs.

The results of Exp. I suggest that degree of association is a powerful factor affecting lexical decisions in the yes–no task. For example, the effect of association appears to be on the order of two or three times larger than the average effect of homography reported by Rubenstein et al. (1970). This effect of association occurred consistently across *S*s, and 11 of the 12 *S*s showed it in excess of 30 msec. In Exp. II, another group of *S*s performed the same–different task to further study the generality of the effect.

Experiment II

Method

Subjects

The *S*s were 12 high school students who served as paid volunteers. They had not been in Exp. 1, but were drawn from the same population.

Stimuli

The same set of test stimuli was used as in Exp. I. In addition, 16 pairs of words, 16 pairs of nonwords, and 32 pairs involving a word and a nonword were constructed as practice stimuli. Most of these practice stimuli also had been used in Exp. 1.

Apparatus

The same apparatus was used as in Exp. I.

Procedure and design

The procedure and design were similar to those used in Exp. I, except for the following modifications. The *S* pressed a "same" key with his right index finger if the stimulus involved either two words or two nonwords, otherwise pressing a "different" key with the left index finger. The complete session lasted about 1 hr. and included a short instruction period, two blocks of 32 practice trials, and six blocks of 32 test trials. Two lists of 192 test stimuli each were constructed. For each list, two random orders of presentation were obtained, subject to constraints like those used in Exp. I. Each of these List × Order combinations was then used for three of the *S*s. During the test trial blocks, each *S* was presented 48 pairs of nonwords, 96 pairs involving a word and a nonword, 24 pairs of associated words, and 24 pairs of unassociated words from the total set of test stimuli. Half of the trials therefore required "same" responses. Because the same–different task was somewhat more difficult than the yes–no task, each *S* was given $3.50 at the start of the session.

Results

The results were analyzed in the same way as Exp. I. Table 2 summarizes mean RTs of correct responses and mean percent errors averaged over *S*s. "Same" responses averaged 117 ± 18 msec. faster for pairs of associated words than for pairs of unassociated words, $F(1, 11) = 42.6, p < .001$. "Same"

364

Table 2 Mean reaction times (RTs) of correct responses and mean percent errors in the same–different task

Type of stimulus pair		Correct response	Proportion of trials	Mean RT (msec.)	Mean % errors
Top string	Bottom string				
word	associated word	same	.125	1,055	2.4
word	unassociated word	same	.125	1,172	8.7
nonword	nonword	same	.25	1,357	8.9
word	nonword	different	.25	1,318	11.6
nonword	word	different	.25	1,386	12.0

responses averaged 185 ± 29 msec. slower for pairs of nonwords than for pairs of unassociated words, $F (1, 11) = 40.7, p < .001$. "Different" responses averaged 68 ± 25 msec. faster when the word was displayed above the nonword, $F (1, 11) = 7.3, p < .025$.

The error rate for pairs of associated words was significantly less than the error rate for unassociated words, $F (1, 11) = 16.6, p < .01$. The difference between error rates for pairs of unassociated words and pairs of nonwords was not significant, $F (1, 11) < 1.0$. For pairs involving a word and a nonword, the error rate did not depend significantly on whether the word was displayed above or below the non-word, $F (1, 11) < 1.0$.

A comparison of mean RTs in the yes–no task (Exp. I) versus mean RTs in the same–different task revealed the following: "Yes" responses to pairs of words averaged 216 ± 68 msec. faster than "same" responses to pairs of words, $F (1, 22) = 10.2, p < .01$. The effect of association on "same" responses to pairs of words did not differ significantly from its effect on "yes" responses, $F (1, 22) = 1.4, p > .20$. "No" responses to pairs involving a word and a nonword averaged 357 ± 74 msec. faster than "different" responses, $F (1, 22) = 23.6, p < .001$. For pairs involving a word and a nonword, the effect of the word's display position on RT interacted significantly with the task, $F (1, 22) = 76.4, p < .001$.

Discussion

As a framework for explaining our results, we tentatively propose a model involving two separate, successive decisions. According to this model, stimulus processing typically begins with the top string of letters in the display. The first decision is whether the top string is a word and the second is whether the bottom string is a word. If the first decision is negative in the yes–no task, we presume that processing terminates without the second decision and *S* responds "no." Otherwise, both decisions are made and *S*'s response corresponds to the second decision's outcome. It is assumed that in the same–different task, both decisions are normally made regardless of the outcome of the first. After both decisions, their outcomes are compared. If the outcomes match, S responds "same"; otherwise, he responds "different."

Now let us consider the RTs and error rates of yes–no responses. The *serial-decision model* explains why "no" responses are faster when the top string is a nonword. This happens because only the first decision is made, whereas both decisions are made when the top string is a word. The model also explains why "no" responses are about equally fast for pairs where only the top string is a nonword, as compared to pairs where both strings are nonwords; i.e., for either kind of pair, only the first decision is ordinarily made. An occasional reversal in the order of stimulus processing, beginning with the bottom rather than top string, might account for the slightly faster responses to pairs of nonwords.

The relatively high error rate for pairs involving a word above a nonword suggests that processes preceding "yes" responses sometimes terminate prematurely after the first decision. In these cases, S may feel that discovering a word in the top position is sufficient evidence for responding "yes," without making the second decision. This behavior would not be too unreasonable, given the relative frequencies of the various types of stimuli. Such premature termination of stimulus processing, together with an occasional reversal in the processing order, would also explain why "no" responses were most accurate for pairs of nonwords.

The RTs from the same–different task do not provide direct evidence for testing the proposed serial-decision model because both lexical decisions are assumed to be made before all same–different responses. However, the relative invariance of the association effect across the yes–no and same–different tasks suggests that similar processes occur in both tasks. An additional operation, which compares the outcomes of the two lexical decisions for a match, would explain why responses were somewhat slower in the same–different task than in the yes–no task.

Several factors in the present experiments may have induced Ss to process the strings of letters serially. For example, Ss were encouraged to perform with high accuracy and were allowed to move their eyes in examining the stimulus display. Under other circumstances, e.g., with brief stimulus presentation and/or a more relaxed error criterion, Ss might process two or more words in parallel.

If the serial-decision model is valid for the present experiments, then one can use the yes–no data to estimate the time taken in deciding that a string of letters is a word. In particular, let T_{nw} represent the mean RT to respond "no" to a nonword displayed above a word. Let T_{wn} represent the mean RT to respond "no" to a nonword displayed below a word. Then with certain assumptions (cf. Sternberg, 1969), the difference $T_{wn} - T_{nw}$ is a measure of the mean time to decide that the top string is a word. From the results of Exp. I, an estimate of this difference is 183 ± 14 msec. An occasional reversal in the order of stimulus processing would make this difference an underestimate of the true mean.

One can also estimate approximately how much time is required to compare the outcomes of the two decisions before same–different responses. For example, suppose the mean RT of "yes" responses (Exp. I) is subtracted from the mean RT of "same" responses to pairs of words (Exp. II). Then with certain assumptions, the difference of 216 ± 68 msec. is an estimate of the comparison time when the two decisions match. On the other hand, suppose the mean RT of "no" responses to a word displayed above a nonword is subtracted from the corresponding mean RT for "different" responses. Then the difference of 231 ± 76 msec. is an estimate of the comparison time when the two decisions do not match.

What kind of operation occurs during each of the two proposed decisions? One possibility is that visual and/or accoustic features of a string of letters are used to compute an "address" in memory (Norman, 1969; Schiffrin & Atkinson, 1969). A lexical decision about a string might then involve accessing and checking some part of the contents of the string's computed memory location (cf. Rubenstein et al., 1970). Given this model, memory locations would be computed for both words and nonwords, although the contents of nonword locations might differ qualitatively from those of word locations. In essence, we are therefore suggesting that both words and nonwords may have locations "reserved" for them in long-term memory.

The effect of association on RT does not necessarily imply that the meaning of a word is retrieved to make a lexical decision. To understand why, consider the following elaboration of the serial-decision model, which may explain the effect. First, suppose that long-term memory is organized semantically, i.e., that there is a structure in which the locations of two associated words are closer than those of two unassociated words. Evidence from other studies of semantic memory suggests that this assumption is not totally unreasonable (Collins & Quillian, 1969; Meyer, 1970). Let L_1 and L_2 denote the memory locations examined in the first and second decisions, respectively. Second, suppose that the time taken to make the second decision depends on where L_2 is relative to L_1. In particular, let us assume that the time taken accessing information for the second decision varies directly with the "distance" between L_1 and L_2. Then responses to pairs of associated words would be faster than those to pairs of unassociated words. This follows because the proximity of associated words in the memory structure permits faster accessing of information for the second decision. The argument holds even if the accessed information is (a) sufficient *only* to determine whether a string is a word and (b) does not include aspects of its meaning.

If our second assumption above is correct, then any retrieval operation R_2 that is required sufficiently soon after another operation R_1 will generally depend on R_1. This would mean that human long-term memory, like many

367

bulk-storage devices, lacks the property known in the computer literature as *random access* (cf. McCormick, 1959, p. 103). Recently, Meyer (1971) has collected data in other tasks that are consistent with this notion.

There are several ways in which this dependence between retrieval operations might be realized. One possibility is that retrieving information from a particular memory location produces a passive "spread of excitation" to other nearby locations, facilitating later retrieval from them (Collins & Quillian, 1970; Warren, 1970). A second speculative possibility is that retrieving information from long-term memory is like retrieving information from a magnetic tape or disk. In this latter model, facilitation of retrieval would occur because (*a*) information can be "read out" of only one location during any given instant, (*b*) time is required to "shift" readout from one location to another, and (*c*) shifting time increases with the distance between locations.

The present data do not provide a direct test between this *location-shifting model* and the *spreading-excitation model*. However, the location-shifting model may explain one result that is difficult to account for in terms of spreading excitation. In particular, consider the following argument about the finding that "different" responses were faster when a word was displayed above a nonword. We previously have argued that processing normally begins with a decision about the top string and then proceeds to a decision about the bottom one. Let us now assume that memory is organized by familiarity as well as by meaning, with frequently examined locations in one "sector" and infrequently examined locations in another sector. Recently, Swanson and Wickens (1970) have collected data supporting a similar assumption that Oldfield (1966) has made. Suppose further that before each trial, a location is preselected in the sector where familiar words are stored, which would be optimal under most circumstances (cf. Oldfield, 1966). Then the response to a word displayed above a nonword would require only one major shift between memory locations in the familiar and unfamiliar sectors. This shift would occur after the first decision, changing readout from the familiar to the unfamiliar sector.[2] In contrast, the response to a nonword displayed above a word would require two major shifts, i.e., one from the familiar to the unfamiliar sector before the first decision and one returning to the familiar sector before the second decision. This would make "different" responses slower when the nonword is displayed above the word. Moreover, the assumption that the starting location is in the familiar sector fits with the finding that lexical decisions are generally faster for familiar than for unfamiliar words (Rubenstein et al., 1970); i.e., a major shift between locations is required to access potential information about an unfamiliar word, whereas such a shift would not be required for a familiar one.

The effect of association on "same" responses to pairs of words (Exp. II) is also relevant to a recent finding by Schaeffer and Wallace (1969). In their study, *S*s were presented with a pair of words and required to respond "same" if both words belonged to the semantic category LIVING THINGS or if both belonged to the category NONLIVING THINGS. Otherwise, Ss responded "different." Reaction time of "same" responses varied inversely with the semantic similarity of the words in the pair; e.g., "same" responses to a stimulus like TULIP-PANSY were faster than "same" responses to a stimulus like TULIP-ZEBRA. In contrast, Schaeffer and Wallace (1970) found that the RT of "different" responses varied directly with semantic similarity. They attributed the effects of similarity on both "same" and "different" responses to a process that compares the meanings of the words in a stimulus.

The effects of association in Exp. I and II possibly could have been caused by such a comparison process, rather than by the retrieval mechanisms discussed above. However, if the "meaning" of a word is represented by the semantic categories to which it belongs, then there seemingly is a difference between the same–different task of Exp. II and the one studied by Schaeffer and Wallace (1969, 1970). Logically, Exp. II did not require Ss to compare the meanings of the items in a stimulus; i.e., Ss did not have to judge whether both strings belonged to the same semantic category, e.g., LIVING THINGS. Instead, Exp. II only required comparing the items' lexical status. Moreover, a comparison of meanings would have been impossible for those pairs involving at least one nonword, since the nonword would have no meaning in the usual sense. One might therefore argue that Ss did not compare the meanings of items in Exp. II. The argument is reinforced by the fact that Exp. I (yes–no task), which logically did not require comparing the strings in any way, produced an effect of association like the one observed in Exp. II.

Our reasoning suggests, furthermore, that the findings of Schaeffer and Wallace (1969, 1970) may not have resulted solely from a comparison of word meanings. Rather, their findings could have been caused at least in part by a retrieval process like the one we have proposed. This point is supported by the magnitudes of the similarity effects they observed, which averaged 176 msec. for facilitating "same" responses (Schaeffer & Wallace, 1969) and 120 msec. for inhibiting "different" responses (Schaeffer & Wallace, 1970). In particular, consider the following detailed argument. Suppose that judgments in their task involved two components: an initial retrieval process similar to the one we have proposed, which might be necessary to access word meanings, and a process that compares word meanings (cf. Schaeffer & Wallace, 1970). Suppose further that our experiments required only the first process. One might then expect that whenever both of these processes are used in "same" judgments, they would both be facilitated by semantic similarity. However, when they are used in "different" judgments, similarity would inhibit the comparison process while still facilitating the retrieval process. This would explain why the effect of association on "same" responses in Exp. II (117 msec.) was less than the effect of similarity on "same" responses in the study by Schaeffer and Wallace (1969). Moreover, it would also explain their finding that semantic similarity inhibited "different" responses less than it facilitated "same" responses. Unfortunately, the argument is partially weakened by at least one fact; i.e., their results for "same" versus "different" responses were obtained in separate experiments using somewhat different semantic categories and test words.

Regardless of whether spreading excitation, location shifting, comparison of meanings, or some other process is involved, the effects of association appear limited neither to semantic decisions nor to same–different judgments. At present we do not have ways to test all the possible explanations of these effects. However, procedures like the ones we have described may provide a way to study relations between retrieval operations that are temporally contiguous. We may therefore be able to learn more about both the nature of individual memory processes and how they affect one another.

Notes

1　This paper is a report from work begun independently by the two authors at Bell Telephone Laboratories and the State University of New York at Stony Brook, respectively. We thank S. Sternberg, T. K. Landauer, and Alexander Pollatsek for their helpful comments, A. S. Coriell for preparing the apparatus, and G. Ellis and B. Kunz for running Ss.
2　Here we are invoking our earlier proposal that both words and nonwords may have locations reserved for them in memory. We are assuming that from the viewpoint of retrieval, a nonword that is similar to English may be treated as a very unfamiliar word whose location is examined infrequently.

References

BOUSFIELD, W. A., COHEN, B. H., WHITMARSH, G. A., & KINCAID, W. D. *The Connecticut free associational norms.* (Tech. Rep. No. 35) Storrs, Conn.: University of Connecticut, 1961.

COLLINS, A. M., & QUILLIAN, M. R. Retrieval time from semantic memory. *Journal of Verbal Learning and Verbal Behavior*, 1969, **8**, 240–247.

COLLINS, A. M., & QUILLIAN, M. R. Facilitating retrieval from semantic memory: The effect of repeating part of an inference. In A. F. Sanders (Ed.), *Attention and performance III.* Amsterdam: North-Holland Publishing Company, 1970.

KUCERA, H., & FRANCIS, W. N. *Computational analysis of present-day American English.* Providence, R. I.: Brown University Press, 1967.

LANDAUER, T. K., & FREEDMAN, J. L. Information retrieval from long-term memory: Category size and recognition time. *Journal of Verbal Learning and Verbal Behavior*, 1968, **7**, 291–295.

MCCORMICK, E. M. *Digital computer primer.* New York: McGraw-Hill, 1959.

MEYER, D. E. On the representation and retrieval of stored semantic information. *Cognitive Psychology*, 1970, **1**, 242–300.

MEYER, D. E. Dual memory-search of related and unrelated semantic categories. Paper presented at the meeting of the Eastern Psychological Association, New York, April 1971.

MEYER, D. E., & ELLIS, G. B. Parallel processes in word recognition. Paper presented at the meeting of the Psychonomic Society, San Antonio, November 1970.

NORMAN, D. A. Comments on the information structure of memory. In A. F. Sanders (Ed.), *Attention and performance III*. Amsterdam: North-Holland Publishing Company, 1970.

OLDFIELD, R. C. Things, words and the brain. *Quarterly Journal of Experimental Psychology*, 1966, **18**, 340–353.

RUBENSTEIN, H., GARFIELD, L., & MILLIKAN, J. A. Homographic entries in the internal lexicon. *Journal of Verbal Learning and Verbal Behavior*, 1970, **9**, 487–494.

SCHAEFFER, B., & WALLACE, R. Semantic similarity and the comparison of word meanings. *Journal of Experimental Psychology*, 1969, **82**, 343–346.

SCHAEFFER, B., & WALLACE, R. The comparison of word meanings. *Journal of Experimental Psychology*, 1970, **86**, 144–152.

SCHIFFRIN, R. M., & ATKINSON, R. C. Storage and retrieval processes in long-term memory. *Psychological Review*, 1969, **76**, 179–193.

SWANSON, J. M., & WICKENS, D. D. Preprocessing on the basis of frequency of occurrence. *Quarterly Journal of Experimental Psychology*, 1970, **22**, 378–383.

STERNBERG, S. Memory scanning: Mental processes revealed by reaction-time experiments. *American Scientist*, 1969, **57**, 421–457.

WARREN, R. E. Stimulus encoding and memory. Unpublished doctoral dissertation, University of Oregon, 1970.

WINER, B. J. *Statistical principles in experimental design*. New York: McGraw-Hill, 1962.

36

CONTEXT-DEPENDENT MEMORY IN TWO NATURAL ENVIRONMENTS

On land and underwater

Duncan R. Godden and Alan D. Baddeley

Source: *British Journal of Psychology*, 66 (1975): 325–331.

In a free recall experiment, divers learnt lists of words in two natural environments: on dry land and underwater, and recalled the words in either the environment of original learning, or in the alternative environment. Lists learnt underwater were best recalled underwater, and vice versa. A subsequent experiment shows that the disruption of moving from one environment to the other was unlikely to be responsible for context-dependent memory.

The philosopher John Locke cites the case of a young man who learned to dance in a room containing an old trunk. Unfortunately, however, 'the idea of this remarkable piece of household stuff had so mixed itself with the turns and steps of all his dances, that though in that chamber he could dance excellently well, yet it was only while that trunk was there; nor could he perform well in any other place unless that or some other trunk had its due place in the room' (Locke, cited in Dennis, 1948, p. 68).

The belief that what is learnt in a given environment is best recalled in that environment has of course been a useful standby for detective story writers from Wilkie Collins onwards, although the empirical evidence for such a belief is somewhat equivocal. Farnsworth (1934) and Pessin (1932) were both unable to obtain a context-dependent memory effect. A later study by Jensen *et al.* (1971) was more successful, but a recent unpublished study by Hitch (personal communication) failed to observe any effect. An alternative approach to the context-dependent phenomenon utilizes a retroactive interference (RI) design in which material learned in one environment is followed by a second set of material presented in either the same or a different environment, which in turn is followed by a recall test on the original material. This final test itself may be in the initial environment or in the interpolated environment. Using this design, Bilodeau & Schlosberg (1951) found that an interpolated list caused only half as much RI when it was learned in a room differing markedly from that in which original learning took place. Comparable results were obtained by Greenspoon & Ranyard (1957), and by Zentall (1970). However, Strand (1970) has presented evidence suggesting that the inferior retention observed when the recall environment is different results not from the different context *per se*, but from the disruption that occurs when the subject moves from one environment to the other. She required the subjects in her control conditions, in which learning and recall were in the same environment, to leave the room and have a drink of water from a drinking fountain before beginning the recall phase of the experiment. Under these conditions she found no reliable difference between subjects who learned the interfering material in the same and those who learned in a different environment.

The evidence for context-dependent memory is therefore far from convincing. Furthermore, a number of the studies which have obtained effects have used extremely artificial environments, suggesting that any effect observed may not generalize beyond the conditions under which the experiment was run. Dallett & Wilcox (1968), in one of their conditions, required their subjects to stand with their heads inside an oddly shaped box containing flashing lights of different colours (two subjects had to be excused due to nausea), while in a further study Rand & Wapner (1967) strapped their subjects to a board which was then rotated so as to keep the subject either supine or erect. As Brunswik (1956) has pointed out, it is important for the psychologist to check the 'ecological validity' of his results by ensuring that they are applicable to the real world, and are not limited to the artificial conditions of the psychological laboratory. The experiments to be described are therefore concerned with investigating the phenomenon of context-dependent memory in two natural environments. Egstrom *et al.* (1972) observed that divers had considerable difficulty in recalling material learnt under water, and since recognition memory was not impaired in this way, they suggested that the defect was probably due to a context-dependent memory effect rather than to differential learning underwater. Unfortunately, since the appropriate controls were not included, such a conclusion was purely speculative. However, the underwater environment does present a particularly good example of a natural environment which differs dramatically from that on the surface. The diver underwater is weightless, has restricted vision, and subjectively is in an environment which is as different from the surface as any he is ever likely to experience. Divers were therefore asked to learn word lists both on land and underwater and subsequently recalled either on land (Dry) or underwater

(Wet). Each diver performed under all four possible conditions: DD (Learn Dry, Recall Dry); DW (Learn Dry, Recall Wet); WW and WD. Should the phenomenon of context-dependent memory exist under these conditions, performance when learning and recall took place in the same environment (DD and WW) should be significantly better than when recall took place in a different environment to that of learning (DW and WD).

Experiment I

Method

Subjects

Eighteen subjects were tested, comprising 13 male and five female members of a university diving club.

Apparatus

Five lists of words, each consisting of 36 unrelated, different, two- and three-syllable words chosen at random from the Toronto word bank, were constructed and subsequently recorded on tape (see *Procedure*).

Two Diver Underwater Communication (DUC) sets were used. A DUC set consists of a surface-to-diver telephone cable, terminating in a bone transducer, which, placed on the diver's mastoid, enables both surface-to-diver and diver-to-surface communication. The two DUC sets were slightly amended such that taped material, monitored by the surface operator, could be presented directly to the subject using a cassette tape-recorder. Twin transducers on each set allowed two separate pairs of subjects to be tested during the same period. Weighted formica boards, sealed with fablon, enabled subjects to record responses in pencil both above and underwater. Subjects used standard SCUBA breathing apparatus and diving equipment of various designs dictated by personal preference.

Procedure

All instructions and stimuli for each experimental session were recorded on tape. Efficient auditory perception of stimuli by a submerged diver using SCUBA apparatus is seriously impaired by the noise of his breathing. The presentation of the material was therefore grouped, so as to allow the diver to adopt a comfortable breathing rate which did not interfere with his auditory perception. Thus, each list was presented in blocks of three words. Within each block, the words were spaced at 2 sec. intervals. Between each block, a 4 sec. interval enabled subjects to exhale, inhale and hold their breath in readiness for the presentation of the next block, and so on.

Each tape began with an explanation of this breathing procedure, followed by a 'breathing pattern' section, to ensure that subjects were breathing correctly and in rhythm before the first word of the list appeared. This section consisted of nine spoken presentations of the letter z, in three blocks of three, and with identical spacings to those of the words in the list itself. Immediately after each block of z's, subjects heard the command 'breathe'. The presentation of the word list followed on naturally in rhythm, and the command to breathe was then dropped.

On each tape (one for each of the 16 condition/list combinations), the relevant list was presented twice. Between the first and second presentations, a gap of 10 sec. allowed subjects a short rest with unconstrained breathing. The second presentation was again preceded by the breathing pattern section.

To eliminate possible primary memory effects, the second presentation of each list was followed by 15 digits which subjects were required to copy at a rate of two seconds per digit. This was followed by the next instruction (e.g. 'Ascend to the shore station'), and a 4 min. delay. This recurred in all conditions and was necessary to enable subjects to comply safely with the relevant instruction. They were then instructed to write down in any order as many of the words from the list as they could remember. Two minutes were allowed for this, after which the session was terminated.

The original 16 subjects were split at random into four groups of four. Prior to the first experimental session, all subjects underwent a practice session, comfortably seated around a table. During this, they first practised the breathing technique, then the task itself, using a practice list.

Pairings of the remaining four lists $L_1 \ldots L_4$ with the four conditions, and the temporal orderings of the conditions for each of the four groups, were arranged according to a Graeco-Latin square design. Subjects experienced one condition per diving session, and the sessions were separated by approximately 24 hr. The design was such that each group experienced conditions and lists in different orders, that a given condition/list pair was never administered to more than one group, and that lists and conditions had equal representation on each experimental session.

Testing took place at open water sites near Oban, Scotland, in most cases as soon as subjects returned from their scheduled dive for the day. The latter consideration helped to ensure that subjects began each session in roughly the same state, that is, wet and cold. They were tested in pairs which remained the same across all sessions.

Subjects in environment D (Dry) sat by the edge of the water, masks tipped back, breathing tubes removed, and receivers in place. In environment W (Wet), subjects dived to approximately 20 ft., taking with them their formica board and two pencils, and with their receivers in position. Heavy weighting enabled them to sit on the bottom, and the session began after a verbal signal to the surface operator signified their readiness.

Due to a series of technical difficulties, two subjects were eventually dropped from the programme. They were subsequently replaced by another pair who were tested at a freshwater site.

Results

Mean recall scores and standard deviations are shown in Table 1. An analysis of variance showed there to be no significant main effect on recall performance due to either the environment of learning or that of recall. The interaction between the effect of learning and recall environment was, however, highly significant ($F = 22.0$; d.f. = 1, 12; $P = < 0.001$). Thus the effect on recall of the environment of recall depended on the environment of original learning. No other interactions proved significant. Finally, to look in more specific detail at the data, a Wilcoxon matched-pairs, signed-ranks test showed that, for learning in environment D, recall in environment D was better than recall in environment W ($P < 0.005$) while for learning in environment W, recall in W was better than recall in D ($P < 0.025$). There was no significant difference in recall between conditions DD and WW, nor between conditions DW and WD.

Discussion

The results of Expt. I are clearly in line with the context-dependent memory hypothesis: what was learned under water was best recalled under water and vice versa. Before accepting a context-dependent interpretation, however, some possible shortcomings of the experiment should be considered. The divers were on a pleasure-diving holiday at the time of the experiment, and it is entirely due to their good will in agreeing to participate, and tolerance in accepting the subsequent demands of the experiment that the latter was completed at all. Nevertheless, since the divers were in no way committed to the experiment, some limitations on what could reasonably be done were experienced. Thus, there was no control over the time of day at which subjects were

Table 1 Mean number of words recalled in Expt. I as a function of learning and recall environment

Learning environment	Recall environment					
	Dry			Wet		
	Mean recall score	S.D.		Mean recall score	S.D.	Total
Dry	13·5	5·8		8·6	(3·0)	22·1
Wet	8·4	3·3		11·4	(5·0)	19·8
Total	21·9	—		20·0	—	—

tested. In addition the experiment had to be run each day at the diving site chosen by the subjects, rather than at a constant location. Diving expeditions are notoriously difficult to organize and run smoothly; in an equipment-intensive operation which depends strongly on such local conditions as weather, fitness, etc., something will usually disrupt planned routine. Some divers may not, for medical reasons, dive each day. A dive may have to be aborted due to equipment failure, and so on. These problems were experienced to some degree, as was the unexpected. One diver was nearly run over during an underwater experimental session by an ex-army, amphibious DUKW. Thus it proved impossible to complete the session in four successive days, and the time between sessions varied both within and between subjects. None the less, under realistic open water conditions, and even subject to the above problems, a highly significant interaction between the environment of learning and that of recall emerged.

Before concluding that this result reflects the effect of context-dependent memory three alternative explanations should be considered. The first of these assumes differential cheating between the four conditions, with subjects in the WW group copying items down before the recall signal. Unfortunately, since it was not practicable to combine monitoring of both the subject and the shore station, this is a logical possibility. It is, however, unlikely for the following reasons; (1) had this been the case, higher level of WW performance might have been expected unless subjects were cheating in a particularly restrained manner; (2) it would be difficult to cheat without the awareness and connivance of one's diving partner; and (3) this particular group of subjects had virtually all had previous involvement in an underwater research project of their own, several were in fact research scientists, and social pressures against cheating would be considerable. Nevertheless, differential, restrained collaborative cheating remains a possible explanation. The second alternative explanation assumes that subjects rehearse during the unfilled interval between presentation and test, the degree of rehearsal being greater in the WW and DD conditions than in WD and DW, where subjects might be expected to be distracted by the procedure of getting into or out of the water. Thirdly, there has been a suggestion (Strand, 1970) that context-dependent effects may not be due to environmental change *per se*, but instead to disruption caused by taking the subject from one environment to the other in the context-change conditions. Thus further discussion of the apparent context-dependent effect found here will be postponed until after the report of the next experiment.

Experiment II

This tests both the differential rehearsal and disruption hypotheses by comparing the standard DD condition used in Expt. I with a modified DD condition in which subjects are required to enter the water and dive during the 4 min.

delay between presentation and the subsequent dry test. Both the differential rehearsal and disruption hypotheses should predict poorer retention in this condition, whereas a context-dependent hypothesis would not predict a decrement, since both learning and recall occur in the same environment.

Method

Subjects

Sixteen members of the Scottish Sub-Aqua Club served as voluntary subjects.

Apparatus

Subjects when in the water breathed using a snorkel tube, since this was administratively more convenient than SCUBA equipment. For the limited diving involved the two types of equipment may be regarded as equivalent. All other apparatus including word lists was the same as for Expt. I.

Procedure

As before, stimuli and instructions were all presented via tape. In condition n (non-disrupted), tapes employing the relevant lists under condition DD for Expt. I were used. For condition d (disrupted), the disruption instruction (to enter the water, swim a short distance, dive to approximately 20 ft., and return to the original position) was dubbed on to copies of the above tapes.

Subjects were assigned randomly to four groups as they volunteered. Prior to the experimental session, subjects practised the task and were then tested at an open water diving site near Oban, Scotland, immediately on their return from their scheduled day's dive.

A within-subject design was adopted. Groups 1 and 2 experienced condition n on the first session while groups 3 and 4 were presented first with condition d. List A occurred on the first session and List B on the second, for groups 1 and 3; List B was used on the first session and List A on the second, for groups 2 and 4. The two sessions were separated by approximately 24 hr.

Insufficient volunteers were found at Oban to complete the design. Consequently, a further three subjects from Stirling University were tested on a subsequent occasion at a freshwater site.

Results

In condition n, the mean number of words recalled was 8·44 ($\sigma = 4\cdot1$), while condition d produced a mean recall score of 8·69 ($\sigma = 3\cdot2$). The marginal difference, in the opposite direction to that predicted by the disruption hypothesis, did not approach significance.

Discussion

Scores obtained in Expt. II were lower than those obtained during the comparable DD conditions of Expt. I. Two possible reasons for this arise. Considerable background noise from other nearby diving groups persisted at a relatively constant rate throughout the experiment; this was not generally the case in Expt. I. Furthermore, most of the volunteers, unlike Expt. I subjects (largely medical students), were unfamiliar with testing situations and experimental procedures. Whatever the reason, the criticism might arise that possible effects of disruption might be masked by a floor effect. However, the two mean scores, both between 8 and 9, represent about 25 per cent recall, a reasonable level at which one might expect an effect to be measurable if it exists. Secondly, if 'high scorers' are identified as those subjects who scored higher than the mean under either condition, it is found that this subgroup recalled a mean of 10·1 words in condition *n* and 10·4 in condition *d*, suggesting that the absence of a disruption effect characterizes both high and low scores. Thus it can be concluded that under open water conditions similar to those for Expt. I, disruption was not a significant factor.

Conclusions

The effect of the environment or context of recall on performance depends upon the environment of learning. Recall is better if the environment of original learning is reinstated. This is unlikely to be due to disruption, and one can be reasonably confident that it is a truly context-dependent phenomenon. The results were obtained under real conditions, away from the laboratory, and using natural environments. The open water setting for the project limited the design such that two separate experiments were needed. However, within the limitations thus imposed, it appears that the phenomenon of context-dependent memory not only exists, but is robust enough to affect normal behaviour and performance away from the laboratory.

Acknowledgements

We acknowledge the invaluable help rendered by the Clydebank, East Kilbride, and Stirling University Sub-Aqua Clubs. In particular we would like to thank the United London Hospitals Diving Group. The experiment was supported by a grant from the Medical Research Council.

References

BILODEAU, I. M. & SCHLOSBERG, H. (1951). Similarity in stimulating conditions as a variable in retroactive inhibition. *J. exp. Psychol.* **41**, 119–204.

Brunswik, E. (1956). *Perception and the Representative Design of Psychological Experiments*. Berkeley: University of California Press.

Dallett, K. & Wilcox, S. G. (1968). Contextual stimuli and proactive inhibition. *J. exp. Psychol.* **78**, 475–480.

Dennis, W. (ed.) (1948). *Reading in the History of Psychology*. New York: Appleton-Century-Crofts.

Egstrom, G. H., Weltman, G., Baddeley, A. D., Cuccaro, W. J. & Willis, M. A. (1972). Underwater work performance and work tolerance. Report no. 51, Bio-Technology Laboratory, University of California, Los Angeles.

Farnsworth, P. R. (1934). Examinations in familiar and unfamiliar surroundings. *J. soc. Psychol.* **5**, 128–129.

Greenspoon, J. & Ranyard, R. (1957). Stimulus conditions and retroactive inhibition. *J. exp. Psychol.* **53**, 55–59.

Jensen, L. C., Harris, K. & Anderson, D. C. (1971). Retention following a change in ambient contextual stimuli for six age groups. *Dev. Psychol.* **4**, 394–399.

Pessin, J. (1932). The effect of similar and dissimilar conditions upon learning and relearning. *J. exp. Psychol.* **15**, 427–435.

Rand, G. & Wapner, S. (1967). Postural status as a factor in memory. *J. verb. Learn. verb. Behav.* **6**, 268–271.

Strand, B. Z. (1970). Change of context and retroactive inhibition. *J. verb. Learn. verb. Behav.* **9**, 202–206.

Zentall, T. R. (1970). Effects of context change on forgetting in rats. *J. exp. Psychol.* **86**, 440–448.

37

EFFECT OF DEPRESSION ON THE SPEED OF RECALL OF PLEASANT AND UNPLEASANT EXPERIENCES

Geoffrey G. Lloyd and William A. Lishman

Source: *Psychological Medicine*, 5 (1975): 173–180.

Synopsis

An experiment is described in which depressed patients were asked to recall pleasant or unpleasant experiences from their past life in response to a standard series of stimulus words. The ratio between the time for recall of pleasant and unpleasant experiences was found to fall progressively with increasing severity of depression or of 'neuroticism' and to be significantly related to each. Among patients who scored relatively low on depression or neuroticism pleasant memories were recalled more speedily than unpleasant; among those who scored high this relationship was reversed. Possible mechanisms to account for these findings are discussed.

It has long been held that pleasant experiences are usually recalled with greater facility than unpleasant ones. This observation is, of course, fundamental to Freud's theory of repression and is commented upon by him in *The Psychopathology of Everyday Life* (Freud, 1901):

'The tendency to forget what is disagreeable seems to me to be a quite universal one; the capacity to do so is doubtless developed with different degrees of strength in different people'.

In a later chapter of the same book Freud urges further investigation into this phenomenon:

'The extent and unwillingness to remember distressing impressions would seem to deserve the most careful psychological examination; moreover, we cannot separate from this wider context the question of what special conditions make this forgetting, that is universally aimed at, possible in individual cases'.

There are now many reports of attempts to verify this observation experimentally. Although there are some conflicting results, the bulk of the evidence, which has been reviewed by Beebe-Center (1932), Rapaport (1942), and Lishman (1972a), suggests that for normal subjects pleasant experiences are recalled more readily than unpleasant experiences. It has also been shown (Lishman, 1972a) that this tendency is more marked in older subjects and in those with high extraversion and low neuroticism scores on the Eysenck Personality Inventory.

Few investigations have been carried out into the effect of depression on the association between the readiness of recall of an experience and its hedonic tone—that is, its pleasantness or unpleasantness. Washburn et al. (1926) found that those subjects who recalled a greater than average number of unpleasant experiences, and recalled them more speedily than pleasant experiences, were more likely to be judged by their friends and themselves as being of depressed and pessimistic temperament. Sharp (1938) studied a heterogeneous group of 'psychoneurotic' and 'mildly psychotic' patients. Using paired associates, she showed pleasant material to be recalled more easily than unpleasant material after initial learning, but this facility did not differ from that shown by a group of normal controls on the same test. No attempt was made to distinguish those patients who were depressed, so no conclusions regarding the interaction of memory, hedonic tone, and depression can be drawn from Sharp's study. Lishman (1972b) tested a group of psychiatric inpatients suffering from affective disorder and found a tendency for the association between hedonic tone and recall to diminish with increasing depression when the latter was assessed clinically. This tendency did not reach statistical significance and was not confirmed when more standardized measures of depression were used. The numbers involved, however, were small because many of the patients found it difficult to master the particular technique employed and those with the more severe degrees of depression could not be tested.

The present paper describes the use of a simpler technique for investigating the situation in a group of depressed patients. It is applicable to patients with a wide range of severity of depression, and permits retesting after recovery by a parallel form of the test. The technique has already been described in detail, and was shown to be a reasonably valid means of assessing the relationship between hedonic tone and memory in the healthy volunteer subjects upon whom it was standardized (Lishman, 1974).

Method

Subjects

These were all inpatients in the adult departments of the Bethlem Royal and Maudsley Hospitals for whom admission to hospital had been thought necessary entirely or largely because of marked depression of mood. The nature of the study was explained to the patients and their participation invited if they were considered suitable for the study after discussion with their own doctor, perusal of the notes, and clinical interview. All patients were under the age of 60 years and none had received electroconvulsive therapy during the six months before testing. No patient was included who had a history of epilepsy or evidence of brain damage, or if at any time there had been reason to suspect schizophrenia.

Technique

The technique consisted essentially of obtaining measures, in each patient, of the time taken for the recall of a series of 'real life personal experiences', some with pleasant and some with unpleasant affective connotations. Recalls were elicited in response to a predetermined list of stimulus words. In response to some words the subject was required to recall a pleasant experience from his past life, and in response to others an unpleasant experience, so that the relative speeds of recall in the two categories could be compared.

The word lists employed are shown in Table 1. They are derived from those previously reported (Lishman, 1974) but a few words have been interchanged between one list and the other; this further balancing was undertaken so that 24 words would be available for use in each list in the present experiment.

Each word was presented singly by reading it aloud to the subject, who was requested to recall an experience associated with the particular word. The subject was instructed that recall of any experience was acceptable as long as it was brought to mind by the stimulus word in question, and as long as it was a definite experience from his memory store and not merely a current thought association. This distinction was illustrated by examples until the point had been thoroughly grasped. The experience had to be specific and to have affected the subject directly or indirectly, but it did not matter how long ago it had occurred. The recall of an experience was signalled by the subject tapping on a desk, and the time between presentation and recall was measured on a stop-watch to the nearest tenth of a second. If no experience could be recalled within 15 seconds of presentation the time for that

Table 1 Word lists used in experiments

List (1)	List (2)
table	touching
walking	scissors
face	car
shop	water
pink	black
long	house
leaving	high
animal	working
green	red
city	food
wall	chair
round	small
child	pen
hand	hearing
	doctor
window	
loud	blue
watching	money
white	soft
friend	leg
fast	street
clothes	yellow
paper	entering
talking	hot
brown	door

particular word was taken as 15.0 seconds. After each word the subject was asked to search his memory store afresh so that the same experience, or a related one, was not recalled in response to a different stimulus word. The method was rehearsed during a preliminary practice period and when the rules had been established the experiment proper was commenced. All subjects were tested individually by one or other of the authors, each having observed the other in action initially so that the technique could be strictly standardized.

At the first test session the subjects were all requested to recall pleasant memories from list (1) and unpleasant memories from list (2). The words were presented in groups of five, alternating between pleasant and unpleasant groups. The subjects were not required to report on the content of the memory in case this might lead to avoidance of emotionally charged material. They were, however, asked to indicate whether the memory was 'mildly' or 'very' pleasant to recall (or unpleasant, as the case might be). It was decided in advance that each subject had to obtain recalls in response to at least two-thirds of all the words administered, and to at least half of each list considered individually; if these criteria were not achieved the results for that particular subject were not utilized further.

When all 48 words had been presented, form A of the Eysenck Personality Inventory (Eysenck and Eysenck, 1964) was administered with instructions amended for use with depressed patients, as suggested by Kendell and DiScipio (1968). It had then been the intention to test the re-recall of the memories some 15 minutes later by presenting the words again in random order, as in the standardization experiment (Lishman, 1974), but it soon became apparent that few subjects were able to re-recall sufficient memories for this part of the experiment to be pursued. Instead, on completion of their tests a small subgroup of nine subjects was asked to report, with prompting if necessary, roughly how long ago each recalled experience had occurred— for example, one week, two years, etc. This, as described below, was to investigate one possible source of artefact in the results. Finally, each subject completed the Beck Depression Inventory (Beck *et al.*, 1961).

Where possible, when it seemed to the patient's own doctor that there had been an improvement in the patient's symptoms, the test was repeated some weeks or months later. At this second session unpleasant memories were requested in response to list (1) and pleasant memories in response to list (2), and form B of the Eysenck Personality Inventory was completed instead of form A. Otherwise the technique was as already described.

Results at first test session

Forty-four patients were invited to participate in the study and 43 agreed to do so. Of these, three proved unable to cooperate with the detailed requirements of the test situation when observed during preliminary practice, and a further four were unable to obtain a sufficient number of recalls to satisfy the criteria previously stipulated. The results therefore pertain to the remaining 36 patients.

There were 17 men and 21 women, ranging in age from 19 to 59 with a mean of 30.64 years (SD ± 11.26). On the Eysenck Personality Inventory, extraversion scores ranged from 0 to 15 (mean 8.39, SD ± 4.52), and neuroticism scores from 6 to 24 (mean 15.78, SD ± 4.65). The patients were therefore, on average, less extraverted and more neurotic than Eysenck's normal standardization sample (E = 12.07, SD ± 4.37; N = 9.07, SD ± 4.78; Eysenck and Eysenck, 1964). The depression scores on the Beck Inventory ranged from 9 to 50 (Mean 26.03, SD ± 9.66; range for the questionnaire 0–63). For the group as a whole, 83% of the pleasant memories and 83% of the unpleasant memories were recalled before the cut-off point of 15 seconds. Unpleasant memories were recalled slightly more rapidly than pleasant memories, the mean time for unpleasant memories (U) being 6.53 seconds and for pleasant memories (P) 6.99 seconds. The ratio of the time taken to recall unpleasant memories to the time taken to recall pleasant memories (U/P) was calculated for each patient. A ratio less than unity indicates that unpleasant memories were recalled more quickly than pleasant ones; for the group as a whole this ratio was 0.979.

Relationships between variables

The relationships between the ratio U/P and depression and neuroticism respectively are displayed in Figs 1 and 2 where the results for each patient are charted separately. There is a progressive diminution of U/P with increasing values of both depression and neuroticism. Furthermore, it can be seen that the less severely depressed patients have tended, like healthy subjects, to obtain U/P ratios in excess of unity—that is, to recall pleasant experiences more quickly than unpleasant experiences—whereas the great majority of the more severely depressed patients have shown a reversal in this respect, obtaining U/P ratios smaller than unity as a result of recalling unpleasant experiences more quickly than pleasant experiences. Thus it appears that, as depression increases in severity, the normal relationship between the hedonic tone of recalled experiences and the speed of their recall becomes not only

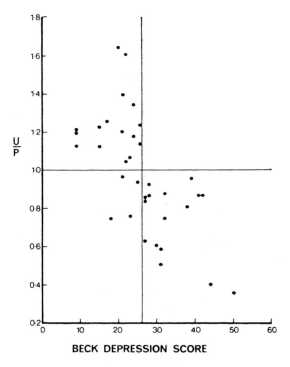

Figure 1 Relationship between U/P ratios and Beck depression scores (vertical line indicates mean depression score for the group).

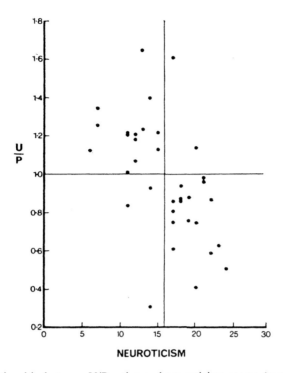

Figure 2 Relationship between U/P ratios and neuroticism scores (vertical line indicates mean neuroticism score for the group).

diminished but, in the severely depressed patients, reversed. Neuroticism shows a broadly similar set of relationships.

Pearson product-moment correlation coefficients were calculated to further investigate the relationships between the different variables. The correlation matrix is shown in Table 2. It can be seen that U/P is inversely correlated with scores on both depression and neuroticism to a highly significant extent ($P < 0.001$). The relationship between U/P and neuroticism is mainly determined by a prolongation of the time taken for the recall of pleasant experiences as neuroticism increases, whereas the effect of increasing depression is perhaps mainly to decrease the recall time for unpleasant experiences. No significant correlations were obtained between U/P and the other variables of age, sex, and extraversion.

Depression and neuroticism, however, were themselves highly inter-correlated ($r = 0.496$) so partial correlation coefficients were calculated. When the effect of neuroticism was held constant, the correlation coefficient between depression and U/P remained significant ($r = -0.498$, $P < 0.01$). Similarly, when the effect of depression was held constant the correlation coefficient between neuroticism and U/P remained significant ($r = -0.357$, $P < 0.05$).

Table 2 Correlation coefficients between age, sex, extraversion (E), neuroticism (N), severity of depression (D), and time to recall of pleasant (P) and unpleasant (U) experiences

	Age	Sex	E	N	D	P	U	U/P
Age	1.000	−0.043	−0.167	−0.184	−0.092	0.026	0.229	0.191
Sex		1.000	−0.141	0.192	0.257	0.169	0.061	−0.076
E			1.000	−0.085	−0.074	−0.297	−0.102	0.229
N				1.000	0.496†	0.517†	−0.038	−0.555‡
D					1.000	0.289	−0.384*	−0.635‡
P						1.000	0.499*	−0.481†
U							1.000	0.479†
U/P								1.000

* $P < 0.05$. † $P < 0.01$. ‡ $P < 0.001$.

When the results of the subjects tested by each author were analysed separately the relationship between depression and U/P was seen to be of a similar order for both groups. For the 25 subjects tested by G.G.L. $r = −0.55$ ($P < 0.01$) and for the 11 subjects tested by W.A.L. $r = −0.77$ ($P < 0.01$).

Time of origin of experiences

In view of the finding that undesirable life events appear to be more frequent in the six months before a depressive illness (Paykel *et al.*, 1969), a small group of nine subjects was asked to state, as accurately as possible, how long ago each recalled experience had occurred. This was done only after the recall phase of the experiment had been completed so that the subject would not be influenced into recalling experiences from any particular period. Of the experiences which could be dated, the percentage occurring during the previous one, six, and 12 months was calculated, and also the proportion of both pleasant and unpleasant experiences during these periods. The results are shown in Table 3. They do not indicate any tendency for more unpleasant than pleasant experiences

Table 3 Time of origin of experiences*

Recalls	Previous 4 weeks (no.) (%)	Recalled from: Previous 6 months (no.) (%)	Previous 12 months (no.) (%)
All	31/278 = 11.2	89/278 = 32.0	121/278 = 43.5
Pleasant	18/140 = 12.9	51/140 = 36.4	70/140 = 50.0
Unpleasant	13/138 = 9.4	38/138 = 27.5	51/138 = 37.0

* Means for nine subjects.

to have been recalled from the specified periods before testing; nor could any relationship be observed, on more detailed analysis, between the severity of the depression and the time period from which recalls had been made.

Intensity of emotion

For all subjects considered together 57.5% of the pleasant experiences were deemed by the subjects to be 'very' pleasant to recall, and of the unpleasant experiences 64.0% were deemed to be 'very' unpleasant. When the percentages for each subject were determined individually, it was found that the excess of unpleasant memories experienced at the higher level of intensity increased significantly with both depression ($r = 0.527$, $P < 0.001$) and neuroticism ($r = 0.395$, $P < 0.02$).

Results at second test session

Eighteen subjects, five men and 13 women, were available for retesting at intervals ranging from two weeks to six months after their original examination. The ages of this group ranged from 19 to 59 years (mean 30.94; SD ± 11.07); their extraversion scores ranged from 5 to 16 (mean 11.39; SD ± 3.78) and their neuroticism scores from 7 to 23 (mean 15.50; SD ± 4.13). The mean score on the Beck Depression Inventory had fallen to 17.33 (SD ± 12.31). The mean time taken to recall pleasant experiences was 5.89 seconds and that taken to recall unpleasant experiences was 6.03 seconds, giving a U/P ratio for the group of 1.031.

When the product-moment correlation coefficients were calculated, it was found that only depression and U/P were significantly related ($r = -0.540$, $P < 0.05$). The relationship between neuroticism and U/P showed a similar tendency to that found at the initial test ($r = -0.448$) but this now failed to reach the 0.05 level of statistical significance.

It had been expected that those subjects who had shown a change in their depression scores might show a change in the U/P ratios in the opposite direction. In other words, a decrease in depression was expected to be accompanied by a relative increase in the U/P ratio. This was not borne out by the results, there being no significant correlation between change in depression and change in U/P ratio ($r = -0.164$). However, it can be seen from Table 4 that the change in U/P ratios was in the expected direction in all eight cases whose depression scores fell from above to below the original mean of 26.03. In fact, in five of these this changed from below unity to above unity.

Discussion

In contrast with normal subjects, this group of depressed hospital inpatients, taken as a whole, has not shown a tendency for pleasant memories to be

Table 4 Results of retesting in 18 patients

Subject	Change in D	Change in U/P
3	−8 (9→1)	−0.061
8	−8 (20→12)	−0.396
9	−12 (21→9)	−0.132
15	−8 (23→15)	+0.152
16	−20 (24→4)	−0.239
17	−13 (24→11)	−0.280
18	+9 (25→34)	+0.097
21*	−10 (27→17)	+0.183
22*	−7 (27→20)	+0.339
23*	−3 (27→24)	+0.201
24*	−17 (28→11)	+0.116
25*	−16 (28→12)	+0.056
27*	−22 (31→9)	+0.576
29*	−30 (32→2)	+0.276
30*	−15 (32→17)	+0.176
31	+1 (38→39)	+0.113
32	−3 (39→36)	−0.100
33	−2 (41→39)	+0.059

* Cases whose Beck Depression Scores fell from above to below the mean on retesting (see text).

recalled more speedily than unpleasant memories. When viewed in relation to severity of depression, however, a highly significant relationship emerges, in that increasing depression is associated with a progressively diminishing ratio between the speed of recall of unpleasant and pleasant memories. Among the less severely depressed patients pleasant memories have been recalled more speedily than unpleasant memories, whereas among the more severely depressed patients this relationship is reversed. The changeover appears to occur at about the mean level of severity of depression for the group as a whole. Increasing neuroticism, which in this group of subjects is itself highly intercorrelated with severity of depression, shows a similar set of relationships.

Depression appears to exert its effect mainly by the speeding up of recall of unpleasant memories, whereas neuroticism appears to act by prolonging the recall of pleasant memories. This aspect of the findings, in depressed patients, is in line with results previously obtained by a different experimental technique (Lishman, 1972b) in which depressed patients were observed to recall more material of negative hedonic tone than non-depressed patients after a prior learning experience. It is also in keeping with what one would expect from clinical observation of such patients. The finding of a *reversal* of hedonic selectivity in the more severely depressed patients, rather than merely a diminution of hedonic effect, has not previously emerged, and is probably attributable in the present study to the use of a simple technique which has been applicable to subjects with severe degrees of depression. The effect of neuroticism—namely, to prolong the time taken for the recall of pleasant memories—is similar to that found in the standardization study of the present technique on healthy subjects (Lishman, 1974). In the standardization study, speedier recall of unpleasant than pleasant memories was very rarely encountered, but the range of neuroticism in the subjects did not extend to the values encountered here. Age and extraversion have had no demonstrable effect in the present investigation.

Various mechanisms must be considered to account for the relatively speedier recall of unpleasant memories in a high proportion of the present subjects. The association with neuroticism suggests that, at least in part, it may be linked with enduring personality characteristics, and confirms the importance of personality factors in hedonic selectivity as previously suggested (Lishman, 1972a, 1974). However, on retesting the patients, neuroticism did not preserve a significant relationship with U/P, although the relationship was still in the same direction.

A preponderance of previous life experiences of a particular hedonic tone could well account for the more rapid recall of memories with similar hedonic tone. There is evidence (Flügel, 1925) that for healthy, normal subjects experiences judged to be pleasant outnumber experiences judged to be unpleasant in everyday life. It could be argued that the group studied here had been exposed to an excess of previous life experiences which were considered to be unpleasant and that this accounted for the speedier recall of these experiences. The results do not rule out this possibility completely but it must be considered unlikely since, when less depressed, the subjects retested showed a slight tendency as a group to recall pleasant memories more quickly, even though they were recalling from a pool of life experiences similar to that at the first test.

The temporal relationship of the experiences recalled might also be expected to influence their speed of recall. If the unpleasant experiences which were recalled had occurred more recently than the pleasant, then this fact alone might determine the speedier recall of the former. That this explanation is unlikely is indicated by the results in Table 3 of those subjects who were able to date their experiences when requested to do so. When the proportion of experiences occurring in specified periods before testing is examined, it is seen that there is no tendency for more unpleasant than pleasant experiences to have been recalled from the more recent past.

Another factor which might influence speed of recall is the intensity of the hedonic tone attached to the memory. In this study the intensity of the emotion was only roughly assessed by asking the subject to judge it as very or mildly pleasant (or unpleasant). More unpleasant experiences were judged as being of the higher intensity than were pleasant experiences, and this excess was significantly correlated both with depression and with neuroticism.

Greater intensity of hedonic tone attached to unpleasant memories may thus be partly responsible for their speedier recall by both depressives and neurotics.

Finally, the effect of the 'mental set' of the subject must be considered, since McGeoch (1952) has suggested that this determines hedonic selectivity. During periods of depression the recall process might be directed preferentially towards unpleasant experiences which would therefore appear in consciousness more quickly than pleasant experiences. There might also be more mental rehearsal of those memories having negative hedonic tone, since it is a common clinical observation that depressives tend to be preoccupied with unpleasant past events. After recovery from depression, this selectivity might be reversed and recall directed towards pleasant experiences. This study provides some support for this suggestion, in that all those subjects whose depression scores fell from above to below the mean for the group showed a decreased tendency towards speedier recall of unpleasant memories when retested, and five out of the eight actually showed a reversal in their hedonic selectivity.

One must consider the question of whether the disturbance of hedonic selectivity of memory found in depressed subjects is a phenomenon secondary to the depressive process, or an enduring characteristic of those individuals who are prone to depressive illness. The presently available evidence suggests that both factors are operative. With regard to the influence of depression, we may note that there is a regular relationship between the degree of depression at the time of testing and the diminution of U/P, which would seem unlikely if it were imposed by premorbid personality characteristics alone; moreover this relationship remains significant after partialling out the effects of 'neuroticism'. Similarly, there are indications that hedonic selectivity tends to return towards normal as the depression resolves.

References

Beck, A. T., Ward, C. H., Mendelson, M., Hock, J., and Erbaugh, J. (1961). An inventory for measuring depression. *Archives of General Psychiatry*, **4**, 561–571.

Beebe-Center, J. G. (1932). *The Psychology of Pleasantness and Unpleasantness.* Reprinted 1965. Russell and Russell: New York.

Eysenck, H. J., and Eysenck, S. B. G. (1964). *Manual of the Eysenck Personality Inventory.* University of London Press: London.

Flügel, J. C. (1925). A quantitative study of feeling and emotion in everyday life. *British Journal of Psychology*, **15**, 318–355.

Freud, S. (1901). *The Psychopathology of Everyday Life.* Reprinted 1966. Benn: London.

Kendell, R. E., and DiScipio, W. J. (1968). Eysenck Personality Inventory scores of patients with depressive illnesses. *British Journal of Psychiatry*, **114**, 767–770.

Lishman, W. A. (1972a). Selective factors in memory. Part I: age, sex and personality attributes. *Psychological Medicine*, **2**, 121–138.

Lishman, W. A. (1972b). Selective factors in memory. Part 2: affective disorder. *Psychological Medicine*, **2**, 248–253.

Lishman, W. A. (1974). The speed of recall of pleasant and unpleasant experiences. *Psychological Medicine*, **4**, 212–218.

McGeoch, J. A. (1952). *The Psychology of Human Learning*. 2nd edn. revised by A. I. Irion. Longmans: New York.

Paykel, E. S., Myers, J. K., Dienelt, M. N., Klerman, G. L., Lindenthal, J. J., and Pepper, M. P. (1969). Life events and depression. A controlled study. *Archives of General Psychiatry*, **21**, 753–760.

Rapaport, D. (1942). *Emotions and Memory*. Williams and Wilkins: Baltimore.

Sharp, A. A. (1938). An experimental test of Freud's doctrine of the relation of hedonic tone to memory revival. *Journal of Experimental Psychology*, **22**, 395–418.

Washburn, M. F., Booth, M. E., Stocker, S., and Glicksmann, E. (1926). A comparison of directed and free recalls of pleasant and unpleasant experiences, as tests of cheerful and depressed temperaments. *American Journal of Psychology*, **37**, 278–280.

38

MOOD AS A MEDIATOR OF PLACE DEPENDENT MEMORY

Eric Eich

Source: *Journal of Experimental Psychology: General*, 124(3) (1995): 293–308.

Converging evidence from 3 studies suggests that how well information transfers from one environment to another depends on how similar the environments feel rather than on how similar they look. Thus, even when target events are encoded and retrieved in the same physical setting, memory performance suffers if the attending affective states differ. Conversely, a change in environment produces no performance decrement if, whether by chance (Experiments 1 and 2) or by design (Experiment 3), the mood at encoding matches the mood at retrieval. These observations imply that place dependent effects are mediated by alterations in affect or mood, and that data that appear on the surface to demonstrate place dependent memory may, at a deeper level, denote the presence of mood dependent memory. Discussion focuses on prospects for future research aimed at clarifying the relations among moods, places, and memory.

A problem of continuing concern in the analysis of place dependent memory has been the apparent capriciousness of the phenomenon. Although several studies have established that events encoded in a particular physical setting or environment are most retrievable in that environment, others have shown no sign of place dependence using similar or even identical methods (for reviews, see Bjork & Richardson-Klavehn, 1989; Roediger & Guynn, in press; Smith, 1988; Underwood, 1977).

Although widely recognized and well researched, the problem of unreliability has thus far resisted resolution. Current conjecture is that place dependence is regulated by a broad range of factors, including (a) characteristics of the to-be-remembered or target events (Wilhite, 1991); (b) the manner in which they are encoded (McDaniel, Anderson, Einstein, &

O'Halloran, 1989); (c) the nature of the retrieval test (Smith, Glenberg, & Bjork, 1978); (d) whether the events are construed as being casually related to, rather than simply contiguous with, a given environment (Fernandez & Glenberg, 1985); (e) whether the events are envisioned as interacting with the environment or as isolated visual images (Eich, 1985); (f) the ease with which participants, at retrieval, can mentally reinstate the original encoding context (Smith, 1979); and (g) the duration of the retention interval (Smith, 1988). Although clearly plausible and probably contributory, these factors provide only a partial understanding of why place dependence sometimes comes, sometimes goes. In aid of acquiring a fuller understanding, the present research focuses on yet another factor that may play a pivotal role in the occurrence of the phenomenon. In essence, the idea is that place dependent effects in memory are mediated by alterations in affect or mood, meaning that how well information transfers from one environment to another depends on how similar the environments feel rather than on how similar they look. More succinctly, the *mood mediation hypothesis* states that place dependent memory (PDM) represents a special—and rather subtle—case of mood dependent memory (MDM).

On first impression, it seems inane to invoke MDM as an explanation for PDM. After all, although it would be fair to say that *place* dependence "has the qualities of a will-o-the-wisp" (Kihlstrom, 1989, p. 26) and that it "presents more problems than solutions" (Ellis & Hunt, 1989, p. 280), these remarks, in fact, have been made in reference to *mood* dependence—and for good reason. Paralleling the recent history of research on PDM, clear and convincing demonstrations of MDM, which were commonplace in the 1970s, became a rare commodity in the 1980s (see Bower, 1981, 1987, 1992). Moreover, attempts to replicate positive MDM results have seldom succeeded, even when undertaken by the same investigator using similar materials, tasks, and mood-modification techniques (e.g., Bower & Mayer, 1989). This is why the comments cited earlier were made, and this is also why it is of immediate interest to ask, How can one precarious phenomenon possibly provide clues to another?

The answer comprises three points. One is that recent research suggests that the unreliability of mood dependence may be more apparent than real. For example, in each of three studies reported by Eich, Macaulay, and Ryan (1994), participants were asked to generate, from autobiographical memory, specific real-life events that were called to mind by common-word probes. Participants attempted, 2 or 3 days later, to freely recall the gist of as many of these events as possible. All three studies revealed MDM, such that significantly more events were recalled when the mood at testing—either pleasant or unpleasant—matched the mood at event generation than when there was a mismatch. On the basis of these and related results (Beck & McBee, in press; Bower, 1992; Eich & Metcalfe, 1989; Macaulay, Ryan, & Eich, 1993), it has been proposed (Eich, 1995) that, under conditions in which participants experience strong and stable moods, take responsibility for generating the target events themselves, and also assume responsibility for generating the cues required for event retrieval, robust and reliable evidence of mood dependence is apt to emerge. In addition to strengthening the case for mood dependence, these results suggest new ways of studying place dependence. Indeed, all three of the PDM experiments reported here entailed the same autobiographical event generation and recall tasks that were invented to investigate MDM (Eich et al., 1994, Experiment 2).

The second point is that the mood mediation hypothesis may shed some light on why certain studies have succeeded in demonstrating PDM, whereas certain others have failed. To clarify, consider an experiment by Eich (1985) in which participants, while seated in one of two distinctively decorated rooms, were read a long list of unrelated nouns. During the encoding session, participants in the *integrated imagery condition* were instructed to visualize every object as being conjoined with a particular feature of their environment (e.g., "I imagine a diamond-shaped *kite* lying on top of the table located in the corner of the room"). In contrast, participants in the *isolated imagery condition* were asked to picture each object as existing by itself (e.g., "I imagine a big blue *kite* sailing on the sky"). Two days later, during the retrieval session, half of the participants in each imagery condition returned to the original room, and half were taken to the other office (i.e., matched vs. mismatched encoding/retrieval environments). On arrival, participants were greeted first with a surprise test of object free recall and then with a test of object recognition memory.

Different patterns of results were predicted for the two tests. Regarding recognition, data from several sources indicate that place dependent effects—like mood dependent effects—seldom emerge when participants are supplied with specific, tangible reminders such as the copy cues provided in a test of recognition memory (see Eich, 1980; Smith, 1988). Accordingly, no reliable evidence of PDM was expected to emerge in recognition of either integrated or isolated imagery items—and none was found.

Regarding recall, it was reasoned that contextual associations (i.e., connections in memory between individual objects and the environmental context in which they are envisaged) are more likely to be formed when the participant is given instructions for generating integrated rather than isolated images. If so, then a change in context should have a greater adverse effect on the recall of objects visualized as interacting with the environment than on the recall of objects visualized as being isolated entities. The results, however, revealed that place dependent effects in recall were not simply enhanced by asking participants to generate integrated item/environment images but were clearly contingent on these instructions: Whereas a mismatch between encoding/retrieval environments significantly impaired the recall of integrated imagery items, it had no appreciable impact on the recall of isolated imagery items.

The failure to find place dependence in the recall of isolated images seemed surprising in view of earlier evidence that the environmental context experienced during encoding can become connected to the target items, even when participants are neither requested nor required to make such contextual associations. For example, in an experiment by Godden and Baddeley (1975), scuba divers learned a word list while they were sitting either at the bottom of a Scottish lake or at the edge of the water. It is important to note that the participants were not specifically told to associate the words with the learning environment. That they nevertheless did so is suggested by the fact that, on average, about 46% more words were freely recalled when learning and testing environments matched than when they mismatched, a finding indicative of place dependence. Similarly, in a study by Smith et al. (1978, Experiment 3), a mismatch between encoding/retrieval rooms was shown to significantly reduce the free recall of words that participants had previously sorted into various conceptual categories, a task, much like the isolated imagery technique used in Eich (1985), that required participants to attend to every target item but did not demand that they mentally link the targets to the encoding environment. If it is the case, as these and related results imply (see Smith, 1988), that connections between the target items and the environment in which they are encoded can be acquired automatically or without any specific intent or special effort on the part of participants, why then were such contextual associations not created when participants in Eich's (1985) study were instructed to generate an isolated image of every target?

The mood mediation hypothesis suggests an answer. As noted by Eich (1985, p. 769):

> Although the environments used in this [Eich's] study were designed to have highly distinctive appearances, they were not intended to induce different affects, and it seems unrealistic to suppose that a subject's mood or psychological state would have been appreciably altered by the transition from one environment to another. It is, however, entirely possible—even probable—that subjects in Godden and Baddeley's (1975) study experienced a profound change of psychological state, as well as one of physical setting, when, for example, they learned a list of words while weightlessly suspended in water, and were later tested for recall while on land. It is also possible that subjects in Smith et al.'s (1978) card sorting study experienced a similar change of both internal state and external surround, especially when they carried out the sorting task in the morning within an austere storeroom stocked with electronic equipment, and completed retention testing in the afternoon within a comfortable if cluttered office decorated with posters, plants, and colorful drapery. In short, it is possible that what both Godden and Baddeley (1975)

and Smith et al. (1978) demonstrated was not *environmental* context dependent memory, but rather *experiential* context dependence, of the kind customarily associated with alterations of a person's affective, circadian, or pharmacological state.

Without too much stretching, the mood mediation hypothesis can be seen to apply to other situations as well. For example, even though university classrooms differ in their size, shape, and other perceptual properties, they probably feel much the same to an undergraduate toiling over a midterm test. This supposed affective similarity may be one of several reasons why Saufley, Otaka, and Bavaresco (1985), in an elegant series of naturalistic studies, found no reliable differences in the examination results of students tested under matched versus mismatched classroom conditions.

Alternatively, a study by Dallett and Wilcox (1968) may represent another case of correlated physical settings and psychological states. In a successful attempt to show that a change of context improves memory performance by reducing proactive interference, Dallett and Wilcox (1968) had each participant learn and recall several lists of words either while he sat before an ordinary memory drum or while he

> stood with his head inside a large [trapezoid-shaped] box, his neck in a foam-rubber-padded U-shaped cutout in the floor of the box, with a curtain to eliminate peripheral stimuli behind him. The room was darkened, and the interior of the box lighted with flashing red and green lights. . . . The inside of the box was painted white, with green and black lines added, converging to a false vanishing point which did not coincide with the perspective of the walls [none of which were parallel]. Some of these painted lines were "connected" to black strings hung across the interior of the box. Half of one wall was covered by furry red patches made of a nylon bathmat. After constructing the box and using it, it seemed to the [experimenters] that a great deal of its effect came from the changing illumination; a red 40-w. bulb flashed at a rate of approximately 80/min, while a green bulb flashed at approximately 18/min. These were the only lights in the box. (pp. 475–476)

That the "box environment" felt as well as looked different from the "drum environment" is suggested by Dallett and Wilcox's (1968, p. 476) understatement that "the [subjects] generally agreed that the box was highly unusual, and on two occasions [subjects] had to be excused because of nausea."

Having tried to make an indirect case for the mood mediation hypothesis, I must now add three caveats. First, although the hypothesis seems well suited to some earlier studies of place dependence, it cannot accommodate them all. As an example, Fernandez and Glenberg (1985, Experiment 8) were unable to replicate the positive PDM results reported by Smith (1979, Experiment 1), despite their use of virtually identical materials, tasks, and environments. If Smith's participants felt different in one setting versus another (a very big "if"), then so too should have those tested by Fernandez and Glenberg. Second, as suggested at the outset, mood mediation is but one of several factors that may play key parts in the expression of place dependent effects. Thus, for example, even a radical change in both environmental and experiential contexts is unlikely to impair performance if retention is tested in the presence of observable cues of reminders. This is why Godden and Baddeley (1980), in a second scuba diver study, found no evidence of place dependence in recognition memory, and also why free recall was the test of choice in each of the three experiments related here. Third, and most critical, in none of the studies cited earlier or any other published PDM report of which I am aware were participants required to rate the similarity (or dissimilarity) between their feelings at retrieval and those experienced at encoding. Consequently, all of the preceding claims about how physical settings and psychological states were correlated in certain studies, but not in others, can be considered only armchair conjectures, not data-based conclusions.

This last comment leads to the last point, which is that the mood mediation hypothesis has a number of specific, testable implications. The simplest of these was investigated in the initial study, which involved two sessions held 2 days apart. During the first session, one group of participants generated autobiographical events in response to neutral-noun probes (à la Eich et al., 1994, Experiment 2) while seated in a small, windowless, dimly lit office. During the second session, these participants were taken to a spacious and scenic Japanese garden, where they were asked to do two things: first, freely recall the gist of the events that they had generated earlier; second, rate the subjective similarity of the two environments—that is, how similar [or dissimilar] did they feel during event recall, relative to how they felt during event generation. A second group of participants did exactly the same, except that they generated events in the garden and recalled them in the office.

Because all participants undertook event recall in a setting that looked very different from the one they had encountered during event generation, the overall level of recall should be about the same in both groups. The issue of chief concern is whether participants (in either group) who feel the same during both sessions fare better in recall than do those who feel differently. A positive relation between subjective similarity and event recall would constitute correlational evidence for the mood mediation hypothesis, which would at least make a start toward assessing its true merit.

General method

Certain aspects of methodology common to all three studies are addressed first. Specific details and special circumstances are then considered on a study-by-study basis.

Environments

Each experiment was conducted in three locations termed the *homeroom*, the *outside environment*, and the *inside environment*. Participants were escorted by the research assistant from one site to another, and as they walked they often talked about matters (e.g., classes, hobbies, and movies) unrelated to the experiment.

The homeroom was a 3.9 × 3.1 m office on the ground floor of the Kenny Building, which houses the Department of Psychology at the University of British Columbia (UBC). Ordinarily used to accommodate two graduate students, the office was refurnished for this project with a pair of armless desk chairs, a cedar credenza, and an oak conference table at which the participant and the research assistant sat on opposite sides.

Directly ahead of the participant was a large, blue-framed window overlooking part of a courtyard; sunlight entering this window provided the sole source of room illumination. To the participant's left was a set of oak bookshelves; to the right were the credenza, a corkboard, and a large wall-mounted calendar; behind were a yellow door and a blackboard. Apart from the window frame and the door, all painted surfaces were white, as was the tile floor and panel ceiling. As its name suggests, the homeroom was where the participant and the assistant met at the start of each session. The homeroom was also where informed consent was obtained, where instructions for the upcoming task of autobiographical event generation were given, and where (in Experiments 2 and 3) the participant provided baseline ratings of current mood; details on these task instructions and mood ratings are reviewed later.

The outside (O) environment was a stunningly scenic section of the Nitobe Memorial Garden, a 2.2 hectare hedge-enclosed area on the UBC campus located about 800 m (6-min walking distance) from the Kenny Building. The participant and assistant sat side by side on a picnic blanket spread over a grassy knoll (if the ground was wet, they moved to a nearby stone bench). The knoll overlooked a koi pond and a ceremonial teahouse and was surrounded on all sides by trees, flowering shrubs, and small running streams. Open to UBC personnel and the general public year-round, the garden attracts about 300 visitors on a typical midsummer day (when most of the participants were tested). The grassy knoll where testing took place was a quiet, secluded site well off any of the main walking trails, selected so as to minimize distractions. All testing that was completed in the O environment occurred under pleasant weather conditions, with moderate temperatures (averaging about 25°C), low humidity, calm or light winds, and clear to partly cloudy skies.

The inside (I) environment, like the homeroom, was located on the ground floor of the Kenny Building; the distance separating them was roughly 60 m (less than a minute's walk away). The I environment, however, was a smaller room (3.0 × 2.6 m) and it had no windows; two lamps, each containing a 40-W soft-light bulb, afforded a low level of illumination. Principal pieces of furniture were a leather recliner chair (occupied by the participant), an adjoining oak end table, a pine desk (at which the assistant sat), and a large black storage cabinet made of metal. The walls and ceiling were white; the flooring was an Aztec-style rug in earth tones. The wall to the participant's right was mostly covered by the storage cabinet and a beige curtain (closed to conceal a one-way mirror); all of the other walls held brass-framed prints by M. C. Escher. In overall appearance and atmosphere, the I environment might best be described as tasteful but subdued, even somber.

Event generation task

The main task undertaken during the first session of each study was *auto-biographical event generation*. Participants in Experiments 1 and 2 performed this task in either the I or the O environment; those in Experiment 3 always did so in O.

While walking from the homeroom to the site of event generation, the assistant informed the participants that, on arrival, she would need about 5 min to set things up and check on her materials. The purpose of this interlude was to give participants a chance to become familiar with their new setting—and possibly "soak up" its atmosphere—while the assistant, sitting nearby, busied herself making notes, collating forms, and so forth. The reason for telling them in advance about this brief break was to keep them from becoming miffed over an unexplained delay in the proceedings. After this 5-min acclimation period, the protocol for event generation was quickly reviewed, participants' current mood was assessed (in Experiments 2 and 3), and then the task was begun.

The task materials consisted of 32 common, unrelated, affectively neutral nouns, such as *ship* and *street*, selected from the Brown and Ure (1969) word norms. The materials were divided into two 16-item lists that were assigned at random to equal numbers of participants in each study.

At the outset of the task, participants were asked to treat each list item as a probe for generating, from autobiographical memory, a specific episode or event from any time in their personal past. List items or "probes" were read to the participants by the assistant. On hearing a given probe, participants were asked to say okay as soon as they thought of a suitably specific event (i.e., one that they could describe in detail and date with precision). If the participants failed to generate such an event within 2 min, then that probe was skipped and the next one was presented. If they succeeded, then the assistant, after logging event generation latency (in seconds), asked them to recount the particulars of the event: where and when (month and year) it occurred, who was involved, and so forth. All of these details were transcribed by the assistant.

Next, participants rated (a) the *emotionality* of the event at the time it occurred, (b) the personal significance or *importance* of the event when it happened, and (c) the *vividness* with which they recollect the event now. Ratings of original emotionality were made on a 9-point scale ranging from *extremely negative* (−4) to *extremely positive* (4); ratings of original importance and current vividness were made on 5-point scales ranging from *not at all important/vague recollection* (1) to *extremely important/vivid recollection* (5). To simplify matters, the assistant provided participants with a set of index cards containing these three scales. Participants made their ratings verbally, and the assistant wrote them down.

The procedures just outlined were identical to those used in Eich et al.'s (1994, Experiment 2) research on MDM, and they were used here to achieve two ends. One was to enhance long-term event retention: Although the participants did not know it at the time, the events that they generated today would be the targets of a surprise test of free recall given 2 days later. By describing, dating, and rating every event, participants were forced to focus on their autobiographical recollections and to process them in a deep, elaborative manner. Such processing should have, in turn, fostered a respectable level of free-recall performance (or at least should have precluded the possibility of a severe floor effect).

The second purpose was to discover what, if any, differences exist between events generated in the O and I environments. Assuming that the former locale is more pleasing—affectively as well as aesthetically—than is the latter, it is plausible to predict that O-generated events would be rated higher in original emotionality (i.e., as more positive experiences) than would I-generated events. This prediction derives from prior studies showing that participants who have been deliberately induced to feel happy—whether through hypnotic suggestions, radiant music, cheerful imagery, or some other mood-modification technique—typically generate more positive autobiographical events, and fewer negative ones, than do participants who have been induced to feel sad (see Blaney, 1986; Bower, 1981; Eich et al., 1994; Singer & Salovey, 1988). Data pertinent to this prediction and to other possible differences between O versus I events (in generation latency, current vividness, and other measures) are included in the accounts of Experiments 1 and 2.

At the conclusion of the first session, participants were discharged and requested to return to the homeroom 2 days later to carry on with the research. As noted earlier, participants were not told that their ability to freely recall the events that they had generated would be assessed at that time.

Event recall task

The main task undertaken during the second session of each experiment was *autobiographical event recall*. This task was performed in the I environment by half of the subjects in each study, and in the O environment by the other half. Like event generation, the task of event recall began following a 5-min acclimation period of which the participants had been apprised in advance.

The assistant reminded the participants that they had generated as many as 16 autobiographical events in response to common-word probes while in a particular environment (either the I or O in Experiments 1 and 2 and always O in Experiment 3). She then asked them to recall, in any order, the gist of as many of these events as possible. Participants were told that they need not give detailed replies; indeed, it was sufficient—even preferable—for them to recall only the probe that had triggered a given recollection. The assistant kept a written record of the participants' spoken responses.

Immediately after recall (in Experiment 1), or shortly thereafter (in Experiments 2 and 3), participants were asked, *How similar did you feel during the test of event recall in comparison with how you felt 2 days ago, during the test of event generation?* The assistant transcribed the responses, which were made on an 11-point *subjective similarity scale* (printed on an index card given to the participant) ranging from *not at all similar* (0) to *extremely similar* (10).

After making these ratings, all participants completed a questionnaire that solicited their views on the study's aims and methods (i.e., what the experiment was about and what it was trying to show); questionnaires given to participants in Experiments 1 and 3 included other, more specialized items discussed later. After recording the spoken responses, the assistant debriefed the participants, asked them not to divulge the details of the project with friends who might later participate, and paid them for their participation.

Participant recruitment and selection

Participants were recruited by means of sign-up sheets posted around the UBC campus. On initial telephone contact, all prospective participants were told that (a) the specific study in which they would serve was part of a larger project aimed at exploring the effects of various campus environments on various cognitive processes, such as those involved in recollecting events of the personal past; (b) they would be tested individually throughout the course of the study, which would be divided into two 30–60-min sessions spaced 2 days apart; and (c) they would receive $25 (Canadian dollars) on completion of the second session. In addition, potential participants in Experiments 2 and 3 were informed that a self-report measure of current mood would be administered on several occasions over the course of the study. It was explained that periodic mood measurement was a standard practice in research on autobiographical memory; the possibility that their mood might shift in different surroundings was not explicitly raised or even implied. Potential participants in Experiment 3 were also told that, during the second session, they would be randomly assigned to one of two mood-induction procedures: one designed to foster feelings of happiness or one meant to impart a state of sadness. Accordingly, participants were advised against volunteering if the prospect of becoming sad, even temporarily, caused them concern.

One hundred twenty-eight UBC undergraduates—95 women and 33 men averaging 22.8 years of age (range = 17 to 44 years)—served as participants in the three studies (ns = 32, 48, and 48 in Experiments 1, 2, and 3, respectively). Criteria for participant selection included 1st-year or 2nd-year standing, fluency in English, and no prior participation in research involving either autobiographical memory or experimentally induced moods. Most of the participants (93, or 73%) were enrolled in summer session courses at UBC and were tested from the middle of May through the end of August; the remaining participants (35, or 27%) were fall semester students who were tested between early September and middle October, while the weather was still good. Sixteen of the 128 participants replaced individuals who began but did not complete a given study because (a) they failed to return as scheduled for the second session (2 cases), (b) recall testing was interrupted by visitors to the Nitobe Garden (1 case), or (c) recall testing that was to have been completed in the garden had to be canceled due to inclement weather (13 cases).

Experiment 1

Method

Participants (n = 32) were randomly assigned in equal numbers to one of two conditions: O/I or I/O. The letter to the left of the slash mark signifies the environment where participants undertook autobiographical event generation; the letter to the right symbolizes the environment where, 2 days later, participants completed autobiographical event recall.

After expressing their views on the study's aims and methods, participants in Experiment 1 were asked to describe, in their own terms, the moods they had experienced during the event generation and event recall tasks. The intent here was to obtain a rough idea of whether the participants did indeed feel different (presumably better) being outside than they did being inside, as I had assumed they would.

Results

Event generation

As a means of assessing performance on this task, six dependent measures were derived for each participant: (a) number of events generated (maximum = 16), (b) mean event generation latency (in seconds), (c) median event age (months since the event occurred), (d) mean event emotionality (range = −4 to 4), (e) mean event importance (range = 1 to 5), and (f) mean event vividness (range = 1 to 5). The resulting scores were then averaged over participants to yield the summary data shown in Table 1.

None of the six measures revealed a reliable difference between events generated in the I as opposed to the O environment, $Fs(1, 30) < 2.41$, $ps > .10$. For the most part, these negative results seem unsurprising when considered in the context of a study conducted by Eich et al. (1994, Experiment 2). In that study, participants undertook the identical event generation task while experiencing either a *very pleasant* (P) or a *very unpleasant* (U) mood, affects that had been instilled through a combination of music and imagery. No appreciable difference was found between P mood and U mood subjects in five of the six measures of generation performance listed earlier (i.e., number of events generated, generation latency, event age, event

Table 1 Number of Events Generated (EvG), Event Generation Latency (EvL), Event Age (EvA), and Ratings of Event Emotionality (EvE), Importance (EvI), and Vividness (EvV) as a Function of Generation Environment

Generation environment	n	Measure					
		EvG	EvL	EvA	EvE	EvI	EvV
		Experiment 1					
I	16	16.0	9.2	64.0	0.49	2.58	3.24
O	16	16.0	10.1	41.5	0.68	2.81	3.38
		Experiment 2					
I	24	15.7	6.7	39.9	0.49	2.67	3.57
O	24	15.4	8.5	29.0	0.45	2.65	3.44
		Experiment 3					
O	48	15.9	7.8	82.8	1.06	2.79	3.34

Note. I = inside, O = outside. *n* = number of participants per mean score. Maximum number of events generated = 16. Event generation latency is indicated in seconds; event age is indicated in months. Ratings of event emotionality reflect a 9-point scale ranging from *extremely negative* (−4) to *extremely positive* (4). Ratings of event importance and event vividness reflect a 5-point scale ranging from *not at all important/vague recollection* (1) to *extremely important/vivid recollection* (5).

importance, and event vividness). Thus, even if one assumes that participants were in a better mood when tested in the O than in the I environment, both groups would be expected to perform similarly with respect to these same five measures, which they did.

Under this same assumption, however, O-environment participants should have produced significantly higher (i.e., more positive) ratings of event emotionality than their I-environment counterparts, which they did not. As noted earlier, several studies entailing an explicit manipulation of mood have shown that participants generate more positive autobiographical events, and fewer negative ones, when tested in a pleasant as opposed to an unpleasant mood. Given that positive and negative events are comparable in intensity (see Eich et al., 1994, Table 3, for supporting data), this translates into a reliable advantage in event emotionality of P-mood over U-mood conditions, an advantage that has been taken as evidence of mood congruence in autobiographical memory (see Blaney, 1986; Bower, 1981). Accordingly, the absence of a reliable difference in event emotionality between O-environment and I-environment participants is puzzling, presuming, once again, that the former were in a better mood than were the latter. For now, I wish only to make note of the puzzle; a possible solution to it is presented in the General Discussion section.

Event recall and subjective similarity

Given that all participants experienced a change in environment between the occasions of event generation and event recall and assuming that one locale was no more helpful or harmful to task performance than the other, the overall level of recall should have been about the same in the I/O and O/I conditions. This was the case: Mean recall (based on 16 generated events) was 44% in the former condition and 43% in the latter.[1]

Additional evidence of comparability between conditions was gained by examining the recall performance of participants who had generated at least one positive event (i.e., an event rated between 1 and 4 on the scale of event emotionality), one neutral event (rated at 0), and one negative event (rated between −1 and −4); 23 of the 32 participants (11 I/O and 12 O/I) met this standard. In the I/O condition, the mean percentages of positive, neutral, and negative events recalled were 50%, 31%, and 45%, respectively; the corresponding values for the O/I condition were 44%, 46%, and 40%. A 2 × 3 (Generation Environment × Event Type) analysis of variance (ANOVA) showed both simple effects, and their interaction, to be insignificant ($Fs < 1$).

Asked to assess how they felt during event recall relative to how they felt during event generation, participants in the I/O and O/I conditions produced similar ratings of subjective similarity ($Ms = 4.69$ and 4.88, respectively), $F < 1$.

The upper panel of Figure 1 plots each participant's subjective similarity rating in relation to the percentage of total events recalled (i.e., positive, neutral, and negative types combined). The overall correlation was positive and significant ($r = .38$, $p < .05$), with both conditions contributing about equally ($rs = .44$ and $.37$ in the I/O and O/I conditions, respectively). Thus, even though all participants undertook event recall in an environment that plainly looked different from the one they had inhabited during event generation, they varied considerably in how similar they felt on the two occasions. Those who felt the most similar recalled the most events. This, in a nutshell, is the foremost result of the first study.

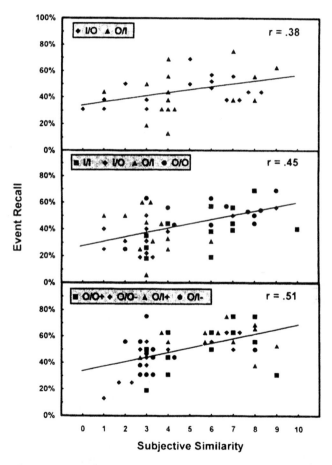

Figure 1 Individual-participant relation between event recall and ratings of subjective similarity: Experiments 1, 2, and 3 (upper, center, and lower panels, respectively). I = inside; O = outside. + = positive mood induction; − = negative mood induction.

Questionnaire responses

Before being asked to describe their moods during event generation and recall, 7 participants surmised—correctly—that the study was seeking to show a connection between affective states and physical settings, such that people would feel different when tested in the garden than when tested in the office.[2]

After being asked to verbalize their moods, 16 of the 32 participants reported feeling happier in the O than in the I environment; how much more cannot be gauged with confidence given the concise and occasionally cryptic nature of many of the participants' replies. Being outside made 4 participants feel more alert or energetic, whereas it made 2 others feel more anxious or agitated. One participant each said that he or she felt either more serene, sadder, or sleepier while in the garden as opposed to the office. The remaining 7 participants claimed that they felt basically the same in both environments. Although most of these participants acknowledged the garden's aesthetic appeal, it appeared not to have moved them emotionally, for better or for worse.

Experiment 2

Rationale

This study sought to achieve four aims. One was to replicate the positive relation between event recall and subjective similarity seen in the first study. A second was to discover whether more events are recalled when generation and recall environments match (conditions I/I and O/O) than when they mismatch (conditions I/O and O/I).

The third objective, which was predicated on the success of the second, was to determine whether the advantage in recall of matched over mismatched conditions is more accurately construed as an instance of PDM or one of MDM. In other words, is the key to recall how similar the generation and recall environments look or, instead, how similar they feel?

Finally, in an effort to measure the moods experienced in the O and I environments, all participants were administered the Positive and Negative Affect Schedule (PANAS) at regular intervals throughout the course of the study. Developed and validated by Watson, Clark, and Tellegen (1988), the PANAS consists of 20 emotion-relevant adjectives such as *attentive* and *irritable*. In the present study, participants were instructed to respond to each item on the basis of how they were feeling "right now." The assistant read aloud the items and recorded the participants' spoken responses, which were made on a 5-point scale ranging from *very slightly or not at all* (1) to *extremely* (5).

The sum of ratings on the 10 odd-numbered items provided an index of Positive Affect (PA), and the sum of ratings on the 10 even-numbered items served as a measure of Negative Affect (NA); thus, the minimum and maximum values of both PA and NA were 10 and 50, respectively. According to Watson et al. (1988, p. 1063):

> Positive Affect . . . reflects the extent to which a person feels enthusiastic, active, and alert. High PA is a state of high energy, full concentration, and pleasurable engagement, whereas low PA is characterized by sadness and lethargy. In contrast, Negative Affect . . . is a general dimension that subsumes a variety of aversive mood states, including anger, contempt, disgust, guilt, fear, and nervousness, with low NA being a state of calmness and serenity.

It was remarked earlier that, among participants in Experiment 1 who perceived a difference in their moods in the O and I environments, most reported feeling happier and more alert in the former locale than in the latter. Because these feelings are more representative of Positive than of Negative Affect, participants in Experiment 2 may be expected to have higher PA when tested in the garden as opposed to the office but to have roughly equivalent levels of NA in either setting. Regardless of whether or not this expectation is confirmed, the PANAS data should prove useful in interpreting the participants' ratings of subjective similarity. For example, if a person experiences high PA during event generation and low PA during event recall, is he or she apt to report feeling very different on the two occasions (as signified by a low rating of subjective similarity)? Alternatively, or in addition, are ratings of subjective similarity inversely related to changes in NA? Data pertinent to these and related questions are discussed shortly.

Method

Participants ($n = 48$) were assigned randomly and in equal numbers to one of four conditions: two in which event generation and recall environments matched (I/I and O/O) and two in which they mismatched (I/O and O/I).

Participants rated their current mood, via the PANAS, on six occasions: (a) in the homeroom, moments after the completion of informed consent and about 5 min before they were escorted to the I or O environment (the intervening time was taken up with instructions and practice on the event generation task). This rating is coded as GSB, for generation session baseline; (b) immediately before and (c) immediately after event generation (ratings BEG and AEG, respectively); (d) in the homeroom, 2 days later, just prior to departure for the recall environment (either I or O). The symbol RSB, short for recall session baseline, denotes this rating; and finally, (e) immediately before and (f) immediately after event recall (ratings BER and AER, respectively).

In view of these repeated PANAS ratings, there seemed little point in asking participants to verbally describe the moods they had experienced during event generation and recall, as had been done at the conclusion of Experiment 1. Accordingly, the only question posed at the end of Experiment 2 concerned the participants' opinions on the aims and methods of the study.

Results

Event generation

Inspection of Table 1 suggests that in this study, as in the earlier one, events generated in the I environment were indistinguishable from those generated in the O environment; this was so for all six measures of task performance, $Fs(1, 46) < 2.11$, $ps > .10$. Here, as before, the most puzzling outcome was that O-generated events were not rated as higher in emotionality than were I-generated events ($Ms = 0.45$ and 0.49, respectively). As noted earlier, discussion of this problem is deferred to the General Discussion section.

Positive and negative affect

Table 2 presents the mean ratings of PA recorded on six occasions by participants in each of the four generate/recall conditions. Two points merit

Table 2 Ratings of Positive Affect as a Function of Generate/Recall Condition and Rating Occasion

Generate/recall condition	n	Rating occasion					
		GSB	BEG	AEG	RSB	BER	AER
		Experiment 2					
I/I	12	31.6	28.2	29.9	27.9	25.9	26.5
I/O	12	31.8	31.3	31.6	27.5	29.8	27.7
O/I	12	28.0	30.3	28.8	27.2	24.6	26.8
O/O	12	26.7	29.1	29.1	23.3	25.6	27.7
		Experiment 3					
O/O+	12	27.3	33.4	27.4	24.7	27.2	26.9
O/O−	12	28.9	31.0	30.3	30.0	24.6	25.8
O/I+	12	32.6	38.5	36.4	32.9	36.3	35.1
O/I−	12	28.4	32.7	30.2	27.1	19.8	22.4

Note. O = outside environment, I = inside environment. n = number of participants per mean rating. + = positive mood induction; − = negative mood induction. GSB = generation session baseline; BEG = before event generation; AEG = after *event generation*; RSB = recall session baseline; BER = before event recall; AER = after event recall.

making in regard to these data. First, as one would anticipate, there were no reliable differences among conditions in ratings of PA made at the outset of either the generation or the recall session (ratings GSB and RSB), $Fs(3, 44)$ < 2.09, ps > .10, for the main effect of condition and the Condition × Rating interaction. Average PA, however, was significantly lower at the second baseline than at the first (M GSB rating = 29.5, M RSB rating = 26.5), $F(1, 44) = 8.25$, p < .01, probably because the experiment was no longer a novel endeavor.

Second, both the O and I environments had a significant but somewhat transient effect on ratings of PA. To clarify, consider the left panel of Figure 2. The first pair of bars represents the mean difference between before generation and generation baseline ratings of PA (i.e., BEG – GSB). Whereas participants who undertook the generation task in the garden showed a net gain of 2.3 points, those who did so in the office showed a net loss of 2.0 points. Each of these values differed reliably from zero, $ts(23)$ > 2.36, ps < .05, and the difference between them was likewise significant, $t(46)$ = 3.55, p < .01.

Similar results arose when ratings of PA taken just before the recall task were compared with the corresponding baseline scores (i.e., BER – RSB). As indicated by the third set of bars, PA increased an average of 2.3 points among participants tested in the garden and decreased an average of 2.3 points among those tested in the office. Once again, the difference between

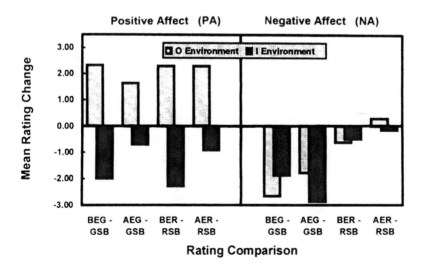

Figure 2 Change in Positive Affect (PA) and Negative Affect (NA) as a function of rating environment (I = inside, O = outside) and rating comparison (GSB = generation session baseline, BEG = before event generation, AEG = after event generation, RSB = recall session baseline, BER = before event recall, AER = after event recall): Experiment 2.

these figures was significant, $t(46) = 5.48$, $p < .01$, and each differed reliably from zero, $ts(23) > 3.63$, $ps < .01$. Thus, at the *start* of both event generation and event recall, O-environment participants felt better than they had at baseline, while I-environment participants felt worse.

The situation was different, however, at the *end* of these tasks. As shown in the second pair of bars, after generation (AEG) ratings of PA were 1.6 points higher than baseline among O-environment participants, and 0.9 points lower among I-environment participants. Neither of these values differed from zero, $ts(23) < 1.43$, $ps > .10$, indicating a return to near-baseline levels of PA. Turning to the fourth set of bars, it can be seen that while O-environment participants experienced significantly higher PA after recall (AER) than at baseline (RSB); mean net gain of 2.3 points, $t(23) = 2.28$, $p < .05$, I-environment participants ended recall only slightly below where they had begun (mean net loss of 0.9 points), $t(23) = 1.15$, $p > .10$.

It may be that the very act of generating or recalling autobiographical events takes people out of the mood that their environment had originally engendered. It is also conceivable that the diminishing differences between posttask and baseline PA ratings (especially among I-environment participants) reflect a regression to the mean or, perhaps, a form of mood management (see Clark & Isen, 1982; Parrott & Sabini, 1990; Singer & Salovey, 1988; Wegener & Petty, 1994). Whatever the reason, it should be noted that although both the garden and (particularly) the office lost some of their hold on mood, they did not lose it all: Relative to baseline ratings, PA was marginally higher for O-environment than for I-environment participants at the conclusion of the generation task, $t(46) > 1.75$, $p < .10$, and significantly higher on completion of the recall task, $t(46) = 2.52$, $p = .01$.

Mean ratings of NA appear in Table 3, following the format used in Table 2. As was true of PA, ratings of NA were lower at the second baseline than at the first (*M* GSB rating = 15.3, *M* RSB rating = 12.9), $F(1, 44) = 8.87$, $p < .01$, possibly for the same reason (i.e., familiarity with the experimental protocol). Unlike PA, however, ratings of NA did not discriminate reliably between the O and I environments: None of the four rating comparisons indicated in the right panel of Figure 2 revealed a significant difference between garden-based and office-based participants, $ts(46) < 1$.

Irrespective of environment, ratings of NA taken either before or after the generation task were lower than those registered at baseline (BEG − GSB = −2.3, AEG − GSB = −2.4). In contrast, neither before-recall nor after-recall ratings differed appreciably from the baseline average (BER − RSB = −0.6, AER − RSB = 0.1). The discrepancy between these patterns may be illusory: Given the earlier observation that baseline NA was reliably lower at recall than at generation, ratings of NA had less room to fall over the course of the former task as compared with the latter.

Table 3 Ratings of Negative Affect as a Function of Generate/Recall Condition and Rating Occasion

Generate/recall condition	n	Rating occasion					
		GSB	BEG	AEG	RSB	BER	AER
		Experiment 2					
I/I	12	15.1	12.6	12.6	13.4	13.1	13.3
I/O	12	16.3	15.1	13.1	12.3	12.5	13.8
O/I	12	13.3	11.5	12.3	12.1	11.4	12.1
O/O	12	16.3	12.8	13.7	14.0	12.5	13.1
		Experiment 3					
O/O+	12	16.0	11.8	12.8	12.6	10.5	11.6
O/O−	12	16.3	13.0	13.4	12.5	18.1	16.1
O/I+	12	18.6	13.4	13.3	15.7	15.0	15.2
O/I−	12	14.5	11.7	11.5	14.2	18.6	14.3

Note. O = outside environment, I = inside environment. *n* = number of participants per mean rating. + = positive mood induction; − = negative mood induction. GSB = generation session baseline; BEG = before event generation; AEG = after event generation; RSB = recall session baseline; BER = before event recall; AER = after event recall.

Event recall and subjective similarity

Table 4 presents both the mean percentage of total events recalled in each generate/recall condition and the corresponding mean rating of subjective similarity. Regarding recall, a 2 × 2 (Generation Environment × Recall Environment) ANOVA showed a slight overall advantage of O over I generation (*M*s = 45% and 37%, respectively), $F(1, 44) = 3.28, p < .10$, perhaps reflecting the elevated level of PA experienced in the garden. More important, the ANOVA revealed a reliable interaction, $F(1, 44) = 5.33, p < .05$. On average, participants recalled more events when generation and recall environments matched (*M* = 46%) than when they mismatched (*M* = 36%), a clear-cut case of place dependence.

Or is it? Referring to Table 4, it can be seen that ratings of subjective similarity mirrored the pattern set by event recall, such that participants felt more similar when generation and recall environments matched than when they mismatched (*M*s = 5.95 and 3.37, respectively), $F(1, 44) = 18.76, p < .01$, for the Generation Environment × Recall Environment interaction and $F < 1$ for the main effects.

The center panel of Figure 1 contains additional data linking the two measures. Among participants in the O/I condition, event recall tended to increase as subjective similarity decreased ($r = -.32$), a strange result, especially considering that O/I participants in Experiment 1 showed the

Table 4 Total Event Recall (EvR) and Ratings of Subjective Similarity (SjS) as a Function of Generate/Recall Conditions

Generate/recall condition	n	EvR (%)	SjS
	Experiment 2		
I/I	12	40	5.83
I/O	12	34	3.50
O/I	12	38	3.25
O/O	12	52	6.08
	Experiment 3		
O/O+	12	52	5.75
O/O–	12	44	4.00
O/I+	12	59	6.33
O/I–	12	46	3.42

Note. O = outside environment, I = inside environment. *n* = number of participants per mean score. + = positive mood induction; – = negative mood induction. Ratings of subjective similarity reflect an 11-point scale ranging from *not at all similar* (O) to *extremely similar* (10).

opposite pattern ($r = .37$). In each of the other three conditions, however, event recall was directly related to subjective similarity (I/I = .54, I/O = .62, O/O = .43). Polling all participants together produced a positive correlation ($r = .45, p < .01$) similar in size to the one found in the first study ($r = .38$).

Given that event recall covaried with subjective similarity, the question arises: Was it the confluence of feelings, or instead the equivalence of environments, that contributed to the advantage in recall of matched over mismatched environments?

Two pieces of evidence provide a tentative answer. One is that the correlation between event recall and generate/recall condition (coded 1 for matched environments and –1 for mismatched environments) declined from a modest .32 to a meager .09 when ratings of subjective similarity were partialed out. In contrast, controlling for the effects of condition had little impact on the relation between event recall and subjective similarity: Both the zero-order correlation and the partial correlation between these measures were reliable ($rs = .45$ and .35, respectively), $ts(46) > 2.53$, $ps < .05$. Thus, similarity of feelings accounted for more of the variance in recall than did similarity in settings.

The second piece of relevant evidence appears in Figure 3. The light bars represent participants who, at recall, felt moderately to extremely similar to the way they felt at generation (i.e., subjective similarity scores between 5 and 10). Unsurprisingly, most of these *high subjective similarity* participants had been tested under matched rather than mismatched environmental conditions ($ns = 16$ and 3, respectively). Participants with *low subjective similarity* (i.e., scores ranging from 0 to 4) are represented by the dark bars; all but 8 of these 29 participants came from either the I/O or the O/I condition.

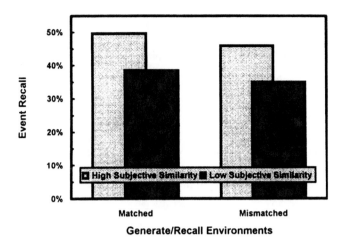

Figure 3 Event recall as a function of generate/recall environment (matched vs. mismatched) and subjective similarity (high vs. low): Experiment 2.

Comparison of the two outermost bars offers a clear view of PDM, with event recall averaging 50% under matched conditions and 35% under mismatched. Note, however, that this comparison involves participants whose ratings of subjective similarity were characteristic of their condition (i.e., high if matched and low if mismatched). Participants with atypical similarity scores showed no sign of PDM. Indeed, as the two innermost bars indicate, participants who experienced similar feelings in different environments fared a bit better in recall than did those who experienced different feelings in the same environment (*M*s = 46% and 38%, respectively). Whether this pattern of correlational data can be reproduced through experimental manipulations of both affective states and physical settings was the principal issue pursued in the next study.

Positive and negative affect as predictors of subjective similarity

Why do some people report higher ratings of subjective similarity than do others? An answer was sought by deriving two scores for each participant in Experiment 2. One measure, coded |PA|, was defined as the absolute difference between (a) the average of the PA ratings recorded before and after the event generation task (BEG and AEG ratings) and (b) average PA based on ratings taken before and after the event recall task (BER and AER ratings). The other measure, designated as |NA|, was defined in the same way, except that ratings of NA replaced those of PA.

Multiple regression using both |PA| and |NA| to predict subjective similarity produced a marginally significant solution (multiple $R = .34$), $F(2, 45)$

415

= 2.91, $p < .10$. Although the beta weight associated with |PA| was reliable (−.33), $t(46) = 2.35$, $p < .05$, the corresponding value for |NA| was not (−.08), $t < 1$. Thus, participants who experienced a substantial between-tasks shift in level of PA, but not necessarily NA, tended to report low ratings of subjective similarity.

Given the correlation between |PA| and subjective similarity on one hand and the connection between subjective similarity and event recall on the other, it is plausible to predict that |PA| would be negatively related to recall. It was to a modest degree ($r = −.26$, $p < .10$), but, like the effect of matched versus mismatched environments on retention performance, the relation between |PA| and event recall was reduced to insignificance once the effects of subjective similarity were taken into account (partial $r = −.13$, $p > .10$).

Questionnaire responses

In Experiment 1, only 22% of the participants (7 of 32) deduced the experimental hypothesis that different environments elicit different feelings or moods. This figure jumped to 40% (19 of 48) in Experiment 2, a probable consequence of the repeated PANAS assessments, which could have clued participants to a probable connection between affective reactions and environmental settings.

Experiment 3

Rationale

By showing that shifts in mood state, as reflected in ratings of subjective similarity, are correlated with recall performance, the two preceding studies provided indirect support for the mood mediation theory of PDM. The purpose of the present study was to put the theory to a direct experimental test.

The reasoning behind Experiment 3 was as follows. Suppose that participants generate autobiographical events while in the O environment (the Nitobe Garden). Given the affect descriptions solicited in the first study and the PANAS data collected in the second, it can be assumed that the participants would perform the generation task in a reasonably good mood.

Now suppose that, 2 days later, participants are tested for event recall under one of four conditions defined by the factorial combination of (a) same versus different setting and (b) same versus different mood. Thus, in one condition (abbreviated as O/O+), participants return to the garden for testing. Before beginning recall, these participants are asked to spend several minutes thinking glad thoughts while listening to mirthful music so as to instill a moderately positive mood—one similar to the mood they presumably experienced in the same setting 2 days earlier. In a second condition

(O/O–), recall in the garden is preceded by a period in which participants ponder gloomy thoughts while listening to melancholic music. The intent here is to nurture the development of a moderately negative mood that will contrast with the way these participants felt "naturally" when last in the garden. In the other two conditions, participants are tested for recall in the I environment (the windowless office). Whereas some of these participants (condition O/I+) first undergo the positive mood induction just sketched, others (condition O/I–) experience the negative mood induction.

If memory is truly and simply place dependent, then recall should be higher when tested in the original than in the substitute setting, irrespective of testing mood. More to the point, participants in either the O/O+ or O/O– conditions should show an advantage in recall over those assigned to either the O/I+ or O/I– conditions. If what really matters, instead, is how similar participants feel at generation and recall rather than how similar the task environments look, then recall performance in either the O/O+ or O/I+ conditions should surpass that seen in either O/O+ or O/I–. Yet a third possibility is that the helpful effects of similar physical settings are offset by the harmful effects of dissimilar psychological states, or vice versa. If so, then in terms of recall performance, the order of conditions would be O/O+ > O/O– = O/I+ > O/I–. However the data turn out, this study should provide a more decisive test of the mood mediation idea than can possibly be achieved through correlational analyses alone.

Method

Participants (n = 48) were randomly assigned in equal numbers to the four generate/recall conditions cited earlier. As in Experiment 2, participants rated their current mood, via the PANAS, on six occasions: twice in the homeroom (to establish baselines for event generation and recall), both before and after generation, and both before and after recall. The method by which moods were modified at recall was similar to the *continuous music technique* used in recent research on mood congruent and mood dependent memory (e.g., Eich et al., 1994; Eich & Metcalfe, 1989). Specifically, participants were asked to entertain either elating or depressing thoughts about factual or fictional incidents while mood-appropriate music played softly in the background (selections of such "happy" pieces as Boccherini's *Minuet in G* and Pachelbel's *Canon in D* or of such "sad" works as Albinoni's *Adagio in G Minor* and Sibelius's *Violin Concerto: Second Movement*; see Eich et al., 1994, for detailed instructions and a more complete list of recordings). The music, once started, did not stop until the after-recall PANAS had been completed (hence the term *continuous* music technique). A high-grade portable cassette deck with detachable speakers was used in the garden; although small in size, its acoustic qualities rivaled those of the much larger stereo system that sat atop a table in the office.

Pilot testing had shown that 10 min of happy ideation plus lively music produced a net increase in PA similar to that seen by comparing the baseline and before-recall ratings made by O-environment participants in the second study. Preliminary research had also revealed that the net decrease in PA displayed by I-environment participants in that same study could be approximated by 10 min of sad ideation linked with languorous music. Accordingly, every participant in Experiment 3 was allotted 10 min for the induction of either a positive or negative state. After this period, participants rated their current mood in the familiar fashion and then proceeded to the test of event recall.

After assessment of the subjective similarity between their feelings at recall and generation but before they were debriefed, participants were asked to share their thoughts on the study's aims and methods. Participants in Experiment 3 were also asked, *How real or genuine was the mood you experienced during the test of recall?* Participants were encouraged to answer with utmost candor and to frame their response in terms of an 11-point scale ranging from *totally artificial* (0) to *extremely realistic* (10). The assistant kept a written record of the participants' spoken responses.

Results

Event generation

Inexplicably, events generated in the present study tended to be older and to have more positive emotionality than those generated in the same (O) environment in either of the previous studies (see Table 1). In terms of the number of events generated, mean generation latency, and average ratings of event importance and vividness, the results were similar across experiments, as one would expect.

Positive and negative affect

Mean ratings of PA and NA are summarized in Tables 2 and 3, respectively. Data gathered during the generation session were similar to those culled from O-environment participants in the second study (see Figure 2). Thus, averaging across conditions, PA increased by 4.6 points moving from the baseline to the before-generation rating, whereas NA decreased by 3.9 points; both of these values differed reliably from zero, $ts(47) > 6.30$, $ps < .01$. Although differences between after-generation and baseline ratings were smaller (PA = 1.8, NA = −3.6), both were at least marginally significant, $ts(47) > 1.89$, $ps < .10$.

PA ratings taken during the recall session were analyzed in the context of a $2 \times 2 \times 2$ mixed design. The between-subjects variables were recall environment (I versus O) and recall mood (positive vs. negative); the within-subject

418

variable was rating comparison: the difference between before-recall and baseline ratings (BER − RSB) versus the difference between after-recall and baseline scores (AER − RSB).

Results of the analysis were negative ($ps > .10$) in all respects except two. First, there was a marked main effect of recall mood, $F(1, 44) = 34.17$, $p < .01$, such that PA increased an average of 2.6 points after the positive mood induction and decreased an average of 5.4 points after the negative mood induction. Second, there was a marginally significant Recall Mood × Rating Comparison interaction, $F(1, 44) = 3.69$, $p < .10$. Relative to their baseline ratings, positive mood participants reached a higher level of PA before rather than after the test of recall (mean net gains of 3.0 and 2.2, respectively), whereas negative mood participants experienced lower PA before recall than after its completion (mean net losses of 6.3 and 4.5 points, respectively).

A similar 2 × 2 × 2 mixed-design analysis was applied in NA ratings registered during the recall session, and the results were the mirror image of those found for PA. Specifically, there was a significant main effect of recall mood, $F(1, 44) = 10.81$, $p < .01$, with positive mood participants showing a decrease in NA of 1.1 points and negative mood participants showing an increase of 3.4 points. The Recall Mood × Rating Comparison interaction was also reliable, $F(1, 44) = 11.55$, $p < .01$, indicating that the difference between before-recall and baseline ratings of NA (means of −1.4 and 5.0 among positive and negative mood participants, respectively) was greater than the difference between after-recall and baseline scores (corresponding means of −0.8 and 1.8).

Considered collectively, the PANAS data suggest that the mood-modification techniques used in this study worked well in three respect. First, participants who received the positive mood induction experienced an increase in PA and a decrease in NA, whereas those given the negative mood induction reacted in the opposite manner. Second, although changes in both PA and NA were particularly pronounced before the test of recall, after-task ratings of either measure showed sizable differences between positive and negative mood participants. Third, given that none of the analyses reported earlier revealed a reliable main or interactive effect of recall environment, it would appear that moods induced in the garden were just as positive—or negative—as those instilled in the office.

Event recall and subjective similarity

As can be inferred from Table 4, it made no difference in terms of memory performance whether participants were tested for recall in the same (O) environment in which they had generated the target events or in the contrasting (I) context (Ms = 48% and 52% under matched and mismatched environmental conditions, respectively), $F(1, 44) = 1.06$, $p > .10$. What did matter was whether participants were tested in a positive or a negative mood, $F(1, 44) = 5.47, p < .05$, with recall being higher in the former case ($M = 55\%$) than in the latter ($M = 45\%$). This was true regardless of setting (interaction $F < 1$).

What accounts for the advantage in recall of positive over negative moods? My preferred answer is that the advantage reflects a form of MDM: Putting people into a positive mood increased the correspondence between their generation and recall states, which in turn increased the likelihood of recall. Consistent with this interpretation, data plotted in the lower panel of Figure 1 reveal a robust relation between event recall and ratings of subjective similarity at the level of individual participants ($r = .51, p < .01$). Moreover, the group averages appearing in Table 4 show that subjective similarity, like event recall, was affected solely by mood at recall (positive = 6.04, negative = 3.71), $F(1, 44) = 17.55, p < .01$.

An alternative—and arguably simpler—explanation is that a positive mood is generally more conducive to recall than is a negative mood. On this account, the advantage in recall of positive over negative moods is precisely what it seems to be—a significant main effect—and not a subtle sign of mood dependence.

There are three problems with this proposal. One is that no main effect of recall environment was evident in Experiment 2, even though the PANAS data indicated that participants were in a better mood when tested in the garden than when tested in the office. A second, related difficulty is that none of the three studies reported by Eich et al. (1994) demonstrated an overall difference in recall between participants tested in a *very pleasant* or *very unpleasant* mood; affects that were both more extreme and more enduring than those experienced by participants in the present experiment.

The third problem concerns the memory performance of two very small and very unusual groups of participants in the current study. One group consisted of participants ($n = 5$) who, despite being tested for recall in a negative mood, felt at least moderately similar to the way they felt during event generation (i.e., subjective similarity scores between 5 and 10). The other group comprised participants ($n = 8$) who felt less than moderately similar (i.e., scores ranging from 0 to 4), even though they were tested in a positive mood.

In terms of event recall, the negative mood group outperformed the positive mood group by a margin of 56% to 46%. Although the difference was insignificant, $t(11) = 1.40, p > .10$, its direction was the reverse of the pattern predicted by the main effect proposal. The data make sense, however, when viewed from the perspective of mood dependence.

Positive and negative affect as predictors of subjective similarity

Regressing ratings of subjective similarity on absolute differences in PA and NA (i.e., |PA| and |NA|, as defined earlier) yielded a reliable multiple correlation (.53), $F(2, 45) = 8.92$, $p < .01$. As in Experiment 2, subjective similarity was predictable on the basis of |PA|, $\beta = -.45$, $t(46) = 3.45$, $p < .01$, but not |NA|, $\beta = -.18$, $t(46) = 1.34$, $p > .10$. Also replicating the earlier results, the correlation between |PA| and event recall, which was modest to begin with ($r = -.23$, $p = .11$), became vanishingly small when the effects of subjective similarity were partialed out ($r = .01$). In contrast, the correlation between subjective similarity and event recall was considerable ($r = .49$) even when both |PA| and |NA| were controlled.

Questionnaire responses

Almost all participants said that the study had something to do with mood and memory, a reasonable if vague response given that participants made their comments shortly after they had been tested for recall in an experimentally induced mood. Only 25% of the participants (12 of 48) specifically stated that moods might be altered by the environment, a figure that seems suspiciously low considering the frequency with which their current mood had been measured with the PANAS. As was remarked in reference to Experiment 2 (wherein 40% of the participants drew the same deduction), awareness of a connection between moods and environments may be enhanced by virtue of repeated PANAS assessments. It is conceivable, then, that some (perhaps many) participants in Experiment 3 were cognizant of a mood–environment connection but simply did not bother to mention it because they had something more salient to talk about (viz., their recently induced mood). Accordingly, the low rate of mood–environment awareness found in the current study is ambiguous at best and potentially misleading at worst.

Much clearer were the results concerning the genuineness of the participants' mood at recall. Only 3 of the 48 participants (6%) claimed that the mood they had been induced to feel seemed contrived or artificial (i.e., a rating below 5 on the 0 to 10 genuineness scale). The mean ratings for positive and negative moods (7.00 and 6.96, respectively) were equally impressive.

General discussion

Place dependent and mood dependent memory have much in common. Both phenomena relate directly to the enduring issue of how changing contexts— or "altered stimulating conditions," to use McGeoch's (1942) preferred phrase—affect learning and remembering. Both are operationally defined as an interaction between encoding/retrieval contexts, where contexts refer to either two different environments or two contrasting moods. Place dependence, like mood dependence, is more apt to occur when target events are retrieved in the absence than in the presence of observable cues or reminders. And as subjects of scientific inquiry, both phenomena have had mercurial histories, with the mostly positive results reported in the 1970s giving way to mostly negative results in the 1980s, leading theorists in the 1990s to wonder whether either PDM or MDM even exists.

To this list can now be added another point of commonality. In line with the mood mediation hypothesis introduced earlier, the results of the present research suggest that how well information transfers from one environment to another depends not on how similar the environments look but on how similar they feel. Thus, even when target events are encoded and retrieved in the same physical setting, memory performance suffers if the attending psychological states differ. Conversely, a change in environmental context produces no performance deficit if, whether by chance (Experiments 1 and 2) or by design (Experiment 3), the mood at encoding matches the mood at retrieval. These observations imply that place dependent effects in memory are mediated by alterations in affect or mood, and that data that appear on the surface to demonstrate PDM (e.g., the advantage in event recall of matched over mismatched environments seen in Experiment 2) may, at a deeper level, manifest MDM.

Although the results reported here strengthen the case for mood mediation, they do not negate its shortcomings, of which there are several. To reiterate a point raised in the introduction, the hypothesis seems plausible when applied to several prior studies of place dependence (e.g., Dallett & Wilcox, 1968; Godden & Baddeley, 1975; Saufley et al., 1985; Smith et al., 1978), but it offers no new insight into why some other studies either succeeded or failed to find the phenomenon (e.g., Fernandez & Glenberg, 1985; Smith, 1979). Also, mood mediation is but one of several factors that play pivotal roles in the occurrence of PDM. Thus, as noted earlier, even a radical change in both physical setting and affective state is unlikely to impair memory performance if observable cues or reminders are available to aid retrieval. Finally, there may be at least two ways of producing "pure" place dependent effects in memory—effects that do not necessarily involve shifts in affective state or mask what are actually mood dependent effects. One is to make memory more context bound by instructing participants, at encoding, to imagine each target item as being integrated with a particular feature of the physical environment rather than as an isolated entity (as in Eich, 1985). The other is to make it especially hard for participants, at retrieval, to mentally reinstate what the encoding environment looked like (as in Smith, 1979; but see Fernandez & Glenberg, 1985). In either case, a change in physical setting may impair memory performance, even if there is no concomitant change in mood.

Despite these shortcomings, the mood mediation idea seems promising enough to warrant further inquiry. Perhaps the most important issue to pursue is how participants decide whether they feel more or less the same at retrieval, relative to how they felt at encoding. One possibility is that similarity ratings reflect an attribution process: Depending on whether they think they did well or poorly on the test of recall, participants adjust their similarity ratings up or down. There are two problems with this intuitively appealing account. First, it is improbable that participants can accurately divine what number or percentage of events corresponds to the average level of recall in any given generate/recall condition. Second, when asked to speculate on the aims of the present research, only 12 participants out of a total of 128 (9%) indicated even an elementary understanding of either MDM or PDM or inferred that memory performance might depend on the similarity of generate/recall feelings.

A more plausible possibility is that participants whose mood at generation differs most markedly from their mood at recall are those likely to report low ratings of subjective similarity. In support of this notion, similarity ratings recorded in Experiments 2 and 3 were negatively correlated with the absolute difference in levels of positive affect experienced during the generation and recall tasks (the measure referred to earlier as |PA|). However, considering the modest size of these correlations (beta weights of −.33 and −.45 in Experiments 2 and 3, respectively), it is clear that something else is involved. It may be that different environments elicit different feelings that are not captured by the PA scale: feelings more somatic than cognitive in nature, such as the sensation of a soft summer breeze winding through the Nitobe Garden. Such feelings may contribute to participants' sense of subjective similarity without the experimenter knowing what these feelings are or even that they exist. Accordingly, an important task for future research is to find better ways of monitoring a participant's on-line reactions to his or her environment and to figure out what particular properties of an environment make the most impact on mood.

A second issue that merits further study relates to a puzzling null result realized in the first two studies. Given that participants were in a better mood when tested for event generation in the garden than when tested in the office, and in view of earlier reports of mood congruence in autobiographical memory (see Blaney, 1986; Bower, 1981), it was predicted that O-environment participants would produce higher ratings of event emotionality (reflecting predominantly pleasant recollections) than would I-environment participants. Neither Experiment 1 nor 2, however, evinced an appreciable difference between environments in mean event emotionality (see Table 1). Although this may merely mean that the moods evoked by either environment were too weak to have an effect, there is another, more interesting possibility.

According to Parrott and Sabini (1990), a common characteristic of studies showing mood congruence is that participants' moods are manipulated in a deliberate, explicit manner (through hypnotic suggestions, music plus imagery, or some other means). Participants in such studies are aware not only that their mood has been altered, but also that their mood is pertinent to the experimental task they will be asked to perform and that they should try to maintain the mood throughout the course of the task. Under these circumstances, cooperative participants will continue to focus on ideas and images that coincide with the positive or negative tone of the targeted mood—a strategy that would promote the occurrence of mood *congruent* memory.

Suppose, however, that moods were manipulated in a much more subtle manner, such as by approaching participants on either a sunny or a cloudy day and asking them to recollect a specific episode or event from their personal past. This is what Parrott and Sabini (1990) did in their second study and, replicating Cunningham (1979), they found that participants reported being in a better mood if the sky was clear rather than overcast. Given the tactfulness of the manipulation, Parrott and Sabini reasoned that the participants would probably not make a connection between their mood and the autobiographical memory task. Lacking awareness of this connection, participants need not try to maintain their mood. On the contrary, they may attempt to regulate their mood by recalling events that are incompatible with it so that they end up feeling not so bad or—paradoxically—not too good either. Consistent with these conjectures, autobiographical events recollected on sunny days were more negative in tone than were those retrieved on cloudy days—a result that Parrott and Sabini interpreted as evidence of mood *incongruent* memory. This result, together with similar findings from four other studies, led Parrott and Sabini (1990, p. 333) to conclude that mood incongruence "occurs when subjects do not try to induce their moods and are unaware of the relevance of their moods to the experiment."

Although Experiments 1 and 2 in the present series were not designed to test this "awareness" hypothesis, their results seem relevant on two accounts. First, in these experiments, as in Parrott and Sabini's (1990) studies, the moods in which participants generated autobiographical events were manipulated in an indirect, covert fashion.[3] Second, on the basis of the participants' statements about the aims and methods of these experiments, it was possible to separate participants into two groups: those who recognized that different environments might evoke different moods and those who were unaware of an affect—environment connection (see Footnote 2 and related text).

In Table 5, mean ratings of event emotionality are given for every combination of participant group (aware vs. unaware) and generation environment (O versus I). A 2 × 2 ANOVA of the data from Experiment 1 revealed negligible main effects, $Fs(1, 28) < 2.11$, $ps > .10$, and a marginally significant interaction, $F(1, 28) = 3.24$, $p < .10$. Among the few participants who were cognizant of a connection between moods and environments, those tested for event generation in the garden rated their events as higher (more positive) in

Table 5 Ratings of Event Emotionality (EvE) as a Function of Participant Group (Aware vs. Unaware of an Affect-Environment Connection) and Generation Environment

Participant group	Generation environment	n	EvE
	Experiment 1		
Aware	O	2	1.00
Aware	I	5	−0.10
Unaware	O	14	0.63
Unaware	I	11	0.75
	Experiment 2		
Aware	O	10	0.80
Aware	I	9	0.58
Unaware	O	14	0.20
Unaware	I	15	0.43

Note. O = outside, I = inside. *n* = number of participants per mean rating. Ratings of event emotionality reflect a 9-point scale ranging from *extremely positive* (−4) to *extremely negative* (4).

emotionality than did those tested in the office ($Ms = 1.00$ and $−0.10$, respectively), $F(1, 28) = 3.26, p < .10$. Assuming that the former participants were in a better mood than were the latter, this result is suggestive of mood congruence in autobiographical memory. Among participants who appeared unaware of an affect-environment connection, however, the effect of environments on event emotionality was trivial ($F < 1$), and, even at that, the effect was in the direction of mood incongruence, with O-environment participants producing a slightly lower average rating than their I-environment peers ($Ms = 0.63$ and 0.75, respectively).

Although the data from Experiment 2 showed similar trends toward both mood congruence (among aware participants) and mood incongruence (among unaware participants), none of the differences were reliable ($ps > .10$), and the critical Participant Group × Generation Environment interaction did not approach significance ($F < 1$). But if one is willing to consider combining the results from the two studies and to redo the analysis adding experiment as a variable, then the only notable effect that emerges is the Participant Group × Generation Environment interaction, $F(1, 72) = 3.90$, $p = .05$; neither the main effect of experiment nor any of its interactions are significant, $Fs(1, 72) < 2.14, ps > .10$.

On balance, then, the present results tend to support Parrott and Sabini's (1990) claim that autobiographical memories can either coincide or conflict with the mood in which they are retrieved, depending on whether or not the mood is perceived as being relevant to the task. Moreover, the results suggest a possible solution to the puzzle of why no evidence of mood congruence, in the form of an advantage in event emotionality of O-generated over

I-generated events, was forthcoming from either of the first two experiments. In light of Table 5, it looks as though participants in these studies did show mood congruence—provided they were aware of a connection between their moods and the environment in which they were tested. However, this effect was countered by a trend toward mood incongruence by unaware participants, culminating in the null results cited in Table 1.

To draw this discussion to a close, consider a third inviting issue for future research. The issue relates to an idea proposed by Bower (1981) in connection with drug dependent memory: the observation that events encoded in a particular pharmacological state (e.g., alcohol intoxication) are more retrievable in the same state than in a different drug context (e.g., sobriety). Bower identified several similarities between drug dependent and mood dependent memory, including the fact that both phenomena are more often found using nominally noncued tests of retention (e.g., free recall) rather than prompted procedures (e.g., cued recall or recognition memory). In addition, drugs that elicit the effect most reliably—centrally acting agents including alcohol, amphetamine, and barbiturates such as Demerol—also engender radical changes in emotion. On the basis of these similarities, Bower (1981, p. 146) surmised that "drugs achieve their state dependent effects by virtue of their impact on moods."

To date, only one study (Eich & Birnbaum, 1988) has been reported that speaks to this issue. Although long overlooked, Bower's (1981) idea now seems particularly primed for investigation, seeing as how the present research suggests that environments achieve their own form of state dependence by virtue of their impact on moods. Theorists have been struggling for years with the problem of how context affects learning and remembering (see Davies & Thomson, 1988; Roediger & Guynn, in press). Were it possible to reduce three seemingly distinct phenomena—drug dependent, place dependent, and mood dependent memory—into one (MDM), the problem would instantly be made more manageable, and ultimately more solvable.

Notes

Preparation of this article was aided by grants from the (American) National Institute of Mental Health (R01-MH48502) and the (Canadian) Natural Sciences and Engineering Research Council (37335). My thanks to Kimberly Daum, Mary Drew, and Dawn Layzell for their expert experimental assistance.

1 Participants were credited with recalling a given event if they recalled its exact corresponding probe (e.g., *ship*) or a specific word or phrase they had mentioned while describing the event to the assistant (e.g., *ferry boat*). Instances of the latter were uncommon, accounting for less than 2% of all of the events recalled in any of the three studies reported here.

2 After being briefed on the study's methods but not its aims or results, two colleagues independently read transcripts of the participants' questionnaire responses and decided whether each participant was or was not aware of an

affect–environment connection. The colleagues concurred on 88% (28 of 32) of their choices; I settled split decisions. The same procedure was applied in Experiments 2 and 3, and in each case the concordance rate between judges exceeded 90%.

3   Experiment 3 is not considered in this context because (a) it did not involve an analogous manipulation (all participants undertook the generation task in the garden) and (b) it was unclear whether participants were or were not aware of an affect–environment connection (as noted in the *Questionnaire responses.* section).

References

Beck, R. C., & McBee, W. (in press). Mood dependent memory for generated and repeated words: Replication and extension. *Cognition & Emotion.*

Bjork, R. A., & Richardson-Klavehn, A. (1989). On the puzzling relationship between environmental context and human memory. In C. Izawa (Ed.), *Current issues in cognitive processes: The Tulane Flowerree Symposium on Cognition* (pp. 313–344). Hillsdale, NJ: Erlbaum.

Blaney, P. H. (1986). Affect and memory: A review. *Psychological Bulletin, 99,* 229–246.

Bower, G. H. (1981). Mood and memory. *American Psychologist, 36,* 129–148.

Bower, G. H. (1987). Commentary on mood and memory. *Behavior Research and Therapy, 25,* 443–455.

Bower, G. H. (1992). How might emotions affect learning? In S.-A. Christianson (Ed.), *Handbook of emotion and memory* (pp. 3–31). Hillsdale, NJ: Erlbaum.

Bower, G. H., & Mayer, J. D. (1989). In search of mood-dependent retrieval. *Journal of Social Behavior and Personality, 4,* 133–168.

Brown, W. P., & Ure, D. M. J. (1969). Five rated characteristics of 650 word association stimuli. *British Journal of Psychology, 60,* 233–249.

Clark, M. S., & Isen, A. M. (1982). Toward understanding the relationship between feeling states and social behavior. In A. H. Hastorf & A. M. Isen (Eds.), *Cognitive social psychology* (pp. 73–108). New York: Elsevier.

Cunningham, M. R. (1979). Weather, mood, and helping behavior: Quasi-experiments with the sunshine samaritan. *Journal of Personality and Social Psychology, 37,* 1947–1956.

Dallett, K., & Wilcox, S. G. (1968). Contextual stimuli and proactive inhibition. *Journal of Experimental Psychology, 78,* 475–480.

Davies, G. M., & Thomson, D. M. (Eds.). (1988). *Memory in context: Context in memory.* Chichester, England: Wiley.

Eich, E. (1980). The cue-dependent nature of state-dependent retrieval. *Memory & Cognition, 8,* 157–173.

Eich, E. (1985). Context, memory, and integrated item/context imagery. *Journal of Experimental Psychology: Learning, Memory, and Cognition, 11,* 764–770.

Eich, E. (1995). Searching for mood dependent memory. *Psychological Science, 6,* 67–75.

Eich, E., & Birnbaum, I. M. (1988). On the relationship between the dissociative and affective properties of drugs. In G. M. Davies & D. M. Thomson (Eds.), *Memory in context: Context in memory* (pp. 81–93). Chichester, England: Wiley.

Eich, E., Macaulay, D., & Ryan, L. (1994). Mood dependent memory for events of the personal past. *Journal of Experimental Psychology: General, 123,* 201–215.

Eich, E., & Metcalfe, J. (1989). Mood dependent memory for internal versus external events. *Journal of Experimental Psychology: Learning, Memory, and Cognition, 15*, 443–455.

Ellis, H. C., & Hunt, R. R. (1989). *Fundamentals of human memory and cognition* (4th ed.). Dubuque, IA: William C. Brown.

Fernandez, A., & Glenberg, A. M. (1985). Changing environmental context does not reliably affect memory. *Memory & Cognition, 13*, 333–345.

Godden, D. R., & Baddeley, A. D. (1975). Context-dependent memory in two natural environments: On land and underwater. *British Journal of Psychology, 66*, 325–331.

Godden, D. R., & Baddeley, A. D. (1980). When does context influence recognition memory? *British Journal of Psychology, 71*, 99–104.

Kihlstrom, J. F. (1989). On what does mood-dependent memory depend? *Journal of Social Behavior and Personality, 4*, 23–32.

Macaulay, D., Ryan, L., & Eich, E. (1993). Mood dependence in implicit and explicit memory. In P. Graf & M. E. J. Masson (Eds.), *Implicit memory: New directions in cognition, development, and neuropsychology* (pp. 75–94). Hillsdale, NJ: Erlbaum.

McDaniel, M. A., Anderson, D. C., Einstein, G. O., & O'Halloran, C. M. (1989). Modulation of environmental reinstatement effects through encoding strategies. *American Journal of Psychology, 102*, 523–548.

McGeoch, J. A. (1942). *The psychology of human learning*. New York: Longmans, Green.

Parrott, W. G., & Sabini, J. (1990). Mood and memory under natural conditions: Evidence for mood incongruent recall. *Journal of Personality and Social Psychology, 59*, 321–336.

Roediger, H. L., & Guynn, M. J. (in press). Retrieval processes. In E. L. Bjork & R. A. Bjork (Eds.), *Memory: Volume 10 of the Academic Press handbook of perception and cognition*. New York: Academic Press.

Saufley, W. H., Otaka, S. R., & Bavaresco, J. L. (1985). Context effects: Classroom tests and context independence. *Memory & Cognition, 13*, 522–528.

Singer, J. A., & Salovey, P. (1988). Mood and memory: Evaluating the network theory of affect. *Clinical Psychology Review, 8*, 211–251.

Smith, S. M. (1979). Remembering in and out of context. *Journal of Experimental Psychology: Human Learning and Memory, 5*, 460–471.

Smith, S. M. (1988). Environmental context-dependent memory. In G. M. Davies & D. M. Thomson (Eds.), *Memory in context: Context in memory* (pp. 13–33). Chichester, England: Wiley.

Smith, S. M., Glenberg, A., & Bjork, R. A. (1978). Environmental context and human memory. *Memory & Cognition, 6*, 342–353.

Underwood, B. J. (1977). *Temporal codes for memories*. Hillsdale, NJ: Erlbaum.

Watson, D., Clark, L. A., & Tellegen, A. (1988). Development and validation of brief measures of Positive and Negative Affect: The PANAS Scales. *Journal of Personality and Social Psychology, 54*, 1063–1070.

Wegener, D. T., & Petty, R. E. (1994). Mood management across affective states: The hedonic contingency hypothesis. *Journal of Personality and Social Psychology, 66*, 1034–1048.

Wilhite, S. C. (1991). Evidence of a negative environmental reinstatement effect. *British Journal of Psychology, 82*, 325–342.

39

ENCODING SPECIFICITY AND RETRIEVAL PROCESSES IN EPISODIC MEMORY[1]

Endel Tulving and Donald M. Thomson

Source: *Psychological Review*, 80 (1973): 352–373.

Recent changes in pretheoretical orientation toward problems of human memory have brought with them a concern with retrieval processes, and a number of early versions of theories of retrieval have been constructed. This paper describes and evaluates explanations offered by these theories to account for the effect of extralist cuing, facilitation of recall of list items by non-list items. Experiments designed to test the currently most popular theory of retrieval, the generation-recognition theory, yielded results incompatible not only with generation-recognition models, but most other theories as well: under certain conditions subjects consistently failed to recognize many recallable list words. Several tentative explanations of this phenomenon of recognition failure were subsumed under the encoding specificity principle according to which the memory trace of an event and hence the properties of effective retrieval cue are determined by the specific encoding operations performed by the system on the input stimuli.

The current transition from traditional associationism to information processing and organizational points of view about human memory manifests itself in many ways. One of the clearest signs of change has to do with the experimental and theoretical separation between storage and retrieval processes. In an important early paper, Melton (1963), for instance, pointed out that "the principal issues in theory of memory ... are about either the storage or the retrieval of traces [p. 4]." Only 10 years before Melton made the statement, it would have puzzled most students of verbal learning. At that time memory was still a matter of acquisition, retention, transfer, and interference of associations betwen stimuli and responses. While everyone was aware of the logical distinction between acquisition and retention on the one hand and retention and recall on the other hand, these distinctions shaped neither experiment nor theory. At the level of conceptual analysis, the mechanism of recall was included in the concept of association; at the level of experimental operations, recall was observable behavior whose measurable aspects simply served to provide evidence about strength of associations. Moreover, the act of recall was empirically neutral in that it did not affect the state of the system; it was theoretically uninteresting because it could not be studied independently of acquisition.

The last 10 or 15 years have changed the ideational framework for studying memory. Today the orienting attitudes clearly include the notion that both recall and recognition are more or less complex retrieval operations or processes that can be studied and analyzed in some sense separately of storage operations or processes. Retrieval operations complete the act of remembering that begins with encoding of information about an event into the memory store. Thus, remembering is regarded as a joint product of information stored in the past and information present in the immediate cognitive environment of the rememberer. It is also becoming increasingly clear that remembering does not involve a mere activation of the learned association or arousal of the stored trace by a stimulus. Some sort of a more complex interaction between stored information and certain features of the retrieval environment seems to be involved in converting a potential memory into conscious awareness of the original event and corresponding behavior.

Relations between the effects of the past and present inputs and the interaction of the memory trace with the retrieval environment constitute the domain of theories of retrieval. Although the important issues are not yet entirely clear, many questions do seem to be central to the understanding of retrieval processes and are likely to come more directly under experimental and theoretical scrutiny. What, for instance, determines the high degree of selectivity of retrieval, the fact that at any given moment a person can only remember one discrete event? Is the output mode of the memory system different from the input mode? Can information be retrieved at the same time that some other information is stored, or does storage always involve retrieval, and retrieval storage? How do we conceptualize the nature of the effect of a retrieval cue on stored information? Does it activate the trace, does it elicit it directly or indirectly, does it provide access to it, does it restrict the size of the search set, does it somehow complement the information contained in the trace, or what? Is there a fundamental difference between recall and recognition, or do these two retrieval operations differ only in terms of the nature of retrieval cues present at output? What controls retrieval in a situation in which no specific cues seem to be present, such as in free recall? What makes some stimuli effective cues for retrieval of a given event and others not?

Since the separation of the total act of remembering into storage and retrieval processes has only recently been translated into experimental observations and theoretical speculations, there are as yet no theories of retrieval that provide satisfactory answers to these and many other possible questions one might want to ask. The development of these theories is one of the important objectives of research on memory. But a modest beginning has been made, and it is the purpose of the present paper to examine and describe the early state of the art.

In the first part of the paper, we describe a familiar phenomenon that has recently been brought into the laboratory and that has become the source of a minor theoretical controversy. This is the so-called extralist cuing effect, facilitation of recall of a list item by a retrieval cue that was not explicitly a part of the input list. We summarize and briefly evaluate seven theories that have been advanced to explain the effect. In the second major section of the paper, we present some new data from experiments that were initially designed to test the most popular and widely accepted explanation of the extralist cuing effect, the generation-recognition theory. Somewhat unexpectedly, the results of the experiments showed large superiority of recall over recognition, a state of affairs that cannot occur according to the generation-recognition theory as well as most other extant theories of retrieval. In the third and final section, we consider several possible interpretations of the new data and subsume them, together with other data already in the literature, under the encoding specificity principle: What is stored is determined by what is perceived and how it is encoded, and what is stored determines what retrieval cues are effective in providing access to what is stored.

The present analysis applies to memory for simple events of the kind frequently used in laboratory studies. A familiar word or some other object is presented as a member of an unfamiliar collection or list, and the subject's task is to remember that he saw that particular word or object in that particular list in that particular situation. In such a list-item task, the subject may be instructed to retrieve the whole set of presented items, some particular subset thereof, or a single item. At the time of retrieval, he is given general instructions as to the set or subset of items to be retrieved, and sometimes the instructions are supplemented with specific cues. The cues may be units of material that were presented as a part of the input list (intralist cues). They may also be items not explicitly present at the time of the study (extralist cues). An intralist cue to aid retrieval of List Item B may be another List Item A, or it may be a literal copy of the Target Item B. In the former case, it is customary to refer to the subject's task as that of cued recall; in the latter we say that the task is one of recognition. (Despite the apparent differences in the nature of these two kinds of cues, we assume that the processes involved are essentially the same in both cases, and we make no theoretical distinction between recall and recognition. The subject's task is the same in both cases, namely to utilize the information provided in the retrieval environment to select some specific stored information.)

The paper is about retrieval processes in episodic rather than semantic memory. The distinction between these two memory systems has been described in detail elsewhere (Tulving, 1972). It forms part of the general background of the present analysis. Briefly, episodic memory is concerned with storage and retrieval of temporally dated, spatially located, and personally experienced events or episodes, and temporal-spatial relations among such events. Appearance of a word in a to-be-remembered list in an experimental task is such an event. (In typical laboratory experiments the spatial co-ordinates of events to be remembered are held constant, hence the focus on their temporal dates and relations only.) Semantic memory is the system concerned with storage and utilization of knowledge about words and concepts, their properties, and interrelations. Thus, episodic information about a word refers to information about the event of which the word is the focal element, or one of the focal elements, while semantic information about a word is entirely independent of the word's occurrence in a particular situation or its temporal co-occurrence with some other words.

We agree with the widely held pretheoretical assumption that the central representation of the to-be-remembered event, the memory trace, is a multidimensional collection of elements, features, or attributes (e.g., Bower, 1967; Norman & Rumelhart, 1970; Posner & Warren, 1972; Underwood, 1969; Wickens, 1970). We also assume, along with many other contemporary students of memory (e.g., Bower, 1967, 1972; Martin, 1968, 1972; Melton & Martin, 1972; Underwood, 1969, 1972; Wickens, 1970) that an encoding process intervenes between the perception of an event and the creation of the corresponding trace, a process of as yet unknown nature that converts the stimulus energy into mnemonic information. The concern with retrieval processes in the present paper necessarily means that we must take an interest in the nature of stored information and in conditions determining the format of this information, that is, in encoding processes. It makes little sense to talk about retrieval without knowing something, or at least making some assumptions, about what it is that is being retrieved.

One term that we will use rather frequently in the paper is "effectiveness of retrieval cues." By this we mean the probability of recall of the target item in the presence of a discretely identifiable retrieval cue. Effectiveness, as thus defined, can always be expressed in absolute terms, but for certain reasons it is more convenient to describe the effectiveness of any specific cue in relation to the basic reference level of retrieval observed in absence of any specific cues. An effective cue, in this sense, is one whose presence facilites recall in comparison with free or nominally noncued recall.[2]

Effectiveness of extralist retrieval cues: seven theories

Effectiveness of extralist cues as an empirical phenomenon is well documented. An early experiment by Postman, Adams, and Phillips (1955), experiments by Bilodeau and his associates (e.g., Bilodeau, 1967; Bilodeau & Blick, 1965; Fox, Blick, & Bilodeau, 1964), as well as an experiment of Bahrick's (1969) have all shown that strong extraexperimental associates of list items, when presented to the subject as recall aids, increase the probability of correct responses. Names of conceptual categories of list words as extralist cues have been used by Hudson and Austin (1970), Tulving and Psotka (1971), and Wood (1967). Light (1972) has shown that homonyms and synonyms facilitate recall of list words. Greater effectiveness of two than of one associative extralist cue has been reported by McLeod, Williams, and Broadbent (1971). In a continuous study–test paradigm, Bregman (1968) studied the effectiveness of semantic, phonetic, and graphemic cues at different retention intervals. Finally, extralist associates have been shown to be effective cues when the subject expects a free-recall test but not when he expects to be tested for list words with other cues (Thomson & Tulving, 1970).

We can identify at least seven theories of retrieval that have been or could be proposed to account for the effectiveness of extralist cues, provided that we use the term "theory" in the sense of its most modest dictionary meaning, as "an idea or a set of ideas about something."

To make the discussion a bit simpler, we occasionally use a concrete example in lieu of more general and abstract terminology. In this example, CHAIR is one of the word events that is presented for study, and *table*, a word not shown in the input list, serves as an effective retrieval cue. The question to be answered then is this: Why does *table* facilitate the recall of CHAIR as the target word?

Guessing from semantic memory

Even if the subject does not have the foggiest notion that CHAIR occurred in the list—the stored information has been completely wiped out, or he never saw the word in the list—he can, if he chooses to guess, or is so instructed by the experimenter (e.g., Bahrick, 1969; Fox, Blick, & Bilodeau, 1964; Freund & Underwood, 1970), boost the correspondence between the input list and his output protocol by thinking of and producing words semantically related to the cue word *table* and thus create the appearance of recalling the specific word event from the list.

Although the possibility of semantic guessing is sometimes mentioned in connection with the interpretation of extralist cuing effects (e.g., Freund & Underwood, 1970), and although it is difficult to deny that some subjects in some episodic memory experiments may utilize information from semantic memory only, the theory cannot be taken seriously for at least two reasons. First, subjects on their own seldom resort to the strategy of semantic guessing in an episodic memory task, as evidenced by the fact that in most extralist cuing experiments a large majority of recall errors consists of plain omissions. Second, the magnitude of cuing effects is usually (*a*) considerably greater than one could expect on the basis of guessing from semantic memory, regardless of what strategy the subject might follow in such guessing, and (*b*) independent of, or even inversely related to, the probability of choosing the correct response on the basis of semantic information alone (e.g., Bahrick, 1969; McLeod et al., 1971).

Convergence of episodic and semantic associations

Some theorists are not interested in subjects' memories for particular events but rather in changes in probabilities of particular responses. One might say they are not interested in memory but in learning. In their pretheoretical scheme of things, Word A is identical with Word A, regardless of the situations in which they occur. For instance, "chair" as a response indicating memory for a particular word event in an experimental task and "chair" as a response to the word *table* in the free-association test are lumped together into the same response class. The changes in the probability of emission of responses of this class then constitute behavioral happenings of experimental and theoretical interest.

Given this type of orienting framework, the following simple explanation of extralist cuing effects can be and has been advocated. A semantic association exists between *table* and CHAIR prior to the experiment. Another association is created between CHAIR, or the corresponding response, and the general contextual stimuli present in the experiment. In the noncued recall test, only the contextual association is reactivated, while in the cued test both the contextual association derived from the experimental input and the specific association with *table* originating outside the experiment converge upon the response CHAIR, producing a higher probability of the correct response in the cued situation.

Such a theory of convergence of experimental and extraexperimentally acquired associations has been proposed by Bilodeau and his associates (e.g., Bilodeau, 1967; Bilodeau & Blick, 1965) to account for their own observations in extralist cuing experiments. It tacitly assumes that the activation of the extraexperimental association between the cue and the target word at the time of recall is independent of what happened at the time of presentation of the target word for study. The demonstration that encoding operations performed on a target word affect the effectiveness of extralist cues would be incompatible with the theory. Such experimental findings are described later in this paper.

434

Increments in trace strength

A theory closely related to the idea of convergent associations holds that presentation of the cue at recall increases the trace strength of the target word, perhaps through the mechanism of elicitation of implicit associative responses. Many theorists assume that the trace of a word can be "strengthened" through repeated presentation of the word for study. They may also find it not too difficult to imagine that the target word could occur as an implicit associate to the cue at recall and that such a covert repetition of the target word would also "strengthen" the trace. Such cue-produced strengthening of originally subliminal traces might thus be responsible for the heightened recallability of target words in the cued test.

The theory of increased trace strength differs from that of convergent associations principally in that it does not require the assumption that retrieval of CHAIR depends on associative connections between it and *table*, or between it and the experimental context. The theory can, therefore, be extended to recognition tests of trace "strength," in which the role of associative connections among items is thought to be minimal.

This theory has been considered by Broadbent (1973, p. 90) in a discussion of effectiveness of extralist retrieval cues and rejected on the basis of data from an unpublished study by Wingrove and Giddings showing lack of facilitative effect of extralist cues in recognition tests of target items. Similarly, data from earlier experiments of ours, designed to study the effect of context on recognition of list words (Thomson, 1972; Tulving & Thomson, 1971), showed that the presence of the cue word *table* inhibits recognition of the target word CHAIR if CHAIR occurred in the input list by itself, a finding quite contrary to the theory of increased trace strength.

Restricted search set

William James's rich legacy includes a colorful metaphor of retrieval as a search process:

> We make search in our memory for a forgotten idea, just as we rummage our house for a lost object. In both cases we visit what seems to us the probable *neighborhood* of that which we miss. We turn over the things under which, or within which, or alongside of which, it may possibly be; and if it lies near them, it soon comes to view [James, 1890, p. 654].

Current conceptualizations of retrieval as search (e.g., Atkinson & Shiffrin, 1968; Norman, 1968; Shiffrin, 1970; Shiffrin & Atkinson, 1969; Yntema & Trask, 1963) have been as much influenced by the developments in computer technology as they have been by William James. These search theories reject the possibility that retrieval of information about the occurrence of any specific event entails the examination of the entire contents of memory. Rather, they assume that search for desired information always takes place in a more or less narrowly circumscribed region of the memory store, the search set. In any given situation the size and nature of the search set is specified by the information available to the retrieval system at the beginning of the search, including specific retrieval cues, and it may be modified as search proceeds. In this scheme, an extralist retrieval cue, for reasons that we have already met in the previous theories, creates a search set more restricted than would otherwise be the case, and since the success of search is, other things being equal, an inverse function of the size of the search set, cued recall is higher than noncued recall.

Search-set theories assume that search sets are smaller in recognition than in recall tests. Probability that a learned item would be recognized, therefore, cannot be smaller than the probability of the item's recall. Experimental data inconsistent with this prediction of search theories are described below.

Generation-recognition models

At the present time the most widely accepted theories of retrieval are various versions of the generate-test model of information processing. The generation-recognition models assume that retrieval of stored information consists of two successive or overlapping stages: (*a*) implicit generation of possible response alternatives and (*b*) recognition of one of the generated alternatives as meeting certain criteria of acceptability. The generation phase is frequently guided by semantic information the system possesses about the cue word: given *table* as cue, the implicitly generated responses consist of words semantically related to it, including CHAIR. The operations in the recognition phase, on the other hand, can be successful only to the extent that relevant episodic information is available. The generated response alternative CHAIR would be identified as the desired word if its internal representation carries an appropriate "occurrence tag" (Mandler, 1972) or "list marker" (Anderson & Bower, 1972), information about the membership of the word in a particular list in a particular situation.

Effective retrieval cues of all sorts, including extralist cues, facilitate recall (to follow the reasoning of generation-recognition models) because they reduce the probability that the desired information, although available in the memory store, cannot be found. Cued recall, in this view, produces a higher level of retrieval than does noncued recall for the same reason that recognition is higher than recall. Bahrick (1969), in one of the most explicit accounts of the workings of the generation-recognition mechanism, said that a cue or a prompt

> is likely to produce a hierarchy of responses as a result of past learning. . . . One of these responses is likely to be the training response.

436

S is thus unburdened of the search strategy involved in unaided recall tasks. He continues to produce responses associated with the prompt until he can identify one of them as the response presented during training. This portion of the prompted recall task functionally approximates a recognition task [Bahrick, p. 217].

In Bahrick's formal model (1970), the probability of recall of the target item in response to the extralist cue is the product of the probability of its implicit generation and the probability of its recognition.

Many other contemporary thinkers advocate, or at least approvingly mention, the generation-recognition model as an appropriate explanation of cuing effects (e.g., Bower, 1970; Bower, Clark, Lesgold, & Winzenz, 1969; Fox & Dahl, 1971; Kintsch, 1970; Murdock, in press; Norman, 1968; Shiffrin & Atkinson, 1969; Slamecka, 1972; Underwood, 1972). The terminology used by different theorists is not always the same, but the basic ideas are identical. For instance, Shiffrin and Atkinson (1969, p. 187) referred to the generation part of the process as search and recovery, and to the recognition phase as response generation. Underwood (1972) talked about response production and evaluation of the response for correctness "by the attributes used in making such recognition decisions [p. 11]" and Bower (1970), in explaining the effectiveness of rhyming cues, assumed that the subject implicitly generates "the plausible candidate-responses" among which "he needs only to recognize the one that has recently occurred in the list context [p. 22]."

Anderson and Bower's (1972) theory of recognition and retrieval processes deals with free recall, but it could be extended to cover extralist cuing effects without introducing any additional mechanisms. In this theory the generation of potential response items takes the form of activation of previously marked word nodes in an associative network, through pathways also appropriately marked during the presentation of the list. The marking of the pathways between the extralist cue node and the target node—a necessary condition for recall in the model—could be assumed to result from the attempt to link the target node to other list-item nodes in the input phase of the trial.

All versions of the generation-recognition theories subscribe to two closely related assumptions. One is the assumption of transsituational identity of words: every word has but a single representation in memory, or at most a few representations, corresponding to its dictionary meaning or meanings. Perception, encoding, or use of the word in any one of a wide variety of situations and contexts, including list-item experiments, leads to the kind of activation and modification of its internal representation that is thought of as the addition of a list marker or an occurrence tag.

The other assumption is that of "automatic access": long-term memory is a self-addressing storage system in which the location of each unit of information is determined by the nature and contents of the information

(Kintsch, 1970; Norman, 1968; Shiffrin & Atkinson, 1969). When a to-be-remembered word is presented for study in a list-item task, its meaning and other properties determine into what part of the memory store it is entered. When the same word occurs again—as a repeated study item, as an implicit response generated by an associated cue word, as an "old" test item in the recognition test, or in some other way—automatic access to the same memory location takes place, permitting the system, among other things, to examine the location for the presence of previously stored episodic information.

The generation-recognition models provide plausible accounts of effects of extralist cues. They are also consistent with a large number of experimental results showing absence of differences in recognition of learned material between experimental conditions that do produce differences in recall (e.g., Kintsch, 1970; McCormack, 1972). But these models cannot handle situations in which an otherwise effective retrieval cue, such as *table*, fails to facilitate recall of a target item with which it is closely related semantically, such as CHAIR. They are also incompatible with findings showing recall to be higher than recognition. These kinds of data are described presently.

Mediation by input-generated implicit associative responses

According to a widely accepted assumption, when a word is presented for study, it activates many existing associations (e.g., Underwood, 1965). For instance, when the to-be-remembered word CHAIR is presented for study, the implicit associative responses made to it include the word *table*. When at recall the word *table* is presented as a cue, it elicits the word CHAIR, and the backward version of the implicit associative response thus revived adds its strength to whatever other associations are elicited by general contextual stimuli responsible for the recall of CHAIR under noncued conditions. The theory is rather similar to the theory of convergent experimental and preexperimental associations, except that it makes the critical assumption of the necessity of the experimental updating of the preexperimental association.

This theory was mentioned as a possible explanation of extralist cuing results by Freund and Underwood (1970). Although these authors rejected it, since they thought their own data did not demonstrate a "true" extralist cuing effect, the theory is quite plausible within the framework of current associative views of memory. Indeed, Postman et al. (1955) interpreted their extralist cuing data along the lines of this theory, and it has been used to account for data from other kinds of experiments that are related to cuing studies (e.g., Cramer, 1970; Puff, 1966). The theory is also highly compatible with a well-known principle according to which probability of recall of an item is a direct function of the similarity between the recall situation and the original learning environment (e.g., Hollingworth, 1928; Melton, 1963).

438

Encoding specificity principle

The encoding specificity principle is the final idea about retrieval and extra-list cuing effects we discuss. In its broadest form the principle asserts that only that can be retrieved that has been stored, and that how it can be retrieved depends on how it was stored. In its more restricted senses, the principle becomes less truistic and hence theoretically more interesting. For instance, we assume that what is stored about the occurrence of a word in an experimental list is information about the specific encoding of that word in that context in that situation. This information may or may not include the relation that the target word has with some other word in the semantic system. If it does, that other word may be an effective retrieval cue. If it does not, the other word cannot provide access to the stored information because its relation to the target word is not stored.

Thus, the effectiveness of retrieval cues depends on the properties of the trace of the word event in the episodic system. It is independent of the semantic properties of the word except insofar as these properties were encoded as a part of the trace of the event. The distinction between semantic characteristics of words as lexical units and words as to-be-remembered events can be readily demonstrated with homographs—for instance, if VIOLET is encoded and stored as a color name, it normally cannot be retrieved as an instance of the category of flowers, or girls' names—but the same principle presumably holds for all verbal items. The cue *table* facilitates recall of the target word CHAIR if the original encoding of CHAIR as a to-be-remembered word included semantic information of the kind that defines the relation between two objects in the same conceptual category. Most intelligent subjects in episodic memory experiments routinely encode to-be-remembered words semantically, and hence words meaningfully related to target items will serve as effective retrieval cues.

A recent application of the encoding specificity principle to the interpretation of effectiveness of retrieval cues appeared in a study by Tulving and Osler (1968); one of its more interesting implications was explicitly tested in three experiments by Thomson and Tulving (1970); and its bearing on results from intralist cuing experiments has been discussed by Postman (1972). Since the principle asserts that it is the encoded trace of the target word rather than the characteristics of the target word in semantic memory that determines the effectiveness of extralist retrieval cues, as well as all other cues, it can be experimentally contrasted with theories that attribute the effectiveness of extralist cues to their preexperimental relations with target words. Such contrasts, however, are possible only under special conditions.

Logic of experimental comparison between theories

The main difference between the generation-recognition models of retrieval and the encoding specificity principle that is subject to test lies in the encoding stage of an item's processing as the locus of the effect of cues. According to the generation-recognition models the encoding stage is not important, as long as it does not disturb the capacity of the extralist cue to produce the target item as an implicit response. According to the encoding specificity principle, the target item must be encoded in some sort of reference to the cue for the cue to be effective.

Both theories can account equally well for the finding that a given cue in fact is effective. Thus, for instance, if *table* does facilitate the recall of the target word CHAIR, it is possible that an implicit response "chair" was made to the cue at retrieval and subsequently recognized. It is also possible that the target CHAIR was semantically encoded at the time of presentation in a specific way that rendered the cue word *table* effective. Experiments in which specific encoding conditions are unknown cannot provide critical data for evaluation of theories that differ in claims that they make about the importance of these conditions. Specific encoding operations performed on an input usually are not identifiable, but they can be experimentally manipulated through instructions and other means. Attempts to determine the nature of specific encoding operations in a particular situation through subjects' introspections (e.g., Light, 1972) are not likely to be any more successful than have been most other attempts to gain theoretical knowledge about mental processes from observations of this sort.

To contrast the encoding specificity principle with other theories, some experimental control over encoding of target items must be exercised. Thus, for instance, the target word CHAIR could be presented, and the subject induced to encode it in the specific context of another word such as *glue* that is semantically unrelated or only vaguely related to the otherwise effective cue word *table*. If CHAIR is encoded in relation to *glue*, it is less likely to be encoded at the same time in relation to *table*, and hence, according to the encoding specificity principle, the effectiveness of the extralist cue *table* should now be reduced. According to the generation-recognition models, on the other hand, the effectiveness of *table* as an extralist cue should not be impaired, as long as the semantic relation between *table* and CHAIR is intact.

The comparison of effectiveness of extralist cues under conditions in which the subjects were free to encode the target item in any way they wished and in which they were induced to encode the target item in the context of a specific list cue was undertaken by Thomson and Tulving (1970). Target words such as CHAIR were presented either alone or in the context of list cues such as *glue*, and the effectiveness of extralist cues such as *table* was observed under the two types of encoding condition. The results showed that extralist cues did facilitate recall of target words, but only if the target words appeared in the list as single items. In this case (Experiment II, Groups 1 and 3) cued recall was on the order of 70% as compared with the values in the neighborhood of 45% in the nominally noncued test. Under the conditions in which the target word occurred at input with, and was presumably stored in some relation to another word (Experiment II, Groups 5 and 6), cuing with extra-list cues resulted in a much lower recall level of some 23%. Noncued recall of target words encoded in presence of specific list cues (Experiment II, Group 4) was approximately 30%. These data seem to be more compatible with the encoding specificity principle than with the generation-recognition theory. It is not known, however, to what extent the pairing of target words with specific list cues at input may have reduced the capacity of extralist cues to produce targets as implicit responses, and therefore the results of the Thomson and Tulving experiment are not entirely unequivocal.

We next report data from three experiments in which the two phases of retrieval as envisioned by generation-recognition theories, generation and recognition, could be directly observed. The experiments were patterned after the Thomson and Tulving study, except that we did not test the effectiveness of extralist retrieval cues under conditions where target words were presented in absence of any specific intralist context. Previous experiments have made it quite clear that extralist associates of target words would be quite effective retrieval cues under these conditions. This kind of result, as we have seen, would not distinguish among theories.

When retrieval cues fail: three experiments

In the experiments to be described, subjects studied a list of target words, such as CHAIR, each presented in the company of a specific input cue, such as *glue*. Since the subjects expected to be tested with these cues, they presumably encoded target words in an appropriate relation to the input cue. After studying the list, the subjects were asked to produce free association responses to strong extraexperimental associates of target words such as *table*. The probability of generation of target words (CHAIR) in response to the extralist cues was one observation of interest. Next, subjects were asked to identify those generated words that they remembered having seen in the input list, their success in doing so being another observation of interest. Finally, a cued recall test involving input cues (*glue*) was given to the subjects in an attempt to estimate the extent to which information about target words (CHAIR) was available in the memory store.

General method

In all three experiments the same procedure was used up to a critical point in time when different treatments and tests were administered to subjects. The procedure common to all experiments follows.

Every subject was shown and tested on three successive lists. The sole purpose of the first two lists was to induce subjects to encode each target word with respect to, or in the context of, another word. The word pairs in these two set-establishing lists were comparable to weak-cue input lists used by Thomson and Tulving (1970). The target words, each paired with its cue word, were shown visually, one at a time, at the rate of three seconds/pair. Immediately at the end of the presentation of the list the subjects were provided with 24 haphazardly ordered input cue words on a recall sheet and instructed to write down the target words. Three minutes were given for the recall of the list. The mean number of words recalled for these two lists were 14.3 and 17.6 in Experiment 1; 15.7 and 18.3 in Experiment 2; and 14.4 and 17.7 in Experiment 3.

The third list in each experiment was the critical list, providing the data of interest. This list, too, consisted of 24 cue-target pairs, with the material presented exactly as in the first two lists.

The target words in the third list in each experiment were those designated as such in Table 1. The two sets, A and B, were used equally frequently with

Table 1 Materials used in the construction of critical lists in experiments 1, 2, and 3

List A			List B		
Weak cue	*Strong cue*	*Target word*	*Weak cue*	*Strong cue*	*Target word*
ground	hot	COLD	hope	low	HIGH
head	dark	LIGHT	stem	long	SHORT
bath	want	NEED	whiskey	lake	WATER
cheese	grass	GREEN	moth	cat	FOOD
stomach	small	LARGE	cabbage	square	ROUND
sun	night	DAY	glass	soft	HARD
pretty	sky	BLUE	country	closed	OPEN
cave	dry	WET	tool	finger	HAND
whistle	tennis	BALL	memory	fast	SLOW
noise	blow	WIND	covering	lining	COAT
glue	table	CHAIR	barn	clean	DIRTY
command	woman	MAN	spider	eagle	BIRD
fruit	bloom	FLOWER	crust	bake	CAKE
home	bitter	SWEET	deep	bed	SLEEP
grasp	infant	BABY	train	white	BLACK
butter	rough	SMOOTH	mountain	leaf	TREE
drink	tobacco	SMOKE	cottage	hate	LOVE
beat	ache	PAIN	art	boy	GIRL
cloth	lamb	SHEEP	adult	labor	WORK
swift	stop	GO	brave	strong	WEAK
lady	king	QUEEN	door	color	RED
blade	scissors	CUT	roll	carpet	RUG
plant	insect	BUG	think	dumb	STUPID
wish	soap	WASH	exist	human	BEING

two subgroups of subjects in each of the three experiments; otherwise, all subjects in a given experiment were treated identically. In Table 1, each target word is accompanied by two cue words, one "weak" and the other one "strong." These triplets were selected from free-association norms (Bilodeau & Howell, 1965; Riegel, 1965) to conform to the following criteria: (*a*) the target word is a low-frequency (mean of 1% for the whole set) associate to its weak cue; (*b*) the target word is a high-frequency associate to its strong cue (mean of 52%), and (*c*) weak and strong cues of a given target word are not associatively related to each other in the norms.

The 24 pairs of words in critical lists consisted of weak cues and their corresponding target words. The strong cue words were not shown at the time of the presentation and were used only as extralist retrieval cues in the subsequent test phase. For instance, subjects tested with List A saw the pairs, *ground* COLD, *head* LIGHT, *bath* NEED, and so on, one pair at a time, for all 24 pairs, the cue word appearing in lower-case letters above the capitalized target word. The same instructions that had been given to the subjects in the first two lists were routinely repeated: their task was to remember the capitalized words, but paying attention to cues might help them at the time of the subsequent test. No mention was made of any change in the procedure between Lists 2 and 3. Each pair was again shown visually for three seconds. After all 24 pairs had been presented once, subjects received different treatments in different experiments, as described below.

Experiment 1

After the presentation of the third, critical list—henceforth referred to as "the list"—all 40 subjects, undergraduates at Yale University, were given the same four successive tasks.

First, each subject received a sheet of paper listing 12 extralist cues corresponding to one half of the to-be-remembered word from the list. For instance, subjects tested with List A were given the words *hot, dark, want,* and so on. They were told that each of the listed cue words was related to one of the capitalized words in the list that they had just studied, and that their task was to write down as many of the capitalized words as they remembered, each one beside its related cue word. Three minutes were allowed for this task. The mean number of target words recalled in this extralist-cue test was 1.8 (15%).

Second, subjects were given the remaining 12 extralist cues, briefly told about the free association procedure, instructed to look carefully at each cue word, produce free associates to each mentally, and then, "if one of the words you generate as a free association is a word from the list that you have just studied," to write it down beside its stimulus word. Again, three minutes were given for this task. The mean number of target words recalled in this test was 3.6 (30%). This figure was significantly higher than the 15% recall level in the first phase.

Third, all 24 extralist cue words, that is, the cues that the subjects had just seen in the first and second phase of testing, were presented to the subjects once more, listed on a sheet of paper, together with instructions to "write down all the words that you can generate as free associations" to these stimulus words. Beside each stimulus word were six blank spaces for up to six responses. Twelve minutes were allowed for this task. Each subject generated, on the average, 104 free association responses to the 24 stimulus words, a mean of 4.4 response words. Among the 104 responses thus generated there were, on the average, 17.7 (74% of the 24) words matching the target words of the list. Of these words, 70% were given by subjects as the primary response to the stimulus words. Thus, the proportion of target words generated as primary responses to the high-frequency stimuli was 52% (70% of the 74%), matching the normative data exactly.

Fourth, the subjects were instructed to look over all their generated responses and to circle all words that they recognized as target words from the list they had learned last. They were given as much time as they needed for this task. The mean number of words circled was 4.2, out of the maximum of 17.7, producing a hit rate of 24%. The percentage of false positives, circled words that were not target words from the list, was 4.5%.

A fifth task in Experiment 1 was an afterthought whose relevance became clear after we had tested and seen the results from 30 subjects. It was administered to the final 10 subjects. (Their performance on the first four tasks was not distinguishable from that of the first 30 subjects.) These 10 subjects were provided, on two sheets of paper, with the 24 input cues from the list and were instructed to recall the capitalized words from the list they had seen last. The mean number of target words recalled on this cued recall test was 15.2, for a hit rate of 63%. Further analysis of the data from these 10 subjects revealed that in their fourth and fifth tasks, they both recognized and recalled a total of 43 words; recognized but did not recall 4 words; and recalled but did not recognize 69 words.

These data can be summarized as follows: (a) Pairing of to-be-remembered words at input with cue words associatively unrelated to subsequently presented extralist cues has no adverse effect on subjects' ability to utilize these extralist cues in generating target words from semantic memory. (b) Regardless of whether subjects are or are not instructed to use the generate-recognize strategy, under conditions where cues are switched from input to output, the level of their recall performance in presence of extralist cues does not materially exceed that expected under noncued conditions (cf. Thomson & Tulving, 1970). (c) Under the experimental conditions as described, subjects cannot recognize many generated copies of target words, although they can produce these words in presence of what appear to be more effective cues, context items from the input list. The recognition hit rate of 24% contrasted with the hit rate of 63% in the cued recall test.

Experiment 2

One purpose of Experiment 2 was to replicate Experiment 1; another was to find out to what extent the low hit rate in the recognition of generated free association responses was attributable to the source of the recognition test items. In Experiment 1, each subject generated the "old" items and distractors for the recognition test. In Experiment 2 this procedure was replicated with one half of the list items, while for the other half of the list the source of "old" test items and distractors for a given subject was the free association protocol of a yoked subject.

Twenty-two subjects, undergraduate students of both sexes at Yale University, participated in this experiment. Again, they were divided into two groups for the sole purpose of using both Lists A and B, as shown in Table 1, in the critical, third list position. Otherwise, all subjects were administered an identical sequence of tasks.

Each subject was again first tested with two successive set-establishing lists, and then the third list was presented, as in Experiment 1. Following the presentation of the list, subjects were given five successive tasks.

1. They were asked to generate and write down six free association responses to each of the 12 extralist cue words corresponding to the target words. The mean number of words generated was 54 per subject, of which 9.6 (80% of the 12) matched target words in the list. Primary responses coincided with target words 53% of the time.

2. Subjects were asked to examine all the words they had generated in the free association test and to write down, on a separate piece of paper, all those words they recognized as target words from the list. On the average, 1.8 target words were thus recognized, for a hit rate of 18%. The false positive rate was 2.8%.

3. Each subject was given the free associates generated by another subject to the remaining 12 extralist cues, and instructed to perform the same kind of recognition test on these words that they had performed on their own. This time the 22 subjects correctly identified 51 out of the total of 204 copies of target words, for a hit rate of 25%, a score not significantly different from the 18% hit rate of subjects' own generated responses, $t = 1.18$, $df = 21$.

4. Subjects were asked to write down, beside each of the recognized target words from the second set (yoked subjects' free association responses), the corresponding input cues they remembered from the list. The 22 subjects could provide 36 (71%) such cues for the 51 targets.

5. Finally, all subjects were given all 24 original input cues from the list and were asked to recall as many target words as they remembered. The mean number of words recalled on this test was 14.1, for a hit rate of 59%. Again, as in Experiment 1, there were very few words that were recognized in the second task but not recalled in the fifth task (a total of 5 for all

22 subjects), and there were numerous words recalled in the fifth task but not recognized, although generated, in the second task (total of 73 for 22 subjects).

The results of Experiment 2 thus confirmed the results of Experiment 1: when provided with strong extraexperimental associates of target words as stimuli, subjects generated many responses matching the target words but they did rather poorly in identifying these as target words from the list. In Experiment 2, the hit rate in the recognition test of generated target words was, on the average, 22%, while the false positive rate was 2.8%. The source of the "old" test words and distractor items in the recognition test—whether the subject's own semantic memory or that of another subject—did not seem to be an important determinant of the recognition performance under these conditions, although the confounding of order of tests with experimental treatment may have contributed to the absence of a significant difference between the two conditions. Subjects also remembered a sizable proportion of input cues for the target words they correctly identified from among those generated by their yoked partners. Finally, the data from Experiment 2 confirmed those from Experiment 1 in showing that a low hit rate in the recognition test on generated target words did not prevent subjects from doing reasonably well in recalling these words in presence of the original input stimuli. The mean recognition hit rate of 22% in Experiment 2 again contrasted starkly with the cued-recall hit rate of 59%.

While the data in these experiments were averaged over all target words in the two critical lists, A and B, as shown in Table 1, it may be of some interest that large differences in recognition of individual words occurred. The words in both lists in Table 1 are ordered from least to most recognizable, on the basis of data in Experiments 1 and 2. Target words at the top of each list (COLD, LIGHT, HIGH, SHORT, WATER) were never recognized, even though each was generated by anywhere from 13 to 21 subjects; words in the middle (BALL, WIND, CHAIR, MAN, FLOWER, SLOW, COAT, DIRTY) showed individual hit rates of .14 to .16; words at the bottom (QUEEN, CUT, BUG, WASH, STUPID, BEING) were correctly recognized over 50% of the time.

Experiment 3

A possible interpretation of the very low recognition hit rates of generated to-be-remembered words in Experiments 1 and 2 might be provided by invoking the concept of "high criterion": for reasons unknown, the subjects adopt a very cautious attitude in the recognition test and check off only those words that they are extremely confident about as being identical with target words from the list. While the observed false positive rates, in relation to the observed hit rates, are sufficiently high to weaken the force of this argument, we made a more direct attempt to evaluate this interpretation in Experiment 3.

Fourteen subjects, from the same source as those in Experiments 1 and 2, served in this experiment. Again, they were divided into two groups for the sole purpose of counterbalancing materials in the critical test conditions. The materials and other conditions of the experiment were identical with those used in Experiments 1 and 2.

Subjects were again given two set-establishing lists first. The third list was then presented under the same instructions and conditions as Lists 1 and 2, and followed by three tasks. First, subjects were provided with two sheets of paper, listing the 24 extralist cues corresponding to the target words from the list. They were instructed to write down four free association responses to each of the 24 cue words, words that the cue words "made them think of."

Second, a forced-choice recognition test was given. Subjects were instructed to look at the four words they had generated for each of the stimulus words and circle the word that appeared to be the most likely member of the set of target words in the last list they had learned, guessing whenever necessary. In addition, the subjects were asked to indicate their confidence in the correctness of the response, on a scale on which the three values, 1, 2, and 3, were labeled as "guessing," "reasonably sure," and "absolutely sure."

The 14 subjects generated a total of 221 target words in the free association test, or an average of 15.8 (66%) of the possible 24. The proportion of target items among primary responses was 46%, only a little less than the normative value of 52%. In what was effectively a four-alternative forced-choice recognition test, the subjects correctly circled 118 out of the 221 copies of target words and failed to recognize the other 103 words, for a hit rate of 53%. Of the 118 to-be-remembered words correctly circled in the recognition test, 47 were labeled as guesses, while the remaining 71 were given confidence ratings of 2 or 3. The standard guessing correction yields a corrected recognition score of 38%. Alternatively, if we consider only those to-be-remembered words as recognized for which the subjects gave confidence ratings of 2 or 3, we obtain a recognition score of 71/221, or 32%.

In the third and final task, subjects were tested for recall of target words in presence of their original input cues, as in Experiments 1 and 2. The mean number of target words recalled was 14.2, for a hit rate of 61%, considerably higher than the recognition scores of 32% or 38%.

The major finding in Experiment 3 was that the failure to recognize recallable words also occurs, perhaps in a somewhat attenuated form, under the conditions of the forced-choice recognition test. It rules out the response bias as the sole explanation of the similar results obtained under free-choice recognition procedure in Experiments 1 and 2.

General results

A summary of the data from the three experiments, together with those from Experiment II in the Thomson and Tulving (1970) paper, is presented in Table 2. Table 2 shows probability of recall of target words in presence of

Table 2 Probability of recall of the target word in the presence of three kinds of retrieval cues

Cue	Tulving & Thomson (1970)[a] Exp. II	Exp. 1	Exp. 2	Exp. 3
Input cue	.65	.63	.59	.61
Extraexperimental associate	.23	.15, .30	—	—
Copy of target	—	.24	.22	.32, .38

[a] Data are from Group 6, Experiment II, by Thomson and Tulving (1970).

three kinds of specific cues: (*a*) input cues, (*b*) copies of target words generated by subjects in free association tests, and (*c*) strong preexperimental associates of target words used as extralist retrieval cues.

The importance of the data pertaining to recall in presence of input cues is twofold: the observed levels of recall in various experiments indicate the extent of effectiveness of input cues in relation to other cues, and they provide a lower-bound estimate of the availability of information about target words in memory. The data thus constitute a critical link in the argument that takes us from the results to the general conclusion of the experiments: conditions can be created in which information about a word event is available in the memory store in a form sufficient for the production of the appropriate response and yet a literal copy of the word is not recognized. This phenomenon of recognition failure was a striking one. Ignoring words that could be both recalled and recognized and those that could be neither recognized nor recalled—response categories defining theoretically uninteresting outcomes— we found, in Experiments 1 and 2, that the number of words that were recalled but not recognized exceeded the number of words that could be recognized but not recalled by a ratio of approximately 15:1.

The phenomenon of recognition failure of recallable items is not a novel one. Other experiments have been reported in which learned materials were recalled at higher levels than they were recognized (Bahrick & Bahrick, 1964; Lachman & Field, 1965; Lachman, Laughery, & Field, 1966). But in these experiments the subjects were given only a limited amount of time to make the recognition judgments, and it is not known to what extent the outcome was a consequence of time pressure. It is quite likely that if the subjects in the Lachman and Field (1965) experiment, for instance, in which the learned material was a meaningful prose passage, would have been given more time, they might have been able to recognize all words that they could recall, simply by reproducing each word as an element of the learned passage and matching it with the test word. This strategy may not have been feasible under the conditions of Lachman and Field's recognition task in which subjects only had 1.5 seconds to make the decision about each word.

Failure of recognition of generated words

The recognition failure of recallable words is an empirical phenomenon that cannot occur according to the two-process theory of recall and recognition (Kintsch, 1970) and other versions of the generation-recognition model of retrieval (e.g., Bower et al., 1969; Murdock, in press; Norman, 1968; Shiffrin & Atkinson, 1969; Slamecka, 1972; Underwood, 1972). Recovery of information through two bottlenecks (generation and recognition) in a recall situation cannot be more effective than that through only one of the two (recognition). Since the experimental data show that under certain conditions generation and recognition produce a higher level of retrieval than recognition alone, existing generation-recognition models require revision.

The phenomenon of recognition failure of recallable words violates the two critical assumptions on which generation-recognition models are based, the assumption of transsituational identity of words and the assumption of automatic access to the internal representation of a word. If a word had only one representation in memory, and if that representation were modified by the appearance of the word in an experimental list, then recognition could fail only because of loss or deterioration of the relevant list or occurrence information. If recall also depended upon an intact list marker, its level could never exceed that of recognition. In our experiments, the copy of the recallable target word that was not recognized may have provided automatic access to some internal representation of the word, or to some specific location in the memory store, but the information about the membership of the word in a particular list was apparently not stored in that location. The question thus is not whether the occurrence of a stimulus word, produced in whatever fashion, provides automatic access but rather automatic access to what?

One might perhaps argue that the conditions of our experiments lie outside the boundaries of the domain of the generation-recognition models, and that in "normal" experimental situations the models do rather faithfully represent the retrieval process. In that case we need to be told what the domain of the generation-recognition models is, and what kind of a model would account for the data that show strong associates of target words to be ineffective cues. In this connection it is helpful to remember that the procedure we used rendered many recallable words not recognizable, but it did not seem to affect the ability of subjects to successfully generate copies of target words in response to extralist cues. The failure of retrieval as envisaged by the two-process theory had its source in the recognition phase and not the generation phase.

A plausible modification of the generation-recognition models that would bring them into line with the phenomenon of recognition failure of recallable words would involve making the assumptions that (a) the pairing of the target word with another word at input creates a specific semantic meaning for the target word, and (b) this specific meaning is stored with the "core" representation of the word and marked with a list tag. The input cue may provide access to the appropriate location in the memory store, because of its list-specific association with the marked sense of the target word. But a copy of the target word may fail to do so, because it would be interpreted in a different sense in absence of the input cue, and thus provide access to an incorrect storage location.

A generation-recognition model thus modified would become in many ways quite similar to the encoding specificity principle in its general orientation. In the modified version the requirement would be relinquished that a given lexical item be represented in only one location. It remains to be seen whether it would be possible to retain some other basic features of these models, such as the assumption that episodic information is stored in the same system as semantic information, that occurrence of the to-be-remembered word in a list results in modification of the existing representation of the word in the memory store, and that recall, but not recognition, involves generation of alternatives other than the desired target words.

The phenomenon of recognition failure creates difficulties not only for extant versions of generation-recognition models but for most other theories of retrieval as well. Apart from the encoding specificity principle, to which we will return in the final section of the paper, the theory that seems to be most readily reconcilable with the data is that of mediation by implicit associative responses. The theory represents a special case of the principle of reinstatement of stimulus conditions and we will briefly consider it as such. This principle states that the success of retrieval depends on the completeness with which stimulating conditions present at input are reinstated at the time of attempted retrieval (Hollingworth, 1928; Melton, 1963). Since the stimulating conditions present at input could be thought to include unobservable processes of the kind that have been labeled implicit associative responses, presentation at the time of the recall of extralist retrieval cues that match implicit associative responses would produce a greater degree of similarity between the test and study conditions than that prevailing in the noncued test situation. While the principle of reinstatement of stimulus conditions does provide a plausible interpretation of the effectiveness of extralist retrieval cues, it cannot account for the phenomenon of recognition failure observed in our experiments. Given that the input consists of a compound stimulus such as glue-CHAIR, and given that the subject clearly knows that his memory will be tested for the target word CHAIR, why should the stimulating conditions be "more completely" reinstated when the glue part of the compound rather than the CHAIR part is presented at test? Thus the theory of mediation by implicit associative responses and the principle of reinstatement of stimulus conditions do not explain the phenomenon of recognition failure any more readily than do generation-recognition models.

Encoding and retrieval

In this last section of the paper, we consider some possible tentative explanations of the phenomenon of recognition failure, relate the phenomenon to other relevant data reported in the literature, and suggest an overall pretheoretical framework within which this phenomenon as well as other problems of retrieval could be experimentally and theoretically analyzed. The demonstrative nature of our own experiments precludes an enlightened interpretation of the failure of extralist associates and copies of target items as retrieval cues, but some possibilities for interpretation should be mentioned.

Recognition failure: tentative interpretations

One may wish to approach the phenomenon of recognition failure of recallable words in terms of the concept of asymmetry of associations between the input cue and the target item. The data show and imply that the "forward" association between the cue and the target in our experiments was stronger than the "backward" association between the target and the cue: given the cue, the target word could be recalled without difficulty in many cases; given the target word, the input cue could be recalled only infrequently. Thus, it would be possible to argue that the recognition failure of target words was a result of the weak association between the target and the cue. If that association had been stronger, the input cue could have been retrieved given the target word, and the target word itself recognized in the presence of the cue.

If one adopted this approach, the problem would become that of explaining the asymmetry of the associations between the input cue and the target word. One would also have to keep in mind an equally plausible alternative line of reasoning: backward association appears to be weaker than the forward association whenever the target word is not as readily recognized as the cue word. Recognition of the stimulus item, which depends on the consistent encoding of the item at input and at test, can be thought of as a necessary condition for associative recall (Martin, 1968, 1972). The difficulty here lies in the uncertainty of whether to account for failure of recognition in terms of a weak association or to interpret the apparent weak association in terms of the recognition failure.

Another approach to the problem of interpretation of the phenomenon of recognition failure could begin with the distinction between nominal and functional memory units. This distinction has often been made in discussions of associative and organizational processes in memory (e.g., Asch, 1969; Köhler, 1947; Tulving, 1968). A verbal unit may be designated as an independent to-be-remembered item by the experimenter, but the processing system, that is the subject, may treat it as a part of a larger functional unit. For instance, a subject shown a list of words under instructions to remember them could do reasonably well if he were asked to recall the letter bigrams he

451

saw in the list. He would "recall" the bigrams by retrieving information about the words and construct the units designated by the experimenter in a post-retrieval operation; he would not store bigrams in the same sense as he stores words. Even under intentional learning conditions, subjects are known to have great difficulty in recognizing bigrams they can readily recall as parts of integrated words (Watkins, 1973). Recognition failure of words that were recalled quite well in response to the specific input cues in our experiments may also have come about because the "old" test item in the recognition test did not match the functional memory unit, the complex consisting of the input cue and the target word. If the whole unit had been presented for recognition, the subjects probably would not have had any great difficulty.

While the explanation of the phenomenon of recognition failure in terms of the distinction between nominal and functional memory units is incomplete as long as we do not know exactly what are the functional units in any given situation, the notion might provide some guidelines for identification of more appropriate units of analysis than those defined by the experimenter. For instance, it may be reasonable to claim that a functional memory unit is one which, among other things, must be recognized if it is to be recalled. Thus, if a nominal unit could be recalled as a part of a larger complex but could not be recognized outside the complex, it would not correspond to a functional unit. The recall-cum-recognition criterion could be combined with other rules for identification of functional units, for instance, that they are activated and emitted in an all-or-none fashion (Mandler, 1967b).

Another closely related interpretation of recognition failure could be based on the Gestalt concept of "embeddedness." It is easy to demonstrate failure of perception of a figure embedded in a larger complex, and similar demonstrations have been reported in memory situations. Koffka (1935, p. 622), for instance, discussed an experiment by Harrower (1933) in which punch lines of jokes could not be recognized as readily when they appeared embedded in a meaningful passage than when they were presented as a part of a collection of unrelated statements. Winograd, Karchmer, and Russell (1971) interpreted their data demonstrating effectiveness of retrieval cues in recognition memory by assuming that under certain conditions nominal elements are compounded into a unitary representation. The principle of embedding would also apply to the results of an earlier demonstration of recognition failure of recallable words (Tulving, 1968b) in which the to-be-remembered words could be encoded by subjects as second halves of compound words, for example, air-PORT; house-HOLD; sand-HOG. In our present experiments the encoding operation performed on the input pairs also may have produced tightly knit compounds. The well-known Gestalt principle that properties of elements change when these elements become parts of larger wholes would then explain why copies of target words were not particularly effective in providing access to the trace created by the compound of the input cue and the target word. Thus, CHAIR may have been as difficult to retrieve from the "*glue*-CHAIR" complex stored in memory as it would be difficult for a person to recognize HIT as an "old" item when the stored unit is "architecture" or POT when the stored complex is "hippopotamus." The embedded part can be discerned easily enough in a perceptual display of the whole, both before the whole has been stored in and after it has been retrieved from memory, but its identification may be impossible after storage and before retrieval.

The major problem with the explanation of the recognition failure in terms of the concept of embedding has to do with the assumed difference in the recognition of input cues and target words: Why is the input cue not embedded in the cue-target complex in the same way as the target word is? Data reported elsewhere (Thomson, 1972) show the same pattern we are assuming here and create the same problem of interpretation: right-hand members of weakly associated input pairs were not as well recognized as left-hand members when the test word was presented alone.

Given the fact that the target word can be more readily recalled in presence of the input cue than in presence of its own literal copy, it is possible to think of the input cue as a "control element" or "code" that governs the access to the complex of stored information about the target word. The concept of "control element" has been used by Estes (1972) and the closely related concept of "code" by Johnson (1970) in theoretical accounts of processing of serial information. In the present context, we think of anything that controls retrieval of a particular memory unit at a particular time as a control element of that unit. A retrieval cue that is not only effective but also necessary for the recovery of certain stored information (an access cue) would be such a control element.

Recent experiments by Martin (1971) and Slamecka (1972) have produced rather striking demonstrations of the role that control elements play in determining access to stored information. While the two experiments were different in both conception and method, they did make one and the same point: certain stored items can be retrieved only through the activation of certain other items. The latter can be regarded as control elements for the former. In Martin's experiment, subjects learned groups of words consisting of a three-word compound stimulus and a single response word. A subsequent recall test showed that one stimulus word as a cue provided access to another one only through the response word. In Slamecka's study, subjects learned lists of words belonging to conceptual categories. In the recall test, one item in a given category provided access to other items in the same category only through the control element of the category label. These experiments, as well as those of Johnson's (1970) on chunking, do not only illustrate the part that control elements and codes play in retrieval, but they also point to the important distinction between experimenter-designated retrieval cues and control elements. The two are not always the same.

Although the data from our own experiments can be interpreted to reflect the role of input cues as control elements, this interpretation fails to tell us exactly what determined the identity of control elements in our situation. Why were the input cues, and not the target items, control elements; why not both?

Still another tentative interpretation of our findings could be advanced under the label of the hypothesis of complementary information. It can be briefly stated as follows. The address of an event stored in episodic memory is essentially temporal, defined in terms of the event's temporal relations to other experienced events. The specification of the address is frequently sufficient for the homunculus to read out the contents of that address. Failure of retrieval of desired information in a situation in which only the temporal address is given may sometimes come about because the information stored at that address is fuzzy or incomplete. An effective retrieval cue then is one that provides the missing information. Thus, the retrieval information complements the information available in the trace and permits the homunculus to read the trace without difficulty. According to this formulation, a copy of the list cue presented in the final cued tests in our experiments did contain information that was lacking in the stored traces, while extralist cues and copies of target items did not. The complementary information hypothesis does not say why the list cue, and not the target item, carried the necessary additional information, and therefore it is as incomplete as all others we have considered.

Encoding specificity

These tentative interpretations of the recognition failure we have briefly considered have not explained the phenomenon, but they have suggested questions that may provide some guidance and direction to future research. At the present time, it is possible only to point once more to the encoding specificity principle as a general answer to the questions. What produced the asymmetry of associations between list cues and target items in our experiments? What determined the functional memory units and their relations to the nominal units? Why was one of the two nominal units embedded in the whole complex more readily recognized when it appeared alone than was the other? Why did the list cue serve the function of a control element or code of the stored cue-target trace while the target item did not? Why was the information contained in the input cue sufficient to complement the stored information while that in the extralist cue and the copy of the target item was not?

A general answer to all these questions is provided by the encoding specificity principle: Specific encoding operations performed on what is perceived determine what is stored, and what is stored determines what retrieval cues are effective in providing access to what is stored.[3]

In our experiments, encoding of target words was influenced by the list cues present at input and by the subjects' expectations that they would be tested with those cues. But it was influenced by other things as well, factors that cannot as yet be adequately identified or labeled. We have referred to the totality of conditions determining the encoding of a perceived item as its cognitive environment (Tulving & Thomson, 1971), and we think of encoding operations as some sort of an interaction between the perceptual input and its cognitive environment. The terms are ill defined, and the concepts do not explain too much at this time. Yet they serve to remind us that something else besides the properties of a presented item determines how well the item is remembered and that an important research problem is to find out what this something else is and how it works. Specific encoding of input materials in our studies was responsible for asymmetry of associations, embeddedness, control elements, and the nature of effective retrieval information. The same material in other situations, however, in a different cognitive environment, could have been encoded in ways in which access routes to the stored information would have been different.

It has been known for a long time, of course, that how well a thing is remembered does not depend only on what it is, but also on how it is stored in memory. Ancient orators knew it when they used the method of loci to ensure that they would know the right thing to say at the right time (Yates, 1966), Gestalt psychologists knew it when they kept telling others that the properties of an element depended on the company the element kept in a larger whole, Bartlett (1932, p. 188) emphasized the importance of the "conditions of the prior perception" in determining recall and recognition, and a long tradition of research on incidental and intentional learning has converged on the conclusions that what is learned depends on what happens in the learning situation (Postman, 1964).

In recent research the effects of encoding operations on what is stored, the memory trace, have been studied in a variety of settings and using a number of different techniques and paradigms (Craik & Lockhart, 1972). One method has been to change the context of an item. It has been found that repetition of a to-be-remembered item may or may not facilitate its recall, depending upon its intralist context (e.g., Asch, 1969; Murdock & Babick, 1961), on its semantic interpretation as biased by context (e.g., Bobrow, 1970), and on its membership in the same or different higher order unit (e.g., Bower et al., 1969). Similarly, recognition of a previously seen list word has been shown to be influenced by its presentation and test contexts (e.g., DaPolito, Barker, & Wiant, 1972; Light & Carter-Sobell, 1970; Thomson, 1972; Tulving & Thomson, 1971; Winograd & Conn, 1971).

In another type of experiment, encoding has been manipulated by asking the subjects to do different things with the material when it is presented. Thus, for instance, Mandler (1967a) had one group of subjects sort words into conceptual categories while another group was exposed to the same words under instructions to study and remember them. In a subsequent free-recall test, both groups did equally well. In Hyde and Jenkins' (1969) experiment, subjects in one group made judgments about semantic properties of words, while in another group they studied the same set of words in expectation of a recall test. Both groups recalled the same number of words and did considerably better than a third group that had made judgments about graphemic properties of words prior to the test. A particularly effective manipulation of input in terms of encoding operations performed on the presented items has been described by Craik (1973). Words were presented tachistoscopically, always for the same short duration, and the subjects were instructed to answer different questions about each presented word, such as, "Is it printed in capital or lower-case letters?" or "Does it belong to the category of fruits?" Large differences in subsequent recall of these words were observed, depending upon the encoding operation performed at input. These and other similar studies (e.g., Gardiner, 1972; Johnston & Jenkins, 1971; Paivio & Csapo, 1972; Schulman, 1971) thus provide convincing evidence about the important role that encoding operations play in determining subsequent retrievability of perceived items.

Differences in recall and recognition of identical material stored under different encoding conditions do not simply reflect established differences in "strength" of traces. The concept of trace strength makes little sense and has little value if: (a) strength must be estimated from observed levels of recall or recognition and (b) these observed levels vary with specific conditions of retrieval. A number of recent experiments supplement common sense in demonstrating that recall and recognition of items stored under identical encoding conditions are influenced, sometimes greatly influenced, by the nature of information present in the retrieval environment. These experiments (e.g., Bahrick, 1969; Light, 1972; McLeod et al., 1971; Tulving, 1968b; Tulving & Pearlstone, 1966; Tulving & Psotka, 1971; Winograd & Conn, 1971) clearly suggest that a stored trace of an item is more accessible through certain cues than others. Memory traces may be said to vary in strength, or quality, or durability, but more importantly they vary in the specificity of code they carry as to the effectiveness of various kinds of retrieval information that govern the recovery of the stored information (Earhard, 1969).

Thus, research has shown that it is possible to hold constant the to-be-remembered item and observe large differences in its recall and recognition depending upon its encoding conditions, and that it is possible to hold constant the encoding conditions of the item and observe large differences in its recall and recognition depending upon retrieval conditions. These two basic sources of variability of recall, encoding and retrieval conditions, usually interact in the sense that a cue effective in one situation may or may not be effective in another. The new data we described in this paper strongly imply such an interaction, and other data already in the literature in fact demonstrate it (e.g., Earhard, 1969; Frost, 1972; Ghatala & Hurlbut, 1973; Lauer & Battig, 1972; Mikula, 1971; Thomson, 1972; Thomson & Tulving, 1970; Tulving & Osler, 1968; Tulving & Thomson, 1971; Tversky, in press; Winograd et al., 1971).

All these data suggest that the effectiveness of a particular cue depends on how the to-be-retrieved item was encoded at input. The recognition failure of recallable words represents an extreme case of the general principle that encoding determines the trace, and the trace determines the effectiveness of retrieval cues. The trace itself is simply the link between encoding conditions and the retrieval environment and, from the point of view of psychological analyses of memory, need have no more reality than is implied by the relation between encoding and retrieval.

The formulation of the encoding specificity principle is so general that it covers all known phenomena of episodic memory and retrieval and in a weak sense provides an understanding of them. More detailed conceptual analyses of the relation between encoding and retrieval processes may also be fruitfully undertaken within the same general paradigm.

Notes

1   This research was supported by the National Science Foundation Grant 24171X.
    The paper was written during the first author's residence as a Fellow at the Center for Advanced Study in the Behavioral Sciences in Stanford, California.
2   Subjects may retrieve items through schemes other than those suggested by the experimenter, and match the item to the cue after retrieval has occurred. Such cases could distort and inflate the absolute measures of effectiveness, and this is why measures relative to the noncued base line are preferred. One can then talk about inhibiting effects of specific cues, although it only means that cues assumed to be present in the nominally noncued situation are more effective in absolute terms than those the subject attempts to use at the experimenter's request (e.g., Earhard, 1969; Postman, Adams, & Phillips, 1955; Slamecka, 1969).
3   Although we have emphasized the importance of encoding conditions at input, we do not wish to imply that once an event has been encoded its trace does not undergo further changes. Among many possible modifications of stored information, those produced through active recoding of the trace are most relevant to determining its subsequent retrievability in different retrieval environments. For our present purposes, encoding processes are considered always to subsume recoding processes that occur prior to the act of explicit retrieval of interest.

References

ANDERSON, J. R., & BOWER, G. H. Recognition and retrieval processes in free recall. *Psychological Review*, 1972, **79**, 97–123.

ASCH, S. E. Reformulation of the problem of association. *American Psychologist*, 1969, **24**, 92–102.

ATKINSON, R. C., & SHIFFRIN, R. M. Human memory: A proposed system and its control processes. In K. W. Spence & J. T. Spence (Eds.), *The psychology of learning and motivation*. Vol. **2**. New York: Academic Press, 1968.

BAHRICK, H. P. Measurement of memory by prompted recall. *Journal of Experimental Psychology*, 1969, **79**, 213–219.

BAHRICK, H. P. A two-phase model for prompted recall. *Psychological Review*, 1970, **77**, 215–222.

BAHRICK, H. P. & BAHRICK, P. O. A re-examination of the interrelations among measures of retention. *Quarterly Journal of Experimental Psychology*, 1964, **16**, 318–324.

BARTLETT, F. C. *Remembering: A study in experimental and social psychology.* Cambridge, England: University Press, 1932.

BILODEAU, E. A. Experimental interference with primary associates and their subsequent recovery with rest. *Journal of Experimental Psychology*, 1967, **73**, 328–332.

BILODEAU, E. A., & BLICK, K. A. Courses of mis-recall over long-term retention intervals as related to strength of preexperimental habits of word association. *Psychological Reports*, 1965, **16** (Monogr. Suppl. 6).

BILODEAU, E. A., & HOWELL, D. C. *Free association norms.* (Catalog No. D210.2: F87) Washington, D. C.: U.S. Government Printing Office, 1965.

BOBROW, S. A. Memory for words in sentences. *Journal of Verbal Learning and Verbal Behavior*, 1970, **9**, 363–372.

BOWER, G. H. A multicomponent theory of the memory trace. In K. W. Spence & J. T. Spence (Eds.), *The psychology of learning and motivation.* Vol. 1. New York: Academic Press, 1967.

BOWER, G. H. Organizational factors in memory. *Cognitive Psychology*, 1970, **1**, 18–46.

BOWER, G. H. Stimulus-sampling theory of encoding variability. In A. W. Melton & E. Martin (Eds.), *Coding processes in human memory.* Washington, D. C.: Winston, 1972.

BOWER, G. H., CLARK, M. C., LESGOLD, A. M., & WINZENZ, D. Hierarchical retrieval schemes in recall of categorized word lists. *Journal of Verbal Learning and Verbal Behavior*, 1969, **8**, 323–343.

BREGMAN, A. S. Forgetting curves with semantic, phonetic, graphic, and contiguity cues. *Journal of Experimental Psychology*, 1968, **78**, 539–546.

BROADBENT, D. E. *In defence of empirical psychology.* London: Methuen, 1973.

CRAIK, F. I. M. A "levels of analysis" view of memory. In P. Pliner, L. Krames, & T. M. Alloway (Eds.), *Communication and affect: Language and thought.* New York: Academic Press, 1973.

CRAIK, F. I. M., & LOCKHART, R. S. Levels of processing: A framework for memory research. *Journal of Verbal Learning and Verbal Behavior*, 1972, **11**, 671–684.

CRAMER, P. Magnitude and selectivity as independent factors in semantic generalization. *Journal of Verbal Learning and Verbal Behavior*, 1970, **9**, 509–524.

DAPOLITO, F., BARKER, D., & WIANT, J. The effects of contextual changes on the component recognition. *American Journal of Psychology*, 1972, **85**, 431–440.

EARHARD, M. Storage and retrieval of words encoded in memory. *Journal of Experimental Psychology*, 1969, **80**, 412–418.

ESTES, W. K. An associative basis for coding and organization. In A. W. Melton & E. Martin (Eds.), *Coding processes in human memory.* Washington, D. C.: Winston, 1972.

FOX, P. W., BLICK, K. A., & BILODEAU, E. A. Stimulation and prediction of verbal recall and misrecall. *Journal of Experimental Psychology*, 1964, **68**, 321–322.

FOX, P. W., & DAHL, P. R. Aided retrieval of previously unrecalled information. *Journal of Experimental Psychology*, 1971, **88**, 349–353.

FREUND, J. S., & UNDERWOOD, B. J. Restricted associates as cues in free recall. *Journal of Verbal Learning and Verbal Behavior*, 1970, **9**, 136–141.

FROST, N. Encoding and retrieval in visual memory tasks. *Journal of Experimental Psychology*, 1972, **95**, 317–326.

GARDINER, J. M. Studies of word retrieval in human memory. Unpublished doctoral dissertation, University of London, 1972.

GHATALA, E. S., & HURLBUT, N. L. Effectiveness of acoustic and conceptual retrieval cues in memory for words at two grade levels. *Journal of Educational Psychology*, 1973, **64**, 347–352.

HARROWER, M. R. Organization in higher mental processes. *Psychologische Forschung*, 1933, **17**, 56–120.

HOLLINGWORTH, H. L. *Psychology: Its facts and principles*. New York: Appleton, 1928.

HUDSON, R. L., & AUSTIN, J. B. Effect of context and category name on the recall of categorized word lists. *Journal of Experimental Psychology*, 1970, **86**, 43–47.

HYDE, T. S., & JENKINS, J. J. Differential effects of incidental tasks on the organization of recall of a list of highly associated words. *Journal of Experimental Psychology*, 1969, **82**, 472–481.

JAMES, W. *Principles of psychology*, New York: Holt, 1890.

JOHNSON, N. F. The role of chunking and organization in the process of recall. In G. H. Bower (Ed.), *The psychology of learning and motivation*. Vol. 4. New York: Academic Press, 1970.

JOHNSTON, C. D., & JENKINS, J. J. Two more incidental tasks that differentially affect associative clustering in recall. *Journal of Experimental Psychology*, 1971, **89**, 92–95.

KINTSCH, W. Models for free recall and recognition. In D. A. Norman (Ed.), *Models of human memory*. New York: Academic Press, 1970.

KOFFKA, K. *Principles of Gestalt psychology*. New York: Harcourt, Brace & World, 1935.

KÖHLER, W. *Gestalt psychology*. New York: Liveright, 1947.

LACHMAN, R., & FIELD, W. H. Recognition and recall of verbal material as a function of degree of training. *Psychonomic Science*, 1965, **2**, 225–226.

LACHMAN, R., LAUGHERY, K. R., & FIELD, W. H. Recognition and recall of high frequency words following serial learning. *Psychonomic Science*, 1966, **4**, 225–226.

LAUER, P. A., & BATTIG, W. F. Free recall of taxonomically and alphabetically organized word lists as a function of storage and retrieval cues. *Journal of Verbal Learning and Verbal Behavior*, 1972, **11**, 333–342.

LIGHT, L. L. Homonyms and synonyms as retrieval cues. *Journal of Experimental Psychology*, 1972, **96**, 255–262.

LIGHT, L. L., & CARTER-SOBELL, L. Effects of changed semantic context on recognition memory. *Journal of Verbal Learning and Verbal Behavior*, 1970, **9**, 1–11.

MANDLER, G. Organization and memory. In K. W. Spence & J. T. Spence (Eds.), *The psychology of learning and motivation*. Vol. 1. New York: Academic Press, 1967. (a)

MANDLER, G. Verbal learning. In, *New directions of psychology, III*. New York: Holt, Rinehart & Winston, 1967. (b)

MANDLER, G. Organization and recognition. In E. Tulving & W. Donaldson (Eds.), *Organization of memory*. New York: Academic Press, 1972.

MARTIN, E. Stimulus meaningfulness and paired-associate transfer: An encoding variability hypothesis. *Psychological Review*, 1968, **75**, 421–441.

MARTIN, E. Stimulus component independence. *Journal of Verbal Learning and Verbal Behavior*, 1971, **10**, 715–721.

MARTIN, E. Stimulus encoding in learning and transfer. In A. W. Melton & E. Martin (Eds.), *Coding processes in human memory*. Washington, D. C.: Winston, 1972.

MCCORMACK, P. D. Recognition memory: How complex a retrieval system? *Canadian Journal of Psychology*, 1972, **26**, 19–41.

MCLEOD, P. D., WILLIAMS, C. E., & BROADBENT, D. E. Free recall with assistance from one and from two retrieval cues. *British Journal of Psychology*, 1971, **62**, 59–65.

MELTON, A. W. Implications of short-term memory for a general theory of memory. *Journal of Verbal Learning and Verbal Behavior*, 1963, **2**, 1–21.

MELTON, A. W., & MARTIN, E. (Eds.). *Coding processes in human memory*. Washington, D. C.: Winston, 1972.

MIKULA, G. Der Einfluss mnemotechnischer Hilfen auf das Erlernen und Behalten verbalen Materials. *Psychologische Forschung*, 1971, **34**, 312–324.

MURDOCK, B. B. *Human short-term memory*. Potomac, Md.: Lawrence Earlbaum Associates, in press.

MURDOCK, B. B., JR., & BABICK, A. J. The effect of repetition on the retention of individual words. *American Journal of Psychology*, 1961, **74**, 596–601.

NORMAN, D. A. Toward a theory of memory and attention. *Psychological Review*, 1968, **75**, 522–536.

NORMAN, D. A., & RUMELHART, D. E. A system for perception and memory. In D. A. Norman (Ed.), *Models of human memory*. New York: Academic Press, 1970.

PAIVIO, A., & CSAPO, K. Picture superiority in free recall: Imagery or dual coding? (Research Bulletin No. 243) London: University of Western Ontario, Department of Psychology, 1972.

POSNER, M. I., & WARREN, R. E. Traces, concepts, and conscious constructions. In A. W. Melton & E. Martin (Eds.), *Coding processes in human memory*. Washington, D. C.: Winston, 1972.

POSTMAN, L. Short-term memory and incidental learning. In A. W. Melton (Ed.), *Categories of human learning*. New York: Academic Press, 1964.

POSTMAN, L. A pragmatic view of organization theory. In E. Tulving & W. Donaldson (Eds.), *Organization of memory*. New York: Academic Press, 1972.

POSTMAN, L., ADAMS, A., & PHILLIPS, L. W. Studies in incidental learning: II. The effects of association value and of the method of testing. *Journal of Experimental Psychology*, 1955, **49**, 1–10.

PUFF, C. R. Clustering as a function of the sequential organization of stimulus word lists. *Journal of Verbal Learning and Verbal Behavior*, 1966, **5**, 503–506.

RIEGEL, K. F. Free associative responses to the 200 stimuli of the Michigan restricted association norms. (USPHS Tech. Rep. No. 8, Grant MH 07619) Ann Arbor: University of Michigan, 1965.

SCHULMAN, A. J. Recognition memory for targets from a scanned word list. *British Journal of Psychology*, 1971, **62**, 335–346.

SHIFFRIN, R. M. Memory search. In D. A. Norman (Ed.), *Models of human memory*. New York: Academic Press, 1970.

SHIFFRIN, R. M., & ATKINSON, R. C. Storage and retrieval processes in long-term memory. *Psychological Review*, 1969, **76**, 179–193.

SLAMECKA, N. J. Testing for associative storage in multitrial free recall. *Journal of Experimental Psychology*, 1969, **81**, 557–560.

SLAMECKA, N. J. The question of associative growth in the learning of categorized material. *Journal of Verbal Learning and Verbal Behavior*, 1972, **11**, 324–332.

THOMSON, D. M. Context effects in recognition memory. *Journal of Verbal Learning and Verbal Behavior*, 1972, **11**, 497–511.

THOMSON, D. M., & TULVING, E. Associative encoding and retrieval: Weak and strong cues. *Journal of Experimental Psychology*, 1970, **86**, 255–262.

TULVING, E. Theoretical issues in free recall. In T. R. Dixon & D. L. Horton (Eds.), *Verbal behavior and general behavior theory*. Englewood Cliffs, N. J.: Prentice-Hall, 1968. (a)

TULVING, E. When is recall higher than recognition? *Psychonomic Science*, 1968, **10**, 53–54. (b)

TULVING, E. Episodic and semantic memory. In E. Tulving & W. Donaldson (Eds.), *Organization of memory*. New York: Academic Press, 1972.

TULVING, E., & OSLER, S. Effectiveness of retrieval cues in memory for words. *Journal of Experimental Psychology*, 1968, **77**, 593–601.

TULVING, E., & PEARLSTONE, Z. Availability versus accessibility of information in memory for words. *Journal of Verbal Learning and Verbal Behavior*, 1966, **5**, 381–391.

TULVING, E., & PSOTKA, J. Retroactive inhibition in free recall: Inaccessibility of information available in the memory store. *Journal of Experimental Psychology*, 1971, **87**, 1–8.

TULVING, E., & THOMSON, D. M. Retrieval processes in recognition memory: Effects of associative context. *Journal of Experimental Psychology*, 1971, **87**, 116–124.

TVERSKY, B. Encoding processes in recognition and recall. *Cognitive Psychology*, in press.

UNDERWOOD, B. J. False recognition produced by implicit verbal response. *Journal of Experimental Psychology*, 1965, **70**, 122–129.

UNDERWOOD, B. J. Attributes of memory. *Psychological Review*, 1969, **76**, 559–573.

UNDERWOOD, B. J. Are we overloading memory? In A. W. Melton & E. Martin, (Eds.), *Coding processes in human memory*. Washington, D. C.: Winston, 1972.

WATKINS, M. J. When is recall spectacularly higher than recognition? *Journal of Experimental Psychology*, 1973, in press.

WICKENS, D. D. Encoding categories of words: An empirical approach to meaning. *Psychological Review*, 1970, **77**, 1–15.

WINOGRAD, E., & CONN, C. P. Evidence from recognition memory for specific encoding of unmodified homographs. *Journal of Verbal Learning and Verbal Behavior*, 1971, **10**, 702–706.

WINOGRAD, E., KARCHMER, M. A., & RUSSELL, I. S. Role of encoding unitization in cued recognition memory. *Journal of Verbal Learning and Verbal Behavior*, 1971, **10**, 199–206.

WOOD, G. Category names as cues for the recall of category instances. *Psychonomic Science*, 1967, **9**, 323–324.

YATES, F. A. *The art of memory*. Chicago: University of Chicago Press, 1966.

YNTEMA, D. B., & TRASK, F. P. Recall as a search process. *Journal of Verbal Learning and Verbal Behavior*, 1963, **2**, 65–74.

40

FUNCTIONAL ASPECTS OF RECOLLECTIVE EXPERIENCE

John M. Gardiner

Source: *Memory & Cognition*, 16(4) (1988): 309–313.

The functional relationship between recognition memory and conscious awareness was examined in two experiments in which subjects indicated when recognizing a word whether or not they could consciously recollect its prior occurrence in the study list. Both levels of processing and generation effects were found to occur only for recognition accompanied by conscious recollection. Recognition in the absence of conscious recollection, although less likely, was generally reliable and uninfluenced by encoding conditions. These results are consistent with dual-process theories of recognition, which assume that recognition and priming in implicit memory have a common component. And they strengthen the case for making a functional distinction between episodic memory and other memory systems.

The function of conscious awareness in memory has gained a fresh importance in contemporary memory research. This importance stems largely from two related sets of findings: neuropsychological findings from studies with amnesic patients and findings of related patterns of functional dissociation from studies with memory-unimpaired adults. Both sets of findings can be described in terms of the distinction that has been made between *explicit* and *implicit* memory tests (Graf & Schacter, 1985; see Schacter, 1987, for a recent review). Explicit memory tests are those in which subjects are asked to remember, in the sense of being able consciously to recollect, prior events and experiences. Such tests include conventional episodic memory tests such as recognition and recall. Implicit memory tests are those in which the conscious recollection of prior events and experiences is not required. Such tests include perceptual identification, lexical decision, and word-stem and word-fragment completion. The priming effects observed in these implicit memory tests (superior performance on items that have been previously encountered in the experiment) are the hub of both related sets of findings. Despite their very poor performance in explicit memory tests, amnesic patients have often been found to exhibit normal or near-normal priming effects, and, in memory-unimpaired adults, priming effects typically have been found either to be uninfluenced by variables, such as levels of processing, that have large effects in explicit memory, or to be influenced in opposite ways by such variables. Unquestionably, therefore, there are fundamental differences in the nature of the memory observed in tests of explicit and implicit memory, and the function of conscious awareness is pivotally important to these differences.

Memory theorists have advocated two alternative conceptualizations of the differences between explicit and implicit memory. Some theorists have proposed that these differences reflect the operation of functionally distinct memory systems. One such proposal distinguishes between procedural and declarative memory (Squire, 1982; Squire & Cohen, 1984). Another distinguishes between three memory systems – procedural, semantic, and episodic memory (Tulving, 1983, 1985a). According to these theories, the neuro-psychological findings are interpreted as evidence that the amnesic syndrome is selective in that it damages particular memory systems and spares others. Similarly, functional dissociations between explicit and implicit memory performance in memory-unimpaired adults are interpreted as evidence that different memory systems are tapped by the two sorts of test.

Other theorists have argued against a memory systems approach and have proposed instead that the differences between explicit and implicit memory performance are more appropriately conceptualized in terms of a process analysis that is based on a more unitary view of memory representation. These theorists typically distinguish between two sorts of processing, or kinds of encoded information, such as between conceptually driven and data-driven processing (Jacoby, 1983; Roediger & Blaxton, 1987) or between the elaboration and integration of stimulus information (Graf & Mandler, 1984; Mandler, 1980). According to these theories, the neuropsychological findings are interpreted as evidence that memory is impaired with respect to one sort of processing (or kind of information) and that the other sort of processing remains relatively intact. Similarly, functional dissociations between explicit and implicit memory performance in memory-unimpaired adults are interpreted as evidence that different sorts of processing are more or less appropriate for the different types of test. Furthermore, on the strength of findings that certain variables also have parallel effects on recognition memory performance and on priming (e.g., Jacoby & Dallas, 1981), theorists of this persuasion have argued additionally that recognition and priming have a component in common, and that recognition therefore entails both sorts of processing (but see Squire, Shimamura, & Graf, 1985; Watkins & Gibson, in press).

The purpose of the present article is to describe some findings that are of interest in relation to these issues and that involve a different empirical approach. This approach makes use of a technique suggested by Tulving (1985b) for measuring, rather than manipulating, the nature of subjects' conscious awareness during the memory test. Tulving (1985b) described two experiments in which he required subjects to put an "R," for "remember," next to items in the test whose prior occurrence in the study list they could consciously recollect and a "K," for "know," next to items they recalled or recognized on some other basis. One experiment showed that the proportion of "remember" responses decreased systematically from uncued through cued recall. Another, recognition memory, experiment showed that the proportion of "remember" responses decreased over a 1-week retention interval and that it was positively correlated with subjects' rated confidence in the accuracy of their responses. These demonstrations show that subjects can make meaningful judgments about their conscious experience in memory tests. They also support Tulving's (1983, 1985a, 1985b) conception of retrieval as a joint product of encoding and retrieval information, which in turn gives rise to feelings of conscious recollection.

In contrast to Tulving's (1985b) emphasis on retrieval factors, the focus of the present article is on the influence of encoding factors on subjects' conscious experience. More particularly, the purpose of this study was to determine the functional relationship between two well-known episodic memory phenomena—levels of processing and generation effects—and conscious experience in recognition memory.

No very strong grounds seem to exist for predicting a particular form for this relationship, and at least some possible relationships would not be of much interest. For example, one relatively uninteresting, but quite plausible, possibility is that "remember" and "know" responses might similarly be influenced by encoding conditions, but with "know" responses being generally less likely. This outcome would be expected if "remember" and "know" measures were merely equivalent to confidence ratings, because there is evidence that such encoding conditions affect recognition of words for which subjects give low confidence ratings, as well as words for which they give high confidence ratings (see, e.g., Slamecka & Graf, 1978). Also, this outcome could all too readily be interpreted in terms of the simple notion that "remember" and "know" responses reflect nothing more or other than strong and weak memory traces.

Tulving's (1983, 1985a, 1985b) proposal of separate procedural, semantic, and episodic memory systems suggests a more interesting possibility. According to this proposal, different kinds of conscious awareness are postulated for each system and recollective experience is a *defining* property of episodic memory, which implies that there should be an essentially perfect correlation between recollective experience and such episodic memory phenomena as levels of processing and generation effects. In this eventuality, recognition memory in the absence of conscious recollection may be linked with priming effects in implicit memory tests, and the overall results would be consistent with dual-process theories of recognition that maintain that recognition and priming have a common component.

Experiment 1

In Experiment 1, encoding conditions were manipulated by giving the subjects incidental learning instructions and orienting tasks that involved encoding either at a phonemic or at a semantic level. Following many previous demonstrations of levels of processing effects (see, e.g., Craik & Tulving, 1975), recognition memory performance was expected to be superior after the semantic orienting task. The subjects were instructed in the test that when recognizing a word they were to indicate whether they were able consciously to recollect its prior occurrence in the study list ("remember") or whether they recognized it on some other basis ("know"). The point of the experiment was to relate the levels of processing effect to the nature of subjects' conscious awareness in the recognition test.

Method

Subjects

The subjects were 32 undergraduates at The City University, London; most were students in an introductory laboratory course. They were tested in small groups, they participated in the experiment without pay, and they were allocated arbitrarily to one of the two between-subjects conditions.

Design

All subjects were presented with a list of 36 words; 16 subjects had to produce a semantic associate for each word, and 16 subjects had to produce a rhyming word. The subjects were told that these tasks were for the collection of normative free association data. One hour later the subjects were given a recognition test consisting of the 36 words from the study list together with 36 lure words. They were required to circle words they recognized from the study list and indicate whether or not their recognition was accompanied by conscious recollection. Target words and lure words were yoked across groups, and within each group target words for half the subjects were lure words for the other half.

Procedure

The 72 words used in the experiment were all common one-syllable or two-syllable nouns. They were divided arbitrarily into two sets of 36 for use as target words and lure words. Study lists were presented in booklets with one words per page. For one group of subjects, the first page of the booklet consisted of instructions to write down next to each word the first word that came to mind that rhymed with the given word, or a word that sounded very much like it. For the other group of subjects, the instructions were to write down next to each word the first word that came to mind that was semantically or meaningfully related to the given word. The subjects were told that the tasks were typical free association tasks used for collecting normative data. The orienting tasks were self-paced, but no systematic difference in their duration was observed; subjects typically took about 5 sec/item. There was then a 1-h retention interval during which subjects attended a practical class.

The order of words in the study list was randomized separately for each subject, but the words in the recognition test were presented in a single constant order, typed in three columns of 24 words each. In this test the subjects were told to work carefully down each column in turn, drawing a circle around each word that they recognized from the study list. In addition, the test was immediately preceded by instructions explaining that at the time they recognized each word, they were also to write an "R," for "remember," if their recognition of the word was accompanied by a conscious recollection of its prior occurrence in the study booklet or a "K," for "know," if they did not consciously recollect the word's occurrence in the study booklet but recognized it on some other basis. "Remember" was defined in these instructions as the ability to become consciously aware again of some aspect or aspects of what happened or what was experienced at the time the word was presented (e.g., aspects of the physical appearance of the word, or of something that happened in the room, or of what one was thinking or doing at that time). "Know" responses were defined as the recognition that the word was in the booklet but the inability to recollect consciously anything about its actual occurrence or what happened or what was experienced at the time of its occurrence. To further illustrate this distinction, the instructions pointed out that if asked one's own name, one would typically respond in the "know" sense, that is, without becoming consciously aware of anything about a particular event or experience; however, when asked what movie one saw last, one would typically respond in the "remember" sense, that is, becoming consciously aware again of some aspects of the particular experience. One subject failed to write any "R" and "K" responses in the test, and this subject was replaced.

Results

The data were analyzed separately in terms of the probability of "remember" and "know" responses for correct recognition judgments and for false positive errors (i.e., in each case the overall mean probability of making a recognition judgment is the sum of the separate mean probabilities of

466

"remember" and "know" responses). These data are summarized in Figure 1. As Figure 1 shows, there was a strong levels of processing effect, but this effect occurred only for words whose recognition was accompanied by conscious recollection. Recognition in the absence of such recollective experience was less likely, but far from negligible, and it was quite uninfluenced by level of processing. These observations are supported by the results of an analysis of variance (ANOVA) carried out on individual subjects' correct recognition scores, with levels of processing and response type as factors.[1] Both the main effect of levels [$F(1,30) = 16.74$, $p < .001$, $MSe = .01$] and that of response type [$F(1,30) = 92.97$, $p < .001$] were significant, as was the interaction between them [$F(1,30) = 5.02$, $p < .05$, $MSe = .03$ in each case]. The extremely low false positive rates precluded any statistical analyses of those data, but in both the associate group and in the rhyme group 14 of 16 subjects made more "know" responses to target words than they did to lure words ($p < .001$ by sign test), with two ties in each case.

Experiment 2

In Experiment 2, encoding conditions were manipulated by giving subjects a list of words, half of which had to be generated in the context of a given rule and half of which had to be read. Following many previous demonstrations of generation effects (see e.g., Slamecka & Graf, 1978), recognition memory performance was expected to be superior after the generate task. The subjects were given instructions in the test that were similar to those given in Experiment 1. The point of the experiment was to relate the generation effect to the nature of the subjects' conscious awareness in the test. In addition, however, Experiment 2 was designed to provide further information about the effects of retention interval, so recognition tests were given at two retention intervals, 1 h and 1 week, with a different group of subjects assigned to each retention interval.

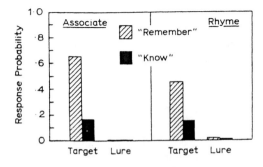

Figure 1 Response probability as a function of levels of processing.

Method

Subjects

The subjects were 40 undergraduate students at The City University, London, who were allocated arbitrarily into one of two equal groups, tested individually, and were paid for their participation in the experiment.

Design

All subjects studied a list of 24 common pairs of opposites, 12 of which were generated and 12 read. Half the subjects were given a recognition test 1 h later, and half were given the test 1 week later. In the test, the 24 target words were mixed with 24 lure words, and the subjects were required to indicate whether or not each recognition judgment was accompanied by conscious recollection. Within each retention interval group, the 48 words used in the experiment were fully rotated across presentation and test conditions.

Procedure

A set of 48 common pairs of opposites was compiled, with one member of the pair designated the stimulus, the other the response. The pairs were selected on the basis of pretrials, which indicated that given the stimulus and the first letter of the response, successful generation of the designated target was guaranteed. The 48 pairs were arbitrarily split into two sets of 24 for use as the alternate study lists. Half the subjects in each group studied one list, half the other. Within each list, but across subjects, each word pair was used equally often in generate and read conditions. Each word pair was printed on a separate card. In the generate condition only the first letter of the target word was printed; in the read condition the target word was printed in full. The cards were presented at a 5-sec rate, and the subjects were told the "rule" was opposites and were instructed to say aloud the response words in each case, whether generated or read, and to study them for a subsequent memory test, the nature of which was not specified. A separate random order of items within the list was used for each subject.

The recognition test consisted of all 48 response words, arranged in a constant random order of three columns with 16 words in each. The tests were given 1 h or 1 week after the study session. Some of the subjects in the 1-h group attended a lecture during that time, but for the most part the retention interval was unfilled. The test instructions given were similar to those given in Experiment 1. Two subjects in the 1-week retention interval group failed to comply with the instructions, and data from these subjects were excluded from analysis; to balance the numbers, data from two corresponding subjects in the 1-h retention interval group were also excluded.

468

Results

The data were analyzed in the same manner as in Experiment 1 and are summarized in Figure 2. As Figure 2 shows, there were large generation effects, and these effects occurred only for words whose recognition was accompanied by conscious recollection of their prior occurrence in the study list. The generation effect seems attenuated but still present after a 1-week retention interval, and the decline in recognition performance after a 1-week interval, like the generation effect itself, seems similarly confined to words whose recognition was accompanied by recollective experience. False positive rates were somewhat greater in Experiment 2 than in Experiment 1, and after 1 week increased somewhat, especially for recognition judgments made in the absence of recollective experience: for these "know" responses, there was little apparent difference between false positive and hit rates.

The foregoing observations are supported by the results of an ANOVA carried out on individual subjects' correct recognition scores, with generate versus read conditions, retention interval, and response type as factors. All main effects were significant: $F(1,34) = 35.23$, $p < .001$, $MSe = .01$, for the generation effect; $F(1,34) = 6.35$, $p < .05$, $MSe = .03$, for retention interval; and $F(1,34) = 39.63$, $p < .001$, $MSe = .06$, for response type. The interaction between encoding conditions and response type was significant $[F(1,34) = 29.47, p < .001, MSe = .02]$, as were those between response type and retention interval $[F(1,34) = 6.90, p < .05, MSe = .06]$ and between encoding conditions and retention interval $[F(1,34) = 7.10, p < .05, MSe = .01]$. The three-way interaction was not significant $[F(1,39) = 2.06, MSe = .02]$.

The results of a comparable ANOVA on false positive responses showed only a significant effect of retention interval $[F(1,34) = 19.38, p < .001, MSe = .01]$, with $F < 1$ for the main effect of response type, and $F(1,34) = 2.66$ for the interaction between response type and retention interval ($MSe = .01$ in each case). At the 1-week retention interval, only 9 of 16 subjects made more "know" responses to target words than they did to lure words; there were

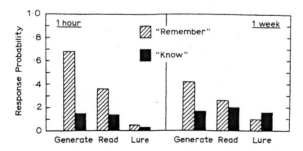

Figure 2 Response probability as a function of generate versus read conditions and retention interval.

two ties. At the 1-h retention interval, 15 of 16 subjects made more "know" responses to target words than they did to lure words, again with two ties ($p < .001$ by sign test). After 1 week, therefore, in contrast with 1 h, subjects were unable in the absence of conscious recollection reliably to distinguish target words from lures.

General discussion

Both levels of processing and generation effects were found to occur only for words whose recognition was accompanied by conscious recollection. Recognition in the absence of recollective experience, although less likely, was generally reliable, and it was completely uninfluenced by encoding conditions. The clear-cut nature of this dissociation argues against the possibility that "remember" and "know" responses simply reflect strong and weak traces, for even weak traces should be influenced to some extent by encoding conditions. Rather, it suggests some correspondence with functional dissociations previously observed in studies that have manipulated conscious awareness by comparing performance in explicit and in implicit memory tests (see Schacter, 1987). Of additional interest in this connection is the finding in Experiment 2 that recognition memory in the absence of conscious recollection does not appear to persist for as long as a week.[2]

More particularly, the overall results are consistent with the assumption that recognition memory may entail two processes, one of which may also give rise to priming effects in implicit memory tests (see, e.g., Graf & Mandler, 1984; Jacoby & Dallas, 1981; Mandler, 1980). The "implicit" component is assumed by these theorists to reflect data-driven, rather than conceptually driven, processing, or stimulus integration rather than elaboration, and to be dependent mainly on prior exposure to the stimulus. Speculatively, the results suggest that "know" responses may be a relatively pure measure of this component, whereas "remember" responses may be primarily a measure of the "explicit" component, which reflects conceptual or elaborative processing. If this is so, it should be possible to establish further, convergent links between these measures and the two sorts of processing.

From the standpoint of Tulving's (1983, 1985a, 1985b) distinction between procedural, semantic, and episodic memory systems, conscious recollection is a defining property of episodic memory. The case for making a functional distinction between episodic memory and other memory systems is therefore materially strengthened by evidence that such staple episodic memory phenomena as levels of processing and generation effects are indeed truly episodic, as defined and measured by the nature of subjects' conscious awareness. "Know" responses, by this account, may reflect semantic memory priming or even, perhaps, a form of procedural memory. If this is so, it should be possible to use these measures to examine directly the interface between episodic and other memory systems.

Thus it seems that these measures of consciousness in memory may usefully supplement our understanding of explicit and implicit memory performance. It is also quite possible, however, that there may turn out to be a more optimal way of measuring explicit and implicit components of conscious awareness, and some priority in future research should be given to further elucidating the nature of the measures per se. Further evidence on the relation between these measures and confidence ratings would, for example, clearly be desirable. So, too, would evidence about whether there is any *necessary* correlation between the proportion of "remember" and "know" responses and level of performance. For the moment, these matters, and other related issues that might well be raised, are left unresolved. But at least the present study—together with that of Tulving (1985b)—seems to offer a promising beginning.

Notes

I am grateful to Endel Tulving for helpful discussion, and to Rosalind Java and Gerard Whittaker for their help with data collection and analysis.

1   The treatment of response type as an independent variable in this analysis is questionable, and perhaps this factor is more properly regarded as a dependent variable. On the other hand, one might suggest that the analysis is not unreasonable, even if its legitimacy is somewhat questionable, and it seems unlikely that any alternative statistical approach would lead to very different conclusions about the pattern of results observed.
2   It is intriguing that this finding is associated with an increase in the proportion of "know" responses to lures, but it is not easy to see what this might signify.

References

CRAIK, F. I. M., & TULVING, E. (1975). Depth of processing and the retention of words in episodic memory. *Journal of Experimental Psychology: General*, **104**, 268–294.

GRAF, P., & MANDLER, G. (1984). Activation makes words more accessible, but not necessarily more retrievable. *Journal of Verbal Learning & Verbal Behavior*, **23**, 553–568.

GRAF, P., & SCHACTER, D. L. (1985). Implicit and explicit memory for new associations in normal and amnesic subjects. *Journal of Experimental Psychology: Learning, Memory, & Cognition*, **11**, 501–518.

JACOBY, L. L. (1983). Remembering the data: Analyzing interactive processes in reading. *Journal of Verbal Learning & Verbal Behavior*, **22**, 485–508.

JACOBY, L. L., & DALLAS, M. (1981). On the relationship between autobiographical memory and perceptual learning. *Journal of Experimental Psychology: General*, **3**, 306–340.

MANDLER, G. (1980). Recognizing: The judgment of previous occurrence. *Psychological Review*, **87**, 252–271.

ROEDIGER, H. L., III., & BLAXTON, T. A. (1987). Retrieval modes produce dissociations in memory for surface information. In D. S. Gorfein & R. R. Hoffman

(Eds.), *Memory and cognitive processes: The Ebbinghaus Centennial Conference* (pp. 349–379). Hillsdale, NJ: Erlbaum.

SCHACTER, D. L. (1987). Implicit memory: History and current status. *Journal of Experimental Psychology: Learning, Memory, & Cognition*, **13**, 501–518.

SLAMECKA, N. J., & GRAF, P. (1978). The generation effect: Delineation of a phenomenon. *Journal of Experimental Psychology: Human Learning & Memory*, **4**, 592–604.

SQUIRE, L. R. (1982). The neuropsychology of human memory. *Annual Review of Neuroscience*, **5**, 241–273.

SQUIRE, L. R., & COHEN, N. J. (1984). Human memory and amnesia. In G. Lynch, J. L. McGaugh, & N. M. Weinberger (Eds.), *Neurobiology of memory* (pp. 3–64). New York: Guilford Press.

SQUIRE, L. R., SHIMAMURA, A. P., & GRAF, P. (1985). Independence of recognition memory and priming effects: A neuropsychological analysis. *Journal of Experimental Psychology: Learning, Memory, & Cognition*, **11**, 37–44.

TULVING, E. (1983). *Elements of episodic memory*. New York: Oxford University Press.

TULVING, E. (1985a). How many memory systems are there? *American Psychologist*, **40**, 385–398.

TULVING, E. (1985b). Memory and consciousness. *Canadian Psychologist*, **26**, 1–12.

WATKINS, M. J., & GIBSON, J. M. (in press). On the relation between perceptual priming and recognition memory. *Journal of Experimental Psychology: Learning, Memory, & Cognition*.

Part 9

SERIAL POSITION EFFECTS

41

TWO STORAGE MECHANISMS
IN FREE RECALL[1]

Murray Glanzer and Anita R. Cunitz

Source: *Journal of Verbal Learning and Verbal Behavior*, 5 (1966): 351–360.

Two experiments were carried out to test the hypothesis that the bimodal serial position curve in free recall is produced by output from two storage mechanisms—short-term and long-term. Experimental operations were applied that were predicted to have a distinct effect on each of these mechanisms, and the changes in the serial position curve were observed. In the first experiment, presentation rate and repetition of individual words were varied in order to affect long-term storage and thereby affect the beginning sections of the serial position curve. Presentation rate has the predicted effect of differentially raising the beginning section of the serial position curve. It does not affect the end section. Repetition, however, did not have any effect that could not be ascribed to presentation rate. It could not, therefore, be used to demonstrate independently the predicted differential effect. In the second experiment, delay between end of list and recall was varied in order to affect short-term storage and, thereby, the end section of the serial position curve. The predicted effect was clearly demonstrated. The results make it possible to systematize a number of findings in the literature.

In a free-recall task, *S* is presented with a series of words, which he then tries to recall. He is permitted to recall the words in any order that he wishes. The data obtained from this task characteristically show a pronounced serial position effect. The plot of the probability of recall as a function of the position of the word in presentation is U-shaped, with the beginning peak usually lower than the end peak.

The hypothesis proposed here is that the U-shaped serial position curve consists of two curves, each curve representing output from a separate storage mechanism. One is a long-term storage mechanism, the other is a short-term storage mechanism. It follows from the assumption of a long-term and short-term storage mechanism that the material recalled from the beginning of the list should be primarily output from long-term storage, that from the end of the list primarily output from short-term storage. From the initial decline in the serial position curve and the preceding statement, it may be further asserted that the capacity of long-term storage is limited. The more items that are already in, the less likely that there will be place for a new item. By definition, the short-term storage mechanism is limited not with respect to capacity but with respect to the amount of time it can hold an item.

The proposal then is to view the usual serial position curve as a composite of two output curves—one, declining from beginning to end of list, represents output from long-term storage. The other, rising from beginning to end of list, represents output from short-term storage. The amount of overlap between the two curves in a given set of data cannot be specified at present. It is, in part, the aim of this study to develop information on this point.

The distinction between long-term and short-term storage has been developed in the work of Hebb (1949) and Broadbent (1958). Experimental work on short-term storage has been carried out by a number of investigators, starting from the work of Broadbent (1958), Brown (1958), Conrad (1957), and Peterson and Peterson (1959). This work, including a study using a two-factor approach (Waugh, 1960) that has points of similarity with the one used here, has been concerned almost wholly with fixed-order recall.[2] Surveys of the developments in the area and the theoretical questions involved may be found in recent papers by Melton (1963) and Postman (1964).

In order to support the view proposed above, the attempt will be made here to separate the two hypothesized curves. This will be done by means of experimental operations which have a differential effect on the beginning and end sections of the serial position curve. As will be pointed out subsequently, some of these differential effects have already been demonstrated in the literature.

There are well-established procedures that are used to produce long-term storage. These are rote-learning procedures. The variables that affect the efficiency of rote learning—presentation rate, number of presentations, meaningfulness, etc.—suggest the operations that should have their effect on the beginning section of the serial position curve. Short-term storage should, by definition, be affected primarily by the amount of time which has elapsed since presentation. This variable, amount of time elapsed, should therefore have its effect on the end section of the serial position curve.

The aim of this study is, then, to test the hypothesis that there are two distinct storage mechanisms that produce the serial position curve in free recall. The strategy is to use variables which should have one effect on one storage mechanism and a different effect (either no effect or an opposed effect) on the other storage mechanism. These variables should give predictable changes in the shape of the serial position curve.

Experiment I

The purpose of this experiment was to change the shape of the beginning of the serial position curve by affecting, primarily, the efficiency of long-term storage. The two main variables used were interval between successive items, or presentation rate, and repetition of items in the list. Since an increase in the interval between items usually facilitates rote learning, an increase should raise the beginning but not the end section of the serial position curve. By the same reasoning, repeated presentation of an item should have the same effect.

Method

There were five main experimental treatments generated by two experimental variables—spacing, or the interval between successive words (S), and number of presentations of each word in the list (P): single spacing and presentation (1S/P)—each word presented once at a 3-sec rate; double spacing (2S)— each word presented once at a 6-sec rate; triple spacing (3S)—each word presented once at a 9-sec rate. There was a further subdivision of the 2S and 3S treatments noted below.

Parallel to the 2S and 3S conditions, were the 2P and 3P conditions: 2P— each word presented twice in succession, all at a 3-sec rate; 3P—each word presented three times in succession, all at a 3-sec rate. (A new word, however, appeared only every 6 or 9 sec.) Since the number of different words in each list was always the same, the total time taken to present a 2P and 2S list was the same. Similarly, the total time taken to present a 3P and 3S list was the same. The S conditions, depending on the location of the additional inter-item intervals, were further subdivided into SA and SB conditions. If the 1S/P condition[3] is taken and an additional 3-sec interval is inserted after each word, a 2SA (after) condition is obtained. If the additional 3-sec interval is inserted before each word, a 2SB (before) condition is obtained. Similar placements of an additional 6-sec interval produce a 3SA and 3SB condition. The effect of these placements made a difference only at the beginning and end of the lists. In 2SA and 3SA an additional interval occurred between the last word of the list and the signal for recall; in 2SB and 3SB the additional interval occurred between the ready signal and the first word.

The main reason for using the two forms of the 2S and 3S conditions was to determine the source of possible differences between the 2S versus 2P, and 3S versus 3P conditions. If only one form of the S conditions had been used, differences between the S and corresponding P conditions might be interpreted as a result of differences in the interval between the first presentation of a repeated word and its recall, or differences in the interval between the last presentation of a repeated word and its recall. (If the 2S condition is viewed as identical with the 2P condition except for the elimination of one of the two presentations of each word, then elimination of the second member of each pair gives the 2SA condition, while elimination of the first member of each pair gives the 2SB condition. Similarly, elimination of the last two presentations of each repeated word in the 3P condition gives the 3SA condition, while elimination of the first two presentations of each repeated word gives the 3SB condition.) A secondary reason for using the two forms of the S condition was to obtain further information on the effect of delays without an interpolated task on recall.

Procedure

All Ss were presented with two 5-word practice lists and eight 20-word main lists consisting of common one-syllable nouns, drawn from the Thorndike-Lorge (1944) AA lists. The lists, recorded on tapes, were composed of the same words in the same order. They varied for the groups only in the presentation rate, number of repetitions of the individual words, or location of the interitem intervals.

The lists were presented in succession to the Ss during the course of a single session. After each list the Ss had 2 min during which they wrote the words that they recalled, in booklets. Each list was preceded by a ready signal, and followed by a bell that signalled the end of the list and start of the recall period. The Ss were tested in groups of 20.

Subjects

The Ss were 240 Army enlisted men. There were 40 Ss in each of the following conditions: 1S/P, 2SA, 3SA, 2P and 3P. There were 20 Ss in 2SB and in 3SB.

Results

In scoring the lists, a word was considered correct if it was (a) the same as a list word, (b) a homonym, or (c) a recognizable misspelling of either. Thus, if the word "night" was given, "knight" or "nite" would both be scored correct. Repetitions of a word were not counted. The mean number correct for the eight lists at each serial position was computed for each S. These twenty means for each S form the basic data used in the analyses discussed below.

The serial position curves for the alternate forms of the spaced lists (2SA and 2SB; 3SA and 3SB) were examined to determine whether the placing of the interval at the end of the list had any effect. No marked or systematic differences were apparent in the curves. Analysis of variance of the data for

478

the four groups found no significant effect of the placement of the interval (F < 1) and no significant interaction of this variable with the serial position effect, $F(19,2204) = 1.19$, $p > .10$. The interpretation of these findings will be discussed subsequently. Since, however, the variable of interval placement had neither an overall effect nor an effect on the shape of the serial position curve, the subsequent analyses of the data combine groups 2SA and 2SB into one group, and groups 3SA and 3SB into another group. The experimental conditions are therefore reduced to five: 1S/P, 2S, 3S, 2P, and 3P.

Examination of the serial position curves for these conditions (Fig. 1) shows a clear and systematic effect of spacing and a similar but less clear effect of repetition. The curve for the 1S/P condition appears in both the top and bottom half of the figure. As spacing increases, the probability of recall is raised in all but the last few positions of the curve. The end peak remains unaffected. As repetition increases, there is a similar effect in going from the 1S/P condition to the 2P condition, but no further systematic change in going from 2P to 3P. Comparison of the curves in the top half of Fig. 1 with those of the bottom half indicates that repetition has little or no effect beyond that of the spacing between new words.

The data were analyzed by analysis of variance with the five main treatments (1S/P, 2S, 2P, 3S, 3P) as a between-subjects variable and serial position as a within-subjects variable. The four degrees of freedom associated with treatments were then broken down into three components: (a) The general effect of spacing the interval between new words, whether or not repetition occurred between the new words. This was evaluated by comparing 1S/P, 2S + 2P, and 3S + 3P ($df = 2$); (b) The effect of repetitions of the words in addition to the effect of spacing *per se*. This was evaluated by comparing 2S + 3S and 2P + 3P ($df = 1$); (c) The interaction of spacing and repetition ($df = 1$).

The overall effect of treatments is significant, $F(4,235) = 2.69$, $p < .05$. The effect of spacing is significant, $F(2,235) = 4.61$, $p < .025$, but neither the additional effect of repetition ($F < 1$) nor the interaction of spacing with repetition, $F(1,235) = 1.34$, $p > .10$, is significant. The within-subjects effect of serial position is highly significant, $F(19,4465) = 236.66$, $p < .001$. Reduction of the degrees of freedom to 1 and 235, giving a lower-bound, conservative test for a repeated measurements design (Greenhouse and Geisser, 1959), leaves this effect significant at the .001 level. The interaction of spacing with serial position is significant at the .005 level, $F(38,4465) = 1.79$, but is no longer significant under the conservative test, with degrees of freedom reduced to 2 and 235. The remaining interactions are negligible.

The conservative test of the interaction between spacing and serial position is actually doubly conservative, since it does not focus on the specific differences expected under the hypothesis of two storage mechanisms. To focus on the predicted effects, a separate test was made of the effect of the three spacing conditions (1S/P versus 2S + 2P versus 3S + 3P) on the sum of

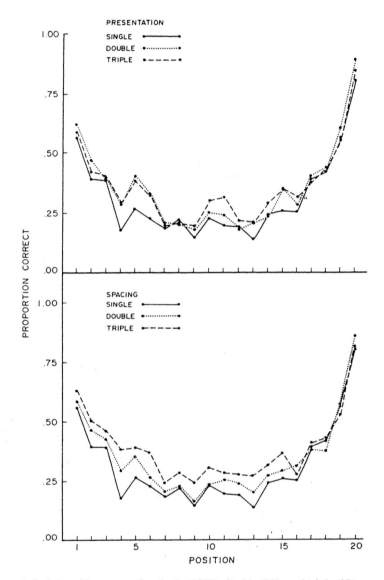

Figure 1 Serial position curves for single (1S/P), double (2P), and triple (3P) presentation above; for single (1S/P), double (2S), and triple (3S) spacing, below. Each point represents the mean for eight lists and either 40 or 60 Ss.

correct responses for successive groups of five serial positions. The degrees of freedom for each of these tests are 2/235. For the first five positions $F = 23.46$, $p < .001$; for the second five, $F = 16.21$, $p < .001$; for the third five $F = 22.00$, $p < .001$. For the last five positions, however, the effect of spacing is not significant—$F = 1.71$, $p > .10$.

It might be argued that absence of significant differences in the last section of the curves is due to a ceiling effect since the probability of recall of the last word is approximately .85. The probabilities of recall for words 15 through 19, however, run lower than the probabilities for positions 1 through 5, which do show significant differences. Comparing the sums for positions 15 through 19 gives an $F = 1.80$, $p > .10$. The ceiling effect cannot, therefore, account for the absence of differences at the end of the curve.

Discussion

The results indicate that spacing, i.e., the rate at which new words are presented, affects the shape of the serial position curve. These results agree with findings of an experiment by Murdock (1962), in which 20-word lists were given at presentation rates of a word every 1 sec and a word every 2 sec. The curves obtained for the two conditions are very similar to those on the bottom of Fig. 1, with the spacing affecting all of the positions except the last few. The presence of a regular ordering of the spacing conditions up to and including the 15th position suggests that the items are still being recruited for long-term storage well towards the end of the list.

It had been expected that adding repetition of the words in the intervals between new words would increase the differences between the serial position curves. This was clearly not so. The repetition, indeed, seems to counteract the spacing effect.

The absence of a repetition effect is surprising for two reasons. First, a preliminary check of the accuracy with which Ss could hear the words in the repeated and corresponding spaced lists indicated, as might be expected, that the Ss heard the words in the repeated lists with slightly more accuracy. The check was carried out by presenting the lists to four groups of Ss drawn from the same population as the experimental groups. Four groups, consisting of 14 to 15 Ss each, listened to the 2S, 2P, 3S, and 3P lists and recorded each new word as they heard it. The interval between the successive words gave the Ss ample time to record each new word. Comparison of the total number correctly recorded in each group indicated a tendency for more words to be recorded accurately by the groups that heard the lists with repeated words. The tendency, however, did not attain statistical significance, $F(1,55) = 3.80$, $.05 < p < .10$.

The absence of a repetition effect is also surprising because in the repeated conditions the Ss had 2 or 3 presentations to learn each word. Viewing the successive repetitions as learning trials leads to the expectation that the probability of recall of a particular word be higher in the repetition condition than in the corresponding spacing condition. It is clear both from the statistical analysis and the curves in Fig. 1 that nothing like this occurred. The curve for the 3P condition actually lies slightly lower than the curve for the 3S condition.

There are several possible reasons for the absence of this effect. One is that simple repetition without active participation by the S may not be effective for learning the words in these lists. Another possible reason is that the particular form of repetition used here—immediately successive repetition—generates effects that counter the effects of learning.

There are two aspects of the data that give information on the effects of delay when no interpolated task is imposed. One is the absence of any effect of spacing on the end peak of the serial position curve. If simple amount of time between presentation and recall were effective, then it would be expected that all points in the end peak would be lowered as spacing increased from 1S/P to 2SA to 3SA. There was no evidence for such an effect. Similarly, it would be expected that all points in the end peak, except the last one, would be lowered as spacing increased from 1S/P to 2SB to 3SB. Again, there was no evidence for such an effect. This is interpreted here as indicating that passage of time without an interpolated task has no effect on short-term storage. The finding is in line with other findings in the literature on fixed-order recall (Brown, 1958).

Another aspect of the data that indicates that pure passage of time does not cause loss in short-term storage is the absence of differences between the 2SA and 2SB conditions, and also between the 3SA and 3SB conditions. In the 2SA and 3SA conditions, there were additional delay periods between end of list and recall. As was noted earlier, these additional delays had no effect. The relevance of these findings to the development of an effective delay procedure will be discussed further in Exp. II.

In summary, the results with the variable that was effective in the experiment—spacing or presentation rate—support the hypothesis. There is an effect on the beginning but not on the end section of the serial position. The results with a second variable, repetition, did not have any overall effect beyond that of spacing and therefore did not furnish any further information for the evaluation of the hypothesis.

Experiment II

The purpose of the second experiment was to study the separate output of the hypothesized short-term storage mechanism. The strategy again was to introduce a variable that would have a different effect on long-term and short-term storage and thus have a different effect on the beginning and end peak of the serial position curve. The variable selected was delay between the end of the list and start of recall.

Before determining the form in which this delay would be imposed, the effects of pure delay, i.e., delay without an interpolated task, were investigated further. The weight of evidence from the fixed-order recall experiments indicates that pure delay has no effect on short-term storage. The subsidiary evidence in Exp. I on the effects of pure delay also indicated that it had no effect. The effects of pure delay were, however, examined further because the interpretation of predicted differential effect of delay would be simplest if no interpolated task were used. There was reason to believe that the free recall task differed sufficiently from the fixed-order recall tasks that had been used, to make it worthwhile to investigate the effects of pure delay on the free-recall task. Moreover, even for the fixed-order recall task there is at least one instance in which pure delay results in a drop in total amount recalled (Anderson, 1960).

A pilot study was, therefore, carried out in which two groups of Ss were each given four 30-word lists, one group with no delay before recall, the other group with 30-sec delay. There was no interpolated task during the delay. A significant reduction of the end peak was found with 30-sec delay, $F(1,233) = 37.00$, $p < .001$. There was no marked effect of delay on the beginning peak, $F(1,233) = 2.67$, $p > .10$. The effect on the end peak was, however, small in magnitude, with the serial position curve showing a clear end peak after a 30-sec delay.

It was therefore decided to require the Ss to carry out a minimal task during the delay periods used in this experiment. It was expected that, under these conditions, as the amount of delay increased, the height of the end peak would decrease but the beginning peak would remain unaffected.

Method

Subjects. The Ss were 46 Army enlisted men.

Materials and Equipment. The words were shown on a screen, with an automatic slide projector. The words were 240 AA monosyllabic nouns drawn from the Thorndike-Lorge list (1944). Each word was printed in black on a light blue background.

Procedure

The S was first shown three 5-word practice lists, and then fifteen 15-word lists. Each word was shown for 1 sec with a 2-sec interval between successive words. The E read each word as it appeared. After the last word in each list, the symbol #, or a digit from 0 to 9 was shown. If the cross-hatch symbol appeared, E said "write," and the S immediately started writing all the words he could recall in his test booklet. If a number appeared, the S started counting out loud from that number until E said "write." While the S was counting, E would measure either 10 or 30 sec with a stop watch before telling him to write. Each of the delay conditions was used with each of the three practice lists and with five of the main lists. The Ss were individually tested. For each S the words were assigned at random to the lists and order of the delay conditions within the three practice lists and within the fifteen main lists was assigned at random. This meant that each S received a different set of lists and a different sequence of delay conditions.

After each list, the *S* was given a minimum of 1 min and a maximum of 5 min to complete his recall of each list. After the completion of each session *E* went over the booklet with the *S* to make sure that all the words were legible.

Results

The results are summarized in Fig. 2. Each curve represents 5 lists recalled by the 46 *S*s. The 10-sec delay was sufficient to remove most of the end peak. With a 30-sec delay there is no trace at all of the end peak.[4]

Analysis of variance was carried with positions, and delay interval as within-subjects variables. Both variables and their interaction are significant at the .001 level or better—position $F(14,630) = 24.87$, delay interval, $F(2,90) = 19.75$, and their interaction, $F(28,1260) = 2.29$. Evaluation of the *F*s with reduced degrees of freedom, here 1 and 45, leaves the effect of position and delay interval both significant at the .001 level. The interaction, however, is not significant, under this conservative test. Since, however, the effect was specifically predicted for the end peak, a separate analysis was made of the effect of the delay condition on the sum of correct responses for successive sets of five positions in the curves. The degrees of freedom for these tests are 1/45. For the first five positions, $F = 3.60$, $p > .05$; for the second five

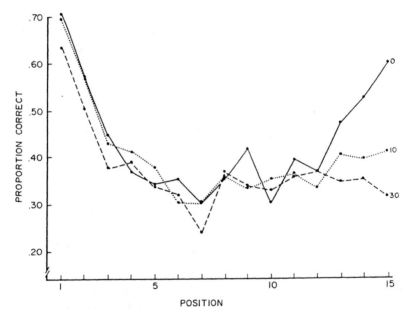

Figure 2 Serial position curves for 0-, 10-, and 30-sec delay. Each point represents the mean for five lists and 46 *S*s.

positions $F = 1.44$, $p > .10$. The effect of delay is significant only in the last five positions—$F = 22.42$, $p < .001$.

There is one characteristic of the no-delay curve that makes it differ from the usual serial position curve—the end peak is lower than the beginning peak. This may be due to the special characteristics of this experiment, in which S was exposed to delay conditions that lowered the efficiency of recall of items from the end of the list. This could have led to a strategy for handling the lists that emphasized the beginning items of the list.

Discussion

The results of Exp. II give further support to the hypothesis of two distinct storage mechanisms. Again, it was demonstrated that an experimental operation had a predicted, differential effect on the peaks of the serial position curve.

The hypothesis furnishes a simple explanation for the serial position curve in free recall. It also furnishes a basis for further assertions about free recall which are supported by findings in the literature. Or, to say the same thing another way, the hypothesis makes it possible to systematize a number of findings in the literature:

(1) Word frequency, a variable that has an effect on rote learning, and, therefore, presumably on long-term storage, should have an effect on the beginning peak of the serial position curve. This assertion is supported by recent findings by Sumby (1963).
(2) Linguistic constraints in the words of the list, a variable that has an effect on rote learning, and therefore, presumably, on long-term storage should have an effect on the beginning peak of the curve. This assertion is supported by findings by Deese and Kaufman (1957).
(3) Requiring the S to recall the items in forward order should depress the end peak of the serial position curve. By requiring sequential recall, E imposes a delay with an interpolated task—recall of the early list items. This permits the loss of items from short-term storage. This assertion is supported by findings by Deese (1957) and Raffel (1936).

The approach used here is not presented as a complete theory for free recall. A complete theory would permit derivation of the exact form of each of the hypothesized component curves. Once such a derivation is available then it would be possible to move away from the gross distinction between short-term and long-term storage. In a complete theory, the derivation of the output curve for long-term storage would, moreover, be based on specific assumptions about the processing involved in long-term storage. This would make it possible to move away from the simple identification of long-term storage variables with those affecting rote learning. The assumptions should also permit derivation of the characteristics of recall under more complex conditions than those considered here—for example, repeated presentations of the same word list.

The attempt to build a complete theory could, of course, be based on a variety of other constructs. For example, an approach could be developed by using inhibition or interference constructs—more specifically the constructs of proactive and retroactive inhibition. Using these constructs to build towards a complete theory leads to some complexities which will be briefly pointed out here.

The application of these constructs to account for the asymmetrical, bimodal shape of the usual serial position curve would require the specification of two functions, one relating amounts of PI to each position in the list, the other relating amounts of RI to each position in the list. If RI is considered simply as a function of the number of items following a given position, and PI simply as a function of the number of items preceding a given position, then the two functions might reasonably be expected to be monotonic. Two monotonic functions of this type and a simple rule for summing the inhibitory effects will not produce the standard type of U-shaped curve such as those in Fig. 1. By using values from Fig. 1, the difficulty may be summarized as follows. The probability of recall of the first list word is approximately .60. The probability of recall of the last list word is approximately .85. It may be assumed that there has been a reduction of .40 at the first position due to RI and a reduction of .15 at the last position due to PI. The probability of recall at the middle position is approximately .25. Within an inhibitory theory, this would be viewed as a reduction of .75 at those positions. The middle positions would be expected, if the RI and PI position functions are monotonic and if their effect is combined by addition, to have much higher probabilities of recall than those actually obtained. There are two ways of coping with this problem. One way is to move away from a simple additive system[5] allowing, for example, for interaction effects. The other way is to move away from simple functions. For example, PI for a position may be considered to be a function of both the number of items preceding the position, and the number of items following the position (time elapsing before recall).

Other complexities develop in applying inhibitory constructs to account for the systematic effects found in the experiments reported above. It is possible to use the PI construct to explain the effect of delay in Exp. II by assuming that PI is a function of both number of preceding items and the time that elapses during the delay interval. The statement of the relations involved might go as follows: Earlier items which have been extinguished recover during the delay interval and then interfere with the recall of items from the end of the list. This statement implies, however, that the effect of delay should merely alter the proportion of early and late items recalled. For every late item that is proactively blocked there should be an early item in its stead. At the very least it could be expected that there should be some increase in the probability of recall of the early items. There is no evidence at all of such an increase. The only change that occurs is that the number of items from the end of the list decreases. Again, additions or alterations can be made to handle the obtained results. Again, however, the theoretical structure grows rather complex.

Notes

1   This investigation was supported by the U. S. Army Medical Research and Development Command, Department of the Army, under Research Contract DA-49-193 MD-2496. William H. Clark assisted in running Experiment I. Thelma Taub carried out part of the statistical analysis.
2   The task used by Peterson and Peterson (1959) is viewed here as a fixed-order recall task, since S was required to recall the letters of the trigram in the order that they had been presented.
3   In the 1S/P condition, each list was preceded by a spoken ready signal 4 sec before the first word; it was followed by a bell signalling the start of the recall period, 3 sec after the last word. These intervals were increased, as indicated, in the SA and SB conditions. In the P conditions the intervals used in the 1S/P condition were used.
4   Since the submission of this paper, similar results have been reported by Postman, L. and Phillips, L. W., *Quart. J. exp. Psychol.* 1965, **17**, 132–138.
5   More technically, the simple additive system referred to here would be called a linear system, in which $f(RI) + f(PI) = f(RI + PI)$.

References

ANDERSON, N. S. Poststimulus cuing in immediate memory. *J. exp. Psychol.*, 1960, **60**, 216–221.

BROADBENT, D. E. *Perception and communication.* New York: Pergamon, 1958.

BROWN, J. Some tests of the decay theory of immediate memory. *Quart. J. exp. Psychol.*, 1958, **10**, 12–21.

CONRAD, R. Decay theory of immediate memory. *Nature*, 1957, **179**, 831–832.

DEESE, J. Serial organization in the recall of disconnected items. *Psychol. Rep.*, 1957, **3**, 577–582.

DEESE, J., AND KAUFMAN, R. A. Serial effects in recall of unorganized and sequentially organized verbal material. *J. exp. Psychol.*, 1957, **54**, 180–187.

GREENHOUSE, S. W., AND GEISSER, S. On methods in the analysis of profile data. *Psychometrika*, 1959, **24**, 95–112.

HEBB, D. O. *The organization of behavior.* New York: Wiley, 1949.

MELTON, A. W. Implications of short-term memory for a general theory of memory. *J. verb. Learn. verb. Behav.*, 1963, **2**, 1–21.

MURDOCK, B. B., JR. The serial position effect of free recall. *J. exp. Psychol.*, 1962, **64**, 482–488.

PETERSON, L. R., AND PETERSON, M. J. Short term retention of individual verbal items. *J. exp. Psychol.*, 1959, **58**, 193–198.

POSTMAN, L. Short-term memory and incidental learning. In A. W. Melton (Ed.), *Categories of human learning.* New York: Academic Press, 1964. Pp. 145–201.

RAFFEL, G. Two determinants of the effect of primacy. *Amer. J. Psychol.*, 1936, **48**, 654–657.

SUMBY, W. H. Word frequency and serial position effects. *J. verb. Learn. verb. Behav.*, 1963, **1**, 443–450.

THORNDIKE, E. L., AND LORGE, I. *The teacher's word book of 30,000 words.* New York: Bureau of Publications, Teachers College, Columbia University, 1944.

WAUGH, N. C. Serial position and the memory span. *Amer. J. Psychol.*, 1960, **73**, 68–79.

42

A TEMPORAL DISTINCTIVENESS THEORY OF RECENCY AND MODALITY EFFECTS

Arthur M. Glenberg and Naomi G. Swanson

Source: *Journal of Experimental Psychology: Learning, Memory, and Cognition*, 12 (1986): 3–15.

A temporal distinctiveness theory of contextually cued retrieval from memory is presented and applied to recency and modality effects. According to this theory, one part of the mnemonic trace of an item is a representation of the item's time of presentation. Time of presentation may be encoded with a coarse grain (so that it is consistent with a wide range of times) or with a fine grain (so that it is consistent with a narrow range of times). Retrieval proceeds by constructing temporally defined search sets that include representations of items consistent with the temporal bounds of the search set. The temporal width of the search set increases as the retention interval increases. Recency effects arise from retrieval of recently presented items from narrow search sets that include representations of few items; within the context of the search set, these items are distinctive and recalled well. Superiority in recall of recently presented auditory information in comparison with recently presented visual information is attributed to differences in the grain of time of presentation representations for aurally (fine grain) and visually (coarse grain) presented information. Four experiments confirm qualitative and quantitative predictions of the theory, including the prediction of auditory superiority at the beginning of the list when the initial items are temporally distinct.

An episodic memory for an event is defined as one for which the rememberer can specify the context in which the event was experienced. Consonant with this definition, virtually all theories of episodic memory propose that context is represented in memory and plays an important role in remembering.

Nonetheless, other than declaring that representation of context specifies location and time, few theorists have attempted to develop the concept (however, see Baddeley, 1982). Part of the problem has been in developing procedures for experimentally disentangling effects of context from other memory mechanisms so that theories of context can be tested.

The distractor paradigm developed by Whitten and Bjork (1972; Bjork & Whitten, 1974) is appropriate for studying contextually cued recall. Pairs of to-be-remembered (TBR) words are separated from one another by distractor-filled interpresentation intervals (IPIs), and the last TBR pair is followed by a distractor-filled retention interval (RI). Appropriate distractor tasks preclude formation of associations between pairs at different serial positions, requiring reliance on contextually cued mechanisms of recall. This paradigm produces a long-term recency effect—best recall of the most recent information even after a considerable filled RI (Bjork & Whitten, 1974; Glenberg et al., 1980). The size of the recency effect is logarithmically related to the ratio of the IPI to the RI over a two-thousand fold change in the duration of the intervals (Glenberg, Bradley, Kraus, & Renzaglia, 1983). Clearly long-term recency is a general phenomenon of contextually cued retrieval from memory. Interestingly, the size of the recency effect is also affected by presentation modality of TBR items. Auditory presentation enhances the recency effect relative to visual presentation—a long-term modality effect (J. M. Gardiner & Gregg, 1979; Glenberg, 1984).

In this article we present a search-set theory of how one type of context—temporal context—can be used to cue recall. In short, we propose that temporally cued remembering requires the creation of a search set that specifies the time at which an event occurred and that recall involves sampling from the search set. Although search set theories are not new (e.g., Shiffrin, 1970), two novel aspects of this theory are that the search sets are specified in the temporal domain (leading to a definition of temporal distinctiveness as an explanatory construct) and that the temporal search set changes during the course of recall. This temporal distinctiveness theory is based on work by J. M. Gardiner (1983) and Glenberg (1984) and is related to Shiffrin's (1970) work. The specific emphasis of this article is application of the distinctiveness theory to the long-term modality effect. Toward that end, we present four experiments that test qualitative predictions of the theory. A specific mathematical model is included in the Appendix. Quantitative predictions from this model are illustrated in Figures 2–5 and verify the qualitative claims we make in the text.

Modality effects

Superior recall of recent information presented aurally compared with recent information presented visually, defines the modality effect. Interest in modality effects is due, at least in part, to the claim that the effect reveals characteristics of basic information processing mechanisms such as echoic memory (O. C. Watkins & M. J. Watkins, 1980). Although data we present contraindicate the echoic memory explanation, we agree that modality effects reveal basic mechanisms—in preview, mechanisms of temporal coding.

Because the modality effect seemed to last but a few seconds, some explanations of the modality effect emphasized sensory storage mechanisms, for example, Precategorical Acoustic Store (PAS; Crowder & Morton, 1969). More recent data has uncovered situations that greatly extend the duration of the modality effect (e.g., O. C. Watkins & M. J. Watkins, 1980), but in which the underlying basis of the effect may still be sensory (echoic).

The echoic position has been weakened considerably by data reported by Gardiner and Gregg (1979). They contrasted recall of information presented aurally (read off a screen by the subject) or visually (read silently) when each to-be-remembered item was preceded and followed by 10–20 s of overtly counting backward. The overt counting backward following each item (including the last) should have eliminated sensory information. Nonetheless, a large, long-term, modality effect was observed. In addition, Glenberg (1984, Experiment 4) found that a redundant auditory suffix did not reduce the auditory superiority found by using the Gardiner and Gregg procedure.

Other accounts of the long-term modality effect have also been disconfirmed. It is unlikely that the effect is due to conscious rehearsal strategies because it is found by using incidental learning procedures (Glenberg, 1984). The effect is not the result of differences in output order between the auditory and visual modalities because the effect can be found in serial as well as free recall (Gardiner, 1983; Glenberg, 1984). Finally, it seems unlikely that the effect reflects a special long-term representation that decays within 20–40 s (thus confining the auditory superiority to the end of the list), because the size of the effect is changed little by increasing the retention interval within this range (Glenberg, 1984).

Temporal distinctiveness theory

Glenberg (1984) proposed a retrieval account of long-term modality effects. On that account auditory superiority results from interference in recall of visual items due to visual information encoded during the distractor task. Recent evidence has demonstrated a long-term modality effect in the absence of visual interference, however. Glenberg, Eberhardt, and Belden (1985) eliminated visual interference in the Bjork and Whitten distractor paradigm by (a) restricting the subject's visual field to a small portion of a monitor which displayed the visual TBR stimuli, (b) using an auditory distractor task, and (c) obtaining oral recall. Even under these conditions a long-term modality effect was found. In this article the retrieval account is modified to take into consideration these new data as well as arguments advanced by Gardiner (1983).

The first encoding assumption of temporal distinctiveness theory is that the cognitive representation of a TBR event includes a component specifying the temporal context in which the event was presented (time of presentation), similar to Yntema and Trask's (1963) time tags. The second assumption is adapted from Gardiner (1983). It is that the time of presentation is specified more completely (to a finer grain) for events experienced predominantly by audition than for those experienced predominantly through vision. That is, following auditory presentation, the representation of time of presentation specifies a narrow temporal region centered on the actual time of presentation; following visual presentation, however, the representation of time of presentation is consistent with a wide temporal region.

Consistent with this assumption are data reviewed by Gardiner (1983), including the results of an experiment reported by Metcalfe, Glavanov, and Murdock (1981). Metcalfe et al. presented words in the same list at different spatial locations; recall order was to conform to either temporal order or spatial order. Auditory superiority was only found when recall was by temporal order. Apparently, the auditory mode codes temporal information more effectively than does the visual mode. There is also some evidence from the time perception literature consistent with this assumption (Sebel & Wilsoncroft, 1983). Additional support for this assumption is provided by the results of Experiments 1–4, which demonstrate a greater sensitivity to manipulation of temporal factors with auditory presentation than with visual presentation.

The second encoding assumption is illustrated in Figure 1. The functions represent the degree to which the encoded time of presentation is consistent with various possible presentation times. The theory does not specify the exact shape of the function; for illustrative purposes and ease of computation exponential functions were chosen. Thus, for a TBR item presented at Time t_i, the consistency function, $c(t_i, t_j)$, gives the consistency of the representation of the time of presentation of TBR item i, (t_i), with any other Time t_j.

$$c(t_i, t_j) = \lambda \exp(-\lambda |t_i - t_j|). \tag{1}$$

In the theory the only difference between auditory and visual presentation is in the value of the parameter λ; λ_a is larger than λ_v, so that the consistency functions are narrower for auditory than for visual presentations.

In the paradigm that produces the long-term modality effect, the TBR items are unrelated to one another and the distractor activity during the IPIs discourages formation of associations or relations between events presented at different serial positions. In addition, the distractor activity during the RI empties working memory. Under these conditions retrieval proceeds by defining multiple temporal search sets. Each search set specifies a temporal domain during which some (or all) of the TBR items had been presented.

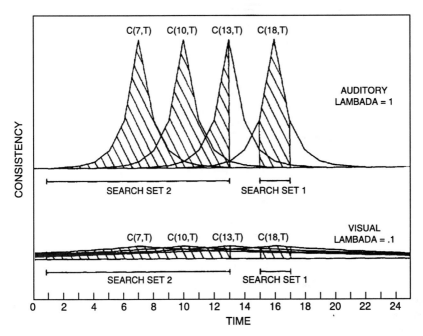

Figure 1 Each curve represents the consistency [$c(t_i, t_j)$ on the ordinate] of the representation of time of presentation for an item encoded at time t_i (on the abscissa) with other times (t_j). [The curves near the top of the figure are for auditory presentation, those near the bottom are for visual presentation. The parameter values (see Appendix) used to generate this figure were $\lambda_a = 1$, $\lambda_v = .1$, $t_i - t_4 - w_1 = 1.5$, and $w_2 = 5$.]

Traces are included in a search set to the extent that the temporal component of the trace (time of presentation) is consistent with the domain of the search set. The use of the search set terminology is close to that of Shiffrin (1970), although our concern here is exclusively with temporally defined search sets.

Two assumptions guide the use of these temporally defined search sets. First, the boundaries of a search set must be expanded to sample information presented temporally distant from the recall test. Recall of recently presented information may be accomplished by constructing a search set with relatively constrained or narrow boundaries; recall of temporally distant information requires construction of a search set with a large temporal extent. Two search sets are illustrated in Figure 1.

Evidence consistent with this assumption was presented by Bellezza (1982, Experiment 5). In a continuous task, subjects attempted to recall the kth word previous to the current word ($k = 1, 20$). Bellezza noted a positive correlation between k and the variance of the deviations between the positions of the recalled word and the correct position. Bellezza suggested that

493

errors result from drawing incorrect responses from a search set centered on item k. The increase in the variance of the positions of the errors implies an increase in the width of the search set as k, the retention interval, increases.

The second retrieval assumption is that the greater the number of representations included in a search set, the less likely any one of them is to be recalled. The degree to which any item is represented in a search set is given by the area under the consistency curve bounded by the search set. Degree of membership in a search set is indicated by cross-hatching in Figure 1. Probability of retrieving an item from the search set is given by the degree to which that item is represented in the search set divided by the sum of memberships of all items in the search set (plus a noise factor, described in the Appendix). This is a cue-overload assumption (O. C. Watkins & M. J. Watkins, 1975), and it is common to many models of retrieval (e.g., Raaijmakers & Shiffrin, 1981).

This last assumption provides a precise way of defining temporal distinctiveness: It is the membership of a given item in a search set divided by the sum of the memberships of all items within that search set. Thus the assertion that aurally presented items are temporally more distinct than visually presented items (Gardiner, 1983) is given greater meaning. Indeed, the theory explains why temporally distinctive auditory items have only been found at the end of the list. The end-of-list search set, being close to the recall test, is temporally narrow and few auditory TBR items are included in the search set. Each is distinctive and recalled well. Search sets focused on midlist or beginning of the list positions are temporally more extensive. Because more representations are included, none are distinctive.

Finally, recall of a specific item is found by combining the probabilities of retrieving the item from multiple search sets. Details are given in the Appendix.

These assumptions generate a number of predictions, some of which are discussed next, and some in the General Discussion. The paradigm that produces the long-term modality effect also generates a long-term recency effect (Bjork & Whitten, 1974; Glenberg et al., 1983, 1980). This recency effect reflects the changing width of the search set. Recall of recently presented items is from constrained search sets (e.g., search set 1 in Figure 1), which contain few TBR items so retrieval is likely. Recall from other serial positions requires larger search sets (e.g., search set 2 in Figure 1) from which few items are recalled. Long-term primacy effects are also found (e.g., Bjork & Whitten, 1974; Gardiner & Gregg, 1979), but these primacy effects are completely attributable to extra rehearsal given the first few items in the list (Glenberg et al., 1980) and need not be incorporated into the distinctiveness account of retrieval.

Importantly, the theory also accounts for major characteristics of the long-term modality effect. Because the end-of-list search set is temporally constrained, the representations of only a few aurally presented items are consistent with the search set, and so they are recalled well. Following visual presentation, the end-of-list search set, although temporally constrained, is consistent with many visually presented items (because $\lambda_v < \lambda_a$). The inclusion of many visual items in the search set reduces recall of the visually presented items.

Recall of items presented in the middle and early parts of a list generally show no auditory superiority or sometimes a small advantage for visually presented information (Glenberg, 1984; Glenberg, Eberhardt, & Petersen, in press; Whitten, 1979). According to the theory, recall of these items requires the construction of search sets with wide boundaries so that many representations are consistent with the search set. For both modalities these search sets are overloaded, and the differences in recall between the two modalities greatly reduced. Thus auditory superiority is confined to the end of the list.

Experiment 1

Gardiner (1983), Gardiner and Gregg (1979), and Glenberg (1984) have attributed the robustness of the auditory superiority found in the long-term modality paradigm to the substantial, filled IPI. In standard paradigms, where the IPI is short (i.e., 0 s), the auditory superiority effect is relatively labile. For example, Engle and Roberts (1982) reported that it was eliminated by a 15-s retention interval filled with an auditory task. In the long-term paradigm, where the IPI is substantial, the auditory superiority is robust. For example, Glenberg (1984) reported a substantial, long-term modality effect when the 8-s IPI and the 40-s RI were filled with an auditory distractor task. The basis of the temporal distinctiveness position is that the filled IPI produces temporally distinct representations. Nonetheless, this attribution has not been directly tested. Experiment 1 provides such a test.

The temporal distinctiveness theory predicts that recall of the last item should increase as its temporal separation from its predecessors increases. As the last item becomes temporally separated, it is more likely to be the only item in the end-of-list search set. Although this reasoning holds for both aurally and visually presented items, the effect (over the temporal ranges used in this experiment) should be much larger for auditory presentation. Temporal separation of the last visually presented item need not greatly increase its temporal distinctiveness: The time of presentation of visual midlist items is represented with such a coarse grain (λ_v is so small), that visual midlist items will be included in the end-of-list search set centered on the last item even when the last item is temporally separated from the midlist items (see Figure 1).

In the experiment, lists of five pairs of TBR words were presented both aurally and visually. The fifth pair was isolated from the previous four pairs by a distractor-filled interval of 0 s, 10 s, or 20 s. This last pair was followed by a 20-s filled retention interval. For auditory presentation, we expect a large increase in recall with increases in the length of the isolating interval. For visual presentation the increase should be much smaller.

Method

Subjects

The 20 subjects were students enrolled in introductory psychology courses at the University of Wisconsin-Madison. In addition, six subjects were eliminated because of equipment failure. All subjects received course credit for participation.

Materials and design

In addition to two practice lists, subjects studied and recalled 18 lists of five-word pairs. There were three lists in each of the six conditions formed by the factorial combination of two levels of modality of presentation (auditory and visual) and three levels of length of the isolating interval (0 s, 10 s, and 20 s).

The word pairs were formed from unrelated five-letter, one- and two-syllable, common concrete English nouns. Each pair was presented for a total duration of 2.5 s. During that time subjects performed an orienting task, determining which word referred to a larger object. If the pair was presented visually, the correct response was a key press on the same side as the larger object. For auditory presentation, subjects were to press the left-hand key if the first word was the larger, or the right-hand key if the second was the larger. This task was designed to produce equivalent processing of each pair and to discourage rehearsal of pairs across serial positions.

Distractor problems consisted of the visual presentation of 2 numbers in word form (e.g., twenty-three, six). The task was to add the two digits in the first number (2 and 3) and determine if the sum was equal to the second number. The second number differed from the correct sum by −1, 0, or 1. Subjects responded by pressing the left-hand button when the sum did not equal the second number and the right-hand button otherwise. Distractor problems were presented for 2 s each. Performance on this task was monitored and difficulty of the problems adjusted to keep each subject's average performance at 80% correct (see Glenberg, 1984, for details on the adjustment scheme). The mathematical aspect of the distractor task was designed to prevent rehearsal by requiring utilization of working memory capacity. In addition, subjects were required to say "bla" 2–4 times a second while solving the mathematics problems. This articulatory suppression task was designed to prevent rehearsal via an articulatory loop.

Each list consisted of a 2-s visual ready signal, a variable interval of distractor activity, five-word pairs, 20 s of distractor activity, and a visual recall signal. Also, separating the fourth and fifth word pairs was 0, 10, or 20 s of distractor problems (the isolating interval). The variable interval of distractor activity at the beginning of the list was 24 s, 14 s, or 4 s for the 0-s, 10-s, or 20-s isolating intervals, respectively. Thus each list required the same total time. Subjects were allowed 45 s for written free recall at the end of each list.

The assignment of word pairs to lists was randomized for each subject, as was the order of the lists (within the constraint that one list representing each of the six conditions occurred in each third of the experiment). The distractor problems and the visually presented word pairs were presented on a TV monitor controlled by an Apple II+ computer. The auditory pairs were prerecorded and played back using an Instavox RA-12 unit. This device records an analog signal on a large floppy disk. Playback is of tape-recorder quality with a maximum of 400-ms search time between stimuli.

Before receiving the 18 experimental lists, subjects practiced on (a) the distractor task, (b) a list containing aurally presented pairs, and (c) a list containing visually presented pairs. The pairs on the practice lists consisted of four-letter nouns.

Results and discussion

The results in Figure 2 confirm the qualitative predictions of the temporal distinctiveness theory. Increasing the temporal isolation of the last auditory TBR item increased recall of that item—presumably by decreasing the probability that representations of other items are included in the end-of-list search set. The increase in recall is much smaller, or absent, for visual TBR items—presumably because visual presentations produce coarse-grained representations of temporal context. In this case, many representations are included in the end-of-list search set and recall suffers. Greatly increasing the duration of the isolating interval should eventually lead to improvement in recall of the isolated visual TBR items.

These conclusions are, for the most part, supported by the statistical analyses. In an analysis over all five serial positions there were main effects for modality of presentation, $F(1, 19) = 18.90$, $MS_e = 1.78$, serial position, $F(4, 76) = 59.98$, $MS_e = 1.25$, and length of the isolating interval, $F(2, 38) = 7.51$, $MS_e = .71$. The last effect indicates improved recall as the length of the isolating interval increased. In addition, the Modality × Serial Position interaction was significant, $F(4, 76) = 30.73$, $MS_e = 1.70$. In an analysis of the last serial position, the linear component of the modality by length of isolating interval interaction indicates whether the size of modality effect increases as the length of the isolating interval increases. The linear component did not quite reach conventional levels of significance, $F(1, 38) = 3.31$, $MS_e = 1.24$, $p = .076$. Nonetheless, Experiment 2 includes a replication of the 0-s and 20-s isolating interval conditions (labeled *5P* and *1P*, respectively, in that experiment) in which the interaction is significant ($p = .016$). Thus we are willing to accept the interaction as a real effect.

The mathematical model developed in the Appendix accounts for the major quantitative trends in the data, notably the large effect of the isolating

EXPERIMENT 1
DURATION OF ISOLATING INTERVAL

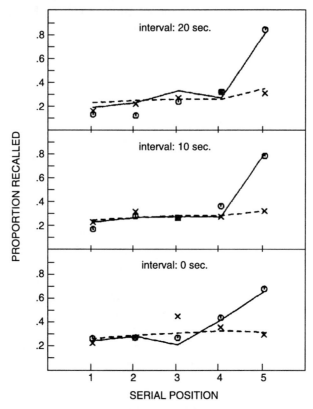

Figure 2 Data are from Experiment 1. [Recall of auditory pairs is illustrated by circles; Xs are for visual presentation. The lines illustrate the fit of the distinctiveness model (solid lines for aural presentation, broken lines for visual, $\lambda_a =$ 11.8, $\lambda_v = .06$, $w_1 = 16.84$, $w_2 = 3.29$, $n = .076$, $d = .17$, RMSE = .05; see the Appendix for explanation of the parameter values)].

interval on the last aurally presented TBR item. It also accounts for the virtual absence of an effect on the last visually presented item. Nonetheless, the fit of the model is only fair (RMSE = .05). Undoubtedly the fit could be improved by either (a) decreasing the error variability in the data by collecting more data (each point in Figure 2 is based on only 60 subject-pairs), or (b) using different mathematical functions to represent the basic processes in the theory such as the consistency curves. Given our poor understanding of the underlying causes of the basic processes, however, this would just be an exercise in curve-fitting. For the present, the mathematical model should be thought of as a convenient device for demonstrating that the theory can accommodate the major qualitative trends in the data.

O. C. Watkins and M. J. Watkins (1980) and M. J. Watkins and Todres (1980) have claimed that echoic (sensory) information can last many seconds (at least 20). Might the results of Experiment 1 be explained by a long-lasting echoic representation? For two reasons, the answer is no. First, sensory information representing the last TBR item should have been disrupted by the overt repetition of "bla" during the retention interval. Second, an unelaborated echoic information account cannot explain the improvement in recall of the last item as a function of the duration of the preceding interval.

Experiment 2

Temporal distinctiveness means that few representations are included in a temporally defined search set. The temporal distinctiveness explanation of the results of Experiment 1 can be tested further by manipulating the number of representations included in the search set. In Experiment 2, the isolating interval (20 s of distractor activity) occurred either before the first, third, or fifth serial positions, so that (nominally) 5, 3, or 1 pairs (Conditions 5P, 3P, or 1P) are isolated at the end of the list. The first and last of these conditions provide replication of the major effects of Experiment 1. Condition 3P is critical: Because the last aurally presented item in Condition 3P is not distinctive, its recall should be well below recall of the last aurally presented item in Condition 1P.

An alternative account of the results from Experiment 1 is that an isolating interval always increases recall of items presented immediately after the interval (perhaps because of some sort of release from proactive interference, cf. Loess & Waugh, 1967). On this account, recall of pairs presented in serial position 3 of Condition 3P should be elevated; indeed, one might expect auditory superiority at this serial position.

Method

Subjects

The 20 subjects were from the same population as those in Experiment 1. Two subjects were replaced for failure to follow instructions.

Materials and design

This experiment differed from Experiment 1 in but one respect. The independent variable, length of the isolating interval, was replaced with another independent variable, number of pairs isolated at the end of the list (1P, 3P, or 5P). In all other respects (e.g., amount of practice, number of lists, types

499

of distractor activity, etc.) the experiments were identical. Twenty seconds of additional distractor activity occurred before the first pair (Condition 5P), the third pair (Condition 3P), or the last pair (Condition 1P).

Results and discussion

The data of major interest are in Figure 3. The data in the figure make it clear that the size of the modality effect depends on temporal distinctiveness. As the number of traces consistent with the end-of-list search set increases (from Condition 1P, to Condition 5P), the size of the modality effect decreases. The effect is due almost exclusively to recall following

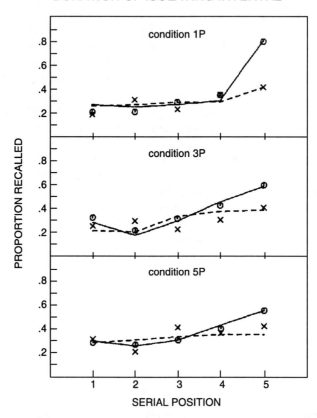

Figure 3 Data are from Experiment 2. (Recall of auditory pairs is illustrated by circles; Xs are for visual presentation. The lines illustrate the fit of the distinctiveness model; solid lines for aural presentation, broken lines for visual, $\lambda_a = .27$, $\lambda_v = .07$, $w_1 = 21.99$, $w_2 = 1.46$, $n = .053$, $d = .24$, RMSE $= .05$).

auditory presentation. Apparently, the grain of the time of presentation representation for visually presented items is so coarse that the location of the isolating interval has little effect on the number of visually presented items included in the end-of-list search set.

These conclusions are supported by statistical analysis. In an analysis including all serial positions, there were main effects of modality of presentation, $F(1, 19) = 5.39$, $MS_e = 3.15$, serial position, $F(4, 76) = 35.25$, $MS_e = 1.63$, as well as interactions between modality and serial position, $F(4, 76) = 5.06$, $MS_e = 2.52$, and number of isolated pairs and serial position, $F(8, 152) = 2.02$, $MS_e = 1.78$. The three-factor interaction just failed to reach standard levels of significance, $F(8, 152) = 1.90$, $MS_e = 1.71$, $p = .06$. This failure is not critical because the omnibus interaction term includes serial positions for which the distinctiveness theory predicts no effects. An analysis of the last serial position indicated significant effects for modality, $F(1, 19) = 33.51$, $MS_e = 1.88$, and the critical Modality × Number of Isolated Pairs interaction, $F(2, 38) = 3.57$, $MS_e = 1.76$.

Two other analyses are of interest. First, the interaction between modality and number of isolated pairs is also significant when condition 3P is removed, $F(1, 38) = 6.39$. This comparison replicates the isolation effect observed in Experiment 1; that is, the modality effect is larger when the last serial position is isolated (Condition 1P) by 20 s of distractor activity than when it is not (Condition 5P).

The last analysis concerns recall of the pair in serial position 3 of condition 3P. This item is proceeded by an isolating interval, but it is not temporally distinctive (a search set centered on this item will include others). As the distinctiveness theory predicts, this pair is recalled no better than the pairs in positions 2 or 4, nor is the modality difference at this serial position significant.

As is verified in Figure 3, the mathematical model does a good job of capturing the major trends in the data.

Experiment 3

Suppose that the very first of a list of TBR items is temporally separated from the others on the list. Because the search set enlarges with temporal distance from the recall test, the separating interval will have to be very large to create a temporally distinctive representation (one that shares the beginning-of-list search set with few other representations). Nonetheless, if an appropriately large interval is used, the first aurally presented item can be made temporally distinctive. (Referring to Figure 1, the consistency function for the first item would be shifted far to the left so that a search set centered on it would include few other items.) Using the same intervals, however, the first visually presented item will be less distinctive: Because λ_v is small, the beginning-of-list search set will include many visually presented items. Put simply, if the first TBR item is temporally isolated, recall of the aurally presented items should exceed recall of the visually presented items at both the end and the beginning of the list. Note that confirmation of this prediction requires reversal of the often found visual superiority at the beginning of a list (Glenberg, 1984; Whitten, 1979).

Because a primary goal of this work is developing an explanation for the long-term recency and long-term modality effects, this experiment (and the next) were conducted by using a variant of the Bjork and Whitten (1974) procedure similar to that used by Gardiner and Gregg (1979) and Glenberg (1984). Subjects were presented with lists of four TBR pairs. The last pair was followed by a filled 10-s RI. Each pair was preceded by a filled 4-s IPI. When the first TBR pair was to be temporally isolated, an additional 36 s of distractor activity was inserted between the first and second TBR pairs. When the first pair was not isolated, the first pair was preceded by a total of 40 s of distractor activity.

Method

Subjects

The 30 subjects were men and women from the University of Wisconsin-Madison community who were paid for their participation.

Material and procedure

Each subject studied and recalled 12 lists of four word pairs. Successive groups of 4 lists included 2 auditory and 2 visual lists. Orthogonally, in two of the lists, the pair presented first was preceded by a 4-s filled interval and followed by a 40-s filled interval (isolating it from the rest of the list), and in two of the lists the first pair was preceded by a 40-s filled interval and followed by a 4-s filled interval. The third and fourth pairs were always preceded by a 4-s filled interval, and the fourth pair was always followed by a 10-s filled interval.

The pairs were a subset of those used in Experiments 1 and 2. Presentation of the pairs and the nature and timing of the distractor task were also as described for Experiments 1 and 2.

Before studying the 12 experimental lists, subjects received practice on (a) the distractor task, (b) a list presented visually, and (c) a list presented aurally.

Results and discussion

Figure 4 presents the major results. An analysis of variance (ANOVA) confirmed the main effects for modality, $F(1, 29) = 59.49$, $MS_e = 1.20$, serial position, $F(3, 87) = 36.59$, $MS_e = 2.06$, and isolation of the first serial position,

EXPERIMENT 3
ISOLATION OF FIRST SERIAL POSITION

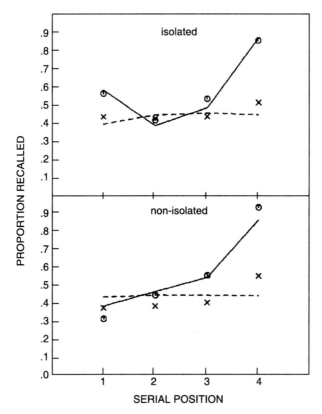

Figure 4 Data are from Experiment 3. (Recall of auditory items is represented by circles; recall of visually presented items is represented by Xs. The lines illustrate fit of the distinctiveness model: solid lines for aural presentation; broken lines for visual, $\lambda_a = .66$, $\lambda_v = .007$, $w_1 = 12.55$, $w_2 = 1.39$, $n = .01$, $d = .58$, RMSE = .05).

$F(1, 29) = 4.79$, $MS_e = 1.05$. In addition, modality and serial position interacted, $F(3, 87) = 13.60$, $MS_e = 1.68$, and isolation and serial position interacted, $F(3, 87) = 4.39$, $MS_e = 1.62$. Most important, however, the three-factor interaction was also significant, $F(3, 87) = 3.16$, $MS_e = 1.32$. Recall after auditory presentation exceeded recall after visual presentation in the last serial position and also in the first serial position when it was isolated. A series of t tests (protected against inflation of Type 1 error rate by the significant F) confirmed in three ways the predictions of the temporal distinctiveness theory regarding the isolated items. (a) For the auditory lists, recall of the first pair in isolated lists exceeded recall of the first pair in nonisolated lists, $t(29) = 4.12$, $SE = 36$. (b) Also for auditory lists, recall of the isolated item exceeded recall of the item presented in the second serial position in both isolated and nonisolated lists, $ts = 2.56$ and 2.00, respectively. In these two comparisons, the item recalled best had a considerably longer retention interval. (c) Critically, recall of the isolated item following aural presentation exceeded recall of the isolated item following visual presentation, $t = 2.09$. Thus auditory superiority can be found at locations other than the end of the list, when these locations result in temporal distinctiveness at retrieval. Again, the mathematical model accounts for major trends in the data, including auditory superiority in the beginning of the list.

Experiment 4

Auditory superiority in the first serial position, when it is temporally isolated, is consistent with the retrieval theory. Clearly, the auditory superiority in the first serial position cannot be attributed to labile echoic mechanisms; presentation of the following pairs as well as the articulatory suppression task should have overwritten any long-lived sensory information. This pattern of results is, however, consistent with the hypothesis that the interval following the isolated item can be used to recode echoic information into a more permanent format. The two accounts make different predictions regarding Experiment 4. In this experiment, the isolating interval is placed between the third and fourth pairs of a six-pair list. On the recoding account, recall of the pair in the third serial position should be elevated when the isolating interval follows it because of the opportunity for recoding during the interval. On the temporal distinctiveness theory, however, the effect of the isolating interval should be much diminished compared with Experiment 3; the beginning-of-list search set should now contain representations of multiple pairs, and recall should be poor.[1]

Method

The 30 subjects were from the same population as sampled in Experiment 3. Details of the method are the same as for Experiment 3 except for an increase in list length (from 4 to 6 pairs), and the location of the isolating interval (between serial positions 3 and 4 in the present experiment).

Results and discussion

The data of major interest are presented in Figure 5. The main effects for modality, serial position, and isolation were all significant, $F(1, 29) = 36.19$, $MS_e = 1.26$, $F(5, 145) = 116.12$, $MS_e = 1.62$, and $F(1, 29) = 5.54$, $MS_e = .341$, respectively. In addition, the Modality × Serial Position interaction was

EXPERIMENT 4
ISOLATION OF FIRST THREE POSITIONS

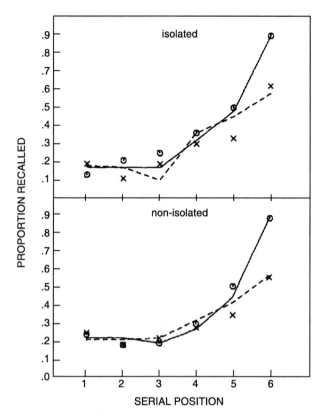

Figure 5 Data are from Experiment 4. (Recall of auditory items is represented by circles; recall of visually presented items is represented by Xs. The lines illustrate fit of the distinctiveness model: solid lines for aural presentation; broken lines for visual, $\lambda_a = 15.11$, $\lambda_v = .24$, $w_1 = 12.19$, $w_2 = 6.78$, $n = .18$, $d = .88$, RMSE = .05).

significant, $F(5, 145) = 14.90$, $MS_e = 1.48$, reflecting auditory superiority at the end of the list. Unlike Experiment 3, however, neither the Isolation × Position nor the Isolation × Position × Modality interactions were significant, $ps > .14$.

In Experiment 3, the effect of the isolating interval passed three statistical tests. The data from Experiment 4 fail all three. (a) For the auditory lists, recall of the pair preceding the isolating interval (serial position 3), did not exceed recall of the corresponding nonisolated item, $t(29) = 1.19$, $SE = .31$. (b) Also for the auditory lists, recall of the pair preceding the isolating interval did not exceed recall of the pair in serial position 2, $t = .87$, and was significantly less than the pair in serial position 4, $t = -2.17$. (c) Recall of the pair preceding the isolating interval did not differ between the auditory and visual lists, $t = 1.08$. An isolating interval does not, by itself, produce an enhancement in recall (Experiments 2 and 4). Only when the isolation results in temporally distinctive presentations (Experiments 1 and 3) does recall improve.

General discussion

We have defined temporal distinctiveness as the presence of few traces in a temporally defined search set and proposed temporal distinctiveness as an explanation of long-term modality effects. Data from all four experiments are well accounted for by this view. In Experiment 1, as the length of the isolating interval between the fourth and the fifth TBR pairs increased, recall of the fifth aurally presented pair increased, increasing the size of the modality effect. Theoretically, lengthening the isolating interval decreases the number of traces in the end-of-list search set, thus increasing temporal distinctiveness (and recall) of the last TBR pair. In Experiment 2, the location of the isolating interval was manipulated. As the number of traces consistent with the end-of-list search set increased the modality effect decreased.

In Experiments 3 and 4, temporal distinctiveness at the beginning of the list was manipulated. When a 40-s interval isolated the first TBR pair from the second, auditory superiority in recall was found for the first pair (Experiment 3). When the number of traces consistent with the beginning-of-list search set was increased to three so that none were distinctive, the beginning-of-list modality effect was eliminated (Experiment 4).

No other currently proposed account of modality effects can provide a consistent explanation for these findings. Theories based on echoic properties are most seriously challenged by beginning-of-list effects because echoic attributes of items at the beginning of the list should be overwritten by succeeding presentations. The end-of-list effects are also difficult for echoic theories; it is not clear how an echoic theory could account for an increase in recall as a function of the length of the preceding interval (Experiment 1) or the location of the isolating interval (Experiment 2). Even allowing echoic theories an additional assumption unrelated to echoic properties (e.g., release from proactive interference), why should this additional factor apply to auditory but not visual presentation?

Application to other long-term phenomena

The temporal distinctiveness theory can be applied to other phenomena associated with the long-term modality effect. Glenberg (1983) and Gregg and Gardiner (1984) have investigated conditions under which phonemic and semantic similarity between TBR items disrupts the long-term modality effect.

The temporal distinctiveness position suggests two reasons for similarity effects. First, similar items may cue one another during study (study-phase retrieval) so that they are rehearsed together, thus forming traces that are not temporally distinct. Second, the dimension of similarity provides the subject with a retrieval cue other than that afforded by the temporal search set. If subjects use retrieval cues other than the temporal context, modality effects resulting from temporal distinctiveness will be attenuated. Consistent with these suggestions, Glenberg (1983) reported that the size of the long-term modality effect increased with length of the IPIs separating unrelated TBR pairs (similar to the results of Experiment 1). However, the size of the long-term modality effect was little affected by the length of the IPI for phonemically and semantically related TBR pairs. Greene and Crowder (1984a) developed a similar interpretation for the disruption of the long-term recency effect by semantic similarity.

Aldridge and Farrell (1977) failed to find a long-term modality effect. In their experiment, subjects memorized word triplets separated by intervals of counting backward. Gardiner and Gregg (1979) used single-word TBR items, whereas Glenberg (1984) and Experiments 1–4 used word-pairs. At first blush, the difference between word-triples and word-pairs does not appear significant. However, in our work with pairs, we have always had the subjects engage in some sort of orienting task that requires comparison of the words within a pair (e.g., the relative size judgment task used in Experiments 1–4), thereby creating a unitized representation at each serial position. Thus in experiments that produce a modality effect, a unitized representation is created to represent information presented at each serial position. In Aldridge and Farrell (1977), however, three separate representations could have been created at each serial position. In this case, traces of three items (the last triplet) would be consistent with the end-of-list search set. The situation is similar to condition 3P in Experiment 2, except that the three words in the Aldridge and Farrell experiment were temporally even less distinct than the three pairs in Experiment 2. Under these conditions, the absence of a long-term modality effect based on temporal distinctiveness is not surprising.

A little discussed, but often found, concomitant of auditory superiority in the recency portion of a list is visual superiority in the primacy portion of a list. Using the long-term paradigm, the visual superiority is evident in some of Gardiner and Gregg's (1979) experiments, in Glenberg (1984), and Glenberg et al. (in press), although, curiously, not in Experiments 1–4. Visual superiority in the primacy portion of a list is also found with standard free recall (e.g., Craik, 1969) and serial recall (e.g., M. J. Watkins, O. C. Watkins, & Crowder, 1974) procedures. Whitten (1979) discussed several parametric manipulations over which the visual superiority is robust. The temporal distinctiveness theory, although not sufficiently developed to predict exactly when visual superiority will occur, does suggest an explanation. Because time of presentation is represented so coarsely, visually presented initial items can be retrieved from search sets centered on initial items or midlist items. On the other hand, aurally presented initial items are only retrieved from search sets centered on the initial items. Thus, the occurrence of visual superiority in the beginning of the list depends on the tradeoff between temporal distinctiveness (which favors auditory presentation) and sampling from multiple retrieval sets (which favors visual presentation). One factor that will influence this tradeoff is the retrieval strategy. If subjects form multiple search sets, visual superiority in primacy is favored. When subjects choose to form few search sets (as in Experiments 1–4) visual superiority in primacy is reduced.[2]

The temporal distinctiveness theory was developed as an explanation of long-term modality effects. Nonetheless, as implicit in the preceding discussion, it seems to have wider applicability. For example, the theory explains major aspects of the long-term recency effect (Bjork & Whitten, 1974; Glenberg et al., 1983; Glenberg et al., 1980). Recall of the most recently presented items is based on retrieval from relatively constrained search sets, which include few representations and is, therefore, higher than recall of midlists items, which require retrieval from temporally wider search sets containing more representations. Also, the theory provides a compelling explanation of the ratio effect, that the size of the long-term recency effect increases with the ratio of the IPI to the RI (Glenberg et al., 1983). Increasing the IPI tends to temporally isolate the most recent items so that they are recalled from search sets containing few representations, and recall is high. On the other hand, increasing the RI requires construction of search sets having wider boundaries so that more representations are included and recall suffers.

Extensions of distinctiveness theory

Temporal distinctiveness theory can account for effects of various postlist events on recall by assuming that search sets are specialized for specific types of information as well as specific temporal domains. Thus events temporally coextensive with the search set can be excluded on the basis of distinctive features. There is evidence for specificity of temporal search sets in regard to three types of features, familiarity, modality, and semantic category membership.

Data on the long-term modality effect reported in Glenberg (1984, Experiment 4) and Glenberg et al. (in press) demonstrate that episodically well-learned, or familiar, postlist events can be excluded from a search set. In both studies (which used the distractor paradigm), TBR pairs were followed by a suffix pair that was not to be recalled and that was repeated after each list. Early in the experimental session, before the suffix was well-learned, the suffix greatly reduced the modality effect. Later in the session, the disruption was much less severe. A similar conclusion (also using the distractor

508

procedure) was reached by Huang and Glenberg (1985, Experiment 1). They compared recall of auditory items followed by a well-learned auditory suffix with a no-suffix control condition (rather than visual presentation). The well-learned suffix did not significantly decrease recall. These effects contrast with effects produced by nonredundant suffixes that cannot become well-learned. In Glenberg (1984, Experiment 5) and Huang and Glenberg (1985, Experiment 3), following auditory TBR items with a nonredundant suffix severely reduced recall. Thus familiarity with the suffix is one factor that can influence entry into a search set.

Suffix familiarity may interact with other variables such as temporal spacing of the suffix and TBR items. In Glenberg (1984) and Huang and Glenberg (1985) the suffixes were separated by distractor activity from the last TBR items. Balota and Engle (1981) used a standard paradigm in which the redundant suffix immediately followed the last TBR item. They found that when the suffix was not well-learned it disrupted recall (as in Huang & Glenberg, 1985). A well-learned suffix minimally disrupted recall of preterminal items temporally separated from the suffix (also as in Huang & Glenberg). However, the well-learned suffix did disrupt recall of terminal TBR items temporally adjacent to the suffix.

There is also evidence that search sets are at least partially modality-specific. In Glenberg (1984, Experiment 5) a nonredundant visual suffix had little apparent affect on recall of auditory TBR items. In Huang and Glenberg (1985, Experiment 3) a visual nonredundant suffix did not reduce recall of auditory TBR items (compared with a no-suffix control).

A number of lines of evidence converge on the conclusion that entry into a temporally defined search set depends, at least in part, on distinctive semantic features. Ayres, Jonides, Reitman, Egan, and Howard (1979) demonstrated that the negative effects of an auditory suffix on recall of aurally presented materials can be attenuated when the suffix is classified as a musical sound (muted trumpet) in comparison with a classification as a speech sound (syllable "wa"). A related effect was demonstrated by Salter (1975) and Routh and Frosdick (1978): When a list of TBR items from one category (e.g., letters) ends with a single item from a different category (e.g., digits), the distinctive last item is immune to interference from a suffix from the original category.

Baddeley and Hitch (1977) suggested that ordinal retrieval from categorically defined search sets is the basis for the long-term recency effect. Although it has been demonstrated that categorical distinctiveness is not sufficient to produce a long-term recency effect (Glenberg, Bradley, Kraus, & Renzaglia, 1983)—presumably temporal distinctiveness is a necessary condition—M. J. Watkins and Peynircioglu (1983) demonstrated that categorical distinctiveness does play a role. They presented a mixed list of events from three categories (e.g., riddles, objects, sounds) for free recall. They found three recency effects, one for each category of events in the list. Apparently, search sets can be category specific, whereas the temporal spacing within each category (produced by the mixed-list design) generates the recency effect.

Without further modification, the temporal distinctiveness theory may be pushed to account for salient characteristics of modality effects found in standard free recall and serial recall paradigms. (Indeed, Gardiner, 1983, proposed temporal distinctiveness as a general account of modality effects.) Of course, the distinctiveness theory can account for the auditory superiority in the recency portion of the list. It seems likely that the theory can also account for mixed-list modality effects, a variety of suffix effects, as well as the visual superiority often found in the primacy portion of lists. Rather than exhaustively listing modality phenomena consistent with the distinctiveness theory, we note the correspondence between the distinctiveness theory and four characteristics of modality differences that O. C. Watkins and M. J. Watkins (1980) attribute to echoic memory. First, Watkins and Watkins note that whatever produces modality differences lasts for many seconds. As demonstrated by Experiments 1 and 2, distinctiveness theory can accommodate modality differences found after a 20-s filled retention interval. Second, whatever produces modality differences is used directly at recall. Watkins and Watkins propose that it is echoic information that is used directly at recall; we propose that fine-grained encoding of time of presentation (large λ) is translated into temporal distinctiveness at the time of recall. Third, Watkins and Watkins propose that aspects of mnemonic representations that result in modality differences are not distinct from other aspects of representations. Our proposal that encoding of time of presentation underlies the modality effect is consistent with this third claim.

Watkins and Watkins's fourth claim is based primarily on unpublished research and so is harder to evaluate. A gloss of this claim is that whatever produces modality differences "forms an integral aspect of the subject's immediate recall capabilities" (p. 274). Because the temporal distinctiveness theory can be applied to many uncued recall phenomena associated with both immediate and delayed recall, we can endorse at least some of the implications of this fourth claim.

Two modality related phenomena are, at first glance, inconsistent with the temporal distinctiveness account. The first is the change in the modality effect with cued recall and list discrimination (recognition) procedures. Murdock (1968, Experiment 1) reported auditory superiority throughout a list when recall of an item presented in serial position n was cued by the item in position $n - 1$. One interpretation of this finding is that the cue provides extra information in regard to the temporal domain to be searched. This extra information may be used to construct a midlist search set without the necessity of increasing the temporal extent of the search set (in terms of the mathematical model, providing a cue increases w_1). With these relatively constrained search sets auditory superiority would be expected throughout the list.

Murdock (1968, Experiment 2) reported the results from an experiment in which subjects attempted to discriminate items in the current list from lures drawn from the previous list. The distinctiveness theory suggests a process account of this task: The copy cue on the recognition test should provide access to the representation of the item, including the component encoding time of presentation. The response (target or lure) depends on how consistent the time of presentation component is with the current list as opposed to the previous list. For both auditory and visual words presented in the latter part of the list, the time of presentation components should be consistent with the temporal extent of the current list (but not the previous list), and performance should be relatively accurate for both presentation modalities. A different prediction is made regarding the words presented earlier in the list. Following visual presentation, the time of presentation components of the first few items should be consistent with the temporal extent of the current list and the previous list. Thus it should be difficult to decide if a visual item presented early in the list was presented in the current list or the previous one. Following auditory presentation the time of presentation components for the first few items should be consistent with the current list, but, because the consistency functions are narrow, not with the previous list. Thus it should be relatively easy to discriminate auditory words presented early in the list from auditory items presented in the previous list. In fact, Murdock reported just this interaction: In the list discrimination task, auditory superiority was observed for the primacy items with little difference between auditory and visual presentations for the recency items.

A second phenomenon apparently inconsistent with the distinctiveness account concerns output order in free recall. Nilsson, Wright, and Murdock (1975, 1979) reported a "lag" analysis of output order. This analysis requires a tabulation of the relative frequencies of recalling an item after n other presentations and recalls have intervened between an item's presentation and its recall. Based on the shapes of these distributions, Nilsson et al. (1975, 1979) suggested that (a) following visual presentation subjects appear to begin free recall in a backward serial order, and (b) following auditory presentation subjects appear to begin recall a few items back in the list and then continue in a forward order. If this claim is correct, then it does represent a challenge for the distinctiveness account. However, we note that Nilsson et al. (1975) indicate that claims based on lag analyses are not conclusive "since a given lag distribution can arise in several different ways" (p. 433).

It is clear that distinctiveness theory requires further theoretical development. As of now we have no clues as to why auditory presentation leads to a more fine-grained encoding of time of presentation than visual presentation. Some possibilities have been suggested by psychologists investigating modality effects. For example, temporal coding may be related to primary linguistic mode of presentation (Shand & Klima, 1981) or changing-state stimuli (Campbell & Dodd, 1980). An examination of the literature on time perception (e.g., Fraisse, 1984) also seems to be a likely source of ideas regarding temporal coding. Polzella, DaPolito, Huisman, and Dayton (1977) suggest differences in the abilities of the cerebral hemispheres to code time that might be related to modality differences. Whatever the mechanism, it should accommodate the recent findings that mouthing stimuli and lip-reading stimuli act much like auditory presentation (Greene & Crowder, 1984b; Nairne & Walters, 1983). Perhaps all these presentation modes tap a single temporal coding mechanism.

Likewise, we have little more than intuition as to why search sets become temporally more extensive with increases in the retention interval, or how inevitable this might be. One possibility (related to Glenberg et al., 1983) is that constructing a temporal search set uses components of the temporally changing context that are available at the test to represent various temporal intervals. Many specific (local) contextual components available at the test may be relevant to (associated with) recently experienced events, hence the recent temporal context can be precisely specified (width:small). Only the general (global) contextual components available at the test may be associated with events experienced in the more distant past, and so the temporal context of the distant past is specified less precisely (width:large). The dependence on the global contextual components to specify the distant past may be peculiar to the laboratory where there is little to distinguish between events. In a more naturalistic setting rememberers may, for some time periods, be able to reconstruct the distant past quite precisely, and thus improve recall.

Conclusions

Recency and modality effects have generated much research because it was believed that the effects tapped basic cognitive processes—recency effects revealed the operation of short-term store, and modality effects revealed characteristics of echoic sensory memory. As we have demonstrated here, these beliefs are no longer tenable. Nonetheless, the effects are important. Indeed, they seem to be revealing not special memory stores but a general retrieval process based on the operation of temporally defined search sets.

Appendix

At this stage in its development, the temporal distinctiveness theory described in the text provides a qualitative account of the long-term modality effect. Because we have little information regarding the basic processes that generate the consistency functions or moderate the width of the search set, we have no strong commitment to particular mathematical functions to represent those processes. Nonetheless, quantification of the theory serves the useful purpose of demonstrating that the theory can at least predict (fit) the major trends in the data. This Appendix provides one set of equations that make this demonstration explicit.

The consistency function was given in the text as Equation 1. The theory specifies that the width of the search set is an increasing function of the distance between the TBR items and the retention test. A function that works well is given in Equation 2. Width, is the width of the search set

$$\text{width}_j = w_2 \times \ln(t_i - t_j - w_1) \qquad (2)$$

centered on Time t_j, when the recall test is at Time t_i. The w_1 parameter is included to allow for the possibility that subjects can adequately recover or reinstate the temporal context w_1 seconds preceding the test so that widening of the search set does not begin until that point. The w_2 parameter is a scaling parameter.

Recall of item i from a search set depends (in part) on the degree to which that item's time of presentation is consistent with the search set, that is, the membership of the item in the search set. Membership of item i in a search set centered on item j, m_{ij}, is given by the area under the consistency function bounded by the search set. This area can be found by integrating separately the two halves of the consistency function and evaluating the integrals over the bounds of the search set. Define L_{ij} as the lower bound of the search set centered at Time t_j relative to the consistency function for an item presented at t_i, and U_{ij} as the upper bound.

$$L_{ij} = t_j - \frac{\text{width}_j}{2} - t_i,$$

$$U_{ij} = t_j + \frac{\text{width}_j}{2} - t_i.$$

After integrating the consistency function, membership of item i in a search set centered at Time t_j is evaluated as

$$m_{ij} = \begin{cases} [1 - \exp(-\lambda|U_{ij}|)] + [1 - \exp(-\lambda|L_{ij}|)] \\ \quad \text{when} \quad L_{ij} < O \quad \text{and} \quad U_{ij} > O, \\[6pt] [1 - \exp(-\lambda|U_{ij}|)] - [1 - \exp(-\lambda|L_{ij}|)] \\ \quad \text{when} \quad L_{ij} > O \quad \text{and} \quad U_{ij} > O, \\[6pt] -[1 - \exp(-\lambda|U_{ij}|)] + [1 - \exp(-\lambda|L_{ij}|)] \\ \quad \text{when} \quad L_{ij} < O \quad \text{and} \quad U_{ij} < O. \end{cases}$$

As described in the text, retrieving an item from a search set is a function of its distinctiveness, membership of the item in the search set (m_{ij}) relative to the sum of the memberships of all L items in the search set. We also allow for the possibility that the search set contains, in addition to TBR items, noise (e.g., representation of a subject's thoughts during the list) that might decrease distinctiveness. Because the amount of noise should increase with the extent of the search set, the noise parameter (n) is multiplied by width$_j$. Thus the probability of retrieving item i from a search set centered on item j given a list of L TBR items is

$$r_{ij} | L = \frac{m_{ij}}{\text{width}_j \times n + \sum_{i-1}^{L} m_{ij}}. \tag{3}$$

The remaining problem is to choose the number and locations of search sets; at this point in its development the theory does not specify either. Most likely, the choice is strategic depending on such factors as the list length, motivation, and past successes in retrieval from the list (cf. Raaijmakers & Shiffrin, 1981). For the data reported in this article, a retrieval strategy was chosen empirically by (a) running simulations of the mathematical model with a free parameter for each serial position indexing the probability of locating a search set at that serial position; and (b) searching for commonalities in the parameter values across experiments. As it turned out, the retrieval strategy was amazingly consistent across the four experiments and can be captured by one free parameter d. The probability of drawing from a search set centered on position j, draw$_j$, is

$$\text{draw}_j = \begin{cases} d + (1 - d)/2 & \text{for } j = 1, \\ 0 & \text{for } 1 < j < L - 2, \\ d & \text{for } j = L - 2, \\ d + (1 - d)/2 & \text{for } j = L - 1, \\ 1 & \text{for } j = L. \end{cases} \tag{4}$$

Finally, probability of recalling an item from a list of length L is a function of the independent probabilities of recalling an item from the various search sets

$$p_l | L = 1 - \prod_{j-1}^{L} (1 - [r_{ij} | L][\text{draw}_j]). \tag{5}$$

The six free parameters (λ_a, λ_v, w_1, w_2, n, and d) were estimated by the program BESTFIT (see Wilkinson & Koestler, 1983, for a description of the program), which minimized the sum of square of errors between the observed recall proportion and the predictions from Equation 5. The values of the parameters and the RMSEs are presented in the figure captions. Although there is considerable variability among the parameter estimates, two consistent trends appear. First, λ_a is always much larger than λ_v, the smallest ratio of the two quantities is 4.03. Second, the w_1 parameter is close to the maximum (the length of the retention interval plus the presentation time of the TBR item).

Notes

The research reported in this article was supported in part by Biomedical Research Support Grant 131153, University of Wisconsin Graduate School Grant 130614, and National Science Foundation Grant BNS-8416300.

Experiments 1 and 2 formed part of Naomi Swanson's master's thesis research. The data from Experiments 1–3 were presented by Arthur M. Glenberg in a paper entitled "Temporally Defined Memory Search" at the May 1984 symposium on Retrieval Processes in Human Memory (H. L. Roediger III, Moderator) conducted at the meeting of the Mid-western Psychological Association, Chicago.

1　The contrast between Experiments 3 and 4 provides conditions analogous to those in Experiment 2. In that experiment we manipulated the size of the *end-of-list* search set; in Experiment 4 we increased the size of the *beginning-of-list* search set relative to Experiment 3. It should be noted, however, that the contrast between Experiment 3 (beginning-of-list search set of one item) and Experiment 4 (beginning-of-list search set of three items) is confounded by changes in the list length (from four to six). We introduced this confound to keep a constant number (three) of TBR pairs between the isolated pairs and the recall test. If we had used a four-pair list in Experiment 4, changing the size of the beginning-of-list search set from one to three pairs would have decreased the number of pairs following the beginning-of-list search set from three to one, respectively. This was not a problem in Experiment 2 because no pairs followed those in the search set of interest, the end-of-list search set.

2　On the basis of the parameters estimated for the mathematical model presented in the Appendix, the expected number of search sets were 2.34, 2.48, 3.16, and 3.76 in Experiments 1–4, respectively.

References

Aldridge, J. W., & Farrell, M. T. (1977). Long-term recency effects in free recall. *American Journal of Psychology, 90*, 475–479.

Ayres, T. J., Jonides, J., Reitman, J. J., Egan, J. C., & Howard, D. A. (1979). Differing suffix effects for the same physical suffix. *Journal of Experimental Psychology: Human Learning and Memory, 5*, 315–321.

Baddeley, A. D. (1982). Domains of recollection. *Psychological Review, 89*, 708–729.

Baddeley, A. D., & Hitch, G. (1977). Recency re-examined. In S. Dornic (Ed.), *Attention and performance* (Vol. 6, pp. 647–667). New York: Erlbaum.

Balota, D. A., & Engle, R. W. (1981). Structural and strategic factors in the stimulus suffix effect. *Journal of Verbal Learning and Verbal Behavior, 20*, 346–357.

Bellezza, F. S. (1982). Updating memory using mnemonic devices. *Cognitive Psychology, 14*, 301–327.

Bjork, R. A., & Whitten, W. B. (1974). Recency-sensitive retrieval processes in long-term free recall. *Cognitive Psychology, 6*, 173–189.

Campbell, R., & Dodd, B. (1980). Hearing by eye. *Quarterly Journal of Experimental Psychology, 32*, 85–99.

Craik, F. I. M. (1969). Modality effects in short-term storage. *Journal of Verbal Learning and Verbal Behavior, 8*, 658–664.

Crowder, R. G., & Morton, J. (1969). Precategorical acoustic storage (PAS). *Perception & Psychophysics, 5*, 365–377.

Engle, R. W., & Roberts, J. S. (1982). How long does the modality effect persist? *Bulletin of the Psychonomics Society, 19*, 343–346.

Fraisse, P. (1984). Perception and estimation of time. *Annual Review of Psychology, 35*, 1–36.

Gardiner, J. M. (1983). On recency and echoic memory. *Philosophical Transactions of the Royal Society of London, 302*, 267–282.

Gardiner, J. M., & Gregg, V. H. (1979). When auditory memory is not overwritten. *Journal of Verbal Learning and Verbal Behavior, 18*, 705–719.

Glenberg, A. M. (1983, November). *Phonemic and category similarity disrupt the long-term modality effect.* Paper presented at the meeting of the Psychonomic Society, San Diego, CA.

Glenberg, A. M. (1984). A retrieval account of the long-term modality effect. *Journal of Experimental Psychology: Learning, Memory, and Cognition, 10*, 16–31.

Glenberg, A. M., Bradley, M. M., Kraus, T. A., & Renzaglia, G. J. (1983). Studies of the long-term recency effect: Support for a contextually guided retrieval hypothesis. *Journal of Experimental Psychology: Learning, Memory, and Cognition, 9*, 231–255.

Glenberg, A. M., Bradley, M. M., Stevenson, J. A., Kraus, T. A., Tkachuk, M. J., Gretz, A. L., Fish, J. H., & Turpin, B. M. (1980). A two-process account of long-term serial position effects. *Journal of Experimental Psychology: Human Learning and Memory, 6*, 355–369.

Glenberg, A. M., Eberhardt, K., & Belden, T. (1985). *The role of visual interference in producing the long-term modality effect.* Manuscript submitted for publication.

Glenberg, A. M., Eberhardt, K., & Petersen, G. (in press). Differential influence of recall modality and post-list instruction modality on the long-term modality effect. *American Journal of Psychology.*

Greene, R. L., & Crowder, R. G. (1984a). Effects of semantic similarity on the long-term recency effect. *American Journal of Psychology, 97*, 441–449.

Greene, R. L., & Crowder, R. G. (1984b). Modality and suffix effects in the absence of auditory stimulation. *Journal of Verbal Learning and Verbal Behavior, 23*, 371–382.

Gregg, V. H., & Gardiner, J. M. (1984). Phonological similarity and enhanced auditory recency in longer term free recall. *Quarterly Journal of Experimental Psychology, 36A*, 13–27.

Huang, S., & Glenberg, A. M. (1985). *A test of echoic and retrieval accounts of long-term modality effects.* Manuscript submitted for publication.

Loess, H., & Waugh, N. (1967). Short-term memory and intertrial interval. *Journal of Verbal Learning and Verbal Behavior, 6*, 455–460.

Metcalfe, J., Glavanov, D., & Murdock, M. (1981). Spatial and temporal processing in the auditory and visual modalities. *Memory & Cognition, 9*, 351–359.

Murdock, B. B., Jr. (1968). Modality effects in short-term memory: Storage or retrieval? *Journal of Experimental Psychology, 77*, 79–86.

Nairne, J. S., & Walters, V. L. (1983). Silent mouthing produces modality-and suffix-like effects. *Journal of Verbal Learning and Verbal Behavior, 22*, 475–483.

Nilsson, L.-G., Wright, E., & Murdock, B. B. Jr. (1975). The effects of visual presentation method on single-trial free recall. *Memory & Cognition, 3*, 427–433.

Nilsson, L.-G., Wright, E., & Murdock, B. B. Jr. (1979). Order of recall, output interference, and the modality effect. *Psychological Research, 41*, 63–78.

Polzella, D. F., DaPolito, F., Huisman, M. C., & Dayton, C. V. (1977). Cerebral asymmetry in time perception. *Perception & Psychophysics, 21*, 1187–1192.

Raaijmakers, J. G. W., & Shiffrin, R. M. (1981). Search of associative memory. *Psychological Review, 88*, 93–134.

Routh, D. A., & Frosdick, R. M. (1978). The basis and implications of the restoration of a recency effect in immediate serial recall. *Quarterly Journal of Experimental Psychology, 30*, 201–220.

Salter, D. (1975). Maintaining recency despite a stimulus suffix effect. *Quarterly Journal of Experimental Psychology, 27*, 433–443.

Sebel, A. J., & Wilsoncroft, W. E. (1983). Auditory and visual differences in time perception. *Perceptual and Motor Skills, 57*, 295–300.

Shand, M. A., & Klima, E. S. (1981). Non-auditory suffix effects in congenitally-deaf signers of American Sign Language. *Journal of Experimental Psychology: Human Learning and Memory, 7*, 464–474.

Shiffrin, R. M. (1970). Memory search. In D. A. Norman (Ed.), *Models of human memory* (pp. 375–447). New York: Academic Press.

Watkins, M. J., & Peynircioglu, Z. F. (1983). Three recency effects at the same time. *Journal of Verbal Learning and Verbal Behavior, 22*, 375–384.

Watkins, M. J., & Todres, A. K. (1980). Suffix effects manifest and concealed: Further evidence for a 20-second echo. *Journal of Verbal Learning and Verbal Behavior, 19*, 46–53.

Watkins, O. C., & Watkins, M. J. (1975). Build-up of proactive inhibition as a cue-overload effect. *Journal of Experimental Psychology: Human Learning and Memory, 1*, 442–452.

Watkins, O. C., & Watkins, M. J. (1980). The modality effect and echoic persistence. *Journal of Experimental Psychology: General, 109*, 251–277.

Watkins, M. J., Watkins, O.C., & Crowder, R. G. (1974). The modality effect in free and serial recall as a function of phonological similarity. *Journal of Verbal Learning and Verbal Behavior, 13*, 430–447.

Whitten, W. B., II (1979, May). *A new look at modality effects in free recall.* Paper presented at the Midwestern Psychological Association meeting, Chicago, IL.

Whitten, W. B., & Bjork, R. A. (1972, April). *Test events on learning trials: The importance of being imperfect.* Paper presented at the Midwestern Mathematical Psychology meeting, Bloomington, IN.

Wilkinson, A. C., & Koestler, R. (1983). Repeated recall; A new model and tests of its generality from childhood to old age. *Journal of Experimental Psychology: General, 112*, 3, 423–451.

Yntema, D. B., & Trask, F. P. (1963). Recall as a search process. *Journal of Verbal Learning and Verbal Behavior, 2*, 65–74.

43

A RECENCY-BASED ACCOUNT OF THE PRIMACY EFFECT IN FREE RECALL

Lydia Tan and Geoff Ward

Source: *Journal of Experimental Psychology: Learning, Memory, and Cognition*, 26 (2000): 1589–1625.

Seven experiments investigated the role of rehearsal in free recall to determine whether accounts of recency effects based on the ratio rule could be extended to provide an account of primacy effects based on the number, distribution, and recency of the rehearsals of the study items. Primacy items were rehearsed more often and further toward the end of the list than middle items, particularly with a slow presentation rate (Experiment 1) and with high-frequency words (Experiment 2). Recency, but not primacy, was reduced by a filled delay (Experiment 3), although significant recency survived a filled retention interval when a fixed-rehearsal strategy was used (Experiment 4). Experimenter-presented schedules of rehearsals resulted in similar serial position curves to those observed with participant-generated rehearsals (Experiment 5) and were used to confirm the main findings in Experiments 6 and 7.

In the free-recall task, participants are presented with a list of unrelated items and, immediately after a cue signaling the end of the list, are asked to recall these items in any order that they wish. A U-shaped serial position curve is typically obtained: Recall performance is excellent for the first items and the last items in the list (advantages known as the primacy and recency effects, respectively) and poor for the middle list items (sometimes known as the asymptote).

The traditional account of the U-shaped serial position curve is that it is composed of two separate components. According to this viewpoint (e.g., Atkinson & Shiffrin, 1968), the primacy effect reflects the advantage in processing (e.g., in terms of the number of rehearsals) given to the first items in the list, resulting in the selective transfer of the early items into a stable long-term memory store (LTS). By contrast, the recency effect reflects the direct output of a temporary and highly accessible short-term store (STS) of limited capacity.

Well-cited evidence shows that the recency effect is consistent with the direct output of a fragile STS. For example, a period of distractor activity immediately after the end of the list and preceding recall abolishes the recency effect but does not greatly reduce performance on earlier list items (e.g., Postman & Phillips, 1965). Furthermore, the size of the recency effect does not appear to be affected by variables known to affect long-term learning and retention, such as the age or the intelligence of the participants (see Glanzer, 1972, for a review).

There is also strong evidence that selective rehearsal is linked to the primacy effect. Rundus (1971) used the overt rehearsal technique, in which participants were encouraged to rehearse aloud during presentation of the words. He showed that the first items in the list received far more rehearsals than the middle and last items, suggesting that the probability of recalling the primacy items was influenced by the number of rehearsals they had received. Fischler, Rundus, and Atkinson (1970) and Glanzer and Meinzer (1967) provided additional evidence for a link between selective rehearsal and the primacy effect. They presented each participant with a sequence of words for free recall and instructed them to rehearse only the item that was currently being presented. Under these fixed-rehearsal conditions, the number of rehearsals was equated across the stimuli, and the primacy effect was greatly attenuated. Finally, many factors might reasonably be argued to reduce the opportunity for rehearsal, resulting in reduced primacy. For example, the primacy effect is reduced when free recall is performed (a) at a fast presentation rate (Glanzer & Cunitz, 1966; Wixted & McDowell, 1989), (b) under concurrent articulatory suppression (Richardson & Baddeley, 1975), (c) with a filled interval between each item in the list (Bjork & Whitten, 1974; Glenberg, 1984; Glenberg et al., 1980; Tzeng, 1973), and (d) under incidental learning conditions (Baddeley & Hitch, 1977; Glenberg et al., 1980; Glenberg, 1984; Marshall & Werder, 1972).

However, there are problems with these traditional accounts of recency and primacy effects in free recall. Recency effects are observed when recalling lists of words after a filled delay when a distractor task follows each word in the list (a methodology known as the continuous distractor paradigm,[1] e.g., Bjork & Whitten, 1974; Glenberg, 1984; Glenberg et al., 1980; Tzeng, 1973). Similarly, recency effects are unaffected by a concurrent six-digit memory load that must be maintained throughout the presentation of the list (Baddeley & Hitch, 1974, 1977). Furthermore, recency effects may be obtained when recalling events separated by days or weeks or months (Baddeley & Hitch, 1977; Pinto & Baddeley, 1991). Clearly, an STS interpretation of recency cannot account for recency effects over these extended and filled time periods.

There are also problems with a rehearsal interpretation of the primacy effect. As Crowder (1982) and Baddeley (1990) pointed out, a large number of studies demonstrated that recall performance is not always improved by extra rehearsals. For example, when the extra rehearsals are massed together in a block, there may be little difference in performance between those stimuli that have received many rehearsals and those that have not (e.g., Craik & Watkins, 1973; Glenberg, Smith, & Green, 1977; Rundus, 1977; Woodward, Bjork, & Jongeward, 1973).

More recent theories of recency and primacy have attempted to explain these problematic findings. For example, the difficulties associated with explaining the recency effect in free recall have been largely overcome by abandoning the distinction between STS and LTS. In accounts of this type, episodic memory is considered to be a continuum; memories for items in the short term and the long term are represented within the same memory mechanism. One influential empirical finding is that the probability that a recency item will be successfully recalled can be predicted using the *ratio rule* (e.g., Bjork & Whitten, 1974; Crowder, 1976), which posits that the probability of recall is proportional to the ratio $(\Delta t/T)$ of the interpresentation interval (Δt) and the retention interval (T). One interpretation of this finding, consistent with viewing episodic memory as a continuum, is that the ratio rule reflects the discriminability of the recency items: the greater the relative discriminability of an item, the higher is its probability of recall (Glenberg, 1984, 1987). This principle is commonly illustrated using a spatial metaphor in which items presented at regular intervals are considered to be a series of regularly spaced telegraph poles. The spatial distance between the poles can be thought of as representing the interpresentation interval (Δt) and the spatial distance between the last pole, and the viewer can be thought of as representing the retention interval (T). Through perspective, near telegraph poles will be more discriminable because they will appear larger and more widely spaced from their neighbors, whereas distant poles will appear smaller and more clustered together near the horizon.

According to the ratio rule, recency is eliminated in standard free recall with a filled retention interval because increasing the retention interval (T) reduces the critical $\Delta t/T$ ratio. By the same logic, recency reappears in the continuous distractor paradigm, because the insertion of a filled distractor between each stimulus item increases the interpresentation interval (Δt), and so increases the critical $\Delta t/T$ ratio. The ratio rule can account for recency effects in a large number of experimental data sets (e.g., Crowder, 1993; Crowder & Neath, 1991; Glenberg, 1984, 1987; Glenberg et al., 1980; Glenberg & Swanson, 1986; Neath & Crowder, 1990), including immediate and delayed free recall, the continuous distractor paradigm, and studies using incidental learning. Although the ratio rule appears to have been reasonably well received in the literature, the exact mechanism underpinning the empirical results appears to be more controversial (e.g., Baddeley, 1986; Baddeley & Hitch, 1993; Crowder, 1993). One explanation of the ratio rule is the contextual retrieval hypothesis (Glenberg et al., 1980, pp. 363–364). According to this account, recall is determined by how well the stored encoding context of an item can be reactivated by the temporal cues presented at test. It is assumed that each word in the list is encoded with a background context that varies as the experiment continues. Accordingly, the test context will be more similar to recent experimental contexts than earlier experimental contexts, such that the recall of any study context is inversely proportional to the retention interval (T). Recall is also proportional to a second factor: the specificity of the contextual cue. The specificity of the retrieved contextual cue to a particular target word is greatest when the interpresentation interval (Δt) is large. Hence, this version of the ratio rule predicts that recall will be proportional to the $\Delta t/T$ ratio. Alternative accounts explain the ratio rule in terms of the temporal distinctiveness (e.g., Crowder, 1993) or the priming (e.g., Baddeley, 1986; Baddeley & Hitch, 1993) of list items, and it is unclear as to which of these accounts best explains the empirical findings.

Although the ratio rule satisfactorily accounts for most recency effects, it has not been successfully used to explain the large and reliable primacy effects commonly found in free recall. This is because the ratio rule solely predicts extended recency functions and thus inaccurately predicts that the primacy items (by definition the earliest in the list) will show the lowest levels of recall. Nevertheless, there have been some attempts to predict primacy using the notion of distinctiveness.

According to Murdock's (1960) conception of stimulus distinctiveness, items at the extremes of a list are considered to be more distinctive, and hence more memorable, than intermediate items. This in itself predicts primacy and recency but does not account for the effect of temporal variables on list learning. Neath (1993) proposed a temporal distinctiveness account of primacy effects to explain recency effects and some primacy effects. According to his temporal distinctiveness theory, the earliest list items may be highly temporally distinctive, despite having the greatest retention intervals, because there are no list items preceding the first. Neath (1993) proposed that the temporal distinctiveness of an item may be calculated as a function of the summed temporal distances from the other items in the presentation group and that this function is of mnemonic significance. According to Neath's formula, primacy effects should be obtained after a short interval, even in the absence of rehearsal. In support of this approach, Neath et al. showed that, after a short delay, permacy effects can be obtained in the recognition of unnameable visual patterns, such as snowflakes and kaleidoscope slides (e.g., Neath, 1993; Knoedler, Hellwig, & Neath, 1999; Neath & Knoedler, 1994). It should be noted that such findings have not always extended to other materials, such as unfamiliar faces and block matrix patterns (Kerr, Avons, & Ward, 1999), and may in some methodologies be the result of response bias (Kerr, Ward, & Avons, 1998). Furthermore, Neath's (1993) temporal distinctiveness theory has been combined with the perturbation theory (e.g., Estes, 1972; Lee & Estes, 1977; Nairne, 1990, 1991, 1992) to form the positional distinctiveness model (Nairne, Neath, Serra, & Byun, 1997), which can provide a satisfactory account of some serial position curves of free recall. It should be pointed out that Nairne et al. (1997) modeled very short lists (typically of six letters) and that the primacy effects obtained in these studies were largely restricted to only a single item. It is, therefore, uncertain whether the model can account for the long and extended primacy effects typically found with lists of longer length. Nevertheless, converging evidence indicates that relatively small, yet significant, one- or two-item primacy effects may be found in the absence of selective rehearsal. For example, a small, but significant one- or two-item primacy effect has been observed in experiments in which the rate of presentation is so fast that rehearsal is unlikely (Wixted & McDowell, 1989, Experiment 1) and in some experiments using the continuous distractor technique (e.g., Watkins, Neath, & Sechler, 1989). A one- or two-item primacy effect has also been observed in some experiments that require that participants rehearse only the currently presented item (e.g., Glanzer & Meinzer, 1967). It, therefore, appears possible that some primacy effects in free recall may be enhanced by the temporal or positional distinctiveness (Nairne et al., 1997; Neath, 1993) of the first items in the list, particularly after a filled delay.

Alternative accounts of primacy have paid closer attention to the distribution of rehearsals in free recall rather than the temporal distinctiveness of the first items. For example, Brodie et al. (Brodie, 1975; Brodie & Murdock, 1977; Brodie & Prytulak, 1975) examined free recall with and without a filled delay under different rates of presentation using the overt rehearsal methodology (Rundus, 1971; Rundus & Atkinson, 1970). Rather than concentrating on simply the number of rehearsals, Brodie et al. examined the distribution of rehearsals. They argued that it was inappropriate to plot serial position curves as a function of the order of presentation (referred to as the *nominal order*). Rather, it was more appropriate to rank order the words in terms of when each word had been most recently rehearsed (referred to as the *functional order*). When the traditional U-shaped nominal serial position curve was replotted in terms of functional order, large and extended recency effects were found, and the primacy effect was virtually abolished (Brodie, 1975; Brodie & Murdock, 1977; Brodie & Prytulak, 1975). This reanalysis suggests that the additional rehearsal given to the early items in a list results in more recent rehearsals, such that the earliest items in the list (the "primacy" items) are rehearsed to the end of the list, resulting in superior recall (because of their recency positions). In fact, a similar relationship can be observed in Rundus' (1971) data. Although commentators tended to concentrate on

Figure 1, Rundus' Figure 2 shows a pattern of results clearly consistent with a recency-based explanation of the primacy effect: List items that were rehearsed to the end of the list were better recalled than the other items.

Modigliani and Hedges (1987) provided further evidence that the earliest items in the list receive selective rehearsal. They performed a free-recall experiment with immediate (Experiment 1) and delayed (Experiment 2) free recall, using the overt rehearsal technique. They demonstrated that the early items in the list were more likely to receive more rehearsals, were more likely to be rehearsed to the end of the list, and were more likely to receive distributed rehearsals. They showed that recall was affected by all three of these factors: Recall improved if a word had received at least one distributed rehearsal, recall improved with an increased number of rehearsals, and recall improved with a reduced retention interval between last rehearsal and test. A *distributed rehearsal* was defined as a class of rehearsal in which a word was rehearsed for one or more rehearsal sets, then dropped from rehearsal, and finally returned to the rehearsal set again. These were contrasted with immediate and consecutive rehearsals, in which a word was rehearsed for one (immediate rehearsal) or more (consecutive rehearsal) rehearsal sets but once dropped from rehearsal was not again later rehearsed. Interestingly, the advantage for distributed rehearsals appeared greatest with a filled distractor period at the end of the list (Experiment 2).

The results of Modigliani and Hedges (1987), Rundus (1971), and Brodie and colleagues suggest an alternative way of extending the ratio rule to explain the primacy effect in free recall. Using the telegraph pole metaphor, rehearsal can be argued to increase the discriminability of an item in three ways. First, the rehearsal of an item will lead to an increase in the number of instantiations of telegraph poles representing the item in episodic memory, providing more opportunities for a rehearsed item to be recalled. Second, rehearsal will lead to more recent instantiations of a given item, reducing the retention interval (T) of the most recent rehearsals, thereby increasing the critical ratio ($\Delta t/T$) for these items. Finally, if retrieval at free recall involves the sampling of different points in the study phase, then distributed rehearsals will increase the probability of recall over massed rehearsals, because distributed rehearsals may be accessed by many different retrieval cues. The advantage for distributed rehearsals over single or massed rehearsals has been shown by Glanzer (1969), and it is interesting to note that this advantage appears to increase with a filled delay (Modigliani & Hedges, 1987). With immediate testing, the probability of successfully recalling the most recent items is very high, and so an item will be most successfully recalled if its rehearsals occur most recently. With delayed testing, the recall advantage for the most recent items is considerably smaller (because T has increased for all items), and so an item may be most successfully recalled if there are multiple, widely spaced instantiations of the item throughout the list. It may, therefore, be expected that recall will be greater for distributed

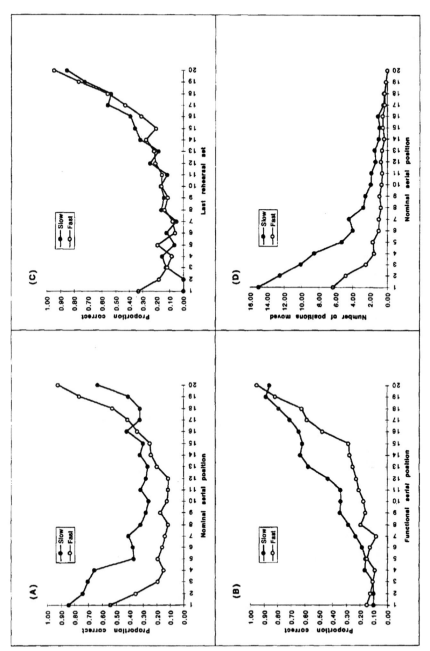

Figure 1 Experiment 1: Mean proportion of correct responses as a function of nominal serial position (A), functional serial position (B), and last rehearsal set to which an item was rehearsed (C). Mean number of rehearsal sets moved by the nominal serial position of the list items (D).

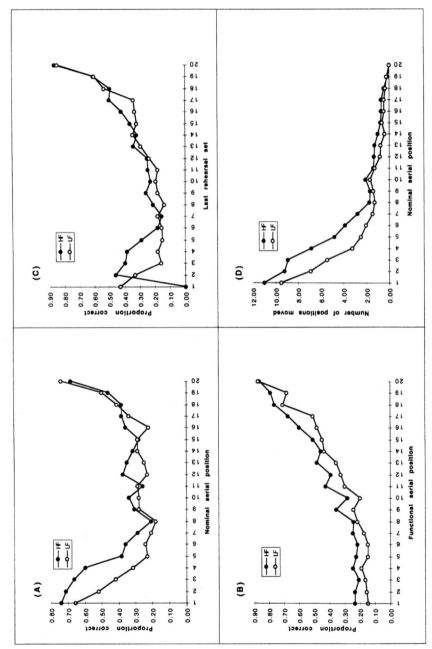

Figure 2 Experiment 2: Mean proportion of correct responses as a function of nominal serial position (A), functional serial position (B),

rather than immediate and consecutive rehearsals, especially after a retention interval.

The purpose of the seven experiments described in the present study is to examine whether accounts that use the ratio rule (e.g., the context encoding hypothesis or temporal distinctiveness hypothesis discussed previously) can be extended to account for primacy effects and recency effects in the free recall of unrelated items. This research is of importance because there is currently no account of free recall that attempts to explain both the extended primacy effects and the recency effects of the free-recall serial position curve. The first two experiments address the question of whether the differential effect of presentation rate (Experiment 1) and word frequency (Experiment 2) on the primacy portion of the serial position curve may be explained in terms of the selective rehearsal of the early items. Experiment 3 examines the effect of a filled retention interval on primacy and recency, investigating the possibility that early items may be selectively and covertly rehearsed during the distractor interval. Experiment 4 examines the effect of the selective rehearsal of primacy items on the recall of recency items with immediate testing and a filled delay. Experiment 5 examines the role of rehearsal in free recall, investigating whether the characterstic U-shaped serial position curves are the result of actively selecting and rehearsing the items or are the consequence of participants' schedules of rehearsals. Finally, Experiments 6 and 7 provide confirmatory evidence that the number, distribution, and recency of rehearsals are important factors influencing recall from lists of experimenter-generated schedules of rehearsals.

Experiment 1

One of the major arguments for a dual-store account of memory has been the demonstration that certain variables differentially affect the primacy and recency portion of the serial position curve. For example, Glanzer and Cunitz (1966) showed that a faster presentation rate reduces free recall for items in the prerecency positions but does not affect the recency portion of the serial position curve. According to the dual-store model, this occurs because rapidly presented items are given less opportunity for rehearsal and are, therefore, less likely to enter the LTS than items presented slowly, leading to a lower level of recall for the prerecency items during a fast presentation rate. The recency items, on the other hand, remain unaffected because they are largely recalled from STS rather than LTS.

However, an alternative explanation is possible based on an extension of the ratio rule. According to this account, a slow presentation rate may permit participants to rehearse more of the early items further down the list, resulting in more instantiations of the primacy items, which will be more distributed and more recent at the time of recall. According to the extension of the ratio rule, all three of these factors will tend to increase recall performance.

The aim of Experiment 1 was to examine whether this explanation could account for the effect of presentation rate on the primacy effect. Three detailed analyses of the distribution of rehearsals permit such an examination. The first analysis is derived from the studies of Brodie and Murdock (1977). They examined the effect of fast (1.25 s/item) and slow (5 s/item) presentation rates on free recall and obtained a typical U-shaped serial position curve when recall was plotted by nominal order (the standard serial position curve), with the expected increase in the primacy and middle portion of the curve for slow compared with fast presentation rates. However, when recall was replotted by functional order, there was an abolition of the primacy effect and a reversal in the effect of presentation rate. That is, when their data were replotted by functional serial order, it was the recency and middle portions of the curve, and not the primacy portion, that was increased by a slower presentation rate. A second analysis of the rehearsals is derived from Rundus (1971), who plotted recall probability as a function of the rehearsal set to which items were last rehearsed. Again, he obtained essentially pure recency with no primacy. A third analysis of the rehearsals directly examined the claim that a slow presentation rate permits participants to rehearse early items further down the list than is possible in a fast presentation rate condition. The analysis compares the mean number of additional positions to which words in each input serial position were rehearsed for each presentation rate condition.

The overt rehearsal procedure (e.g., Rundus, 1971; Rundus & Atkinson, 1970), in which participants were asked to rehearse out loud during list presentation, was used to record participants' rehearsals.

Method

Participants

Forty students from the University of Essex participated in this experiment.

Materials and apparatus

The materials for each participant consisted of 130 words: a practice list of 10 words and six experimental lists of 20 words each. The words for each list were selected from a pool of monosyllabic nouns, which were generated from the Oxford Psycholinguistic Database (Quinlan, 1992), with frequencies of occurrence of 10 to 50 per million based on the Kučera and Francis (1967) norms. A tape recorder was used to record participants' rehearsal protocols.

Design

The experiment used a mixed-subjects design. Presentation rate was a between-subjects variable with two levels: fast (1.25 s/word) and slow (5 s/

word). The within-subjects variable was the serial position of the items in the lists.

Procedure

Twenty participants were randomly assigned to each of the two presentation rate conditions (fast and slow). Participants were tested individually and informed that they would be shown a practice list of 10 words followed by six lists of 20 words for free recall. Each trial began with a warning tone, followed after 3 s by a series of 20 words. The words were presented individually in the middle of the computer screen for 1 s. The interpresentation interval for the slow presentation rate condition was 5 s, and the interpresentation interval for the fast presentation rate condition was 1.25 s. Participants were instructed to read each word aloud as it was presented on the screen. They were also instructed to use the interval between words to rehearse aloud any words from the current list that came to mind as they were studying the list. A series of beeps signaled the beginning of the recall period, and this sounded either 1.25 s or 5 s (depending on the relevant presentation rate condition) after presentation of the last word of each list. All participants were given 1 min to write down as many words from the list as they could recall in any order they wished. A tape recorder was used to record the participants' rehearsals.

Results

The same data are considered in four different analyses. The nominal serial position curves are the standard serial position curves that plot recall performance by the presentation order. The functional serial position curves are the serial position curves used by Brodie et al. (1975, 1977). Each word in the list is rank ordered in terms of when it was last rehearsed and has its own unique functional serial position. It effectively provides a subjective rank ordering of the items that were most recently experienced.[2] The serial position plot by last rehearsal set (last R) plots recall performance as a function of the rehearsal set to which a word was most recently rehearsed. Rundus (1971) used this measurement in his Figure 2. A rehearsal set refers to any one of the 20 interpresentation intervals in a list during which the participants' rehearsals occurred. More than one word may be rehearsed to the same last R set. Finally, the fourth analysis examines the mean number of additional positions to which words in each input serial position were rehearsed.

Nominal serial position

The proportion of items recalled at each serial position for each presentation rate is shown in Figure 1A. A 2 × 5 mixed-design analysis of variance

(ANOVA) with presentation rate (slow or fast) as a between-subjects factor and nominal serial position (Serial Position [SP] 1–4, 5–8, 9–12, 13–16, or 17–20) as a within-subjects factor revealed a significant main effect of presentation rate, $F(1, 38) = 26.54$, $MSE = .029$, $p < .001$, a significant main effect of serial position, $F(4, 152) = 95.50$, $MSE = .010$, $p < .001$, and also a significant interaction, $F(4, 152) = 56.67$, $MSE = .001$. Simple main effects revealed that the effect of presentation rate was significant ($p < .001$) at all serial positions except SP 13–16 ($p > .05$). Inspection of Figure 1A shows that a slow presentation rate resulted in significantly increased recall over the fast presentation condition in the primacy and middle portions of the nominal serial position curve but also led to a reduced level of recall in the recency portion of the curve.

For the slow presentation rate condition, Tukey honestly significant difference (HSD) pairwise comparisons revealed significant differences between the mean correct recall of the early items (SP 1–4) and every other serial position ($p < .001$) and between the late items (SP 17–20) and the middle items (SP 9–12, $p < .001$, and SP 13–16, $p < .05$). For the fast presentation rate condition, Tukey HSD pairwise comparisons revealed significant differences between the late items (SP 17–20) and all other items ($p < .001$), between the early items (SP 1–4) and the middle items (SP 5–8 and 9–12, $p < .001$), and between items in SP 13–16 and SP 5–8 ($p < .05$) and SP 9–12 ($p < .01$).

Functional serial position

The proportion of items recalled at each functional serial position for each presentation rate is shown in Figure 1B. A 2 × 5 mixed-design ANOVA with presentation rate (slow or fast) as a between-subjects factor and functional serial position (SP 1–4, 5–8, 9–12, 13–16, or 17–20) as a within-subjects factor revealed a significant main effect of presentation rate, $F(1, 38) = 26.08$, $MSE = .029$, $p < .001$, a significant main effect of functional serial position, $F(4, 152) = 223.48$, $MSE = .013$, $p < .001$, and also a significant interaction, $F(4, 152) = 10.46$, $MSE = .013$, $p < .001$. Further analysis revealed that the effect of presentation rate was significant ($p < .001$) at functional SP 9–12 and SP 13–16. Thus, the serial position curves for both the fast and slow presentation rates showed exclusive recency; recall performance in the middle serial positions was greater for the slow presentation rate than for the fast presentation rate. Tukey's HSD revealed that for the slow presentation rate all serial positions were significantly different ($p < .001$) from all other serial positions, except for the difference between SP 1–4 and SP 5–8, which was not significant. For the fast presentation rate, SP 13–16 and SP 17–20 were significantly different from each other ($p < .001$) and from all other SP (all at least $p < .01$).

Last rehearsal set (Last R)

Figure 1C plots the proportion of items successfully recalled as a function of the rehearsal set to which the items were last rehearsed. Inspection of Figure 1C shows that the proportion of items successfully recalled is an increasing function of the last rehearsal set to which an item was rehearsed. There also appears to be little difference between the fast and slow presentation conditions.

A 2×9 mixed-subject ANOVA, with presentation rate (slow or fast) as a between-subjects factor and last R (Rehearsal Set [RS] 1–6, 7–8, 9–10, 11–12, 13–14, 15–16, 17–18, 19, 20) as a within-subjects factor was performed. Grouping last R in this manner provided a fine grain of analysis while ensuring an approximately equal number of observations in each group. The analysis showed a main effect of last R, $F(8, 304) = 205.95$, $MSE = .016$, $p < .001$, but not of presentation rate. The Presentation Rate × Last R interaction also failed to reach significance ($p > .05$). Tukey's HSD pairwise comparisons revealed pure recency with no primacy; RSs 15–16, 17–18, 19, and 20 were significantly different (at least $p < .01$) from each other (and all other rehearsal sets), and RS 13–14 were significantly different from all other rehearsal sets except RS 11–12.

Table 1 shows the frequencies of items that were last rehearsed at each rehearsal set. Inspection of Table 1 shows clearly that early items in the list were almost always rehearsed during later rehearsal intervals, such that there were relatively few words that were not last rehearsed beyond the early rehearsal sets. Therefore, it should be noted that the data for these early rehearsal sets are less reliable than those for the later rehearsal sets shown in Figure 1C. It is also apparent that there are higher frequencies of words rehearsed to later rehearsal sets in the slow-presentation condition compared with the fast-presentation condition. This trend can be seen more clearly in Figure 1D.

Number of positions moved

Figure 1D illustrates the mean number of positions that an item was rehearsed down the list as a function of its nominal-serial position for both presentation rates. As can be seen, the number of positions moved decreases with nominal serial position for both presentation rates. In addition, the early words in the slow condition were rehearsed further down the list than the corresponding words in the fast condition. The number of positions moved down the list by an item was analyzed by a 2×5 mixed ANOVA, with presentation rate (fast or slow) as a between-subjects factor and nominal serial position (SP 1–4, 5–8, 9–12, 13–16, 17–20) as a within-subjects factor. There was a significant main effect of presentation rate, $F(1, 38) = 119.58$,

Table 1 Frequency of words that were last rehearsed at each rehearsal set in experiments 1 and 2

		Last rehearsal set																		
Experiment		1	2	3	4	5	6	7	8	9	10	11	12	13	14	15	16	17	18	19	20
1																					
	Slow	2	2	10	39	55	96	82	106	104	130	98	124	116	125	136	136	163	204	291	378
	Fast	27	33	75	115	135	112	133	120	132	133	120	119	129	161	123	122	132	147	135	182
2																					
	HF	1	13	10	62	75	105	103	126	126	117	133	126	117	127	115	168	154	176	215	328
	LF	21	27	50	76	117	129	130	114	120	108	131	122	129	127	125	149	134	164	172	253

Note. HF = high frequency; LF = low frequency.

$MSE = 2.640$, $p < .001$, and nominal serial $F(4, 152) = 292.03$, $MSE = 1.238$, $p < .001$. The Presentation Rate × Nominal serial position interaction was also significant, $F(4, 152) = 78.14$, $MSE = 1.238$, $p < .001$. The difference in the distance items moved down the list was significant at all but the final serial positions, mirroring the between-group difference in recall of the earlier items; the effect of presentation rate was significant at nominal SPs 1–4, 5–8, and 9–12 (at at least $p < .001$). Tukey HSD pairwise comparisons revealed that, for the slow condition, the number of rehearsal sets moved for each serial position was significantly different ($p < .001$) from every other serial position, except SP 13–16, which was not significantly different from SP 9–12 and SP 17–20. For the fast condition, only SP 1–4 was significantly different from all other serial positions ($p < .001$).

Discussion

The results from Experiment 1 show typical U-shaped nominal serial position curves for both the fast and slow presentation rates. There is also the standard finding of increased primacy in the slow condition compared with the fast condition (e.g., Brodie & Murdock, 1977; Glanzer & Cunitz, 1966). The three further analyses reveal that this familiar pattern of results may be reinterpreted in terms of the recency with which individual words were rehearsed in each of the two conditions. These analyses reveal that early and middle words were rehearsed further down the list in the slow-presentation condition compared with the fast-presentation condition and that the serial position curves can be replotted by functional serial position and by last R to produce curves showing pure recency, with little or no primacy. The results are consistent with Rundus' (1971) finding that early items receive more rehearsals than later items and with Brodie and Murdock's (1977) claim that the selective rehearsal of early items to terminal serial positions aids recall. In addition, the functional serial position curves are essentially identical to those obtained by Brodie and Murdock (1977), a result that demonstrates that our measure of functional serial position is indeed a close approximation to their measure.

A recency-based account of primacy can explain these results. When words are presented at a slow rate, there is more opportunity for rehearsal; thus, more early list items are rehearsed toward the end of the list. Items that are rehearsed more often will provide more opportunities for recalling that word, will be distributed more widely throughout the list, and will also tend to be rehearsed more recently. All three factors may help increase recall performance. When the data are plotted by nominal serial position (see Figure 1A), one sees this effect as strong and extended primacy effects for both presentation rate conditions, with greater primacy for the slow-presentation condition. When the data are replotted by functional serial position (Figure 1B), this effect is seen as strong and extended recency effects for both conditions (because the mechanism for recall is recency based). There is also a differential effect of presentation rate on the recency portion of the serial position curves (because more items can be rehearsed to later rehearsal sets in the slow-presentation condition compared with the fast-presentation condition). Finally, when the data are replotted by last R (Figure 1C), there is no effect of presentation rate on the serial position curves. Although this may be simply a coincidence, it could alternatively be a manifestation of the ratio rule. The ratio rule predicts that the probability of recall is directly proportional to the ratio of the interpresentation interval and the retention interval ($\Delta t/T$). If this rule is applied to the probability of sampling from a particular rehearsal set, then the ratio for the slow presentation rate (5/5) is the same as that for the fast presentation rate (1.25/1.25). Application of the ratio rule to the level of rehearsal sets, therefore, predicts an equivalent probability of sampling across these conditions. Regardless of the exact interpretation of these analyses, it is clear that the probability of recall is strongly sensitive to the recency with which an item has been rehearsed: Items that are rehearsed toward the end of the list are more likely to be recalled.

Finally, our results differ in one way from the traditional data found in free recall when presentation rate is manipulated. We found increased recency with the fast condition compared with the slow condition. This contrasts with the typically reported finding of a lack of an effect of presentation rate on the recency portion of the nominal serial position curve (e.g., Glanzer & Cunitz, 1966). In fact, our results are similar to those obtained by Brodie et al. (Brodie, 1975; Brodie & Murdock, 1977; Brodie & Prytulak, 1975), who observed a similar although not significant crossover at the end of the serial position curve in their studies. This may reflect the difficulty in recalling recency items in the slow condition that are embedded in rehearsals of earlier (primacy) items. In the fast condition, the recency items may be more easily recalled because they are embedded in far fewer rehearsals of earlier items. The recency items in the fast condition can be considered to be more temporally distinctive than the corresponding items in the slow condition. This explanation is consistent with the recency effects observed in Experiment 4.

Experiment 2

The aim of Experiment 2 was to examine the effect of word frequency on free recall. Word frequency has, like presentation rate, been shown to affect the beginning but not the middle and ending portions of the serial position curve (Raymond, 1969; Sumby, 1963). High-frequency (HF) words occurring in early list positions are generally better recalled than the corresponding low-frequency (LF) words. Most studies of the word frequency effect in free recall have shown a recall advantage for pure HF lists in comparison to pure LF lists (e.g., DeLosh & McDaniel, 1996). The advantage for HF words has been thought by some researchers to result from a greater degree of organizational and associative processing for these words (e.g., Gregg, 1976; Sumby, 1963).

DeLosh and McDaniel (1996) proposed the order-encoding hypothesis to explain the word frequency effect in free recall. The order-encoding hypothesis makes two assumptions. First, free-recall performance is based on contributions from both individual item information and relational/order information. Although the free-recall task does not appear to require order information, there are clear order effects both in terms of the serial position curves and also in terms of the output order of recall (e.g., Howard & Kahana, 1999; Kahana, 1996; Laming, 1999; Wixted, Ghadisha, & Vera, 1997). These findings suggest that, although order information is not required in successful free recall, it is nonetheless an influential factor. Second, although order information is usually encoded, resources are lured away from processing order information if the item is particularly distinctive. In the case of frequency effects, DeLosh and McDaniel (1996) argued that participants encode the item information associated with HF words more easily than for LF words and so can process the HF words more effectively for order than the LF words.

A third possibility, stemming from the extension of the ratio rule, is that HF and LF words are differentially rehearsed in free recall. It may be that HF words are rehearsed more often, are more widely distributed, and are rehearsed further toward the end of the list than LF words. According to the extention of the ratio rule, all three of these factors will tend to increase recall performance; hence, HF words will tend to be recalled more often than LF words, particularly for items in early list positions. This third possibility need not be incompatible with the two earlier accounts. For example, one reason why HF words may be more easily rehearsed than LF words is that HF words may be more easily brought to mind because they have more elaborative associations (cf. Gregg, 1976; Sumby, 1963). Alternatively, rehearsal may offer a candidate mechanism for the encoding of order/relational information in DeLosh and McDaniel's (1996) order-encoding hypothesis.

Method

Participants

Forty students from the University of Essex participated in this experiment. None had taken part in Experiment 1.

Materials and apparatus

A total of 260 monosyllabic nouns were selected from the Oxford Psycholinguistic Database (Quinlan, 1992), and frequency counts were based on Kučera and Francis' (1967) word frequency norms. Half of the words were of HF (occurrence greater than 100 per million) and half were of LF (occurrence less than 4 per million). From this item pool, six HF lists and 6 LF lists of 20 items each and two 10-word practice lists were constructed, one for each condition. The order and composition of each list were assigned randomly and were different for each participant. A tape recorder was used to record participants' rehearsal protocols.

Design

There were two independent variables. Word frequency was a between-subjects independent variable with two levels (high and low), and serial position was a within-subjects variable.

Procedure

All participants were given practice at free recall with a list of 10 words, followed by six further tests of free recall with the experimental lists of 20 words each. Equal numbers of participants were randomly assigned to the HF and LF conditions. The words were presented one at a time in the center of the computer screen for 1 s, with a rehearsal interval of 3 s after each word. The participants were instructed to read each word aloud as it was presented on the screen and, additionally, to use the 3-s rehearsal interval to rehearse aloud any words from the current list that came to mind as they were studying the list. After the last rehearsal interval, a series of beeps signaled the beginning of the recall period, during which participants were given 1 min to write down as many words from the list as they could recall in any order they wished.

Results

The results were analyzed using the same four procedures used in Experiment 1.

Nominal serial position

The proportion of items recalled at each nominal serial position for each word frequency is shown in Figure 2A. A 2 × 5 mixed-design ANOVA with word frequency (high or low) as a between-subjects factor and nominal serial position (SP 1–4, 5–8, 9–12, 13–16, or 17–20) as a within-subjects factor was performed. This revealed a significant main effect of word frequency, $F(1, 38) = 9.00$, $MSE = .033$, $p < .01$, a significant main effect of nominal serial position, $F(4, 152) = 36.83$, $MSE = .021$, $p < .001$, and a significant interaction between word frequency and nominal serial position, $F(4, 152) = 3.22$, $MSE = .021$, $p = .01$. Further analysis revealed that the effect of frequency was significant at SP 1–4, $F(1, 190) = 17.72$, $MSE = .024$, $p < .001$, and approached significance at SP 5–8, $F(1, 190) = 3.75$, $MSE = .024$, $p = .05$. For the HF words, Tukey HSD pairwise comparisons of the main effect of nominal serial position revealed a significant difference between the mean correct recall of the early items (SP 1–4) and every other serial position ($p < .001$) and between the late items (SP 17–20) and items in SP 5–8, 9–12 ($p < .01$), and 13–16 ($p < .05$). For the LF words, Tukey HSD pairwise comparisons revealed a significant difference between the mean correct recall of the early items (SP 1–4) and all other items ($p < .001$), except those in SP 17–20, and between the recall of the late items (SP 17–20) and items in SP 5–8, 9–12, and 13–16 ($p < .001$).

The results show the standard effect of word frequency on free recall: The recall advantage of HF words is limited to the primacy portion of the nominal serial position curve.

Functional serial position

The proportion of items recalled at each functional serial position for each word frequency is shown in Figure 2B. A 2 × 5 mixed-design ANOVA with word frequency (high or low) as a between-subjects factor and functional serial position (SP 1–4, 5–8, 9–12, 13–16, or 17–20) as a within-subjects factor revealed a significant main effect of word frequency, $F(1, 38) = 8.93$, $MSE = .033$, $p < .01$, and a significant main effect of functional serial position, $F(4, 152) = 131.34$, $MSE = .015$, $p < .001$. The interaction between word frequency and functional serial position was not significant. Tukey HSD pairwise comparisons of the main effect of functional serial position revealed that all functional serial positions were significantly different from all other functional serial positions ($p < .001$), except for SP 1–4 and SP 5–8, which were not significantly different from each other.

Last rehearsal set

Figure 2C illustrates the mean probability of recall plotted as a function of the last R set to which an item was rehearsed. For purposes of statistical analysis, last R was grouped in two ways. The first method of grouping provided a finer grain of analysis, whereas the second method resulted in a more balanced number of observations within each level.

In the first analysis, recall was analyzed by a 2 × 8 mixed ANOVA with word frequency (HF or LF) as a between-subjects factor and last R (RS 1–6, 7–8, 9–10, 11–12, 13–14, 15–16, 17–18, 19–20) as a within-subjects factor. The analysis revealed a main effect of last R, $F(7, 266) = 79.93$, $MSE = .020$, $p < .001$, but no effect of word frequency ($p > .05$). The interaction between the two variables was also not significant ($p > .05$). Analysis revealed that the probability of recall of an item was primarily affected by the recency of its last rehearsal. Tukey HSD pairwise comparisons of the means revealed that rehearsal sets 17–18 and 19–20 were significantly different from each other and from all other rehearsal sets (all at least $p < .05$). There was also a significant difference between RS 15–16 and all other rehearsal sets except 13–14 (all at least $p < .05$). RS 13–14 was also significantly different from RS 1–6, 7–8, and 11–12 (all at least $p < .05$).

In the second analysis with more equally balanced groups, recall was analyzed by a 2×7 mixed ANOVA, with word frequency (HF or LF) as a between-subjects factor and last R (RSs 1–7, 8–10, 11–12, 13–15, 16–17, 18–19, 20) as a within-subjects factor. This analysis similarly revealed a main effect of last R, $F(6, 228) = 140.17$, $MSE = .018$, $p < .001$, but not of word frequency ($p > .05$). The interaction between the two variables was also not significant ($p > .05$). Recall was similarly shown to be recency based; Tukey HSD pairwise comparisons revealed significant differences between rehearsal sets 13–15, 18–19, and 20 and all other rehearsal sets (all at least $p < .01$). Rehearsal sets 16–17 were also significantly different from all other rehearsal sets ($p < .001$) except rehearsal sets 13–15.

Inspection of Figure 2C shows that, with the exception of the first few rehearsal sets, the probability of recalling an item was primarily affected by the recency of its last rehearsal. Although recall appeared to be superior in the first few rehearsal sets, the primacy effects did not reach significance. Table 1 provides the frequencies (number of rehearsals) on which the last R function is based for both HF and LF items. It should be noted that the proportions of words correctly recalled in these early rehearsal sets were based on far fewer observations than the other rehearsal sets.

Number of positions moved

Figure 2D shows the mean number of positions that an item was transferred down the list via rehearsal as a function of its nominal serial position. It can be seen that the mean number of rehearsal sets moved by an item decreases with serial position, and that the early HF words were rehearsed further down the list than the early LF items.

The mean number of rehearsal sets moved was analyzed by a 2×5 mixed ANOVA, with word frequency (HF or LF) as a between-subjects factor and nominal serial position (SP 1–4, 5–8, 9–12, 13–16, 17–20) as a within-subjects factor. There was a significant main effect of both word frequency, $F(1, 38) = 6.86$, $MSE = 7.22$, $p < .05$, and nominal serial position, $F(4, 152) = 100.59$, $MSE = 3.52$, $p < .001$. The Word Frequency $\times$ Nominal serial position interaction was also significant, $F(4, 152) = 3.54$, $MSE = 3.52$, $p < .01$. Further analyses revealed a significant effect of word frequency at nominal serial positions 1–4 ($p < .001$) and 5–8 ($p < .05$).

Discussion

The results from Experiment 2 suggest that the increased primacy associated with HF words in the nominal serial position curves may be explained by the fact that HF words occurring early in the list tend to be rehearsed more often, are more widely distributed, and are rehearsed further down the list than corresponding LF words. The results are clearly consistent with an extension of the ratio rule that takes into account the rehearsals of all items. Such an account predicts that all three factors will increase the probability of recall of HF words compared with LF words, particularly at the early serial positions.

One possible reason why HF words were more frequently rehearsed is that they were more easily accessible because of the high levels of associative and organizational processing that they elicit (cf. Gregg, 1976; Sumby, 1963). The results are also consistent with the proposal that rehearsal is a candidate mechanism for encoding order/relational information in the DeLosh and McDaniel (1996) Order-encoding hypothesis. Furthermore, the results from Experiment 2 are consistent with the recency-based explanation of primacy discussed in Experiment 1. When the data in Experiment 2 were reanalyzed in terms of functional serial position and by last R, the probability of recall was strongly sensitive to recency and there was little or no indication of primacy (Figures 2B and 2C).

There are several potential explanations for the slight primacy observed in the last R plot. The first is that this effect is genuine, indicating the advantage in temporal distinctiveness that the first few items enjoy solely by virtue of their early serial positions (e.g., Murdock, 1960; Neath, 1993; Wixted & McDowell, 1989). An alternative explanation is that it occurs as a result of item-item associations. An item that was rehearsed to the end of the list may have been rehearsed earlier with an item that was quickly dropped from rehearsal. It is, therefore, possible that following the recall of the items that were rehearsed most recently, a few earlier associated items were cued, such that the level of recall of these items remained high even though they were dropped from rehearsal very early on. A third alternative is that participants rehearse some early items covertly. In this case, items that were actually rehearsed to the end of the list and so are, correctly, recency items are interpreted as primacy items because the critical rehearsals were not recorded. This explanation can be supported by the finding that participants in some studies reported that they selectively fail to overtly vocalize all their rehearsals of the first items in a list (e.g., Brodie & Prytulak, 1975). Whatever the cause of the slight primacy advantage in the last R plots, it is important to note that they are the result of a relatively small number of words (see Table 1). We can, therefore, conclude that the vast majority of words can be successfully accounted for by an extension of the ratio rule that takes into account the number, distribution, and recency of the rehearsals of the study items.[3]

Experiment 3

Experiments 1 and 2 have been discussed with respect to an extension of the ratio rule that takes into account the number, distribution, and recency of the rehearsals of the study items. However, the results have been replotted only by the functional serial position, the recency of the last rehearsal of an item, and the number of serial positions moved. These three analyses emphasize the importance of the recency of the last rehearsal with immediate testing but ignore the importance of the number of rehearsals and the distribution of earlier rehearsals.

There are clearly problems with a model of primacy based solely on the recency of the last rehearsal of an item. If primacy was solely attributable to the recency of participants' rehearsals, then it might be expected that the insertion of a distractor period after the end of the list and before recall would affect primacy as much as it does recency. However, this is known not to be the case. In experiments in which a distractor period follows list presentation, recency, but not primacy, is eliminated (e.g., Glanzer & Cunitz, 1966; Postman & Phillips, 1965). Although this evidence was originally taken to be evidence for a temporary and labile STS, we have seen in the introduction that it is only theories that underpin the ratio rule (e.g., Baddeley & Hitch, 1993; Crowder, 1993; Glenberg, 1984, 1987; Glenberg & Swanson, 1986; Glenberg et al., 1980) that can account for the level of recency in the full range of different temporal and distractor conditions.

However, before ruling out recency mechanisms based solely on the last rehearsal of an item, it is worth investigating the extent to which the distractor task truly prevents rehearsal. The distractor tasks used in delayed-recall experiments tend to be fairly simple, such as forward (Glanzer & Cunitz, 1966) or backward (Postman & Phillips, 1965) counting by 1s. It is, therefore, possible, as Poltrock and MacLeod (1977) suggested, that primacy effects after a filled retention interval may be due to covert rehearsal during the distractor task. If the early items were selectively rehearsed throughout the distractor period, then the early list items, but not the recency items, would be recently rehearsed at the time of recall. There is some evidence for this possibility. Glenberg et al. (1980) found that increasing the difficulty of the distractor task during the interpresentation interval in a continuous distractor task paradigm greatly reduced recall in the primacy and middle portions of the serial position curve, such that primacy was reduced from four items to two items. However, this argument should not be overplayed: Modest but significant primacy effects have been reported in situations in which rehearsal is unlikely, such as incidental learning followed by free recall (e.g., Baddeley & Hitch, 1977; Pinto & Baddeley, 1991) and under extremely demanding continuous distractor conditions (e.g., Watkins, Neath, & Sechler, 1989).

Nevertheless, Experiment 3 investigated the effect of two different distractor tasks on free recall to test this hypothesis (which we can call the covert selective rehearsal hypothesis). Both distractor tasks involved counting: The easy task required participants to count forward by 1s, and the other task, which was presumed to be more difficult, required participants to count backward by 3s. The covert selective rehearsal hypothesis predicts that if participants can engage in covert rehearsal of items from the list while performing the distractor task, then they should selectively rehearse more early items covertly during the easy distractor task than during the difficult distractor task. Selective covert rehearsal would, therefore, lead to better recall for the early items in the easy distractor condition than in the difficult distractor condition and to worse recall in both these conditions compared with one requiring immediate recall with no distractor interval.

Method

Participants

Thirty students from the University of Essex participated. None had participated in the previous experiments.

Materials and apparatus

The materials and apparatus were the same as those used in Experiment 1.

Design

There were two independent variables: Distractor condition was a between-subjects variable with three levels (no distractor, easy distractor, and hard distractor), and serial position was a within-subjects variable.

Procedure

Ten participants performed free recall with no distractor task, 10 performed free recall with an easy distractor task, and 10 performed free recall with a hard distractor task. The participants were randomly assigned to their respective distractor conditions. The experimental procedure in the no distractor condition was equivalent to that used in Experiment 2. The experimental procedure in the two distractor conditions was also equivalent to that used in Experiment 2, except that participants in the easy distractor condition were presented with an additional random digit (between 0 and 9) immediately after the end of the list. They were required to count forward by 1s out loud from that number until they heard a series of beeps signaling the beginning of the recall period. The hard distractor condition differed from the easy distractor condition in that the participants were presented with a random three-digit number (instead of a single digit). They were told to count backward by 3s out loud from that number until they heard a series of beeps signaling the beginning of the recall period. The distractor period in each distractor condition lasted 30 s. At the end of the experiment, participants in the easy distractor and hard distractor conditions were asked to rate the difficulty of the distractor task that they performed on a scale of 1 (*extremely easy*) to 9 (*extremely difficult*).

Results

The results were analyzed using two of the four procedures used in Experiment 1. Analysis of participants' ratings of the two tasks revealed that the hard distractor task was rated as significantly more difficult than the easy distractor task, $t(18) = 3.36, p < .01$.

Nominal serial position

Figure 3A shows the proportion of correct responses as a function of nominal serial position for each of the three distractor conditions. A 3×5 mixed ANOVA with distractor condition (no distractor, easy distractor, or hard distractor) as a between-subjects factor and nominal serial position (SP 1–4, 5–8, 9–12, 13–16, or 17–20) as a within-subjects factor revealed that there was a significant main effect of serial position, $F(4, 108) = 24.31$, $MSE = .016, p < .001$, but no significant main effect of distractor condition ($p > .05$). There was also a significant interaction between distractor condition and serial position, $F(8, 108) = 3.59$, $MSE = .016, p = .001$. Further analysis revealed that the effect of distractor condition was significant only at SP 17–20, $F(2, 135) = 7.54$, $MSE = .025, p < .001$, confirming the traditional effect of distractor task on recency.

In line with conventional findings, marked recency was found in the no distractor condition, whereas the recency effect was abolished in the easy distractor and hard distractor conditions. It can also be seen that there was no effect of distractor task on the primacy portion of the curve. If anything, performance on the primacy items was improved by the filled interval, and the hard distractor condition resulted in greater primacy than the easy distractor condition. These results are contradictory to the predictions of the covert selective rehearsal hypothesis and, as such, provide evidence that the selective rehearsal of early items during the distractor interval was not responsible for the intact primacy effect after a filled delay.

Number of positions moved

Figure 3B illustrates the mean number of positions that an item was transferred down the list as a function of its nominal (input) serial position for all three distractor conditions. It can be seen that the number of positions moved by an item decreased with serial position. The difference between an item's nominal serial position and the last rehearsal set to which it was rehearsed was analyzed by a 3 × 5 mixed ANOVA, with distractor condition (no distractor, easy distractor, or hard distractor) as a between-subjects factor and nominal serial position (SP 1–4, 5–8, 9–12, 13–16, 17–20) as a within-subjects factor. There was a significant main effect of serial position, $F(5, 135) = 117.46$, $MSE = .946$, $p < .001$, but not of distractor condition ($p > .05$). The Distractor Condition × Serial Position interaction was not significant ($p > .05$). Further analysis of the main effect of serial position revealed a significant difference between SP 1–6 and all other serial positions ($p < .001$), between SP 7–9 and SP 16–18 ($p < .01$) and SP 19–20 ($p < .001$), between SP 10–12 and SP 19–20 ($p < .001$), and between SP 13–15 and SP 19–20 ($p < .05$).

Discussion

The results from Experiment 3 show that models of primacy that are based solely on the recency of the last rehearsal of an item are inadequate. Primacy effects, but not recency effects, survived a filled delay, and there was no evidence that participants engaged in covert rehearsal of the early list items during the distractor interval. The rejection of the covert selective rehearsal hypothesis necessitates that the most simple, recency-based explanations of primacy must be rejected. This is because, in the absence of covert selective rehearsal, a mechanism based solely on the recency of the last instantiation of an item must predict that both recency and primacy should be reduced with an increase in retention interval. It is difficult to argue that participants in different conditions (distractor condition was a between-subjects factor) were using different rehearsal strategies, because there appears to be little or no significant difference in the pattern of rehearsals of participants across conditions (see Figure 3B).

The results of Experiment 3, therefore, suggest that more than one factor is important in determining recall. Experiment 4 investigated whether an extension of the ratio rule, which considered the number and distribution of rehearsals as well as the recency of the rehearsals, could account for the pattern of performance with both immediate and delayed testing.

Experiment 4

In Experiment 4, the participants' rehearsal strategy and the retention interval were manipulated. Participants were either required to adopt a fixed-rehearsal strategy in which they rehearsed only the item that was currently being presented or were free to rehearse any item they wished. After the end of the list, they were tested either immediately or after a period of distractor activity.

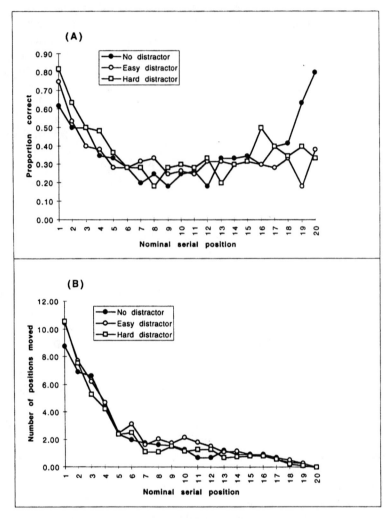

Figure 3 Experiment 3: Mean proportion of correct responses as a function of nominal serial position (A) Mean number of rehearsal sets moved by the nominal serial position of the list items (B).

The first aim of Experiment 4 was to test the predictions of an extension of the ratio rule that considers the number, distribution, and recency of the rehearsals of the items. According to this account, the probability of recalling any instantiation of an item will depend on the ratio of the interval between that item and its nearest neighbors (the interpresentation interval) and its retention interval. In the free-rehearsal conditions, the early items are rehearsed frequently, the rehearsals are widely distributed, and the items are rehearsed toward the end of the list. In the fixed-rehearsal conditions, all items are rehearsed to the same extent, the rehearsals are less widely distributed, and the items are not rehearsed toward the end of the list. Therefore, according to the extension of the ratio rule, recall of early items should be far greater in the free-rehearsal than the fixed-rehearsal conditions. By contrast, the recency items in the free-recall conditions are rarely rehearsed, and they are embedded within rehearsals of earlier items, whereas the recency items in the fixed-recall conditions are rehearsed as often as any other item, and they are not embedded within rehearsals of earlier items. According to the extension of the ratio rule, recall of later items should be greater in the fixed-rehearsal than the free-rehearsal conditions.

The extension of the ratio rule further predicts that, after a filled retention interval, performance on both rehearsal conditions will decrease. This is largely because the critical ratio determining recall ($\Delta t / T$) will be decreased with a filled retention interval (because T has increased). However, the extension of the ratio rule again predicts less primacy and greater recency in the fixed-rehearsal condition compared with the free-rehearsal condition.

A second aim of Experiment 4 was to investigate the level of primacy in the fixed-rehearsal condition. In Experiments 1 and 2, there were small, although not significant, primacy effects in the analysis by last R. One possibility was that these effects were genuine, reflecting the greater temporal distinctiveness of the first one or two items (Murdock, 1960; Neath, 1993; Wixted & McDowell, 1989). However, interpretation of the finding was complicated because there were relatively few data points in the early last R positions. The fixed-rehearsal strategy condition of Experiment 4 allowed a more systematic investigation of these primacy effects. Because the participants were instructed to rehearse only the currently presented item, the nominal serial position is equivalent to the plot by last R, and the frequencies across the serial positions should be equivalent.

Method

Participants

Forty students from the University of Essex participated. None had taken part in the previous experiments.

Materials

We drew from the Oxford Psycholinguistic Database (Quinlan, 1992) 250 monosyllabic nouns with frequencies of occurrence of 10 to 50 per million based on Kučera and Francis's (1967) word-frequency norms. From this item pool, 12 experimental lists of 20 words each and a practice list of 10 words were constructed. A tape recorder was used to record participants' rehearsal protocols.

Design

There was one between-subjects variable and two within-subjects variables. Rehearsal strategy was a between-subjects variable with two levels (fixed rehearsal or free rehearsal). Retention interval was a within-subjects variable with two levels (immediate or delayed recall). Serial position was also a within-subjects variable.

Procedure

One half of the participants were assigned at random to each of the two types of rehearsal condition. Those participants in the free-rehearsal condition were instructed to read each word aloud as it was presented on the screen and, additionally, to use the interval between words to rehearse aloud any words from the current list that came to mind as they were studying the list. Those participants in the fixed-rehearsal condition were instructed to read each word aloud as it was presented on the screen and to continue rehearsing only that word aloud at a fairly constant rate until the next word appeared on the screen. All participants were presented with a practice list of 10 words requiring delayed recall, followed by 12 experimental lists, each of 20 words. Half of the lists required immediate recall, and the other half required delayed recall. The lists were presented in a random order, and participants were not told whether immediate or delayed recall was required until the end of each list. The words were presented one at a time in the center of the computer screen for 1 s, with a rehearsal interval of 3 s occurring between words. In the immediate-recall condition, a series of beeps after the last rehearsal interval signaled the beginning of the recall period. In the delayed-recall condition, a random digit between 0 and 9 appeared on the screen after the last rehearsal interval. Participants were told to count forward by 1s out loud from that number. After 30 s, they heard a series of beeps signaling the beginning of the recall period. During the recall period, participants were given 1 min to write down as many words from the list as they could recall in any order they wished. The participants' overt rehearsals during list presentation were recorded using a tape recorder.

Results

Nominal serial position

Figure 4A shows recall performance as a function of the nominal serial position for each of the four experimental conditions. A 2 (rehearsal type) × 2 (retention interval) × 5 (serial position) mixed ANOVA, with rehearsal type (free or fixed) as a between-subjects factor and retention interval (immediate or delayed) and serial position (SP 1–4, 5–8, 9–12, 13–16, 17–20) as

546

within-subjects factors was performed. This revealed a significant main effect of retention interval, $F(1, 38) = 55.90$, $MSE = .006$, $p < .001$, and a significant main effect of serial position, $F(4, 152) = 45.55$, $MSE = .020$, $p < .001$, but not of rehearsal type. The Rehearsal Type × Serial Position interaction, $F(4, 152) = 12.20$, $MSE = .020$, $p < .001$, and the Retention Interval × Serial Position interaction were significant, $F(4, 152) = 33.12$, $MSE = .011$, $p < .001$. The Rehearsal Type × Retention Interval interaction was not significant. The three-way interaction between Rehearsal Type × Retention Interval × Serial Position was also not significant. Simple main effects revealed that there was an effect of rehearsal type at SP 1–4, $F(1, 190) = 20.78$, $p < .001$, and SP 17–20, $F(1, 190) = 11.26$, $p = .001$. The effect of retention interval at SP 17–20 was also significant, $F(1, 190) = 176.13$, $MSE = .010$, $p < .001$. To determine whether there was any primacy in the fixed-rehearsal conditions, the results from the first set of four words from these conditions were subjected to a planned linear contrast analysis. This revealed a significant primacy advantage, $F(1, 57) = 7.55$, $p < .01$ for the immediate-fixed rehearsal condition but not for the delayed fixed rehearsal condition ($p > .05$).

From Figure 4A, it can be seen that there were different levels of recency across the four conditions; the two fixed-rehearsal conditions showed more recency than the corresponding free-rehearsal conditions.

Number of positions moved

Figure 4B shows the number of positions that an item was transferred down the list as a function of its input serial position. In line with the previous findings, the number of positions moved by an item is seen to decrease with serial position. The difference between an item's nominal serial position and the last rehearsal set to which it was rehearsed was analyzed by a 2 × 5 ANOVA, with retention interval (immediate or delayed) and nominal serial position (SP 1–4, 5–8, 9–12, 13–16, 17–20) as within-subjects factors. There was a significant main effect of serial position, $F(4, 76) = 42.21$, $MSE = 5.34$, $p < .001$. There was no main effect of retention interval ($p > .05$), and the two-way interaction was not significant ($p > .05$). Tukey pairwise comparisons on the main effect of nominal serial position revealed significant differences between SP 1–4 and all other serial positions ($p < .001$) and between SP 5–8 and SP 13–16 ($p < .05$) and SP 17–20 ($p < .01$).

Discussion

The results from Experiment 4 show that the primacy effect was greatly attenuated in the fixed-rehearsal conditions compared with the free-rehearsal conditions (Figure 4A). This finding replicates previous studies with fixed rehearsal (e.g., Fischler et al., 1970; Glanzer & Meinzer, 1967) and is consistent with other results that implicate a distributed selective rehearsal account

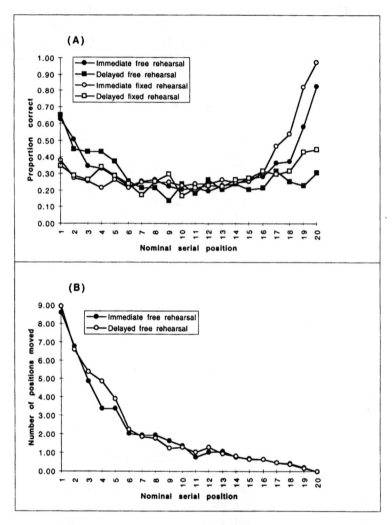

Figure 4 Experiment 4: Mean proportion of correct responses as a function of nominal serial position (A). Mean number of rehearsal sets moved by the nominal serial position of the list items (B).

of primacy effects (e.g., Modigliani & Hedges, 1987). The fact that a small yet significant primacy effect is obtained in the immediate fixed condition also suggests that the primacy items enjoy a small recall advantage by virtue of the additional temporal distinctiveness of their early list positions (e.g., Murdock, 1960; Wixted & McDowell, 1989).

The results also demonstrate that a period of distractor activity greatly reduces the recency effect but has little or no effect on the primacy effect.

This finding is consistent with the results of Experiment 3 and Glanzer and Cunitz (1966). This finding also provides further evidence that the recall of primacy items after a delay is less sensitive to the recency of the most recent rehearsal and more sensitive to the number and distribution of rehearsals, an issue that is returned to in Experiment 7.

The results also show that recency was increased in the fixed-rehearsal compared with the free-rehearsal conditions for both immediate and delayed recall. This result suggests that the large and extended recency effects found with standard (free) rehearsal instructions provide an underestimate of the recall advantage associated with the last items in the list. Under free-rehearsal conditions, the recency items are embedded within rehearsals of the early list items. They receive relatively few additional rehearsals and must be retrieved from a mass of rehearsals of earlier items. By contrast, the recency items in the fixed conditions are not embedded within rehearsals of early list items. They receive the same number of additional rehearsals as all the other items and must be retrieved from a mass of rehearsals of repeated recency items. This pattern of results is consistent with a recency-based account of episodic memory such as extensions to the ratio rule. However, the increase in recency with fixed-rehearsal conditions in Experiment 4 is difficult to reconcile with a traditional STS account of recency because, according to these accounts, a recency effect should be abolished by a period of distractor activity regardless of the type of rehearsal used.

Therefore, the results from Experiment 4 may be explained by an extension of the ratio rule that considers the number, distribution, and recency of the rehearsals of the study items. At immediate testing, recall performance appears to be greatly sensitive to the recency of the last rehearsal of an item. However, after a filled delay, it is the distribution and number of rehearsals that best predict recall. The hypothesis was able to predict all but a small primacy effect in the immediate fixed-rehearsal condition, suggesting that a recency-based account of memory incorporating the ratio rule can account for the majority of primacy effects in free recall. It is interesting to note that the recency effect is also reduced with a slow presentation rate such as in Experiment 2 and in Brodie and Murdock (1977). Under these conditions, the recency items are embedded within very large numbers of rehearsals of earlier items, and so the difficulty in accessing the recency items is increased. It appears that the reduction in recency for the slow presentation condition in Experiment 2 may be a more exaggerated form of the reduction in recency between fixed and free recall in Experiment 4.

Experiment 5

The main conclusion from the results of Experiments 1 to 4 is that the primacy effect in free recall may be caused by a recency-based mechanism acting on the number, distribution, and recency of the study items and their rehearsals. One aim of Experiment 5 was to confirm this conclusion. Each participant in Experiment 5 was presented with a schedule of words that directly reflected the subjective distribution of study items and rehearsals of a participant in Experiment 2. If the primacy effect in free recall was caused by a recency-based mechanism acting on the distribution of study items and their rehearsals, then it should be possible to reproduce essentially the same nominal U-shaped serial position curves.

A second aim was to examine the role of rehearsal in determining the serial position curve. If rehearsal acts only as a mechanism for repeating and reordering items, then there should be little difference between the results of Experiment 2 and Experiment 5. If, however, rehearsal involves the active selection and maintenance of items, then one might expect a recall advantage in Experiment 2, in which rehearsal is more active, compared with Experiment 5, in which the schedule of rehearsals was passively presented to participants.

These two aims were addressed in Experiment 5 by comparing performance across three experimental conditions. Participants in the HF condition received presentation schedules that directly reflected the content and order of rehearsals of participants in the HF condition of Experiment 2. Participants in the LF condition received presentation schedules that directly reflected the content and order of rehearsals of participants in the LF condition of Experiment 2. Finally, participants in the LF/HF condition received the words in the LF condition of Experiment 2 but the order of rehearsals of participants in the HF condition of Experiment 2. A third and final aim of Experiment 5 was to determine whether the difference in presentation schedules associated with HF and LF words could solely account for the effects of word frequency in free recall.

Method

Participants

Sixty students from the University of Essex participated in this experiment. None had taken part in the previous experiments.

Materials

Twenty different presentation schedules were constructed for each experimental condition. For the HF and LF conditions, the presentation schedules directly reflected the content and distribution of rehearsals of the 20 participants in the respective HF and LF conditions of Experiment 2. For the LF/ HF condition, the presentation schedules directly reflected the content of the LF words in Experiment 2 with the distribution of rehearsals of each of the 20 participants in the HF condition of Experiment 2.

Design

There were two independent variables. Presentation schedule was a between-subjects variable with three levels (HF, LF, or LF/HF). Serial position was a within-subjects variable.

Procedure

All participants were given practice at free recall with a list of 10 words, followed by six further tests of free recall with the experimental lists each of 20 words. Twenty participants received HF words with a HF schedule of rehearsals, 20 participants received LF words with a LF schedule of rehearsals, 20 participants received LF words with a HF schedule of rehearsals. The participants were randomly assigned to their respective experimental conditions.

The presentation schedules directly reflected the individual participants' subjective schedules in Experiment 2. All words were presented one at a time in the center of the computer screen. The initial presentation of each word was for 1 s. The presentation time for each word that was rehearsed in the rehearsal interval was calculated by dividing the 3-s rehearsal interval equally by the number of rehearsed words in that rehearsal interval. The screen was cleared between each rehearsal, such that two rehearsals of the same item could be differentiated from a single rehearsal (there was the briefest "flash" between presentations of the two rehearsals). The participants were instructed to read each word aloud as it was presented on the screen and to continue to rehearse the word while it remained on the screen. After the last rehearsal interval, a series of beeps signaled the beginning of the recall period, during which participants were given 1 min to write down as many words from the list as they could recall in any order they wished.

Results

The results were first analyzed using three of the four procedures used in Experiment 2. The analysis by the number of positions an item was transferred down the list was not included because the distribution of rehearsals in Experiment 5 was based on the results of Experiment 2 (which are displayed in Figure 2D). An additional comparison of the proportion of items recalled at each nominal serial position was made between Experiments 2 and 5.

Nominal serial position

The proportion of items recalled at each nominal serial position for each word frequency is shown in Figure 5A. A 3×5 mixed-design ANOVA with presentation schedule (HF, LF, or LF/HF) as a between-subjects factor, and

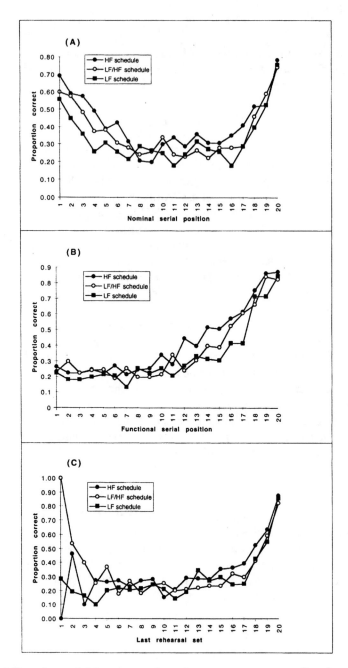

Figure 5 Experiment 5: Mean proportion of correct responses as a function of nominal serial position (A), functional serial position (B), and last rehearsal set
to which an item was rehearsed (C). HF = high frequency; LF = low
frequency.

nominal serial position (SP 1–4, 5–8, 9–12, 13–16, or 17–20) as a within-subjects factor was performed. This revealed a significant main effect of presentation schedule, $F(2, 57) = 9.49$, $MSE = .020$, $p < .001$, and of nominal serial position, $F(4, 228) = 47.44$, $MSE = .020$, $p < .001$. The interaction between presentation schedule and nominal serial position was not significant ($p > .05$). Planned pairwise comparisons of the main effect of presentation schedule revealed significant differences between the HF and LF/HF conditions, $t(38) = 2.30$, $p < .05$, between the HF and LF conditions, $t(38) = 4.35$, $p < .001$, and between the LF/HF and LF conditions, $t(38) = 2.05$, $p < .05$.

Functional serial position

The proportion of items recalled at each functional serial position for each word frequency is shown in Figure 5B. A 3 × 5 mixed-design ANOVA with presentation schedule (HF, LF, or LF/HF) as a between-subjects factor and functional serial position (SP 1–4, 5–8, 9–12, 13–16, or 17–20) as a within-subjects factor revealed a significant main effect of presentation schedule, $F(2, 57) = 9.49$, $MSE = .020$, $p < .001$, and a significant main effect of functional serial position, $F(4, 228) = 208.87$, $MSE = .013$, $p < .001$. The interaction between presentation schedule and functional serial position was not significant ($p > .05$). Tukey pairwise comparisons of the main effect of presentation schedule revealed a significant difference between the HF schedule and LF schedule ($p < .001$). Tukey pairwise comparisons of the main effect of functional serial position revealed that SP 13–16 and SP 17–20 were significantly different from each other and from all other functional serial positions (all $p < .001$).

Last rehearsal set

Figure 5C illustrates recall plotted as a function of the last R to which an item was rehearsed. For purposes of statistical analysis, last R was grouped in two ways. The first method of grouping provided a finer grain of analysis, whereas the second resulted in a more balanced number of observations within each level.

In the first analysis, recall was analyzed by a 2 × 8 mixed ANOVA presentation schedule (HF or LF) as a between-subjects factor and last R (Rehearsal Intervals 1–6, 7–8, 9–10, 11–12, 13–14, 15–16, 17–18, or 19–20) as a within-subjects factor. The analysis revealed a main effect of last R, $F(7, 399) = 124.91$, $p < .001$, but no effect of presentation schedule ($p > .05$). The interaction between the two variables was also not significant ($p > .05$). The probability of recall of an item was primarily affected by the recency of its last rehearsal. Tukey HSD pairwise comparisons of the means revealed that RSs 17–18 and 19–20 were significantly different from each other and from all other rehearsal sets (all at least $p < .01$). There was also a significant difference between RS 15–16 and all other rehearsal sets except RS 13–14 (all at least $p < .05$). RS 13–14 was also significantly different from RS 11–12 ($p < .05$).

In the second analysis with more equally balanced groups, recall was analyzed by a 2 × 7 mixed ANOVA, with presentation schedule (HF or LF) as a between-subjects factor and last R (Rehearsal Intervals 1–7, 8–10, 11–12, 13–15, 16–17, 18–19, or 20) as a within-subjects factor. This analysis similarly revealed a main effect of last R, $F(6, 342) = 226.79$, $MSE = .016$, $p < .001$, but not of presentation schedule ($p > .05$). The interaction between the two variables was also not significant ($p > .05$). Recall was similarly shown to be recency based, with Tukey HSD pairwise comparisons revealing that RSs 18–19 and 20 were significantly different from each other and from all other rehearsal sets (all $p < .001$). Rehearsal set 16–17 was also significantly different from all other rehearsal sets (all at least $p < .05$) except rehearsal set 13–15. There was also a significant difference between RSs 11–12 and 13–15 ($p < .01$).

Inspection of Figure 5C shows that, with the exception of the first few rehearsal sets, the probability of recall of an item was primarily affected by the recency of its last rehearsal. Although recall appeared to be superior in the first few rehearsal sets, the primacy effects did not reach significance. The frequencies (number of rehearsals) on which the last R function is based are identical to those of Experiment 2 and are shown in Table 1. (The frequencies for the LF/HF schedule were the same as those for the HF schedule.) It should be noted that the proportions of words correctly recalled in the early rehearsal sets were based on relatively few observations.

Role of rehearsal

A comparison of the results of the HF and LF schedules in Experiment 5 with the corresponding conditions in Experiment 2 was performed. Figure 6 shows that the serial position curves for Experiments 2 and 5 are very similar for both HF words (Figure 6A) and LF words (Figure 6B). This was confirmed by two 2 × 5 mixed ANOVAs on each type of word frequency, with experiment (Experiment 2 or Experiment 5) as a between-subjects factor and serial position (SP 1–4, 5–8, 9–12, 13–16, or 17–20) as a within-subjects factor. These analyses revealed significant effects only of serial position, $F(4, 152) = 38.83$, $MSE = .022, p < .001$, and $F(4, 152) = 28.22$, $MSE = .020, p < .001$, for HF and LF words, respectively. There was no significant effect of experiment and no significant Experiment × Serial Position interaction ($p > .05$).

Discussion

The results from Experiment 5 demonstrate that the U-shaped serial position function in free recall can adequately be explained in terms of the number,

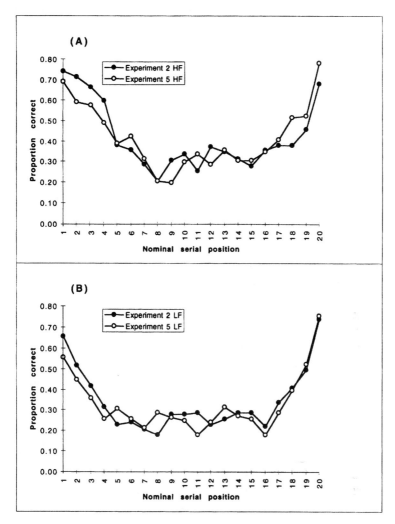

Figure 6 Experiments 2 and 5: Mean proportion of correct responses as a function of nominal serial position for the high-frequency (A) and low-frequency (B) words. HF = high frequency; LF = low frequency.

distribution, and recency of rehearsals. When the participants in Experiment 5 were presented with the schedules of rehearsals of participants in Experiment 2, essentially the same patterns of results were obtained. The fact that typical U-shaped serial position curves were found in Experiment 5 supports the main conclusion from the results of Experiments 1 to 4: that the primacy effect in free recall is caused by a recency-based mechanism acting on the distribution of study items and their rehearsals (Figure 5A). The fact that there was essentially no difference between the results of Experiment 5 and those of Experiment 2 (see Figure 6A and 6B) suggests that the main causal effect of rehearsal in these experiments is limited to repeating, reordering, and redistributing the study items throughout the list. There appears to be no additional advantage to rehearsal based on actively selecting and rehearsing the items.

The finding that the HF schedule resulted in superior performance to the LF schedule suggests that one factor that causes frequency effects in free recall is the differential distribution of rehearsals in the two conditions. However, it is possible that a second factor is also important. If the presentation schedule was the only factor responsible for frequency effects, then one would have expected the LF words with the HF schedule to be recalled as well as the HF words and far better than the LF words. The results illustrated in Figure 5A reveal that the situation is not so clear-cut: Performance in this third condition was somewhere in between the performance in the HF and LF conditions. One possible reason for this is that the standard HF advantage reflects not only superior presentation schedules but also factors associated with the items themselves. For example, HF words may result in greater item–item associations, may be more easily generated than LF words, or may result in a greater degree of organizational and associative processing (e.g., Gregg, 1976; Sumby, 1963). Alternatively, the LF words may be harder to encode than the HF words (e.g., Delosh & McDaniel, 1996). According to this interpretation, the LF items were presented at a faster than optimal rate in the LF words with HF schedule condition, and this offset some of the advantage of the HF schedule. The finding that there is an HF advantage that is independent of rehearsal schedule is further supported by a second examination of Experiment 2. An HF advantage was also observed in the functional serial position curves in Experiment 2, in which the recency positions of the most recently rehearsed items are equated. Although the results clearly suggest that a second factor may be responsible for some frequency effects in free recall, they nevertheless demonstrate that the distribution and recency of rehearsals are a highly significant factor in explaining frequency effects in free recall.

Experiment 6

The main claim that we wish to make from the results of Experiments 1 to 4 is that the primacy effect may be largely explained by a recency-based account of episodic memory, which operates on the episodic memory for the items and their rehearsals. Specifically, we have argued that it is the number, distribution, and recency of the items and their rehearsals that determine free-recall performance. However, it could be argued that much of the evidence presented so far might yet be explained in terms of a model of primacy and recency that takes into account only the number of rehearsals that each item receives. A reanalysis of the data from Experiments 1 to 4 (Table 2)

Table 2 Mean frequency of rehearsals of words at each nominal serial position in experiments 1 to 4

Experiment	Nominal serial position																			
	1	2	3	4	5	6	7	8	9	10	11	12	13	14	15	16	17	18	19	20
1																				
Slow	14.78	11.91	9.63	7.51	5.45	4.27	4.47	3.38	3.28	2.78	2.80	2.75	2.86	2.63	2.51	2.67	2.19	2.26	1.84	1.68
Fast	4.40	3.73	2.75	2.13	2.01	1.73	1.78	1.73	1.76	1.63	1.65	1.71	1.58	1.54	1.56	1.55	1.47	1.44	1.31	1.21
2																				
HF	9.26	8.17	7.54	6.11	4.30	3.82	3.23	2.62	2.52	2.68	2.29	2.19	2.44	2.18	2.02	2.02	2.03	1.88	1.60	1.42
LF	7.02	6.15	4.85	3.38	2.71	2.39	1.93	1.91	1.88	1.98	1.95	1.68	1.66	1.48	1.55	1.54	1.48	1.43	1.39	1.11
3																				
Immediate free recall	6.52	5.72	4.90	3.48	2.70	2.65	2.65	2.28	2.48	2.27	1.93	1.92	2.13	2.18	2.22	2.05	1.97	1.87	1.68	1.47
Easy distractor free recall	8.95	7.48	5.75	4.60	3.13	3.35	2.45	2.60	2.53	2.55	2.70	2.37	2.10	2.27	2.12	2.13	2.00	1.78	1.62	1.25
Hard distractor free recall	7.48	6.17	4.42	3.67	2.95	2.75	1.98	1.90	2.25	1.92	2.12	2.32	1.92	1.83	2.07	2.12	2.20	1.63	1.48	1.42
4																				
Immediate free recall	6.18	5.54	4.53	3.47	3.40	2.44	2.34	2.38	2.31	2.08	1.75	1.89	2.03	1.89	1.81	1.71	1.68	1.66	1.54	1.23
Delayed free recall	7.05	5.88	4.73	4.01	3.23	2.62	2.38	2.29	2.09	2.10	2.03	2.06	1.84	1.87	1.79	1.71	1.68	1.58	1.47	1.20
Immediate fixed recall	4.71	4.67	4.65	4.65	4.70	4.53	4.54	4.50	4.52	4.55	4.62	4.60	4.54	4.51	4.53	4.52	4.53	4.56	4.59	4.52
Delayed fixed recall	4.86	4.73	4.56	4.62	4.71	4.58	4.56	4.60	4.60	4.58	4.53	4.59	4.51	4.61	4.63	4.47	4.53	4.53	4.63	4.60

Note. HF = high frequency; LF = low frequency.

confirms that the primacy items in all free-recall conditions received the greatest number of rehearsals ($p < .01$) and that the primacy items in the slow and HF conditions are rehearsed more than their fast and LF counterparts ($p < .01$, in each comparison). Furthermore, it is items that have received more rehearsals that survive a filled retention interval (Experiments 3 and 4, $p < .01$) and provide greater recency (Experiment 4, $p < .01$).

One response is to demonstrate that, with immediate testing, recall is a function of both the number of rehearsals and the recency of the last rehearsal. Figure 7 shows the data in Experiments 1 to 4 when they are replotted as a function of both the number of rehearsals and the recency of the last rehearsals. The data show separate recency curves for each level of number of rehearsals, suggesting that some advantage in the primacy items arises because of the increased number of rehearsals and that some advantage in the primacy items also arises because of the recency of the most recent rehearsal. Note that it is not solely the number of rehearsals that causes the superior recall performance of the earlier items. Rather, episodic memory is recency based for all numbers of rehearsal: The traditional advantage of primacy items stems from both the number of rehearsals and the recency of the most recent rehearsal.

These analyses may be easily explained by a recency-based explanation of primacy that extends the ratio rule, if we argue that each rehearsal represents an additional potential item that can be recalled. Clearly, such an account predicts that recall will be heavily recency based, but it also predicts that as the number of rehearsals of an item increases so there will be greater opportunities to recall earlier rehearsals of that item as well as the most recent.

One difficulty with the post hoc analysis reported in Figure 7 is that there is a highly uneven distribution of data points across the different levels of numbers of rehearsals and the recency of last rehearsal, making statistical analyses difficult. Importantly, there are very few data points representing the circumstances in which an item receives many rehearsals (and so should do very well according to number of rehearsal accounts) but is not rehearsed toward the end of the list (and so should do less well according to our account). This situation was remedied in Experiment 6. It made use of the findings from Experiment 5, in which experimenter-presented schedules of repetitions were shown to result in similar levels of performance to those obtained from the participants' own rehearsals in Experiment 2. Using experimenter-generated schedules of words, it was possible to completely counterbalance the number of repetitions of different items and the recency of the last presentation of these items. Specifically, different words were presented once, twice, four times, or eight times, and the most recent presentation occurred either in the first, second, third, or fourth quarter of the list.

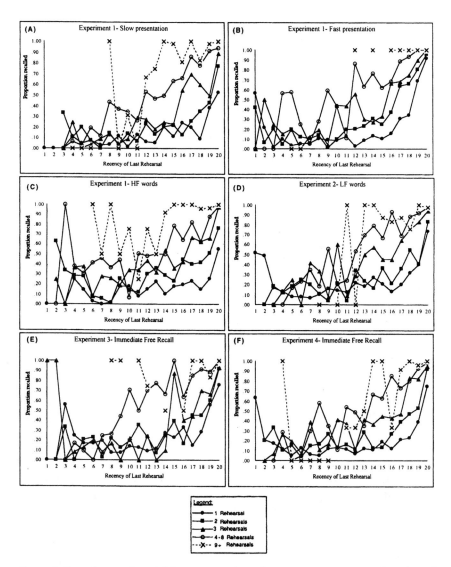

Figure 7 Experiments 1 to 4: Mean proportion of correct responses as a function of last rehearsal for each level of number of rehearsals. These are plotted for slow (A) and fast (B) presentations in Experiment 1, for the high-frequency (C) and low-frequency (D) words of Experiment 2, and for the immediate free-recall conditions of Experiments 3 (E) and 4 (F). HF = high frequency; LF = low frequency.

Method

Participants

Twenty-eight students from the University of Essex participated in this experiment. None had taken part in any of the previous experiments.

Materials

Four hundred two-syllable words were selected from the Quinlan (1992) database. The stimuli were all of medium frequency; rates of occurrence were between 30 and 120 per million.

Design

There were two independent variables. Number of presentations was a within-subjects variable with four levels (one, two, four, and eight). The serial position of the most recent presentation was also a within-subjects variable with four levels (the most recent presentation occurred within the first quarter, the second quarter, the third quarter, or the final quarter of the list, Q1–Q4, respectively).

Procedure

Participants were presented with 10 lists of 160 words. The words appeared one at a time at a constant rate of 1 every second (each item was displayed for 750 ms and there was a 250-ms interstimulus interval). Each list consisted of 40 different words: 8 words were presented once, 10 words were presented twice, 11 words were presented four times, and 11 words were presented eight times. The organization of the total list consisted of four quarters of 40 words each, and the order of the words was carefully controlled. Within each quarter, there were 15 different types of trials, reflecting the different possible combinations of number of presentations, distribution of presentations, and recency of last presentation. For example, in the first quarter, the different types of stimuli were two instances of words that were presented only once in total (Q1), four instances of words that were presented twice in total (once in this quarter and once again in a same or different quarter [Q1Q1, Q1Q2, Q1Q3, Q1Q4]), four instances of words that were presented four times in total (twice in this quarter and twice again in the same or different quarter [Q1Q1Q1Q1, Q1Q1Q2Q2, Q1Q1Q3Q3, Q1Q1Q4Q4]), one instance of a word that was presented four times in total (once in each quarter [Q1Q2Q3Q4]), four instances of words that were presented eight times in total (four in this quarter and four again in the same or different quarter [Q1 × 8, Q1 × 4 Q2 × 4, Q1 × 4 Q3 × 4, Q1 × 4 Q4 × 4]), and finally one instance of a word that was presented eight times in total (twice in each quarter [Q1 Q1 Q2 Q2 Q3 Q3 Q4 Q4]). Both the order of these different types of trial within each quarter and the allocation of words to different types of trial were assigned at random.

The participants were instructed that they would see a long series of words at a fast rate. They were told to read each word aloud as it was presented and not to rehearse earlier items. A musical trill signaled the end of the list, and participants were given 45 s to write down as many words as possible. After recall, there was a brief period when participants could rest, if needed, before continuing onto the next list.

Results

The mean proportions of words recalled for each type of trial are presented in Table 3.

As can be seen, recall increased with the number of presentations, and recall also increased with the recency of the most recent presentation. There

Table 3 Mean proportion of correct responses for each trial type in experiment 6

Trial type	Last presented Q1	Last presented Q2	Last presented Q3	Last presented Q4
		One presentation		
	.028	.060	.096	.166
		Two presentations		
Q1	.076	.104	.116	.232
Q2		.104	.116	.212
Q3			.116	.232
Q4				.296
		Four presentations		
Q1	.124	.144	.116	.232
Q2		.128	.196	.212
Q3			.176	.232
Q4				.468
Q1Q2Q3Q4				.336
		Eight presentations		
Q1	.200	.236	.272	.560
Q2		.244	.300	.572
Q3			.304	.588
Q4				.636
Q1Q2Q3Q4				.428

Note. The different trial types refer to different combinations of number of presentations, recency of most recent presentation, and distribution or spacing of the presentations. Q1 = first quarter; Q2 = second quarter; Q3 = third quarter; Q4 = fourth quarter.

appeared to be very little effect of when an item was first presented within each last-presentation quarter. As a result, the data were collapsed across different types of trial that shared the same recency of last presentation and number of presentations. A 4×4 within-subjects ANOVA, with number of presentations as a within-subjects factor (levels: one, two, four, and eight) and the recency of the last presentation as the second within-subjects factor (levels: Q1, Q2, Q3, and Q4) was performed. This revealed a significant main effect of number of presentations, $F(3, 72) = 142.4$, $MSE = .007$, $p < .0001$, a significant main effect of recency of last presentation, $F(3, 72) = 79.81$, $MSE = .011$, $p < .0001$, and a significant interaction, $F(9, 216) = 9.28$, $MSE = .006$, $p < .0001$. Figure 8 shows the mean proportions of correct responses for each level of number of presentations and recency of last presentation.

An analysis of the simple main effects revealed significant effects of each variable at every level of the other ($p < .001$). Tukey pairwise comparisons revealed that the interaction was caused by the greater increase in recall with more recent last presentations for those items presented eight times compared with those presented one, two, and four times.

Discussion

The results from Experiment 6 confirmed the findings from the post hoc analyses of Figure 7, and showed that recall performance in free recall with

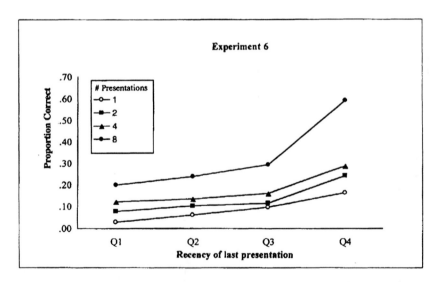

Figure 8 Experiment 6: Mean proportion of correct responses as a function of number of presentations and the recency of the last presentation. Q1 = first quarter; Q2 = second quarter; Q3 = third quarter; Q4 = fourth quarter.

immediate testing is greatly affected by both the number of repetitions and the recency of the most recent rehearsal. These results are clearly in line with a recency-based account of primacy: Primacy items in standard free recall can be likened to the items that have many repetitions, including those occurring toward the last quarters of the list.

Experiment 7

The claim from Experiments 1 to 4 was that it was the number, distribution, and recency of the rehearsals that were important factors in determining recall performance in free recall. The post hoc analyses in Figure 7 and the experimental results in Experiment 6 suggest a role for the number and recency of rehearsals, but there is little evidence from Experiment 6 that the distribution or spacing of the rehearsals makes a significant difference. One reason why the effect of spacing may not have been detected in Experiment 6 is that even those items that are least well spaced (i.e., those in which the repetitions occur in the same quarter) are distributed over as many as 40 items. Experiment 7 investigated the effect of spacing directly, using experimenter-generated schedules of stimuli that were presented only once or twice and that were presented in massed or distributed schedules. The reduction in the number of repetitions allowed for shorter lists and more data to be collected at each serial position. The first aim of Experiment 7 was to determine whether recall performance is affected by the number, the recency, and the distribution of rehearsals.

The second aim of Experiment 7 was to investigate the effect of retention interval on recall performance. In Experiments 3 and 4, a filled retention interval affected the recency items but did not decrease performance on the primacy items (indeed there was a small but nonsignificant increase in performance on these items). One argument made in the discussions of Experiments 3 and 4 was that, after a filled delay, performance was based less on the recency of the last rehearsal and more on the number and distribution of rehearsals. Experiment 7 provided an opportunity to examine the effects of retention interval on items that were last presented at different positions throughout the list and that were presented once, presented twice in close succession (massed items), or presented twice after a more considerable interval (distributed items).

Method

Participants

Forty students from the University of Essex participated in this experiment. None had taken part in any of the previous experiments.

Materials

The words were the same as those used in Experiment 6.

Design

There were two independent variables. Retention interval was a between-subjects factor with two levels (immediate and delayed). The combination of number of presentations and serial position of the presentations (i.e., the trial type) was a within-subjects factor. The different possible trial types were single presentations at each of four serial positions (Q1, Q2, Q3, and Q4), and items presented twice that were presented with every combination of quarters (Q1Q1, Q1Q2, Q1Q3, Q1Q4, Q2Q2, Q2Q3, Q2Q4, Q3Q3, Q3Q4, and Q4Q4).

Procedure

The participants were presented with 18 lists of 24 words, which were presented at a rate of 2 s per word (each item was displayed for 1.5 s with a 500-ms interstimulus interval). Each list consisted of 14 different words: 4 words were presented once and 10 words were presented twice. The organization of the total list consisted of four quarters of 6 words each, and the order of the words was carefully controlled. Within each quarter, there were five different types of combinations of number of presentations, distribution of presentations, and recency of most recent presentation. For example, in Q1 the different types of stimuli were one instance of a word that was presented only once (Q1) and four instances of words that were presented twice in total, once in this quarter and once again in a same or different quarter (Q1Q1, Q1Q2, Q1Q3, Q1Q4). The order of these different types of stimuli within each quarter and the allocation of words to different types of trial were assigned such that each type of stimulus was last rehearsed equally often in every serial position in that quarter. The instructions and procedure were otherwise identical to those of Experiment 6.

Results

The mean proportions of words recalled for each type of trial are presented in Table 4. With immediate recall, performance increased with the number of presentations and with the recency of the most recent presentation. The distributed items were also recalled overall more often than the massed items. After a delay, there was a similar pattern of results, except that the recall performance of all the different types of items that were last rehearsed to the end of the list was greatly reduced. There was also a small increase in performance of many of the nonrecency items after a delay.

Table 4 Mean proportion of correct responses for each trial type in experiment 7 with immediate and delayed testing

Trial type	Last presented Q1	Last presented Q2	Last presented Q3	Last presented Q4
		One presentation		
Immediate recall	.200	.161	.242	.561
		Two presentations		
Q1	.250	.344	.417	.767
Q2		.231	.347	.681
Q3			.333	.653
Q4				.756
		One presentation		
Delayed recall	.227	.203	.191	.308
		Two presentations		
Q1	.311	.329	.481	.558
Q2		.303	.404	.439
Q3			.341	.455
Q4				.487

Note. The different trial types refer to different combinations of number of presentations, recency of most recent presentation, and distribution or spacing of the presentations. Q1 = first quarter; Q2 = second quarter; Q3 = third quarter; Q4 = fourth quarter.

The data were collapsed across trial types, which shared the same recency of last presentation (Q1, Q2, Q3, and Q4) and schedule (1 presentation, 2 presentations-massed, and 2 presentations-distributed) for each retention interval. Figure 9 plots recall performance as a function of the recency of the last presentation, the type of schedule, and the retention interval.

The data were analyzed using two separate ANOVAs, the first examining the effects of schedule (one presentation, two presentations massed) across all four serial positions, the second examining the effects of all three schedules (one presentation, two presentations massed, two presentations distributed) across the last three serial positions. A $2 \times 2 \times 4$ mixed ANOVA was performed with retention interval (immediate or delayed) as a between-subjects factor and schedule (one presentation or two presentations massed) and recency of last presentation (Q1, Q2, Q3, and Q4) as the within-subjects factors. This revealed a near significant main effect of retention interval, $F(1, 38) = 3.278$, $MSE = .050$, $p < .10$, a significant main effect of schedule, $F(1, 38) = 119.05$, $MSE = .009$, $p < .0001$, and a significant main effect of recency of last presentation, $F(3, 114) = 76.74$, $MSE = .021$, $p < .0001$. There were also significant two-way interactions between retention interval and recency of last presentation, $F(3, 114) = 21.04$, $MSE = .021$, $p < .0001$, and between schedule and recency of last presentation, $F(3, 114) = 7.37$, $MSE = .008$,

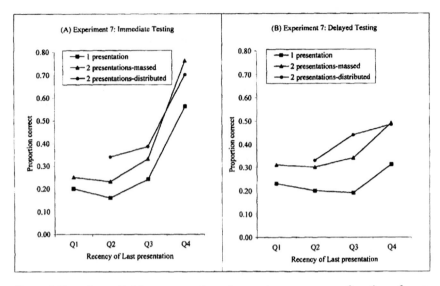

Figure 9 Experiment 7: Mean proportion of correct responses as a function of number and spacing of presentations and the recency of the last presentation
with immediate testing (A) and after a filled delay (B). Q1 = first quarter;
Q2 = second quarter; Q3 = third quarter; Q4 = fourth quarter.

$p < .001$. The other two-way interaction and the three-way interaction did
not approach significance ($p > .05$). An analysis of the simple main effects on
the interaction between retention interval and recency of last presentation
revealed that the effect of retention interval was to reduce performance on all
the recency (Q4) items but not on the other items. There was also a far
greater effect of recency of last presentation with immediate compared with
delayed testing, although both significant main effects were still highly significant ($p < .0001$), showing that a reduced but significant recency effect
survived a filled delay. An analysis of the simple main effects on the interaction between schedule and recency of last presentation revealed that all
simple main effects were highly significant ($p < .0001$), although the
magnitude of the effect of schedule was not quite as large at the earliest
presentation, Q1 items ($p < .001$).

A $2 \times 3 \times 3$ mixed ANOVA was also performed with retention interval
(immediate or delayed) as a between-subjects factor and schedule (one presentation, two presentations massed, or two presentations distributed), and
recency of last presentation (Q2, Q3, and Q4) as the within-subjects factors.
This revealed a significant main effect of retention interval, $F(1, 38) = 6.65$,
$MSE = .064$, $p < .05$, a significant main effect of schedule, $F(2, 76) = 91.52$,
$MSE = .010$, $p < .0001$, and a significant main effect of recency of last
presentation, $F(2, 76) = 141.6$, $MSE = .019$, $p < .0001$. There were also

significant two-way interactions between retention interval and recency of last presentation, $F(2, 76) = 36.36$, $MSE = .019$, $p < .0001$, and between schedule and recency of last presentation, $F(4, 152) = 4.94$, $MSE = .044$, $p < .001$. The other two-way interaction did not approach significance ($p > .05$), but the three-way interaction just reached significance, $F(4, 152) = 2.80$, $MSE = .009$, $p < .05$. An analysis of the simple main effects on the three-way interaction revealed that there were significant simple main effects of retention interval on the recency (Q4) items in all schedules but not on any of the prerecency items. There were also significant simple main effects of schedule at all retention intervals and recency of last presentations (all $p < .001$). Distributed items were better recalled than massed items in prerecency portions of the serial position curve, although there was no difference between massed and distributed items at Q4 for both immediate and delayed testing. There were significant simple main effects of recency of last presentation at all retention intervals and schedules (all $p < .001$), except the delayed one-presentation condition, which only just reached significance ($p < .05$). This shows that there was still a significant but reduced recency effect after a filled delay in at least two of the three schedules.

The analyses show that, with the exception of the most recent items, items that were presented twice in different quarters (distributed) were recalled better than those that were presented twice in the same quarter (massed), which, in turn, were recalled better than items that were presented once. The analyses also showed that the effect of a retention interval is to reduce recall of all items that are presented at the end of the list, including those presented once, those presented twice in the last quarter of the list, and those presented twice in different quarters of the list. There was also a reduced recency effect after the filled delay in at least two of three schedules. There was also a small but nonsignificant increase in recall of many nonrecency items with a retention interval.

Discussion

The results from Experiment 7 showed that recall performance in free recall is affected by the distribution of presentations as well as the number of presentations and the recency of the most recent presentation. This result finally confirms that all three factors are important in determining recall both at immediate testing and after a filled delay. The results also show that there was still a significant (albeit reduced) recency effect after a filled delay. An STS account correctly predicts that there would be no reduction in primacy with a filled delay but incorrectly predicts that there would be no recency effect after a delay.

The results also demonstrate that after a filled delay there was a significant reduction in all the items that were presented in the final quarter. It is important to note that the reduction with delay for the items that were also presented early in the list (e.g., Q1Q4, Q2Q4, Q3Q4) is equivalent to the reduction with delay for those items that were only presented in the final quarter (Q4, Q4Q4). That is, both recency items and primacy items that were repeated at the end of the list are detrimentally affected with a filled retention interval. At first glance, this finding is difficult to reconcile with the traditional result that a filled retention interval reduces recall of recency and not primacy items. However, a closer look at the data in Table 4 provides a clue as to why the primacy items might survive a filled delay in free recall. Six of the seven early and early-middle list items that were not rehearsed to the end of the list (Q1, Q2, Q1Q1, Q1Q3, Q2Q2, Q2Q3, but not Q1Q2) actually improved slightly after a filled delay. That is, the average proportion of nonrecency early and early-middle items actually increased from .28 to .32 after a filled delay. This suggests that the preserved primacy effect in free recall is caused by the slight (although not significant) improvement with delay of early and early-middle items that are not rehearsed to recency positions. It is the increased performance on these items that offsets the large and significant decrease with delay of early and early-middle items that are rehearsed to recency positions. Possible explanations for this effect are discussed in the General discussion.

General discussion

We have attempted to outline an account of the U-shaped serial position curve of free recall in which both the primacy and the recency effects are the result of a recency-based mechanism that satisfies the ratio rule. The ratio rule predicts that the probability that an item will be recalled in free recall will be inversely proportional to the retention interval (i.e., it is recency based) and proportional to the interitem presentation interval. Out extension of this account is to assume that every rehearsal leads to a copy of that item in memory, which may itself be accessed by a mechanism consistent with the ratio rule. Rehearsal will, therefore, result in the repetition, the reordering, and the redistribution of the items throughout the list. Our account predicts that it is the number, distribution, and recency of the rehearsals of an item that will determine its probability of being subsequently recalled. All three factors are considered to be important. With immediate testing, the recency of the most recent instantiation is the most dominant factor. The most recently rehearsed items are highly accessible, leading to better recall. With delayed testing, the retention interval (T) is increased and the recency of the most recent instantiation becomes far less important in determining recall. However, there are still advantages for items that are repeated many times and for those items with instantiations that are widely spaced.

We believe that our extension of the ration rule can adequately explain the effects of presentation rate (Experiment 1) and at least partly explain the effects of word frequency (Experiment 2) on the primacy portion of the nominal serial position curve. Furthermore, the extension of the ratio rule can be successfully applied to account for the effect of massed (fixed rehearsal) and distributed (free rehearsal) conditions on immediate and delayed recall (Experiments 3 and 4). In addition, the extension of the ratio rule can successfully account for the serial position curves of participants who are presented with the schedule of rehearsals of items generated from other participants' rehearsals (Experiment 5). Finally, the results of Experiments 6 and 7 confirm that recall in free recall is sensitive to the number, the recency, and the distribution of participants' rehearsals. We believe that this recency-based explanation of primacy provides a simple and elegant explanation of the serial position curves in free recall. It can account for the empirical findings of Brodie and Murdock (1977), Modigliani and Hedges (1987), and Rundus (1971, Figure 2) and unites the evidence implicating the role of distributed and selective rehearsal in the primacy effect with ratio rule accounts of the recency effect.

One prediction that arises from our assumption that episodic memory is viewed as a continuum is that all items (both recency and primacy items) that are rehearsed to the end of the list will be less well remembered after a filled delay. This is because our account is based on the absolute discrimination of the study items (and their rehearsals). If we assume that the items are presented and rehearsed at a constant rate (such that Δt is a constant), then our account is based largely on the recency ($1/T$) of each instantiation. It seems reasonable to expect with a model of this type that there would be an effect of retention interval (an increase in T) on all items, with recency items most greatly reduced and primacy items slightly reduced overall with delay. A close examination of the results of Experiment 7 reveal that indeed all the items that are presented or rehearsed to recency positions (including the primacy items) are very well remembered at immediate testing but are less well remembered after a filled delay. In addition, items that are repeated and that are more widely spaced continue to be recalled overall more often than single presentations and those that are presented under massed schedules. However, these findings coexist with the traditional finding that primacy items are relatively unaffected by retention interval, a result replicated by the slight increases in primacy with retention interval found in Experiments 3 and 4. The results of Experiment 7 suggest that the stability of the primacy effect with a filled retention interval is the result of small and nonsignificant increases with delay in the performance of early and early-middle items that were not rehearsed to the end of the list. This unexpected finding is difficult to explain in terms of the absolute discrimination of the study items (and their rehearsals), and our discussion of this result can be divided into four lines of argument.

First, it is possible that the stability or even increase in primacy with a filled retention is an atypical result. It is worth noting that in two of the most well-cited articles examining the effect of retention interval on free recall (e.g., Glanzer & Cunitz, 1966; Postman & Phillips, 1965), the primacy effect is slightly reduced with a filled retention interval. This result is entirely compatible with an account based on the absolute discrimination of the study items. This suggests that, in some circumstances or instances, our proposed account may not be too far from the mark. However, it should also be noted that in three of our studies as well as others (e.g., Howard & Kahana, 1999) there is absolutely no reduction in primacy and there may even be an increase.

Second, it is possible that the stability or even increase in primacy with a filled retention is the typical result. This finding could be explained if there was competition between the primacy and the recency items. Suppose that the effect of retention interval is to decrease recall of all items but that the recency items are more affected than the primacy items. Suppose also that there is competition between items such that the recall of items is affected in part by the recall of the other items in the list. This combination of factors predicts that when the recall of the recency items is relatively good (such as with immediate testing), the primacy items are less well remembered. Similarly, when the recall of recency items is reduced (such as with delayed testing), the recall of the primacy items is relatively increased. This may be enough to return the primacy items to their original absolute level after a delay (and may even be enough to lead to a slightly greater level of recall).

Competition between items could be due to competition for retrieval from memory. One modification to our recency-based account is to assume that recall is based on the relative discrimination of the study items (and their rehearsals). According to this modification, the probability of recalling a given item (or rehearsal) will be dependent on the discriminability of that item (related to $1/T$) divided by the discriminability of all the items in the list. This formula successfully predicts that the effect of increasing the retention interval will be to reduce performance greatly on recency items and increase performance slightly on the primacy items. In fact, many theories of free recall (both dual store and distinctiveness) use a relative measure in the recall formula. For example, the retrieval process in the search of associative memory (SAM) model (e.g., Gillund & Shiffrin, 1984) includes a component of retrieval (called sampling), which is determined by the relative associative strength of an item. Specifically, the probability that an item will be sampled is determined by the associative strength of the target item (given the available cues) divided by the associative strength of all the items (given the same cues). A relative measure is also used by many models that are influenced by SAM (e.g., Wixted et al., 1997). Similarly, Neath (1993) proposed that the distinctiveness of an item is related to the discriminability of that item compared with all the others in the list (his model was for items that were not easily rehearsed) before being normalized (to give a relative measure).

Competition between items could also be the result of output interference. At its simplest, the recall of one item could increase the difficulty in recalling the next because the second item must be recalled after an increase in the retention interval, an increase in the amount of retroactive interference, and a reduction in the remaining recall period. It is well known that the order of recall can play a large role in determining the relative sizes of the primacy and recency effects in free recall (e.g., Dalezman, 1976), and more recent work confirmed that there are serial position effects that affect the order of recall (e.g., Howard & Kahana, 1999; Kahana, 1996; Laming, 1999; Wixted et al., 1997).

Our final two responses involve considering the alternatives to a recency-based model of episodic memory. We have consistently found only the smallest advantage in recall performance for items that were presented at the beginning of the list but that were not later rehearsed. This suggests that only a small portion of the primacy effect can be explained in terms of distinctiveness (e.g., Murdock, 1960; Neath, 1993; Wixted & McDowell, 1989) of the items. However, an additional alternative is to consider whether an STS/LTS account of episodic memory can better account for our results.

Perhaps the most explicit and most well-developed dual store model is the search of associative memory model, SAM (e.g., Gillund & Shiffrin, 1984; Raaijmakers & Shiffrin, 1981). According to SAM, STS and LTS possess qualitatively different properties and the formulas for determining which items are rehearsed and which items are recalled are very different. LTS is assumed to be a permanent store of almost unlimited capacity, whereas STS acts as a limited-capacity buffer with a capacity of r items (where r is typically approximately 4). The direct output of items from the STS rehearsal buffer is responsible for the recency effect. The STS rehearsal buffer also serves the purpose of encoding items into LTS. Specifically, the greater the amount of time that an item spends in the STS rehearsal buffer, the greater is the increase in the strength of the associations in LTS (a) between that item and the encoding context, (b) between that items with other items in the rehearsal buffer, and (c) between that item with itself. The increase in strength of these associations is also greatest when there are fewest items in the buffer (such as at the start of the list) compared with when the rehearsal buffer is full. The formula for displacing items in STS when the rehearsal buffer's capacity is exceeded is very different to the formula for retrieving items from LTS. Retrieval from LTS requires first sampling and then recovery. As noted earlier, sampling from LTS is determined by the relative associative strength of an item compared with the associative strength of all the other items in the list, using first the context as a cue and then the context and recalled items as cues. Recovery from LTS is assumed to be a function of the absolute strength of that item. Note that the primacy effect can be explained by the fact that the associative strengths of the first items are greatest as a result of their tendency to receive more rehearsals than later items and more effective rehearsals (because they are often rehearsed before the capacity of the buffer is full).

A number of results in this article may be less elegantly explained by SAM. First, throughout the article, we have seen that the primacy items are better recalled in free recall because they are rehearsed more often, are rehearsed more recently, and are rehearsed with more distributed schedules. It is difficult to see how SAM can account for the long and extended recency curves shown throughout the article, especially within curves of equivalent numbers of rehearsals (e.g., Figures 7 and 8). Second, there are instances in which a reduced yet significant recency effect survives a filled interval which is assumed to abolish the recency effect (the fixed presentation condition in Experiment 4, and in at least two of the three schedules in Experiment 7). These two methodological conditions can be added to others such as the continuous distractor techniques and long-term recency methodologies which result in significant (though reduced) recency over filled retention intervals.

Finally, the hypothetical role of STS as a rehearsal buffer can be considered. According to SAM, the probability that an item will be displaced from STS when the capacity is exceeded is not linked to the relative strength of the items in the list. Rather, different versions of SAM propose that items in the buffer are displaced either with equal probability (e.g., Raaijmakers & Shiffrin, 1981) or by a formula which tends to displace older items rather than more recent items (Gillund & Shiffrin, 1984). A further post hoc analysis on Experiments 1 to 4 sheds some light on the role of rehearsal in free recall.[4]

According to SAM, the items that are rehearsed in the STS rehearsal buffer should be insensitive to the relative strength of the items in LTS and be affected only by the nominal serial position of the items and the capacity of participants' rehearsal buffers. Figure 10 plots the proportion of items from different nominal serial positions that are rehearsed (at least once) at four different rehearsal sets throughout the list (rehearsal sets 4, 7, 14, and 20) for each of the immediate free-recall conditions in Experiments 1 to 4. The full tables are available in the Appendix. There are two main points of interest from these analyses. First, the shape of the serial position curves of the rehearsals appears to change as the later items are encoded. Early in the list (at rehearsal set 4), all early list items appear to be rehearsed with equal probability. Then, at rehearsal set 7, there is a tendency for earlier items to be rehearsed more often than later items ($p < 0.01$). That is, items that have entered the rehearsal set earlier are more resistant to displacement than later items (cf. opposite prediction of SAM). Interestingly, the shape of the serial position curve in these rehearsal sets tends to resemble the primacy-dominated curves observed in immediate serial recall, with one- or perhaps two-item recency. Finally, at later rehearsal sets (rehearsal sets 14 and 20), there is a tendency for extended recency effects ($p < 0.01$), with reduced primacy (the serial position curves tend to resemble free recall serial position curves). Note that at each rehearsal set there is at least one-item recency; this

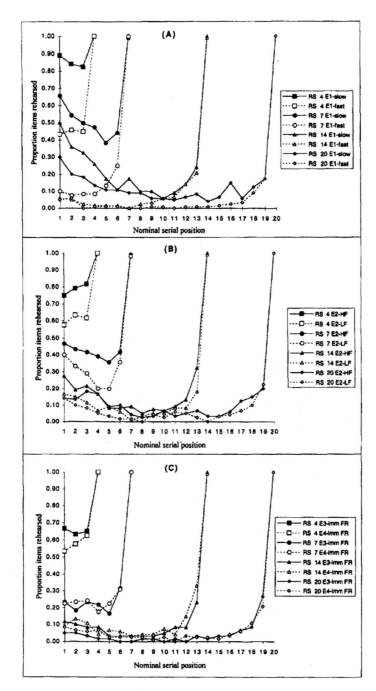

Figure 10 Experiments 1 to 4: Mean proportion of items rehearsed as a function of nominal serial position during rehearsal sets (RS) 4, 7, 14, and 20. These are plotted for slow and fast presentations in Experiment 1 (A), for the high-frequency (HF) and low-frequency (LF) words of Experiment 2 (B), and for the immediate free-recall conditions of Experiments 3 and 4 (C).

is due in part to the instructions given to our participants to read the current item aloud first before rehearsal of any earlier items.

A second point of interest is that the effects of traditional LTS variables such as frequency and presentation rate are also present in the rehearsal buffer. Early HF items and early items presented at a slow rate are more likely to be retained in the rehearsal sets than their LF and fast rate counterparts (p at least <0.1 for every serial position curve). When this result is combined with the finding that it is the earliest items (those that have been previously rehearsed the most) that are most resistant to displacement from the rehearsal set, it suggests that the probability that an item is rehearsed is similar to the probability that an item will be recalled. In effect, rehearsals can be argued to be very similar to short retrieval periods at different list lengths from episodic memory. That is, the probability that an item is rehearsed at a given rehearsal set is itself a function of the number, distribution, and recency of earlier rehearsals. These findings plotted in Figure 10 question the qualitatively different role given to rehearsal in STS and retrieval from LTS in theories such as SAM. One possible solution would be to modify the formula used by SAM for the displacement of items from the STS rehearsal buffer to that used in the retrieval of LTS items. Although such a change in formula may help model these results, the modification would greatly reduce the necessity for qualitatively different STS and LTS memory stores.

Overall, we believe that our extension of the ratio rule can adequately explain most of the empirical results in this article, and where there are problems, alternative modifications can be suggested that are in line with the assumptions that we have stated. It is also possible that our account (which assumes that both primary and recency items in free recall are rehearsed toward the end of the list) can help account for other empirical findings in free recall. For example, in tests of final free recall, participants are given an unexpected free-recall test of all the items in preceding lists. In these tests, the performance of items from all nominal serial position curves is reduced, but the recency items in the list are most severely affected compared with all the other items, a result known as the negative recency effect (e.g., Craik, 1970). According to our account, early and middle list items receive more rehearsals (some toward the very end of the list), and so they are affected less by the retention interval (see Brodie & Murdock, 1977, Experiment 1 for data on this issue).

The use of the overt rehearsal technique (in Experiments 1 to 4) and the methodology using experimenter-generated lists of words (in Experiments 5 to 7) has also allowed us to see how free-recall performance is affected by the number, distribution, and recency of the rehearsals. We have seen that increasing the number of rehearsals increases the probability of recall and that this effect is greatly exaggerated when the rehearsals are rehearsed toward the end of the list (e.g., see Figures 7, 8, and 9). It could be argued that our results and those of Rundus (1971), Brodie (1975), and Modigliani and Hedges (1987) contrast with the effects of rehearsal in other paradigms. For example, Greene (1987) reviewed the effects of maintenance rehearsal on human memory. A large number of studies are reviewed from five different paradigms. These included the directed forgetting paradigm (e.g., Woodward et al., 1973), rehearsal interval experiments (e.g., Craik & Watkins, 1973, Experiment 2), the copying paradigm (e.g., Meunier, Kestner, Meunier, & Ritz, 1974), the scanning paradigm (e.g., Craik & Watkins, 1973, Experiment 1), and the distractor paradigm (e.g., Glenberg et al., 1977; Naveh-Benjamin & Jonides, 1984a, 1984b; Rundus, 1977, 1980). In these studies, participants viewed lists of items, and immediately after the presentation of each item they were given the opportunity to rehearse that item for an amount of time that varied from item to item. At the end of the experiment, the participants were presented with an unexpected final free-recall task. In many, but not all, of the studies, there was little or no systematic effect of the number of rehearsals on subsequent final free recall, but increasing rehearsals did increase recognition performance. However, there is an important methodological difference between the overt rehearsal methodology and those paradigms reviewed by Greene (1987). In the latter, an increase in the number of rehearsals led to an increased number of massed rehearsals, whereas in the overt rehearsal technique, an increase in the number of rehearsals led to an increased number of distributed rehearsals. Our emphasis on the additional effects of the distribution and recency of the rehearsals (rather than relying solely on the number of rehearsals) may help explain these two rather different findings.

We have tended to be theoretically neutral with respect to the mechanism underpinning the ratio rule. We prefer the context encoding account (Glenberg et al., 1980) of the ratio rule (e.g., Glenberg, 1984, 1987), but because we have not experimentally manipulated the experimental context, we accept that the combination of rehearsal and recency may alternatively be explained by the many other interpretations of the ratio rule (Bjork & Whitten, 1974), such as temporal (Crowder & Neath, 1991) or priming (e.g., Baddeley & Hitch, 1993) accounts. Indeed, it seems likely that many different theoretical accounts of episodic memory will be able to account for these effects of repetition, recency, and spacing.

We also believe that our account enhances and extends the significance of the ratio rule in explaining serial position curves in methodologies traditionally associated with the STS. The ratio rule has already been used to account for the slope of the Brown–Peterson distractor task (e.g., Baddeley, 1976 [pp. 127–130], 1990 [pp. 47–50]; Crowder, 1989, 1993). It can also account for the slope of the recency effect in free recall under immediate, delayed, and continuous distractor conditions (e.g., Baddeley, 1986 [pp. 156–164]; Baddeley & Hitch, 1993; Crowder, 1989, 1993). Furthermore, it elegantly accommodates additional empirical facts arising from manipulations of interstimulus/

intertrial intervals and retention intervals in the Brown–Peterson distractor task (Peterson & Gentile, 1963; Loess & Waugh, 1967; Turvey, Brick, & Osborn, 1970) and free recall (Crowder & Neath, 1991). Because the ratio rule essentially predicts recency, it would also have little difficulty explaining the Waugh and Norman (1965) digit probe task and the Hockey (1973) running memory span task. In addition, it predicts, accurately, that there should be little effect of increasing the presentation rate on recall in these tasks because, as the rate of presentation increases, so the ratio of interstimulus interval/retention interval remains constant.

Table 5 presents a summary of the components of traditional short-term memory tasks that can be explained by the ratio rule. On the basis of the results of the current experiments, we have added the asymptote and primacy effects in free recall to the already impressive list of methodologies that can be explained by these recency-based episodic memory mechanisms. It is interesting to note that the only component of these traditional short-term memory methodologies that has not yet been explained in terms of the ratio rule is immediate serial recall. Of course, logically, the ratio rule offers an explanation as to why performance on the memory span could be limited. As the number of items in the list increases, so the recall performance of the first item in the list will decrease dramatically if rehearsal is prevented, because $\Delta t/T$ will result in an ever decreasing fraction. However, as yet the ratio rule has little to say about the large primacy and reduced recency effects in the serial position curves for immediate serial recall as well as the well-established effects of variables such as phonological similarity, articulatory suppression, word length, and unattended noise. These effects are well modeled by specialist models of immediate serial recall (e.g., Burgess & Hitch, 1992, 1999; Henson, 1998; Page & Norris, 1998), which are typically thought to be separate cognitive mechanisms from those underpinning recency effects in free recall (e.g., Baddeley, 1986). This is not least because there is well-cited

Table 5 Summary of the components of short-term memory tasks can be explained in terms of the ratio rule

Methodologies traditionally associated with STS	Ratio rule explanation
Brown–Peterson task	✓
Digit probe task	✓
Running memory span task	✓
Primacy: immediate free recall	✓
Asymptote: immediate free recall	✓
Recency: immediate free recall	✓
Recency: delayed free recall	✓
Recency: CDT free recall	✓
Immediate serial recall	???

Note. STS = short-term memory store; CDT = Continuous Distractor Task.

neuropsychological evidence for a dissociation in performance between immediate serial recall and other episodic memory tasks (e.g., Shallice, 1988), and so it appears that the ratio rule cannot as yet account for the serial position curves in immediate serial recall.

In conclusion, this study has provided evidence that the primacy effect in free recall is the result of at least two factors. One major factor is the operation of a recency-based retrieval mechanism acting on the number, distribution, and recency of rehearsals. This mechanism is also assumed to underpin the ratio rule account of recency effects. A second factor is the additional distinctiveness of the first items in the list. It is likely that this advantage may be limited to the first one or two items. We have also provided additional evidence that some advantages of highly memorable items (e.g., HF words) are also due to their schedule of rehearsals, although our evidence also suggests that some advantage is due to the nature of the items themselves. Finally, we demonstrate the importance of considering the subjective serial position of items in the list (in addition to the experimental input order of the items) when constructing and evaluating theories of episodic memory.

Notes

Experiments 1 to 5 and 7 were conducted as part of Lydia Tan's doctoral thesis under the primary supervision of Geoff Ward. We acknowledge the comments and feedback provided by the Department of Psychology Memory Club, University of Essex, United Kingdom, especially those of S. E. Avons. Experiments 1 to 4 were presented at the XVI Annual Conference of the British Psychological Society Cognitive Psychology Section, York, United Kingdom, September 1999.

1   As one of our reviewers suggested, the continuous distractor paradigm may be more appropriately named the continual distractor paradigm because the participants in this methodology are distracted continually (i.e., regularly) rather than continuously (e.g., they are not distracted during the presentation of to-be-remembered items). Although we note and agree with this point, we nevertheless have chosen to retain the term continuous distractor paradigm because of its established use in the literature.

2   The functional serial positions reported here are only very close approximations to the participants' actual functional serial order in that the functional order of items that shared identical last rehearsal sets was determined by randomly allocating the words to neighboring functional serial positions.

3   In fact, to anticipate the findings from Experiment 4, it appears that the effect is genuine but small.

4   We thank Michael Kahana for suggesting this reanalysis.

Appendix

Table A1 Experiment 1: slow presentation rate

	Nominal serial position																			
RS	1	2	3	4	5	6	7	8	9	10	11	12	13	14	15	16	17	18	19	20
1	1.00																			
2	0.83	1.00																		
3	0.87	0.85	1.00																	
4	**0.89**	**0.84**	**0.83**	**1.00**																
5	0.76	0.74	0.68	0.64	1.00															
6	0.69	0.69	0.61	0.60	0.56	1.00														
7	**0.66**	**0.54**	**0.50**	**0.48**	**0.38**	**0.44**	**0.99**													
8	0.57	0.50	0.43	0.36	0.33	0.28	0.40	1.00												
9	0.57	0.45	0.43	0.30	0.28	0.21	0.33	0.31	1.00											
10	0.53	0.47	0.38	0.25	0.20	0.23	0.28	0.24	0.34	0.99										
11	0.50	0.39	0.38	0.33	0.21	0.11	0.20	0.15	0.17	0.19	1.00									
12	0.40	0.34	0.38	0.33	0.18	0.10	0.16	0.16	0.15	0.15	0.28	0.99								
13	0.39	0.38	0.34	0.25	0.18	0.14	0.18	0.13	0.13	0.11	0.22	0.28	1.00							
14	**0.50**	**0.36**	**0.33**	**0.26**	**0.18**	**0.11**	**0.18**	**0.10**	**0.10**	**0.06**	**0.09**	**0.14**	**0.24**	**1.00**						
15	0.45	0.32	0.29	0.21	0.13	0.15	0.15	0.09	0.12	0.04	0.11	0.11	0.22	0.24	0.99					
16	0.32	0.28	0.34	0.24	0.14	0.10	0.10	0.06	0.12	0.08	0.06	0.08	0.14	0.15	0.27	1.00				
17	0.38	0.28	0.24	0.18	0.17	0.14	0.13	0.09	0.07	0.08	0.07	0.09	0.12	0.13	0.13	0.23	1.00			
18	0.35	0.29	0.23	0.22	0.13	0.09	0.12	0.03	0.09	0.06	0.07	0.06	0.10	0.10	0.12	0.22	0.25	1.00		
19	0.38	0.29	0.23	0.18	0.16	0.12	0.16	0.07	0.08	0.06	0.08	0.06	0.08	0.08	0.08	0.12	0.08	0.26	1.00	
20	**0.30**	**0.20**	**0.18**	**0.13**	**0.11**	**0.11**	**0.09**	**0.09**	**0.06**	**0.06**	**0.05**	**0.07**	**0.08**	**0.04**	**0.07**	**0.15**	**0.06**	**0.13**	**0.18**	**1.00**

Note. Data points in bold are plotted in Figure 10A. RS = rehearsal set.

Table A2 Experiment 1: fast presentation rate

Nominal serial position

RS	1	2	3	4	5	6	7	8	9	10	11	12	13	14	15	16	17	18	19	20
1	0.99																			
2	0.52	0.99																		
3	0.56	0.57	1.00																	
4	**0.43**	**0.46**	**0.45**	**1.00**																
5	0.25	0.23	0.24	0.27	0.99															
6	0.21	0.17	0.13	0.14	0.23	0.98														
7	**0.10**	**0.08**	**0.08**	**0.08**	**0.13**	**0.25**	**1.00**													
8	0.10	0.10	0.04	0.06	0.11	0.09	0.21	0.99												
9	0.11	0.10	0.08	0.02	0.08	0.10	0.15	0.24	1.00											
10	0.12	0.07	0.04	0.03	0.03	0.05	0.06	0.11	0.18	0.99										
11	0.06	0.06	0.03	0.02	0.02	0.01	0.03	0.05	0.08	0.19	0.98									
12	0.06	0.08	0.04	0.03	0.01	0.02	0.03	0.03	0.07	0.08	0.22	0.99								
13	0.07	0.05	0.04	0.03	0.03	0.01	0.01	0.01	0.03	0.04	0.11	0.18	0.99							
14	**0.06**	**0.05**	**0.03**	**0.02**	**0.02**	**0.02**	**0.00**	**0.03**	**0.03**	**0.06**	**0.07**	**0.14**	**0.21**	**0.99**						
15	0.05	0.00	0.02	0.01	0.03	0.01	0.00	0.00	0.03	0.02	0.02	0.06	0.09	0.16	0.98					
16	0.04	0.04	0.01	0.00	0.00	0.00	0.03	0.02	0.03	0.01	0.01	0.03	0.03	0.09	0.20	0.99				
17	0.05	0.01	0.01	0.00	0.01	0.00	0.01	0.00	0.03	0.00	0.01	0.02	0.03	0.02	0.08	0.13	1.00			
18	0.03	0.03	0.01	0.01	0.04	0.01	0.01	0.02	0.03	0.01	0.00	0.01	0.02	0.02	0.07	0.13	0.17	1.00		
19	0.03	0.03	0.01	0.00	0.00	0.00	0.02	0.00	0.00	0.00	0.00	0.01	0.01	0.01	0.01	0.03	0.07	0.14	1.00	
20	**0.05**	**0.06**	**0.00**	**0.01**	**0.01**	**0.01**	**0.00**	**0.00**	**0.01**	**0.01**	**0.00**	**0.01**	**0.01**	**0.01**	**0.02**	**0.03**	**0.03**	**0.09**	**0.18**	**1.00**

Note. Data points in bold are plotted in Figure 10A. RS = rehearsal set.

Table A3 Experiment 2: high-frequency words

| | Nominal serial position | | | | | | | | | | | | | | | | | | | |
RS	1	2	3	4	5	6	7	8	9	10	11	12	13	14	15	16	17	18	19	20
1	1.00																			
2	0.79	1.00																		
3	0.78	0.82	1.00																	
4	**0.75**	**0.79**	**0.82**	**1.00**																
5	0.75	0.71	0.67	0.69	1.00															
6	0.53	0.50	0.49	0.53	0.58	0.99														
7	**0.47**	**0.43**	**0.42**	**0.39**	**0.36**	**0.42**	**0.99**													
8	0.36	0.36	0.33	0.31	0.23	0.33	0.43	1.00												
9	0.33	0.34	0.34	0.24	0.23	0.24	0.27	0.32	0.99											
10	0.23	0.23	0.31	0.22	0.13	0.20	0.17	0.17	0.31	1.00										
11	0.24	0.26	0.27	0.20	0.17	0.13	0.13	0.13	0.17	0.32	1.00									
12	0.28	0.19	0.19	0.15	0.12	0.12	0.09	0.08	0.11	0.18	0.26	1.00								
13	0.26	0.18	0.22	0.16	0.05	0.08	0.10	0.07	0.09	0.11	0.16	0.23	1.00							
14	**0.28**	**0.19**	**0.22**	**0.17**	**0.08**	**0.08**	**0.09**	**0.05**	**0.08**	**0.07**	**0.09**	**0.13**	**0.33**	**1.00**						
15	0.28	0.21	0.19	0.17	0.09	0.08	0.07	0.03	0.08	0.05	0.08	0.08	0.17	0.16	1.00					
16	0.22	0.18	0.18	0.17	0.07	0.09	0.08	0.03	0.06	0.08	0.03	0.14	0.13	0.23	0.33	1.00				
17	0.23	0.13	0.18	0.14	0.09	0.09	0.05	0.04	0.03	0.12	0.08	0.06	0.08	0.10	0.18	0.22	1.00			
18	0.18	0.16	0.17	0.20	0.09	0.07	0.05	0.03	0.04	0.08	0.06	0.05	0.07	0.08	0.08	0.13	0.28	1.00		
19	0.13	0.13	0.16	0.15	0.13	0.10	0.06	0.04	0.03	0.08	0.05	0.05	0.07	0.06	0.05	0.09	0.16	0.27	1.00	
20	**0.14**	**0.13**	**0.18**	**0.17**	**0.09**	**0.10**	**0.04**	**0.03**	**0.03**	**0.07**	**0.03**	**0.05**	**0.07**	**0.03**	**0.03**	**0.06**	**0.13**	**0.15**	**0.20**	**1.00**

Note. Data points in bold are plotted in Figure 10B. RS = rehearsal set.

Table A4 Experiment 2: low-frequency words

	Nominal serial position																			
RS	1	2	3	4	5	6	7	8	9	10	11	12	13	14	15	16	17	18	19	20
1	0.99																			
2	0.61	0.99																		
3	0.62	0.64	1.00																	
4	**0.58**	**0.63**	**0.62**	**1.00**																
5	0.51	0.48	0.40	0.46	1.00															
6	0.43	0.43	0.36	0.33	0.36	1.00														
7	**0.40**	**0.33**	**0.29**	**0.20**	**0.36**	**0.98**														
8	0.33	0.25	0.22	0.14	0.08	0.16	0.26	0.98												
9	0.28	0.19	0.15	0.08	0.09	0.09	0.08	0.23	0.98											
10	0.25	0.16	0.17	0.11	0.09	0.05	0.08	0.13	0.20	1.00										
11	0.27	0.23	0.14	0.10	0.08	0.09	0.06	0.12	0.13	0.28	0.99									
12	0.19	0.16	0.12	0.05	0.05	0.05	0.04	0.04	0.09	0.10	0.31	1.00								
13	0.21	0.13	0.11	0.08	0.08	0.06	0.03	0.08	0.03	0.06	0.11	0.22	0.99							
14	**0.17**	**0.15**	**0.12**	**0.07**	**0.09**	**0.06**	**0.01**	**0.03**	**0.05**	**0.05**	**0.08**	**0.08**	**0.18**	**0.99**						
15	0.18	0.16	0.14	0.07	0.04	0.03	0.03	0.01	0.02	0.08	0.06	0.05	0.12	0.20	0.99					
16	0.15	0.12	0.11	0.07	0.06	0.05	0.03	0.05	0.03	0.04	0.06	0.00	0.06	0.10	0.23	1.00				
17	0.13	0.13	0.09	0.05	0.04	0.03	0.02	0.03	0.00	0.04	0.05	0.02	0.06	0.03	0.07	0.23	0.99			
18	0.15	0.12	0.11	0.05	0.03	0.06	0.03	0.01	0.06	0.07	0.05	0.03	0.03	0.02	0.03	0.08	0.17	0.98		
19	0.12	0.09	0.07	0.03	0.03	0.02	0.03	0.03	0.03	0.06	0.03	0.03	0.03	0.01	0.04	0.05	0.10	0.20	0.99	
20	**0.14**	**0.10**	**0.08**	**0.05**	**0.03**	**0.02**	**0.02**	**0.00**	**0.04**	**0.03**	**0.06**	**0.05**	**0.03**	**0.00**	**0.03**	**0.04**	**0.07**	**0.10**	**0.23**	**1.00**

Note. Data points in bold are plotted in Figure 10B. RS = rehearsal set.

Table A5 Experiment 3: immediate free recall

Nominal serial position

RS	1	2	3	4	5	6	7	8	9	10	11	12	13	14	15	16	17	18	19	20
1	1.00																			
2	0.72	1.00																		
3	0.67	0.77	1.00																	
4	**0.67**	**0.63**	**0.65**	**1.00**																
5	0.50	0.53	0.53	0.48	1.00															
6	0.25	0.23	0.23	0.22	0.33	1.00														
7	**0.23**	**0.18**	**0.23**	**0.22**	**0.17**	**0.32**	**1.00**													
8	0.25	0.18	0.20	0.08	0.25	0.28	0.40	0.98												
9	0.15	0.12	0.10	0.10	0.08	0.17	0.17	0.20	1.00											
10	0.13	0.12	0.18	0.07	0.12	0.10	0.08	0.18	0.30	1.00										
11	0.15	0.12	0.10	0.08	0.02	0.10	0.08	0.10	0.15	0.22	1.00									
12	0.10	0.08	0.13	0.03	0.05	0.03	0.05	0.05	0.10	0.17	0.28	1.00								
13	0.22	0.12	0.12	0.10	0.03	0.07	0.07	0.02	0.12	0.08	0.08	0.27	1.00							
14	**0.12**	**0.10**	**0.08**	**0.08**	**0.03**	**0.03**	**0.03**	**0.03**	**0.03**	**0.05**	**0.08**	**0.08**	**0.23**	**1.00**						
15	0.10	0.07	0.03	0.02	0.00	0.05	0.07	0.05	0.02	0.05	0.02	0.07	0.10	0.25	1.00					
16	0.08	0.08	0.07	0.07	0.05	0.02	0.00	0.00	0.03	0.05	0.02	0.02	0.10	0.12	0.27	1.00				
17	0.08	0.05	0.03	0.10	0.00	0.00	0.07	0.00	0.03	0.03	0.02	0.02	0.08	0.13	0.18	0.30	1.00			
18	0.07	0.08	0.10	0.03	0.00	0.00	0.00	0.05	0.02	0.03	0.02	0.02	0.12	0.08	0.13	0.17	0.25	1.00		
19	0.12	0.07	0.12	0.03	0.00	0.02	0.00	0.03	0.02	0.02	0.02	0.00	0.03	0.05	0.08	0.12	0.13	0.25	1.00	
20	**0.05**	**0.05**	**0.03**	**0.02**	**0.02**	**0.00**	**0.00**	**0.02**	**0.02**	**0.00**	**0.02**	**0.00**	**0.03**	**0.02**	**0.03**	**0.03**	**0.07**	**0.08**	**0.27**	**1.00**

Note. Data points in bold are plotted in Figure 10C. RS = rehearsal set.

Table A6 Experiment 4: immediate free recall

Nominal serial position

RS	1	2	3	4	5	6	7	8	9	10	11	12	13	14	15	16	17	18	19	20
1	0.98																			
2	0.57	1.00																		
3	0.62	0.64	0.98																	
4	**0.53**	**0.58**	**0.63**	**1.00**																
5	0.39	0.39	0.43	0.47	1.00															
6	0.33	0.38	0.32	0.31	0.48	1.00														
7	**0.23**	**0.23**	**0.24**	**0.18**	**0.23**	**0.31**	**1.00**													
8	0.20	0.17	0.19	0.13	0.17	0.21	0.35	1.00												
9	0.24	0.20	0.13	0.09	0.16	0.08	0.12	0.28	1.00											
10	0.13	0.10	0.14	0.07	0.12	0.09	0.13	0.17	0.31	1.00										
11	0.16	0.12	0.13	0.08	0.11	0.04	0.08	0.13	0.18	0.28	1.00									
12	0.12	0.14	0.09	0.08	0.12	0.03	0.05	0.08	0.09	0.11	0.25	0.99								
13	0.14	0.10	0.11	0.04	0.08	0.03	0.06	0.09	0.08	0.10	0.08	0.22	1.00							
14	**0.09**	**0.13**	**0.11**	**0.04**	**0.07**	**0.06**	**0.03**	**0.04**	**0.04**	**0.08**	**0.04**	**0.15**	**0.33**	**0.99**						
15	0.12	0.12	0.06	0.06	0.07	0.01	0.06	0.07	0.04	0.06	0.04	0.08	0.15	0.24	1.00					
16	0.09	0.11	0.07	0.05	0.05	0.01	0.03	0.05	0.08	0.03	0.03	0.04	0.10	0.12	0.28	1.00				
17	0.12	0.07	0.06	0.08	0.08	0.03	0.03	0.04	0.08	0.03	0.03	0.05	0.06	0.10	0.13	0.26	1.00			
18	0.12	0.12	0.08	0.05	0.08	0.03	0.03	0.03	0.03	0.04	0.01	0.03	0.04	0.08	0.08	0.10	0.21	0.99		
19	0.11	0.08	0.08	0.08	0.07	0.05	0.03	0.03	0.05	0.04	0.02	0.02	0.03	0.03	0.04	0.05	0.11	0.29	1.00	
20	**0.08**	**0.07**	**0.06**	**0.07**	**0.03**	**0.03**	**0.03**	**0.03**	**0.01**	**0.03**	**0.00**	**0.03**	**0.03**	**0.03**	**0.02**	**0.04**	**0.06**	**0.11**	**0.21**	**1.00**

Note. Data points in bold are plotted in Figure 10C. RS = rehearsal set.

References

Atkinson, R. C., & Shiffrin, R. M. (1968). Human memory: A proposed system and its control processes. In K. W. Spence & J. T. Spence (Eds.), *The psychology of learning and motivation* (Vol. 2, 89–195). New York: Academic Press.

Baddeley, A. D. (1976). *The psychology of memory*. New York: Basic Books.

Baddeley, A. D. (1986). *Working memory*. Oxford, England: Clarendon Press.

Baddeley, A. D. (1990). *Human memory: Theory and practice*. Hove, England: Lawrence Erlbaum.

Baddeley, A. D., & Hitch, G. J. (1974). Working memory. In G. Bower (Ed.), *Recent advances in learning and motivation, Vol. VIII* (pp. 47–90). London: Academic Press.

Baddeley, A. D., & Hitch, G. J. (1977). Recency re-examined. In S. Dornic (Ed.), *Attention and performance VI* (pp. 647–667). Hillsdale, NJ: Erlbaum.

Baddeley, A. D., & Hitch, G. (1993). The recency effect: Implicit learning with explicit retrieval? *Memory & Cognition, 21*, 146–155.

Bjork, R. A., & Whitten, W. B. (1974). Recency-sensitive retrieval processes in long-term free recall. *Cognitive Psychology, 6*, 173–189.

Brodie, D. A. (1975). Free recall measures of short-term store: Are rehearsal and order of recall data necessary? *Memory & Cognition, 3*, 653–662.

Brodie, D. A., & Murdock, B. B. (1977). Effect of presentation time on nominal and functional serial-position curves of free recall. *Journal of Verbal Learning and Verbal Behavior, 16*, 185–200.

Brodie, D. A., & Prytulak, L. S. (1975). Free recall curves: Nothing but rehearsing some items more or recalling them sooner? *Journal of Verbal Learning and Verbal Behavior, 14*, 549–563.

Burgess, N., & Hitch, G. (1992). Toward a network model of the articulatory loop. *Journal of Memory and Language, 31*, 429–460.

Burgess, N., & Hitch, G. (1999). Memory for serial order: A network model of the phonological loop and its timing. *Psychological Review, 106*, 551–581.

Craik, F. I. M. (1970). The fate of primary memory items in free recall. *Journal of Verbal Learning and Verbal Behavior, 9*, 143–148.

Craik, F. I. M., & Watkins, M. J. (1973). The role of rehearsal in short-term memory *Journal of Verbal Learning and Verbal Behavior, 12*, 599–607.

Crowder, R. G. (1976). *Principles of learning and memory*. Hillsdale, NJ: Erlbaum.

Crowder, R. G. (1982). The demise of short-term memory. *Acta Psychological 50*, 291–323.

Crowder, R. G. (1989). Modularity and dissociations in memory systems. In H. L. Roediger & F. I. M. Craik (Eds.), *Varieties of memory and consciousness: Essays in honor of Endel Tulving*. Hillsdale, NJ: Erlbaum.

Crowder, R. G. (1993). Short-term memory: Where do we stand? *Memory & Cognition, 21*, 142–145.

Crowder, R. G., & Neath, I. (1991). The microscope metaphor in human memory. In W. E. Hockley & S. Lewandowsky (Eds.), *Relating theory and data: Essays in human memory in honour of Bennet B. Murdock*. Hillsdale, NJ: Erlbaum.

Dalezman, J. J. (1976). Effects of output order on immediate, delayed, and final free recall performance, *Journal of Experimental Psychology: Human Learning and Memory, 2*, 597–608.

DeLosh, E. L., & McDaniel, M. A. (1996). The role of order information in free recall: Application to the word-frequency effect. *Journal of Experimental Psychology: Learning, Memory, and Cognition, 22*, 1136–1146.

Estes, W. K. (1972). An associative basis for coding and organization in memory. In A. W. Melton & E. Martin (Eds.), *Coding processes in human memory* (pp. 161–190). Washington, DC: Winston.

Fischler, I., Rundus, D., & Atkinson, R. C. (1970). Effects of overt rehearsal procedures on free recall. *Psychonomic Science, 19*, 249–250.

Gillund, G., & Shiffrin, R. M. (1984). A retrieval model for both recognition and recall. *Psychological Review, 91*, 1–67.

Glanzer, M. (1969). Distance between related words in free recall: Trace of the STS. *Journal of Verbal Learning and Verbal Behavior, 8*, 105–111.

Glanzer, M. (1972). Storage mechanisms in recall. In G. H. Bower (Ed.), *The psychology of learning and motivation: Advances in research and theory, Vol. V* (pp. 129–193). New York: Academic Press.

Glanzer, M., & Cunitz, A. R. (1966). Two storage mechanisms in free recall. *Journal of Verbal Learning and Verbal Behavior, 5*, 351–360.

Glanzer, M., & Meinzer, A. (1967). The effects of intralist activity on free recall. *Journal of Verbal Learning and Verbal Behavior, 6*, 928–935.

Glenberg, A. M. (1984). A retrieval account of the long-term modality effect. *Journal of Experimental Psychology: Learning, Memory and Cognition, 10*, 16–31.

Glenberg, A. M. (1987). Temporal context and recency. In D. S. Gorfein & R. R. Hoffman (Eds.), *Memory and learning: The Ebbinghaus centennial conference.* Hillsdale, NJ: Lawrence Erlbaum.

Glenberg, A. M., Bradley, M. M., Stevenson, J. A., Kraus, T. A., Tkachuk, M. J., Gretz, A. L., Fish, J. H., & Turpin, B. M. (1980). A two-process account of long-term serial position effects. *Journal of Experimental Psychology: Human Learning and Memory, 6*, 355–369.

Glenberg, A. M., Smith, S. M., & Green, C. (1977). Type I rehearsal: Maintenance and more. *Journal of Verbal Learning and Verbal Behavior, 16*, 339–352.

Glenberg, A. M., & Swanson, N. G. (1986). A temporal distinctiveness theory of recency and modality effects. *Journal of Experimental Psychology: Learning, Memory and Cognition, 12*, 3–15.

Greene, R. L. (1987). Effects of maintenance rehearsal on human memory. *Psychological Bulletin, 102*, 403–413.

Gregg, V. (1976). Word frequency, recognition and recall. In J. Brown (Ed.), *Recall and recognition* (pp. 183–216). London: Wiley.

Henson, R. N. A. (1998). Short-term memory for serial order: The start-end model of serial recall. *Cognitive Psychology, 36*, 73–137.

Hockey, R. (1973). Rate of presentation in running memory and direct manipulation of input-processing strategies. *Quarterly Journal of Experimental Psychology, 25*, 104–111.

Howard, M. W., & Kahana, M. J. (1999). Contextual variability and serial position effects in free recall. *Journal of Experimental Psychology: Learning, Memory and Cognition, 25*, 923–941.

Kahana, M. J. (1996). Associative retrieval processes in free recall. *Memory & Cognition, 24*, 103–109.

Kerr, J. R., Avons, S. E., & Ward, G. (1999). The effect of retention interval on serial position curves for item recognition of visual patterns of faces. *Journal of Experimental Psychology: Learning, Memory, and Cognition, 25,* 1475–1494.

Kerr, J., Ward, G., & Avons, S. E. (1998). Response bias in visual serial order memory. *Journal of Experimental Psychology: Learning, Memory, and Cognition, 24,* 1316–1323.

Knoedler, A. J., Hellwig, K. A., & Neath, I. (1999). The shift from recency to primacy with increasing delay. *Journal of Experimental Psychology: Learning, Memory, and Cognition, 25,* 474–487.

Kučera, H., & Francis, V. W. (1967). *Computational analysis of presentday American English.* Providence, RI: Brown University Press.

Laming, D. (1999). Testing the idea of distinct storage mechanisms in memory. *International Journal of Psychology, 34,* 419–426.

Lee, C. L., & Estes, W. K. (1977). Order and position in primary memory for letter strings. *Journal of Verbal Learning and Verbal Behavior, 16,* 395–418.

Loess, H., & Waugh, N. C. (1967). Short-term memory and inter-trial interval. *Journal of Verbal Learning and Verbal Behavior, 6,* 455–460.

Marshall, P. H., & Werder, P. R. (1972). The effects of the elimination of rehearsal on primacy and recency. *Journal of Verbal Learning and Verbal Behavior, 11,* 649–653.

Meunier, G. F., Kestner, J., Meunier, J. A., & Ritz, D. (1974). Overt rehearsal and long-term retention. *Journal of Experimental Psychology, 102,* 913–914.

Modigliani, V., & Hedges, D. G. (1987). Distributed rehearsals and the primacy effect in single-trial free recall. *Journal of Experimental Psychology: Learning, Memory, and Cognition, 13,* 426–436.

Murdock, B. B. (1960). The distinctiveness of stimuli. *Psychological Review, 67,* 16–31.

Nairne, J. S. (1990). A feature model of immediate memory. *Memory & Cognition, 18,* 251–269.

Nairne, J. S. (1991). Positional uncertainty in long-term memory. *Memory & Cognition, 19,* 332–340.

Nairne, J. S. (1992). The loss of positional certainty in long-term memory. *Psychological Science, 3,* 199–202.

Nairne, J. S., Neath, I., Serra, M., & Byun, E. (1997). Positional distinctiveness and the ratio rule in free recall. *Journal of Memory and Language, 37,* 155–166.

Naveh-Benjamin, M., & Jonides, J. (1984a). Cognitive load and maintenance rehearsal. *Journal of Verbal Learning and Verbal Behavior, 23,* 494–507.

Naveh-Benjamin, M., & Jonides, J. (1984b). Maintenance rehearsal: A two-component analysis. *Journal of Experimental Psychology: Learning, Memory, and Cognition, 10,* 369–385.

Neath, I. (1993). Distinctiveness and serial position effects in recognition. *Memory & Cognition, 21,* 689–698.

Neath, I., & Crowder, R. G. (1990). Schedules of presentation and temporal distinctiveness in human memory. *Journal of Experimental Psychology: Learning, Memory, and Cognition, 16,* 316–327.

Neath, I., & Knoedler, A. J. (1994). Distinctiveness and serial position effects in recognition and sentence processing. *Journal of Memory & Language, 33,* 776–795.

Page, M. P. A., & Norris, D. (1998). The primacy model: A new model of immediate serial recall. *Psychological Review, 105*, 761–781.

Peterson, L. R., & Gentile, A. (1963). Proactive interference as a function of time between tests. *Journal of Experimental Psychology, 70*, 473–478.

Pinto, A. Da C., & Baddeley, A. D. (1991). Where did you park your car? Analysis of a naturalistic long-term recency effect. *European Journal of Cognitive Psychology, 3*, 297–313.

Poltrock, S. E., & MacLeod, C. M. (1977). Primacy and recency in the continuous distractor paradigm. *Journal of Experimental Psychology: Human Learning and Memory, 3*, 560–571.

Postman, L., & Phillips, L. W. (1965). Short-term temporal changes in free recall. *Quarterly Journal of Experimental Psychology, 17*, 132–138.

Quinlan, P. T. (1992). *The Oxford psycholinguistic database.* Oxford, England: Oxford Electronic Publishing, Oxford University Press.

Raaijmakers, J. G. W., & Shiffrin, R. M. (1981). Search of associative memory. *Psychological Review, 88*, 93–134.

Raymond, B. (1969). Short-term and long-term storage in free recall. *Journal of Verbal Learning and Verbal Behavior, 8*, 567–574.

Richardson, J. T. E., & Baddeley, A. D. (1975). The effect of articulatory suppression in free recall. *Journal of Verbal Learning and Verbal Behavior, 14*, 623–629.

Rundus, D. (1971). Analysis of rehearsal processes in free recall. *Journal of Experimental Psychology, 89*, 63–77.

Rundus, D. (1977). Maintenance rehearsal and single-level processing. *Journal of Verbal Learning and Verbal Behavior, 16*, 665–681.

Rundus, D. (1980). Maintenance rehearsal and long-term recency. *Memory & Cognition, 8*, 226–230.

Rundus, D., & Atkinson, R. C. (1970). Rehearsal processes in free recall: A procedure for direct observation. *Journal of Verbal Learning and Verbal Behavior, 9*, 99–105.

Shallice, T. (1988). *From neuropsychology to mental structure.* Cambridge, England: Cambridge University Press.

Sumby, W. H. (1963). Word frequency and serial position effects. *Journal of Verbal Learning and Verbal Behavior, 1*, 443–450.

Turvey, M. T., Brick, P., & Osborn, J. (1970). Proactive interference in short-term memory as a function of prior-item retention interval. *Quarterly Journal of Experimental Psychology, 22*, 142–147.

Tzeng, O. J. L. (1973). Positive recency effect in a delayed free recall. *Journal of Verbal Learning and Verbal Behavior, 12*, 436–439.

Watkins, M. J., Neath, I., & Sechler, E. S. (1989). Recency effect in recall of a word list when an immediate memory task is performed after each word presentation. *American Journal of Psychology, 102*, 265–270.

Waugh, N. C., & Norman, D. A. (1965). Primary memory. *Psychological Review, 72*, 89–104.

Wixted, J. T., Ghadisha, H., & Vera, R. (1997). Recall latency following pure- and mixed-strength lists: A direct test of the relative strength model of free recall. *Journal of Experimental Psychology: Learning, Memory, and Cognition, 23*, 523–538.

Wixted, J. T., & McDowell, J. J. (1989). Contributions to the functional analysis of single-trial free recall. *Journal of Experimental Psychology: Learning, Memory, and Cognition, 15*, 685–697.

Woodward, A. E., Jr., Bjork, R. A., & Jongeward, R. H., Jr. (1973). Recall and recognition as a function of primary rehearsal. *Journal of Verbal Learning and Verbal Behavior, 12*, 608–617.